2019 上海统计年鉴

Shanghai Statistical Yearbook

上　海　市　统　计　局

国家统计局上海调查总队

SHANGHAI MUNICIPAL STATISTICS BUREAU

SURVEY OFFICE OF THE NATIONAL BUREAU OF STATISTICS IN SHANGHAI

中国统计出版社

China Statistics Press

《上海统计年鉴—2019》编辑委员会

主　　编　周　亚　朱章海

副 主 编　汤汇浩　肖永培　李　炜　施　方
阮大成　沈丽华　周学文　庄龙德
孙德麟　冯瑶钧　吴展敏　程　英

编　　委　（按姓氏笔画）
丁　俊　王　静　王建军　王震颖
朱静蕾　刘　慧　杨建忠　宋丽琛
张玲玲　陆立萍　陈永奇　周　蓉
甄明霞　熊　玲

责任编辑　钟　钰　熊　威

执行编辑　曹美芳

编辑人员　（按姓氏笔画）
于国斌　马向科　王莉芳　叶寅松
朱　冰　朱羽飞　刘　纲　孙　颖
孙杭麟　孙轶男　苏振宇　李　刚
李　珍　李国娟　何佳伟　宋　玉
张　凤　张　源　张庆华　陈　巍
陈汤斌　陈骁冬　金慧莲　周群艳
郑尉梅　钟　华　钟晓韵　钱　萍
钱国光　徐　平　栾　璇　曹月勤
屠孟樵　韩　君　谢蕾蕾　戴伟慧

英文翻译　陈君君

光盘设计　史江旭

EDITORIAL BOARD

Editor-in-Chiefs: Zhou Ya　Zhu Zhanghai

Deputy Editor-in-Chiefs:
Tang Huihao　Xiao Yongpei　Li Wei　Shi Fang
Ruan Dacheng　Shen Lihua　Zhou Xuewen　Zhuang Longde
Sun Delin　Feng Yaojun　Wu Zhanmin　Cheng Ying

Editorial Board (in order of strokes of Chinese surname)
Ding Jun　Wang Jing　Wang Jianjun　Wang Zhenying
Zhu Jinglei　Liu Hui　Yang Jianzhong　Song Lichen
Zhang Lingling　Lu Liping　Chen Yongqi　Zhou Rong
Zhen Minxia　Xiong Ling

Chief Copy Editors　Zhong Yu　Xiong Wei

Executive Copy-Editor　Cao Meifang

Editorial Staff (in order of strokes of Chinese surname)
Yu Guobin　Ma Xiangke　Wang Lifang　Ye Yinsong
Zhu Bing　Zhu Yufei　Liu Gang　Sun Ying
Sun Hanglin　Sun Yinan　Su Zhenyu　Li Gang
Li Zhen　Li Guojuan　He Jiawei　Song Yu
Zhang Feng　Zhang Yuan　Zhang Qinghua　Chen Wei
Chen Tangbin　Chen Xiaodong　Jin Huilian　Zhou Qunyan
Zheng Weimei　Zhong Hua　Zhong Xiaoyun　Qian Ping
Qian Guoguang　Xu Ping　Luan Xuan　Cao Yueqin
Tu Mengqiao　Han Jun　Xie Leilei　Dai Weihui

English Translator　Chen Junjun

CD-ROM Design　Shi Jiangxu

编者说明

一、《上海统计年鉴—2019》是一本信息高度密集的资料工具书。本书收录了2018年上海的经济和社会等各方面的统计数据，以及重要年份和改革开放以来的主要统计数据。

二、全书内容分为24个篇目，即：1. 综合；2. 人口；3. 从业人员和工资；4. 国民经济核算；5. 财政收支；6. 能源与环境；7. 固定资产投资；8. 对外经济贸易和旅游；9. 价格水平；10. 人民生活；11. 城市建设；12. 农业；13. 工业；14. 建筑业；15. 服务业；16. 交通运输、邮政和信息传输；17. 批发、零售和住宿、餐饮；18. 金融业；19. 房地产业；20. 科学技术；21. 教育；22. 卫生、社会保障和社会福利业；23. 文化和体育；24. 法律、公证和其他。为便于读者正确地使用资料，各篇目还附有简要说明和主要统计指标解释。

三、本年鉴数据除特别说明外，是由上海市统计局和国家统计局上海调查总队通过年报调查收集。因年鉴编辑期间第四次经济普查数据尚未公布，本年鉴2018年国民经济核算、工业、投资等数据采用快报数。

四、资料中所使用的度量衡单位均采用国际统一标准计量单位，金额除特别标明外，均以人民币计量。

五、本年鉴总量指标计算所采用的价格均为现行价格。

六、本年鉴部分数据合计数或相对数由于单位取舍不同产生的计算误差均未作机械调整。

七、本年鉴表中的符号使用说明：

"…"表示数据不足本表最小计量单位数；

"空格"表示该项统计数据不详或无该项数据；

"#"表示其中的主要项。

八、《上海统计年鉴》公开出版以来，受到了国内外广大读者的关心和支持，对本年鉴的内容和编辑工作提出了许多宝贵的意见，对此我们深表谢意。限于我们的水平，欢迎读者继续对年鉴的不足之处给予批评和指正，帮助我们进一步改进年鉴的编辑工作，以期更好地为广大读者服务。

EDITOR'S NOTE

Ⅰ. Shanghai Statistical Yearbook 2019 contains comprehensive statistics of Shanghai's social and economic development in 2018 and selected data of some important years and of the period since China adopted the policy of reform and opening to the outside world.

Ⅱ. The book is composed of 24 parts viz.1. General Survey; 2. Population; 3. Employment and Wages; 4. National Economic Accounting; 5. Fiscal Revenue and Expenditure; 6. Energyand Environment Protection; 7. Investment in Fixed Assets; 8. Foreign Economic Relations, Trade and Tourism; 9. Prices; 10. Living Standards; 11. Urban Construction; 12. Agriculture; 13. Industry; 14. Construction; 15. Serviec; 16. Transportation, Posts and Information Transmission; 17. Wholesale and Retail, Hotels and Catering Services; 18. Finance; 19. Real Estate; 20. Science and Technology; 21. Education; 22. Health, Social Security and Social Welfare; 23. Culture, Sports; 24. Laws, Notary and others. In order to make readers using materials correctly, brief introduction and explanations of major statistical indicators are attached after every chapter.

Ⅲ. Main part of the data in this yearbook are investigated and collected by Shanghai Municipal Statistical Bureau and Survey Office of the National Bureau of Statistics in Shanghai, except those with special notes. Because of the data of the Fourth China Economic Census were not released during the editing period, and related data of National Economic Accounting, Industry and Investment are from monthly or quarterly report.

Ⅳ. The international standard unit of measurement is applied in this book. All amounts are denominated in RMB, except those with special notes.

Ⅴ. The prices used for calculating of gross indicators in this yearbook are current prices.

Ⅵ. Statistical discrepancies in this book due to rounding are not adjusted.

Ⅶ. Marks in this book: ··· means not large enough to be rounded into the least unit of measurement; blank space means data are not available; # indicates major item in a category.

Ⅷ. Previous editions of Shanghai Statistical Yearbook have won wide acclaim among the readers. In order to get further improvement in the yearbook editing, we welcome all candid comments and criticism from our readers.

目录 CONTENTS

第一篇 CHAPTER 1 综合 GENERAL SURVEY

目录
CONTENTS

第二篇 CHAPTER 2 人口 POPULATION

第三篇 CHAPTER 3 从业人员和工资 EMPLOYMENT AND WAGES

第四篇 CHAPTER 4 国民经济核算 NATIONAL ECONOMIC ACCOUNTING

目录
CONTENTS

第五篇 CHAPTER 5 财政收支 FISCAL REVENUE AND EXPENDITURE

第六篇 CHAPTER 6 能源与环境 ENERGY AND ENVIRONMENT PROTECTION

第七篇 CHAPTER 7 固定资产投资 INVESTMENT IN FIXED ASSETS

目录 CONTENTS

目录
CONTENTS

第九篇 CHAPTER 9 价格水平 PRICES

第十篇 CHAPTER 10 人民生活 LIVING STANDARDS

目录

CONTENTS

第十一篇 CHAPTER 11 城市建设 URBAN CONSTRUCTION

第十二篇 CHAPTER 12 农业 AGRICULTURE

目录
CONTENTS

第十三篇 CHAPTER 13 工业 INDUSTRY

第十四篇 CHAPTER 14 建筑业 CONSTRUCTION

目录

CONTENTS

第十七篇 CHAPTER 17 批发、零售和住宿、餐饮 WHOLESALE AND RETAIL, HOTELS AND CATERING SERVICES

第十八篇 CHAPTER 18 金融业 FINANCE

目录

CONTENTS

目录
CONTENTS

第二十一篇 CHAPTER 21 教 育 EDUCATION

第二十二篇 CHAPTER 22 卫生、社会保障和社会福利业 HEALTH, SOCIAL SECURITY AND SOCIAL WELFARE

目录

CONTENTS

第二十三篇 CHAPTER 23 文化和体育 CULTURE AND SPORTS

目录
CONTENTS

第二十四篇 CHAPTER 24 法律、公证和其他 LAWS, NOTARY AND OTHERS

第一篇

CHAPTER 1

综 合

GENERAL SURVEY

简要说明

本篇章主要内容和资料来源

一、综合资料主要包括上海市行政区划、国民经济和社会发展综合资料两部分。分别由上海市民政局、上海市统计局和国家统计局上海调查总队编辑整理。

二、行政区划资料，由上海市民政局根据上海市政府批准的、截止到上一年末上海市区划变更情况汇总整理并提供。

三、国民经济和社会发展综合资料是抽取全书的精华，通过对各篇章主要统计指标及其速度、结构、比例和效益等的加工计算，来反映国民经济和社会发展的总体情况。

BRIEF INTRODUCTION

Main Contents and Sources of Data

1. This chapter consists of two parts: divisions of Shanghai administrative areas and summary data on the national economy and social development, which are compiled by the Shanghai Municipal Civil Affairs Bureau, Shanghai Municipal Statistics Bureau and the Survey Office of the National Bureau of Statistics in Shanghai.

2 . Data on divisions of administrative areas in Shanghai, are prepared and provided by the Shanghai Municipal Civil Affairs Bureau on the basis of the changes in the divisions of administrative areas as approved by the Shanghai municipal government at the end of the previous year.

3. The summary data on the national economy and social development reflect on the overall situation of the economy and social development by presenting further processed statistics including growth, structure, ratio, and efficiency data derived from other chapters.

表 1.1　行政区划(2018)
ADMINISTRATIVE DIVISION

单位:个 (unit)

地　区	District	镇 Towns	乡 Township	街道办事处 Urban Sub-district Office	居民委员会 Neighbourhood Committees	村民委员会 Village Committees
全　市	**Total**	**107**	**2**	**105**	**4 416**	**1 572**
浦东新区	Pudong New Area	24		12	961	362
黄 浦 区	Huangpu			10	177	
徐 汇 区	Xuhui	1		12	303	
长 宁 区	Changning	1		9	185	
静 安 区	Jing'an	1		13	267	1
普 陀 区	Putuo	2		8	259	7
虹 口 区	Hongkou			8	206	
杨 浦 区	Yangpu	1		11	301	
闵 行 区	Minhang	9		4	449	118
宝 山 区	Baoshan	9		3	382	104
嘉 定 区	Jiading	7		3	214	143
金 山 区	Jinshan	9		1	106	124
松 江 区	Songjiang	11		6	259	85
青 浦 区	Qingpu	8		3	141	184
奉 贤 区	Fengxian	8		2	125	175
崇 明 区	Chongming	16	2		81	269

注：本表数据由上海市民政局提供。
Note: Data in this table are provided by Shanghai Civil Affairs Bureau.

表 1.2　主要气象指标(2018)
MAIN CLIMATE INDICATORS

指　标	Indicators	2018	指　标	Indicators	2018
平均气温（℃）	Annual Average Temperature（℃）	17.7	蒸发量(毫米)	Evaporation（mm）	1 129.6
极端最高气温（℃）	Utmost Highest Air Temperature（℃）	37.4	降水量(毫米)	Precipitation(mm)	1 407.9
极端最低气温（℃）	Utmost Lowest Air Temperature（℃）	-7.0	降雨日(天)	Annual Rainy Days(day)	134
日照时间（小时）	Annual Sunshine Time（h）	1 839.1	无霜期(天)	Frost-free Period(day)	281

表 1.3　各月主要气象指标(2018)
MAIN CLIMATE INDICATORS OF EVERY MONTH

月　份	Month	平均气温(℃) Annual Average Temperature（℃）	极端最高气温(℃) Utmost Highest Air Temperature(℃)	极端最低气温(℃) Utmost Lowest Air Temperature(℃)	平均最高气温(℃) Average Maximum temperature(℃)	平均最低气温(℃) Average Minimum temperature(℃)
1 月	Jan.	4.3	14.2	-7.0	7.2	1.7
2 月	Feb.	5.3	20.1	-5.9	9.5	1.4
3 月	Mar.	12.1	26.3	0.4	17.2	7.7
4 月	Apr.	17.5	30.0	3.1	22.7	12.6
5 月	May.	22.3	36.4	11.1	26.4	18.6
6 月	Jun.	25.2	37.1	17.3	29.1	21.8
7 月	Jul.	29.3	37.4	25.0	32.9	26.5
8 月	Aug.	29.4	35.9	24.3	32.4	26.9
9 月	Sep.	25.9	34.0	18.8	29.1	23.2
10 月	Oct.	18.8	25.9	8.0	22.4	15.0
11 月	Nov.	14.4	22.2	5.3	18.1	11.0
12 月	Dec.	8.2	21.6	-3.2	11.2	5.6

表 1.3 续表 continued

月　份	Month	日照时间（小时） Annual Sunshine Time(h)	降水量(毫米) Precipitation (mm)	降雨日(天) Annual Rainy Days (day)	蒸发量(毫米) Evaporation (mm)
1 月	Jan.	87.4	96.3	10	59.4
2 月	Feb.	135.8	67.6	8	61.9
3 月	Mar.	165.5	75.5	11	77.1
4 月	Apr.	204.2	84.4	8	99.8
5 月	May.	143.2	171.6	16	107.3
6 月	Jun.	175.3	57.2	11	119.2
7 月	Jul.	223.5	122.8	11	139.0
8 月	Aug.	216.4	249.4	11	143.0
9 月	Sep.	144.8	193.3	13	113.6
10 月	Oct.	177.0	35.5	6	105.3
11 月	Nov.	107.8	97.8	12	51.4
12 月	Dec.	58.2	156.5	17	52.6

注：本页资料由上海市气象局提供。
Note: Data on this page are provided by Shanghai Meteorological Bureau.

表 1.4　中国(上海)自由贸易试验区主要经济指标(2018)
MAIN ECONOMIC INDICATORS OF THE CHINA(SHANGHAI) PILOT FREE TRADE ZONE

指　标	Indicators	单　位	Unit	2018
税收总额	Taxes	亿元	100 million yuan	2 680.20
一般公共预算收入	General Budgetary Revenue	亿元	100 million yuan	648.16
外商直接投资合同项目	Foreign Direct Investment Projects	个	unit	1 049
外商直接投资合同金额	Contracted Capital of Foreign Direct Investment	亿美元	100 million USD	100.38
外商直接投资实际到位金额	Foreign Direct Investment Actually Absorbed	亿美元	100 million USD	67.70
新增内资企业注册户数	New Domestic Funded Enterprises Registered	个	unit	5 939
新增内资企业注册资本	Registered Capital of New Domestic Funded Enterprises	亿元	100 million yuan	2 052.90
全社会固定资产投资总额	Total Investment in Fixed Assets	亿元	100 million yuan	638.07
规模以上工业总产值	Gross Output Value of Industry	亿元	100 million yuan	4 965.00
社会消费品零售额	Total Retail Sales of Consumer Goods	亿元	100 million yuan	1 515.67
商品销售总额	Commodity Sales	亿元	100 million yuan	40 874.86
服务业营业收入	Revenue of Service Industry	亿元	100 million yuan	5 723.97
外贸进出口总额	Total Value of Imports and Exports	亿元	100 million yuan	14 600.00
#出　口	Exports	亿元	100 million yuan	4 542.50
发明专利授权数	Invention Patent Certified	个	unit	5 029
期末监管类金融机构	Regulatory Financial Institutions	个	unit	887
跨境人民币结算总额	Total Cross-border Settlement in RMB	亿元	100 million yuan	25 518.88
跨境人民币境外借款金额	Overseas Borrowing of Cross-border RMB	亿元	100 million yuan	5.38

①自贸区按注册地口径统计，统计范围为 120.72 平方公里。
②一般公共预算收入按开发区财力结算口径。
❶The statistics of China (shanghai) Pilot Free Trade Zone follow registration place, and statistical range covers 120.72 square kilometers.
❷The statistics of general public budget revenue follow the financial settlement standard of Development Zone.

表 1.5 主要年份社会经济主要指标
MAJOR SOCIAL AND ECONOMIC INDICATORS IN MAIN YEARS

指 标	Indicators	1990	2000	2010	2017	2018
人口与就业	**Population and Employment**					
人 口	**Population**					
年末常住人口(万人)	Year-end Resident Population (10 000 persons)	1 334.00	1 608.60	2 302.66	2 418.33	2 423.78
年末户籍人口(万人)	Year-end Registered Population (10 000 persons)	1 283.35	1 321.63	1 412.32	1 455.13	1 462.38
就 业	**Employment**					
城镇登记失业率(%)	Registered Unemployment Rate in Urban Areas (%)	1.5	3.5	4.2	3.9	3.57
宏观经济	**Macro Economy**					
国民经济核算	**National Economic Accounts**					
上海市生产总值(亿元)	Gross Domestic Product (100 million yuan)	781.66	4 812.15	17 436.85	30 632.99	32 679.87
# 第一产业	Primary Industry	34.24	76.68	117.79	110.78	104.37
第二产业	Secondary Industry	505.60	2 231.93	7 376.81	9 330.67	9 732.54
第三产业	Tertiary Industry	241.82	2 503.54	9 942.25	21 191.54	22 842.96
# 工 业	Industry	469.83	2 022.53	6 689.90	8 392.84	8 694.95
人均生产总值(元)(按常住人口计算)	Per Capita Gross Domestic Product (yuan) (Calculated by Resident Population)	5 911	30 307	77 275	126 634	134 982
经济增长贡献率(%)	Contribution Rate of Economic Growth (%)					
# 第一产业	Primary Industry	2.5	0.6	-0.3	…	…
第二产业	Secondary Industry	57.1	55.8	69.1	25.5	8.4
第三产业	Tertiary Industry	40.4	43.6	31.2	74.5	92.0
# 工 业	Industry	52.8	54.8	66.5	25.9	7.9
固定资产投资	**Investment in Fixed Assets**					
全社会固定资产投资总额(亿元)	Total Investment in Fixed Assets (100 million yuan)	227.08	1 869.67	5 317.67	7 246.60	7 623.69
# 房地产开发	Investment in Real Estate	8.16	566.17	1 980.68	3 856.53	4 033.18

表 1.5 续表 1 continued

	指　标 Indicators	1990	2000	2010	2017	2018
财　政	**Public Finance**					
一般公共预算收入(亿元)	General Budgetary Revenue (100 million yuan)	166.99	497.96	2 873.58	6 642.26	7 108.15
一般公共预算支出(亿元)	General Budgetary Expenditure (100 million yuan)	75.56	622.84	3 302.89	7 547.62	8 351.54
价　格	**Price**					
居民消费价格指数(上年=100)	Consumer Price Index (preceding =100)	106.3	102.5	103.1	101.7	101.6
商品零售价格指数(上年=100)	Retail Price Index (preceding =100)	104.8	96.4	101.7	100.9	101.6
产　业	**Industries**					
农　业	**Agriculture**					
农业总产值(亿元)	Gross Output Value of Agriculture (100 million yuan)	68.16	216.50	296.24	292.61	289.58
工　业	**Industry**					
工业总产值(亿元)	Gross Output Value of Industry (100 million yuan)	1 642.75	7 022.98	31 038.57	36 094.36	36 451.84
建筑业	**Construction**					
建筑业总产值(亿元)	Gross Output Value of Construction (100 million yuan)	75.62	631.64	4 300.19	6 426.42	7 112.32
交通运输、邮政业和信息传输	**Transportation, Post and Information Transmission**					
货物运输量(万吨)	Freight Transportation Volume (10 000 tons)	22 848	47 954	81 023	97 257	107 387
旅客发送量(万人次)	Passenger Departures (10 000 person-times)	3 835	6 893	13 456	20 855	21 497
港口货物吞吐量(万吨)	Port Cargo Freight Throughput (10 000 tons)	13 959	20 440	65 339	75 051	73 048
国际标准集装箱吞吐量(万 TEU)	International Container Throughput Capacity (10 000 TEU)	45.60	561.20	2 906.90	4 023.31	4 201.02
年末固定电话用户(万户)	Year-end Installed Telephones (10 000 households)	45.69	549.00	931.80	690.95	663.19
批发和零售	**Wholesale and Retail**					
社会消费品零售总额(亿元)	Total Retail Sales of Consumer Goods (100 million yuan)	333.86	1 865.28	6 186.58	11 745.96	12 668.69
批发零售业商品销售总额(亿元)	Sales of Commodities of Wholesale and Retail (100 million yuan)	1 305.41	7 474.81	48 659.55	113 133.19	119 461.28

表 1.5 续表 2 continued

指 标	Indicators	1990	2000	2010	2017	2018
对外经济贸易	**Foreign Trade**					
上海关区进出口总额(亿美元)	Total Trade Value Through Customs (100 million USD)	172.89	1 093.11	6 846.45	8 814.67	9 715.23
进口额	Imports	86.27	477.39	2 613.05	3 647.91	4 090.77
出口额	Exports	86.62	615.72	4 233.40	5 166.76	5 624.46
上海市进出口总额(亿美元)	Total Value of Foreign Trade Imports and Exports (100 million USD)	74.31	547.10	3 688.69	4 761.23	5 156.49
进口额	Imports	21.10	293.56	1 880.85	2 824.42	3 084.79
出口额	Exports	53.21	253.54	1 807.84	1 936.81	2 071.70
外商直接投资	**Foreign Direct Investment**					
合同项目（个）	Number of Contracts (item)	203	1 814	3 906	3 950	5 597
合同金额（亿美元）	Contractual Foreign Capital (100 million USD)	2.14	63.90	153.07	401.94	469.37
实到金额（亿美元）	Foreign Investment Actually Absorbed (100 million USD)	1.77	31.60	111.21	170.08	173.00
国际旅游	**International Tourism**					
国际旅游入境人数（万人次）	Number of Overseas Tourists Through Shanghai Custom (10 000 persons-times)	89.30	181.40	851.12	873.01	893.71
国际旅游(外汇)收入（亿美元）	Foreign Exchange Earnings from International Tourism (100 million USD)	2.31	16.13	64.05	68.10	73.71
金 融	**Finance**					
金融机构存款余额(亿元)	Saving Deposits Balance of Financial Institutions (100 million yuan)	851.51	9 349.83	52 190.04	112 461.74	121 112.33
金融机构贷款余额(亿元)	Loan Balance of Financial Institutions (100 million yuan)	1 106.80	7 254.26	34 154.17	67 182.01	73 272.35
有价证券成交总额(亿元)	Total Volume of Priced Securities Trading (100 million)		49 901	398 396	3 063 862	2 646 249
#股 票	Stocks		31 374	304 312	511 243	403 184
原保险保费收入（亿元）	Premium of Primary Insurance (100 million yuan)	8.99	127.23	883.86	1 587.10	1 405.79
原保险赔付支出（亿元）	Payment of Primary Insurance (100 million yuan)	2.22	36.44	194.54	548.93	581.56
教育、科技、文化	**Education, Science&Technology and Culture**					
教 育	**Education**					
在校学生数（万人）	Students Enrollment (10 000 persons)					
普通高等学校	Regular Institutions of Higher Education	12.13	22.68	51.57	51.49	51.78
普通中学	Regular Secondary Schools	48.31	79.54	59.44	57.06	59.07
普通小学	Primary Schools	110.19	78.86	70.16	78.49	80.02
每万人拥有大学生(人)	Number of College and University Students Per 10 000 Persons (person)	90	141	224	213	214

表 1.5 续表 3 continued

指　标	Indicators	1990	2000	2010	2017	2018
科　技	**Science and Technology**					
科技成果（项）	Achievements in Science and Technology (item)	2 092	1 102	2 318	2 028	1 618
研究与试验发展经费内部支出（亿元）	Expenditures on R&D (100 million yuan)	10.13	76.73	481.70	1 205.21	1 359.20
研究与试验发展经费支出相当于上海市生产总值比例(%)	R&D Expenditure as Percentage of Gross Domestic Product (%)	1.30	1.59	2.76	3.93	4.16
文　化	**Culture**					
出版数量	Number of Publications					
图　书（亿册）	Books (100 million copies)	2.98	2.54	2.89	4.23	4.81
期　刊（亿册）	Periodicals (100 million copies)	1.73	1.85	1.78	0.94	0.85
报　纸（亿份）	Newspapers (100 million copies)	16.16	16.77	15.90	9.13	8.17
故事影片产量（部）	Feature Films Produced(film)	16	10	19	67	75
家庭、生活、环境	**Family, Living and Environment**					
家　庭	**Household**					
家庭总户数（万户）	Total Households (10 000 households)	415.28	475.73	519.27	546.13	551.95
平均每户家庭人口（人）	Average Persons per Household (person)	3.09	2.78	2.72	2.66	2.65
婚　姻	**Marriages and Divorces**					
准予登记结婚（万对）	Marriage Registration Permitted (10 000 couples)	10.77	9.31	13.03	10.87	10.37
离婚件数（万件）	Divorce (10 000 cases)	1.64	3.18	4.67	5.72	5.41
住　宅	**Housing**					
城镇居民人均住房建筑面积（平方米）	Construction Area per Capita of Urban Residents (sq.m)			32.6	36.7	37.0
生　活	**Living**					
全市居民人均可支配收入(元)	Per Capita Annual Disposable Income of Residents (yuan)				58 988	64 183
全市居民人均消费支出(元)	Per Capita Annual Consumption Expenditure of Residents (yuan)				39 792	43 351
城镇常住居民人均可支配收入(元)	Per Capita Annual Disposable Income of Urban Households (yuan)				62 596	68 034
城镇常住居民人均消费支出(元)	Per Capita Annual Consumption Expenditures of Urban Households (yuan)				42 304	46 015
农村常住居民人均可支配收入(元)	Per Capita Annual Disposable Income of Rural Households (yuan)				27 825	30 375
农村常住居民人均消费支出(元)	Per Capita Annual Consumption Expenditure of Rural Households (yuan)				18 090	19 965
个人存款(住户存款)余额（亿元）	Household Deposits (100 million yuan)		2 627.07	16 249.29	25 763.20	28 569.24

注：城镇居民人均住房建筑面积由市住房和城乡建设管理委员会提供。
Note: Construction Area per Capita of Urban Residents data are provided by Shanghai Municipal Housing and Urban-Rural Construction Management Committee.

表 1.5 续表 4 continued

	指 标 Indicators	1990	2000	2010	2017	2018
工 资	Wages					
城镇单位就业人员平均工资（元）	Average Wages of Employees in Urban Units (yuan)					105 176
卫 生	Health Care					
医 院（个）	Quantity of Hospitals (unit)	462	459	306	363	364
医 生（万人）	Doctors (10 000 persons)	5.82	4.99	5.13	6.83	7.49
医院床位数（万张）	Quantity of Hospital Beds (10 000 beds)	6.21	7.31	8.48	11.59	12.90
每万人拥有医生（人）	Quantity of Doctors Per 10 000 Persons (person)	44	31	22	28	31
城市建设	Urban Construction					
自来水售水量（亿立方米）	Total Quantity of Water Supply (100 million cu.m)	12.25	19.75	24.44	24.52	24.35
用电量（亿千瓦时）	Electricity Power Consumption (100 million kwh)	264.74	559.51	1 295.87	1 526.77	1 566.66
天然气销售总量（亿立方米）	Sales of Natural Gas (100 million cu.m)		2.16	42.66	77.20	85.44
年末出租车运营总数（辆）	Year-end Operating Taxi Vehicles (vehicle)	11 298	42 943	50 007	46 397	41 881
运营公交车辆数（辆）	Total Number of Operating Public Transportation Vehicles (vehicle)	6 264	17 939	17 455	17 461	17 513
道路长度（公里）	Length of Roads (km)	1 631	6 641	16 687	18 546	18 423
人均公园绿地面积（平方米）	Per Capita Park Green Areas (sq.m)	1.0	4.6	13.0	8.1	8.2
建成区绿化覆盖率（%）	Coverage Rate of Urban Green Areas (%)	12.4	22.2	38.2	39.1	39.4
森林覆盖率（%）	Coverage Rate of Forest(%)	5.5	9.2	12.6	16.2	16.9
环境保护投资相当于上海市生产总值比例（%）	Investment on Environment Protection as Percentage of Gross Domestic Product (%)	2.06	2.97	2.96	3.10	3.00
环境空气质量优良率（%）	Rate of Good Ambient Air Quality (%)		80.8	92.1	75.3	81.1
火灾、交通事故	Fires and Traffic Accidents					
火灾发生数（万起）	Quantity of Fires (10 000 units)	0.21	0.52	0.57	0.42	0.39
火灾损失额（万元）	Loss of Fires (10 000 yuan)	1 868	1 919	22 949	7 823	6 367
交通事故发生数（万起）	Quantity of Traffic Accidents (10 000 units)	0.76	4.13	0.22	0.07	47.28
交通事故损失额（万元）	Loss of Traffic Accidents (10 000 yuan)	1 345	20 391	967	363	27 487

注：本表总量指标中的价值量指标均按当年价格计算。从 2018 年起，交通事故统计口径扩大范围，包含走简易程序处理的事故，以前只包含走一般程序处理的事故。

Note: The data in value terms in the table are calculated at current prices. Since 2018, the scope of traffic accident statistics which only including accidents handled by general procedures before has been expanded, and the accidents handled by simple procedures are also included.

表 1.6　主要年份社会经济主要指标发展速度
GROWTH RATE OF MAJOR SOCIAL AND ECONOMIC INDICATORS IN MAIN YEARS

单位:%

指　标	Indicators	2018 年比下列各年增长 Indicator's Growth Rate Between 2018 and Year Below			
		1990	2000	2010	2017
年末常住人口	Year-end Residnet Population	81.7	50.7	5.3	0.2
上海市生产总值	Gross Domestic Product	15.9 倍	4.3 倍	75.2	6.6
第一产业	Primary Industry	-9.3	-28.5	-22.6	-6.9
第二产业	Secondary Industry	11.5 倍	3.1 倍	34.5	1.8
第三产业	Tertiary Industry	22.6 倍	5.2 倍	1.0 倍	8.7
全社会固定资产投资总额	Total Investment in Fixed Assets	32.6 倍	3.1 倍	50.9	5.2
一般公共预算收入	General Budgetary Revenue	41.6 倍	13.3 倍	1.5 倍	7.0
一般公共预算支出	General Budgetary Expenditure	109.5 倍	12.4 倍	1.5 倍	10.7
农业总产值	Gross Output Value of Agriculture	16.1	-26.6	-20.9	-2.3
工业总产值	Gross Output Value of Industry	20.6 倍	4.3 倍	21.7	1.3
货物运输量	Freight Transportation Volume	3.7 倍	1.2 倍	32.5	10.4
旅客发送量	Passenger Departures	4.6 倍	2.1 倍	59.8	3.1
港口货物吞吐量	Port Freight Throughput	4.2 倍	2.6 倍	11.8	-2.7
社会消费品零售总额	Total Retail Sales of Consumer Goods	36.9 倍	5.8 倍	1.0 倍	7.9
上海关区进出口总额	Total Trade Value Through Customs	55.2 倍	7.9 倍	41.9	10.2
进口额	Imports	46.4 倍	7.6 倍	56.6	12.1
出口额	Exports	63.9 倍	8.1 倍	32.9	8.9
上海市进出口总额	Total Value of Foreign Trade Imports and Exports	68.4 倍	8.4 倍	39.8	8.3
进口额	Imports	145.2 倍	9.5 倍	64.0	9.2
出口额	Exports	37.9 倍	7.2 倍	14.6	7.0
外商直接投资	Foreign Direct Investment				
合同项目	Number of Contracts	26.8 倍	2.1 倍	43.3	41.7
合同金额	Contractual Foreign Capital	124.2 倍	6.3 倍	2.1 倍	16.8
实到金额	Foreign Investment Actually Absorbed	96.7 倍	4.5 倍	55.6	1.7
全市居民人均可支配收入	Per Capita Annual Disposable Income of Residents				8.8
全市居民人均消费支出	Per Capita Annual Consumption Expenditures of Residents				8.9
城镇常住居民人均可支配收入	Per Capita Annual Disposable Income of Urban Households				8.7
城镇常住居民人均消费支出	Per Capita Annual Consumption Expenditures of Urban Households				8.8
农村常住居民人均可支配收入	Per Capita Annual Disposable Income of Rural Households				9.2
农村常住居民人均消费支出	Per Capita Annual Consumption Expenditures of Rural Households				10.4
城市基础设施投资额	Urban Infrastructure Investment	38.5 倍	3.1 倍	24.5	9.3
医　生	Doctors	28.7	50.1	46.0	9.7
普通高等学校在校学生	Student Enrollment of Institutions of Higher Education	3.3 倍	1.3 倍	0.4	0.6

注：本表速度指标中，上海市生产总值及三次产业、工业总产值、农业总产值均按可比价格计算。
Note: The growth rates of the following indicators are calculated by comparable prices: Gross Domestic Product and three industries, gross output value of agriculture and Industry.

表 1.6 续表 continued

单位:%

指 标	Indicators	平均每年增长 Indicators' Average Annual Growth Rate		
		1991~2018	2001~2018	2011~2018
年末常住人口	Year-end Resident Population	2.2	2.3	0.6
上海市生产总值	Gross Domestic Product	10.6	9.7	7.3
第一产业	Primary Industry	-0.3	-1.8	-3.2
第二产业	Secondary Industry	9.4	8.1	3.8
第三产业	Tertiary Industry	12.0	10.7	9.4
全社会固定资产投资总额	Total Investment in Fixed Assets	13.4	8.1	5.3
一般公共预算收入	General Budgetary Revenue	14.3	15.9	12.0
一般公共预算支出	General Budgetary Expenditure	18.3	15.5	12.3
农业总产值	Gross Output Value of Agriculture	0.5	-1.7	-2.9
工业总产值	Gross Output Value of Industry	11.6	9.7	2.5
货物运输量	Freight Transportation Volume	5.7	4.6	3.6
旅客发送量	Passenger Departures	6.4	6.5	6.0
港口货物吞吐量	Port Freight Throughput	6.1	7.3	1.4
社会消费品零售总额	Total Retail Sales of Consumer Goods	13.9	11.2	9.4
上海关区进出口总额	Total Trade Value Through Customs	15.5	12.9	4.5
进口额	Imports	14.8	12.7	5.8
出口额	Exports	16.1	13.1	3.6
上海市进出口总额	Total Value of Foreign Trade Imports and Exports	16.3	13.3	4.3
进口额	Imports	19.5	14.0	6.4
出口额	Exports	14.0	12.4	1.7
外商直接投资	Foreign Direct Investment			
合同项目	Number of Contracts	12.6	6.5	4.6
合同金额	Contractual Foreign Capital	21.2	11.7	15.0
实到金额	Foreign Investment Actually Absorbed	17.8	9.9	5.7
医 生	Doctors	0.9	2.3	4.8
普通高等学校在校学生	Student Enrollment of Institutions of Higher Education	5.3	4.7	0.1
城市基础设施投资额	Urban Infrastructure Investment	14.0	8.2	2.8

表 1.7 主要年份社会经济发展结构指标
STRUCTURAL INDICATORS OF SOCIAL AND ECONOMIC DEVELOPMENT IN MAIN YEARS

单位:%

指 标	Indicators	1990	2000	2010	2017	2018
户籍人口性别结构	Structure of Sex					
男	Male	50.4	50.4	49.8	49.6	49.5
女	Female	49.6	49.6	50.2	50.4	50.5
上海市生产总值产业结构	Industrial Structure of GDP					
第一产业	Primary Industry	4.4	1.6	0.7	0.3	0.3
第二产业	Secondary Industry	64.7	46.4	42.3	30.5	29.8
第三产业	Tertiary Industry	30.9	52.0	57.0	69.2	69.9
上海市生产总值所有制结构	Ownership Structure of GDP					
公有制经济	Public State-owned	95.4	71.4	50.7	48.6	48.6
国有经济	State-owned	71.2	55.1	45.5	45.2	45.3
集体经济	Collective-owned	24.2	16.3	5.2	3.4	3.3
非公有制经济	Non-state-owned	4.6	28.6	49.3	51.4	51.4
全社会固定资产投资所有制结构	Ownership Structure of Total Investment					
国有经济	State-owned	84.7	44.4	42.0	30.3	29.0
非国有经济	Non-State-owned	15.3	55.6	58.0	69.7	71.0
一般公共预算收入	General Budgetary Revenue					
#增值税	Value-added Tax		18.8	13.5	37.0	36.9
营业税	Business Tax		30.9	32.5	-	-
企业所得税	Enterprise Income Tax		20.7	21.1	21.1	21.4
个人所得税	Personal Income Tax		12.1	9.1	10.4	10.8
农业总产值结构	Structure of Gross Output Value of Agriculture					
#种植业	Planting	42.7	41.5	54.0	50.0	51.8
畜牧业	Animal Husbandry	44.4	40.3	22.2	20.9	16.7
渔 业	Fishery	11.8	17.5	18.3	20.0	19.4
货物运输总量结构	Structure of Freight Transportation					
铁 路	Railways	5.5	2.2	1.2	0.5	0.4
公 路	Roadways	38.2	59.1	50.5	40.9	36.9
水 运	Waterways	56.3	38.5	47.9	58.2	62.3
民用航空	Civil Aviation	0.1	0.2	0.5	0.4	0.4
社会消费品零售总额结构	Structure of Retail Sales of Consumer Goods					
吃	Food	42.6	39.8	25.9	20.8	20.3
穿	Clothing	15.7	13.4	13.6	15.4	16.5
用	Articles	41.1	46.0	51.9	58.4	57.4
烧	Fuels	0.6	0.8	8.6	5.5	5.8
上海市出口总额结构	Structure of Exports					
#一般贸易	General Trade		40.1	35.0	44.0	46.4
加工贸易	Processing Trade		58.3	55.5	40.9	38.3
外商直接投资实到金额投资方式结构	Foreign Direct Investment Structure of Foreign Investment Actually Absorbed					
#合资企业	Joint Ventures	61.0	40.9	16.0	17.4	19.6
合作企业	Coopraive Enterprises	37.9	9.5	1.5	0.9	0.1
独资企业	Sole-foreign Enterprises	1.1	49.6	81.6	76.3	75.8

表 1.7 续表 continued

单位:%

	指 标 Indicators	1990	2000	2010	2017	2018
金融机构境内存款结构	Structure of Domestic Deposits of Financial Institutions					
住户存款	Household Deposits				24.0	24.8
非金融企业存款	Non Financial Enterprise Deposits				45.9	46.6
广义政府存款	General Government Deposits				14.1	13.8
非银行业金融机构存款	Deposits of Non Banking Financial Institutions				16.0	14.8
金融机构境内贷款结构	Structure of Domestic Loans of Financial Institutions					
#住户贷款	Household Loans				31.2	32.1
非金融企业及机关团体贷款	Loans of Non Financial Enterprise and Non-profit Institutions				68.3	67.4
非银行业金融机构贷款	Loans of Non Banking Financial Institutions				0.5	0.5
在校学生结构	Structure of Students Enrollment					
大学生	University and College Students	7.1	12.5	28.5	27.5	27.1
中学生	Secondary Students	28.3	43.9	32.8	30.5	31.0
小学生	Primary Students	64.6	43.6	38.7	42.0	41.9
全市居民消费支出构成	Consumption Structure of Residents					
#食品烟酒	Food, Cigarettes and Liquors				25.1	24.7
衣 着	Clothing				4.4	4.7
居 住	Residence				34.5	32.8
生活用品及服务	Living Goods and Services				4.6	4.8
交通通信	Transportation and Communication				10.2	11.3
教育文化娱乐	Education, Culture and Entertainment				11.8	11.6
城镇常住居民消费支出构成	Consumption Structure of Urban Residents					
#食品烟酒	Food, Cigarettes and Liquors				24.7	24.1
衣 着	Clothing				4.3	4.7
居 住	Residence				34.9	33.4
生活用品及服务	Living Goods and Services				4.6	4.8
交通通信	Transportation and Communication				10.0	11.1
教育文化娱乐	Education, Culture and Entertainment				12.0	11.9
农村常住居民消费支出构成	Consumption Structure of Rural Residents					
#食品烟酒	Food, Cigarettes and Liquors				33.8	–
衣 着	Clothing				5.1	–
居 住	Residence				26.1	–
生活用品及服务	Living Goods and Services				5.2	–
交通通信	Transportation and Communication				13.1	–
教育文化娱乐	Education, Culture and Entertainment				6.7	–
卫生机构数结构	Structure of Health Care Institutions					
#医 院	Hospitals	6.0	10.4	9.4	7.1	6.9
卫生技术人员结构	Structure of Medical Professionals					
#医 生	Doctors	49.2	46.6	37.9	36.3	36.3
护 士	Nurses	27.6	34.4	41.3	44.7	45.3

①2015 年起，存贷款分类进行了调整，故与往年数据不可比。
②2013 年起，卫生机构数中新增村卫生室数据，故与往年数据不可比。
③2018 年住户调查进行样本轮换，自 2018 年一季度起，本市不发布农村常住居民收支结构数据。
❶The statistic of deposits and Loans has been adjusted since 2015, so the data are not comparable with the previous years.
❷The Number of Health Care Institutions has contained the data of village health rooms since 2013, so it can not be comparable with the previous years.
❸Sample rotation was carried out in household survey in 2018. Since the first quarter of 2018, the data of income and expenditure structure of rural residents are not released.

表 1.8 国民经济主要指标比上年增长（1978~2018）
GROWTH RATE OF MAJOR NATIONAL ECONOMIC INDICATORS OVER PRECEDING YEAR

单位:%

年 份 Year	上海市 生产总值 Gross Domestic Product	一般公共 预算收入 General Budgetary Revenue	一般公共 预算支出 General Budgetary Expenditure	工 业 总产值 Gross Output Value of Industry	全社会固定资产 投资总额 Total Investment in Fixed Assets
1978	15.8	14.6	51.4	12.1	55.1
1979	7.4	2.1	4.0	8.6	27.5
1980	8.4	1.2	-29.1	6.5	27.7
1981	5.6	-0.2	-0.6	3.7	20.2
1982	7.2	-3.6	8.5	4.7	30.7
1983	7.8	-6.9	8.3	7.0	6.5
1984	11.6	4.8	35.4	9.9	21.5
1985	13.4	12.4	51.9	13.5	28.5
1986	4.4	-2.6	28.2	5.5	23.9
1987	7.5	-5.8	-8.9	6.7	26.8
1988	10.1	-4.3	22.3	10.5	31.7
1989	3.0	3.3	11.3	3.0	-12.4
1990	3.5	0.1	3.1	4.0	5.7
1991	7.1	5.1	13.9	14.1	13.7
1992	14.8	5.7	10.4	20.2	38.4
1993	15.1	30.6	36.1	20.1	83.0
1994	14.5	-27.7	52.3	18.2	71.8
1995	15.0	29.6	36.0	17.4	42.6
1996	13.1	26.9	27.9	15.5	21.9
1997	12.8	22.1	25.2	14.5	1.3
1998	10.3	11.3	12.1	7.8	-0.6
1999	10.4	10.1	13.7	10.5	-5.5
2000	11.0	15.3	14.0	13.5	0.7
2001	10.5	24.6	16.6	16.4	6.7
2002	11.4	16.1	20.9	14.6	9.6
2003	12.3	24.9	25.6	31.4	12.1
2004	14.3	24.5	26.6	20.3	25.8
2005	11.5	28.7	19.0	13.9	14.8
2006	12.8	11.6	9.2	13.9	10.8
2007	15.2	31.4	21.4	15.7	13.6
2008	9.7	13.3	18.9	8.1	8.3
2009	8.4	7.7	15.3	3.2	9.2
2010	10.2	13.1	10.5	22.9	0.8
2011	8.3	19.4	18.5	6.6	0.3
2012	7.5	9.2	6.9	-0.3	3.7
2013	7.9	9.8	8.2	4.3	7.5
2014	7.1	11.6	8.7	1.6	6.5
2015	7.0	13.3	19.5	-0.5	5.6
2016	6.8	10.3	11.7	0.7	6.3
2017	6.9	9.1	9.1	6.5	7.3
2018	6.6	7.0	10.7	1.3	5.2

表 1.8 续表 continued

单位:%

年 份 Year	社会消费品零售总额 Total Retail Sales of Consumer Goods	上海市进出口总额 Total Value of Foreign Trade Import and Export	# 出口总额 Export	外商直接投资合同金额 Contracted Foreign Direct Investment	外商直接投资实到金额 Foreign Investment Actually Absorbed	港口货物吞吐量 Port Freight Throughput
1978	9.8	30.4	30.3			30.6
1979	26.2	28.2	27.0			5.0
1980	17.8	16.2	16.1			1.6
1981	10.3	-7.9	-10.8	1.0 倍	…	-1.7
1982	1.2	-6.2	-5.3	1.8 倍	…	7.7
1983	12.1	6.3	1.2	1.8 倍	2.7 倍	2.4
1984	22.9	6.3	-1.7	3.1 倍	1.5 倍	9.5
1985	40.1	17.6	-6.3	56.4	1.2 倍	12.2
1986	13.5	0.6	6.6	-68.9	58.1	11.6
1987	14.4	15.2	16.1	35.8	1.2 倍	1.8
1988	31.3	20.8	10.7	28.7	71.7	3.8
1989	12.0	8.3	9.3	6.6	15.9	9.6
1990	0.7	-5.3	5.7	20.9	-58.1	-4.4
1991	14.4	8.2	7.9	30.4	-1.1	5.2
1992	21.7	21.3	14.2	5.7 倍	6.2 倍	11.0
1993	45.4	30.5	12.6	1.0 倍	84.1	8.0
1994	23.5	24.6	23.0	42.3	39.4	-5.8
1995	25.9	19.9	27.5	0.2	0.6	-0.1
1996	19.7	17.0	14.3	8.4	45.1	-1.0
1997	14.1	11.2	11.2	-8.4	2.0	…
1998	11.0	26.6	8.4	9.9	-24.3	-0.1
1999	8.1	23.2	17.7	-29.8	-16.2	13.7
2000	8.3	41.7	35.0	55.7	3.7	9.7
2001	8.1	11.3	9.0	15.4	39.0	8.1
2002	9.3	19.3	16.0	43.4	14.5	19.4
2003	9.1	54.7	51.2	23.5	30.1	19.8
2004	10.5	42.4	51.6	12.6	11.8	19.8
2005	12.1	16.5	23.4	18.3	4.7	16.9
2006	13.3	22.1	25.2	5.4	3.8	21.3
2007	14.8	24.4	26.7	2.0	11.4	4.5
2008	18.2	13.8	17.7	15.1	27.3	3.6
2009	13.9	-13.8	-16.2	-22.3	4.5	1.8
2010	18.7	32.8	27.4	15.1	5.5	10.4
2011	16.2	18.6	16.0	31.3	13.3	11.4
2012	9.1	-0.2	-1.4	11.1	20.5	1.1
2013	9.1	1.1	-1.2	11.6	10.5	5.5
2014	8.7	5.6	3.0	26.8	8.3	-2.6
2015	8.9	-3.2	-6.3	86.5	1.6	-5.0
2016	8.0	-3.4	-6.4	-13.5	0.3	-2.2
2017	7.3	9.7	5.6	-21.2	-8.1	6.9
2018	7.9	8.3	7.0	16.8	1.7	-2.7

表1.9　上海社会经济主要指标占全国比重(2018)
PERCENTAGE OF THE NATIONAL TOTAL OF SHANGHAI'S MAJOR SOCIAL AND ECONOMIC INDICATORS

指　标	Indicators	全　国 Country	上　海 Shanghai	上海占全国比重(%) Percentage of the National Total(%)
生产总值(亿元)	Gross Domestic Product (100 million yuan)	900 309.50	32 679.87	3.6
#第一产业	Primary Industry	64 734.00	104.37	0.2
第二产业	Secondary Industry	366 000.90	9 732.54	2.7
第三产业	Tertiary Industry	469 574.60	22 842.96	4.9
#工　业	Industry	305 160.20	8 694.95	2.8
港口货物吞吐量(亿吨)	Port Freight Throughput (100 millions tons)	133.44	7.30	5.5
社会消费品零售总额(亿元)	Total Retail Sales of Consumer Goods (100 million yuan)	380 986.90	12 668.69	3.3
上海关区进出口总额(亿美元)	Total Trade Value Through Customs (100 million USD)	46 224.20	9 715.23	21.0
进口额	Imports	21 357.30	4 090.77	19.2
出口额	Exports	24 866.80	5 624.46	22.6
外商直接投资实到金额(亿美元)	Foreign Direct Investment Actually Absorbed (100 million USD)	1 349.70	173.00	12.8
国际旅游入境人数(万人次)	Number of International Tourists (10 000 person-times)	14 119.83	893.71	6.3
研究与试验发展经费支出(亿元)	Expenditures on R&D (100 million yuan)	19 657.00	1 359.20	6.9
图书出版量(亿册)	Books Published (100 million copies)	95	4.81	5.1
期　刊(亿册)	Periodicals (100 million copies)	24	0.85	3.5
报纸出版量(亿份)	Newspapers Published (100 million copies)	340	8.17	2.4
医　生(万人)	Doctors (10 000 persons)	358	7.49	2.1
医院床位数(万张)	Beds in Hospitals (10 000 beds)	656	12.90	2.0

注：全国港口货物吞吐量为沿海规模以上主要港口货物吞吐量数据。
Note: National Port freight throughput refers to freight throughput of major coastal ports above the set scale.

表 1.10　各时期社会经济主要指标
MAJOR SOCIAL AND ECONOMIC INDICATORS OF EACH PERIOD

时　期	Period	上海市生产总值（亿元）Gross Domestic Product (100 million yuan)	其中 of which 第一产业 Primary Industry	第二产业 Secondary Industry	第三产业 Tertiary Industry	一般公共预算收入（亿元）General Budgetary Revenue (100 million yuan)
"一五"时期	"First Five-year Plan" Period	293.26	12.56	163.89	116.81	14.93
"二五"时期	"Second Five-year Plan" Period	568.99	21.03	412.70	135.26	304.28
1963～1965		304.94	17.28	220.81	66.85	172.51
"三五"时期	"Third Five-year Plan" Period	657.06	37.64	487.88	131.54	374.19
"四五"时期	"Fourth Five-year Plan" Period	918.76	42.75	708.84	167.17	633.79
"五五"时期	"Fifth Five-year Plan" Period	1 309.61	49.26	1 004.23	256.12	797.56
"六五"时期	"Sixth Five-year Plan" Period	1 871.24	74.20	1 349.98	447.06	846.92
"七五"时期	"Seventh Five-year Plan" Period	3 162.79	132.52	2 105.23	925.04	846.96
"八五"时期	"Eighth Five-year Plan" Period	8 036.26	213.47	4 709.33	3 113.46	1 006.06
"九五"时期	"Ninth Five-year Plan" Period	19 311.48	365.76	9 526.30	9 419.42	1 962.85
"十五"时期	"Tenth Five-year Plan" Period	35 345.98	412.41	16 733.40	18 200.17	4 792.94
"十一五"时期	"Eleventh Five-year Program" Period	70 388.13	542.80	30 459.14	39 386.19	11 499.22
"十二五"时期	"Twelfth Five-year Program" Period	112 089.49	651.84	41 033.53	70 404.12	21 674.31

表 1.10 续表 continued

时　期	Period	一般公共预算支出（亿元）General Budgetary Expenditure (100 million yuan)	工业总产值（亿元）Gross Output Value of Industry (100 million yuan)	全社会固定资产投资总额（亿元）Total Investment in Fixed Assets (100 million yuan)	上海市出口总额（亿美元）Total Exports Value (100 million USD)	社会消费品零售总额（亿元）Retail Sales of Consumer Goods (100 million yuan)
"一五"时期	"First Five-year Plan" Period	12.25	512.03	19.29	17.46	121.02
"二五"时期	"Second Five-year Plan" Period	60.79	1 069.50	55.60	31.00	145.82
1963～1965		19.28	596.63	20.29	20.12	79.50
"三五"时期	"Third Five-year Plan" Period	39.41	1 334.94	34.77	43.08	153.86
"四五"时期	"Fourth Five-year Plan" Period	86.78	1 894.01	95.79	92.86	200.62
"五五"时期	"Fifth Five-year Plan" Period	111.30	2 550.91	151.44	150.33	302.07
"六五"时期	"Sixth Five-year Plan" Period	138.52	3 509.15	412.74	180.08	576.32
"七五"时期	"Seventh Five-year Plan" Period	327.68	6 498.13	1 020.34	226.96	1 383.16
"八五"时期	"Eighth Five-year Plan" Period	775.11	17 308.90	3 994.67	403.31	3 408.52
"九五"时期	"Ninth Five-year Plan" Period	2 421.50	29 776.04	9 620.86	880.57	7 874.26
"十五"时期	"Tenth Five-year Plan" Period	5 762.87	59 716.74	13 261.11	2 724.27	12 261.12
"十一五"时期	"Eleventh Five-year Program" Period	12 925.94	124 634.89	23 804.15	7 495.49	23 225.42
"十二五"时期	"Twelfth Five-year Program" Period	24 001.72	168 202.99	28 338.39	10 280.86	43 018.18

表 1.11　各时期社会经济主要指标平均增长率
GROWTH RATE OF MAJOR SOCIAL AND ECONOMIC INDICATORS OF EACH PERIOD

单位:%

时　期	Period	上海市生产总值 Gross Domestic Product	其中 of which 第一产业 Primary Industry	第二产业 Secondary Industry	第三产业 Tertiary Industry	一般公共预算收入 General Budgetary Revenue
“一五”时期	“First Five-year Plan” Period	13.8	3.3	18.4	8.3	12.6
“二五”时期	“Second Five-year Plan” Period	1.6	1.3	4.2	-3.1	57.2
1963~1965		17.0	11.6	21.8	5.6	12.3
“三五”时期	“Third Five-year Plan” Period	8.7	3.3	9.7	5.6	9.7
“四五”时期	“Fourth Five-year Plan” Period	6.6	-1.6	7.2	6.2	6.4
“五五”时期	“Fifth Five-year Plan” Period	8.4	0.9	8.6	8.6	5.1
“六五”时期	“Sixth Five-year Plan” Period	9.1	4.3	8.3	12.3	1.1
“七五”时期	“Seventh Five-year Plan” Period	5.7	1.2	5.0	7.9	-1.6
“八五”时期	“Eighth Five-year Plan” Period	13.3	1.4	14.0	13.0	6.0
“九五”时期	“Ninth Five-year Plan” Period	11.5	3.4	9.8	15.5	17.0
“十五”时期	“Tenth Five-year Plan” Period	12.0	-1.4	13.1	11.3	23.6
“十一五”时期	“Eleventh Five-year Program” Period	11.2	-0.1	10.2	12.3	14.9
“十二五”时期	“Twelfth Five-year Program” Period	7.6	-0.9	4.3	9.8	13.9

表 1.11 续表 continued

单位:%

时　期	Period	一般公共预算支出 General Budgetary Expenditure	工业总产值 Gross Output Value of Industry	全社会固定资产投资总额 Total Investment in Fixed Assets	上海市出口总额 Total Exports Value	社会消费品零售总额 Retail Sales of Consumer Goods
“一五”时期	“First Five-year Plan” Period	12.3	14.5	23.1	30.6	5.6
“二五”时期	“Second Five-year Plan” Period	0.6	4.9	26.5	4.2	1.2
1963~1965		25.2	18.8	31.4	11.4	-0.1
“三五”时期	“Third Five-year Plan” Period	11.2	10.2	-3.6	2.5	3.3
“四五”时期	“Fourth Five-year Plan” Period	15.5	7.5	19.4	20.7	8.4
“五五”时期	“Fifth Five-year Plan” Period	-6.3	7.6	-2.4	14.0	11.0
“六五”时期	“Sixth Five-year Plan” Period	19.2	7.7	20.6	-4.7	16.6
“七五”时期	“Seventh Five-year Plan” Period	10.4	5.9	18.7	9.6	14.0
“八五”时期	“Eighth Five-year Plan” Period	28.8	18.0	45.4	16.8	25.8
“九五”时期	“Ninth Five-year Plan” Period	18.4	12.3	6.2	17.0	12.2
“十五”时期	“Tenth Five-year Plan” Period	21.7	19.2	11.9	29.0	9.8
“十一五”时期	“Eleventh Five-year Program” Period	14.7	12.6	10.0	14.8	15.7
“十二五”时期	“Twelfth Five-year Program” Period	13.4	2.3	3.9	1.7	10.4

表 1.12 新中国成立 70 年上海经济社会主要指标
MAJOR SOCIAL AND ECONOMIC INDICATORS OF SHANGHAI OF THE 70 YEARS SINCE THE FOUNDING OF NEW CHINA

指 标	Indicators	1978
上海市生产总值(亿元)	Gross Domestic Product (100 million yuan)	272.81
#第三产业	Tertiary Industry	50.76
第三产业增加值占 GDP 比重(%)	Proportion of Add Value of Tertiary Industry to GDP (%)	18.6
人均生产总值(元)	Per Capita Gross Domestic Product (yuan)	2 485
人均生产总值(美元)	Per Capita Gross Domestic Product (USD)	1 445
一般公共预算收入(亿元)	General Budgetary Revenue (100 million yuan)	169.22
一般公共预算支出(亿元)	General Budgetary Expenditure (100 million yuan)	26.01
全社会固定资产投资总额(亿元)	Total Investment in Fixed Assets (100 million yuan)	27.91
#房地产开发	Investment in Real Estate	
城市基础设施投资(亿元)	Urban Infrastructure Investment (100 million yuan)	
批发零售业商品销售总额(亿元)	Sales of Commodities of Wholesale and Retail (100 million yuan)	303.43
社会消费品零售总额(亿元)	Total Retail Sales of Consumer Goods (100 million yuan)	54.10
关区进出口总额(亿美元)	Total Trade Value Through Customs (100 million USD)	
进口额	Imports	
出口额	Exports	
上海市进出口总额(亿美元)	Total Value of Foreign Trade Imports and Exports (100 million USD)	30.26
进口额	Imports	1.33
出口额	Exports	28.93
服务贸易进出口(亿美元)	Total Value of Service Trade Imports and Exports (100 million USD)	
外商直接投资实际到位金额(亿美元)	Foreign Investment Actually Absorbed (100 million USD)	
国际旅游入境人数(万人次)	Number of Overseas Tourists Through Shanghai Custom (10 000 persons-times)	24.02
国际标准集装箱吞吐量(万 TEU)	International Container Throughput Capacity (10 000 TEU)	
机场旅客吞吐量(万人次)	Passenger Turnover (10 000 person-times)	
民航货物运输量(万吨)	Freight Traffic Volume of Civil Aviation (10 000 tons)	1
邮轮旅客吞吐量(万人次)	Cruise Passenger Throughput (10 000 persons)	

1990	1992	2000	2010	2012	2017	2018
781.66	1 114.32	4 812.15	17 436.85	20 588.98	30 632.99	32 679.87
241.82	402.77	2 503.54	9 942.25	12 361.79	21 191.54	22 842.96
30.9	36.1	52.0	57.0	60.1	69.2	69.9
5 911	8 208	30 307	77 275	86 969	126 634	134 982
1 236	1 488	3 661	11 415	13 778	18 756	20 398
166.99	185.56	497.96	2 873.58	3 743.71	6 642.26	7 108.15
75.56	94.99	622.84	3 302.89	4 184.02	7 547.62	8 351.54
227.08	357.38	1 869.67	5 317.67	5 254.38	7 246.60	–
8.16	12.71	566.17	1 980.68	2 381.36	3 856.53	4 033.18
47.22	84.35	449.90	1 497.46	1 038.61	1 705.22	–
1 305.41	1 802.53	7 474.81	48 659.55	70 021.87	113 133.19	119 461.28
333.86	464.82	1 865.28	6 186.58	7 840.40	11 745.96	12 668.69
172.89	251.45	1 093.11	6 846.45	8 013.10	8 814.67	9 715.23
86.27	131.81	477.39	2 613.05	3 101.54	3 647.91	4 090.77
86.62	119.64	615.72	4 233.40	4 911.56	5 166.76	5 624.46
74.31	97.57	547.10	3 688.69	4 367.58	4 761.23	5 156.49
21.10	32.02	293.56	1 880.85	2 299.51	2 824.42	3 084.79
53.21	65.55	253.54	1 807.84	2 068.07	1 936.81	2 071.70
		79.10	871.42	1 358.22	1 954.70	1 975.03
1.77	12.59	31.60	111.21	151.85	170.08	173.00
89.30	125.31	181.40	851.12	800.40	873.01	893.71
45.60	73.00	561.20	2 906.90	3 252.94	4 023.31	4 201.02
			7 187.74	7 870.84	11 188.52	11 763.43
13	19	88	372.31	337.96	423.18	417.57
				35.03	297.29	275.29

表 1.12 续表 continued

指 标	Indicators	1978
工业总产值(亿元)	Gross Output Value of Industry (100 million yuan)	514.01
用电量(亿千瓦时)	Power Consumption (100 million kwh)	147.09
研究与试验发展经费支出(亿元)	Expenditures on R&D (100 million yuan)	1.32
研究与试验发展经费支出相当于生产总值比例(%)	R&D Expenditure as Percentage of Gross Domestic Product (%)	0.48
发明专利授权量(件)	Patent Certified for Inventions (item)	
技术合同成交额(亿元)	Contracted Value of Technological Contracts (100 million yuan)	
轨道交通运营线路长度(公里)	Length of Operation Lines of Railway Communication	
轨道交通客运总量(亿人次)	Passenger Volume of Railway Communication (100 million person-times)	
常住人口(万人)	Year-end Resident Population (10 000 persons)	1 104.00
从业人员(万人)	Employees (10 000 persons)	698.32
职工工资总额(亿元)	Total Wages of Staff and Workers (100 million yuan)	28.12
职工平均工资(元)	Average Annual Wages of Staff and Workers (yuan)	672
城镇单位就业人员平均工资(元)	Average Wages of Employees in Urban Units	
城镇居民人均住房建筑面积(平方米)	Construction Area per Capita of Urban Residents (sq.m)	
居民消费价格指数(上年=100)	Overall Residents Consumer Price Index (preceding year=100)	100.5
普通高等学校研究生毕业数(万人)	Postgraduates of Institutions of Higher Education (10 000 persons)	9
电影放映场次(万场)	Showing of Films (10 000 times)	35
公共图书馆总藏量(万册、件)	Collection of Public Libraries (10 000 copies)	1 064
博物馆、纪念馆参观人次(万人次)	Visiting Persong-times of Museums and Memorials (10 000 person-times)	56
每万人口医院床位数(张)	Hospital Beds Per 10 000 Persons (bed)	42
环境保护投资(亿元)	Investment on Enviromnent Protection (100 million yuan)	
环境保护投资相当于 GDP 比例(%)	Investment on Environment Protection as Percentage of Gross Domestic Product (%)	
建成区绿化覆盖率(%)	Coverage Rate of Urban Green Areas (%)	8.2
森林覆盖率(%)	Coverage Rate of Forest (%)	
户籍人口期望寿命(岁)	Life Expectancy of Registered Population (year)	73.35

1990	1992	2000	2010	2012	2017	2018
1 642.75	2 429.96	7 022.98	31 038.57	33 186.41	36 094.36	36 451.84
264.74	317.38	559.42	1 295.87	1 353.45	1 526.77	1 566.66
10.13	17.48	76.73	481.70	679.46	1 205.21	1 359.20
1.30	1.57	1.59	2.76	3.31	3.93	4.16
99	98	304	6 867	11 379	20 681	21 331
	15.25	73.90	525.45	588.52	867.53	1 303.20
			452.57	468.19	666.40	704.91
			18.84	22.76	35.38	37.10
1 334.00	1 365.00	1 608.60	2 302.66	2 380.43	2 418.33	2 423.78
787.72	806.91	828.35	1 090.76	1 115.50	1 372.65	1 375.66
146.78	217.21	614.53	3 018.55	5 347.99	10 046.46	
2 917	4 273	15 420	46 757	56 300	85 582	
						105 176
			32.6	33.9	36.7	37.0
106.3	110.0	102.5	103.1	102.8	101.7	101.6
2 953	2 262	5 435	26 843	33 189	40 425	42 462
38	29	18	55	96	337	403
1 586	1 642	5 500	6 809	7 202	7 773	7 894
53	59	165	1 114	1 521	2 268	2 216
47	47	45	37	38	48	53
		141.91	507.54	570.49	923.53	989.19
2.06	1.36	2.97	2.96	2.83	3.10	3.00
12.4	13.2	22.2	38.2	38.3	39.1	39.4
5.5	6.2	9.2	12.6	12.6	16.2	16.9
75.46	75.97	78.77	82.13	82.41	83.37	83.63

表 1.13 主要年份人大情况
BASIC STATISTICS OF SHANGHAI MUNICIPAL PEOPLE'S CONGRESS IN MAIN YEARS

类 别	Types	2000	2010	2017	2018
全国人大代表人数(人)	Quantity of National Congress (person)	68	66	58	58
#女 性	Female	17	17	13	13
全国人大代表提出议案(件)	Proposals Offered by National Congress Representations (case)		21	28	21
市人大代表人数(人)	Quantity of Municipal CongressRepresentatives (person)	865	864	853	856
#女 性	Female	203	244	283	282
市人大常委会组成人员数(人)	Quantity of Municipal Standing Committee (person)	65	64	65	59
#女 性	Female	13	9	13	11
市人大代表提出议案(件)	Proposals Offered by Municipal CongressRepresentatives (case)		78	24	39
区县人大代表人数(人)	Quantity of District Level Congress Representatives (person)	4 944	4 667	4 494	4 449
#女 性	Female	1 451	1 454	1 704	1 775
区县人大常委人数(人)	Quantity of District Level Standing Committee (person)	432	414	544	534
#女 性	Female	67	94	190	178

注：本表数据由市人大代表工作委员会提供。
Note: Data in this Table are provided by Shanghai Committee of People's Congress.

表 1.14 主要年份政协情况
BASIC STATISTICS OF SHANGHAI MUNICIPAL PEOPLE'S POLITICAL CONSULTATIVE CONFERENCE IN MAIN YEARS

类 别	Types	2000	2010	2017	2018
全国政协委员人数(人)	Quantity of National Commissary (person)	104	109	103	109
#女 性	Female	20	18	17	24
市政协委员人数(人)	Quantity of Municipal Commissary (person)	729	817	813	834
#女 性	Female	120	168	188	216
市政协常委人数(人)	Quantity of Municipal Standing Committee (person)	121	132	156	156
#女 性	Female	20	24	32	33
市政协委员提出提案(件)	Proposals Offered by Municipal Commissary (case)	1 197	944	696	737
区县政协委员人数(人)	Quantity of District Level Commissary (person)	4 802	5 280	4 605	4 601
#女 性	Female	1 230	1 459	1 431	1 612
区县政协常委人数(人)	Quantity of District Level Standing Committee (person)	707	709	678	779
#女 性	Female	174	154	203	280

注：本表数据由市政协提供。
Note: Data in this table are provided by Shanghai Municipal People's Political Consultative Conference.

上/海/统/计/年/鉴

主要统计指标解释

■ 行政区划

指国家对行政区域的划分。根据宪法规定，我国的行政区域划分如下：(1)全国分为省、自治区、直辖市；(2)省、自治区分为自治州、县、自治县、市；(3)自治州分为县、自治县、市；(4)县、自治县分为乡、民族乡、镇；(5)直辖市和较大的市分为区、县；(6)国家在必要时设立的特别行政区。

■ 气　候

指地球与大气之间长期能量交换与质量交换所形成的一种自然环境状态，它是多种因素综合作用的结果。气候既是人类生活和生产的环境要素之一，又是供给人类生活和生产的重要资源。气温、降水、湿度等气象要素的多年平均值是用来描述一个地区气候状况的主要参数，而各种气象要素某年、某月的平均值(或总量)则可以反映出该时期天气气候状况的重要特征。

■ 气　温

指空气的温度，一般以摄氏度(℃)为单位表示。气象观测的温度表是放在离地面约1.5米处通风良好的百叶箱里测量的，因此，通常说的气温指的是离地面1.5米处百叶箱中的温度。其统计计算方法为：

月平均气温是将全月各日的平均气温相加，除以该月的天数而得。

年平均气温是将12个月的月平均气温累加后除以12而得。

■ 降水量

指从天空降落到地面的液态或固态(经融化后)水，未经蒸发、渗透、流失而在地面上积聚的深度。其统计计算方法为：

月降水量是将全月各日的降水量累加而得。

年降水量是将12个月的月降水量累加而得。

■ 日照时间

指太阳实际照射地面的时间。其统计方法与降水量相同。

■ 国民经济行业分类

《国民经济行业分类》国家标准于1984年首次发布，1994年对其进行了第一次修订，2002年为第二次修订，2011年为第三次修订。

本年鉴的行业分类除特别说明外均使用2011年修订的行业分类标准。

2011年新行业分类标准立足我国社会经济发展的实际情况，确保国家经济结构和产业结构的完整性、科学性和可观察性；确保国家统计、核算真实的反映我国的经济结构和产业结构。此次修订不仅坚持行业分类的修订原则和国际惯例，同时顺应《国务院关于加快培育和发展战略性新兴产业的决定》要求，准确反映一定时期内国民经济行业的构成状况。

此次修订主要调整如下：

1.调整部门门类名称和顺序。如将“信息传输、计算机服务和软件业”更名为“信息传输、软件业和信息技术服务业”，将“科学研究、技术服务和地址勘查业”更名为“科学研究和技术服务业”，将“居民服务和其他服务业”更名为“居民服务、修理和其他服务业”，将“卫生、社会保障和社会福利业”更名为“卫生和社会工作”。但整体行业门类的数目保持不变，保证了行业分类的延续性。

2.为与联合国分类相对应以及反映我国产业的状况，行业大类由95个调整为96个，新增了“开采辅助活动”、“汽车制造业”、“金属制造、机械和设备修理业”、“房屋建筑业”、“互联网和相关服务”、“机动车、电子产品和日用品修理业”等6大类，减少了“建筑装修业”、“城市公共交通业”、“其他金融活动”、“地址勘查业”等4大类，合并“橡胶制品业”和“塑料制品业”为一个大类。

3.为反映我国日益发展的互联网、信息技术、金融、影视娱乐等产业，行业中类新增了“互联网接入及相关服务”、“信息系统集成服务”、“化纤织造及印染精加工”等中类，取消了“猪的饲养”、“纺织制成品制造”等中类。

4.为与联合国ISIC Rev.4的小类进行转换同时反映我国新兴产业，行业小类增加了“稻谷种植”、“食用菌种植”“葡萄的种植”等小类，取消了“常用有色金属压延加工”、“制帽”、“车辆、飞机及工程机械轮胎制造”等小类。

■ 各个计划时期

表内所用各个“时期”代表的年份如下：恢复时期为1950到1952年；第一个五年计划时期(简称“一五”时期)为1953到1957年；第二个五年计划时期(简称“二五”时

主要统计指标解释

期）为1958到1962年；第三个五年计划时期（简称“三五”时期）为1966到1970年；第四个五年计划时期（简称“四五”时期）为1971到1975年；第五个五年计划时期（简称“五五”时期）为1976到1980年；第六个五年计划时期（简称“六五”时期）为1981到1985年；第七个五年计划时期（简称“七五”时期）为1986到1990年；第八个五年计划时期（简称“八五”时期）为1991到1995年；第九个五年计划时期（简称“九五”时期）为1996到2000年；第十个五年计划时期（简称“十五”时期）为2001到2005年；第十一个五年规划时期（简称“十一五”时期）为2006到2010年；第十二个五年规划时期（简称“十二五”时期）为2011到2015年。

■ 指　数

指数是一种表明社会经济现象动态的相对数。运用指数可以测定不能直接相加和直接对比的社会经济现象的总动态；可以分析社会经济现象总变动中各因素变动的影响程度；可以研究总平均指标变动中各组标志水平和总体结构变动的作用。它是在把各个年份的产值换算成可比价格的基础上，根据定基指数等于相应各个环比指数的连乘积这个换算关系计算出来的。

本年鉴所列的上海市生产总值、工业总产值、农业总产值等指标增长速度，就是分别使用上海市生产总值指数、工业总产值指数、农业总产值指数直接计算的。

■ 平均每年增长速度

在我国计算平均增长速度有两种方法。一种是习惯上经常使用的“水平法”，又称几何平均法，是以间隔期最后一年的水平同基期水平对比来计算平均每年增长（或下降）速度；另一种是“累计法”，又称代数平均法或方程法，是以间隔期内各年水平的总和同基期水平对比来计算平均每年增长（或下降）速度。

在一般正常情况下，两种方法计算的平均每年增长速度比较接近。但在经济发展不平衡，出现大起大落时，两种方法计算的结果差别较大。

本年鉴内所列的平均每年增长速度，均用“水平法”计算。从某年到某年平均增长速度的年份，均不包括基期年在内。如1991-2009年平均增长速度是以1990年为基期计算的，余类推。

SHANGHAI STATISTICAL YEARBOOK

EXPLANATORY NOTES TO MAJOR STATISTICAL INDICATORS

□ Administrative Division

Administrative Division refers to the division of administrative areas by the state. The Constitution of the People's Republic of China stipulates that the administrative areas in China are divided as: 1) The whole country is divided into provinces, autonomous regions and municipalities directly under the central government; 2) Provinces and autonomous regions are divided into autonomous prefectures, counties, autonomous counties and cities; 3) Autonomous prefectures are divided into counties, autonomous counties and cities; 4) Counties and autonomous counties are divided into townships, nationality townships and towns; 5) Municipalities and large cities are divided into districts and counties, 6) The state shall, when necessary, establish special administrative regions.

□ Climate

Climate refers to the natural environmental status formed by the long- term exchange of energy and mass between the earth and the air, and is the results of interaction of many factors. Climate is both one of the environment factors and the important resources for the living and production activities of the human being. The average values across several years of meteorological factors such as temperature, rainfall and humidity are used as important parameters to describe the climate of a region, while the average values (or total values) of a given year or month of meteorological factors reflect the key characteristics of climate for that period of time.

□ Temperature

Temperature refers to the air temperature. It often uses centigrade as the unit. The thermometry used for weather observation is put in a breezy shutter, which is 1.5 meters high from the ground. Therefore, the commonly used temperature refers to the temperature in the breezy shutter 1.5 meters away from the ground. The calculation method is as follows:

Monthly average temperature is the summation of average daily temperature of one month divided by the actual days of that particular month. Annual average temperature is the summation of monthly average of a year divided by 12 months.

□ Volume of Precipitation

Volume of Precipitation refers to the deepness of liquid state or solid state (thawed) water falling from the sky to the ground that has not been evaporated, infiltrated or run off. The calculation method is as follows:

Monthly precipitation is the summation of daily precipitation of a month.

Annual precipitation is the summation of 12 months precipitation of a year.

□ Sunshine Hours

Sunshine Hours refer to the actual hours of sun irradiating the earth. The calculation method is the same as that of the precipitation.

□ Classification of the Sectors of the National Economy

The national standard of <Classification of the Sectors of the National Economy> was first released in 1984, and was revised for the first time in 1994, for the second revision in 2002, and for the third revision in 2011.

Unless otherwise stated, the industry classification used in this yearbook was based on Industrial Classification Standard revised in 2011.

The new industrial classification standard was based on China's social and economic development, to ensure that the national economic structure and industrial structure is integrity, scientific, and observability; to ensure national statistics and accounting reflecting the economic structure and industrial structure integrity. This revision was not only adhere to revision principle of industry classification and international practice, and conformed to the requirement in <State Council on accelerating the cultivation and development of emerging industries of strategic decision>, accurately reflect the composition of national economy industry in a given period.

The revision was mainly adjusted as follows:

1. Adjusting sector category name and order. For example, "information transmission, computer service and software industry" was renamed to "information transmission, software industry and information technology service", "scientific research,

EXPLANATORY NOTES TO MAJOR STATISTICAL INDICATORS

technical service and geological prospecting" was renamed to "scientific research and technical service", "resident service and other services" was renamed to "resident service, repairs and other services", "health, social security and social welfare" was renamed to "health and social work". But the overall number of industry categories remain unchanged, ensuring the continuity of industry classification.

2. In order to correspond with the classification of the United Nations, and reflect the situation of our industry, number of industry categories was adjusted from 95 to 96, six new categories, "mining support activities", "the automotive manufacturing", "metal products, machinery and equipment repair industry", "housing construction", "internet and related services", "motor vehicles, electronics and daily necessities repair industry" were added, and four categories, "building decoration industry", "urban public transport industry", "other financial activities", "geological prospecting" were reduced. "Rubber products manufacturing" and "plastic products manufacturing" were combined into one category.

3. In order to reflect our growing internet, information technology, finance, entertainment and other industries, new medium categories, "internet and related services", "information integration system services", "fiber weaving and dyeing and finishing" were added, "pig breeding", "textile manufactured goods manufacturing" were reduced.

4. In order to convert with ISIC Rev.4 and reflect our emerging industries, new minimal categories, "rice planting", "mushroom cultivation", "grape cultivation" were added, "common non-ferrous metal rolling processing", "hat manufacturing", "vehicles, aircraft and construction machinery tire manufacturing" were reduced.

□ Various Planning Periods

The conventional division of time period in this statistical yearbook is as follows: Rehabilitation Period, 1950-1952; The First Five-Year Plan period (cited as first-five period), 1953-1957; The Second Five-Year Plan period (cited as second-five period), 1958-1962; The Third Five-Year Plan period (cited as third-five period), 1966-1970; The Fourth Five-Year Plan period (cited as fourth-five period), 1971-1975; The Fifth Five-Year Plan period (cited as fifth-five period), 1976-1980; The Sixth Five-Year Plan period (cited as sixth-five period), 1981-1985; The Seventh Five-Year Plan period (cited as seventh-five period), 1986-1990; The Eight Five-Year Plan period (cited as eighth-five period), 1991-1995; The Ninth Five-Year Plan period (cited as ninth-five period),1996-2000;The Tenth Five-Year Plan period (cited as tenth-five period),2001-2005; The eleventh Five-Year Plan period(cited as eleventh-five period),2006-2010; The twelfth Five-Year Plan period (cited as twelfth-five period), 2011-2015.

□ Index

Index refers to the relative figures indicating social and economic phenomena and developments. Index is used to evaluate the overall development of social and economic phenomena which can not be determined by simple addition or direct comparison. It is also used to analyze the outcome of various changes in the general phenomenon movement of social and economic development, and to study the level of each sub-index in the changes of general average index and the role of the changes of the overall structure. It is calculated at the comparable prices conversed from the output value of each year, using the formula of index number with fixed base period equal to the continuous product of its relative chain index .

The increases of Shanghai Gross Domestic Product, industrial output value and agricultural output value compared with the previous year, which are listed in this yearbook, are calculated according to Shanghai GDP index, industrial output value index and agricultural output value index.

□ Average Annual Growth Rate

Two methods for calculating Average Annual Growth Rate are applied in China, one is often called "level approach" or geometry average, which is derived by comparing the growth rate for the last year of the interval with that of the beginning year; the other is called "accumulating approach" or algebraic average or equation method, which is calculated by comparing the total growth rate of each year for the interval with that of base year .

Usually the results calculated by the two methods are fairly close, but they differ sharply when imbalance occurred in economic development with striking fluctuations in growth.

The Average Annual Growth Rates listed in this statistical yearbook are calculated by "level approach". The base years are not listed when the years are listed for average annual growth rates for instance, the average annual growth rate of 1991-2009 is calculated with the base year 1990, and the analogy of this is also for the rest.

第二篇

CHAPTER 2

2019上海统计年鉴 SHANGHAI STATISTICAL YEARBOOK

人 口

POPULATION

简要说明

一、本篇资料的主要内容

本篇资料反映上海市1978-2018年人口方面的基本情况,包括全市及各区的主要人口统计数据,如:1978-2018年全市常住人口数和户籍人口数;2018年各区县常住人口数和外省市来沪常住人口数;1990-2018年户籍人口自然增长和机械增长变动;2018年各区户籍人口年龄构成、计划生育情况;主要年份外籍常住人口数等。

二、本篇的资料来源

本篇资料由上海市统计局人口和就业统计处整理。1982、1990、2000、2010年年末常住人口数据为当年普查数据推算数,其余年份数据为年度人口抽样调查推算数据,部分年份数据根据人口普查数据进行了修订。表2-1中除常住人口数据外,其余数据统计范围均为户籍人口,由市公安局提供。表2-2中行政区划面积由市民政局提供,各区常住人口数和外省市来沪常住人口数根据上海市2018年人口变动抽样调查数据推算。表2-3至表2-6数据统计范围均为户籍人口,由市公安局提供。表2-8数据统计范围为户籍人口,由市卫生和计划生育委员会提供。表2-11由市公安局出入境管理局提供。

三、本篇的统计调查方法

目前由上海市统计局人口和就业统计处实施的人口统计调查有:

在逢“0”的年份进行全国人口普查; 在逢”5”的年份进行全国1%人口抽样调查;其余年份进行全国人口变动情况抽样调查,其样本量约占全市总人口的1.3‰左右。人口抽样调查是以全国为总体,省级单位为次总体,采用分层、多阶段、整群概率比例抽样方法抽取样本。

BRIEF INTRODUCTION

I. Main Contents

Data in this chapter reflect the basic conditions of Shanghai′s population between 1978 and 2018, including data of the city as well as districts under it. For example: there are data of the city’s permanent residents and registered population between 1978 and 2018 permanent residents and residents from other provinces and cities in districts in 2018; changes of registered population’s natural growth and mechanical growth between 1990 and 2018; registered population age structure in districts in 2018 and their conditions of family planning; population of foreign residents in main years.

II. Sources of Data

Data in this chapter are collected, prepared, and provided by the Department of Population and Employment Statistics of the Shanghai Statistics Bureau. Data of permanent residents by the year end for 1982, 1990, 2000 and 2010 are the census year estimates; the rest of the data are estimates from the annual national sample survey on population changes and data for selected years have been revised according to the census results. Data in table 2–1, provided by the Shanghai Public Security Bureau, refer to registered population, with permanent residents in exception. Land area data in table 2–2 are provided by the Shanghai Civil Affairs Bureau, and the data on permanent residents in districts and counties, and residents from other provinces and cities are estimates based on Sample Survey of Population Change in Shanghai in 2018. Data in table 2–3 to table 2–6, provided by the Shanghai Public Security Bureau, all refer to registered population. Data in table 2 – 8, provided by the Shanghai Municipal Commission of Health and Family Planning, refer to registered population. Data in table 2– 11 are provided by the Shanghai Public Security Bureau Exit–Entry Administration.

III. Survey Methodology

The statistical surveys on population which are conducted by the Department of Population and Employment Statistics of the Shanghai Statistics Bureau are as follows:

The national population census is conducted in the year ending with 0; the national 1 percent population sample survey is conducted in the year ending with 5; sample surveys on population changes are conducted in the rest of the years which cover about 1.3 per thousand of the total population of the city. The sample survey on population change takes the whole nation as the population sample with each province, autonomous region or municipality as sub–populations, and the stratified multi–stage systematic PPS cluster sampling scheme is used.

表 2.1 户数、人口、人口密度和户籍人口期望寿命(1978~2018)
TOTAL HOUSEHOLDS,POPULATION,DENSITY OF REGISTERED POPULATION AND LIFE EXPECTANCY

年 份 Year	常住人口 (万人) Year-end Resident Population (10 000 persons)	人口密度 (人/平方公里) Density of Population (person/sq.km)	总户数 (万户) Total Households (10 000 households)	平均每户人口 (人) Average Persons Per Household (person)	年末户籍人口 (万人) Year-end Registered Population (10 000 persons)
1978	1 104.00	1 785	291.69	3.77	1 098.28
1979	1 137.00	1 838	296.71	3.82	1 132.14
1980	1 152.00	1 862	303.87	3.77	1 146.52
1981	1 168.00	1 888	314.56	3.70	1 162.84
1982	1 186.00	1 917	321.71	3.67	1 180.51
1983	1 201.00	1 942	330.60	3.61	1 194.01
1984	1 217.00	1 968	340.78	3.54	1 204.78
1985	1 233.00	1 993	351.72	3.46	1 216.69
1986	1 249.00	1 970	364.92	3.38	1 232.33
1987	1 265.00	1 995	380.19	3.29	1 249.51
1988	1 288.00	2 031	394.95	3.20	1 262.42
1989	1 311.00	2 067	406.82	3.14	1 276.45
1990	1 334.00	2 104	415.28	3.09	1 283.35
1991	1 350.00	2 128	425.84	3.02	1 287.20
1992	1 365.00	2 154	431.67	2.99	1 289.37
1993	1 381.00	2 179	438.69	2.95	1 294.74
1994	1 398.00	2 204	444.38	2.92	1 298.81
1995	1 414.00	2 230	450.76	2.89	1 301.37
1996	1 451.00	2 288	457.49	2.85	1 304.43
1997	1 489.00	2 348	461.40	2.83	1 305.46
1998	1 527.00	2 409	465.72	2.81	1 306.58
1999	1 567.00	2 472	470.11	2.79	1 313.12
2000	1 608.60	2 537	475.73	2.78	1 321.63
2001	1 668.33	2 631	478.92	2.77	1 327.14
2002	1 712.97	2 702	481.77	2.77	1 334.23
2003	1 765.84	2 785	486.06	2.76	1 341.77
2004	1 834.98	2 894	490.58	2.76	1 352.39
2005	1 890.26	2 981	496.69	2.74	1 360.26
2006	1 964.11	3 098	499.54	2.74	1 368.08
2007	2 063.58	3 255	503.29	2.74	1 378.86
2008	2 140.65	3 376	506.64	2.75	1 391.04
2009	2 210.28	3 486	509.79	2.75	1 400.70
2010	2 302.66	3 632	519.27	2.72	1 412.32
2011	2 347.46	3 702	522.01	2.72	1 419.36
2012	2 380.43	3 754	524.31	2.72	1 426.93
2013	2 415.15	3 809	527.52	2.72	1 432.34
2014	2 425.68	3 826	532.55	2.70	1 438.69
2015	2 415.27	3 809	536.76	2.69	1 442.97
2016	2 419.70	3 816	541.62	2.68	1 450.00
2017	2 418.33	3 814	546.13	2.66	1 455.13
2018	2 423.78	3 823	551.95	2.65	1 462.38

①户数和年末户籍人口由市公安局提供。2016 年起，年末户籍人口为公安局公布的 11 月底数据(后表同)。户籍人口期望寿命由市卫生和计划生育委员会提供。

②上海取消农业户口和非农业户口性质区分。

❶The figures of household and year-end registered population are provided by Shanghai Municipal Public Security Bureau. From 2016, the figures of year-end registered population refer to the data of the end of November published by Shanghai Municipal Public Security Bureau (same as follows). The figures of life expendency are provided by Shanghai Municipal Health and Family Planning Commission.

❷Shanghai has cancelled the distinction between agricultural and non-agricultural household accounts.

表2.1 续表 continued

年 份 Year	按性别分 Grouped by Sex		户籍人口期望寿命（岁）Life Expectancy of Registered Population (year)	其 中 of which	
	男 性 Male	女 性 Female		男 性 Male	女 性 Female
1978	542.70	555.58	73.35	70.69	74.78
1979	560.40	571.74	73.14	70.64	75.48
1980	569.30	577.22	73.33	71.25	75.36
1981	578.76	584.08	73.38	71.28	75.47
1982	588.82	591.69	74.04	71.77	76.25
1983	596.67	597.34	73.23	71.15	75.26
1984	602.59	602.19	73.90	71.73	76.17
1985	609.70	606.99	74.27	72.14	76.37
1986	618.88	613.45	74.71	72.54	76.85
1987	628.78	620.73	74.46	72.32	76.60
1988	635.82	626.60	74.63	72.50	76.77
1989	643.51	632.94	74.98	72.85	77.12
1990	647.13	636.22	75.46	73.16	77.74
1991	649.03	638.17	75.79	73.58	77.95
1992	649.97	639.40	75.97	74.04	77.91
1993	652.92	641.82	75.97	74.04	77.91
1994	655.14	643.67	76.26	74.29	78.23
1995	656.48	644.89	76.03	74.11	77.97
1996	657.86	646.57	76.11	74.07	78.21
1997	657.93	647.53	77.20	75.18	79.21
1998	658.22	648.36	77.03	75.06	79.02
1999	661.19	651.93	78.44	76.38	80.53
2000	665.51	656.12	78.77	76.71	80.81
2001	668.32	658.82	79.66	77.47	81.83
2002	672.05	662.18	79.52	77.36	81.63
2003	675.47	666.30	79.80	77.78	81.81
2004	680.38	672.01	80.29	78.08	82.48
2005	683.51	676.75	80.13	77.89	82.36
2006	686.66	681.42	80.97	78.64	83.29
2007	691.08	687.78	81.08	78.87	83.29
2008	695.57	695.47	81.28	79.06	83.50
2009	699.25	701.45	81.73	79.42	84.06
2010	703.57	708.75	82.13	79.82	84.44
2011	706.37	712.99	82.51	80.23	84.80
2012	709.62	717.31	82.41	80.18	84.67
2013	711.93	720.41	82.47	80.19	84.79
2014	714.71	723.99	82.29	80.04	84.59
2015	716.37	726.60	82.75	80.47	85.09
2016	719.35	730.65	83.18	80.83	85.61
2017	721.29	733.84	83.37	80.98	85.85
2018	724.14	738.23	83.63	81.25	86.08

表 2.2 各区土地面积、常住人口及人口密度（2018）
LAND AREA, POPULATION AND DENSITY OF POPULATION IN DISTRICTS

地　区	District	行政区域面积（平方公里）Land Area (sq.km)	年末常住人口（万人）Year-end Resident Population (10 000 persons)	其中 of which 外来人口 Floating People	人口密度（人/平方公里）Density of Population (person/sq・km)
全　市	**Total**	**6 340.50**	**2 423.78**	**976.21**	**3 823**
浦东新区	Pudong New Area	1 210.41	555.02	235.84	4 585
黄 浦 区	Huangpu	20.46	65.38	17.43	31 955
徐 汇 区	Xuhui	54.76	108.44	26.70	19 803
长 宁 区	Changning	38.30	69.40	17.70	18 120
静 安 区	Jing'an	36.88	106.28	26.88	28 818
普 陀 区	Putuo	54.83	128.19	33.98	23 380
虹 口 区	Hongkou	23.48	79.70	15.26	33 944
杨 浦 区	Yangpu	60.73	131.27	27.33	21 615
闵 行 区	Minhang	370.75	254.35	125.00	6 860
宝 山 区	Baoshan	270.99	204.23	83.71	7 536
嘉 定 区	Jiading	464.20	158.89	90.18	3 423
金 山 区	Jinshan	586.05	80.50	27.22	1 374
松 江 区	Songjiang	605.64	176.22	106.11	2 910
青 浦 区	Qingpu	670.14	121.90	71.27	1 819
奉 贤 区	Fengxian	687.39	115.20	57.68	1 676
崇 明 区	Chongming	1 185.49	68.81	13.92	580

表2.3　主要年份户籍人口出生率、死亡率、自然增长率
BIRTH RATE, DEATH RATE AND NATURAL GROWTH RATE OF REGISTERED POPULATION IN MAIN YEARS

年　份 Year	出　生 Birth		死　亡 Death		自然增长 Natural Growth	
	人　数（万人）Population (10 000 persons)	出生率（‰）Birth Rate（‰）	人　数（万人）Population (10 000 persons)	死亡率（‰）Death Rate（‰）	人　数（万人）Population (10 000 persons)	自然增长率（‰）Natural Growth Rate（‰）
1990	13.12	10.25	8.63	6.74	4.49	3.51
1995	7.11	5.47	9.79	7.53	-2.68	-2.06
2000	6.95	5.27	9.45	7.17	-2.50	-1.90
2001	5.76	4.34	9.34	7.05	-3.58	-2.71
2002	6.20	4.66	9.67	7.27	-3.47	-2.61
2003	5.73	4.28	10.07	7.52	-4.34	-3.24
2004	8.09	6.00	9.65	7.16	-1.56	-1.16
2005	8.25	6.08	10.23	7.54	-1.98	-1.46
2006	8.12	5.95	9.80	7.19	-1.68	-1.24
2007	10.08	7.34	10.22	7.44	-0.14	-0.10
2008	9.67	6.98	10.70	7.73	-1.03	-0.75
2009	9.23	6.62	10.67	7.64	-1.44	-1.02
2010	10.02	7.13	10.87	7.73	-0.84	-0.60
2011	10.15	7.17	11.11	7.85	-0.96	-0.68
2012	12.11	8.51	11.74	8.25	0.37	0.26
2013	10.89	7.62	11.67	8.16	-0.78	-0.54
2014	12.41	8.64	11.95	8.32	0.46	0.32
2015	10.59	7.35	12.42	8.62	-1.83	-1.27
2016	13.07	9.04	12.35	8.54	0.72	0.50
2017	11.77	8.10	12.64	8.70	-0.87	-0.60
2018	9.84	6.70	12.57	8.60	-2.73	-1.90

表2.4　主要年份户籍人口迁移
MIGRATION OF REGISTERED POPULATION IN MAIN YEARS

年　份 Year	迁　入 Inflows		迁　出 Outflows		机械增长 Mechanical Increase	
	人　口（万人）Population (10 000 persons)	迁入率（‰）Rate of Inflows（‰）	人　口（万人）Population (10 000 persons)	迁出率（‰）Rate of Outflows（‰）	人　口（万人）Population (10 000 persons)	增长率（‰）Growth Rate（‰）
1990	12.18	9.52	10.72	8.38	1.46	1.14
1995	13.12	10.09	6.47	4.98	6.65	5.11
2000	15.16	11.51	5.32	4.04	9.84	7.47
2001	14.63	11.05	5.56	4.20	9.07	6.85
2002	15.41	11.58	4.38	3.29	11.03	8.29
2003	14.92	11.15	3.69	2.76	11.23	8.39
2004	13.93	10.34	2.74	2.03	11.19	8.31
2005	12.96	9.55	3.46	2.55	9.50	7.00
2006	12.86	9.43	3.50	2.57	9.36	6.86
2007	14.69	10.70	3.95	2.88	10.74	7.82
2008	17.28	12.48	4.29	3.10	12.99	9.38
2009	15.72	11.26	4.77	3.42	10.95	7.84
2010	17.22	12.24	4.97	3.53	12.25	8.71
2011	13.15	9.29	5.33	3.76	7.82	5.53
2012	12.96	8.11	5.89	4.14	7.07	3.97
2013	12.12	8.48	6.06	4.24	6.06	4.24
2014	11.55	8.05	5.78	4.02	5.77	4.03
2015	11.61	8.06	5.32	3.69	6.29	4.37
2016	11.25	7.78	4.64	3.22	6.61	4.57
2017	11.85	8.16	4.17	2.87	7.68	5.29
2018	13.75	9.43	3.92	2.69	9.83	6.74

表 2.5 各区户籍人口迁移(2017~2018)
MIGRATION OF REGISTERED POPULATION IN DISTRICTS

单位:人(persons)

地 区 District		2017 市外迁入 Inflows from Outside of the City	2017 迁往市外 Outflows To the Outside of the City	2018 市外迁入 Inflows from Outside of the City	2018 迁往市外 Outflows To the Outside of the City
全 市	**Total**	**118 513**	**41 656**	**137 503**	**39 206**
浦东新区	Pudong New Area	27 248	6 543	34 763	6 047
黄 浦 区	Huangpu	2 890	692	3 108	800
徐 汇 区	Xuhui	9 832	6 225	10 657	5 885
长 宁 区	Changning	4 280	1 661	5 086	1 585
静 安 区	Jing'an	4 246	904	5 295	903
普 陀 区	Putuo	4 868	1 065	5 585	945
虹 口 区	Hongkou	3 913	1 377	4 460	1 396
杨 浦 区	Yangpu	16 485	8 679	17 043	8 006
闵 行 区	Minhang	15 098	3 994	16 941	3 873
宝 山 区	Baoshan	8 185	2 257	8 415	2 197
嘉 定 区	Jiading	5 735	1 122	6 798	1 071
金 山 区	Jinshan	1 433	187	1 812	150
松 江 区	Songjiang	9 045	5 611	11 189	5 284
青 浦 区	Qingpu	2 431	813	2 772	554
奉 贤 区	Fengxian	1 652	368	2 170	339
崇 明 区	Chongming	1 172	168	1 409	171

表2.6　各区户籍人口年龄构成(2018)
AGE STRUCTURE OF REGISTERED POPULATION IN DISTRICTS

单位:万人(10 000 persons)

地　区	District	合　计 Total	17岁及以下 17 and below	18~34岁 18~34	35~59岁 35~59	60岁及以上 60 and above
全　市	**Total**	**1 462.38**	**176.50**	**247.43**	**536.42**	**502.03**
浦东新区	Pudong New Area	302.94	40.78	52.16	114.79	95.22
黄 浦 区	Huangpu	83.21	8.44	14.43	27.78	32.56
徐 汇 区	Xuhui	92.15	12.55	16.70	30.94	31.95
长 宁 区	Changning	57.89	6.44	10.05	20.09	21.32
静 安 区	Jing'an	92.58	10.45	15.56	31.51	35.05
普 陀 区	Putuo	89.43	10.20	14.27	30.48	34.49
虹 口 区	Hongkou	73.12	7.17	12.47	24.45	29.04
杨 浦 区	Yangpu	107.35	11.60	21.08	35.55	39.11
闵 行 区	Minhang	113.49	17.21	18.86	42.66	34.75
宝 山 区	Baoshan	99.06	12.15	15.84	36.68	34.39
嘉 定 区	Jiading	63.93	8.15	10.02	24.36	21.40
金 山 区	Jinshan	52.35	5.64	7.97	21.84	16.91
松 江 区	Songjiang	64.31	8.90	11.66	25.20	18.56
青 浦 区	Qingpu	48.87	5.66	7.91	19.95	15.35
奉 贤 区	Fengxian	53.85	6.02	8.21	22.30	17.30
崇 明 区	Chongming	67.86	5.15	10.25	27.83	24.63

注：本页数据由市公安局提供，报告期为2018年11月底。
Note: Data on this page are provided by Shanghai Municipal Public Security Bereau, and the report period is at the end of November 2018.

表 2.7 各区户籍老年人口年龄构成(2018)
AGE STRUCTURE OF REGISTERED AGING POPULATION IN DISTRICTS

单位:万人(10 000 persons)

地 区	District	合 计 Total	60~64 岁 60~64	65~79 岁 65~79	80 岁及以上 80 and above
全 市	**Total**	**503.28**	**166.38**	**255.23**	**81.67**
浦东新区	Pudong New Area	95.49	30.79	49.61	15.10
黄 浦 区	Huangpu	32.60	11.72	15.46	5.42
徐 汇 区	Xuhui	32.02	10.26	15.77	5.98
长 宁 区	Changning	21.37	7.27	10.09	4.00
静 安 区	Jing'an	35.09	12.33	16.94	5.82
普 陀 区	Putuo	34.59	12.37	16.80	5.42
虹 口 区	Hongkou	29.06	10.19	13.98	4.89
杨 浦 区	Yangpu	39.23	13.99	18.71	6.53
闵 行 区	Minhang	34.87	10.91	18.36	5.60
宝 山 区	Baoshan	34.56	11.86	17.83	4.88
嘉 定 区	Jiading	21.48	6.67	11.45	3.36
金 山 区	Jinshan	16.92	5.23	9.11	2.58
松 江 区	Songjiang	18.60	5.70	9.96	2.94
青 浦 区	Qingpu	15.39	4.83	8.10	2.46
奉 贤 区	Fengxian	17.34	5.22	9.47	2.65
崇 明 区	Chongming	24.68	7.05	13.59	4.04

注：本页数据由上海市老龄工作委员会提供，报告期为2018年12月底。
Note: The data on this page are provided by the Office of Shanghai Aging Working Committee, and the report period is at the end of December 2018.

表 2.8　各区户籍人口生育基本情况（2017~2018）
FAMILY PLANNING IN DISTRICTS

单位：万人(10 000 persons)

地　区	District	2017 已婚育龄妇女人数 Married Women at Childbearing Age	2017 出生人数 Birth	2018 已婚育龄妇女人数 Married Women at Childbearing Age	2018 出生人数 Birth
全　市	**Total**	**200.92**	**11.77**	**198.73**	**9.84**
浦东新区	Pudong New Area	45.19	2.75	44.53	2.36
黄 浦 区	Huangpu	10.44	0.64	10.07	0.46
徐 汇 区	Xuhui	11.92	0.77	11.66	0.62
长 宁 区	Changning	7.82	0.46	7.51	0.37
静 安 区	Jing'an	11.88	0.74	11.59	0.59
普 陀 区	Putuo	9.75	0.66	9.76	0.56
虹 口 区	Hongkou	9.27	0.52	8.90	0.41
杨 浦 区	Yangpu	13.45	0.80	13.48	0.65
闵 行 区	Minhang	15.76	1.08	15.97	0.92
宝 山 区	Baoshan	13.11	0.76	12.88	0.65
嘉 定 区	Jiading	8.81	0.53	9.15	0.47
金 山 区	Jinshan	8.30	0.35	7.96	0.30
松 江 区	Songjiang	9.01	0.64	8.98	0.53
青 浦 区	Qingpu	7.78	0.37	7.74	0.33
奉 贤 区	Fengxian	8.45	0.36	8.55	0.31
崇 明 区	Chongming	9.98	0.35	10.00	0.31

表2.9 主要年份婚姻情况
MARRIAGE STATISTICS IN MAIN YEARS

年 份 Year	登记结婚（万对）Marriage Registration (10 000 couples)	初 婚（万人）First Marriage (10 000 persons)	再 婚（万人）Remarriage (10 000 persons)	其 中 of which 女 性 Female	离 婚（万对）Divorce (10 000 Couples)	其 中 of which 民政部门批 准 Approved by the Civil Administration	法 院 调 判 Mediated by the Court
1990	10.77	19.49	2.04	1.06	1.64	0.73	0.91
1995	8.40	14.61	2.19	1.09	2.27	0.98	1.29
2000	9.31	15.08	2.89	1.45	3.18	1.76	1.42
2001	9.30	15.23	2.68	1.40	3.15	1.68	1.47
2002	9.10	14.60	3.05	1.40	2.96	1.54	1.42
2003	10.82	17.20	3.97	2.31	3.30	1.98	1.32
2004	12.49	20.27	4.18	2.05	3.63	2.67	0.96
2005	10.27	16.44	4.09	2.05	3.93	3.10	0.83
2006	16.56	27.29	5.83	2.93	4.72	3.78	0.94
2007	12.01	18.10	5.93	2.95	4.69	3.75	0.94
2008	14.16	22.04	6.28	3.17	4.68	3.72	0.96
2009	14.99	23.33	6.65	3.31	4.83	3.92	0.91
2010	13.03	20.10	5.96	2.98	4.67	3.81	0.86
2011	14.89	23.94	5.84	2.90	4.78	3.92	0.86
2012	14.42	22.96	5.88	2.86	5.29	4.42	0.87
2013	14.95	22.17	7.74	3.77	6.96	6.09	0.87
2014	14.19	20.14	8.25	4.06	6.15	5.30	0.85
2015	14.18	19.89	8.47	4.19	6.66	5.83	0.83
2016	12.52	13.79	11.25	4.53	8.26	7.44	0.82
2017	10.87	13.84	7.90	3.92	5.72	5.08	0.64
2018	10.37	14.23	6.51	3.81	5.41	5.18	0.22

表2.10 主要年份涉外婚姻情况
CHINESE-FOREIGN MARRIAGE IN MAIN YEARS

年 份 Year	涉外婚姻（对）Chinese-Foreign Marriage (couple)	在涉外婚姻中的国内公民（人）In Chinese-Foreign Marriage Chinese Citizens (person)	在国内公民中 Among the Chinese Citizens 男 性 Male	女 性 Female
1990	1 345	1 345	136	1 209
1995	3 033	3 030	274	2 756
2000	3 187	3 182	374	2 808
2001	3 447	3 438	399	3 039
2002	2 705	2 690	67	2 623
2003	2 418	2 418	367	2 051
2004	2 636	2 623	417	2 206
2005	2 407	2 385	372	2 013
2006	2 943	2 943	540	2 403
2007	2 495	2 483	109	2 374
2008	2 626	2 553	428	2 125
2009	2 492	2 416	305	2 111
2010	2 231	2 144	414	1 730
2011	2 225	2 125	474	1 651
2012	2 195	2 064	473	1 591
2013	2 054	1 900	430	1 470
2014	1 962	1 817	437	1 380
2015	1 778	1 642	397	1 245
2016	1 684	1 533	433	1 100
2017	1 479	1 347	386	961
2018	1 402	1 269	382	887

注：本页数据由市民政局和市高级人民法院提供。
Note: This table is provided by Shanghai Civil Affairs Bureau and Shanghai Municipal Senior People's Court.

表2.11　主要年份在沪外国常住人口
RESIDENT FOREIGNERS IN SHANGHAI IN MAIN YEARS

单位：人(person)

类　别	Types	2005	2010	2015	2017	2018
总　计	**Total**	**100 011**	**162 481**	**178 335**	**163 363**	**172 076**
居留许可外国人	**Residence Permitted Foreigners**	**95 384**	**159 303**	**175 931**	**157 924**	**164 765**
按国别(地区)分	Grouped by Country and Region					
#日　本	Japan	27 812	35 075	33 440	28 870	29 546
韩　国	Republic of Korea	14 047	21 073	21 178	20 823	21 685
新加坡	Singapore	5 547	7 545	6 421	5 786	6 033
德　国	Germany	4 591	8 023	8 446	7 583	7 736
英　国	United Kingdom	2 904	5 591	6 543	5 993	6 416
加拿大	Canada	4 279	7 306	8 012	7 439	7 476
美　国	United States	14 329	24 358	25 537	21 903	22 051
澳大利亚	Australia	3 729	6 165	7 444	6 995	7 110
法　国	France	4 181	8 238	9 993	8 659	8 936
按类别分	By Types					
#工　作	Work			91 372	79 701	87 525
学　习	Study			16 030	18 985	21 561
团　聚	Reunit			17 112	16 367	25 739
私人事务	Private Transaction			48 915	42 769	29 845
新闻从业人员	Journalists			98	102	95
永久居留外国人	Permanent Resident Foreigners		948	2 404	5 439	7 311

上/海/统/计/年/鉴

主要统计指标解释

■ 人　口

人口数为每年12月31日的年末总人口。根据统计口径的不同，分为户籍人口和常住人口。户籍人口是指在公安部门办理了户籍登记的人口。常住人口是指实际上经常居住在一个地方（住所）的人口，一般都以在其住所居住半年以上者为常住人口。

■ 出生率

出生率（又称粗出生率）指在一定时期内（通常为一年）一定地区的出生人数与同期平均人数（或期中人数）之比，一般用千分率表示。计算公式：

$$出生率=\frac{年出生人数}{年平均人数}\times1000‰$$

出生人数是指活产婴儿，即胎儿脱离母体时(不管怀孕月数)，有过呼吸或其他生命现象。年平均人数是年初、年底人口数的平均数，也可用年中人口数代替。

■ 死亡率

死亡率（又称粗死亡率）指在一定时期内（通常为一年）一定地区的死亡人数与同期平均人数（或期中人数）之比，一般用千分率表示。计算公式：

$$死亡率=\frac{年死亡人数}{年平均人数}\times1000‰$$

■ 人口自然增长率

指在一定时期内（通常为一年）人口自然增加数（出生人数减死亡人数）与该时期内平均人数（或期中人数）之比，一般用千分率表示。计算公式：

$$人口自然增长率=\frac{本年出生人数-本年死亡人数}{年平均人数}\times1000‰$$

$$人口自然增长率=人口出生率-人口死亡率$$

■ 户籍人口期望寿命

指在一定年龄组的死亡率水平下，该年龄组人群日后平均可能继续生存的年（岁）数。通常所说的平均期望寿命是指刚出生的一批人平均一生可能存活的年数。

SHANGHAI STATISTICAL YEARBOOK

EXPLANATORY NOTES TO MAJOR STATISTICAL INDICATORS

□ Population

Population refers to the total population by December 31 every year. According to different statistical approaches, there are two definitions of population named as population with registered residence and population with permanent residence. The former refers to the population with registration in the police while the latter refers to the population that actually reside in a place (residence) permanently, usually longer than half a year.

□ Birth Rate

Birth Rate (or gross birth rate) means the ratio of the number of births in a certain period (usually a year) to the average population in the same period (or mid-year figure). It is usually calculated in terms of permillage and its calculating formula is:

$$\text{Birth Rate}=\frac{\text{Number of Births}}{\text{Average Number of Population}}\times 1000‰$$

Number of Births refers to live births, when babies have showed any vital phenomena regardless of the length of pregnancy.

Average Number of Population is the average of the number of population at the beginning of the year and, at the end of the year and sometimes is substituted for with mid-year population.

□ Death Rate

Death Rate (or Gross Death Rate) refers to the ratio of number of deaths to the average population (or mid-year population) during a certain period of time (usually a year), which is often presented as permillage. Its calculating formula is :

$$\text{Death Rate}=\frac{\text{Number of Deaths}}{\text{Average Number of Population}}\times 1000‰$$

□ Natural Growth Rate of Population

Natural Growth Rate of Population refers to the ratio of natural increase in population (number of births minus number of deaths) in a certain period of time (usually a year) to the average population (or mid-year population) of the same period, which is often presented as permillage. The following formula are applied:

$$\text{Natural Growth Rate of Population}=\frac{\text{Number of Births}-\text{Number of Deaths}}{\text{Average Number of Population}}\times 1000‰$$

Natural Growth Rate of Population = Birth Rate−Death Rate

□ Life Expectancy of Registered Population

Life Expectancy of Registered Population refers to the average age that an age group may possibly live at a certain mortality rate of the group, in the common knowledge, the average age that a group of new-borns may possibly live.

第三篇

CHAPTER 3

2019上海统计年鉴 SHANGHAI STATISTICAL YEARBOOK

从业人员和工资

EMPLOYMENT AND WAGES

简 要 说 明

一、本篇资料的主要内容

本篇资料反映上海市劳动经济方面的基本情况。如:从业人员、城镇登记失业人数和城镇登记失业率,新增就业岗位,离退休、退职职工人数,工资总额,平均工资及离退休、退职人员养老金情况等。

二、本篇资料的统计范围

《劳动统计报表制度》的调查范围为上海市国民经济各行业法人单位及其所属的产业活动单位。上海市人力资源和社会保障局有关统计报表的统计范围为上海市国民经济各行业法人单位及其所属的产业活动单位。

三、本篇的资料来源

1. 从业人员、工资总额等资料是根据《劳动统计报表制度》搜集资料,加工整理汇总取得。

2. 城镇登记失业人数和城镇登记失业率,新增就业岗位,离退休、退职职工人数,离退休、退职人员养老金情况,由上海市人力资源和社会保障局提供。

四、本篇的统计调查方法

本篇资料对规模以上工业、有资质的建筑业、限额以上批发和零售业、限额以上住宿和餐饮业、有开发经营活动的全部房地产开发经营业、规模以上服务业法人单位采取全面调查;除上述范围以外的法人单位采取抽样调查方法。人力资源社会保障的资料采用全面调查方法,由市人力资源社会保障部门收集相关数据资料加工整理取得。

BRIEF INTRODUCTION

I. Main Contents

Data in this chapter reflect the basic conditions of Shanghai's labor economy, such as number of employed people, the urban registered unemployed people and unemployment rate, the number of new jobs, the number of retired people, total wages, average wages and pension situations.

II. Scope and Coverage of Statistics

The Reporting Form System on Labor Statistics covers various corporate units with legal person status and their subordinated business units in Shanghai's economic and social development.

The reporting forms provided by the Shanghai Human Resources and Social Security Bureau cover various corporate units with legal person status and their subordinated business units in Shanghai's economic and social development.

III. Sources of Data

(1) Data on basic conditions including employment and total wages are collected, prepared and compiled through The Reporting Form System on Labor Statistics.

(2) Data on the urban registered unemployed people and unemployment rate, the number of new jobs, the number of retired people and pension situations are provided by the Shanghai Human Resources and Social Security Bureau.

IV. Methodology of Survey

Data of this chapter are from comprehensive surveys on industry above designated size, the construction industry, the wholesale and retail industry above the set scale, the accommodation and catering industry above the set scale, all real estate development business with development and operation activities, service industry corporations above the set scale. Date of other legal entities are from sampling surveys. The data of human resources and social security are from compre hensive surveys, which collected and processed by Shanghai Human Resources and Social Security Bureau.

表 3.1 全社会各行业从业人员(2016~2018)
QUANTITY OF WHOLE SOCIAL EMPLOYEES IN DIFFERENT SECTORS

单位:万人(10 000 persons)

行业	Sectors	2016	2017	2018
总　计	**Total**	**1 365.24**	**1 372.65**	**1 375.66**
按产业分	**Grouped by Industry**			
第一产业	Primary Industry	45.45	42.44	40.83
第二产业	Secondary Industry	448.50	430.51	422.82
第三产业	Tertiary Industry	871.29	899.70	912.01
按行业分	**Grouped by Sector**			
农、林、牧、渔业	Farming, Forestry, Animal Husbandry and Fishery	48.30	46.49	45.31
采矿业	Mining	0.04	0.04	0.04
制造业	Manufacturing	341.82	331.73	322.55
电力、热力、燃气及水的生产和供应业	Electricity, Heat, Gas and Water Production and Supply Industry	4.83	4.57	4.57
建筑业	Construction	106.36	98.90	99.96
批发和零售业	Retail and Wholesale	239.06	240.39	243.92
交通运输、仓储和邮政业	Transportation, Warehousing and Post Industries	89.73	89.39	89.52
住宿和餐饮业	Hoteling and Catering	52.22	55.26	60.89
信息传输、软件和信息技术服务业	Information Transmission, Software and IT Services	48.60	52.47	55.84
金融业	Finance	36.42	35.54	35.32
房地产业	Real Estate	50.01	51.88	51.59
租赁和商务服务业	Leasing and Business Service Industries	133.18	140.13	141.84
科学研究和技术服务业	Scientific and Technical Services	45.75	48.55	50.24
水利、环境和公共设施管理业	Water Conservancy, Environment and Public Facility Management	20.82	21.79	19.53
居民服务、修理和其他服务业	Resident Services, Repairs and Other Services	36.06	37.88	37.40
教　育	Education	37.41	39.24	39.47
卫生和社会工作	Health and Social Work	28.70	30.69	30.40
文化、体育和娱乐业	Culture, Sports and Entertainment	11.42	11.72	11.59
公共管理、社会保障和社会组织	Public Administration, Social Security and Social Organizations	34.51	35.99	35.68

表 3.2 主要年份城镇登记失业人数和城镇登记失业率
QUANTITY OF URBAN REGISTERED UNEMPLOYMENT AND URBAN REGISTERED UNEMPLOYMENT RATE IN MAIN YEARS

指 标	Indicators	2000	2010	2017	2018
城镇登记失业人数(万人)	Registered Urban Unemployment (10 000 persons)	20.08	27.73	22.06	19.41
城镇登记失业率(%)	Registered Urban Unemployment Rate (%)	3.5	4.2	3.9	3.57

表 3.3 主要年份新增就业岗位
NEWLY ADDED WORKING POST IN MAIN YEARS

指 标	Indicators	2003	2010	2017	2018
新增就业岗位(万个)	Newly Added Working Post (10 000 units)	46.20	63.15	57.90	58.17

表 3.4 主要年份离休、退休及退职职工人数
QUANTITY OF RETIRED, RETIRED VETERAN CADRES AND RESIGNED PERSONS IN MAIN YEARS

单位：万人(10 000 persons)

指 标	Indicators	2000	2010	2017	2018
总 计	**Total**	**234.23**	**352.02**	**489.19**	**501.99**
国有单位	State-owned Units	165.55	166.38	164.51	163.03
离 休	Retired Veteran Cadres	3.39	1.82	1.04	0.93
退 休	Retired	161.03	160.53	161.70	160.38
退 职	Resigned	1.13	4.03	1.77	1.72
集体单位	Collective-owned Units	50.22	46.97	47.25	46.78
离 休	Retired Veteran Cadres	0.10	0.04	0.02	0.02
退 休	Retired	48.40	45.15	45.98	45.57
退 职	Resigned	1.72	1.78	1.25	1.19
其他单位	Other Ownership Units	18.46	138.67	277.43	292.18
离 休	Retired Veteran Cadres	0.21	0.68	0.39	0.35
退 休	Retired	18.05	132.29	270.47	285.12
退 职	Resigned	0.20	5.70	6.57	6.71

表 3.5 城镇单位就业人员平均工资(2018)
AVERAGE WAGES OF EMPLOYEES IN URBAN UNITS

单位:元(yuan)

指 标	Indicators	2018
城镇非私营单位就业人员平均工资	Average Wages of Employees in Urban Non-Private Units	140 270
城镇私营单位就业人员平均工资	Average Wages of Employees in Urban Private Units	57 056
城镇单位就业人员平均工资	Average Wages of Employees in Urban Units	105 176

表 3.6 主要年份离退休、退职人员养老金
PENSION FOR NONWORKING STAFF AND WORKERS IN MAIN YEARS

单位:亿元(100 million yuan)

指 标	Indicators	2000	2010	2017	2018
离退休、退职人员养老金	**Pension for Nonworking Staff and Workers**	**205.14**	**783.42**	**2 265.11**	**2 469.00**
离休职工的离休费	Pensions for Retired Veteran Cadres	7.32	11.41	9.68	14.32
退休职工的退休费	Pensions for Retired	195.90	763.44	2 247.58	2 446.80
退职人员的退职生活费	Living Expenses for the Resigned	1.92	8.57	7.85	7.88

表 3.7 离退休、退职人员养老金(2018)
PENSION FOR NONWORKING STAFF AND WORKERS

单位:亿元(100 million yuan)

指 标	Indicators	合 计 Total	国有单位 State-owned Units	集体单位 Collective-owned Units	其他单位 Other Ownership Units
离退休、退职人员养老金	**Pension for Nonworking Staff and Workers**	**2 469.00**	**1 015.79**	**214.60**	**1 238.61**
离休职工的离休费	Pensions for Retired Veteran Cadres	14.32	10.27	0.24	3.81
退休职工的退休费	Pensions for Retired	2 446.80	1 002.92	212.46	1 231.42
退职人员的退职生活费	Living Expenses for the Resigned	7.88	2.60	1.90	3.38

注：本表“其他单位”包括港澳台及外商企业。
Note: “Other Ownership Units” in this table includes foreign invested and HongKong, Macao and Taiwan funded enterprises.

上 / 海 / 统 / 计 / 年 / 鉴

主要统计指标解释

■ 从业人员

指从事一定社会劳动并取得工资或其他形式劳动报酬的人员，包括在岗职工、劳务派遣人员、再就业的离退休人员、私营和个体从业人员、农村从业人员、其他从业人员。这一指标反映了一定时期内全部劳动力资源的实际利用情况，是研究我国基本国情国力的重要指标。

■ 城镇登记失业人员

指有非农业户口，在一定的劳动年龄内(16 岁以上及男 50 岁以下、女 45 岁以下)，有劳动能力，无业而要求就业，并在当地就业服务机构进行求职登记的人员。

■ 城镇登记失业率

指城镇登记失业人员同城镇单位就业人员、城镇私营企业及个体就业人员(扣除使用的农村劳动力、聘用的离退休人员、港澳台及外方人员)和城镇登记失业人员、城镇单位中的不在岗职工之和的比。计算公式为:

城镇登记失业率=城镇登记失业人员/(城镇单位就业人员－使用的农村劳动力－聘用的离退休人员－聘用的港澳台及外方人员＋不在岗职工+城镇私营企业及个体就业人员+城镇登记失业人员) 100%

■ 职工工资总额

指在报告期内直接支付给本单位职工的劳动报酬或生活费。职工工资总额包括在岗职工工资和离岗职工生活费两部分。

■ 职工平均工资

指企业、事业、机关单位的职工在一定时期内平均每人所得的货币工资额。它表明一定时期职工工资收入的高低程度，是反映职工工资水平的主要指标。计算公式为:

职工平均工资=报告期实际支付的全部职工工资总额/报告期全部职工平均人数

SHANGHAI STATISTICAL YEARBOOK

EXPLANATORY NOTES TO MAJOR STATISTICAL INDICATORS

□ Employees

Employees refer to the persons who are engaged in social working and receive wages and other forms of remuneration payment, including total staff and workers, labor dispatched personnel, re−employed retirees, employees in private enterprises and individual economy, employed persons in the rural areas, and other employed persons. This indicator reflects the actual utilization of total labour force during a certain period of time and is often used for the research on China′s economic situation and national power.

□ Registered Urban Unemployment

Registered Urban Unemployment refers to those non−agricultural population within working age (16− 50 years for male and 16− 45 years for females),who are able and willing to work but unemployed and have registered for job in local employment service agencies.

□ Registered Urban Unemployment Rate

Registered Urban Unemployment Rate refers to the ratio of the number of the registered unemployed to the sum of the number of persons employed in various units (minus the rural labour force, retirees, and Hong Kong, Macao, Taiwan and foreign employees they employ) laid−off workers in urban units, urban self−employed individuals and the registered urban unemployed persons . The formula is as follows:

Registered Urban Unemployment Rate = Number of Registered Urban Unemployed Persons ÷ (Number of Persons Employed in Urban Units − rural labour force employed− retirees employed − Hong Kong, Macao, Taiwan and foreign employees + laid−off workers + Self−employed Individuals in Urban Areas + Number of Registered Urban Unemployed Persons) × 100%.

□ Total Wages of Staff and Workers

Total Wages of Staff and Workers refer to the compensation for services of living cost a unit pays to its employees on the payroll, including the living cost paid to those not on duty.

□ Average Wages of Staff and Workers

Average Wages of Staff and Workers refers to the average wage in money terms per person during a certain period of time for staff and workers in enterprises, institutions, and government agencies, which reflects the general level of wage income during a certain period of time and is calculated as follows:

Average Wages of Staff and Workers = Total Wages of Staff and Workers at Reference Time /Average Number of Staff and Workers at Reference Time.

第四篇

CHAPTER 4

国民经济核算

NATIONAL ECONOMIC ACCOUNTING

简要说明

生产总值(简称GDP)核算采取国家和地区分级核算制度,上海市生产总值由上海市统计局核算处核算,主要包括:(1)初步核算数。我国按照季度开展GDP核算,1-4季度GDP的初步核算数即为年度GDP初步核算数,于次年1月20日左右公布;(2)最终核实数,根据专业统计年报、财政决算资料和行政记录资料计算,在次年《上海市统计年鉴》上公布。由于基础资料和核算方法的不同,年度GDP初步核算数和初步核实数会有所差异。除上述核算程序外,在国家开展普查和重点行业调查,或计算方法、分类标准发生变化时,上海市统计局会根据国家统计局的有关要求对GDP当期或历史数据进行调整,并在《上海市统计年鉴》上公布。

本年鉴所公布的GDP核算数据包括:(1)按照当年价格计算的总量;(2)可比增长及指数。GDP总量变动受到价格变化和物量变化共同影响,在比较不同时期的GDP总量时要剔除价格变化的影响,以反映生产活动成果的实际变动。本年鉴公布的GDP及相关指标的增速为剔除价格变动影响的可比增速,并在此基础上计算指数。本篇GDP核算行业分类标准采用《国民经济行业分类》(GB/T 4754-2011),产业划分标准采用《三次产业划分规定》(国统字[2012]108号)。2017年,按照国家统计局对地区GDP进行研发支出核算方法改革的统一要求,将能够为所有者带来经济利益的研发支出不再作为中间消耗,而是作为固定资本形成处理。根据新的核算方法,修订了1995-2016年上海市GDP历史数据。2018年,根据第三次全国农业普查结果修订了2007-2016年上海市GDP历史数据。本年鉴中的数据是修订后的数据。

BRIEF INTRODUCTION

The gross domestic product, or GDP, uses nation-level and city-level classification system for calculation. Shanghai's GDP is produced by the Department of Accounting at the Shanghai Statistics Bureau. It covers (1) Preliminary figure: China calculates quarterly GDP figures, and the yearly preliminary GDP, which is published around January 20 in the following year, equals the preliminary rate for the four quarters combined. (2) Verified figure: it is calculated based on professional statistical report, fiscal accounts data and administrative records, published in the following year's Shanghai Statistical Yearbook. Because of differences in basic information and method of calculation, preliminary figure of the annual GDP and its verified figure may be different. In addition to the above-mentioned calculation procedure, the Shanghai Statistics Bureau modifies related GDP figures when China carries out national census or surveys in key industries, or when calculation methods or classification criteria change. The results will be published on The Shanghai Statistical Yearbook.

GDP data published in this yearbook include: (1) The total output based on the year's prices; (2) Comparable growth and indices. The total output of GDP changes with the prices and volumes, so the comparison of GDP in different periods should exclude the effect of price changes to reflect the actual movement in production activities. Growth of GDP data and related indicators in this yearbook has excluded the effect of price changes and is thus comparable. The indices are based on such comparable data as well. The calculation of GDP on sector classification still uses The Classification of National Economic Sectors (GB/T 4754-2011). Industrial division standard uses Three Industry Classification Regulation (National Statistic Word No.108, 2012). In 2017, according to the unified requirements of reform on R & D expenditure accounting method for regional GDP conducted by the National Bureau of Statistics, the R & D expenditure which will be able to bring economic benefits to the owner is no longer taken as intermediate consumption, but as fixed capital formation. According to the new accounting method, the historical data of GDP in Shanghai during the 1995-2016 years have been revised. In 2018, according to the result of the third national agricultural census, the historical data of GDP in Shanghai during the 2007-2016 years have been revised. The data in this yearbook are the revised data.

表 4.1 上海市生产总值(1978~2018)
GROSS DOMESTIC PRODUCT

年 份 Year	上海市生产总值(亿元) Gross Domestic Product (100 million yuan)	按产业分 Grouped by Industry			按行业分 Grouped by Sector	
		第一产业 Primary Industry	第二产业 Secondary Industry	第三产业 Tertiary Industry	#工 业 Industry	#建筑业 Construction
1978	272.81	11.00	211.05	50.76	207.47	3.58
1979	286.43	11.39	221.21	53.83	216.62	4.59
1980	311.89	10.10	236.10	65.69	230.87	5.23
1981	324.76	10.58	244.34	69.84	237.12	7.22
1982	337.07	13.31	249.32	74.44	240.75	8.57
1983	351.81	13.52	255.32	82.97	246.26	9.06
1984	390.85	17.26	275.37	98.22	263.19	12.18
1985	466.75	19.53	325.63	121.59	311.12	14.51
1986	490.83	19.69	336.02	135.12	318.89	17.13
1987	545.46	21.60	364.38	159.48	336.54	27.84
1988	648.30	27.36	433.05	187.89	399.53	33.52
1989	696.54	29.63	466.18	200.73	432.92	33.26
1990	781.66	34.24	505.60	241.82	469.83	35.77
1991	893.77	34.06	550.64	309.07	514.79	35.85
1992	1 114.32	34.16	677.39	402.77	636.68	40.71
1993	1 519.23	37.82	902.38	579.03	846.71	55.67
1994	1 990.86	47.61	1 148.45	794.80	1 074.37	74.08
1995	2 518.08	59.82	1 430.47	1 027.79	1 318.93	111.54
1996	2 980.75	68.72	1 610.47	1 301.56	1 466.12	144.35
1997	3 465.28	72.03	1 789.72	1 603.53	1 614.13	175.59
1998	3 831.00	73.84	1 889.63	1 867.53	1 687.39	202.24
1999	4 222.30	74.49	2 004.55	2 143.26	1 807.29	197.26
2000	4 812.15	76.68	2 231.93	2 503.54	2 022.53	209.40
2001	5 257.66	78.00	2 431.38	2 748.28	2 194.09	237.29
2002	5 795.02	79.68	2 654.47	3 060.87	2 399.07	255.40
2003	6 762.38	81.02	3 249.43	3 431.93	2 980.43	269.00
2004	8 165.38	83.45	3 947.01	4 134.92	3 646.47	300.54
2005	9 365.54	90.26	4 451.11	4 824.17	4 104.65	346.46
2006	10 718.04	93.81	5 056.43	5 567.80	4 659.17	397.26
2007	12 668.89	102.61	5 674.34	6 891.94	5 254.57	419.77
2008	14 276.79	112.79	6 207.97	7 956.03	5 695.23	512.74
2009	15 287.56	115.80	6 143.59	9 028.17	5 546.27	597.32
2010	17 436.85	117.79	7 376.81	9 942.25	6 689.90	686.91
2011	19 539.07	130.17	8 128.44	11 280.46	7 403.07	725.37
2012	20 558.98	133.26	8 063.93	12 361.79	7 301.05	762.88
2013	22 264.06	131.29	8 147.16	13 985.61	7 368.20	802.13
2014	24 068.20	131.59	8 434.97	15 501.64	7 619.88	843.02
2015	25 659.18	125.53	8 259.03	17 274.62	7 431.36	855.22
2016	28 183.51	114.34	8 406.28	19 662.89	7 555.34	879.81
2017	30 632.99	110.78	9 330.67	21 191.54	8 392.84	970.79
2018	32 679.87	104.37	9 732.54	22 842.96	8 694.95	1 071.75

注：2018 年根据第三次全国农业普查结果对 GDP 历史数据进行了修订(下表同)。
Note: Since 2018, the historical data of GDP has been revised according to the result of the third national agricultural census(same as below).

表 4.2 上海市生产总值比上年增长(1978~2018)
GROWTH RATE OF GROSS DOMESTIC PRODUCT RAISED PRECEDING YEAR

单位:%

年 份 Year	上海市生产总值 Gross Domestic Product	按产业分 Grouped by Industry			按行业分 Grouped by Sector	
		第一产业 Primary Industry	第二产业 Secondary Industry	第三产业 Tertiary Industry	#工 业 Industry	#建筑业 Construction
1978	15.8	27.0	16.6	10.5	15.8	89.7
1979	7.4	-0.7	8.6	3.0	8.8	-2.1
1980	8.4	-0.6	6.0	22.2	6.1	1.7
1981	5.6	0.3	4.9	8.9	4.1	39.2
1982	7.2	26.2	4.6	13.4	4.2	18.7
1983	7.8	平	7.5	9.8	7.5	8.9
1984	11.6	25.3	10.0	14.7	9.7	19.3
1985	13.4	-22.2	14.9	14.7	15.0	11.0
1986	4.4	-0.2	4.0	6.0	3.7	11.7
1987	7.5	-2.7	7.4	8.9	6.8	22.3
1988	10.1	4.6	9.4	12.6	9.3	12.1
1989	3.0	0.3	1.6	7.1	1.9	-4.4
1990	3.5	4.3	2.8	5.3	2.7	5.1
1991	7.1	0.4	6.9	8.6	8.8	-18.7
1992	14.8	0.4	17.2	12.0	17.7	7.7
1993	15.1	-2.7	16.7	13.7	16.9	13.8
1994	14.5	2.9	14.2	16.2	14.2	14.1
1995	15.0	6.4	15.5	14.8	15.0	25.4
1996	13.1	5.0	11.2	18.1	10.4	24.9
1997	12.8	4.2	10.6	17.8	10.2	16.9
1998	10.3	2.2	8.3	14.8	7.8	14.8
1999	10.4	2.1	9.0	13.4	9.7	-0.6
2000	11.0	3.4	9.8	13.5	10.3	3.1
2001	10.5	3.0	12.0	9.5	12.1	10.9
2002	11.4	3.0	12.1	10.9	12.7	6.4
2003	12.3	2.3	16.2	9.0	17.6	1.3
2004	14.3	-5.0	15.0	14.1	16.1	0.9
2005	11.5	-9.7	10.6	12.8	10.6	10.3
2006	12.8	0.8	12.1	13.7	11.9	14.5
2007	15.2	3.7	11.6	18.7	12.2	4.1
2008	9.7	0.7	7.5	11.7	7.6	5.8
2009	8.4	-0.5	3.8	12.3	3.2	11.8
2010	10.2	-5.2	16.5	5.7	17.2	7.9
2011	8.3	0.5	6.6	9.7	7.6	-3.4
2012	7.5	0.5	3.2	10.7	2.9	6.0
2013	7.9	-2.2	6.1	9.1	6.1	5.3
2014	7.1	1.7	4.4	8.9	4.5	3.9
2015	7.0	-4.9	1.3	10.7	0.8	6.9
2016	6.8	-12.4	1.2	9.6	1.0	3.1
2017	6.9	-0.8	5.8	7.5	6.5	-0.5
2018	6.6	-6.9	1.8	8.7	1.9	1.1

表 4.3 上海市生产总值指数(以 1978 年为 100，1978~2018)
INDEX OF GROSS DOMESTIC PRODUCT (1978=100)

年 份 Year	上海市 生产总值 Gross Domestic Product	按产业分 Grouped by Industry 第一产业 Primary Industry	第二产业 Secondary Industry	第三产业 Tertiary Industry	按行业分 Grouped by Sector #工 业 Industry	#建筑业 Construction
1978	100.0	100.0	100.0	100.0	100.0	100.0
1979	107.4	99.3	108.6	103.0	108.8	97.9
1980	116.5	98.7	115.1	125.9	115.4	99.6
1981	123.0	99.0	120.7	137.1	120.1	138.6
1982	131.8	124.9	126.3	155.5	125.1	164.5
1983	142.1	124.9	135.8	170.7	134.5	179.2
1984	158.6	156.5	149.4	195.8	147.5	213.9
1985	179.9	121.7	171.6	224.5	169.6	237.5
1986	187.8	121.5	178.4	238.0	175.9	265.3
1987	201.9	118.2	191.6	259.1	187.9	324.5
1988	222.3	123.7	209.6	291.7	205.4	363.7
1989	229.0	124.1	213.0	312.4	209.3	347.7
1990	237.0	129.4	219.0	329.0	215.0	365.4
1991	253.9	129.9	234.1	357.1	234.0	297.1
1992	291.6	130.4	274.3	399.8	275.4	320.0
1993	335.7	126.9	320.2	454.5	321.9	364.2
1994	384.2	130.6	365.7	528.1	367.6	415.5
1995	442.0	139.0	422.5	606.1	422.9	521.2
1996	500.1	146.0	469.8	715.8	467.0	651.1
1997	564.0	152.1	519.7	843.5	514.8	761.2
1998	622.2	155.5	562.7	968.3	555.2	873.8
1999	686.8	158.8	613.3	1 098.0	608.8	868.8
2000	762.5	164.2	673.7	1 246.3	671.4	895.3
2001	842.8	169.1	754.5	1 364.2	752.7	993.2
2002	938.5	174.2	845.8	1 513.0	848.2	1 057.0
2003	1 054.1	178.2	982.5	1 649.8	997.4	1 071.1
2004	1 204.9	169.3	1 129.5	1 883.2	1 158.3	1 080.7
2005	1 343.2	152.9	1 248.9	2 124.7	1 281.0	1 191.6
2006	1 515.2	154.1	1 399.9	2 415.5	1 433.4	1 364.0
2007	1 745.9	159.9	1 561.8	2 868.2	1 608.5	1 419.5
2008	1 914.9	161.1	1 678.9	3 203.2	1 731.3	1 501.3
2009	2 076.0	160.3	1 742.8	3 597.8	1 786.4	1 678.0
2010	2 288.6	151.9	2 030.3	3 801.4	2 094.2	1 811.0
2011	2 478.9	152.7	2 164.0	4 169.8	2 253.6	1 749.5
2012	2 664.8	153.4	2 232.2	4 616.5	2 318.6	1 855.3
2013	2 874.0	150.1	2 367.5	5 038.7	2 460.6	1 953.9
2014	3 077.9	152.7	2 471.5	5 486.8	2 570.8	2 031.0
2015	3 294.3	145.2	2 503.8	6 073.4	2 591.0	2 170.8
2016	3 519.2	127.3	2 534.8	6 658.6	2 617.1	2 237.7
2017	3 762.2	126.3	2 681.2	7 154.7	2 787.9	2 225.7
2018	4 008.9	117.6	2 730.3	7 776.0	2 841.1	2 250.2

表 4.4 上海市生产总值构成(1978~2018)
STRUCTURE OF GROSS DOMESTIC PRODUCT

单位:%

年 份 Year	上海市 生产总值 Gross Domestic Product	按产业分 Grouped by Industry 第一产业 Primary Industry	 第二产业 Secondary Industry	 第三产业 Tertiary Industry	按行业分 Grouped by Sector #工 业 Industry	 #建筑业 Construction
1978	100.0	4.0	77.4	18.6	76.1	1.3
1979	100.0	4.0	77.2	18.8	75.6	1.6
1980	100.0	3.2	75.7	21.1	74.0	1.7
1981	100.0	3.3	75.2	21.5	73.0	2.2
1982	100.0	3.9	74.0	22.1	71.4	2.6
1983	100.0	3.8	72.6	23.6	70.0	2.6
1984	100.0	4.4	70.5	25.1	67.4	3.1
1985	100.0	4.2	69.8	26.0	66.7	3.1
1986	100.0	4.0	68.5	27.5	65.0	3.5
1987	100.0	4.0	66.8	29.2	61.7	5.1
1988	100.0	4.2	66.8	29.0	61.6	5.2
1989	100.0	4.3	66.9	28.8	62.1	4.8
1990	100.0	4.4	64.7	30.9	60.1	4.6
1991	100.0	3.8	61.6	34.6	57.6	4.0
1992	100.0	3.1	60.8	36.1	57.1	3.7
1993	100.0	2.5	59.4	38.1	55.7	3.7
1994	100.0	2.4	57.7	39.9	54.0	3.7
1995	100.0	2.4	56.8	40.8	52.4	4.4
1996	100.0	2.3	54.0	43.7	49.2	4.8
1997	100.0	2.1	51.6	46.3	46.6	5.1
1998	100.0	1.9	49.3	48.8	44.0	5.3
1999	100.0	1.8	47.5	50.7	42.8	4.7
2000	100.0	1.6	46.4	52.0	42.0	4.4
2001	100.0	1.5	46.2	52.3	41.7	4.5
2002	100.0	1.4	45.8	52.8	41.4	4.4
2003	100.0	1.2	48.1	50.7	44.1	4.0
2004	100.0	1.0	48.4	50.6	44.7	3.7
2005	100.0	1.0	47.5	51.5	43.8	3.7
2006	100.0	0.9	47.2	51.9	43.5	3.7
2007	100.0	0.8	44.8	54.4	41.5	3.3
2008	100.0	0.8	43.5	55.7	39.9	3.6
2009	100.0	0.8	40.2	59.1	36.3	3.9
2010	100.0	0.7	42.3	57.0	38.4	3.9
2011	100.0	0.7	41.6	57.7	37.9	3.7
2012	100.0	0.6	39.2	60.1	35.5	3.7
2013	100.0	0.6	36.6	62.8	33.1	3.6
2014	100.0	0.5	35.0	64.4	31.7	3.5
2015	100.0	0.5	32.2	67.3	29.0	3.3
2016	100.0	0.4	29.8	69.8	26.8	3.1
2017	100.0	0.4	30.5	69.2	27.4	3.2
2018	100.0	0.3	29.8	69.9	26.6	3.3

表 4.5 上海市人均生产总值(1978~2018)
PER CAPITA GROSS DOMESTIC PRODUCT

年 份 Year	上海市 生产总值(亿元) Gross Domestic Product (100 million yuan)	人均生产总值 (按人民币计算)(元) Per Capita Gross Domestic Product (yuan)	人均生产总值指数 Per Capita Gross Domestic Product Index		人均生产总值 (按美元计算)(美元) Per Capita Gross Domestic Product (USD)
			以 1978 年为 100 (1978=100)	以上年为 100 (preceding year=100)	
1978	272.81	2 485	100.0	114.9	1 445
1979	286.43	2 556	105.3	105.3	1 787
1980	311.89	2 725	111.8	106.2	1 829
1981	324.76	2 800	116.5	104.2	1 642
1982	337.07	2 864	123.0	105.6	1 513
1983	351.81	2 947	130.7	106.3	1 492
1984	390.85	3 232	144.0	110.2	1 389
1985	466.75	3 811	161.3	112.0	1 298
1986	490.83	3 956	166.1	103.0	1 146
1987	545.46	4 340	176.2	106.1	1 166
1988	648.30	5 080	191.0	108.4	1 365
1989	696.54	5 362	193.3	101.2	1 424
1990	781.66	5 911	196.6	101.7	1 236
1991	893.77	6 661	207.6	105.6	1 251
1992	1 114.32	8 208	235.6	113.5	1 488
1993	1 519.23	11 061	268.1	113.8	1 920
1994	1 990.86	14 328	303.2	113.1	1 662
1995	2 518.08	17 910	342.3	112.9	2 145
1996	2 980.75	20 808	380.3	111.1	2 502
1997	3 465.28	23 573	417.9	109.9	2 843
1998	3 831.00	25 405	449.2	107.5	3 069
1999	4 222.30	27 293	483.3	107.6	3 297
2000	4 812.15	30 307	522.9	108.2	3 661
2001	5 257.66	32 089	560.0	107.1	3 877
2002	5 795.02	34 277	604.2	107.9	4 141
2003	6 762.38	38 878	659.8	109.2	4 697
2004	8 165.38	45 353	728.4	110.4	5 480
2005	9 365.54	50 282	785.2	107.8	6 138
2006	10 718.04	55 615	855.9	109.0	6 976
2007	12 668.89	62 909	944.1	110.3	8 274
2008	14 276.79	67 916	992.2	105.1	9 779
2009	15 287.56	70 273	1 039.8	104.8	10 287
2010	17 436.85	77 275	1 105.3	106.3	11 415
2011	19 539.07	84 037	1 161.7	105.1	13 013
2012	20 558.98	86 969	1 227.9	105.7	13 778
2013	22 264.06	92 852	1 305.3	106.3	14 992
2014	24 068.20	99 438	1 384.9	106.1	16 188
2015	25 659.18	106 009	1 481.8	107.0	17 020
2016	28 183.51	116 582	1 585.5	107.0	17 551
2017	30 632.99	126 634	1 693.3	106.8	18 756
2018	32 679.87	134 982	1 803.4	106.5	20 398

表 4.6 主要年份上海市生产总值(按所有制分)
GROSS DOMESTIC PRODUCT(BY OWNERSHIP) IN MAIN YEARS

年 份 Year	上海市生产总值 Gross Domestic Product	其 中 of which				
		公有制经济 Public-owned	其中 of which: 国有经济 State-owned	其中 of which: 集体经济 Collective-owned	非公有制经济 Non-public-owned	其中 of which: #私营和个体 Private
绝对值(亿元) Absolute Volume(100million yuan)						
1990	781.66	746.03	556.87	189.16	35.63	22.39
1995	2 518.08	2 059.79	1 500.81	558.98	458.29	195.21
2000	4 812.15	3 436.81	2 652.14	784.67	1 375.34	629.45
2001	5 257.66	3 585.69	2 803.70	781.99	1 671.97	836.78
2002	5 795.02	3 738.81	2 922.57	816.24	2 056.21	1 062.89
2003	6 762.38	4 215.79	3 403.13	812.66	2 546.59	1 267.49
2004	8 165.38	4 870.93	4 128.24	742.69	3 294.45	1 306.25
2005	9 365.54	5 333.69	4 546.17	787.52	4 031.85	1 960.70
2006	10 718.04	5 908.34	5 086.31	822.03	4 809.70	2 301.09
2007	12 668.89	6 789.39	5 962.67	826.72	5 879.50	2 828.07
2008	14 276.79	7 477.13	6 583.09	894.04	6 799.66	3 341.63
2009	15 287.56	7 927.48	7 015.53	911.95	7 360.08	3 604.44
2010	17 436.85	8 839.74	7 925.31	914.43	8 597.11	4 176.61
2011	19 539.07	9 809.18	8 875.60	933.58	9 729.89	4 646.45
2012	20 558.98	10 208.29	9 244.68	963.61	10 350.69	4 936.92
2013	22 264.06	10 932.23	10 014.20	918.03	11 331.83	5 382.44
2014	24 068.20	11 731.29	10 808.33	922.96	12 336.91	5 864.86
2015	25 659.18	12 419.44	11 525.00	894.44	13 239.74	6 346.75
2016	28 183.51	13 625.19	12 653.78	971.41	14 558.32	7 019.27
2017	30 632.99	14 877.55	13 825.50	1 052.05	15 755.44	7 538.12
2018	32 679.87	15 896.97	14 818.99	1 077.98	16 782.90	8 155.27
构 成(%) Composition(%)						
1990	100.0	95.4	71.2	24.2	4.6	2.9
1995	100.0	81.8	59.6	22.2	18.2	7.8
2000	100.0	71.4	55.1	16.3	28.6	13.1
2001	100.0	68.2	53.3	14.9	31.8	15.9
2002	100.0	64.5	50.4	14.1	35.5	18.3
2003	100.0	62.3	50.3	12.0	37.7	18.7
2004	100.0	59.7	50.6	9.1	40.3	16.0
2005	100.0	57.0	48.5	8.5	43.0	20.9
2006	100.0	55.1	47.5	7.6	44.9	21.5
2007	100.0	53.6	47.1	6.5	46.4	22.3
2008	100.0	52.4	46.1	6.3	47.6	23.4
2009	100.0	51.9	45.9	6.0	48.1	23.6
2010	100.0	50.7	45.5	5.2	49.3	24.0
2011	100.0	50.2	45.4	4.8	49.8	23.8
2012	100.0	49.7	45.0	4.7	50.3	24.0
2013	100.0	49.1	45.0	4.1	50.9	24.2
2014	100.0	48.7	44.9	3.8	51.3	24.4
2015	100.0	48.4	44.9	3.5	51.6	24.7
2016	100.0	48.3	44.9	3.4	51.7	24.9
2017	100.0	48.6	45.2	3.4	51.4	24.6
2018	100.0	48.6	45.3	3.3	51.4	25.0

表 4.7 主要年份非公有制经济增加值(按产业分)
ADDED VALUE OF NON-PUBLIC-OWNED (GROUPED BY INDUSTRY) IN MAIN YEARS

单位:亿元(100 million yuan)

年 份 Year	非公有制经济增加值 Added Value of Non-public-owned	其 中 of which			其 中 of which
		第一产业 Primary Industry	第二产业 Secondary Industry	第三产业 Tertiary Industry	#工 业 Industry
1978	2.71	1.64	0.67	0.40	0.40
1990	35.63	9.01	15.22	11.40	13.74
1991	44.72	8.11	22.20	14.41	20.62
1992	73.41	7.65	42.13	23.63	39.85
1993	133.93	8.98	77.02	47.93	72.81
1994	250.63	10.88	154.62	85.13	148.31
1995	458.29	13.29	291.73	153.27	280.47
1996	663.40	14.31	431.78	217.31	414.94
1997	799.74	13.42	512.23	274.09	478.52
1998	950.97	13.26	571.31	366.40	527.61
1999	1 136.54	13.56	646.65	476.33	596.26
2000	1 375.34	14.25	786.71	574.38	728.00
2001	1 671.97	14.77	939.54	717.66	872.50
2002	2 056.21	14.34	1 102.53	939.34	1 021.67
2003	2 546.59	13.04	1 481.64	1 051.91	1 399.53
2004	3 294.45	10.44	1 951.58	1 332.43	1 786.92
2005	4 031.85	11.12	2 266.19	1 754.54	2 091.67
2006	4 809.70	11.41	2 681.04	2 117.25	2 484.04
2007	5 879.50	12.34	3 100.78	2 766.38	2 886.14
2008	6 799.66	13.82	3 361.00	3 424.84	3 103.95
2009	7 360.08	14.06	3 291.09	4 054.93	3 000.32
2010	8 597.11	14.92	4 014.62	4 567.57	3 659.30
2011	9 729.89	16.99	4 447.20	5 265.70	4 066.18
2012	10 350.69	17.47	4 425.96	5 907.26	3 993.52
2013	11 331.83	17.62	4 448.99	6 865.22	4 014.62
2014	12 336.91	18.06	4 643.66	7 675.19	4 188.91
2015	13 239.74	20.73	4 589.05	8 629.96	4 121.22
2016	14 558.32	15.10	4 708.47	9 834.75	4 221.71
2017	15 755.44	12.74	5 230.41	10 512.29	4 691.60
2018	16 782.90	12.01	5 561.45	11 209.44	4 963.46

表 4.8 主要年份旅游产业增加值
VALUE ADDED OF TOURISM INDUSTRY IN MAIN YEARS

指 标	Indicators	2005	2010	2017	2018
增加值(亿元)	**Value Added (100 million yuan)**	**584.26**	**1 360.80**	**1 888.24**	**2 078.64**
按行业分	**Grouped by Sectors**				
# 旅行社服务业	Travel Agency	9.02	17.50	40.55	44.60
旅游住宿业	Hotel	91.78	212.34	208.17	225.12
旅游运输业	Travel Transportation	120.86	159.67	258.94	277.91
邮电通讯业	Post and Telecommunication	25.21	38.60	49.20	50.41
旅游商业	Tourism Commerce	96.17	529.28	624.78	720.26
旅游餐饮业	Catering	68.92	67.17	137.29	156.48
城市交通业	Urban Traffic	45.96	93.18	135.03	151.38
园林文化业	Gardening	92.42	169.98	290.17	307.16
旅游产业增加值占上海市生产总值比重(%)	**Ratio of Value Added of Tourism Industry to GDP (%)**	**6.2**	**7.8**	**6.2**	**6.4**

上／海／统／计／年／鉴

主要统计指标解释

■ 生产总值(原国内生产总值)

指按市场价格计算的一个国家(或地区)所有常住单位在一定时期内生产活动的最终成果。生产总值有三种表现形态,即价值形态、收入形态和产品形态。从价值形态看,它是所有常住单位在一定时期内所生产的全部货物和服务价值超过同期投入的全部非固定资产货物和服务价值的差额,即所有常住单位的增加值之和;从收入形态看,它是所有常住单位在一定时期内所创造并分配给常住单位和非常住单位的初次收入之和;从产品形态看,它是所有常住单位在一定时期内最终使用的货物和服务减去货物和服务的进口价值。在实际核算中,生产总值有三种计算方法,即生产法、收入法和支出法。三种方法分别从不同的方面反映生产总值及其构成。根据国务院和国家统计局有关我国GDP核算和数据发布制度的规定,上海国内生产总值自2004年起更名为“上海市生产总值”,简称“上海市GDP”。

■ 三次产业

三次产业的划分是国际上常用的产业结构分类。第一产业是指产品直接取自自然界的部门,第二产业是指对初级产品进行再加工的部门,第三产业是指为生产和消费提供各种服务的部门。

第一产业是指农、林、牧、渔业(不含农、林、牧、渔服务业)。

第二产业是指采矿业(不含开采辅助活动),制造业(不含金属制品、机械和设备修理业),电力、热力、燃气及水生产和供应业,建筑业。

第三产业即服务业,是指除第一产业、第二产业以外的其他行业。

■ 劳动者报酬

指劳动者因从事生产活动所获得的全部报酬。包括劳动者获得的各种形式的工资、奖金和津贴,既包括货币形式的,也包括实物形式的,还包括劳动者所享受的公费医疗和医药卫生费、上下班交通补贴、单位支付的社会保险费、住房公积金等。对于个体经济来说,其所有者所获得的劳动报酬和经营利润不易区分,这两部分统一作为劳动者报酬处理。

■ 生产税净额

指生产税减生产补贴后的余额。生产税指政府对生产单位从事生产、销售和经营活动以及因从事生产活动使用某些生产要素(如固定资产、土地、劳动力)所征收的各种税、附加费和规费。生产补贴与生产税相反,指政府对生产单位的单方面转移支出,因此视为负生产税,包括政策亏损补贴、价格补贴等。

■ 固定资产折旧

指一定时期内为弥补固定资产损耗按照规定的固定资产折旧率提取的固定资产折旧,或按国民经济核算统一规定的折旧率虚拟计算的固定资产折旧。它反映了固定资产在当期生产中的转移价值。各类企业和企业化管理的事业单位的固定资产折旧是指实际计提的折旧费;不计提折旧的政府机关、非企业化管理的事业单位和居民住房的固定资产折旧是按照统一规定的折旧率和固定资产原值计算的虚拟折旧。原则上,固定资产折旧应按固定资产当期的重置价值计算,但是目前我国尚不具备对全社会固定资产进行重估价的基础,所以暂时只能采用上述办法。

■ 营业盈余

指常住单位创造的增加值扣除劳动者报酬、生产税净额和固定资产折旧后的余额。它相当于企业的营业利润(不包括投资收益)加上生产补贴,但要扣除从利润中开支的工资和福利等。

■ 支出法生产总值

是从最终使用的角度反映一个国家(或地区)一定时期内生产活动最终成果的一种方法,包括最终消费支出、资本形成总额及货物和服务净出口三部分。计算公式为:

支出法生产总值=最终消费支出+资本形成总额+货物和服务净出口

■ 最终消费支出

指常住单位在一定时期内对于货物和服务的全部最终消费支出,也就是常住单位为满足物质、文化和精神生活的需要,从本国经济领土和国外购买的货物和

主要统计指标解释

服务的支出；不包括非常住单位在本国经济领土内的消费支出。最终消费支出分为居民消费支出和政府消费支出。

■ 居民消费支出

指常住住户在一定时期内对货物和服务的全部最终消费支出。居民消费按市场价格计算，即按居民支付的购买者价格计算。购买者价格是购买者取得货物所支付的价格，包括购买者支付的运输和商业费用。居民消费除了直接以货币形式购买货物和服务的消费之外，还包括以其他方式获得的货物和服务的消费支出，即所谓的虚拟消费支出。居民虚拟消费支出包括以下几种类型：单位以实物报酬及实物转移的形式提供给劳动者的货物和服务；住户生产并由本住户消费了的货物和服务，其中的服务仅指住户的自有住房服务；金融机构提供的金融媒介服务；保险公司提供的保险服务。

■ 政府消费支出

指一定时期内政府部门为全社会提供公共服务的消费支出和免费或以较低价格向住户提供的货物和服务的净支出。前者等于政府服务的产出价值减去政府单位所获得的经营收入的价值，政府服务的产出价值等于它的经常性业务支出加上固定资产折旧；后者等于政府部门免费或以较低价格向住户提供的货物和服务的市场价值减去向住户收取的价值。

■ 资本形成总额

指常住单位在一定时期内获得的，并减去处置的固定资产，加上存货的变动，包括固定资本形成总额和存货变动。

■ 固定资本形成总额

指生产者在一定时期内获得的固定资产减处置的固定资产的价值总额。固定资产是通过生产活动生产出来的，且其使用年限在一年以上、单位价值在规定标准以上的资产，不包括自然资产。可分为有形固定资本形成总额和无形固定资本形成总额。有形固定资本形成总额包括一定时期内完成的建筑工程、安装工程和设备工器具购置(减处置)价值，以及土地改良、新增役、种、奶、毛、娱乐用牲畜和新增经济林木价值。无形固定资本形成总额包括矿藏的勘探、计算机软件等获得减处置。

■ 存货变动

指常住单位在一定时期内存货实物量变动的市场价值，即期末价值减期初价值的差额，再扣除当期由于价格变动而产生的持有收益。存货变动可以是正值，也可以是负值，正值表示存货上升，负值表示存货下降。存货包括生产单位购进的原材料、燃料和储备物资等存货，以及生产单位生产的产成品、在制品和半成品等存货。

■ 货物和服务净流出

指货物和服务流出减货物和服务流入的差额。流出包括常住单位向非常住单位出售或无偿转让的各种货物和服务的价值；流入包括常住单位从非常住单位购买或无偿得到的各种货物和服务的价值。地区核算净流出，除包括本地区对外贸易及国外非贸易往来的净出口额，还包括地区间货物和服务流出减流入后的净额。

■ 信息产业

是指与电子信息相关联的各种活动的集合，包括信息产品的制造、销售和信息服务等活动。由于信息产业增加值是依据若干行业的有关资料进行跨行业核算的，因此不宜将其与上海市生产总值中其他行业的增加值进行加总，否则会造成重复计算。

■ 旅游产业

指本市与旅游相关的各行业，为境内外旅游者提供旅游服务的产业。这些服务包括：旅行社服务、交通运输服务、住宿服务、电讯服务、娱乐服务、餐饮服务、商品零售服务等。由于旅游产业增加值是依据相关行业的有关资料进行跨行业核算的，因此不宜将其与上海市生产总值中其他行业的增加值进行加总，否则会造成重复计算。

SHANGHAI STATISTICAL YEARBOOK

EXPLANATORY NOTES TO MAJOR STATISTICAL INDICATORS

□ Gross Regional Product(former Gross Domestic Product)

Gross Regional Product refers to the final products at market prices by (of) all resident units of a country (or region) during a certain period of time. Gross product is expressed in three different forms, i.e value, income, and products respectively. The form of value refers to the total value of all products and services produced by all resident units during a certain period of time minus the total value of input of non-fixed-assets products and services or the summation of the value-added of all resident units; the form of income includes all the income items produced by all resident units and distributed primarily to all resident and non-resident units; the form of product refers to all final goods and services minus the value of imports of goods and services. In the practice of national accounting, it is calculated by three approaches, i.e. product approach, income approach, and expenditure approach, respectively, to reflect Gross Product and its composition of different aspects. According to the regulations of GDP national accounting and data release issued by the State Council and National Bureau of Statistics, since 2004 Shanghai Gross Domestic Product has been renamed as Shanghai Gross Product Value, for short Shanghai GDP.

□ Three Industries

Classification of economic activities into three strata of industry is a common practice in the world. Primary industry refers to extraction of natural resources; secondary industry involves processing of primary products; and tertiary industry provides services of various kinds for production and consumption.

Primary industry includes farming, forestry, animal husbandry, fishery industry (not including the service industry for farming, forestry, animal husbandry and fishery).

Secondary industry includes mining (not including mining auxiliary activities), manufacturing (not including metal products, machinery and equipment repair industry), electricity, gas and water production and supply industry and construction.

Tertiary industry refers to all other industries not included in primary or secondary industries.

□ Labourers Remuneration

Labourers Remuneration refers to the whole payment of various forms earned by the labourers from the productive activities they are engaged in. It includes wages, bonuses and allowances the labourers earned in monetary form and in kind. It also includes the free medical services provided to the labourers and the medicine expenses, traffic subsidies and social insurance, housing fund paid by the employers. As the individual economy is concerned, since the labourers remuneration is not easily distinguished from the operating profit, both are treated as labourers remuneration.

□ Net Taxes on Production

Net Taxes on Production refers to taxes on production less subsidies on production. The taxes on production refers to the various taxes, extra charges and fees levied on the production units on their production, sale and business activities as well as on the use of some factors of production, such as fixed assets, land and labour force in the production activities they are engaged in. In contrast to the taxes on production, the subsidies on production refer to the unilateral government transfer to the production units and are therefore regarded as negative taxes on production. They include subsidies on the loss due to implementation of government policies, price subsidies, etc.

□ Depreciation of Fixed Assets

Depreciation of Fixed Assets refers to the depreciation of fixed assets of a given period, drawn in accordance with the stipulated depreciation rate for the purpose of compensating the wear loss of the fixed assets or the depreciation of fixed assets calculated in a fictitious way in accordance with the stipulated unified depreciation rate in the national economic accounting system. It reflects the value of transfer of the fixed assets in the production of the current period. The depreciation of fixed assets in various enterprises and institutions managed as enterprises refers to the depreciation expenses actually drawn. In government agencies and institutions not managed as enterprises which do not draw the depreciation expenses, as well as for the houses of residents, the depreciation of fixed assets is the imputed depreciation, which is calculated in accordance with

EXPLANATORY NOTES TO MAJOR STATISTICAL INDICATORS

the stipulated unified depreciation rate. In principle, the depreciation of fixed assets should be calculated on the basis of the re-purchased value of the fixed assets. However, there is no actual condition to re- evaluate all the fixed assets in China. Therefore, the above-mentioned methods are temporarily adopted at present.

□ Operating Surplus

Operating Surplus refers to the balance of the value added created by the resident units deducting the labourers remuneration, net taxes on production and the depreciation of fixed assets. It is equivalent to the business profit (excluding income from investment) of the enterprises plus subsidies on production, but the wages and welfare expenses paid from the profits should be deducted.

□ GDP by Expenditure Approach

GDP by Expenditure Approach refers to the method of measuring the final results of production activities of a country (region) during a given period from the perspective of final use. It includes final consumption, total capital formation and net export of goods and services, i.e.:

GDP by expenditure approach = final consumption + total capital formation + net export of goods and services

□ Final Consumption

Final Consumption refers to the total expenditure of resident units on final consumption of goods and services in a certain period, namely the expenditure of the resident units for purchases of goods and services from domestic economic territory and abroad to meet the requirements of material, cultural and spiritual life. It excludes the expenditure of non-resident units on consumption in the economic territory of the country. The final consumption is classified into household consumption and government consumption.

□ Household Consumption

Household Consumption refers to the total expenditure of resident households on the final consumption of goods and services in a certain period of time. The households consumption is calculated at market prices, namely the purchasers prices which the households pay; the purchasers prices of goods are the prices the households pay when they obtain the goods, including the transport and commercial expenses paid by the households. In addition to the consumption of goods and services bought by the households directly with money, the expenditure on goods and services obtained by the households in other ways, i.e. the so-called imputed expenditure on consumption, is also included in the households consumption. The imputation expenditure of the households on consumption includes the following types: (a) the goods and services provided to the households by the units in the form of payment in kind and transfer in kind; (b) the goods and services produced and consumed by the households themselves, in which the services refer only to the services provided by the residential buildings owned by the households; (c) the services of financial intermediary provided by the financial institutions; (d) the insurance services provided by the insurance companies.

□ Government Consumption

Government Consumption refers to the expenditure on the consumption of the public services provided by the government to the whole society and the net expenditure on the goods and services provided by the government to the households free charge or at lower prices in a certain period of time. The former equals to the output value of the government services minus the value of operating income obtained by the government departments. (The output value of the government services equals to its current operating expenditure plus depreciation of fixed assets). The latter equals to the market value of the goods and services provided by the government free of charge or at lower prices to the households minus the value received by the government from the households.

□ Total Capital Formation

Total Capital Formation refers to the fixed assets acquired minus those disposed and the change in inventory, including the total fixed capital assets formation and the changes in inventory.

□ Total Fixed Capital Formation

Total Fixed Capital Formation refers to the value of fixed assets acquired minus those disposed of during a given period. Fixed assets are the assets produced through production activities with specified unit value which could be used for over one year, excluding natural assets. Total fixed capital formation can be categorized into total tangible capital formation and total intangible capital formation. The total tangible capital formation

EXPLANATORY NOTES TO MAJOR STATISTICAL INDICATORS

include the value of the construction projects, installation projects completed and the equipment, apparatus and instruments purchased as well as the value of land improved, the value of draught animals, breeding stock, animals for milk, wool and for recreational purpose, and the newly increased forest with economic value during a given period. The total intangible capital formation includes the prospecting of minerals, the acquisition of computer software minus the disposal of them.

□ Changes in Inventory

Changes in Inventory refers to the market value of the changes in inventory of resident units during a given period, i.e. the difference of value between the beginning and the end of the period minus the current gains due to the change in prices. The changes in inventory can be positive or negative. A positive value indicates the increase in inventory while a negative value indicates the decrease in stock. The inventory includes the raw materials, fuels and reserve materials purchased by the production units as well as the inventory of finished products, semi-finished products, work-in-progress, etc.

□ Net Outflow of Goods and Services

Net Outflow of Goods and Service refers to difference of outflow of goods and service minus inflow of goods and service. The outflow includes the value of various goods and service sold or gratuitously transferred by resident units to non-resident units, and the inflow includes the value of various goods and service sold or gratuitously transferred by non-resident units to resident units. The net outflow of district, include the net outflow of foreign trade or non-trade of local district, and also the difference of outflow minus inflow of goods and service between domestic districts.

□ Information Industry

Information Industry refers to the aggregation of all kinds of activities related to electronic information, including manufactory and distribution of information-related products and information service. As accounted by referring to relevant documents of several industries, the value added of the information industry shall not be counted together with that of other industries in the Shanghai GDP to avoid repetitive computation.

□ Tourism Industry

Tourism Industry refers to those tourism-related industries that provide tourism services to domestic and overseas tourists, including: travel agency service, transportation service, hostelling service, telecommunication service, entertainment service, catering service and retailing service, etc.. As accounted by referring to relevant cross-industry data of several industries, the value added of the tourism industry shall not be counted together with that of other industries in the Shanghai GDP to avoid repetitive computation.

第五篇

CHAPTER 5

财政收支

FISCAL REVENUE AND EXPENDITURE

简要说明

本篇反映上海市地方财政收支和税收收入情况，资料来源于国家税务总局上海市税务局和上海市财政局。

有关财政收支方面的资料，根据财政收支总表、财政收入明细表、财政支出明细表和各区财政收支完成情况表等的数据加工整理编制，其中，地方财政收支由市本级财政收支和区级财政收支组成。有关税收收入方面的资料，根据全市税收收入情况表的数据加工整理编制。

BRIEF INTRODUCTION

The data in this chapter reflect government revenue, expenditure, and tax income situations. The data are collected, provided and complied by Shanghai Municipal Tax Service, State Administration of Taxation and Shanghai Finance Bureau.

Data on government revenue and expenditure are prepared, collected and compiled on the basis of information from the city's balance sheet of government revenue and expenditures, tables of government revenue and expenditure at city level, and tables of government revenue and expenditure at district level. Among them, local fiscal revenue and expenditure is comprised by revenue and expenditure in the city as well as in districts. The data on tax income is prepared, collected and compiled on the base of information on Shanghai's tax income table.

表 5.1 一般公共预算收支(1978~2018)
GENERAL BUDGETARY REVENUE AND EXPENDITURE

单位:亿元 (100 million yuan)

年 份 Year	一般公共预算收入 General Budgetary Revenue	其中 of which 税收收入 Taxes	非税收入 Non-taxes	一般公共预算支出 General Budgetary Expenditure
1978	169.22	51.51	117.71	26.01
1979	172.69	53.73	118.96	27.06
1980	174.73	57.59	117.14	19.18
1981	174.35	62.93	111.42	19.06
1982	167.99	65.79	102.20	20.68
1983	156.39	110.05	46.34	22.39
1984	163.96	137.67	26.29	30.32
1985	184.23	185.76	-1.53	46.07
1986	179.46	177.90	1.56	59.08
1987	168.97	167.26	1.71	53.85
1988	161.62	182.42	-20.80	65.88
1989	166.88	190.21	-23.33	73.31
1990	166.99	183.31	-16.32	75.56
1991	175.53	182.88	-7.35	86.05
1992	185.56	188.61	-3.05	94.99
1993	242.34	252.99	-10.65	129.26
1994	175.33	196.60	-21.27	196.98
1995	227.30	240.06	-12.76	267.89
1996	288.49	308.26	-19.77	342.66
1997	352.33	369.23	-16.90	428.92
1998	392.22	406.73	-14.51	480.70
1999	431.85	427.23	4.62	546.38
2000	497.96	484.00	13.96	622.84
2001	620.24	589.91	30.33	726.38
2002	719.79	657.70	62.09	877.84
2003	899.29	796.87	102.42	1 102.64
2004	1 119.72	1 036.23	83.49	1 395.69
2005	1 433.90	1 238.40	195.50	1 660.32
2006	1 600.37	1 393.97	206.40	1 813.80
2007	2 102.63	1 975.48	127.15	2 201.92
2008	2 382.34	2 223.43	158.91	2 617.68
2009	2 540.30	2 368.45	171.85	2 989.65
2010	2 873.58	2 707.80	165.78	3 302.89
2011	3 429.83	3 172.72	257.11	3 914.88
2012	3 743.71	3 426.79	316.92	4 184.02
2013	4 109.51	3 797.16	312.35	4 528.61
2014	4 871.76	4 219.05	652.71	5 182.65
2015	5 519.50	4 858.16	661.34	6 191.56
2016	6 088.03	5 301.59	786.44	6 918.94
2017	6 642.26	5 865.51	776.75	7 547.62
2018	7 108.15	6 285.04	823.11	8 351.54

注:"营改增"全面推开后,增值税收入中央与地方分成比例调整,2016 年收入根据财政部要求进行同口径调整。

Note: After the implementation of Business Tax Replaced with VAT, the proportion of VAT revenue between the central and local government has been adjusted. In 2016, the revennue was adjusted with same standard according to the requirement of the Ministry of Finance.

表 5.2 主要年份一般公共预算收入
GENERAL BUDGETARY REVENUE IN MAIN YEARS

指 标	Indicators	2010	2015	2017	2018
一般公共预算收入(亿元)	**General Budgetary Revenue (100 million yuan)**	**2 873.58**	**5 519.50**	**6 642.26**	**7 108.15**
#增值税	Value-added Tax	388.62	1 012.80	2 460.39	2 624.82
企业所得税	Enterprise Income Tax	606.05	1 104.08	1 402.30	1 518.71
个人所得税	Personal Income Tax	261.20	487.61	692.46	770.21
契 税	Deed	173.58	270.99	271.55	284.95
#市级收入	Revenue at Municipal Level	1 393.23	2 806.13	3 156.83	3 362.00
区级收入	Revenue at District Level	1 480.35	2 713.37	3 485.43	3 746.15
一般公共预算收入构成(%)	**Compostion of General Budgetary Revenue (%)**	**100**	**100**	**100**	**100**
#增值税	Value-added Tax	13.5	18.3	37.0	36.9
企业所得税	Enterprise Income Tax	21.1	20.0	21.1	21.4
个人所得税	Personal Income Tax	9.1	8.8	10.4	10.8
契 税	Deed	6.0	4.9	4.1	4.0
#市级收入	Revenue at Municipal Level	48.5	50.8	47.5	47.3
区级收入	Revenue at District Level	51.5	49.2	52.5	52.7

注：2016 年实施“营改增”，增值税收入口径有所调整。
Note: Since the “Business Tax Replaced with VAT” was implemented in 2016, the scope of value-added tax revenue has been adjusted.

表 5.3 主要年份区级一般公共预算收支
GENERAL BUDGETARY REVENUE AND EXPENDITURE OF DISTRICTS IN MAIN YEARS

单位:亿元 (100 million yuan)

地区	District	一般公共预算收入 General Budgetary Revenue				一般公共预算支出 General Budgetary Expenditure			
		2010	2015	2017	2018	2010	2015	2017	2018
总计	**Total**	**1 480.35**	**2 713.37**	**3 485.43**	**3 746.15**	**1 955.58**	**3 858.09**	**5 335.81**	**5 559.72**
浦东新区	Pudong New Area	425.40	788.19	996.26	1 066.20	524.06	920.22	1 257.69	1 305.51
黄浦区	Huangpu	64.36	180.88	212.21	225.00	80.73	207.41	263.45	279.66
卢湾区	Luwan	51.30				56.69			
徐汇区	Xuhui	90.43	151.08	186.02	193.52	99.29	173.32	264.52	231.29
长宁区	Changning	72.08	129.94	154.28	162.84	85.50	143.80	183.92	192.09
静安区	Jing'an	65.96	106.24	232.80	246.83	71.43	158.52	312.17	370.55
闸北区	Zhabei	46.30	88.13			68.55	129.16		
普陀区	Putuo	51.97	96.36	108.10	114.05	78.57	124.41	174.46	203.61
虹口区	Hongkou	48.36	90.14	110.11	116.75	74.52	126.82	173.45	184.67
杨浦区	Yangpu	50.07	95.77	119.52	126.71	82.65	162.76	206.18	230.53
闵行区	Minhang	125.30	214.40	278.71	296.80	156.60	344.25	416.06	408.63
宝山区	Baoshan	70.35	127.08	151.11	160.45	114.43	219.23	271.83	301.61
嘉定区	Jiading	82.96	191.36	252.26	269.92	112.84	297.24	370.74	391.45
金山区	Jinshan	30.75	65.50	108.36	124.63	70.98	145.18	234.39	241.66
松江区	Songjiang	77.33	123.11	192.56	204.38	103.55	194.30	288.84	345.09
青浦区	Qingpu	58.95	125.33	188.01	203.10	88.40	179.89	383.95	333.54
奉贤区	Fengxian	40.43	84.89	128.11	151.20	77.12	168.18	312.72	272.83
崇明区	Chongming	28.04	54.98	67.00	83.77	78.21	163.39	221.45	267.01

注：2012 年起，原卢湾区并入黄浦区；2016 年起，原闸北区并入静安区。
Note: Former Luwan District has been merged into Huangpu District since 2012. Former Zhabei District has been merged into Jing'an District since 2016.

表 5.4 主要年份一般公共预算支出
GENERAL BUDGETARY EXPENDITURE IN MAIN YEARS

指 标	Indicators	2010	2015	2017	2018
一般公共预算支出(亿元)	**General Budgetary Expenditure(100 million yuan)**	**3 302.89**	**6 191.56**	**7 547.62**	**8 351.54**
#一般公共服务	General Public Services	226.02	259.84	320.70	367.16
公共安全	Public Security	187.25	269.2	356.12	412.13
教 育	Education	417.28	767.32	874.10	917.99
社会保障和就业	Social Security and Jobs	362.56	543.16	1 061.03	933.39
医疗卫生与计划生育	Medical and Health Care, Family Planning	160.07	303.46	412.18	470.11
城乡社区	Urban and Country Community Affairs	475.47	1 173.88	1 531.42	2 088.33
#市级支出	Expenditure at Municipal Level	1 278.76	2 333.47	2 211.81	2 791.81
区级支出	Expenditure at District (County) Level	2 024.13	3 858.09	5 335.81	5 559.72
一般公共预算支出比重(%)	**Percentage of the General Budgetary Expenditure(%)**	**100**	**100**	**100**	**100**
#一般公共服务	General Public Services	6.8	4.2	4.2	4.4
公共安全	Public Security	5.7	4.3	4.7	4.9
教 育	Education	12.6	12.4	11.6	11.0
社会保障和就业	Social Security and Jobs	11.0	8.8	14.1	11.2
医疗卫生与计划生育	Medical and Health Care, Family Planning	4.8	4.9	5.5	5.6
城乡社区	Urban and Country Community Affairs	14.4	19.0	20.3	25.0
#市级支出	Expenditure at Municipal Level	38.7	37.7	29.3	33.4
区级支出	Expenditure at District (County) Level	61.3	62.3	70.7	66.6

注：自 2014 年开始，计划生育支出从一般公共服务支出中转出，并入原医疗卫生支出，改名为医疗卫生与计划生育支出。
Note: The government takes the expenditure of faminly planning from the expenditure of general public services to the expenditure of medical and health care Since 2014. The name of the item has been changed into the expditure of medical and health care, family planning.

表 5.5 主要年份全市税收总收入
TAXATION IN MAIN YEARS

单位:亿元(100 million yuan)

指 标	Indicators	2010	2015	2017	2018
全市税收总收入	**Taxation**	**8 003.43**	**13 989.51**	**16 213.67**	**17 202.33**
#证券交易印花税	Stamp Tax of Stock Transaction	305.26	1 344.31	476.93	430.22
海关代征	Custom Taxation	2 082.92	2 759.11	3 373.75	3 378.56
国内增值税	Domestic Value Added Tax	1 575.0	2 676.46	4 911.82	5 248.81
国内消费税	Domestic Excise	499.58	825.26	684.40	832.70
企业所得税	Enterprise Income Tax	1 567.31	2 857.32	3 607.88	3 911.25
个人所得税	Personal Income Tax	653.01	1 219.01	1 731.14	1 925.52

上 / 海 / 统 / 计 / 年 / 鉴

主要统计指标解释

■ 一般公共预算收入

一般公共预算收入是指根据现行财政管理体制规定，划归地方财政的税收收入和非税收入。

■ 税收收入

一般公共预算收入中的税收收入主要包括房产税、城镇土地使用税、车船税、土地增值税、耕地占用税、契税等固定收入，以及增值税、企业所得税、个人所得税等共享收入部分。

■ 一般公共预算支出

一般公共预算支出是指按照现行中央政府与地方政府事权的划分，经地方人大批准，用于保障地方经济社会发展的各项财政支出。主要包括一般公共服务，公共安全，教育，科学技术，文化体育与传媒，社会保障和就业，医疗卫生与计划生育，环境保护，城乡社区，农林水事务，交通运输等支出。

SHANGHAI STATISTICAL YEARBOOK

EXPLANATORY NOTES TO MAJOR STATISTICAL INDICATORS

□ General Budgetary Revenue

General Budgetary Revenue refers to the tax revenue and non-tax revenue collected by the local government as defined by the finance management system.

□ Tax Revenue

Tax Revenue of general budgetary revenue mainly includes house property tax, urban land use tax, tax on vehicles and boat operation, land appreciation tax, farm land occupation tax, deed tax, etc and the share part of value added tax, corporate income tax, individual income tax, etc.

□ General Budgetary Expenditure

General Budgetary Expenditure refers to the fiscal expenditure demarcated on the basis of the classification of the affairs administration rights between the central government and local government. It is approved by the local people′s congress and used for the development of local economy and society. Local fiscal expenditure mainly includes the expenditure for general public services, public security, education, science and technology, culture, sport and media, social safety and employment, medical and health care, family planning, environment protection, urban and rural community affairs, agriculture, forestry and water conservancy and transportation, etc.

第六篇

CHAPTER 6

能源与环境

ENERGY AND ENVIRONMENT PROTECTION

简要说明

一、本篇资料的主要内容

本篇主要包含两部分内容:能源生产、消费和环境保护治理。

能源生产、消费的主要内容有能源消耗基本情况,能源消费弹性系数,人均、日均能源消费量,分行业、分主要能源品种的时间序列能源消费量,综合能源平衡表和主要能源品种的单项平衡表,电力建设情况等。

环境保护治理的主要内容有环保投入,工业固体废弃物防治,水环境保护,大气环境保护,环境空气状况、声环境及治理和城市环境卫生情况等。

二、本篇资料的统计范围

本篇资料的统计范围为全社会。

三、本篇的资料来源

能源生产、消费的资料来源: 电力建设情况由市电力公司提供,其他表的数据均来自历年能源平衡表。

环境保护治理的资料来源:环保投入、工业固体废弃物防治、大气环境保护、环境空气状况和声环境及治理由上海市生态环境局提供;水环境保护由上海市水务局和上海市生态环境局提供;城市环境卫生情况是由上海市绿化和市容管理局提供。

四、关于数据口径与计算方法的说明

环境保护治理

1. 2008年起,工业废气排放量按新排放系数计算。

2. 2011年起,烟尘排放总量统计口径变更为烟(粉)尘排放量。

3. 2011年起,废水排放总量中增加了农业源和集中式治理设施排放的废水。

4. 2013年起,环境空气质量优良率以AQI评价。

BRIEF INTRODUCTION

I. Main Contents

Data in this chapter cover mainly energy production, energy consumption, and environment protection and governance.

Energy production and consumption include basic energy consumption situations, elasticity coefficient of energy consumption, average energy consumption per capita, average daily energy consumption, energy consumption in time series by industry and main energy categories, comprehensive energy balance sheet, single balance sheet of main energy categories and electric power construction.

Environment protection and governance include investment in environment protection, prevention of industrial solid waste, water environment protection, air protection, governance of air and acoustic environment, and management of urban sanitation situations.

II. The Scope of Data

The scope of data in this chapter covers the whole city.

III. Sources of Data

Sources of data on energy production and consumption: Data on electric power construction are provided by the Shanghai Electric Power Company, and the rest are collected from the energy balance sheets over the years.

Sources of data on environment protection and governance: Data on investment in environment protection, prevention of industrial solid waste, air protection, and governance of air and acoustic environment are provided by Shanghai Municipal Bureau of Ecology and Environment; data on water environment protection are provided by Shanghai Water Authority and Shanghai Municipal Bureau of Ecology and Environment; data on urban sanitation situations are provided by the Shanghai Greening & City Appearance Bureau.

IV. Notes on Coverage and Compilation of Data

Environment protection and governance

(a) Industrial emission is calculated on new emission coefficient since 2008.

(b) Coverage of dust discharge changes to dust (smoke) discharge since 2011.

(c) Coverage of wastewater discharge started to include agricultural wastewater and wastewater from centralized treatment facilities from 2011.

(d) Ambient air quality is evaluated by AQI since 2013.

表 6.1 主要年份能源消耗基本情况
ENERGY CONSUMPTION IN MAIN YEARS

年 份 Year	能源消费量 (万吨标准煤) Energy Consumption (10 000 tons SCE)	其中 of which #工 业 Industry	电力消费 (亿千瓦时) Electricity Power Consumption (100 million kwh)	其中 of which #工 业 Industry
1990	3 191.06	2 462.21	264.74	220.97
1995	4 392.48	3 439.11	403.27	307.01
2000	5 413.45	3 687.90	559.42	393.13
2001	5 825.80	3 851.75	592.99	413.33
2002	6 114.47	3 929.31	645.71	447.46
2003	6 658.49	4 245.09	745.97	507.00
2004	7 167.16	4 405.55	821.44	555.12
2005	7 730.66	4 692.65	921.97	617.59
2006	8 355.49	4 987.81	990.15	656.10
2007	9 103.30	5 351.93	1 072.38	705.90
2008	9 608.49	5 544.13	1 138.22	727.13
2009	9 759.35	5 472.16	1 153.38	701.59
2010	10 243.26	5 890.93	1 295.87	786.61
2011	10 489.09	5 946.66	1 339.62	805.76
2012	10 573.00	5 798.02	1 353.45	786.25
2013	10 890.39	5 965.53	1 410.61	799.45
2014	10 639.86	5 796.95	1 369.02	785.64
2015	10 930.53	5 745.55	1 405.56	787.03
2016	11 241.73	5 681.86	1 486.02	798.18
2017	11 381.85	5 537.01	1 526.77	798.22
2018	11 453.73	5 360.68	1 566.66	780.21

表 6.1 续表 1 continued

年 份 Year	煤品占能源消费量比重(%) Coal Total (%)	油品占能源消费量比重(%) Petroleum Products Total (%)	天然气占能源消费量比重(%) Natural Gas (%)	净调入电及其他能发电占能源消费量比重(%) Electricity of Outside the city and Other Power(%)	其他能源占能源消费量比重(%) Other Energy (%)
1990	66.13	35.85		-1.98	
1995	69.84	27.09		-0.27	3.33
2000	65.46	33.35	0.61	0.10	0.48
2001	64.25	33.97	0.74	0.92	0.13
2002	61.08	36.31	0.92	1.60	0.09
2003	59.01	37.51	0.97	2.56	0.00
2004	54.33	38.58	1.94	5.05	0.11
2005	50.43	38.95	3.07	7.54	0.01
2006	46.24	40.12	3.38	10.07	0.19
2007	43.81	40.80	3.84	11.48	0.08
2008	44.23	40.37	4.06	11.18	0.17
2009	42.46	41.24	4.46	11.66	0.17
2010	44.84	39.13	5.46	10.38	0.19
2011	44.91	39.31	6.73	8.85	0.20
2012	41.08	40.35	7.80	10.55	0.22
2013	38.96	40.58	8.38	11.82	0.26
2014	35.34	40.21	8.59	15.43	0.43
2015	33.63	41.21	8.93	15.77	0.45
2016	31.29	42.13	8.87	17.12	0.59
2017	29.78	42.96	9.34	17.18	0.74
2018	28.62	41.93	10.41	18.32	0.72

注：由于第四次经济普查，2018 年为初步统计数据；2000~2017 年能源消费量作初步调整，其他能源表相关数据对应调整。

Note: Due to the Fourth Economic Census, data of 2018 are the preliminary statistical data, 2000~2017 annual energy consumption has been preliminarily adjusted, so the data in the following tables are adjusted accordingly.

表 6.2 能源消费弹性系数 (1978~2018)
ELASTICITY OF ENERGY CONSUMPTION

年 份 Year	能源消费 比上年增长 (%) Growth Rate of Energy Consumption over Preceding Year(%)	电力消费 比上年增长 (%) Growth Rate of Electric Power Consumption over Preceding Year(%)	能源消费 弹性系数 Elasticity of Energy Consumption	电力消费 弹性系数 Elasticity of Electric Power Consumption
1978	6.6	10.8	0.42	0.68
1979	1.5	3.0	0.20	0.41
1980	-0.6	3.4		0.40
1981	1.0	6.4	0.18	1.14
1982	2.6	4.4	0.36	0.61
1983	2.5	4.2	0.32	0.54
1984	2.5	4.1	0.22	0.35
1985	4.9	3.9	0.37	0.29
1986	9.0	6.8	2.05	1.55
1987	5.7	4.1	0.76	0.55
1988	1.3	2.5	0.13	0.25
1989	4.4	1.3	1.47	0.43
1990	2.6	5.8	0.74	2.09
1991	8.6	9.0	1.22	1.28
1992	5.5	10.0	0.37	0.67
1993	7.9	9.0	0.52	0.60
1994	5.8	9.1	0.40	0.63
1995	5.2	6.9	0.36	0.48
1996	3.7	6.7	0.28	0.51
1997	3.6	5.5	0.28	0.43
1998	2.5	6.3	0.25	0.61
1999	4.7	3.8	0.46	0.37
2000	6.9	11.6	0.62	1.06
2001	7.6	6.0	0.73	0.57
2002	5.0	8.9	0.43	0.78
2003	8.9	15.5	0.72	1.26
2004	7.6	10.1	0.53	0.71
2005	7.9	12.2	0.68	1.06
2006	8.1	7.4	0.63	0.58
2007	8.9	8.3	0.59	0.55
2008	5.5	6.1	0.57	0.63
2009	1.6	1.3	0.19	0.15
2010	5.0	12.4	0.49	1.22
2011	2.4	3.4	0.29	0.41
2012	0.8	1.0	0.11	0.13
2013	3.0	4.2	0.38	0.53
2014	-2.3	-3.0	-	-
2015	2.7	2.7	0.39	0.39
2016	2.8	5.7	0.42	0.84
2017	1.2	2.7	0.18	0.39
2018	0.6	2.6	0.10	0.39

表 6.3　主要年份能源消费总量
FINAL CONSUMPTION OF ENERGY IN MAIN YEARS

单位：万吨标准煤(10 000 tons SCE)

年　份 Year	能源消费总　量 Energy Consumption	能源终端消费量 Final Consumption of Energy	加工转换投入(－)产出(＋)量 Processing Conversion Input (－) and Output (＋)	损失量 Loss Volume
1990	3 191.06	3 098.82	-52.20	40.04
1995	4 392.49	4 250.44	-1.29	140.75
2000	5 413.45	5 226.81	-3.15	183.49
2001	5 825.80	5 554.41	-60.23	211.16
2002	6 114.47	5 840.35	-55.50	218.62
2003	6 658.49	6 332.88	-82.06	243.55
2004	7 167.16	6 926.24	-22.21	218.71
2005	7 730.66	7 599.84	57.37	188.18
2006	8 355.49	8 196.29	34.47	193.67
2007	9 103.30	8 991.39	96.14	208.05
2008	9 608.49	9 438.48	56.46	226.48
2009	9 759.35	9 649.84	122.71	232.22
2010	10 243.26	10 055.36	60.78	248.69
2011	10 489.09	10 671.97	432.92	250.04
2012	10 573.00	10 715.25	402.53	260.27
2013	10 890.39	10 972.78	355.75	273.37
2014	10 639.86	10 787.07	409.10	261.90
2015	10 930.53	11 034.75	376.62	272.40
2016	11 241.73	11 325.41	366.53	282.85
2017	11 381.85	11 389.41	328.80	321.24
2018	11 453.73	11 477.87	333.68	309.55

表 6.4　平均每人生活用能源(2015~2018)
ANNUAL RESIDENT ENERGY CONSUMPTION PER CAPITA

品　名	Items	2015	2016	2017	2018
生活消费能源总计(千克标准煤)	**Total Resident Energy Consumption (kg of SCE)**	**449.69**	**489.27**	**500.54**	**529.65**
煤炭（千克）	Coal (kg)	12.48	7.95	1.65	1.65
天然气（立方米）	Natural Gas (cu.m)	55.77	58.95	60.02	65.38
液化石油气（千克）	Liquefied Petroleum Gas (kg)	10.42	9.08	7.24	7.22
电力（千瓦时）	Electric Power (kwh)	766.34	900.60	945.80	1 005.96

注：本表按年平均人口数计算。
Note: Data in this table are calculated by average annual population.

表 6.5　平均每天各种能源消费量(2015~2018)
AVERAGE DAILY ENERGY CONSUMPTION BY VARIETY

能源品种	Items	2015	2016	2017	2018
合计(万吨标准煤)	**Total(10 000 tons of SCE)**	**29.95**	**30.80**	**31.18**	**31.38**
煤炭(万吨)	Coal(10 000 tons)	10.58	10.45	10.27	9.80
焦炭(万吨)	Coke(10 000 tons)	1.73	1.64	1.62	1.70
燃料油(万吨)	Fuel Oil(10 000 tons)	1.48	1.61	1.84	1.80
汽油(万吨)	Gasoline(10 000 tons)	1.28	1.32	1.33	1.35
煤油(万吨)	Kerosene(10 000 tons)	1.40	1.60	1.79	1.92
柴油(万吨)	Diesel Oil(10 000 tons)	1.23	1.22	1.21	1.20
天然气(亿立方米)	Natural Gas(100 million cu.m)	0.21	0.22	0.23	0.25
电力(亿千瓦时)	Electricity(100 million kwh)	3.85	4.07	4.18	4.29

表 6.6 主要年份能源终端消费量
FINAL CONSUMPTION OF ENERGY IN MAIN YEARS

单位:万吨标准煤(10 000 tons SCE)

年 份 Year	能源终端消费量 Final Consumption of Energy	其 中 of which			
		第一产业 Primary Industry	第二产业 Secondary Industry	第三产业 Tertiary Industry	生活消费 Living Consumption
1980	2 130.56	71.04	1 655.92	194.64	208.96
1990	3 098.82	58.49	2 387.88	403.47	248.98
1995	4 250.44	77.12	3 339.75	517.06	316.51
1996	4 376.40	102.18	3 291.04	626.39	356.79
1997	4 505.70	90.53	3 312.13	715.32	387.72
1998	4 608.13	91.06	3 261.21	828.86	427.02
1999	4 899.61	98.00	3 467.48	915.48	418.61
2000	5 226.81	103.37	3 593.64	1 068.85	460.94
2001	5 554.41	99.12	3 698.17	1 276.89	480.22
2002	5 840.35	79.85	3 790.50	1 481.13	488.86
2003	6 332.88	75.69	4 045.91	1 669.86	541.42
2004	6 926.24	63.72	4 297.68	1 967.59	597.24
2005	7 599.84	53.96	4 717.72	2 159.62	668.54
2006	8 196.29	53.20	4 990.65	2 412.44	740.01
2007	8 991.39	53.09	5 402.14	2 740.20	795.95
2008	9 438.48	56.02	5 564.11	2 953.44	864.91
2009	9 649.84	57.41	5 581.52	3 106.55	904.36
2010	10 055.36	59.56	5 919.84	3 105.60	970.36
2011	10 671.97	58.10	6 359.03	3 255.72	999.12
2012	10 715.25	57.98	6 178.22	3 423.47	1 055.57
2013	10 972.78	59.75	6 295.57	3 488.41	1 129.05
2014	10 787.07	60.21	6 190.79	3 490.06	1 046.00
2015	11 034.75	59.80	6 117.30	3 769.18	1 088.47
2016	11 325.41	63.01	6 046.32	4 033.27	1 182.80
2017	11 389.41	62.16	5 832.40	4 284.04	1 210.82
2018	11 477.87	61.78	5 672.86	4 460.92	1 282.31

表 6.7 主要年份工业能源终端消费量
FINAL CONSUMPTION OF ENERGY OF INDUSTRY IN MAIN YEARS

年 份 Year	工业能源终端消费量(万吨标准煤) Final Consumption Energy of Industry (10 000 tons SCE)	原 煤(万吨) Coal (10 000 tons)	焦 炭(万吨) Coke (10 000 tons)	燃料油(万吨) Fuel Oil (10 000 tons)	电 力(亿千瓦时) Electric power (100 million kwh)
1980	1 645.20	535.03	211.52	122.41	136.85
1990	2 369.99	596.14	419.24	136.09	209.21
1995	3 297.07	694.31	687.98	154.76	282.87
1996	3 234.63	726.24	637.73	149.69	293.04
1997	3 245.71	698.14	653.75	147.70	309.74
1998	3 186.98	723.59	660.40	132.93	318.12
1999	3 389.09	792.14	658.28	120.21	335.01
2000	3 506.07	733.65	676.06	139.67	362.94
2001	3 586.48	790.51	654.79	136.93	381.64
2002	3 662.21	676.60	571.92	112.19	413.61
2003	3 928.44	675.58	573.94	117.11	464.74
2004	4 172.43	731.30	552.68	118.77	510.67
2005	4 577.48	843.73	603.16	80.94	568.29
2006	4 841.96	869.58	617.92	74.80	604.59
2007	5 253.66	790.10	691.38	91.99	649.82
2008	5 393.68	787.01	684.92	74.98	667.59
2009	5 391.00	825.59	658.32	71.92	641.58
2010	5 732.44	854.71	705.21	43.12	718.63
2011	6 165.57	813.06	706.34	62.86	735.27
2012	5 979.74	730.71	673.17	40.23	714.46
2013	6 089.11	800.15	640.30	35.36	723.07
2014	5 983.21	862.92	654.84	21.22	710.70
2015	5 897.69	709.70	630.75	11.86	711.54
2016	5 810.35	635.79	596.95	8.00	718.45
2017	5 591.59	468.97	571.62	7.90	716.29
2018	5 434.91	484.97	607.79	4.59	704.94

表 6.8 能源平衡表(标准量)(2015~2018)
BALANCE SHEET OF ENERGY(STANDARD EQUIVALENT)

单位:万吨标准煤(10 000 tons SCE)

指 标	Indicators	2015	2016	2017	2018
可供本地区消费的能源量	**Volume of Energy Available for Local Consumption**	**10 933.41**	**11 238.48**	**11 373.84**	**11 456.52**
库存差	Inventory Change	-106.24	-91.99	138.60	-62.52
一次能源生产量	Primary Energy Production	118.80	143.36	184.45	380.78
外省(市)调入量	Inflow from Other Provinces (Autonomous Region and Municipalities)	18 228.74	21 212.66	17 419.64	15 081.94
进口量	Imports	3 561.75	4 606.69	5 588.46	5 582.76
我轮、机在外国加油量	China Airplanes&ships Refueling in Abroad	713.89	776.70	1 000.58	954.69
本市调出量(-)	Outflow from Shanghai (Autonomous Region of Municipality)	-11 036.57	-15 151.01	-12 418.62	-9 751.03
出口量(-)	Exports	-296.46	-0. .41	-260.50	-451.74
外轮、机在我国加油量(-)	Foreign Airplanes&ships Refueling in China	-250.52	-257.51	-278.77	-278.36
加工转换投入(-)产出(+)量	**Processing Conversion Input (-) and Output (+)**	**376.62**	**366.53**	**328.80**	**333.68**
#火力发电	Fuel Power Generation				
供　热	Heating Supply	-31.55	-31.60	-34.35	-32.96
炼　焦	Coke Making	-32.07	-29.83	-20.25	-25.94
炼　油	Oil Refining	4.90	19.66	4.55	26.96
制　气	Gas Making	-0.12			
回收能	Recovery of Energy	465.84	438.00	411.18	419.75
损失量	**Loss Volume**	**272.40**	**282.85**	**321.24**	**309.55**
#运输和输配损失	Loss in Transportation and Distribution	272.40	282.85	321.24	309.55
终端消费量	**Final Consumption**	**11 034.75**	**11 325.41**	**11 389.41**	**11 477.87**
第一产业	Primary Industry	59.80	63.01	62.16	61.78
第二产业	Secondary Industry	6 117.30	6 046.32	5 832.40	5 672.86
工　业	Industry	5 897.69	5 810.35	5 591.59	5 434.91
建 筑 业	Construction	219.61	235.97	240.80	237.95
第三产业	Tertiary Industry	3 769.18	4 033.27	4 284.04	4 460.92
#交通运输、仓储和邮政业	Transportation, Storage and Post	2 024.34	2 230.54	2 456.04	2 520.00
批发、零售贸易业和住宿、餐饮业	Wholesale, Retail Sales and Hotel, Restaurants	546.50	529.35	513.95	534.62
生活消费	Living Consumption	1 088.47	1 182.80	1 210.82	1 282.31
城　镇	Urban	960.51	1 056.04	1 087.41	1 151.77
乡　村	Rural	127.97	126.76	123.41	130.54
平衡差额	**Balance**	**2.87**	**-3.25**	**-8.01**	**2.78**
能源消费总量	**Total Energy Consumption**	**10 930.53**	**11 241.73**	**11 381.85**	**11 453.73**

表 6.9　能源终端消费量(2018)
FINAL CONSUMPTION OF ENERGY (QUANTITY EQUIVALENT)

单位:万吨(10 000 tons)

行　业	Sectors	原　煤 Coal	焦　炭 Coke	燃料油 Fuel Oil
总　计	**Total**	**494.67**	**607.79**	**658.22**
生产消费	**Production Consumption**	**490.67**	**607.79**	**658.22**
第一产业	Primary Industry	0.34		1.61
第二产业	Secondary Industry	486.32	607.79	9.15
# 工　业	Industry	484.97	607.79	4.59
第三产业	Tertiary Industry	4.01		647.46
# 交通运输、仓储和邮政业	Transportation, Storage and Post	0.01		647.46
批发、零售贸易业和住宿、餐饮业	Wholesale, Retail Sales and Hotel, Restaurants	2.00		
生活消费	**Living Consumption**	**4.00**		

表 6.9　续表 1 continued

单位:万吨(10 000 tons)

行　业	Sectors	汽　油 Gasoline	煤　油 Kerosene	柴　油 Diesel Oil
总　计	**Total**	**494.01**	**701.64**	**435.98**
生产消费	**Production Consumption**	**278.30**	**701.64**	**426.49**
第一产业	Primary Industry	14.97		11.50
第二产业	Secondary Industry	41.80	0.54	58.57
# 工　业	Industry	15.06	0.54	32.60
第三产业	Tertiary Industry	221.53	701.10	356.42
# 交通运输、仓储和邮政业	Transportation, Storage and Post	64.73	701.10	190.93
批发、零售贸易业和住宿、餐饮业	Wholesale, Retail Sales and Hotel, Restaurants	63.89		88.15
生活消费	**Living Consumption**	**215.71**		**9.49**

表 6.9　续表 2 continued

行　业	Sectors	其他石油制品(万吨) Other Petroleum Products (10 000 tons)	热　力(万百万千焦) Thermopower (10 000 million KJ)	电　力(亿千瓦时) Electric Power (100 million kwh)
总　计	**Total**	**207.63**	**9 189.22**	**1 491.39**
生产消费	**Production Consumption**	**207.63**	**9 189.22**	**1 247.84**
第一产业	Primary Industry			6.37
第二产业	Secondary Industry	207.63	9 079.22	748.62
# 工　业	Industry	207.63	9 075.60	704.94
第三产业	Tertiary Industry		110.00	492.85
# 交通运输、仓储和邮政业	Transportation, Storage and Post		3.93	54.23
批发、零售贸易业和住宿、餐饮业	Wholesale, Retail Sales and Hotel, Restaurants		23.25	88.83
生活消费	**Living Consumption**			**243.55**

表6.10 煤炭、石油、电力平衡表（2018）
COAL,PETROLEUM,ELECTRICITY BALANCE SHEET

指标	Indicators	煤炭（万吨）Coal (10 000 tons)	石油（万吨）Crude Oil (10 000 tons)	电力（亿千瓦时）Electricity (100 million kwh)
可供本地区消费的能源量	**Total Energy Available for Consumption**	**4 420.24**	**3 320.01**	**1 566.66**
库存差	Inventory Changes in the Year	-1.46	-41.53	
生产量	Energy Production		25.60	856.60
外省（市）调入量	Inflow from Other Provinces	3 295.34	6 183.96	855.37
进口量	Imports	1 550.29	2 723.73	
我轮、机在外国加油量	China Airplanes&ships Refueling in Abroad		662.86	
本市调出量（-）	Outflow from Shanghai	-423.93	-5 736.79	-145.31
出口量（-）	Exports		-308.64	
外轮、机在我国加油量（-）	Foreign Airplanes&ships Refueling in China		-189.18	
消费量	**Total Energy Consumption**	**4 420.62**	**3 318.48**	**1 566.66**
按行业分	**Consumption by Sectors**			
农、林、牧、渔业	Farming, Forestry, Animal Husbandry, Fishery and Water Conservancy	0.34	28.62	6.37
工　业	Industry	4 410.92	956.66	780.21
建筑业	Construction	1.35	76.55	43.68
交通运输、仓储和邮政业	Transport, Storage and Post	0.01	1 619.73	54.23
批发、零售业和住宿、餐饮业	Wholesale, Retail Trade and Hotel, Restaurants	2.00	165.47	88.83
其　他	Others	2.00	217.66	349.79
生活消费	Residential Consumption	4.00	253.79	243.55
按用途分	**Consumption by Usage**			
终端消费	Final Consumption	494.67	3 284.76	1 491.39
#工　业	Industry	484.97	922.94	704.94
用于加工转换	Processing and Conversion	3 887.17	33.72	
损失量	Others Losses	38.78		75.27
平衡差额	**Balanced Difference**	**-0.38**	**1.53**	

表6.11 电力建设情况(2015~2018)
STATISTICS OF ELECTRIC POWER COUSTRUCTION

	指　标 Indicators	2015	2016	2017	2018
发电量(亿千瓦时)	**Electric Power Generated(100 million kwh)**	**821.19**	**832.32**	**865.50**	**856.59**
线损率(%)	Electricity Loss Rate on Lines(%)	6.12	6.06	6.03	5.30
年末发电设备容量(万千瓦)	Power Generating Equipment Capacity (year-end)(10 000kw)	2 343.68	2 370.65	2 399.67	2 446.88
架空线长度(公里)	Length of Overhead Lines(km)	9 928.78	9 641.98	9 880.37	10 096.89
1 000KV(公里)	1 000KV(km)	33.97	147.34	147.34	147.34
750KV(公里)	750KV(km)	106.14	106.14	106.14	106.14
500KV(公里)	500KV(km)	1 504.48	1 149.77	1 149.77	1 151.00
220KV(公里)	220KV(km)	3 467.13	3 453.92	3 601.04	3 716.88
110KV(公里)	110KV(km)	917.68	920.19	993.32	1 028.35
35KV(公里)	35KV(km)	3 899.37	3 509.91	3 528.07	3 592.23
电缆长度(公里)	Length of Cable(km)	10 719.90	12 645.26	13 626.81	14 323.45
500KV(万千伏安)	500KV(10 000kva)	31.26	31.26	60.86	60.86
220KV(万千伏安)	220KV(10 000kva)	655.14	702.24	721.93	820.07
110KV(万千伏安)	110KV(10 000kva)	1 595.09	1 871.78	2 176.27	2 378.41
35KV(万千伏安)	35KV(10 000kva)	8 438.49	10 039.98	10 667.76	11 064.55
公用变电容量(万千伏安)	Public Transformer Capacity(10 000kva)	15 860.69	16 365.25	17 422.64	18 141.59
500KV(万千伏安)	500KV(10 000kva)	5 680.44	5 684.64	6 029.64	6 194.64
220KV-35KV(万千伏安)	220KV-35KV(10 000kva)	10 180.25	10 680.61	11 393.00	11 946.95
用电最高负荷(万千瓦)	Peak Electric Power Consumption Load(10 000kw)	2 981.90	3 138.40	3 268.20	3 094.00

注：本表数据由市电力公司提供。
Note: Data in this table is provided by Shanghai Electric Power Corporation.

表 6.12 主要年份环保投入
INVESTMENT ON ENVIRONMENT PROTECTION IN MAIN YEARS

单位:亿元(100 million yuan)

年份 Year	环境保护投资 Investment on Environment Protection	其中 of which			环境保护投资相当于GDP(%) Investment on Environment Protection as Percentage of Gross Domestic Product(%)
		#工业污染源治理投资 Investment on Industrial Pollution Source Control	其中 of which		
			#治理废水 Treatment of Wastewater	#治理废气 Treatment of Exhaust Gas	
1990					2.06
1995	46.49				1.86
2000	141.91				2.97
2001	152.93				2.94
2002	162.39				2.83
2003	191.53				2.86
2004	225.37				2.79
2005	281.18				3.04
2006	310.85				2.94
2007	366.12				2.93
2008	422.37				3.00
2009	460.42				3.06
2010	507.54				2.96
2011	557.92				2.91
2012	570.49	64.25	4.36	6.59	2.83
2013	607.88	70.40	4.70	17.00	2.81
2014	699.89	260.14	6.84	27.06	2.97
2015	708.83	125.22	3.90	40.93	2.82
2016	823.57	135.29	1.98	50.33	3.00
2017	923.53	146.23	5.81	29.57	3.10
2018	989.19	109.56	8.05	19.30	3.00

表 6.13 主要年份工业固体废弃物防治
PREVENTION AND CURE OF INDUSTRIAL SOLID WASTES IN MAIN YEARS

指标	Indicators	2000	2010	2017	2018
工业固体废弃物产生量(万吨)	Volume of Industrial Solid Wastes Produced (10 000 tons)	1 354.74	2 448.36	1 630.48	1 668.77
#危险废物	Dangerous Wastes	28.32	51.25	110.44	109.04
工业废弃物综合利用量(万吨)	Volume of Industrial Wastes Treated and Utilized (10 000 tons)	1 515.90	2 366.90	1 532.71	1 552.84
#危险废物	Dangerous Wastes	27.05	28.47	24.36	32.60
工业废弃物综合利用率(%)	Ratio of Industrial Wastes Treated and Utilized (%)	93.26	96.16	94.00	93.05
工业固体废物处置量(万吨)	Volume of Industrial Solid Wastes Disposed (10 000 tons)	90.96	93.86	99.98	135.77
#危险废物	Dangerous Wastes	1.08	23.44	85.81	75.35

注：本页数据由上海市环境保护局提供。
Note: Data on this page are provided by Shanghai Environmental Protection Bureau.

表 6.14　水环境保护(1995~2018)
WATER ENVIRONMENT PROTECTION

年份 Year	废水排放总量(亿吨) Total Waste Water Discharged (100 million tons)	其中 of which 工业 Industrial Waste Water	废水化学需氧量排放总量(万吨) Total Emission of Oxygen of Waste Water Needed by Chemistry (10 000 tons)	其中 of which 工业 Industrial Waste Water	污水处理厂数(座) Quantity Sewage Disposal Plants(unit)	污水处理厂污水处理量(万吨) Volume of Sewage Disposed by Sewage Disposal Plants (10 000 tons)
1995	22.45	11.61		12.29	17	14 665
1996	22.85	11.41	27.46	12.16	20	12 876
1997	21.10	9.99	38.55	11.70	22	14 790
1998	20.81	9.00	36.55	9.63	22	15 605
1999	20.28	8.52	34.98	8.92	22	17 479
2000	19.37	7.25	31.87	6.93	27	23 028
2001	19.50	6.80	30.48	5.27	26	29 487
2002	19.21	6.49	32.96	4.78	27	30 658
2003	18.22	6.11	28.38	4.38	30	39 891
2004	19.34	5.64	29.38	3.76	37	95 301
2005	19.97	5.11	30.44	3.66	42	117 833
2006	22.37	4.83	30.20	3.53	43	155 726
2007	22.66	4.76	29.44	3.38	45	152 886
2008	22.60	4.41	26.67	2.76	47	177 090
2009	23.05	4.12	24.34	2.90	51	171 609
2010	24.82	3.67	21.98	2.16	52	189 654
2011	19.86	4.46	24.90	2.74	53	193 354
2012	22.05	4.77	24.26	2.62	53	200 685
2013	22.30	4.54	23.56	2.55	53	203 222
2014	22.12	4.39	22.44	2.48	53	208 145
2015	22.41	4.69	19.88	2.27	53	213 944
2016	22.08	3.66	14.75	1.44	53	267 954
2017	21.20	3.16	14.18	1.29	52	263 703
2018	20.98	2.91	12.05	1.02	51	265 541

①2011 年起，废水排放总量中增加了农业源和集中式治理设施排放的废水。
②2016 年起，废水化学需氧量排放总量不包括农业源排放量。
❶Since 2011, waste water discharged from the agricultural source and centralized treatment facilities has been added in Total Waste Water Discharged.
❷From 2016 wastewater COD (Chemical Oxygen Demand) emissions do not include agricultural source emission.

表6.15 大气环境保护（1995~2018）
ATMOSPHERE ENVIRONMENT PROTECTION

年 份 Year	工业废气排放总量（亿标立方米） Industrial Waste Gas Emission (100 million cu.m)	烟尘排放总量(万吨) Total Emission of Smoke and Dust (10 000 tons)	其中 of which		废气二氧化硫排放总量（万吨） Total Emission of SO_2 (10 000 tons)	其中 of which	
			工 业 Industrial Sector	生活及其他 Residential Sector and Others		工 业 Industrial Sector	生活及其他 Residential Sector and Others
1995	4 625	20.78	13.33	7.45	53.41	38.15	15.26
1996	4 757	15.78	14.77	1.01	51.00	43.30	7.70
1997	4 755	17.08	13.38	3.70	50.85	43.62	7.23
1998	4 912	15.63	10.74	4.89	48.89	39.09	9.80
1999	4 947	13.57	9.00	4.57	40.31	31.09	9.22
2000	5 755	14.12	8.32	5.80	46.49	32.68	13.81
2001	6 964	13.52	6.23	7.29	47.26	30.00	17.26
2002	7 440	10.74	5.60	5.14	44.66	32.49	12.17
2003	7 799	11.54	4.97	6.57	43.54	30.07	13.47
2004	8 834	12.27	5.25	7.02	47.31	34.95	12.36
2005	8 482	11.52	4.95	6.57	51.28	37.52	13.76
2006	9 428	11.29	4.73	6.56	50.80	37.43	13.37
2007	9 591	10.60	4.04	6.56	49.78	36.44	13.34
2008	10 436	10.63	4.06	6.57	44.61	29.80	14.81
2009	10 059	10.18	3.64	6.54	37.89	23.93	13.96
2010	12 969	10.21	4.18	6.03	35.81	26.32	9.49
2011	13 692	8.98	6.64	2.34	24.01	21.01	3.00
2012	13 361	8.71	6.37	2.34	22.82	19.34	3.48
2013	13 344	8.09	6.72	1.37	21.58	17.29	4.29
2014	13 007	14.17	13.14	1.03	18.81	15.54	3.27
2015	12 802	12.07	11.14	0.93	17.08	10.49	6.59
2016	12 669	7.95	7.28	0.67	7.42	6.74	0.68
2017	13 867	4.70	3.03	1.67	1.85	1.27	0.58
2018	13 780	2.81	1.62	1.19	0.99	0.91	0.08

①2008 年起工业废气排放量按新排放系数计算。
②2011 年起，烟尘排放总量统计口径变更为烟(粉)尘排放量。
③2014 年工业粉尘排放量统计口径包括无组织排放量。
④2016 年起，废气二氧化硫排放总量不包括非道路移动源排放量。
❶The Volume of Industrial Exhaust Emission in 2008 was calculated by new emission coefficient.
❷Since 2011, the statistics caliber of Total Emission of Smoke and Dust has been changed to Total Emission of Smoke(Powder) and Dust.
❸The statistics of industrial dust emissions include inorganization emissions in 2014.
❹From 2016 exhaust gas SO_2(sulfur dioxide) emissions do not include non-road moving source emission.

表 6.16 主要年份环境空气状况
AMBIENT AIR CONDITION IN MAIN YEARS

指标	Indicators	2000	2010	2017	2018
中心城区二氧化硫年日平均值（毫克/立方米）	Annual Daily Mean Concentration of SO_2 in Urban Area (mg/m^3)	0.045	0.029	0.012	0.010
中心城区二氧化氮年日平均值（毫克/立方米）	Annual Daily Mean Concentration of NO_2 in Urban Area (mg/m^3)	0.090	0.050	0.044	0.042
中心城区可吸入颗粒平均浓度（毫克/立方米）	Mean Concentration of Inhalable Particulate in Urban Area (mg/m^3)		0.079	0.055	0.051
降水 PH 平均值	Rain PH Value	5.19	4.66	5.12	5.13
酸雨频率(%)	Frequency of Acid Rain (%)	26.0	73.9	47.6	53.8
环境空气质量优良天数(天)	Quantity of Days with Good Ambient Air Quality (day)	295	336	275	296
环境空气质量优良率(%)	Rate of Good Ambient Air Quality (%)	80.8	92.1	75.3	81.1

注：2013 年起，环境空气质量优良率以 AQI 评价。
Note: Since 2013, rate of ambient air quality is evaluated by AQI.

表 6.17 主要年份声环境及治理
ENVIRONMENTAL NOISE AND TREATMENT IN MAIN YEARS

指标	Indicators	2000	2010	2017	2018
区域环境噪声平均等效声级	**Average Equivalent Sound Level of Area Ambient Noise**				
昼间时段(LeqdB(A))	Daytime (LeqdB(A))	56.6	55.8	55.7	54.6
夜间时段(LeqdB(A))	Nighttime (LeqdB(A))	49.2	48.3	48.8	48.3
交通环境噪声平均等效声级	**Average Equivalent Sound Level of Traffic Noise**				
昼间时段(LeqdB(A))	Daytime (LeqdB(A))	70.5	69.8	69.8	69.3
夜间时段(LeqdB(A))	Nighttime (LeqdB(A))	64.1	64.3	65.0	64.9

注：本页数据由上海市环境保护局提供。
Note: Data on this page are provided by Shanghai Environmental Protection Bureau.

表 6.18 城市环境卫生情况(1978~2018)
URBAN ENVIRONMENTAL SITUATION

年 份 Year	垃圾产生量 (万吨) Garbage Produced (10 000 tons)	其 中 of which		清运粪便 (万吨) Night Soil Disposal Cleared (10 000 tons)
		生活垃圾 Residential Garbage	建筑垃圾 Construction Garbage	
1978	214	108	106	418
1979	250	125	126	374
1980	272	131	141	331
1981	272	146	126	329
1982	296	169	127	325
1983	280	166	113	311
1984	308	185	123	272
1985	305	196	109	252
1986	328	226	102	263
1987	325	229	97	262
1988	329	240	89	249
1989	344	250	94	246
1990	382	279	103	243
1991	393	296	97	229
1992	428	301	127	242
1993	488	335	152	234
1994	558	358	200	240
1995	668	372	296	216
1996	736	419	317	217
1997	755	454	301	227
1998	824	470	353	218
1999	767	500	267	172
2000	858	641	217	256
2001	901	644	257	219
2002	760	467	293	238
2003	800	585	215	251
2004	802	610	192	258
2005	777	622	155	254
2006	805	658	146	247
2007	852	702	150	232
2008	841	678	153	220
2009	870	710	160	221
2010	890	732	158	201
2011	1142	704	438	207
2012	11 728	716	11 012	200
2013	13 716	735	12 981	222
2014	15 135	743	14 392	200
2015	10 755	790	9 965	173
2016	7 796	880	6 916	160
2017	6 435	900	5 535	158
2018	8 614	984	7 630	137

①2012 年起，建筑垃圾中增加了工程渣土清运量。
②本页数据由市绿化和市容管理局提供。
❶Since 2012, Construction Garbage Contains Volume of Construction Dregs Clearance.
❷Data on this page are provided by Shanghai Municipal Virescence and Appearance Administration Bureau.

表 6.19 环境卫生设施（1978~2018）
URBAN ENVIRONMENTAL SANITATION

年 份 Year	公共厕所（座）Public lawatories(unit)	生活垃圾收集点(处) Collection Points of Residential Garbage(unit)	废物箱（只）Trash Cans(unit)	倒粪站（座）Excrements Stations(unit)	化粪池（只）Septic Tanks(unit)
1978	706	13 840	2 333	3 303	25 540
1979	696	12 695	3 151	3 382	25 915
1980	713	15 707	3 402	3 445	26 754
1981	740	17 905	2 546	3 464	27 407
1982	760	18 824	2 821	3 484	28 652
1983	778	17 859	2 733	3 467	29 977
1984	798	20 384	3 890	3 481	30 943
1985	952	22 870	5 700	3 470	33 477
1986	950	31 142	5 983	3 537	39 175
1987	978	37 751	6 341	3 587	40 042
1988	992	42 802	5 117	3 342	41 171
1989	1 057	46 149	5 276	3 107	41 349
1990	1 016	46 368	4 921	2 973	43 655
1991	1 033	40 309	4 980	3 006	43 089
1992	1 048	44 752	4 961	2 655	43 694
1993	1 104	46 741	5 756	2 732	43 323
1994	1 100	50 292	6 993	2 739	43 125
1995	1 100	48 563	9 019	2 532	43 151
1996	1 112	51 456	9 522	2 412	38 657
1997	1 120	53 643	12 735	2 207	44 440
1998	1 203	59 498	15 968	2 127	41 760
1999	1 311	66 067	17 326	2 192	44 694
2000	2 215	22 470	23 189	2 045	46 921
2001	2 406	17 694	24 672	1 890	47 500
2002	3 776	26 787	29 517	1 846	49 220
2003	3 468	27 814	31 272	1 709	48 831
2004	3 640	28 649	34 571	1 611	47 579
2005	3 640	28 388	39 539	1 689	47 424
2006	3 746	29 812	44 888	2 253	46 217
2007	5 415	29 538	47 739	2 158	45 841
2008	5 866	29 965	56 485	2 064	45 537
2009	5 633	30 584	67 465	2 257	43 775
2010	6 026	30 645	74 658	1 900	43 170
2011	5 768	30 648	78 213	1 868	42 652
2012	6 340	31 625	82 454	1 837	42 306
2013	6 224	32 018	98 266	1 800	43 887
2014	6 168	32 122	98 857	1 756	43 629
2015	6 197	32 209	94 310	1 729	43 582
2016	6 220	32 257	81 246	1 832	43 983
2017	6 221	32 247	86 246	1 832	43 983
2018	6 061	31 319	80 360	1 627	40 178

上 / 海 / 统 / 计 / 年 / 鉴

主要统计指标解释

能源消费总量

能源消费总量指一定时期内全国(地区)物质生产部门、非物质生产部门和生活消费的各种能源的总和,是观察能源消费水平、构成和增长速度的总量指标。能源消费总量包括原煤和原油及其制品、天然气、电力,但不包括低热值燃料、生物质能和太阳能等的利用。能源消费总量分为三部分,即终端能源消费量、能源加工转换损失量和能源损失量。

(1)终端能源消费量指一定时期内全国(地区)物质生产部门、非物质生产部门和生活消费的各种能源在扣除了用于加工转换二次能源消费量和损失量以后的数量。

(2)能源加工转换损失量指一定时期内全国(地区)投入加工转换的各种能源数量之和与产出各种能源产品之和的差额。它是观察能源在加工转换过程中损失量变化的指标。

(3)能源损失量指一定时期内能源在输送、分配、储存过程中发生的损失和由客观原因造成的各种损失量。不包括各种气体能源放空、放散量。

能源消费弹性系数

能源消费弹性系数反映能源消费增长速度与国民经济增长速度之间比例关系的指标:

$$能源消费弹性系数=\frac{能源消费量年平均增长速度}{国民经济年平均增长速度}$$

电力消费弹性系数

电力消费弹性系数反映电力消费增长速度与国民经济增长速度之间比例关系的指标。计算公式为:

$$电力消费弹性系数=\frac{电力消费量年平均增长速度}{国民经济年平均增长速度}$$

能源加工转换效率

能源加工转换效率指一定时期内能源经过加工转换后,产出的各种能源产品的数量与投入加工转换的各种能源数量的比率。它是观察能源加工转换装置和生产工艺先进与落后、管理水平高低等的重要指标。计算公式为:

$$能源加工转换效率=\frac{加工转换产出量}{加工转换投入量}\times 100\%$$

自然保护区

指对有代表性的自然生态系统、珍稀濒危野生动植物物种的天然分布区、水源涵养区、有特殊意义的自然历史遗迹等保护对象所在的陆地、陆地水体或海域,依法划出一定面积进行特殊保护和管理的区域。以县及县以上各级人民政府正式批准建立的自然保护区为准(包括“六五”以前由部门或“革委会”批准且现仍存在的自然保护区)。风景名胜区、文物保护区不计在内。自然保护区分国家级、省级、地市级和县级。按主管部门分属:环保、林业、农业、地矿、海洋、水利和其他部门。

工业固体废弃物产生量

指报告期内企业在生产过程中产生的固体状、半固体状和高浓度液体状废弃物的总量,包括危险废物、冶炼废渣、粉煤灰、炉渣、煤矸石、尾矿、放射性废物和其他废物等;不包括矿山开采的剥离废石和掘进废石(煤矸石和呈酸性或碱性的废石除外)。酸性或碱性废石指采掘的废石其流经水、雨淋水的pH值小于4或pH值大于10.5者。

危险废物

指列入国家危险废物名录或根据国家规定的危险废物鉴别标准和鉴别方法认定的,具有爆炸性、易燃性、易氧化性、毒性、腐蚀性、易传染疾病等危险特性之一的废物。

工业废弃物综合利用量

指报告期内企业通过回收、加工、循环、交换等方式,从废弃物中提取或者使其转化为可以利用的资源、能源和其他原材料的废弃物量(包括当年利用往年的工业废弃物贮存量),如用作农业肥料、生产建筑材料、筑路等。综合利用量由原产生废弃物的单位统计。

主要统计指标解释

工业废弃物综合利用率

指工业废弃物综合利用量占工业废弃物产生量(包括综合利用往年贮存量)的百分率。计算公式为:

$$工业废弃物综合利用率=\frac{工业废弃物综合利用量}{工业废弃物产生量+综合利用往年贮存量}\times 100\%$$

工业固体废物处置量

指报告期内企业将固体废物焚烧或者最终置于符合环境保护规定要求的场所,并不再回取的工业固体废物量(包括当年处置往年的工业固体废物贮存量)。处置方式有填埋(其中危险废物应安全填埋)、焚烧、专业贮存场(库)封场处理、深层灌注、回填矿井及海洋处置(经海洋管理部门同意投海处置)等。

工业废水排放量

指经过企业厂区所有排放口排到企业外部的工业废水量。包括生产废水、外排的直接冷却水、超标排放的矿井地下水和与工业废水混排的厂区生活污水,不包括外排的间接冷却水(清污不分流的间接冷却水应计算在内)。

工业废水排放达标量

指报告期内废水中各项污染物指标都达到国家或地方排放标准的外排工业废水量,包括未经处理外排达标的,经废水处理设施处理后达标排放的,以及经污水处理厂处理后达标排放的。

工业废水排放达标率

指工业废水排放达标量占工业废水排放量的百分率,计算公式为:

$$工业废水排放达标率=\frac{工业废水排放达标量}{工业废水排放量}\times 100\%$$

工业废气排放量

指企业厂区内燃料燃烧和生产工艺过程中产生的各种排入空气的含有污染物的气体总量,按标准状态〔273K,101 325Pa〕计算。测算公式为:

工业废气排放量 = 燃料燃烧过程中废气排放量 + 生产工艺过程中废气排放量

工业二氧化硫排放总量

指报告期内企业在燃料燃烧和生产工艺过程中排入大气的SO_2总量,计算公式为:

工业二氧化硫排放量 = 燃料燃烧过程中二氧化硫排放量 + 生产工艺过程中二氧化硫排放量

工业烟尘排放量

指企业厂区内燃料燃烧过程中产生的烟气中夹带的颗粒物排放量。

酸雨频率

指酸雨出现的次数占降水出现次数的比例,通常称PH值小于5.6的降水为酸雨。

SHANGHAI STATISTICAL YEARBOOK

EXPLANATORY NOTES TO MAJOR STATISTICAL INDICATORS

□ Total Energy Consumption

Total Energy Consumption refers to the total energy consumption of various forms by material production departments, non- material production departments and households in the country (region) in a given period of time. It is a comprehensive indicator to observe the scale, composition and development of energy consumption. The total energy consumption includes raw coal, crude petroleum and their products, natural gas and electricity, but excludes fuel of low calorific value, bioenergy and solar energy. Total domestic energy consumption can be divided into three parts:

(1) Final Energy Consumption refers to the total energy consumption by material production departments, non-material production departments and households in the country (region) in a given period of time, after deducting the secondary energy consumption and loss during the process of energy conversion.

(2) Loss During the Process of Energy Conversion refers to the total input of various forms for conversion, minus the total output of energy of various forms in the country in a given period of time. It is an indicator to observe the loss that occurs during the process of energy conversion.

(3) Loss refers to the total loss of energy due to mistakes or any objective reasons during the course of energy transport, distribution and storage in a given period of time. The loss of various kinds of gas due to gas discharges and stocktaking is excluded.

□ Elasticity of Energy Consumption

Elasticity Ratio of Energy Consumption is an indicator to show the relationship between the growth rate of energy consumption and the growth rate of the national economy. The formula is:

$$\text{Elasticity of Energy Consumption} = \frac{\text{average annual growth rate of energy consumption}}{\text{average annual growth rate of national economy}}$$

□ Elasticity of Electricity Consumption

Elasticity Ratio of Electricity Consumption is an indicator to show the relationship between the growth rate of electricity consumption and the growth rate of the national economy. The formula is:

$$\text{Elasticity of Electricity Consumption} = \frac{\text{average annual growth rate of electricity consumption}}{\text{average annual growth rate of national economy}}$$

□ Efficiency of Energy Transformation

Efficiency of Energy Transformation refers to the ratio of the total output of energy products after transformation and the total input of energy for transformation in the same reference period .It is an indicator to show the current conditions of energy processing and conversion equipment, production technique and management. The formula is:

$$\text{Efficiency of Energy Transformation} = \frac{\text{output of enery from transformation}}{\text{Input of energy for transformation}} \times 100\%$$

□ Natural Reserves

Natural Reserves refer to all the land, water areas on land and sea areas are under special protection or management due to the possess ion of representative natural ecological system, natural distribution of rare and dying out animal zones, water- resource conservation areas, and natural historical relics. Also included are natural reserves formally approved by people's governments at various levels at and above county level (including those approved before the Sixth-five-year Program and still active natural reserves).Scenic spots and historical sites and zones for preservation of cultural relics are not included. Natural reserves are classified as national level, provincial level, prefecture level and county level ones. They are under the jurisdiction of different departments, such as: environment protection, forestry, agriculture, geological and mining, oceanic and water conservancy and so on.

□ Industrial Solid Wastes Produced

Industrial Solid Wastes Produced refers to total volume of solid, semi- solid and high concentration liquid residues produced by industrial enterprises from production process in a given period of time, including hazardous wastes, slag, coal ash, gangue, tailings, radioactive residues and other wastes, but excluding stones stripped or dug out in mining (gangue and acid or

EXPLANATORY NOTES TO MAJOR STATISTICAL INDICATORS

alkaline stones not included). A stone is acid or alkaline depending on the pH value of the water below 4 or above 10.5 when the stone is in, or soaked by, the water.

□ Hazardous Wastes

Hazardous Wastes refers to those included in the national hazardous wastes catalogue or specified as any one of the following properties in the national hazardous wastes identification standards: explosive, ignitable, oxidizable, toxic, corrosive or liable to cause infectious diseases or lead to other dangers.

□ Industrial Wastes Utilized

Industrial Wastes Utilized refers to volume of wastes from which useful materials can be extracted or which can be converted into usable resources, energy or other materials by means of reclamation, processing, recycling and exchange (including utilizing in the year the stocks of industrial wastes of the previous year). Examples of such utilizations include fertilizers, building materials and road materials. The information shall be collected by the producing units of the wastes.

□ Ratio of Industrial Wastes Utilized

Ratio of Industrial Wastes Utilized refers to the percentage of industrial wastes utilized over industrial wastes produced (including stocks of the previous years). It is calculated as:

Ratio of industrial wastes utilized=volume of industrial wastes utilized / (industrial wastes produced + stock of previous years) ×100%

□ Industrial Solid Wastes Disposed

Industrial Solid Wastes Disposed refers to quantity of industrial solid wastes which are burnt or placed ultimately in the sites meeting the requirements for environmental protection and not salvaged or recycled (including disposition in the year of those wastes of previous years). The disposition includes landfill (Safe landfills should be conducted for hazardous wastes), incineration, containment spaces, deep underground disposal, backfill in mining pits and disposal at sea.

□ Volume of Industrial Waste Water Discharged

Volume of Industrial Waste Water Discharged refers to the volume of industrial waste water discharged, through all outlets, to the outside of industrial enterprises, including waste water produced, direct- cooling water, underground water from mines that does not meet the standard of discharge, and the domestic sewage mixed up with industrial waste water when discharged, but excluding discharged indirect-cooling water.

□ Industrial Waste Water Meeting Discharge Standards

Industrial Waste Water Meeting Discharge Standards refers to volume of industrial waste water discharge which, with or without treatment, reaches national or local standards with regard to all pollutants.

□ Ratio of Standard Waste Water Discharged to the Total Discharge

Ratio of Standard Waste Water Discharged to the Total Discharge refers to the share of the volume of waste water up to the standard for discharge of the total volume. The formula is as follows:

Ratio of Standard Waste Water
Discharged to the Total Discharge

$$\frac{\text{average annual growth rate of electricity consumption}}{\text{average annual growth rate of national economy}} \times 100\%$$

□ Volume of Waste Industrial Gas Emission

Industrial Waste Air Emission refers to discharge into atmosphere of waste air containing pollutants generated from fuel burning and production process in enterprises within a given period of time. It is calculated at standard status (273K, 101325Pa) as:

Industrial waste air emission = emission through fuel burning + emission through production process

□ SO_2 Emission through Industrial Activities

SO_2 Emission through Industrial Activities refers to volume of sulphur dioxide emission from fuel burning and production process by enterprises during a given period of time. It is calculated as:

SO_2 emission through industrial activities = SO_2 emission from fuel burning + SO_2 emission from production process

□ Industrial Soot Emission

Industrial Soot Emission refers to volume of soot in smoke emitted in process of fuel burning in premises of enterprises.

EXPLANATORY NOTES TO MAJOR STATISTICAL INDICATORS

□ Acid Rain Frequency

Acid Rain Frequency refers to the proportion of frequencies of acid rainfall to the total rainfall times. Rainfall is defined as acid rain when the PH value of its rainwater is small than 5.6.

第七篇
CHAPTER 7

固定资产投资
INVESTMENT IN FIXED ASSETS

简要说明

一、本篇资料的主要内容

本篇资料通过对一定时期全社会建造和购置固定资产活动的数量方面的描述，反映报告期内固定资产投资的规模、速度和内部结构情况，固定资产投资的资金来源及房屋施、竣工面积情况等。

二、本篇资料的统计范围

固定资产投资统计的范围包括：城镇和农村非农户建设项目投资，房地产开发投资及农户投资。

三、本篇的资料来源

城镇和农村非农户建设项目投资的统计资料来自上海市统计局投资建设统计处的固定资产投资统计调查；房地产开发投资的统计资料来自上海市统计局投资建设统计处的房地产开发、经营统计调查；农户投资的统计资料来自国家统计局上海调查总队居民收支调查处的农村住户固定资产投资抽样调查。

四、本篇的统计调查方法

除农户固定资产投资统计采用抽样调查方法外，其他均为全面统计报表。

五、统计口径的变化

自1997年起，固定资产投资的统计起点由5万元及以上提高到50万元及以上。

自2011年起，固定资产投资项目的统计起点由计划总投资50万元及以上提高到500万元及以上。

BRIEF INTRODUCTION

I. Main Contents

Statistics in this chapter describe activities on the construction and purchase of fixed assets of the whole society during a given period of time, and reflect the size, growth, internal structure, source of funds of fixed asset investment and floor space of buildings under construction or completed.

II. Scope of Statistics

Statistics the investment in fixed assets cover investments in construction projects of urban and rural non–farm households, investments in real estate development, and investment of farm households.

III. Sources of Data

Data on the investments in construction projects of urban and rural non–farm households are from the surveys of investment in fixed assets from Department of Investment and Construction Statistics of the Shanghai Municipal Bureau of Statistics. Data on the real estate investments are from surveys of real estate development and management conducted by Department of Investment and Construction Statistics of the Shanghai Municipal Bureau of Statistics. Data on the investment of farm households are from surveys of fixed assets investment in rural households conducted by Department of Residents Income and Expenditure Survey of the Survey Office of NBS in Shanghai

IV. Methodology of Data Collection

All data on investment in fixed assets are collected by the system of reporting form with complete enumeration, except data on individual investments in fixed assets in rural areas, which are collected through sample surveys.

V. Changes in Statistical Scope

Since 1997, the cut–off point of statistics of investment in fixed assets is raised from 50000 yuan to 500000 yuan. Since 2011, the cut–off point of projects covered by statistics of investment in fixed assets is raised from an investment of 500000 yuan to 5000000 yuan.

表 7.1 全社会固定资产投资总额(按投资类别分)(1978~2017)
TOTAL INVESTMENT IN FIXED ASSETS(GROUPED BY TYPE OF INVESTMENT)

单位:亿元(100 million yuan)

年 份 Year	本年完成投资合 计 Investment Completed Total	其 中 of which				
		建设项目 Construction Project	其 中 of which		房地产开发 Investment in Real Estate	农户投资 Farmers' Investment
			城 镇 Town	农村非农户 Rural Non-agricultural		
1978	27.91	26.88	23.92	2.96		0.79
1979	35.58	34.39	32.22	2.17		0.94
1980	45.43	43.45	40.44	3.01		1.41
1981	54.60	49.85	45.20	4.65		3.97
1982	71.34	65.97	61.91	4.06		4.32
1983	75.94	70.21	65.26	4.95		4.48
1984	92.30	83.11	76.04	7.07		7.28
1985	118.56	103.16	96.12	7.04		12.00
1986	146.93	132.44	122.64	9.80		10.30
1987	186.30	167.88	154.04	13.84	0.97	12.66
1988	245.27	219.90	197.71	22.19	1.68	16.90
1989	214.76	194.64	177.70	16.94	1.85	14.32
1990	227.08	199.05	184.67	14.38	8.16	15.96
1991	258.30	232.34	208.72	23.62	7.59	14.17
1992	357.38	318.93	263.51	55.42	12.71	17.00
1993	653.91	610.80	505.98	104.82	22.04	5.33
1994	1 123.29	971.68	830.45	141.23	117.43	10.40
1995	1 601.79	1 097.68	958.11	139.57	466.20	13.10
1996	1 952.05	1 238.85	1 080.53	158.32	657.79	20.00
1997	1 977.59	1 322.92	1 156.76	166.16	614.23	16.80
1998	1 964.83	1 361.41	1 224.01	137.40	577.12	12.76
1999	1 856.72	1 325.84	1 191.51	134.33	514.83	5.54
2000	1 869.67	1 284.08	1 122.47	161.61	566.17	10.36
2001	1 994.73	1 354.22	1 181.09	173.13	630.73	9.28
2002	2 187.06	1 430.69	1 262.77	167.92	748.89	6.87
2003	2 452.11	1 544.38	1 374.38	170.00	901.24	6.49
2004	3 084.66	1 903.33	1 722.51	180.82	1 175.46	5.86
2005	3 542.55	2 288.61	1 984.61	304.00	1 246.86	7.08
2006	3 925.09	2 643.53	2 246.93	396.60	1 275.59	5.96
2007	4 458.61	3 145.87	2 775.81	370.06	1 307.53	5.21
2008	4 829.45	3 459.38	3 044.46	414.92	1 366.87	3.20
2009	5 273.33	3 807.62	3 384.31	423.31	1 464.18	1.53
2010	5 317.67	3 334.95	2 858.56	476.39	1 980.68	2.03
2011	5 067.09	2 893.95	2 519.48	374.47	2 170.31	2.83
2012	5 254.38	2 870.04	2 559.12	310.92	2 381.36	2.98
2013	5 647.79	2 824.54	2 544.99	279.55	2 819.59	3.66
2014	6 016.43	2 806.49			3 206.48	3.46
2015	6 352.70	2 880.45			3 468.94	3.31
2016	6 755.88	3 042.65			3 709.03	4.21
2017	7 246.60	3 384.42			3 856.53	5.66

注:自 2011 年起,全社会固定资产投资由建设项目投资、房地产开发投资和农户投资三部分组成;建设项目投资由城镇投资和农村非农户投资两部分组成,其中城镇投资包括原来的基本建设、更新改造、其他投资和城镇私人建房投资;从 2014 年起建设项目取消"城乡分组"。

Note: Since 2011, total investment in fixed assets was composed of construction project investment, investment in real estate development and investment of rural households; construction project investment was composed of investment in urban areas and rural non-agricultural investment, in which investment in urban areas was composed of fundamental construction, renovation, other investments and urban private housing investment. Group of urban and rural construction projects was canceled since 2014.

表 7.2　全社会固定资产投资总额(按经济类型分)(1978~2017)
TOTAL INVESTMENT IN FIXED ASSETS (GROUPED BY ECONOMIC TYPES)

单位:亿元(100 million yuan)

年 份 Year	本年完成投资合 计 Investment Completed Total	其 中 of which			
		#国 有 经 济 State-owned	#集 体 经 济 Collective-owned	#股份制 经 济 Share-holding	#外商、港澳台 经 济 Hong Kong, Macao, Taiwan and Foreign Funded
1978	27.91	23.83	3.20		
1979	35.58	32.08	2.42		
1980	45.43	40.27	3.58		
1981	54.60	45.00	5.43		
1982	71.34	61.62	5.11		
1983	75.94	65.01	6.20		
1984	92.30	75.80	8.98		
1985	118.56	95.92	10.44		
1986	146.93	122.46	13.99		
1987	186.30	154.45	18.65		
1988	245.27	198.68	29.03		
1989	214.76	178.81	21.00		
1990	227.08	192.24	18.29		
1991	258.30	215.61	27.82		
1992	357.38	275.67	64.16		
1993	653.91	419.22	124.18	32.83	61.61
1994	1 123.29	721.37	189.75	76.99	101.78
1995	1 601.79	935.92	247.11	150.17	208.30
1996	1 952.05	1 048.27	239.47	165.57	340.18
1997	1 977.59	1 148.69	257.10	118.80	367.50
1998	1 964.83	1 087.94	208.84	203.81	405.17
1999	1 856.72	986.82	227.19	268.68	325.58
2000	1 869.67	829.98	156.34	421.53	319.05
2001	1 994.73	760.58	136.81	580.75	362.25
2002	2 187.06	742.72	101.33	631.70	369.96
2003	2 452.11	811.85	116.63	647.27	468.20
2004	3 084.66	955.12	146.58	667.52	851.39
2005	3 542.55	1 240.27	131.07	916.27	640.31
2006	3 925.09	1 460.09	159.31	910.31	725.85
2007	4 458.61	1 779.43	121.51	1 169.49	711.35
2008	4 829.45	2 295.74	104.86	1 026.67	748.14
2009	5 273.33	2 618.61	132.30	1 174.81	617.90
2010	5 317.67	2 234.12	183.07	1 200.26	686.95
2011	5 067.09	1 875.48	133.33	1 349.65	726.57
2012	5 254.38	1 855.24	112.41	1 417.80	758.08
2013	5 647.79	1 926.89	102.81	1 601.33	894.47
2014	6 016.43	1 796.22	55.07	1 812.77	1 103.04
2015	6 352.70	1 974.08	53.62	2 124.52	1 164.72
2016	6 755.88	1 844.66	33.85	2 611.71	1 153.48
2017	7 246.60	2 192.32	61.35	2 830.73	1 010.74

表 7.3 全社会固定资产投资主要指标比上年增长（2018）
GROWTH RATE OF MAJOR INDICATORS OF TOTAL INVESTMENT IN FIXED ASSETS

单位：%

指 标	Indicators	2018
本年完成投资合计	**Investment Completed Total**	**5.2**
按隶属关系分	**Grouped by Administrative Relationship**	
中央项目	Central Government Projects	38.8
地方项目	Local Projects	1.5
按构成分	**Grouped by Use of Funds**	
建筑安装工程	Construction and Installation	-3.0
设备工器具购置	Purchase of Equipment and Instruments	36.3
其他费用	Others	7.3
按建设性质分	**Grouped by Type of Construction**	
#新 建	New Construction	-7.2
扩 建	Expansion	8.9
改建和技术改造	Reconstruction and Technical Transformation	29.0
单纯购置	Simply Purchase	47.0
按产业分	**Grouped by Type of Industry**	
第一产业	Primary Industry	209.1
第二产业	Secondary Industry	17.2
第三产业	Tertiary Industry	3.2
按经济类型分	**Grouped by Economic Types**	
国有经济	State-owned	1.0
非国有经济	Non-state-owned	7.0
集体经济	Collective-owned	-73.9
私营经济	Private	26.7
联营经济	Joint Owned	9.9
股份制经济	Share-holding	7.2
港澳台商投资	Hong Kong, Macao and Taiwan Funded	-16.1
外商投资	Foreign Funded	-1.7
其他经济	Others	22.1
新增固定资产（亿元）	**Newly Increased Fixed Assets(100 million yuan)**	**3 599.51**
固定资产交付使用率（%）	Rate of Fixed Assets Transfered and in Use(%)	47.2
房屋建筑面积（万平方米）	**Floor Space of Buildings (10 000 sq.m)**	
施工面积	Floor Space Under Construction	18 757.71
#住 宅	Residential Housing	7 615.04
竣工面积	Floor Space Completed	3 790.92
#住 宅	Residential Housing	1 765.79

表 7.4 地方项目固定资产投资主要指标比上年增长 (2018)
GROWTH RATE OF MAJOR INDICATORS OF LOCAL INVESTMENT IN FIXED ASSETS

单位:%

指　标	Indicators	2018
本年完成投资合计	**Investment Completed Total**	**1.5**
按构成分	**Grouped by Use of Funds**	
建筑安装工程	Construction and Installation	-4.0
设备工器具购置	Purchase of Equipment and Instruments	24.2
其他费用	Others	5.3
按建设性质分	**Grouped by Type of Construction**	
#新　建	New Construction	-10.1
扩　建	Expansion	6.9
改建和技术改造	Reconstruction and Technical Transformation	34.5
单纯购置	Simply Purchase	-3.7
按产业分	**Grouped by Type of Industry**	
第一产业	Primary Industry	61.3
第二产业	Secondary Industry	17.2
第三产业	Tertiary Industry	3.1
按行业分	**Grouped by Sectors**	
#工　业	Industry	20.3
批发和零售业	Wholesale and Retail	-1.4
交通运输、仓储和邮政业	Transportation, Storage, Postal and Telecommunications	-17.6
住宿和餐饮业	Hotel and Catering	72.5
信息传输、软件和信息技术服务业	Transmission of Information, Software and Information Technology Services	8.4
金融业	Finance	48.5
房地产业	Real Estate	3.6
租赁和商务服务业	Leasing and Business Service	-38.6
科学研究和技术服务业	Scientific Research and Technology Service	21.4
水利、环境和公共设施管理业	Water Conservancy, Environment and Public Facility Management	-15.2
居民服务、修理和其他服务业	Residents Service, Repair and Other Services	42.2
教　育	Education	31.8
卫生和社会工作	Health and Social Work	30.8
文化、体育和娱乐业	Culture, Sports and Entertainment	6.2
公共管理、社会保障和社会组织	Public Administration and Social Organizations	35.8
新增固定资产(亿元)	**Newly Increased Fixed Assets (100 million yuan)**	**2 946.98**
固定资产交付使用率(%)	Rate of Fixed Assets Transfered and in Use (%)	44.4
房屋建筑面积(万平方米)	**Floor Space of Buildings (10 000 sq.m)**	
施工面积	Floor Space Under Construction	17 837.50
#住　宅	Residential Housing	7 044.28
竣工面积	Floor Space Completed	3 676.96
#住　宅	Residential Housing	1 690.43

表 7.5 建设项目固定资产投资主要指标比上年增长(2018)
GROWTH RATE OF MAJOR INDICATORS OF INVESTMENT IN FIXED ASSETS OF THE CONSTRUCTION PROJECT

单位:%

指 标	Indicators	全 市 Total	#地 方 Local Projects
本年完成投资合计	**Investment Completed Total**	**5.9**	**-1.2**
按建设性质分	**Grouped by Type of Construction**		
#新 建	New Construction	-7.2	-10.1
扩 建	Expansion	8.9	6.9
改建和技术改造	Reconstruction and Technical Transformation	29.0	34.5
单纯购置	Simply Purchase	47.0	-3.7
按产业分	**Grouped by Type of Industry**		
第一产业	Primary Industry	433.5	138.5
第二产业	Secondary Industry	17.2	17.2
第三产业	Tertiary Industry	0.9	0.8
按行业分	**Grouped by Economic Sectors**		
#工 业	Industry	17.7	20.3
批发和零售业	Wholesale and Retail	0.7	-1.4
交通运输、仓储和邮政业	Transportation, Storage, Postal and Telecommunications	9.6	-17.6
住宿和餐饮业	Hotel and Catering	72.5	72.5
信息传输、软件和信息技术服务业	Transmission of Information, Software and Information Technology Services	14.1	8.4
金融业	Finance	12.6	48.5
房地产业	Real Estate	-2.2	-2.2
租赁和商务服务业	Leasing and Business Service	-37.2	-38.6
科学研究和技术服务业	Scientific Research and Technology Service	10.4	21.4
水利、环境和公共设施管理业	Water Conservancy,Environment and Public Facility Management	-15.1	-15.2
居民服务、修理和其他服务业	Residents Service, Repair and Other Services	56.1	42.2
教 育	Education	31.1	31.8
卫生和社会工作	Health and Social Work	41.9	30.8
文化、体育和娱乐业	Culture,Sports and Entertainment	6.0	6.2
公共管理、社会保障和社会组织	Public Administration and Social Organizations	34.0	35.8
新增固定资产(亿元)	**Newly Increased Fixed Assets(100 million yuan)**	**1 638.39**	**1 027.10**
固定资产交付使用率(%)	Rate of Fixed Assets Transfered and in Use(%)	45.7	36.6
房屋建筑面积(万平方米)	**Floor Space of Buildings (10 000 sq.m)**		
施工面积	Floor Space Under Construction	4 034.04	3 860.27
#住 宅	Residential Housing	44.46	19.38
竣工面积	Floor Space Completed	639.75	615.54
#住 宅	Residential Housing	1.12	1.12

表 7.6 工业各行业固定资产投资主要指标(2018)
MAIN INDICATORS OF INVESTMENT IN FIXED ASSETS OF VARIOUS INDUSTRIES

行业	Sectors	施工项目(个) Projects Under Construction (unit)	本年投产项目(个) Projects Completed and Put into Production (unit)	建成投产率(%) Rate of Projects Completed and Put into Use(%)	本年完成投资合计比上年增长(%) Growth Rate of Construction Transformation Investment(%)
总　计	**Total**	**2 145**	**712**	**33.2**	**17.7**
采矿业	**Excavation**				
开采辅助活动	Mining Support Activities				
制造业	**Manufacturing**	**1 516**	**470**	**31.0**	**14.8**
农副食品加工业	Farm and Sideline Products Processing	23	9	39.1	-7.9
食品制造业	Food Manufacturing	46	12	26.1	-25.7
酒、饮料和精制茶制造业	Wine, Drinks and Purified Tea Manufacturing	10	1	10.0	63.3
烟草制品业	Tabacco Manufacturing	2	1	50.0	-33.5
纺织业	Textile	9	2	22.2	-8.0
纺织服装、服饰业	Textiles and Clothing Industry	16	3	18.8	-19.7
皮革、毛皮、羽毛及其制品和制鞋业	Leather, Fur, Wool Products, and Shoes Manufacturing	2			432.4
木材加工和木、竹、藤、棕、草制品业	Timber Processing and Timber, Bamboo, Rattan, Coir and Straw Products Manufacturing	6	1	16.7	426.6
家具制造业	Furniture Manufacturing	5			-74.4
造纸和纸制品业	Paper-making and Paper Products Manufacturing	18	5	27.8	-45.7
印刷业和记录媒介复制业	Printing and Record Duplicating	26	15	57.7	-18.4
文教、工美、体育和娱乐用品制造业	Culture, Education, Industrial Arts, Sports and Entertainment Goods Manufacturing	10	3	30.0	-63.8
石油加工、炼焦和核燃料加工业	Oil Processing, Coking and Nuclear Fuel Processing	44	27	61.4	-55.1
化学原料和化学制品制造业	Raw Chemical Materials and Chemical Products Manufacturing	117	29	24.8	13.5
医药制造业	Medicine Manufacturing	67	13	19.4	1.8
化学纤维制造业	Chemical Fiber Manufacturing	2	1	50.0	-16.7
橡胶和塑料制品业	Rubber and Plastic Products Manufacturing	54	16	29.6	-21.2
非金属矿物制品业	Non-metallic Mineral Products Manufacturing	34	12	35.3	19.1
黑色金属冶炼和压延加工业	Ferrous Metal Smelting and Rolling Processing Industry	150	90	60.0	18.4
有色金属冶炼和压延加工业	Nonferrous Metal Smelting and Rolling Processing Industry	7	1	14.3	95.2
金属制品业	Metal Products Manufacturing	60	16	26.7	12.6
通用设备制造业	General Equipment Manufacturing	136	34	25.0	-16.3
专用设备制造业	Special Purpose Equipment Manufacturing	81	29	35.8	-20.7
汽车制造业	The Automotive Manufacturing	232	50	21.6	
铁路、船舶、航空航天和其他运输设备制造业	The Railroad, Marine, Aerospace and Other Transportation Equipment Manufacturing	25	5	20.0	5.9
电气机械和器材制造业	Electric Machinery Equipments and Manufacturing	121	35	28.9	14.9
计算机、通信和其他电子设备制造业	Computer, Communications and Other Electronic Equipment Manufacturing	107	29	27.1	71.4
仪器仪表制造业	Instrumentation Manufacturing	19	6	31.6	-23.9
其他制造业	Other Manufacturing	72	21	29.2	16.3
废弃资源综合利用业	Comprehensive Utilization of Waste Resources	13	4	30.8	105.1
金属制品、机械和设备修理业	Metal Products, Machinery and Equipment Repair Industry	2			134.5
电力、热力、燃气及水的生产和供应业	Electricity, Heat, Gas and Water Production and Supply Industry	629	242	38.5	28.0
电力、热力生产和供应业	Power and Heat Production and Supply	587	237	40.4	11.5
燃气生产和供应业	Gas Production and Supply	5	0	0.0	-27.7
水的生产和供应业	Water Production and Supply	37	5	13.5	56.0

注：单纯购置项目固定资产投资不计算施工项目和本年投产项目个数。

Note: The investment in fixed assets of purchasing and preparatory project doesn't be calculated in projects under construction or projects completed and put into production in this year.

表 7.7 主要年份工业六个重点发展行业固定资产投资额
FIXED ASSETS INVESTMENT IN SIX KEY INDUSTRIES IN MAIN YEARS

单位：亿元(100 million yuan)

指 标	Indicators	2010	2015	2017	2018
工业六个重点发展行业	**Six Key Industries**	**730.68**	**556.33**	**552.60**	**555.99**
电子信息产品制造业	Electronic Information Product Manufacturing	219.65	173.28	193.10	183.25
汽车制造业	Automobile Manufacturing	109.68	118.10	130.44	154.50
石油化工及精细化工制造业	Petrochemical and Fine Chemical Products Manufacturing	85.03	67.09	70.90	52.15
精品钢材制造业	Fine Steel Manufacturing	113.79	40.35	38.40	44.92
成套设备制造业	Equipment Complex Manufacturing	176.31	98.30	69.43	82.27
生物医药制造业	Bio-medicine Manufacturing	26.21	59.21	50.33	38.91

注：自 2012 年起固定资产投资项目行业代码采用新的分类标准(GB/T 4754-2011)，本表中的数据参照新行业标准进行相应调整。由于个别投资项目同时属于工业六个重点发展行业中的两类，故各分类投资数直接相加大于合计数。

Note: The industry code of fixed asset investment projects use the new classification standard(GB/T 4754-2011) since 2012, the data in this table was adjusted by the new standard. Individual investment projects belong to two types in Six Key Industries, so the sum of each segment is greater than the total number.

表 7.8 主要年份新增固定资产
NEWLY INCREASED FIXED ASSETS IN MAIN YEARS

年 份 Year	新增固定资产(亿元) Newly Increased Fixed Assets(100 million yuan)	其中 of which: #房地产开发 Investment in Real Estate Development	固定资产交付使用率(%) Rate of Fixed Assets Transferred and in Use(%)
1990	222.99	4.97	98.2
1995	826.94	127.08	51.6
2000	1 493.35	477.39	79.9
2005	2 547.02	1 054.02	71.9
2006	2 680.85	1 058.94	68.3
2007	2 466.68	1 048.47	55.3
2008	2 773.14	994.10	57.4
2009	2 686.43	932.24	50.9
2010	3 179.40	964.27	59.8
2011	2 816.59	1 250.88	55.6
2012	2 911.34	1 388.45	55.4
2013	2 664.81	1 354.75	47.2
2014	2 739.79	1 583.93	45.5
2015	3 281.26	1 890.67	51.7
2016	2 958.65	1 558.72	43.8
2017	3 957.94	2 110.17	54.6
2018	3 599.51	1 955.84	47.2

表 7.9 主要年份固定资产投资资金来源
CAPITAL SOURCES OF FIXED ASSETS INVESTMENT IN MAIN YEARS

单位：亿元(100 million yuan)

指 标	Indicators	2010	2015	2017	2018
到位资金合计	**Total Actual Funds This Year**	**7 997.62**	**10 652.67**	**11 287.40**	**11 345.84**
上年末结余资金	Balance at End of Previous Year	1 440.57	2 472.70	3 105.06	3 182.31
本年实际到位资金	Sub-total Actual Funds this Year	6 557.05	8 179.97	8 182.34	8 163.53
国家预算资金	State Budgetary Funds	624.91	501.61	811.59	825.70
国内贷款	Domestic Loans	1 568.79	2 050.79	2 013.01	1 988.20
债 券	Bonds	10.06	0.50	18.72	4.30
利用外资	Foreign Investment	239.18	130.13	18.76	12.28
#外商直接投资	Foreign Direct Investment	139.72	85.36		
自筹资金	Self-Financed Capital	2 764.91	3 010.99	2 834.87	3 150.43
其他资金	Other Capital	1 349.21	2 485.96	2 485.39	2 182.62
本年各项应付款合计	The Total Payment of This Year	997.93	1 661.63	1 536.84	1 494.77
#工程款	Project Funds	438.19	867.08	701.12	709.02

注：自 2012 年起，国家预算资金和自筹资金统计口径调整，历年指标数据已做相应调整；自 2017 年起，利用外资取消其中外商直接投资指标。

Note: The Statistical caliber of state budget funds and self-financing was adjusted since 2012, and data over the years have been adjusted accordingly.Since 2017, the Foreign Investment has abolished the indicator of Foreign Direct Investment.

表 7.10 全社会房屋施工面积、竣工面积(1985~2018)
TOTAL FLOOR SPACE OF CONSTRUCTION AND COMPLETED BUILDINGS

年 份 Year	施 工 面 积 (万平方米) Floor Area of Construction (10 000 sq.m)	其中 of which #住 宅 Residential Housing	其中 of which 占全社会房屋施工面积比重(%) As Percentage of Total Floor Space Of Construction(%)	竣 工 面 积 (万平方米) Floor Area Completed (10 000 sq.m)	房屋建筑面积竣工率(%) Construction Completion Rate (%)
1985	4 162.15	2 651.52	63.7	2 909.58	69.9
1986	4 874.44	2 469.27	50.7	2 493.93	51.2
1987	4 382.40	2 658.05	60.7	2 700.96	61.6
1988	4 369.20	2 667.00	61.0	2 457.34	56.2
1989	3 683.77	2 048.20	55.6	1 941.80	52.7
1990	3 801.46	2 269.06	59.7	2 138.44	56.3
1991	3 611.53	2 157.46	59.7	1 923.92	53.3
1992	4 709.52	2 463.79	52.3	2 608.20	55.4
1993	4 724.30	2 142.39	45.3	2 031.76	43.0
1994	6 720.70	3 520.27	52.4	2 519.09	37.5
1995	10 566.42	6 195.12	58.6	3 093.93	29.3
1996	10 730.85	5 874.26	54.7	3 254.57	30.3
1997	9 955.21	5 450.13	54.7	3 614.19	36.3
1998	9 364.36	5 113.52	54.6	3 364.43	35.9
1999	8 364.48	4 608.49	55.1	3 257.57	38.9
2000	8 636.31	4 804.12	55.6	3 266.52	37.8
2001	8 588.49	5 236.93	61.0	3 215.12	37.4
2002	9 425.42	5 994.70	63.6	3 102.54	32.9
2003	11 023.24	6 974.27	63.3	3 582.34	32.5
2004	12 291.81	7 873.44	64.1	4 932.57	40.1
2005	14 477.85	8 267.24	57.1	4 873.82	33.7
2006	14 596.49	8 085.28	55.4	4 901.46	33.6
2007	14 979.37	7 789.91	52.0	5 068.46	33.8
2008	14 083.52	7 060.19	50.1	3 828.79	27.2
2009	13 553.64	6 581.16	48.6	2 970.92	21.9
2010	15 020.76	7 344.07	48.9	2 776.21	18.5
2011	16 553.86	8 423.11	50.9	2 913.78	17.6
2012	16 874.72	8 350.83	49.5	2 838.97	16.8
2013	17 180.27	8 188.56	47.7	2 698.35	15.7
2014	18 010.06	8 573.04	47.6	2 682.42	14.9
2015	17 885.94	8 443.82	47.2	2 923.42	16.3
2016	17 733.25	8 157.21	46.0	2 840.03	16.0
2017	18 587.63	8 083.44	43.5	3 832.45	20.6
2018	18 757.71	7 615.04	40.6	3 790.92	20.2

表 7.11 全社会住宅投资和竣工面积(1978~2018)
TOTAL INVESTMENT IN RESIDENTIAL HOUSING AND FLOOR SPACE OF BUILDINGS COMPLETED

年 份 Year	住宅投资额 (亿元) Investment in Residential Housing (100 million yuan)	其 中 of which #房地产 Real Estate	占全社会固定资产投资总额比重(%) As Percentage of Total Investment in Fixed Asset(%)	住宅竣工建筑面积(万平方米) Floor Area of Residence Building Completed (10 000 sq.m)	住宅建筑面积竣工率(%) Construction Completion Rate (%)
1978	2.67		9.6	199.61	
1979	3.31		9.3	215.99	
1980	5.82		12.8	304.32	
1981	10.02		18.4	1 380.70	78.3
1982	11.03		15.5	1 363.63	77.7
1983	11.18		14.7	1 347.79	77.2
1984	15.88		17.2	1 788.44	80.9
1985	25.47		21.5	2 112.04	79.7
1986	28.24		19.2	1 790.01	72.5
1987	36.28		19.5	1 874.90	70.5
1988	44.84		18.3	1 758.29	65.9
1989	35.82	1.85	16.7	1 246.58	60.9
1990	42.94	7.26	18.9	1 339.02	59.0
1991	48.92	7.31	18.9	1 160.61	53.8
1992	61.23	11.73	17.1	1 379.18	56.0
1993	77.14	13.96	11.8	1 017.54	47.5
1994	300.65	106.31	26.8	1 349.24	38.3
1995	433.76	280.38	27.1	1 746.82	28.2
1996	466.99	356.01	23.9	1 872.65	31.9
1997	458.22	334.07	23.2	2 179.68	40.0
1998	404.96	320.66	20.6	1 963.51	38.4
1999	378.82	324.49	20.4	1 731.55	37.6
2000	443.90	408.82	23.7	1 724.02	35.9
2001	466.71	439.17	23.4	1 743.90	33.3
2002	584.51	567.76	26.7	1 880.50	31.4
2003	694.30	676.28	28.3	2 280.79	32.7
2004	922.61	900.67	29.9	3 270.43	41.5
2005	936.36	920.84	26.4	2 819.35	34.1
2006	854.15	835.65	21.8	2 746.80	34.0
2007	853.13	837.53	19.1	2 843.62	36.5
2008	871.52	843.63	18.0	1 899.40	26.9
2009	922.81	918.68	17.5	1 522.07	23.1
2010	1 232.96	1 229.83	23.2	1 415.44	19.3
2011	1 403.13	1 398.75	27.7	1 568.83	18.6
2012	1 457.64	1 451.94	27.7	1 626.73	19.5
2013	1 626.95	1 615.51	28.8	1 439.20	17.6
2014	1 730.81	1 724.65	28.8	1 549.64	18.1
2015	1 822.73	1 813.32	28.7	1 617.86	19.2
2016	1 979.85	1 965.43	29.3	1 557.98	19.1
2017	2 159.07	2 152.40	29.8	1 895.64	23.5
2018	2 238.45	2 225.92	29.4	1 765.79	23.2

注：1981 年以前住宅投资额和住宅竣工面积数据不包括城乡私人建房和农村投资，从 1981 年开始为全社会口径。

Note: Before 1981, investments and floor area of residential housing completed in this table didn't cover private-built houses in urban and rural areas and rural investment, the whole society is covered since 1981.

上 / 海 / 统 / 计 / 年 / 鉴

主要统计指标解释

■ 全社会固定资产投资

固定资产投资是国民经济再生产活动的一个重要部分。固定资产投资额是以货币形式表现的在一定时期内建造和购置固定资产的工作量以及与此有关的费用总称。它是反映固定资产投资规模、结构和发展速度的综合性指标。按照现行国家统计制度，全社会固定资产投资包括建设项目投资、房地产开发投资和农户投资。

自1997年起，固定资产投资统计起点为50万元(含50万元)以上项目；自2011年起，固定资产投资统计起点为500万元(含500万元)以上项目。

■ 固定资产投资按国民经济行业分

固定资产投资按国民经济行业分是根据建设项目建成投产后的主要产品或主要用途及社会经济活动性质来确定国民经济行业。一般情况下，一个建设项目或一个企业、事业单位只能属于一种国民经济行业。

■ 固定资产投资按隶属关系分

固定资产投资按隶属关系分是按建设单位或企业、事业、行政单位的主管上级机关确定的。

(1)中央：是指中共中央、人大常委会和国务院各部、委、局、总公司以及直属机构直接领导的建设项目和企业、事业、行政单位。这些单位的固定资产投资计划由国务院各部门直接编制和下达，建设中所需物资、主要设备以及建设中的问题都由中央有关部门安排和解决。

(2)地方：是由省(自治区、直辖市)、地区(州、盟、省辖市)、县(旗、县级市)三级政府及业务主管部门直接领导和管理的建设项目、企业、事业、行政单位。地方项目还包括不隶属以上各级政府及主管部门的建设项目和企业、事业单位，如外商投资企业和无主管部门的企业等。

■ 固定资产投资按构成分

固定资产投资按构成分是按其工作内容和实现方式来划分的，主要分为建筑安装工程，设备、工具、器具购置，其他费用三个部分。

(1)建筑安装工程(建筑安装工作量)：指各种房屋、建筑物的建造工程和各种设备、装置的安装工程。包括各种房屋建造工程；各种用途设备基础和各种工业窑炉的砌筑工程及金属结构工程；为施工而进行的各种准备工作和临时工程以及完工后的清理工作等；铁路、道路的铺设，矿井的开凿及石油管道的架设等；水利工程；防空地下建筑等特殊工程；列入房屋工程预算内的暖气、卫生、通风、照明、煤气等设备的价值及装设油饰工程；列入建筑工程预算内的各种管道(蒸汽、压缩空气、石油、给排水等管道)、电力、电讯电缆导线等的敷设工程；以及各种机械设备的安装工程；为测定安装工程质量，对设备进行的试运工作；房地产开发单位进行的商品房屋开发建设工程、土地开发工程。

在安装工程中，不包括被安装设备本身的价值。

(2)设备、工具、器具购置：指建设单位或企、事业单位购置或自制的，达到固定资产标准的设备、工具、器具的价值。新建单位及扩建单位的新建车间，按照设计或计划要求购置或自制的全部设备、工具、器具，不论是否达到固定资产标准均计入“设备、工具、器具购置”中。

(3)其他费用：指在固定资产建造和购置过程中发生的，除上述几项内容以外的各种应分摊计入固定资产的费用。

■ 固定资产投资的资金来源

固定资产投资的资金来源是根据固定资产投资的资金来源不同，分为国家预算资金、国内贷款、债券、利用外资、自筹资金和其他资金来源。

(1)国家预算资金：自2011年起，按照全国人大和国务院的要求，各级财政的所有资金，包括税收和非税收入，均必须纳入预算管理，我国已不存在预算外资金的概念，因此各级政府用于固定资产投资的财政资金均为预算资金。旧的国家预算内资金的内容和现中央预算资金的内容基本一致。国家预算包括一般预算、政府性基金预算、国有资本经营预算和社保基金预算。各类预算中用于固定资产投资的资金全部作为国家预算资金填报。

(2)国内贷款：指报告期内企、事业单位向银行及非银行金融机构借入的用于固定资产投资的各种国内借款。包括银行利用自有资金及吸收的存款发放的贷款、上级主管部门拨入的国内贷款、国家专项贷款(包括煤代油贷款、劳改煤矿专项贷款等)、地方财政专项资金安排的贷款、国内储备贷款、周转贷款等。

(3)债券：是企业(公司)或金融机构通过发行各种债券，筹集用于固定资产投资的资金。包括由银行代理国

主要统计指标解释

家专业投资公司发行的重点企业债券和基本建设债券。

(4)利用外资：指报告期内收到的用于固定资产投资的国外资金，包括统借统还、自借自还的国外贷款，中外合资项目中的外资，以及对外发行债券和股票等。国家统借统还的外资指由我国政府出面同外国政府、团体或金融组织签订贷款协议、并负责偿还本息的国外贷款。

(5)自筹资金：指固定资产投资单位在报告期收到的，由各企事业单位筹集用于固定资产投资的资金，包括各类企事业单位的自有资金和从其他单位筹集的用于固定资产投资的资金，但不包括各类财政性资金、从各类金融机构借入资金和国外资金。

(6)其他资金来源：指在报告期收到的除以上各种资金之外的用于固定资产投资的资金。包括社会集资、个人资金、无偿捐赠的资金及其他单位拨入的资金等。

■ 固定资产投资按建设性质分

建设项目的性质一般分为新建、改建、扩建和单纯建造生活设施。

(1)新建：一般指从无到有"平地起家"开始建设的企业、事业和行政单位或独立的工程。现有企业、事业、行政单位一般不属于新建。但如有的单位原有基础很小，经过建设后新增的固定资产价值超过该企、事业、行政单位原有固定资产价值(原值)三倍以上的也应作为新建。

(2)改建和技术改造：是指现有企业、事业单位对原有设施进行技术改造或更新(包括相应配套的辅助性生产、生活福利设施)的建设项目。改建项目包括现有企业、事业单位为适应市场变化的需要，而改变企业的主要产品种类(如军工企业转民用品等)的建设项目，原有产品生产作业线由于各工序(车间)之间能力不平衡，为填平补齐充分发挥原有生产能力而增建不增加本企业主要产品设计能力的车间的建设项目。技术改造是指企业、事业单位在现有基础上，用先进的技术代替落后的技术，用先进的工艺和装备代替落后的工艺和装备，以改变企业落后的技术经济面貌，实现以内涵为主的扩大再生产，达到提高产品质量、促进产品更新换代、节约能源、降低消耗、扩大生产规模、全面提高社会经济效益的目的。技术改造具体包括以下内容：机器设备和工具的更新改造；生产工艺改革、节约能源和原材料的改造；厂房建筑和公共设施的改造；保护环境进行的"三废"治理改造；劳动条件和生产环境的改造等。

(3)扩建：指在厂内或其他地点，为扩大原有产品的生产能力(或效益)或增加新的产品生产能力，而增建主要的生产车间(或主要工程)、分厂、独立的生产线。行政、事业单位在原单位增建业务用房(如学校增建教学用房、医院增建门诊部、病房等)也作为扩建。

现有企、事业单位为扩大原有主要产品生产能力或增加新的产品生产能力，增建一个或几个主要生产车间(或主要工程)、分厂，同时进行一些更新改造工程的，也应作为扩建。

(4)单纯建造生活设施：是指企(事)业及行政单位在不扩建、改建生产性工程和业务用房的情况下，单纯建造职工住宅、托儿所、子弟学校、医务室、浴室、食堂等生活福利设施。

■ 新增固定资产

新增固定资产又称交付使用的固定资产，是指已经完成建造和购置过程，并已交付生产或使用单位的固定资产价值。新增固定资产是表示固定资产投资成果的价值量指标，也是反映建设进度、计算固定资产投资效果的必要数据。

■ 固定资产交付使用率

指一定时期新增固定资产与同期完成投资额的比率。该指标是反映固定资产动用速度，衡量建设过程中宏观投资效果的综合指标。由于新增固定资产是较长时期内形成的结果，而投资额则是当年完成的，因此，该指标一般适宜于反映较长时期内固定资产的动用情况。

■ 施工项目

指报告期内正式进行过建筑或安装施工活动的建设项目。凡是报告期内施过工的建设项目，不论施工时间长短，均作为施工项目统计。施工项目个数可以反映一定时期固定资产投资的实际规模，与同期建成投产的建设项目个数相比，可以从建设速度的角度反映固定资产投资的效果。根据建设项目施工活动的不同性质，施工项目又分为：本年新开工项目，以前年度开工跨入本年继续施工项目，本年全部投产项目，以前年度全部停缓建在本年恢复施工的项目和本年进行过施工又在本年内全部停缓建的项目。

■ 全部投产项目

指报告期内按设计文件规定建成主体工程和相应配套的辅助设施，形成生产能力或工程效益，经过验收合格，并且已正式投入生产或交付使用的建设项目。

全部投产的工业项目是指设计文件规定形成生产能力的主体工程及其相应配套的辅助设施全部建成，经负荷试运转，证明具备生产设计规定合格产品的条件，并经过验收鉴定合格或达到竣工验收标准，与生产性工程配套的

主要统计指标解释

生活福利设施可以满足近期正常生产的需要，正式移交生产的建设项目。

■ 建成投产率

指一定时期内全部投产项目个数与同期施工项目个数的比率。该指标是从建设单位建设速度的角度反映投资效果的指标。

■ 房屋建筑面积竣工率

指一定时期内房屋竣工面积占同期房屋施工面积的比率。该指标从房屋建筑施工速度的角度反映投资效果的指标。

SHANGHAI STATISTICAL YEARBOOK

EXPLANATORY NOTES TO MAJOR STATISTICAL INDICATORS

□ Total Investment in Fixed Assets

Investment in Fixed Assets constitutes an important portion of the national economic reproduction. Fixed assets investment is a general term for both the work volume of production and purchase of fixed assets and relevant expenditure, in the form of currency, during a certain period. It is a comprehensive indicator of scale, structure and development speed of fixed assets investment. As stipulated in the current national statistics regulations, the social fixed assets investment includes infrastructure project investment, real estate development investment and farmers′ investment.

From 1997, the fixed assets items only include those with investment of 0.5 million yuan and above. From 2011, the fixed assets items only include those with investment of 5 million yuan and above.

□ Investment in Fixed Assets by Sector

Investment in Fixed Assets by Sector refers to determining the classification of construction projects by the major products or the purpose of the projects when they are put into production or use, and by the nature of their social economic activities. In general, one project or one enterprise or institution can only be classified into one sector.

□ Investment in Fixed Assets by Jurisdiction of Management

Investment in Fixed Assets by Jurisdiction of Management refers to the classification of investment by the competent authorities under which investment is made by construction units, enterprises, institutions or administrative units.

(1) Central investment refers to the investment in projects or by enterprises, institutions or administrative units which are under the direct leadership and management of the CPC Central Committee, the NPC Standing Committee, the State Council and of the national commissions, ministries, agencies and state-owned large corporations. Various ministries and departments of the State Council prepare and implement plans for investment in fixed assets by those departments, and arrange and ensure the supply of materials and key equipment required for the projects.

(2) Local investment refers to the investment in projects or by enterprises, institutions or administrative units which are under the direct leadership and management of departments under the provincial, prefecture and county governments. Also included are projects by foreign-invested enterprises and enterprises without competent managing authorities.

□ Investment in Fixed Assets by Structure

Investment in Fixed Assets by Structure is classified by their contents. It is mainly classified into 3 categories, i.e. construction and installation, purchase of equipment and instrument, and other expenses.

(1) Construction and installation (work volume of construction and installation) refers to the construction of various houses and buildings and installation of various kinds of equipment and instruments. They include construction of various houses; equipment foundations, industrial kilns and stoves, and metal structure work; preparation works for project construction, and clearing up works post project construction; pavement of railways and roads, drilling of mines and putting up of oil pipes; construction of projects of water conservancy; construction of underground air-raid shelters and construction of other special projects; value of equipment for heating, sanitation, ventilation, lighting, gas, painting, etc. that are covered by the budget of housing projects; laying out of various pipelines (for steam, compressed air, petroleum, tap water and sewage) and lines for electric power and for communications; installation of various machinery equipment, testing operation for pre-testing the quality of installation projects, and land and other development work conducted by real estate developers for commercial housing. The value of equipment installed is not included in the value of installation projects.

(2) Purchase of equipment and instruments refers to the total value of equipment, tools, and instruments purchased or self-produced which come up to standards for fixed assets by the construction units or investing enterprises or institutions. Equipment, tools and instruments purchased or self-produced for new workshops by newly established or expanded units are categorized as "purchase of equipment and instruments" no matter whether they come up to the standards for fixed assets.

EXPLANATORY NOTES TO MAJOR STATISTICAL INDICATORS

(3) Other expenses refer to expenses occurring during the construction or purchase of fixed assets other than those mentioned above.

□ Sources of Capital for Investment in Fixed Assets

Sources of capital for Investment in Fixed Assets include state budget funds, domestic loans, bond, foreign investment, self-raised funds, and others.

(1) State state budget funds. Since 2011, according to the requirement of the NPC and the State Council, all levels of financial resources, including tax and non-tax revenue, must be included in the budget management, extra-budgetary didn't exist any longer, all levels of government for fixing asset investment funds are budget funds. The old state budget funds were basically the same with the central budget funds. State budget includes the general budget, the government fund budget, the state capital budget and the social security fund budget. All kinds of budgets for all funds invested in fixed assets were reported as state budget funds.

(2) Domestic loans refers to various funds borrowed by enterprises and institutions from banks and non-bank financial institutions during the reference period for the purpose of investment in fixed assets, including loans issued by banks from their self-owned funds and deposit, loans appropriated by higher responsible authorities, special loans by government (including loan for replacing petroleum with coal, special loan for reform-through-labour coal mines), loans arranged by local government from special funds, domestic reserve loan, and working loan, etc.

(3) Bond refers to company and finance institutions raising funds for investment in fixed assets by issuing various bond, including keystone enterprise bond and infrastructure bond issued by banks as agency of national professional investment company.

(4) Foreign Investment refers to foreign funds received during the reference period for the purpose of investment in fixed assets, including foreign funds borrowed and managed by the government, by individual units, foreign fund in joint venture program, and issue of bonds and stocks at the international financial markets. The foreign funds borrowed and managed by the government refer to foreign loans borrowed by the government from foreign governments, organizations, or financial institutions under official agreements signed by both parties, under which government is responsible for the repayment of both the principal and interests of the foreign loans.

(5) Self-raised funds refers to the fixed asset investment units received during the reporting period, by the enterprises and institutions to raise funds for investment in fixed assets, including various types of enterprises and institutions of its own funds and from other units raised funds for investment in fixed assets, but does not include all kinds of financial funds, borrowed funds from various financial institutions and foreign capital.

(6) Other sources of funding refers to the reporting period, in addition to all of these funds received outside funding for investment in fixed assets. Including social funds raised from individuals, donations, funds and funds transferred from other units.

□ Investment in Fixed Assets by Type of Construction

The construction projects in general can be classified, by the type of construction, into new construction, expansion, reconstruction and construction of living facilities.

(1) New construction in general refers to newly constructed enterprises, institutions, administrative agencies or independent projects from scratch. Construction in the existing enterprises, institutions or agencies is not considered as new construction. In case the asset of the existing unit is quite small, and the value of newly added fixed assets exceeds the original value of assets by three times, the expansion will be considered as new construction.

(2) Reconstruction and technical transformation refers to construction projects by existing enterprises or institutions in innovation or technical transformation of the old facilities (including auxiliary production equipment and welfare facilities). Also considered as Reconstruction and Technical Transformation is the construction of new workshops by the existing enterprises or institutions to change the variety of products to meet the market demand (such as the production of civil products by defense industries), or to bring the designed production capacity into full play through a more balanced production process on production lines. Technical transformation refers to replacement of old technology and equipment by new technology and equipment, in order to expand the reproduction through improvement of technology contents in production, to improve product quality, to promote new products, to save energy, to reduce consumption, to expand the production scale and to improve overall social-eco-

EXPLANATORY NOTES TO MAJOR STATISTICAL INDICATORS

nomic efficiency. Technical transformation contains the following contents: updating of machinery, equipment and tools; reforming production process by using energy or material saving technology; construction of workshops and transformation of public facilities; improvement of working conditions and environment, etc.

(3) Expansion refers to construction of new major production workshop, branch factory or independent production line within a factory or in other locations, for the purpose of increasing the production capacity (or improving efficiency) of the original products. Newly constructed houses for the operation of institutions and administrative organizations (such as the newly constructed buildings for teaching in schools, buildings for clinics or wards in hospitals, etc.) are also classified as expansion.

Also included in the expansion are investments by existing enterprises or institutions in building major production line(s) or branch factory(ies) along with some work on innovation, for the purpose of expending the production capacity of original products or producing new products.

(4) Simply constructing establishment for life refers to enterprises and administrative unit simply construct the employee´s residence, nursery, children school, infirmary, bathroom and eatery, without expanding or rebuilding the productive engineering and operation houses.

□ Newly Increased Fixed Assets

Newly Increased Fixed Assets, also called fixed assets put into operation, refers to the value of fixed assets that has been put into production or handed over to the production units after the completion of the process of construction and purchase. The newly increased fixed asset is an value indicator of the result of investment. It is also the necessary data for reflecting the construction process and the result of investment in fixed assets.

□ Rate of Projects of Fixed Assets Completed and Put into Operation

Rate of Projects of Fixed Assets Completed and Put into Operation refers to the ratio of the newly increased fixed assets to the total investment made in the same period. This is a comprehensive indicator reflecting the speed of the employment of fixed assets and the investment efficiency at the macro-level. As the newly increase fixed assets is the result of a long period while the investment is completed in the current year, this indicator is expected to be used to reflect the employment of fixed assets over a long period of time.

□ Projects under Construction

Projects under Construction refer to projects with construction and installation activities undertaken in the reference period. All projects that have construction activities undertaken during the reference period are reported as projects under construction irrespective of the length of construction work. The number of projects under construction can reflect the actual size of investment in fixed assets during a given period, and when compared with the number of projects completed and put into use during the same period, it demonstrates the results of investment in fixed assets. Depending on the nature of construction activities, projects under construction can also be classified into projects under construction in current year, winding-up projects in current year and stopped or suspended projects in previous years (with preservation work in current year).

□ Projects Completed and Put into Use

Projects Completed and Put into Use Industrial projects refer to the major projects and accessory facilities completed which result in forming production capacity and have been checked and accepted while the living and welfare facilities have been completed and can ensure normal production and formally put into production. Non-industrial projects refer to the major projects and accessory facilities completed which possess the designed capacity and have been checked, accepted and formally put into production.

□ Rate of Construction Projects Completed and Put into Use

Rate of Construction Projects Completed and Put into Use refers to the ratio of the number of construction projects completed and put into use in certain period of time to the number of projects under construction in the same period. This reflects the investment efficiency from the perspective of the speed of projects construction.

□ Completion Rate of Floor Space of Buildings

Completion Rate of Floor Space of Buildings refers to the ratio of the floor space of buildings completed in certain period of time to the floor space of buildings under construction in the same period. This indicator reflects the investment result from the perspective of the speed of construction.

第八篇
CHAPTER 8

2019上海统计年鉴 SHANGHAI STATISTICAL YEARBOOK

对外经济贸易和旅游
FOREIGN ECONOMIC RELATIONS, TRADE AND TOURISM

简要说明

本篇资料综合反映主要年份上海市对外贸易、进出口商品检验、外商直接投资、对外直接投资、对外经济合作和旅游等方面的概况。

一、对外贸易

对外贸易统计范围是按照联合国国际贸易统计原则，采用专门贸易记录制，对凡能引起区域内物质资源存量增加或减少的进出口货物，除制度另有规定外，均列入统计。在按国别（地区）分的进、出口总额表中，出口货物按中华人民共和国关境外最终目的国（地区）统计，进口货物按中华人民共和国关境外原产国(地区)统计。

主要内容包括：上海关区和上海市货物进出口的金额、国别、贸易方式、企业性质、产品类别等项目。

统计资料来源于上海海关，调查方法是全面调查。

二、进出口商品检验

进出口商品检验统计范围是涉及安全、卫生和环境保护等检验、检疫进出口商品目录范围内的所有商品。

主要内容包括：进口和出口商品检验批数、金额，不合格商品检验批数、金额等。

统计资料来源于上海出入境检验检疫局，调查方法是全面调查。

三、服务贸易

服务贸易统计范围包括商业服务，通信服务，建筑及有关工程服务，销售服务，教育服务，环境服务，金融服务，健康与社会服务，与旅游有关的服务，娱乐、文化与体育服务，运输服务等。

统计资料来源于国家外汇管理局上海市分局。调查方法是全面调查。

四、外商直接投资

外商直接投资统计范围是国外及港澳台地区的法人和自然人在中国大陆地区以现金、实物、无形资产、股权等方式投资设立的企业，其中外国投资者在非上市公司中的全部投资及在单个外国投资者所占股权比例不低于10%的上市公司中的投资。

主要内容包括：外商直接投资方式、投资产业和国别地区等情况。

统计资料来源于上海市商务委员会，调查方法是全面调查。

五、对外直接投资

对外直接投资指我国企业、团体等（简称境内投资主体）在国外及港澳台地区以现金、实物、无形资产等方式投资，并以控制国（境）外企业的经营管理权为核心的经济活动。对外直接投资统计范围 主要包括境内投资主体通过直接投资在境外设立的各类公司型企业和非公司型企业。

主要内容包括:对外直接投资的项目数、投资总额。

统计资料来源于上海市商务委员会,调查方法是全面调查。

六、对外经济合作

对外经济合作统计范围是经各级商务主管部门批准的从事对外承包和劳务合作业务并具有法人地位的对外承包、劳务合作企业。

主要内容包括:对外承包工程合同金额、完成营业额和对外劳务合作派出人员等。

统计资料来源于上海市商务委员会,调查方法是全面调查。

七、旅游

旅游统计范围是旅行社、星级饭店和旅游者。

主要内容包括:旅行社接待经营情况、旅游景点和星级饭店基本情况、国际旅游入境人数、国内旅游来沪人数和人均消费支出等。

统计调查方法:国内旅游者来沪人数和人均消费支出指标采取抽样调查方法,其余数据均为全面调查。

统计资料来源于上海市旅游局、上海出入境边防检查总站。

BRIEF INTRODUCTION

Data in this chapter reflect Shanghai′s foreign trade, inspection of imports and exports, foreign direct investment, outbound direct investment, economic cooperation with foreign countries or territories as well as tourism in main years.

I. Foreign Trade

The scope of foreign trade statistics is in accordance with the United Nations′ principles on international trade statistics, i.e.: all imports or exports that will lead to stock changes of material resources with the monitored territory; excluding goods by escape clause.In the table on the total imports and exports classified by countries and regions, the exports are calculated at the Customs of the countries (regions) of destination and the imports are calculated at the Customs of the countries (regions) of origin.

Data on foreign trade include: value of imports and exports through Shanghai ports, imports and exports by countries (regions), mode of trade, nature of trading companies, and product categories.

Sources of data on foreign trade are complied from the Shanghai Customs through a comprehensive reporting system.

II. Inspection of Imports and Exports

The scope of imports and exports inspection includes all commodities that are under the catalog of imports and exports quarantine, related to safety, sanitation and environment protection issues.

Data on inspection of imports and exports include: lot number and value of imports and exports, lot number of ineligible commodities and their value.

Sources of data are from the Shanghai Entry-Exit Inspection and Quarantine Bureau through a comprehensive reporting system.

III. Serice Trade

The scope of service trade includes commercial services, communications services, construction and related engineering services, sales services, educational services, environmental services, financial services, health and social services, tourism-related services, entertainment, cultural and sports services, transport services, etc.

Sources of data are from Shanghai Branch of State Administration of Foreign Exchange through a comprehensive reporting system.

Ⅳ. Foreign Direct Investment

The statistics of foreign direct investment cover the enterprises in the mainland established in the form of cash, physical goods, intangible assets or equity by legal and natural persons from foreign countries and Hong Kong, Macao and Taiwan regions, and also cover all investment of foreign investors in non-listed company and investment in listed companies with a share ratio not less than 10% of a single foreign investor.

Foreign direct investment includes: mode of foreign direct investment, investment by industry and countries (regions).

Sources of data are from the Shanghai Commission of Commerce through a comprehensive reporting system.

Ⅴ. Outbound Direct Investment

Outbound Direct Investment refers to the economic activities that Chinese enterprises or groups (referred to as domestic investors) invest in foreign countries and Hong Kong, Macao and Taiwan regions in the form of cash, physical goods and intangible assets, which take the management right of the enterprises both abroad and outside the border controlled as the core. The scope of Outbound Direct Investment mainly includes various types of corporate and non corporate enterprises established by domestic investors through direct investment abroad.

Data on outbound direct investment includes: number of outbound direct investment projects, total investment of outbound direct investment.

Sources of data are from the Shanghai Commission of Commerce through a comprehensive reporting system.

Ⅵ. Foreign Economic Cooperation

The scope of foreign economic cooperation covers enterprises engaged in contracted projects and labor services cooperation with foreign countries with approvals from the department of commerce at various levels.

Data on foreign economic cooperation include: contracted value of project, its revenue and labor services cooperation.

Data on foreign economic cooperation are from the Shanghai Commission of Commerce through a comprehensive reporting system.

Ⅶ. Tourism

The scope of tourism covers travel agencies, star-rated hotels and tourists.

Data on tourism include: operating conditions of the travel agencies, tourist attractions and star-rated hotels, the number of international tourists, the number of domestic tourists to Shanghai and consumption expenditure per capita.

Methodologies: sample survey method is used for domestic tourists to Shanghai and consumption expenditure per capita, and the rest are through a comprehensive reporting system.

Data are from the Shanghai Tourism Bureau and the Shanghai Entry-Exit Frontier Inspection Station.

表 8.1 主要年份上海关区出口总额
TOTAL EXPORT TRADE VOLUME THROUGH CUSTOMS IN MAIN YEARS

单位:亿美元(100 million USD)

年 份 Year	关区出口总额 Export Trade Volume Through Customs	其中 of which #一般贸易 Ordinary Trade	来料加工装配贸易 Processing and Assembly Trade with Customers' Materials	进料加工贸易 Processing Trade with Imported Materials	对外承包工程货物 Construction Projects in Foreign Countries	出料加工贸易 Outward Processing Trade
1990	86.62	51.39	3.20	30.67	0.41	0.45
1995	256.07	149.16	14.31	90.12	0.63	0.06
2000	615.72	341.02	64.21	205.13	1.25	
2001	680.07	380.43	61.09	228.43	1.26	0.13
2002	818.03	473.13	66.88	266.72	1.44	0.13
2003	1 123.06	618.90	78.81	408.79	1.18	0.12
2004	1 612.68	824.92	126.99	623.27	3.18	0.14
2005	2 124.30	1 057.68	195.83	813.26	6.37	0.16
2006	2 665.65	1 319.56	212.77	1 058.07	9.45	0.14
2007	3 284.80	1 659.44	228.77	1 273.71	20.55	0.17
2008	3 936.50	2 050.49	240.91	1 467.78	53.92	0.23
2009	3 251.28	1 647.82	175.38	1 252.87	69.78	0.13
2010	4 233.40	2 183.98	178.52	1 639.70	60.55	0.09
2011	4 999.64	2 691.93	151.78	1 846.59	77.70	0.11
2012	4 911.56	2 722.62	137.52	1 718.06	72.14	0.12
2013	4 991.29	2 857.73	130.46	1 642.18	80.16	0.11
2014	5 232.12	3 112.37	126.18	1 601.78	85.04	0.05
2015	5 005.80	3 016.20	133.26	1 497.66	67.43	0.04
2016	4 798.74	2 978.08	132.05	1 307.63	73.72	0.07
2017	5 166.76	3 256.88	135.63	1 385.12	84.12	0.03
2018	5 624.46	3 666.32	116.73	1 423.57	88.30	0.12

表 8.2 主要年份上海关区进口总额
TOTAL IMPORT TRADE VOLUME THROUGH CUSTOMS IN MAIN YEARS

单位:亿美元(100 million USD)

年 份 Year	关区进口总额 Import Trade Volume Through Customs	其中 of which #一般贸易 Oridinary Trade	来料加工装配贸易 Processing and Assembly Trade with Customers' Materials	进料加工贸易 Processing Trade with Imported Materials	外商投资企业进口设备 Imported Equipment of Foreign Funded Enterprise	租赁贸易 Leasing Trade
1990	86.27	51.79	2.40	19.70	6.11	
1995	225.30	93.79	13.49	65.96	45.16	0.11
2000	477.39	212.65	44.87	125.13	40.26	2.47
2001	524.81	245.94	47.38	123.39	47.46	2.45
2002	606.98	267.66	48.12	160.91	54.95	1.89
2003	888.95	377.21	54.47	243.24	66.32	2.36
2004	1 213.07	472.16	89.47	338.57	99.72	4.70
2005	1 382.48	502.49	133.69	409.30	74.76	7.85
2006	1 621.89	574.40	122.52	497.41	73.72	23.74
2007	1 924.29	719.30	154.88	528.03	75.22	24.46
2008	2 129.07	848.23	174.86	525.68	76.91	22.21
2009	1 903.61	883.20	121.40	428.62	38.92	4.36
2010	2 613.05	1 209.42	169.36	552.83	43.81	18.56
2011	3 123.50	1 558.35	135.68	610.32	51.18	13.69
2012	3 101.54	1 516.96	123.06	553.38	33.00	10.79
2013	3 130.08	1 628.68	135.19	524.14	23.58	23.68
2014	3 402.43	1 777.08	164.31	568.61	26.63	40.52
2015	3 182.06	1 616.79	155.92	502.04	13.89	23.12
2016	3 127.25	1 674.22	141.84	452.20	9.00	2.87
2017	3 647.91	2 002.06	93.30	594.74	8.79	1.94
2018	4 090.77	2 234.96	61.41	750.68	6.68	2.94

注：自 2009 年起，原口岸进出口商品总额改为上海关区进出口总额。
Note：Since 2009,Total Value of Port Imports and Exports have been changed to Total Trade Volume through Customs.

表 8.3 主要年份按国别(地区)分的上海关区出口总额
TOTAL EXPORT TRADE VOLUME THROUGH CUSTOMS BY COUNTRIES AND REGIONS IN MAIN YEARS

单位:亿美元(100 million USD)

国别(地区)	Country (Region)	2010	2015	2017	2018
总　计	**Total**	**4 233.40**	**5 005.80**	**5 166.76**	**5 624.46**
亚　洲	**Asia**	**1 653.96**	**2 145.10**	**2 191.83**	**2 371.17**
#中国香港	Hong Kong, China	210.46	260.67	252.50	268.03
中国台湾	Taiwan, China	112.52	137.00	149.05	161.37
日　本	Japan	442.82	474.49	435.00	462.24
韩　国	Republic of Korea	138.83	212.30	198.77	213.02
新加坡	Singapore	94.80	117.74	113.33	117.66
马来西亚	Malaysia	73.08	78.47	85.31	95.77
泰　国	Thailand	61.18	99.26	109.65	116.87
菲律宾	Philippines	29.43	49.70	51.96	62.02
巴基斯坦	Pakistan	16.12	32.55	49.13	46.97
科威特	Kuwait	4.05	5.48	7.05	6.94
沙特阿拉伯	Saudi Arabia	19.92	34.23	26.88	26.39
阿联酋	United Arab Emirates	44.97	49.20	42.10	43.55
非　洲	**Africa**	**130.79**	**168.00**	**155.40**	**172.05**
#埃　及	Egypt	12.11	16.43	19.68	23.05
苏　丹	Sudan	4.39	3.20	2.69	1.91
欧　洲	**Europe**	**1 095.67**	**1 033.36**	**1 073.72**	**1 169.54**
#德　国	Germany	214.67	186.34	184.21	204.41
法　国	France	110.42	75.35	79.06	83.79
意大利	Italy	118.34	84.83	86.88	96.37
荷　兰	Netherlands	154.89	167.30	177.77	184.33
英　国	United Kingdoms	117.88	142.14	128.61	132.90
瑞　典	Sweden	20.26	19.52	19.77	21.23
俄罗斯	Russia	59.95	55.68	65.50	74.09
美　洲	**America**	**1 234.11**	**1 510.83**	**1 591.58**	**1 747.64**
#美　国	United States	910.54	1 127.24	1 199.32	1 309.02
加拿大	Canada	74.81	75.11	82.46	88.74
巴　西	Brazil	75.44	76.11	75.74	89.73
智　利	Chile	20.47	25.89	28.16	33.00
大洋洲及太平洋岛屿	**Oceanic and Pacific Island**	**118.87**	**148.52**	**154.07**	**164.05**
#澳大利亚	Australia	95.45	118.27	129.06	140.87
新西兰	New Zealand	9.87	13.50	15.87	17.97

表 8.4　主要年份按国别(地区)分的上海关区进口总额
TOTAL IMPORT TRADE VOLUME THROUGH CUSTOMS BY COUNTRIES AND REGIONS IN MAIN YEARS

单位:亿美元(100 million USD)

国别(地区)	Country (Region)	2010	2015	2017	2018
总　计	**Total**	**2 613.05**	**3 182.06**	**3 647.91**	**4 090.77**
亚　洲	**Asia**	**1 477.09**	**1 599.12**	**1 843.72**	**2 050.69**
#中国香港	Hong Kong, China	17.05	8.97	10.02	20.88
中国台湾	Taiwan, China	210.86	225.94	265.40	290.22
日　本	Japan	473.84	393.87	460.95	502.72
韩　国	Republic of Korea	279.87	346.03	391.90	479.43
新加坡	Singapore	51.61	73.92	106.57	87.58
马来西亚	Malaysia	117.63	120.27	123.89	129.33
泰　国	Thailand	63.19	62.99	74.20	76.65
菲律宾	Philippines	36.47	33.81	34.87	42.31
巴基斯坦	Pakistan	3.24	3.81	3.51	3.30
科威特	Kuwait	0.71	0.47	0.35	0.37
沙特阿拉伯	Saudi Arabia	8.28	14.08	13.50	19.92
阿联酋	United Arab Emirates	1.85	5.38	5.70	7.34
非　洲	**Africa**	**41.85**	**37.10**	**42.07**	**56.89**
#埃　及	Egypt	1.31	0.94	1.52	1.47
南　非	South Africa	16.60	14.04	20.07	22.44
欧　洲	**Europe**	**619.42**	**924.88**	**1 081.72**	**1 208.08**
#德　国	Germany	248.28	297.18	350.45	379.69
法　国	France	53.72	80.22	86.59	96.21
意大利	Italy	51.07	70.69	99.30	96.23
荷　兰	Netherlands	15.19	24.85	27.11	30.36
英　国	United Kingdoms	37.69	70.31	61.48	65.18
瑞　典	Sweden	28.75	34.62	42.42	49.44
俄罗斯	Russia	22.93	34.56	29.76	40.57
美　洲	**America**	**420.66**	**509.48**	**561.83**	**614.98**
#美　国	United States	268.76	344.59	377.16	382.92
加拿大	Canada	27.89	25.09	28.81	37.51
巴　西	Brazil	19.03	21.62	24.02	30.21
智　利	Chile	63.82	57.45	66.20	87.58
大洋洲及太平洋岛屿	**Oceanic and Pacific Island**	**53.73**	**110.72**	**118.01**	**159.13**
#澳大利亚	Australia	45.35	96.07	96.02	133.65
新西兰	New Zealand	8.33	14.40	21.33	25.10
其　他	**Others**	**0.30**	**0.74**	**0.56**	**0.99**

注:其他为无国别数(以下同)。
Note: Others refer to regions without sovereignty(Same as follows).

表 8.5 主要年份上海市进出口总额
TOTAL VALUE OF FOREIGN TRADE IMPORTS AND EXPORTS IN MAIN YEARS

年 份 Year	上海市 进出口总额 (亿美元) Total Value of Foreign Trade Imports and Exports (100 million USD)	上海市 进口总额 (亿美元) Total Value of Foreign Trade Imports (100 million USD)	上海市 出口总额 (亿美元) Total Value of Foreign Trade Exports (100 million USD)	进出口 差 额 (亿美元) Balance (100 million USD)	进出口总额相当于生产总值的比例(%) Foreign Trade Imports and Export as Percentage of Gross Domestic Product(%)	出口总额相当于生产总值的比例(%) Foreign Trade Export as Percentage of Gross Domestic Product(%)
1990	74.31	21.10	53.21	32.11	47.0	33.6
1995	190.25	74.48	115.77	41.29	63.1	38.4
2000	547.10	293.56	253.54	-40.02	94.1	43.6
2001	608.98	332.70	276.28	-56.42	95.9	43.5
2002	726.64	406.09	320.55	-85.54	103.8	45.8
2003	1 123.97	639.15	484.82	-154.33	137.6	59.3
2004	1 600.26	865.06	735.20	-129.86	162.2	74.5
2005	1 863.65	956.23	907.42	-48.81	163.0	79.4
2006	2 274.89	1 139.16	1 135.73	-3.43	169.2	84.5
2007	2 829.73	1 390.45	1 439.28	48.83	169.9	86.4
2008	3 221.38	1 527.88	1 693.50	165.62	156.7	82.4
2009	2 777.31	1 358.17	1 419.14	60.97	124.1	63.4
2010	3 688.69	1 880.85	1 807.84	-73.01	143.2	70.2
2011	4 374.36	2 276.47	2 097.89	-178.58	144.6	69.3
2012	4 367.58	2 299.51	2 068.07	-231.44	134.1	63.5
2013	4 413.98	2 371.54	2 042.44	-329.10	122.8	56.8
2014	4 666.22	2 563.45	2 102.77	-460.68	119.1	53.7
2015	4 517.33	2 547.64	1 969.69	-577.95	109.7	47.8
2016	4 338.05	2 503.38	1 834.67	-668.71	102.3	43.2
2017	4 761.23	2 824.42	1 936.81	-887.60	104.9	42.7
2018	5 156.49	3 084.79	2 071.70	-1 013.09	104.4	42.0

注：1999 年以前外贸进口、出口商品总额为外经贸委统计口径，1999 年以后为海关统计的上海企业进口、出口总额(以下同)。
Note: Before 1999, the figures of Shanghai's foreign trade imports and exports were based on statistics from Shanghai Foreign Trade and Economic Cooperation Commission. Since 1999, the figures representing imports and exports are made by Shanghai enterprises through Shanghai Custom.Same as follows.

表 8.6 主要年份上海市出口总额
TOTAL VALUE OF FOREIGN TRADE EXPORTS IN MAIN YEARS

单位:亿美元 (100 million USD)

指 标	Indicators	2000	2010	2017	2018
出口总额	**Total Value of Exports**	**253.54**	**1 807.84**	**1 936.81**	**2 071.70**
按企业性质分	**Grouped by Different Enterprises**				
#国有企业	State-owned Enterprises	106.78	307.67	228.10	232.76
外商投资企业	Foreign-funded Enterprises	142.61	1 259.74	1 292.95	1 344.15
按贸易方式分	**Grouped by Trade Modes**				
#一般贸易	Original Trade	101.72	632.74	852.48	961.03
加工贸易	Processing Trade	147.83	1 003.74	791.46	794.10
按产品类别分	**Grouped by Different Products**				
#机电产品	Electrical and Mechanical Products	121.43	1 311.14	1 371.58	1 436.83
#高新技术产品	High-tech Products		841.11	841.70	869.59

表 8.7 主要年份按国别(地区)分的上海市出口总额
TOTAL VALUE OF FOREIGN TRADE EXPORTS BY COUNTRIES AND REGIONS IN MAIN YEARS

单位:亿美元 (100 million USD)

国别(地区)	Country (Region)	2000	2010	2017	2018
总　计	**Total**	**253.54**	**1 807.84**	**1 936.81**	**2 071.70**
亚　洲	**Asia**	**129.10**	**725.93**	**873.59**	**956.20**
#中国香港	Hong Kong, China	23.02	134.09	179.64	200.12
中国台湾	Taiwan, China	5.67	56.54	69.24	77.08
日　本	Japan	60.81	196.46	193.49	215.09
韩　国	Republic of Korea	10.59	58.92	63.41	68.78
新加坡	Singapore	7.88	59.01	73.44	69.41
马来西亚	Malaysia	2.59	42.52	36.84	42.70
泰　国	Thailand	2.48	24.14	36.62	42.96
巴基斯坦	Pakistan	0.55	3.08	7.74	8.78
科威特	Kuwait	0.20	1.53	1.99	1.93
沙特阿拉伯	Saudi Arabia	1.14	5.72	8.92	7.13
阿拉伯联合酋长国	United Arab Emirates	1.79	20.67	15.72	15.86
非　洲	**Africa**	**5.63**	**40.98**	**38.09**	**43.46**
#埃　及	Egypt	0.44	3.28	2.74	4.23
苏　丹	Sudan	0.22	1.21	0.73	0.73
阿尔及利亚	Algeria	0.09	1.29	1.37	1.86
摩洛哥	Morocco	0.20	0.97	1.43	2.26
欧　洲	**Europe**	**45.62**	**450.72**	**377.08**	**411.12**
#德　国	Germany	9.48	86.05	63.63	69.37
法　国	France	4.50	60.97	22.28	24.21
意大利	Italy	4.98	36.99	26.52	28.71
荷　兰	Netherlands	6.16	77.61	93.52	97.45
比利时	Belgium	2.95	16.70	12.39	12.11
英　国	United Kingdoms	7.07	43.11	44.72	44.16
俄罗斯	Russia	0.37	21.15	23.98	28.40
美　洲	**America**	**67.82**	**532.30**	**582.14**	**595.88**
#美　国	United States	56.25	409.91	464.57	475.10
加拿大	Canada	4.04	27.80	25.63	27.18
巴　西	Brazil	1.06	26.95	20.05	21.09
古　巴	Cuba	0.07	0.90	0.47	0.74
大洋洲及太平洋岛屿	**Oceanic and Pacific Island**	**5.37**	**57.91**	**65.80**	**65.04**
#澳大利亚	Australia	4.74	45.59	52.95	54.05

表 8.8 主要年份按国别(地区)分的上海市进口总额
TOTAL VALUE OF FOREIGN TRADE IMPORTS BY COUNTRIES AND REGIONS IN MAIN YEARS

单位:亿美元 (100 million USD)

国别(地区)	Country (Region)	2000	2010	2017	2018
总 计	**Total**	**293.56**	**1 880.85**	**2 824.42**	**3 084.79**
亚 洲	**Asia**	**161.59**	**1 041.98**	**1 291.39**	**1 389.38**
# 中国香港	Hong Kong, China	16.68	12.61	3.97	16.98
中国台湾	Taiwan, China	19.44	150.05	179.34	195.08
日 本	Japan	70.43	308.71	329.02	360.29
韩 国	Republic of Korea	20.63	146.41	186.23	198.53
新加坡	Singapore	9.39	39.42	89.83	68.17
马来西亚	Malaysia	6.49	107.75	113.67	114.54
泰 国	Thailand	4.35	53.09	53.86	59.65
菲律宾	Philippines	1.83	33.44	29.97	32.01
科威特	Kuwait	0.22	0.94	0.45	1.78
沙特阿拉伯	Saudi Arabia	0.78	7.23	8.93	16.88
阿拉伯联合酋长国	United Arab Emirates	0.40	2.11	9.88	9.69
非 洲	**Africa**	**1.89**	**28.19**	**43.71**	**55.65**
欧 洲	**Europe**	**63.36**	**400.75**	**855.90**	**927.47**
# 德 国	Germany	26.59	140.61	268.11	264.33
法 国	France	7.95	42.54	71.33	78.05
意大利	Italy	4.81	36.46	79.23	74.09
荷 兰	Netherlands	2.43	11.06	24.14	24.61
比利时	Belgium	2.83	25.08	22.19	21.27
英 国	United Kingdoms	3.76	23.43	62.18	63.45
瑞 士	Switzerland	2.22	29.87	158.98	186.06
瑞 典	Sweden	4.53	15.77	23.29	30.84
美 洲	**America**	**58.60**	**344.63**	**483.03**	**521.12**
# 美 国	United States	40.11	202.75	305.53	293.77
加拿大	Canada	7.03	20.90	26.93	41.70
巴 西	Brazil	4.11	40.89	72.00	90.23
大洋洲及太平洋岛屿	**Oceanic and Pacific Island**	**8.07**	**65.13**	**149.94**	**190.30**
# 澳大利亚	Australia	6.68	56.25	130.45	167.99
新西兰	New Zealand	1.25	7.48	17.93	18.86
其 他	**Others**	**0.05**	**0.17**	**0.44**	**0.87**

表 8.9　服务贸易进出口情况(2018)
TOTAL VALUE OF SERVICE TRADE IMPORTS AND EXPORTS

单位:亿美元 (100 million USD)

指　标	Indicators	进出口 Imports and Exports	其中 of which 出口 Exports	进口 Imports
总　计	**Total**	**1 975.03**	**595.76**	**1 379.27**
运输服务	Transport	325.14	127.24	197.90
旅　行	Travel	919.82	23.23	896.59
建筑服务	Construction	10.88	6.44	4.44
保险和养老金服务	Insurance and Pension Services	15.47	7.32	8.15
金融服务	Financial Service	2.19	0.85	1.33
电信、计算机和信息服务	Telecommunication,Computer and Information Service	129.78	89.69	40.09
专业管理和咨询服务	Professional Management and Advisory Services	287.57	220.16	67.41
技术服务	Technical Service	88.91	53.45	35.46
文化和娱乐服务	Cultural and Recreational Service	8.79	2.75	6.04
知识产权使用费	Charges for the Use of Intellectual Property	97.87	1.96	95.91
其他服务	Other Service	88.62	62.67	25.94

表 8.10　主要年份服务贸易基本情况
BASIC STATISTICS OF SERVICE IN MAIN YEARS

单位:亿美元 (100 million USD)

指　标	Indicators	2005	2010	2017	2018
进出口额	**Total of Service Imports and Exports**	**251.40**	**871.42**	**1 954.70**	**1 975.03**
出口额	Total of Exports	122.30	327.96	524.30	595.76
进口额	Total of Imports	129.10	543.46	1 430.40	1 379.27

表 8.11　主要年份总部经济情况
CONDITIONS OF HEADQUARTERS ECONOMY IN MAIN YEARS

单位：家(unit)

指　标	Indicators	2005	2010	2017	2018
跨国公司地区总部	Regional Headquarters of Multinational Corporations	125	305	625	670
外商投资性公司	Foreign-invested Companies	130	213	345	360
外资研发中心	Foreign Research and Development Centers	173	316	426	441

表 8.12　主要年份外商直接投资情况
FOREIGN DIRECT INVESTMENT IN MAIN YEARS

指　标	Indicators	2000	2010	2017	2018
合同项目(个)	**Number of Contracts (item)**	**1 814**	**3 906**	**3 950**	**5 597**
#合资企业	Joint Ventures	441	445	847	1 014
合作企业	Cooperative Ventures	226	14	7	5
独资企业	Sole-foreign Funded Enterprises	1 146	3 443	3 084	4 566
合同金额(亿美元)	**Contracted Foreign Capital (100 million USD)**	**63.90**	**153.07**	**401.94**	**469.37**
#合资企业	Joint Ventures	13.86	21.54	63.67	91.87
合作企业	Cooperative Ventures	5.86	1.11	-2.04	-2.51
独资企业	Sole-foreign Funded Enterprises	44.14	128.17	333.28	377.19
实到金额(亿美元)	**Foreign Investment Actually Absorbed (100 million USD)**	**31.60**	**111.21**	**170.08**	**173.00**
#合资企业	Joint Ventures	12.94	17.84	29.65	33.85
合作企业	Cooperative Ventures	2.99	1.69	1.58	0.10
独资企业	Sole-foreign Funded Enterprises	15.67	90.71	129.77	131.11

表 8.13 外商直接投资合同项目和金额(2018)
NUMBER OF CONTRACTS SIGNED AND VALUES OF FOREIGN DIRECT INVESTMENT PROJECTS

类　别	Types	合同项目(个) Number of Contracts (item)		合同金额(亿美元) Contracted Foreign Capital (100 million USD)		实到金额(亿美元) Foreign Investment Actually Absorbed (100 million USD)	
		2018	至 2018 年底累计 Total by the End of 2018	2018	至 2018 年底累计 Total by the End of 2018	2018	至 2018 年底累计 Total by the End of 2018
总　计	**Total**	**5 597**	**97 013**	**469.37**	**4 672.59**	**173.00**	**2 404.40**
按投资方式分	**Grouped by Investment Mode**						
# 合资企业	Joint Ventures	1 014	23 470	91.87	911.01	33.85	543.78
合作企业	Cooperative Ventures	5	5 148	-2.51	167.26	0.10	121.75
独资企业	Sole-foreign Funded Enterprises	4 566	68 251	377.19	3 516.96	131.11	1 683.93
按产业分	**Grouped by Industry**						
第一产业	Primary Industry	8	329	0.39	7.66	0.14	4.66
第二产业	Secondary Industry	167	26 831	75.22	1 066.07	18.31	614.68
# 工　业	Industry	137	25 790	74.33	1 040.61	17.84	606.47
第三产业	Tertiary Industry	5 422	69 853	393.76	3 598.86	154.55	1 785.06
按主要国别(地区)分	**Grouped by Country and Region**						
# 中国香港	Hong Kong, China	1 620	31 281	254.58	2 433.35	99.88	1 052.45
中国澳门	Macao, China	16	332	0.27	6.84		2.19
中国台湾	Taiwan, China	914	10 800	8.85	95.27	0.58	50.33
日　本	Japan	231	10 662	10.47	281.04	6.53	215.15
韩　国	Republic of Korea	283	4 253	4.57	51.55	1.26	26.51
新 加 坡	Singapore	274	4 809	48.94	284.60	10.04	151.53
泰　国	Thailand	17	330	0.26	5.55	0.06	3.35
德　国	Germany	133	2 408	7.55	107.75	17.24	84.97
英　国	United Kingdoms	168	1 842	9.68	56.21	2.59	31.52
法　国	France	118	1 216	7.88	52.58	2.58	32.56
意 大 利	Italy	84	1 239	1.06	15.67	0.52	8.77
美　国	United States	390	9 162	13.18	229.76	4.65	147.38
加拿大	Canada	115	1 663	0.14	15.53	0.07	6.46
澳大利亚	Australia	105	1 735	0.83	17.64	0.16	7.40

表 8.14　主要年份引进技术设备实际到货金额
ARRIVED CAPITAL THROUGH IMPORTED TECHNOLOGY AND EQUIPMENT IN MAIN YEARS

单位:万美元(10 000 USD)

国　别(地区)	Country(Region)	2000	2010	2017	2018
总　计	**Total**	**104 558**	**3 903 807**	**6 159 637**	**6 818 455**
#中国香港	Hong Kong, China	10 746	17 414	10 688	12 003
日　本	Japan	10 069	886 132	948 615	1 105 943
德　国	Germany	16 314	814 006	1 405 285	1 331 713
意 大 利	Italy	622	123 823	335 278	201 842
美　国	United States	49 431	427 275	784 589	810 570
瑞　士	Switzerland	1 862	126 605	162 130	210 554
英　国	United Kingdoms	712	85 649	403 744	404 361
瑞　典	Sweden	639	72 594	111 931	153 161
奥 地 利	Austria	1 162	31 804	52 015	69 783
法　国	France	1 926	98 172	121 582	128 584

表 8.15　对外承包工程和劳务合作(2015~2018)
OVERSEAS CONTRACTED PROJECTS AND LABOR SERVICES COOPERATION

指　标	Indicators	2015	2016	2017	2018
对外承包工程	**Overseas Contracted Projects**				
签订合同金额(亿美元)	Value of Contract (100 million USD)	111.00	118.45	108.50	118.97
实际营业额(亿美元)	Actual Business Volume (100 million USD)	74.55	66.56	99.30	75.41
派出人员(人次)	Dispatched Persons (person-time)	5 866	6 497	13 902	8 764
对外劳务合作	**Overseas Labor Services Cooperation**				
派出人员(人次)	Dispatched Persons (person-time)	14 369	15 290	18 935	9 808

表 8.16　对外直接投资情况(2015~2018)
OVERSEAS DIRECT INVESTMENT

指　标	Indicators	2015	2016	2017	2018
投资项目(个)	Number of Projects (unit)	1 338	1 425	608	792
对外直接投资中方投资额(亿美元)	Investment Value (100 million USD)	398.97	366.50	110.83	168.72

注：为规范指标名称，本表名原“海外企业情况”调整为“对外直接投资情况”，指标含义和口径不变。
Note: In order to standardize the name of the index, the original name ENTERPRISES ABROAD is adjusted to OVERSEAS DIRECT INVESTMENT, but the meaning and statistical coverage of the index remain unchanged.

表 8.17　国际会展(2015~2018)
INTERNATIONAL CONFERENCE AND EXHIBITION

指　标	Indicators	2015	2016	2017	2018
举办国际会展个数(个)	International Exhibit(time)	292	287	293	300
国际会展展出总面积(万平方米)	Total Square of International Exhibit(10 000 sq.m)	1 124.06	1 177.47	1 329.16	1 415.30

注：2015 年前，本表数据由上海市会展行业协会提供，2015 年起，本表数据由上海市商务委提供。
Note: Data in this table before 2015 are provided by Shanghai Convention & Exibition Industries Association.Since 2015,data in this table are providede by Shanghai Commossion of Commerce.

表 8.18　主要年份旅行社接待经营情况
TOURISTS RECEIVED BY TOUR AGENCIES IN MAIN YEARS

指　标	Indicators	2010	2015	2017	2018
接待境内外来沪旅游者(万人次)	**Overseas and Domestic Tourists (10 000 person-times)**	**1 239.28**	**816.00**	**831.14**	**801.94**
境外旅游者	Overseas Tourists	158.25	64.16	71.85	59.98
#外国人	Foreigners	147.79	56.15	65.29	54.99
中国香港	Tourists from Hong Kong, China	4.47	3.23	1.70	1.04
中国澳门	Tourists from Macao, China	0.08	1.79	0.29	0.04
中国台湾	Tourists from Taiwan,China	5.91	2.98	4.57	3.91
境内旅游者	Domestic Tourists	1 081.03	751.85	759.29	741.96
出境旅游者(万人次)	**Tourists Going Abroad (10 000 person-times)**	**116.86**	**393.34**	**547.07**	**494.09**
经营和财务状况	Operation and Financial Status				
营业收入(亿元)	Operational Revenues(100 million yuan)	341.88	826.72	1 396.37	1 602.60
利润总额(亿元)	Total Profits(100 million yuan)	4.02	0.31	8.17	7.87

表 8.19 主要年份旅游景点基本情况
BASIC STATISTICS OF SCENIC SPOTS IN MAIN YEARS

指 标	Indicators	2010	2015	2017	2018
A 级旅游景点数(家)	Scenic Spots of A Level and above(unit)	61	98	99	113
#5A 级景点	AAAAA-Level	3	3	3	3
4A 级景点	AAAA-Level	28	51	50	59
红色旅游基地数(个)	Red Travelling Base(unit)	30	34	34	34
#全国红色旅游基地	National Red Travelling Base	8	9	9	12

表 8.20 主要年份国内旅游者来沪人数和人均消费支出
NUMBER OF DOMESTIC TOURISTS VISITING SHANGHAI AND PER CAPITA CONSUMPTION EXPENDITURES IN MAIN YEARS

指 标	Indicators	2005	2010	2017	2018
国内旅游者来沪人数（万人次）	**Number of Domestic Tourists Visiting Shanghai(10 000 person-times)**	**9 012**	**22 432**	**31 845**	**33 977**
外省市来沪旅游人数	Number of Tourists from other Provinces Visiting Shanghai	6 805	11 254.68	15 523	16 209
本市市民在本地旅游人数	Number of Local Tourists	2 207	11 177.37	16 322	17 768
国内旅游者人均消费支出（元）	**Consumption Expenditure Per Person (yuan)**	**1 452**	**1 175**	**1 264**	**1 338**
#长途交通费	Long-distance Traffic Expenditure	176	139	201	183
住宿费	Accommodation Expenditure	219	168	158	146
餐饮费	Food Expenditure	220	153	193	171
购物费	Shopping Expenditure	553	453	411	552
门票费	Ticket Expenditure	96	131	154	144
娱乐费	Entertainment Expenditure	30	42	27	20
市内交通费	Local Traffic Expenditure	88	53	50	45
邮电通信费	Post and Telecommunications Expenditure	37	14	4	6

注：本表为抽样调查资料。
Note: Data in this table are from the sampling survey.

表 8.21 旅游星级饭店基本情况(2018)
BASIC STATISTICS OF STAR-RATED TOURISM HOTELS

指 标	Indicators	合 计 Total	五星级 Five-Star	四星级 Four-Star	三星级 Three-Star	二星级 Two-Star
饭店数(个)	Number of Hotels(unit)	206	72	65	57	12
客房数(万间)	Number of Rooms (10 000 rooms)	5.53	2.87	1.79	0.76	0.11
床位数(万张)	Number of Beds (10 000 beds)	8.39	4.06	2.84	1.31	0.18
客房平均出租率(%)	Average Occupancy Rate (%)	67.0	69.3	66.3	59.5	73.9
营业收入(亿元)	Business Revenues (100 million yuan)	200.97	132.81	53.34	13.17	1.65
平均房价 (元/间天)	Average Room Rates (yuan/room.day)	753	982	554	362	324

表 8.22 主要年份国际旅游入境人数
NUMBER OF OVERSEAS TOURISTS THROUGH SHANGHAI CUSTOM IN MAIN YEARS

指 标	Indicators	2000	2010	2017	2018
国际旅游入境人数(万人次)	**Number of Overseas Tourists Through Shanghai Custom(10 000 person-times)**	**181.40**	**851.12**	**873.01**	**893.71**
#外国人	Foreigner	139.14	665.63	671.21	685.90
#日 本	Japanese	53.76	152.47	116.68	113.23
新加坡	Singaporean	5.29	23.50	23.36	23.77
德 国	German	7.11	29.52	33.65	32.94
法 国	French	5.39	24.86	22.17	22.57
英 国	Briton	1.69	20.94	24.33	24.14
意大利	Italian	1.88	11.49	12.35	12.51
加拿大	Canadian	2.25	20.97	25.08	24.31
美 国	American	13.78	80.79	95.88	98.63
澳大利亚	Australian	3.23	21.33	25.34	25.29
港澳同胞	Hong Kong and Macao Chinese	17.62	77.47	73.64	76.78
台湾同胞	Taiwanese	19.88	108.02	128.16	131.03
平均每天来沪旅游人数(人次/天)	**Average Number of Tourists Visiting Shanghai Everyday (person-time/day)**	**4 970**	**23 382**	**23 918**	**24 485**
来沪旅游者平均逗留天数(天/人)	**Average Time Tourists Staying in Shanghai (day/person)**	**3.92**	**3.51**	**3.30**	**3.70**
国际旅游(外汇)收入(亿美元)	**Foreign Exchange Earnings from International Tourism(100 million USD)**	**16.13**	**64.05**	**68.10**	**73.71**

上 / 海 / 统 / 计 / 年 / 鉴

主要统计指标解释

■ 关区进出口总额

指在上海海关办理进出口申报手续的进出口商品总额。统计方法依据联合国的国际贸易统计原则，反映进出上海而引起物质资源储备增加或减少的商品运动。按上述原则应具备条件：实际进出上海（海关关境），不仅包括经商业交易行为的进出口货品，也包括援助、捐赠等未发生买卖关系的货品价值。出口按离岸价（FOB）统计，进口按到岸价（CIF）统计。

■ 上海市进出口总额

指海关统计中按经营单位即进出口企业在海关注册地的行政区域口径统计的数据，它反映的是上海行政辖区内各类具有进出口经营权企业（外贸企业）的进出口。它不包含外省市外贸企业途经上海口岸由上海海关结关放行及统计的进出口商品，但包含上海外贸企业经由非上海口岸进出口结关放行及统计的商品。

■ 服务贸易

服务贸易是一国的法人或自然人在其境内或进入他国境内向外国的法人或自然人提供服务的贸易行为。服务提供者在其境内向他国家或地区的服务消费者提供的服务，即服务出口；境外服务提供者从其他国家或地区向他国境内的服务消费者提供的服务，即服务进口。

■ 外商直接投资

指外国企业和经济组织或个人（包括华侨、港澳台胞以及我国在境外注册的企业）按我国有关政策、法规，用现汇、实物、技术等在我国境内开办外商独资企业、与我国境内的企业或经济组织共同设立中外合资经营企业、合作经营企业或合作开发资源的投资（包括外商投资收益的再投资）以及企业投资总额内直接投资者对企业的贷款，即外方股东贷款。

反映外商直接投资状况的指标主要有三个：外商直接投资合同项目、外商直接投资合同金额、外商直接投资实际到位金额。

■ 引进技术

指通过贸易途径从国外获得发展我国国民经济和提高技术水平所需要的技术装备。引进方式有：许可证贸易（技术贸易）、生产线（包括成套设备）、单机（包括关键设备）、软硬件结合（同时引进技术和设备）和其他。

■ 对外承包工程

对外承包工程包括各对外承包公司以招标议标承包方式承揽的下列业务：(1) 承包国外工程建设项目。(2) 承包我国对外经济援助项目。(3) 承包我国驻外机构的工程建设项目。(4) 承包我国境内利用外资进行建设的工程项目。(5) 与外国承包公司合营或联合承包工程项目时我国公司分包部分。(6) 以服务成果向业主收费的技术服务项目（包括承担地形地貌测绘；地质资源勘探与普查；建设区域规划；提供设计文件、图纸、生产工艺技术资料和工程技术经济咨询；工程项目的可行性考察、研究和评估；进行技术指导和培训人员等）。(7) 对外承包兼营的房屋开发业务。对外承包工程的营业额是以货币表现的本期内完成的对外承包工程的工作量，包括以前年度签订的合同和本年度新签订的合同在报告期完成的工作量。

■ 对外劳务合作

指以收取工资的形式向业主或承包商提供技术和劳动服务的活动。上海对外承包公司在境外开办的合营企业，上海公司同时又提供劳务的，其劳务部分也纳入劳务合作统计。劳务合作营业额按报告期内向雇主提交的结算数（包括工资、加班费和奖金等）统计。

■ 国际旅游入境人数

指来上海参观、访问、旅行、探亲、访友、休养、考察、参加会议或从事经济、科技、文化、教育、体育、宗教等活动的外国人、华侨、港澳和台湾同胞的人数。不包括来上海常住1年以上的外国专家、留学生等。上海入境的境外旅游人数包括从上海口岸入境的境外旅游人数和从我国其他口岸入境来沪的境外旅游人数。

■ 国际旅游（外汇）收入

指入境旅游的外国人和华侨港澳台同胞在上海旅游过程中发生的一切旅游支出。

SHANGHAI STATISTICAL YEARBOOK

EXPLANATORY NOTES TO MAJOR STATISTICAL INDICATORS

□ Total Trade Volume Through Customs

Total Trade Volume through Customes refers to the aggregate volume of commodities that are conducted declaration procedure through Shanghai's ports. The statistics method follows the international trade statistics principles set by the United Nations. It reflects the fluctuation of Shanghai's material reserves caused by export or import. Requirements involved in the principle is: the commodities refer to those enter or leave Shanghai's ports, including not only the business trading activities but also the commodities value of the aid and donations that haven't been involved in sales . Exports are calculated according to FOB price, and imports are calculated according to CIF.

□ Total Value of Foreign Trade Imports and Exports of Shanghai

Total Value of Foreign Trade Imports and Exports of Shanghai is offered by Customs authorities, covering the operation units, or the enterprises involved in import and export, that have registered in the administrative regions where the Customs operate. It reflects the import and export of all the enterprises with import and export rights (foreign trade enterprises) under the administration of Shanghai Municipality. It excludes those commodities of foreign trade enterprises from out of town that underwent customs clearance at Shanghai ports but includes commodities of foreign trade enterprises of Shanghai that underwent customs clearance in non-Shanghai ports.

□ Service Trade

Service Trade is the trade behaviour in which a legal person or natural person of a country provides services to a foreign legal person or natural person in its territory or in the territoy of another country. Services providede by service providers to service consumers in other countries or regions in their territory, namely service exprot; services provided by service providers abroad from other countries or regions to service consumers in other countries, namely service import.

□ Foreign Direct Investment

Foreign Direct Investment refers to the investments made inside China by foreign enterprises and economic organizations or individuals (including overseas Chinese, compatriots in Hong Kong, Macao and Chinese enterprises registered abroad), in line with the relevant policies and laws of China, for the establishment of wholly foreign-owned enterprises, and joint ventures or development projects launched in China (including re-investment of profits from foreign businesses), and the funds that enterprises borrow from abroad in the total investment of projects which are approved by the relevant departments of the governments and the loans from the direct investors within the total investment of the projects, i.e., foreign shareholders' loans.

There are three main indicators that reflect the status of foreign direct investment: signed contracts of foreign direct investment, contracted foreign capital and foreign investment actually absorbed.

□ Import of Technology

Import of Technology refers to technology and equipments obtained through the trade channel from other countries which are needed for advancing China's national economy and improving its technological level. The import form includes: licensing (technological trade), production lines (including complete plant), single machine (including key equipments), combination of hardware and software (importing technology and equipments simultaneously) and others.

□ Overseas Contracted Projects

Overseas Contracted Projects refer to projects undertaken by Chinese contractors (project contracting companies) through bidding process. They include: (1) overseas civil engineering construction projects financed by foreign investors. (2) overseas projects financed by the Chinese government through its foreign-aid programs. (3) construction projects of Chinese diplomatic missions, trade offices and other institutions stationed abroad. (4) construction projects in China financed by foreign investment. (5) sub-contracted projects to be taken by Chinese contractors through a joint umbrella project with foreign contractor(s). (6) technical assistance projects in the form of service results and chargeable to the owners (such as topographic surveying, geological prospecting, development zone programming, provision of documents, blueprint, materials on

EXPLANATORY NOTES TO MAJOR STATISTICAL INDICATORS

production process, technical consultation, project feasibility studies and evaluation, personnel training, etc.). and (7) housing development projects. The business turnover from international contracting is the work of contracted projects completed during the reporting period, expressed in monetary terms, including completed work on project contracts signed in previous years.

□ Overseas Labor Service Cooperation

Overseas Labor Service Cooperation refers to activities of providing technology and labor services to employers or contractors by collecting salaries and wages. Labor services provided by Shanghai ′s international contrasting corporations to their overseas joint ventures shall be included into the statistics of overseas services. The business turn over of overseas labor services is the settlement price (including salaries, overtime pay and bonuses) submitted to the employers during the reporting period.

□ Number of Overseas Tourists to Shanghai

Number of Overseas Tourists to Shanghai refers to the number of foreigners, overseas Chinese, and compatriots from Hong Kong, Macao and Taiwan coming to Shanghai for sightseeing, visits, tours, family reunions, meeting friends, vacations, study tours, attending meetings and other activities of an economic, scientific and technological, cultural, physical culture and religious nature. This does not include foreign experts and students residing in Shanghai for over 1 year. The number of overseas tourists to Shanghai includes those overseas tourists entering China through Shanghai customs and through customs other than Shanghai.

□ Foreign Exchange Earnings from International Tourism

Foreign Exchange Earnings from International Tourism refer to the total expenditures of foreigners, overseas Chinese, Chinese compatriots from Hong Kong, Macao and Taiwan during their stay in Shanghai.

第九篇
CHAPTER 9

价格水平
PRICES

简要说明

一、本篇资料的主要内容

本篇价格指数资料，反映生产、流通、消费、投资与交易等环节的价格变动趋势和变动幅度。主要包括居民消费价格指数、商品零售价格指数、工业生产者出厂价格指数、工业生产者购进价格指数、固定资产投资价格指数。

二、本篇的资料来源

价格指数编制由国家统计局上海调查总队组织实施，依据国家统计局统一制定的价格统计调查制度，由上海调查总队直接或通过区调查队从基层采集原始价格数据汇总后上报。

三、居民消费、商品零售价格指数

编制居民消费、商品零售价格指数的资料采用抽样调查和重点调查相结合的方法取得，即在全市选择不同经济区域和分布合理的商品销售或服务网点，以及有代表性的商品或服务作为样本，对其市场价格进行定期调查，以样本推断总体。目前，居民消费、商品零售价格调查已涉及全市全部16个区。

1. 价格调查网点的抽选方法：对全市消费市场进行摸底调查、掌握市场的基本情况（经营品种、销售额等指标）基础上，将各种类型的商场（店）、超市、农贸市场、服务网点以销售额（成交额或经营规模）为标志，从高到低排队，依据所需调查点的数量进行等距抽样。选择经营品种齐全、销售额大的商场（店）、超市、农贸市场、服务网点作为价格调查网点。

2. 代表规格品根据全市的消费情况确定，必须遵循以下原则：（1）选择消费量较大的消费项目；（2）价格变动趋势和变动程度有较强的代表性，即选中规格品与未选中规格品的价格变动特征愈相关愈好；（3）在市场销售份额大体相等的情况下，同一基本分类的规格品之间，性质差异愈大愈好，价格变动特征的相关性愈低愈好；（4）生产和销售前景较好；（5）选中的工业消费品必须是合格产品，工业产品包装上必须有注册商标、产地、规格等级等标识。

目前，居民消费价格调查分为8大类，262个基本分类，全市每月共调查约1100种的规格品价格；商品零售价格分为16个大类，229个基本分类，全市每月调查800种以上的规格品价格。

3. 价格调查方法：居民消费、商品零售价格调查是非全面调查，主要方法是定人、定点、定时直接调查。

4. 权数的确定：居民消费价格指数的权数主要根据全市城镇居民家庭消费支出构成确定；商品零售价格指数的权数主要根据全市社会商品零售额资料确定。

5. 指数计算方法：使用链式拉氏公式计算，每5年更换1次基期，目前固定基期为2015年。

6. 居民消费价格调查分类变化说明

2016年，国家统计局参考联合国制定的《按目的划分的个人消费分类》（COICOP）和《居民消费支出分类（2013）》，对CPI调查类别进行了较大调整。八大类调整前分为食品、烟酒、衣着、家庭设备及维修服务、医疗保健和个人用品、交通和通信、娱乐教育文化用品及服务和居住(见表9.4到表9.6),调整后分为食品烟酒、衣着、居住、生活用品及服务、交通和通信、教育文化和娱乐、医疗保健、其他用品和服务(见表9.1到表9.3)。

此次类别结构调整较大,主要是:

(1)调整前"食品"、"烟酒"两类,合并为"食品烟酒"类。其中,调整前"食品"类包括粮食、淀粉及制品、干豆类及豆制品、油脂、肉禽及其制品、蛋、水产品、菜、调味品、糖、茶及饮料、干鲜瓜果、液体乳及乳制品、在外用膳食品和其他食品等16分类,调整后"食品"类包括粮食、薯类、豆类、食用油、菜、畜肉类、禽肉类、水产品、蛋类、奶类、干鲜瓜果类、糖果糕点类、调味品和其他食品类等16分类;

(2)调整前"医疗保健和个人用品"类,调整后此类相关指标被拆分到"生活用品及服务"类、"医疗保健"类和"其他用品和服务"类中;

(3)调整前"娱乐教育文化用品及服务"类,调整后相关指标被拆分到"教育文化和娱乐"类和"其他用品和服务"类中;

(4)调整前"家庭设备用品及维修服务"类,调整后相关指标被拆分到"生活用品及服务"类和"其他用品及服务"类中。

7. 2016年商品零售价格调查分类变化说明

2016年,国家统计局对RPI调查中的类别进行了调整。调整前"食品"类包括粮食、淀粉及制品、干豆类及豆制品、油脂、肉禽及其制品、蛋、水产品、菜、调味品、糖、干鲜瓜果、糕点饼干面包、液体乳及乳制品、在外用膳食品和其他食品等15分类,调整后包括粮食、薯类、豆类、食用油、菜、畜肉类、禽肉类、水产品、蛋类、奶类、干鲜瓜果类、糖果糕点类、调味品、其他食品类和在外餐饮等15分类;调整前"金银珠宝"类,调整后为"金银饰品"类。

四、工业生产者价格指数

工业生产者价格包括工业品第一次出售时的出厂价格和企业作为中间投入的原材料、燃料、动力的购进价格。该项调查采用重点调查的方法,调查对象为规模以上工业法人企业。

1.选择代表企业的原则:(1)按工业行业选择调查企业,各主要中类行业原则上都要有调查企业;(2)大型企业应尽量都选上(或占相当大比重);(3)选择生产正常、稳定的企业作为调查对象;(4)选择企业时要兼顾不同所有制形式。不仅选择国有企业,也要选择非国有企业。根据以上原则上海共选择1000余家工业企业开展工业生产者价格调查。

2.选择代表产品的原则:(1)按工业行业选择基本分类和代表产品;(2)选择对国计民生影响大的产品;(3)选择生产较为稳定的产品;(4)选择有发展前景的产品;(5)选择具有地方特色的产品。

根据《工业生产者价格调查目录》,上海编制工业生产者出厂价格指数选用500余个基本分类(1000余种产品),工业生产者购进价格指数选用了400余个基本分类(近1000种产品)。

3.价格调查方式采用企业网上直报形式。

五、固定资产投资价格指数

固定资产投资价格调查采用重点调查与典型调查相结合的方法。固定资产投资价格调查所涉及的价格是构成固定资产投资额实体的实际购进价格或结算价格。调查的内容包括构成当年建筑工程实体的钢材、木材、水泥、地方材料（如砖、瓦、灰、沙、石等）、化工材料（如油漆等）等主要建筑材料价格；作为活劳动投入的劳动力价格（单位工资）和各种施工机械使用价格；设备、工器具购置和其他费用投资价格。

1. 选择建筑安装工程调查点的原则：（1）样本单位应具有一定覆盖面；（2）投资经济活动代表性强；（3）兼顾不同登记注册类型；（4）选择重点工程；（5）兼顾不同工程类别。

2. 选择其他费用调查点的原则：在选择其他费用调查点时，所遵循的原则与建筑安装工程调查点的原则基本相同，特别是要注意选择那些投资额大的工程。但由于其他费用不易取得，所以在实际操作过程中，应同时在建设单位、施工单位开展重点调查，并辅以典型调查（从管理部门取得资料）。

3. 价格调查方式采用企业报表形式，每季度120余家调查企业上报数据资料。

BRIEF INTRODUCTION

I. Main Contents

Data on price indices in this chapter show the changing trends and the changing rates in the prices of production, trade, consumption, investment and transaction, mainly including consumer price indices, retail price indices, producer price indices, producer purchasing price indices, price indices for investment in fixed assets.

II. Sources of Data

Statistics on price indices, organized and compiled by the Survey Office of the National Bureau of Statistics in Shanghai, are collected from the grassroots units or survey offices in districts in accordance with the scheme of price survey system stipulated by the National Bureau of Statistics, and then statistics are tabulated and reported to the higher agencies.

III. Consumer Price Indices and Retail Price Indices

Data for compilation of the consumer price indices and the retail price indices in Shanghai are collected through a combination of sample surveys and surveys of key units. Areas distributed in the city's economic regions, representative commodities and representative services are selected as samples. Regular surveys are conducted to collect data on their market prices. Population parameters are inferred on the basis of the sample data. At present, 16 districts in Shanghai are all included in the survey of the consumer price indices and the retail price indices.

(1) The selection of sample survey areas: Based on the basic conditions (including product varieties, their sales and etc) the city's consumer market, the city's consumer market, shops, supermarkets, wet markets and service outlets of different varieties are ranked by sales (turnover or scales) and then selected on the number of survey areas needed via systematic sampling method schemes. The price survey areas should be shops, supermarkets, wet markets and service outlets with a wide range of products and big sales.

(2) The goods are selected on the city's consumption conditions, following these principles: (a) goods sold in large quantities; (b) Representative for the price changing trends and the changing rates, which means selected goods are highly relevant with those unselected; (c) Under the conditions of similar market shares, the bigger the differences in nature among goods and the lower the price relevance, the better; (d) Good production and sales outlook; (e) Qualified industrial goods, with registered trademark, origin and grade printed on the packaging.

At present, data are collected on about 1100 specifications each month in the city under 262 basic headings in 8 categories in the consumer price surveys. For the retail price surveys, data are collected on more than 800 specifications each month under 229 basic headings in 16 categories.

(3) Method of data collection: Sample surveys are used for the consumer price indices and the retail price indices, with method of direct survey with fixed people, fixed location and fixed time period.

(4) Determination of the weights: The weights of the consumer price indices are determined according to the composition of the consumption expenditures of Shanghai's urban and rural households. The weights of the retail price indices are determined mainly according to the total retail sales of commodities in the city.

(5) Method of calculation: the approach of the chain Laspyres with base period replaced every 5 years which is 2015 at present.

(6) Classification changes of consumer price survey.

In 2016, the National Bureau of statistics made a great adjustment of the categories of CPI investigation according to the Classification of Individual Consumption according to Purpose(COICOP) and the Classification of Consumer Spending (2013) formulated by the United Nations. 8 categories before the adjustment contain the food, cigarettes and liquors, clothing, home appliances and repair service, medical services and personal aricles, transportation and communication, recreation and education and culture articles , living (see tables 9.4 to 9.6), and after adjustment, they contain the food, cigarettes and liquors, clothing, residence, daily necessities and services, transportation and communication, education and culture and entertainment , medical care , other supplies and services (see tables 9.1 to 9.3).

The category adjustment is great, the main changes contain:

①The original "food" and "cigarettes and liquors" are combined into "food, cigarettes and liquors"; Among them, the "food" category before adjustment includes 16 categories of grain, starch, beans, oil, poultry, eggs, aquatic products, vegetables, condiments, sugar, tea and beverages, fruits, milk, dining out and other foods. The adjusted "food" category includes 16 categories of grain, potatoes, beans, oil, vegetables, meat, poultry, aquatic products, eggs, milk, fruits, confectionery, condiments and others.

②The original "medical services and personal aricles" is split to "daily necessities and services ", "medical care" and "other supplies and services".

③The original "recreation, education and culture articles" is split to "education, culture and entertainment" and "other supplies and services ";

④The original "home appliances and repair service" is split to "daily necessities and services" and "other supplies and services".

(7)Revisions in category of RPI: Since 2016, the National Bureau of Statistics made an adjustment to the category of RPI investigation. Before the adjustment, category of "Food" was divided into Grain, Starch and Its Products, Dry Beans and Bean Products, Oil and Fat, Meat Poultry and Their Products, Eggs, Aquatic Products, Vegetables, Flavoring, Sugars, Dried and Fresh Fruits, Cakes, Biscuits and Bread, Milk and Its Products, Dining Out, and Other Food. After the adjustment, category of "Food" is divided into Grain, Potato, Beans, Edible Oil, Vegetables, Meat, Poultry, Aquatic Products, Eggs, Milks, Dried and Fresh Fruits, Sweets and Cakes, Flavoring, Other Food, and Dining Out. The "Gold and Silver Jewelry" category was adjusted to the"Gold and Silver Ornament" category.

IV. Producer Price Indices

Producer prices include Producer Prices for Industrial Products, which are the prices of manufactured goods when they are sold for the first time, and Purchasing Prices for Industrial Producers,which are prices paid by industrial enterprises when they purchase productive inputs such as raw materials, fuels and power from the market or from other enterprises. Methologically, this is a survey of the key enterprises, which refer to those industrial enterprises avove set scale.

(1) Principles for the selection of representative enterprises: (a) Enterprises to be covered in the survey are selected by industrial sectors. In principle, every second-level classifacation should have representative enterprises; (b) All (or the majority of) large-scale enterprises should be selected; (c) Enterprises selected should be those with normal and stable production. (d) Enterprises selected should include both state-owned enterprises and enterprises of other ownerships. According to these principles, nearly 1000 enterprises in Shanghai are selected for this survey.

(2) Principle for the selection of representative goods: (a) The goods are selected by industrial sectors; (b) The selected goods should have great importance in the national economy and people's living conditions; (c) The production of the goods selected should be stable; (d) The prospects of the goods selected should be promising; (e) The goods selected should be of local specialties.

According to the catalog of Producer Price Suvey, more than 500 basic categories (over 1000 goods) and more than 400 basic categories (nearly 1000 inputs) in Shanghai are selected for the surveys of Producer Price Index for Industrial Products and Purchasing Price index for Industrial Producers respectively.

(3) Online direct reporting method is used for the data collection of Producer Price survey.

V. Price Indices for Investment in Fixed Assets

Data on prices of investment in fixed assets are collected by a program involving the combined use of surveys on key units and surveys on typical units. The prices collected in the surveys of investment in fixed assets are the actual purchasing prices or settlement prices of entities of investment in fixed assets. The survey content includes the prices of main construction materials that constitute the architectural engineering entity in the year, such as steel, timber, cement, local construction materials (such as brick, tile, calcareous ashes, sand, stone, and etc.), chemical materials (such as oil paint, and etc.), the price of labor cost (wages), using price of various construction machinery, the purchasing price of equipment, tools and instruments and the prices of others investments.

1. Principles for selecting the survey points of construction and installation: (1) Sample units should have a good coverage; (2) The economic activity of investment should have strong representativeness; (3) Different types of registration should be considered; (4) Key projects should be selected; (5) Inclusion of various types of projects.

2. Principles for selecting price survey points of other charges or cost: The principles for selecting survey points of others charges or cost is in general the same as that of construction and installation, with special attention to include projects with huge investment value. Since it is not easy to obtain the other charges or cost, during the actual data gathering operations, survey on key construction owner units and building units should be conducted concurrently with survey on typical units (with information from administration units)

3. Enterprises reporting system is used as the method for the price survey. More than 120 enterprises should report their data in each quarter.

表 9.1 居民消费价格和商品零售价格指数(1978~2018)
OVERALL RESIDENTS CONSUMER PRICE INDEX AND RETAIL PRICE INDEX

年 份 Year	居民消费价格指数 Overall Residents Consumer Price Index		年 份 Year	商品零售价格指数 Retail Price Index	
	以上年价格为 100 preceding year = 100	以 1978 年价格为 100 1978 = 100		以上年价格为 100 preceding year = 100	以 1978 年价格为 100 1978 = 100
1978	100.5	100.0	1978	100.1	100.0
1979	100.9	100.9	1979	101.0	101.0
1980	105.9	106.9	1980	106.5	107.6
1981	101.4	108.3	1981	101.5	109.2
1982	100.3	108.7	1982	100.3	109.5
1983	100.2	108.9	1983	100.1	109.6
1984	102.2	111.3	1984	102.2	112.0
1985	115.2	128.2	1985	116.4	130.4
1986	106.3	136.3	1986	106.7	139.1
1987	108.1	147.3	1987	108.8	151.4
1988	120.1	176.9	1988	121.3	183.6
1989	115.9	205.1	1989	116.7	214.3
1990	106.3	218.0	1990	104.8	224.6
1991	110.5	240.9	1991	109.5	245.9
1992	110.0	265.0	1992	109.7	269.8
1993	120.2	318.5	1993	117.5	317.0
1994	123.9	394.6	1994	117.5	372.4
1995	118.7	468.4	1995	113.0	420.9
1996	109.2	511.5	1996	105.0	441.9
1997	102.8	525.8	1997	98.8	436.6
1998	100.0	525.8	1998	95.1	415.2
1999	101.5	533.7	1999	97.3	404.0
2000	102.5	547.0	2000	96.4	389.5
2001	100.0	547.0	2001	98.6	384.0
2002	100.5	549.7	2002	98.7	379.0
2003	100.1	550.1	2003	99.0	375.4
2004	102.2	561.9	2004	100.9	378.8
2005	101.0	567.3	2005	99.4	376.7
2006	101.2	574.2	2006	100.2	377.3
2007	103.2	592.3	2007	102.4	386.5
2008	105.8	626.5	2008	105.3	407.1
2009	99.6	624.0	2009	99.4	404.8
2010	103.1	643.4	2010	101.7	411.7
2011	105.2	676.7	2011	104.1	428.4
2012	102.8	695.9	2012	101.2	433.6
2013	102.3	711.9	2013	100.2	434.3
2014	102.7	730.7	2014	100.9	438.0
2015	102.4	748.4	2015	101.1	442.8
2016	103.2	772.6	2016	100.8	446.3
2017	101.7	785.7	2017	100.9	450.3
2018	101.6	798.3	2018	101.6	457.5

表9.2 居民消费价格指数(2016~2018,以上年价格为100)
CLASSIFIED RESIDENTS CONSUMER PRICE INDEX (PRECEDING YEAR=100)

类别	Types	2016	2017	2018
居民消费价格指数	**Overall Residents Consumer Price Index**	**103.2**	**101.7**	**101.6**
#消费品价格指数	Consumer Goods Price Indices	102.2	101.2	101.6
服务价格指数	Services Items Price Indices	104.5	102.3	101.6
食品烟酒	**Food, Cigarettes and Liquors**	**103.7**	**101.2**	**102.3**
食　品	Food	104.8	100.6	102.5
粮　食	Grain	100.9	101.7	100.3
薯　类	Potatoes	113.0	92.6	105.7
豆　类	Beans	100.4	100.1	105.4
食用油	Edible Oil	99.9	101.5	100.2
菜	Vegetables	110.6	94.9	107.1
畜肉类	Meat	108.3	99.3	98.8
禽肉类	Poultry	101.6	102.1	106.3
水产品	Aquatic Products	107.8	103.5	101.3
蛋　类	Eggs	98.4	98.5	108.6
奶　类	Milk	101.4	99.7	101.3
干鲜瓜果类	Dried and Fresh Fruits	101.8	104.0	102.9
糖果糕点类	Sweet and Pastries	102.3	103.3	101.9
调味品	Flavouring	104.8	105.2	100.4
其他食品	Other Food	102.3	100.7	103.7
茶及饮料	Tea and Beverages	100.8	101.0	103.2
烟　酒	Cigarettes and Liquors	102.2	102.3	101.3
在外餐饮	Dining Out	101.6	102.4	101.9
衣　着	**Clothing**	**100.8**	**100.5**	**98.3**
服　装	Garments	101.3	100.2	98.6
服装材料	Clothing Materials	103.6	100.4	101.8
其他衣着及配件	Other Clothing and Accessories	100.4	100.4	100.8
衣着加工服务费	Garment Processing Service	103.6	103.8	108.3
鞋　类	Shoes	98.8	101.2	95.6

表 9.2 续表 continued

类 别	Types	2016	2017	2018
居　住	**Residence**	**105.1**	**101.7**	**100.2**
租赁房房租	Rent of Rental Housing	107.3	101.8	99.7
住房维修保养及管理	Housing Maintenance and Management	103.1	103.9	105.9
水电燃料	Water, Electricity and Fuels	99.0	101.1	100.6
自有住房	Self-owned House	106.4	101.6	99.5
生活用品及服务	**Daily Necessities and Services**	**101.2**	**101.5**	**101.4**
家具及室内装饰品	Furniture and Interior Decorations	100.2	101.2	103.0
家用器具	Household Appliances	100.4	100.4	99.8
家用纺织品	Home Textiles	101.9	100.3	99.0
家庭日用杂品	Home Daily Groceries	100.5	101.6	102.1
个人护理用品	Personal Care Articles	99.6	100.5	100.4
家庭服务	Family Services	106.6	104.9	103.7
交通和通信	Transportation and Communication	97.0	100.7	104.0
交　通	Transportation	96.8	101.1	105.1
通　信	Communication	97.3	100.0	102.2
教育文化和娱乐	**Education, Culture and Entertainment**	**102.7**	**100.9**	**103.1**
教　育	Education	104.6	104.6	106.9
文化娱乐	Culture and Entertainment	101.6	98.6	100.7
医疗保健	**Medical Care**	**109.0**	**106.6**	**102.4**
药品及医疗器具	Drugs and Medical Devices	110.6	102.2	101.1
医疗服务	Medical Service	107.3	111.6	103.8
其他用品和服务	**Other Supplies and Services**	**103.3**	**102.6**	**102.4**
其他用品类	Other Supplies	104.6	101.0	100.5
其他服务类	Other Services	102.5	103.6	103.6

表 9.3 商品零售价格指数 (2016~2018,以上年价格为 100)
RETAIL PRICE INDEX (PRECEDING YEAR =100)

类别	Types	2016	2017	2018
商品零售价格指数	**Overall Retail Price Index**	**100.8**	**100.9**	**101.6**
食　品	Food	104.1	101.1	102.3
#粮　食	Grain	100.9	101.7	100.3
薯　类	Potato	113.0	92.6	105.7
豆　类	Beans	100.4	100.1	105.4
食用油	Edible Oil	99.9	101.5	100.2
菜	Vegetables	110.6	94.9	107.1
畜肉类	Meat	108.3	99.3	98.8
禽肉类	Poultry	101.6	102.1	106.3
水产品	Aquatic Products	107.8	103.5	101.3
蛋　类	Eggs	98.4	98.5	108.6
奶　类	Milks	101.4	99.7	101.3
干鲜瓜果类	Dried and Fresh Fruits	101.8	104.0	102.9
糖果糕点类	Sweets and Cakes	102.3	103.3	101.9
调味品	Flavoring	104.8	105.2	100.4
其他食品类	Other Food	102.3	100.7	103.7
在外餐饮	Dining Out	101.6	102.4	101.9
饮料、烟酒	Beverages, Tobacco and Liquor	102.0	102.0	101.6
服装、鞋帽	Garments, Shoes and Hats	100.7	100.4	98.0
纺织品	Textiles	102.4	100.3	99.2
家用电器及音像器材	Household Appliances and Audio-video Appliances	99.2	99.6	97.9
文化办公用品	Cultural Office Articles	103.2	100.1	100.4
日用品	Daily Use Articles	100.4	101.0	101.0
体育娱乐用品	Sports and Recreation Goods	99.5	101.2	101.3
交通、通信用品	Transportation and Communication Goods	97.1	98.6	100.4
家　具	Furniture	100.1	101.2	103.2
化妆品	Cosmetics	99.4	100.4	100.4
金银饰品	Gold and Silver Ornament	107.4	101.7	100.6
中西药品及医疗保健用品	Traditional Chinese and Western Medicines	111.0	102.2	101.2
书报杂志及电子出版物	Newspapers and Magazines and Electronic Publications	101.1	99.7	106.0
燃　料	Fuels	95.6	108.2	110.9
建筑材料及五金电料	Building Materials and Hardwares	99.6	100.7	105.3

表 9.4 居民消费价格指数(1991~2015,以上年价格为 100)
OVERALL RESIDENTS CONSUMER PRICE INDEX (PRECEDING YEAR=100)

年 份 Year	居民消费价格指数 Overall Residents Consumer Price Index	食 品 Food	烟 酒 Cigarettes and Liquors	衣 着 Clothing
1991	110.5	113.5	103.0	105.7
1992	110.0	113.4	109.7	109.5
1993	120.2	122.1	110.2	118.6
1994	123.9	131.8	112.0	115.7
1995	118.7	126.1	106.9	108.8
1996	109.2	110.5	100.0	108.7
1997	102.8	100.0	90.3	101.1
1998	100.0	97.8	96.0	94.0
1999	101.5	97.4	100.4	98.3
2000	102.5	98.2	97.2	95.3
2001	100.0	100.3	98.9	98.9
2002	100.5	102.9	98.9	97.5
2003	100.1	101.3	99.8	97.5
2004	102.2	108.3	98.3	94.2
2005	101.0	104.5	99.7	92.1
2006	101.2	102.5	100.2	106.4
2007	103.2	109.4	100.7	101.3
2008	105.8	115.3	101.7	101.6
2009	99.6	102.1	100.8	99.3
2010	103.1	107.7	101.1	98.6
2011	105.2	110.8	101.3	104.3
2012	102.8	105.8	101.4	103.0
2013	102.3	104.4	100.1	100.0
2014	102.7	103.2	101.0	103.7
2015	102.4	102.9	104.2	107.8

表 9.4 续表 continued

年 份 Year	家庭设备用品及维修服务 Home Appliances and Repair Service	医疗保健和个人用品 Medicine, Medical Services and Personal Aricles	交通和通信 Transportation and Communication	娱乐教育文化用品及服务 Recreation, Education and Culture Articles	居 住 Residence
1991	112.5	113.1	108.5	96.9	129.3
1992	102.6	117.3	100.4	96.8	119.0
1993	109.5	114.4	117.0	123.4	134.4
1994	110.9	119.2	117.3	117.6	120.6
1995	103.8	110.0	114.7	116.2	120.3
1996	99.1	106.0	106.1	118.6	109.7
1997	91.4	102.1	115.6	109.6	120.6
1998	92.5	101.9	103.7	106.3	113.6
1999	96.4	101.9	112.4	111.7	105.9
2000	95.7	99.9	110.9	121.5	103.3
2001	97.2	97.4	98.1	102.1	102.3
2002	97.7	97.6	96.9	100.8	100.0
2003	98.4	100.0	96.3	100.3	101.1
2004	97.8	100.0	96.5	99.9	101.6
2005	100.8	100.3	97.5	98.3	102.9
2006	102.7	101.1	97.3	98.2	102.9
2007	103.3	100.2	96.9	97.3	104.5
2008	108.3	103.1	97.5	98.2	102.5
2009	101.5	99.4	97.5	98.0	96.6
2010	101.1	103.7	97.4	100.9	103.5
2011	107.1	104.1	100.2	99.2	105.4
2012	103.5	100.6	100.8	99.3	102.8
2013	101.3	100.0	100.4	100.1	103.9
2014	101.8	100.4	100.1	101.8	104.6
2015	102.9	99.3	97.6	100.3	104.6

表 9.5　主要年份居民消费价格指数 (以上年价格为 100)
CLASSIFIED RESIDENTS CONSUMER PRICE INDEX IN MAIN YEARS(PRECEDING YEAR=100)

类　别	Types	2001	2010	2015
居民消费价格指数	**Overall Residents Consumer Price Index**	**100.0**	**103.1**	**102.4**
#消费品价格指数	Consumer Goods Price Indices	98.6	103.5	102.0
服务项目价格指数	Services Items Price Indices	105.4	102.0	103.2
食　品	**Food**	**100.3**	**107.7**	**102.9**
粮　食	Grain	102.9	112.0	103.0
淀粉及制品	Starch and Its Products	103.6	95.5	103.9
干豆类及豆制品	Dry Beans and Bean Products	95.6	108.7	101.2
油　脂	Oil or Fat	84.5	105.6	98.5
肉禽及其制品	Meat Poultry and Their Products	99.3	104.3	105.3
蛋	Eggs	102.4	106.1	98.0
水产品	Aquatic Products	100.1	116.4	101.3
菜	Vegetables	108.9	111.0	107.5
调味品	Flavoring	99.2	106.5	104.9
糖	Sugars	101.4	103.8	102.2
茶及饮料	Tea and Beverages	98.4	103.9	103.9
干鲜瓜果	Dried and Fresh Fruits	104.3	112.0	96.8
糕点饼干面包	Cakes,Biscuits and Bread	100.5	100.5	101.8
液体乳及乳制品	Milk and Its Products	100.8	102.3	99.2
在外用膳食品	Dining Out	98.0	105.6	104.1
其他食品	Other Food	99.2	105.0	104.2
烟　酒	**Cigarettes and Liquors**	**98.9**	**101.1**	**104.2**
烟　草	Tobacco	99.2	101.0	104.9
酒	Liquors	98.2	101.6	102.5
衣　着	**Clothing**	**98.9**	**98.6**	**107.8**
服　装	Garments	96.4	99.9	107.3
衣着材料	Clothing Materials	98.7	102.9	106.3
鞋袜帽	Shoes, Socks and Hats	106.2	93.6	109.8
衣着加工服务	Garment Processing Service	100.0	107.2	105.5

表 9.5 续表 continued

类别	Types	2001	2010	2015
家庭设备用品及维修服务	**Home Appliances and Repair Service**	**97.2**	**101.1**	**102.9**
耐用消费品	Durable Consumer Goods	94.7	99.6	101.8
室内装饰品	Interior Decorations	101.0	99.2	102.2
床上用品	Bed Articles	100.5	104.2	103.4
家庭日用杂品	Daily Use Household Articles	98.6	99.4	101.4
家庭服务及加工维修服务	Other Daily Use Articles	100.0	108.8	108.5
医疗保健和个人用品	**Medicine, Medical Services and Personal Aricles**	**97.4**	**103.7**	**99.3**
医疗保健	Medicine and Medical Services	96.5	100.8	100.7
个人用品及服务	Personal Articles and Service	99.8	107.1	98.0
交通和通信	**Transportation and Communication**	**98.1**	**97.4**	**97.6**
交　通	Transportation	102.3	98.7	97.3
通　信	Communications	94.4	95.3	98.2
娱乐教育文化用品及服务	**Recreation, Education and Culture Articles**	**102.1**	**100.9**	**100.3**
文娱用耐用消费品及服务	Durable Consumer Goods for Recreational Use	91.2	89.4	95.9
教　育	Education	109.6	101.2	102.5
文化娱乐类	Recreation and Culture Articles	105.2	101.0	100.7
旅　游	Tourism	96.2	115.9	97.9
居　住	**Residence**	**102.3**	**103.5**	**104.6**
建房及装修材料	Construction and Decoration Materials	97.5	102.1	101.4
住房租金	Rents	111.0	106.8	107.3
自有住房	Self-owned House	99.8	103.0	105.5
水、电、燃料	Water, Electricity and Fuels	101.7	103.8	102.4

表 9.6 主要年份商品零售价格指数 (以上年价格为 100)
CLASSIFIED RETAIL PRICE INDEX IN MAIN YEARS (PRECEDING YEAR =100)

类别	Types	2001	2010	2015
商品零售价格指数	**Overall Retail Price Index**	**98.6**	**101.7**	**101.1**
食　品	Food	98.4	107.6	102.8
#粮　食	Grain	100.1	112.0	103.0
淀粉及制品	Starch and Its Products	100.4	95.5	103.9
干豆类及豆制品	Dry Beans and Bean Products	111.3	108.7	101.2
油　脂	Oil and Fat	81.4	105.6	98.0
肉禽及其制品	Meat Poultry and Their Products	100.4	104.2	105.3
蛋	Eggs	110.7	106.1	98.0
水产品	Aquatic Products	90.1	116.1	101.3
菜	Vegetables	107.1	111.0	107.5
调味品	Flavoring	99.5	106.5	104.8
糖	Sugars	104.4	103.8	102.2
干鲜瓜果	Dried and Fresh Fruits	107.3	112.1	96.8
糕点饼干面包	Cakes, Biscuits and Bread	99.8	100.5	101.8
液体乳及乳制品	Milk and Its Products	99.8	102.3	99.2
在外用膳食品	Dining Out	100.7	105.6	104.1
其它食品	Other Food	99.5	105.0	104.2
饮料、烟酒	Beverages, Tobacco and Liquors	98.4	101.9	103.9
服装、鞋帽	Garments, Shoes and Hats	107.7	98.4	107.9
纺织品	Textile Products	98.8	103.9	104.1
家用电器及音像器材	Household Appliances and Audio-video Equipment	95.0	92.4	99.3
文化办公用品	Culture and Office Articles	98.7	97.7	99.2
日用品	Daily Use Articles	99.0	100.3	101.5
体育娱乐用品	Sports and Recreation Articles	99.1	95.9	99.4
交通、通信用品	Transport and Communication Products	97.4	94.0	97.8
家　具	Furniture	90.4	101.1	101.8
化妆品	Cosmetics	100.7	101.0	100.1
金银珠宝	Jewelry	87.2	111.7	95.2
中西药品及医疗保健用品	Traditional Chinese and Western Medicines, Medical and Health Care Articles	98.7	99.8	100.6
书报杂志及电子出版物	Newspapers and Magazines and Electronic Publications	99.5	103.2	101.7
燃　料	Fuels	111.4	112.8	91.2
建筑材料及五金电料	Building Materials and Hardware	101.8	103.3	99.6

表 9.7 工业生产者出厂价格指数（2011～2018，以 2000 年价格为 100）
PRODUCER PRICE INDEX FOR INDUSTRIAL PRODUCTS (2000 = 100)

类别	Types	2011	2012	2013	2014
工业生产者出厂价格指数	**Producer Price Index for Industrial Products**	**102.3**	**100.7**	**98.9**	**97.8**
按轻重工业分	**Grouped by Light or Heavy Industries**				
轻工业	Light Industry	89.5	90.1	89.4	88.6
以农产品为原料	Using Farm Products as Raw Materials	120.4	122.6	122.5	122.3
以非农产品为原料	Using Non-farm Products as Raw Materials	78.3	78.1	76.9	75.8
重工业	Heavy Industry	114.8	112.4	110.2	108.9
采　掘	Mining and Guarrying	272.9	273.2	283.9	290.1
原　料	Raw Material	191.0	189.3	184.8	181.5
加　工	Manufacturing	94.3	92.0	90.3	89.4
按用途分	**Grouped by Use**				
生产资料	Means of Production	106.6	104.6	102.4	101.1
生活资料	Consumer Goods	94.7	94.2	93.4	92.8
#食　品	Food	133.8	138.2	138.1	138.7
衣　着	Clothing	110.5	110.1	110.3	110.7
一般日用品	Non-Durable Consumer Goods	108.5	109.5	106.8	105.9
耐用消费品	Durable Consumer Goods	67.0	64.5	64.3	63.6

表 9.7 续表 continued

类别	Types	2015	2016	2017	2018
工业生产者出厂价格指数	**Producer Price Index for Industrial Products**	**94.0**	**92.9**	**96.2**	**97.8**
按轻重工业分	**Grouped by Light or Heavy Industries**				
轻工业	Light Industry	87.4	87.2	88.2	88.7
以农产品为原料	Using Farm Products as Raw Materials	120.8	121.3	122.6	124.9
以非农产品为原料	Using Non-farm Products as Raw Materials	74.7	74.1	75.1	74.5
重工业	Heavy Industry	104.0	102.5	106.7	108.9
采　掘	Mining and Guarrying	247.2	229.4	253.9	295.9
原　料	Raw Material	157.5	152.5	174.8	188.0
加　工	Manufacturing	87.3	86.4	87.8	88.3
按用途分	**Grouped by Use**				
生产资料	Means of Production	96.1	94.7	99.3	101.6
生活资料	Consumer Goods	92.2	91.9	92.2	92.4
#食　品	Food	137.7	138.1	139.1	140.5
衣　着	Clothing	110.7	112.0	109.9	110.1
一般日用品	Non-Durable Consumer Goods	104.5	105.4	109.9	110.9
耐用消费品	Durable Consumer Goods	63.3	62.4	61.3	61.0

表 9.8 工业生产者出厂价格指数 (2010~2018,以 2000 年价格为 100)(按国民经济行业分)
PRODUCER PRICE INDEX FOR INDUSTRIAL PRODUCTS(GROUPED BY NATIONAL INDUSTRIES, 2000 = 100)

类别	Types	2011	2012	2013	2014
工业生产者出厂价格指数	**Producer Price Index for Industrial Products**	**102.3**	**100.7**	**98.9**	**97.8**
按国民经济行业分	**Grouped by National Economy Industries**				
石油和天然气开采业	Petroleum and Natural Gas Exploiting	272.9	273.2	283.9	290.1
农副食品加工业	Farm and Sideline Products Processing	205.0	213.2	211.1	203.3
食品制造业	Food Manufacturing	133.3	138.2	140.8	143.8
酒、饮料和精制茶制造业	Wine, Beverage and Refined Tea Manufacturing	113.2	119.2	114.3	112.6
烟草制品业	Tabacco Manufacturing	141.2	145.4	146.3	146.3
纺织业①	Textile	108.6	106.8	105.5	103.9
纺织服装、服饰业①	Textile and Garment, Apparel Industry	112.2	111.5	111.6	111.9
皮革、毛皮、羽毛及其制品和制鞋业①	Leather, Fur, Feather and Its Products and Shoemaking Industry	101.0	100.4	102.1	103.7
木材加工和木、竹、藤、棕、草制品业	Timber Processing and Timber, Bamboo, Rattan, Coir and Straw Products Manufacturing	110.7	114.6	114.9	118.0
家具制造业	Furniture Manufacturing	92.9	93.2	93.0	93.0
造纸和纸制品业	Paper-making and Paper Products Manufacturing	100.0	101.1	98.9	97.9
印刷和记录媒介复制业	Printing and Record Duplicating Industry	91.9	91.3	89.5	89.6
文教、工美、体育和娱乐用品制造业①	Stationary, Education ,Industrial Art, Sport and Entertainment Products Manufacturing	108.8	111.8	104.0	98.8
石油加工、炼焦和核燃料加工业	Oil Processing, Coking and Nuclear Fual Processing	325.6	333.1	327.1	311.7
化学原料和化学制品制造业	Raw Chemical Materials and Chemical Products Manufacturing	159.3	154.2	149.3	147.8
医药制造业	Medicine Manufacturing	97.4	99.2	96.5	96.7
化学纤维制造业	Chemical Fiber Manufacturing	132.5	120.8	118.5	114.9
橡胶和塑料制品业①	Rubber and Plastic Products Manufacturing	113.5	113.4	112.6	110.3
非金属矿物制品业	Nonmetal Mineral Products	112.2	107.0	103.9	104.4
黑色金属冶炼和压延加工业①	Smelting and Pressing of Ferrous Metals	190.6	167.7	165.0	161.2
有色金属冶炼和压延加工业	Smelting and Pressing of Nonferrous Metals	225.9	205.6	192.9	185.0
金属制品业①	Metal Products Manufacturing	131.9	130.1	125.2	120.8
通用设备制造业①	General Equipment Manufacturing	94.6	94.0	92.2	91.2
专用设备制造业①	Special Purpose Equipment Manufacturing	95.1	95.7	95.2	96.2
汽车制造业	Automotive Industry		96.3	94.9	94.6
铁路、船舶、航空航天和其他运输设备制造业	Railroads, Ships, Aerospace and other Transportation Equipment Manufacturing Industry		98.5	96.5	95.8
电气机械和器材制造业①	Electric Machinery Equipments and Manufacturing	94.7	92.9	90.5	89.1
计算机、通信和其他电子设备制造业	Computers, Communications and other Electronic Equipment Manufacturing Industry	49.5	49.2	48.4	47.7
仪器仪表制造业①	Instruments and Meters Manufacturing	82.4	81.4	81.2	81.0
其他制造业①	Other Manufacturing	164.6	165.4	165.2	165.4
废弃资源综合利用业	Comprehensive Utilization of Waste Resources	167.8	145.3	132.5	125.9
金属制品、机械和设备修理业	Metal Products, Machinery and Equipment Repair		97.3	96.4	97.6
电力、热力生产和供应业	Production and Supply of Electricity and Thermal Power	112.7	115.4	115.2	116.8
燃气生产和供应业	Production and Supply of Gas	165.4	160.4	150.5	148.7
水的生产和供应业	Production and Supply of Water	179.1	180.5	189.0	223.0

①2012 年起按新口径编制。
②废弃资源和废旧材料回收加工业以 2002 年价格为 100。
❶These in dices have been calaulated according to the new caliber since 2012.
❷The price index of Waste Resources and Materials Recycling and Processing was 100 in 2002.

表 9.8 续表 continued

	类 别 Types	2015	2016	2017	2018
工业生产者出厂价格指数	**Producer Price Index for Industrial Products**	**94.0**	**92.9**	**96.2**	**97.8**
按国民经济行业分	**Grouped by National Economy Industries**				
石油和天然气开采业	Petroleum and Natural Gas Exploiting	247.2	229.4	253.9	295.5
农副食品加工业	Farm and Sideline Products Processing	187.4	189.1	189.9	193.9
食品制造业	Food Manufacturing	144.8	144.8	148.6	151.4
酒、饮料和精制茶制造业	Wine, Beverage and Refined Tea Manufacturing	110.0	109.6	113.5	122.2
烟草制品业	Tabacco Manufacture	146.3	146.4	146.4	147.1
纺织业	Textile	101.7	103.3	111.0	122.0
纺织服装、服饰业	Textile and Garment, Apparel Industry	111.5	114.1	112.8	112.4
皮革、毛皮、羽毛及其制品和制鞋业	Leather, Fur, Feather and Its Products and Shoemaking Industry	104.1	102.2	98.5	99.8
木材加工和木、竹、藤、棕、草制品业	Timber Processing and Timber, Bamboo, Rattan, Coir and Straw Products Manufacturing	119.7	118.7	117.5	116.4
家具制造业	Furniture Manufacturing	93.2	94.4	95.0	95.9
造纸和纸制品业	Paper-making and Paper Products Manufacturing	96.9	96.6	102.7	107.2
印刷和记录媒介复制业	Printing and Record Duplicating Industry	88.5	87.9	88.4	87.9
文教、工美、体育和娱乐用品制造业	Stationary, Education ,Industrial Art, Sport and Entertainment Products Manufacturing	96.3	105.6	109.1	110.8
石油加工、炼焦和核燃料加工业	Oil Processing, Coking and Nuclear Fual Processing	230.3	210.3	240.8	289.6
化学原料和化学制品制造业	Raw Chemical Materials and Chemical Products Manufacturing	129.0	129.3	150.4	154.6
医药制造业	Medicine Manufacturing	98.2	97.7	106.6	107.0
化学纤维制造业	Chemical Fiber Manufacturing	105.4	94.8	109.3	121.0
橡胶和塑料制品业	Rubber and Plastic Products Manufacturing	105.2	102.1	104.1	105.3
非金属矿物制品业	Nonmetal Mineral Products	99.8	96.0	105.2	119.7
黑色金属冶炼和压延加工业	Smelting and Pressing of Ferrous Metals	138.6	134.2	160.2	165.7
有色金属冶炼和压延加工业	Smelting and Pressing of Nonferrous Metals	168.4	157.8	178.3	182.5
金属制品业	Metal Products Manufacturing	115.6	115.4	125.1	129.7
通用设备制造业	General Equipment Manufacturing	90.8	91.4	92.3	94.9
专用设备制造业	Special Purpose Equipment Manufacturing	98.0	99.7	99.6	99.9
汽车制造业 *	Automotive Industry	93.7	92.3	90.5	89.8
铁路、船舶、航空航天和其他运输设备制造业 *	Railroads, Ships, Aerospace and other Transportation Equipment Manufacturing Industry	95.3	94.3	94.6	94.8
电气机械和器材制造业	Electric Machinery Equipments and Manufacturing	87.2	84.3	83.6	82.4
计算机、通信和其他电子设备制造业	Computers, Communications and other Electronic Equipment Manufacturing Industry	47.4	47.1	47.0	46.2
仪器仪表制造业	Instruments and Meters Manufacturing	80.7	81.3	82.5	82.6
其他制造业	Other Manufacturing	168.0	157.2	167.9	167.4
废弃资源综合利用业	Comprehensive Utilization of Waste Resources	93.7	87.0	85.3	85.9
金属制品、机械和设备修理业 *	Metal Products, Machinery and Equipment Repair	95.2	99.2	104.1	101.8
电力、热力生产和供应业	Production and Supply of Electricity and Thermal Power	115.4	111.8	112.2	111.2
燃气生产和供应业	Production and Supply of Gas	149.0	146.0	140.6	138.5
水的生产和供应业	Production and Supply of Water	225.7	225.0	224.6	220.5

注：* 为以 2011 年价格为 100。
Note: The price index symbled " * " was 100 in 2011.

表 9.9 工业生产者出厂价格指数 (2011~2018,以上年价格为 100)
PRODUCER PRICE INDEX FOR INDUSTRIAL PRODUCTS(PRECEDING YEAR =100)

类 别	Types	2011	2012	2013	2014
工业生产者出厂价格指数	**Producer Price Index for Industrial Products**	**102.9**	**98.4**	**98.2**	**98.9**
按轻重工业分	**Grouped by Light or Heavy Industries**				
轻工业	Light Industry	103.9	100.7	99.2	99.1
以农产品为原料	Using Farm Products as Raw Materials	104.6	101.8	99.9	99.8
以非农产品为原料	Using Non-farm Products as Raw Materials	103.3	99.8	98.5	98.6
重工业	Heavy Industry	102.6	97.9	98.0	98.8
采 掘	Mining and Guarrying	115.0	100.1	103.9	102.2
原 料	Raw Material	110.3	99.1	97.6	98.2
加 工	Manufacturing	100.6	97.6	98.1	99.0
按用途分	**Grouped by Use**				
生产资料	Means of Production	102.8	98.1	97.9	98.7
生活资料	Consumer Goods	102.9	99.5	99.2	99.4
#食 品	Food	105.5	103.3	99.9	100.4
衣 着	Clothing	101.9	99.6	100.2	100.4
一般日用品	Non-Durable Consumer Goods	105.1	100.9	97.5	99.2
耐用消费品	Durable Consumer Goods	100.2	96.2	99.7	98.9

表 9.9 续表 continued

类 别	Types	2015	2016	2017	2018
工业生产者出厂价格指数	**Producer Price Index for Industrial Products**	**96.1**	**98.8**	**103.5**	**101.7**
按轻重工业分	**Grouped by Light or Heavy Industries**				
轻工业	Light Industry	98.6	99.8	101.2	100.5
以农产品为原料	Using Farm Products as Raw Materials	98.8	100.4	101.1	101.9
以非农产品为原料	Using Non-farm Products as Raw Materials	98.5	99.2	101.4	99.2
重工业	Heavy Industry	95.5	98.6	104.1	102.0
采 掘	Mining and Guarrying	85.2	92.8	110.7	116.4
原 料	Raw Material	86.8	96.8	114.6	107.5
加 工	Manufacturing	97.7	99.0	101.6	100.6
按用途分	**Grouped by Use**				
生产资料	Means of Production	95.1	98.5	104.9	102.3
生活资料	Consumer Goods	99.3	99.7	100.3	100.2
#食 品	Food	99.3	100.3	100.7	101.0
衣 着	Clothing	100.0	101.2	98.1	100.2
一般日用品	Non-Durable Consumer Goods	98.7	100.9	104.3	100.9
耐用消费品	Durable Consumer Goods	99.6	98.6	98.3	99.4

表 9.10 工业生产者出厂价格指数 (2011~2018,以上年价格为 100)(按国民经济行业分)
PRODUCER PRICE INDEX FOR INDUSTRIAL PRODUCTS(GROUPED BY NATIONAL INDUSTRIES, PRECEDING YEAR=100)

类 别	Types	2011	2012	2013	2014
工业生产者出厂价格指数	**Producer Ex-factory Price Index**	**102.9**	**98.4**	**98.2**	**98.9**
按国民经济行业分	**Grouped by National Economy Industries**				
石油和天然气开采业	Petroleum and Natural Gas Exploiting	115.0	100.1	103.9	102.2
农副食品加工业	Farm and Sideline Products Processing	119.6	104.0	99.0	96.3
食品制造业	Food Manufacturing	106.7	103.7	101.9	102.1
酒、饮料和精制茶制造业	Wine, Beverage and Refined Tea Manufacturing	103.2	105.3	95.9	98.5
烟草制品业	Tabacco Manufacture	100.0	103.0	100.6	100.0
纺织业	Textile	104.3	98.3	98.8	98.5
纺织服装、服饰业	Textile and Garment, Apparel Industry	102.4	99.4	100.1	100.3
皮革、毛皮、羽毛及其制品和制鞋业	Leather, Fur, Feather and Its Products and Shoemaking Industry	100.1	99.4	101.7	101.6
木材加工和木、竹、藤、棕、草制品业	Timber Processing and Timber, Bamboo, Rattan, Coir and Straw Products Manufacturing	106.2	103.5	100.3	102.7
家具制造业	Furniture Manufacturing	102.8	100.3	99.8	100.0
造纸和纸制品业	Paper-making and Paper Products Manufacturing	105.0	101.1	97.8	99.0
印刷和记录媒介复制业	Printing and Record Duplicating Industry	101.4	99.3	98.0	100.1
文教、工美、体育和娱乐用品制造业	Stationary, Education ,Industrial Art, Sport and Entertainment Products Manufacturing	107.0	102.8	93.0	95.0
石油加工、炼焦和核燃料加工业	Oil Processing, Coking and Nuclear Fual Processing	116.7	102.3	98.2	95.3
化学原料和化学制品制造业	Raw Chemical Materials and Chemical Products Manufacturing	110.9	96.8	96.8	99.0
医药制造业	Medicine Manufacturing	103.1	101.8	97.3	100.2
化学纤维制造业	Chemical Fiber Manufacturing	113.6	91.2	98.1	97.0
橡胶和塑料制品业	Rubber and Plastic Products Manufacturing	107.6	99.9	99.3	98.0
非金属矿物制品业	Nonmetal Mineral Products	108.0	95.4	97.1	100.5
黑色金属冶炼和压延加工业	Smelting and Pressing of Ferrous Metals	110.1	88.0	98.4	97.7
有色金属冶炼和压延加工业	Smelting and Pressing of Nonferrous Metals	112.8	91.0	93.8	95.9
金属制品业	Metal Products Manufacturing	103.2	98.6	96.2	96.5
通用设备制造业	General Equipment Manufacturing	98.9	99.4	98.1	98.9
专用设备制造业	Special Purpose Equipment Manufacturing	100.5	100.6	99.5	101.0
汽车制造业	Automotive Industry		96.3	98.5	99.7
铁路、船舶、航空航天和其他运输设备制造业	Railroads, Ships, Aerospace and other Transportation Equipment Manufacturing Industry		98.5	98.0	99.3
电气机械和器材制造业	Electric Machinery Equipments and Manufacturing	100.8	98.1	97.4	98.4
计算机、通信和其他电子设备制造业	Computers, Communications and Other Electronic Equipment Manufacturing Industry	98.1	99.4	98.3	98.5
仪器仪表制造业	Instruments and Meters Manufacturing	101.4	98.8	99.8	99.8
其他制造业	Other Manufacturing	116.3	100.5	99.9	100.1
废弃资源综合利用业	Comprehensive Utilization of Waste Resources	123.2	86.6	91.2	95.0
金属制品、机械和设备修理业	Metal Products, Machinery and Equipment Repair		97.3	99.1	101.2
电力、热力生产和供应业	Production and Supply of Electricity and Thermal Power	100.9	102.4	99.8	101.4
燃气生产和供应业	Production and Supply of Gas	109.0	97.0	93.8	98.8
水的生产和供应业	Production and Supply of Water	110.1	100.8	104.7	118.0

表 9.10 续表 continued

类别	Types	2015	2016	2017	2018
工业生产者出厂价格指数	**Producer Price Index for Industrial Products**	**96.1**	**98.8**	**103.5**	**101.7**
按国民经济行业分	**Grouped by National Economy Industries**				
石油和天然气开采业	Petroleum and Natural Gas Exploiting	85.2	92.8	110.7	116.4
农副食品加工业	Farm and Sideline Products Processing	92.2	100.9	100.4	102.1
食品制造业	Food Manufacturing	100.7	100.0	102.6	101.9
酒、饮料和精制茶制造业	Wine, Beverage and Refined Tea Manufacturing	97.7	99.6	103.6	107.6
烟草制品业	Tabacco Manufacture	100.0	100.1	100.0	100.5
纺织业	Textile	97.9	101.6	107.5	109.8
纺织服装、服饰业	Textile and Garment, Apparel Industry	99.6	102.3	98.9	99.6
皮革、毛皮、羽毛及其制品和制鞋业	Leather, Fur, Feather and Its Products and Shoemaking Industry	100.4	98.2	96.4	101.3
木材加工和木、竹、藤、棕、草制品业	Timber Processing and Timber, Bamboo, Rattan, Coir and Straw Products Manufacturing	101.4	99.2	99.0	99.1
家具制造业	Furniture Manufacturing	100.2	101.3	100.6	101
造纸和纸制品业	Paper-making and Paper Products Manufacturing	99.0	99.7	106.3	104.4
印刷和记录媒介复制业	Printing and Record Duplicating Industry	98.8	99.3	100.6	99.4
文教、工美、体育和娱乐用品制造业	Stationary, Education ,Industrial Art, Sport and Entertainment Products Manufacturing	97.5	109.7	103.3	101.6
石油加工、炼焦和核燃料加工业	Oil Processing, Coking and Nuclear Fual Processing	73.9	91.3	114.5	120.2
化学原料和化学制品制造业	Raw Chemical Materials and Chemical Products Manufacturing	87.3	100.2	116.3	102.8
医药制造业	Medicine Manufacturing	101.5	99.5	109.1	100.4
化学纤维制造业	Chemical Fiber Manufacturing	91.7	89.9	115.3	110.7
橡胶和塑料制品业	Rubber and Plastic Products Manufacturing	95.4	97.1	102.0	101.1
非金属矿物制品业	Nonmetal Mineral Products	95.6	96.2	109.6	113.8
黑色金属冶炼和压延加工业	Smelting and Pressing of Ferrous Metals	86.0	96.8	119.4	103.4
有色金属冶炼和压延加工业	Smelting and Pressing of Nonferrous Metals	91.0	93.7	113.0	102.3
金属制品业	Metal Products Manufacturing	95.7	99.8	108.4	103.7
通用设备制造业	General Equipment Manufacturing	99.6	100.7	101.0	102.8
专用设备制造业	Special Purpose Equipment Manufacturing	101.9	101.7	99.9	100.3
汽车制造业	Automotive Industry	99.0	98.5	98.1	99.1
铁路、船舶、航空航天和其他运输设备制造业	Railroads, Ships, Aerospace and other Transportation Equipment Manufacturing Industry	99.5	98.9	100.3	100.2
电气机械和器材制造业	Electric Machinery Equipments and Manufacturing	97.9	96.7	99.2	98.5
计算机、通信和其他电子设备制造业	Computers, Communications and other Electronic Equipment Manufacturing Industry	99.3	99.4	99.8	98.3
仪器仪表制造业	Instruments and Meters Manufacturing	99.6	100.8	101.5	100.1
其他制造业	Other Manufacturing	101.6	93.6	106.8	99.7
废弃资源综合利用业	Comprehensive Utilization of Waste Resources	74.4	92.9	98.0	100.8
金属制品、机械和设备修理业	Metal Products, Machinery and Equipment Repair	97.5	104.2	104.9	97.8
电力、热力生产和供应业	Production and Supply of Electricity and Thermal Power	98.8	96.9	100.4	99
燃气生产和供应业	Production and Supply of Gas	100.2	98.0	96.3	98.5
水的生产和供应业	Production and Supply of Water	101.2	99.7	99.8	98.2

表 9.11 工业生产者购进价格指数 (2011～2018,以 2000 年价格为 100)
PRODUCER PURCHASING PRCIE INDEX (2000 = 100)

类别	Types	2011	2012	2013	2014
工业生产者购进价格指数	**Producer Purchasing Price Index**	**164.7**	**156.0**	**150.5**	**144.3**
燃料、动力类	Fuels and Power	307.1	303.7	274.5	257.8
黑色金属材料类	Ferrous Metals	208.9	178.0	171.4	153.7
#钢　材	Rolled-steel	158.9	148.7	141.6	135.2
有色金属材料类	Nonferrous Metals	223.0	202.9	188.7	176.2
化工原料类	Chemical Raw Materials	147.3	142.0	138.0	133.6
木材及纸浆类	Wood and Paper Pulps	101.9	100.1	99.6	98.9
建筑材料类及非金属矿类	Building Materials and Nonmetal Minerals	138.7	130.0	128.6	131.6
其他工业原材料及半成品类	Other Industrial Raw and Processed Materials	107.5	104.4	101.6	99.6
农副产品类	Farm and Sideline Products	170.5	174.8	173.9	168.9
纺织原料类	Textile Raw Material	123.0	121.9	122.0	121.9

表 9.11 续表 continued

类别	Types	2015	2016	2017	2018
工业生产者购进价格指数	**Producer Purchasing Price Index**	**130.7**	**127.7**	**139.1**	**146.3**
燃料、动力类	Fuels and Power	176.1	160.8	195.4	228.9
黑色金属材料类	Ferrous Metals	125.6	127.0	149.5	154.3
#钢　材	Rolled-steel	121.0	122.7	143.4	148.6
有色金属材料类	Nonferrous Metals	156.5	155.9	173.2	179.4
化工原料类	Chemical Raw Materials	119.4	116.1	128.8	135.8
木材及纸浆类	Wood and Paper Pulps	98.2	96.5	101.2	105.0
建筑材料类及非金属矿类	Building Materials and Nonmetal Minerals	124.0	121.6	135.6	148.1
其他工业原材料及半成品类	Other Industrial Raw and Processed Materials	96.6	95.6	97.7	98.9
农副产品类	Farm and Sideline Products	158.9	150.0	156.6	157.5
纺织原料类	Textile Raw Material	122.1	123.1	126.4	128.2

表 9.12 工业生产者购进价格指数 (2011~2018,以上年价格为 100)
PRODUCER PURCHASING PRICE INDEX(PRECEDING YEAR =100)

类别	Types	2011	2012	2013	2014
工业生产者购进价格指数	**Producer Purchasing Price Index**	**107.5**	**94.7**	**96.5**	**95.9**
燃料、动力类	Fuels and Power	117.9	98.9	90.4	93.9
黑色金属材料类	Ferrous Metals	110.9	85.2	96.3	89.7
#钢　材	Rolled-steel	105.9	93.6	95.2	95.5
有色金属材料类	Nonferrous Metals	113.8	91.0	93.0	93.4
化工原料类	Chemical Raw Materials	110.5	96.4	97.2	96.8
木材及纸浆类	Wood and Paper Pulps	103.6	98.2	99.5	99.3
建筑材料类及非金属矿类	Building Materials and Nonmetal Minerals	116.0	93.7	98.9	102.3
其他工业原材料及半成品类	Other Industrial Raw and Processed Materials	100.9	97.1	97.3	98.0
农副产品类	Farm and Sideline Products	111.7	102.5	99.5	97.1
纺织原料类	Textile Raw Material	110.6	99.1	100.1	99.9

表 9.12 续表 continued

类别	Types	2015	2016	2017	2018
工业生产者购进价格指数	**Producer Purchasing Price Index**	**90.6**	**97.7**	**108.9**	**105.2**
燃料、动力类	Fuels and Power	68.3	91.3	121.5	117.2
黑色金属材料类	Ferrous Metals	81.7	101.1	117.7	103.2
#钢　材	Rolled-steel	89.5	101.4	116.9	103.6
有色金属材料类	Nonferrous Metals	88.8	99.6	111.1	103.6
化工原料类	Chemical Raw Materials	89.4	97.2	110.9	105.4
木材及纸浆类	Wood and Paper Pulps	99.3	98.3	104.9	103.7
建筑材料类及非金属矿类	Building Materials and Nonmetal Minerals	94.2	98.1	111.5	109.2
其他工业原材料及半成品类	Other Industrial Raw and Processed Materials	97.0	99.0	102.2	101.2
农副产品类	Farm and Sideline Products	94.1	94.4	104.4	100.5
纺织原料类	Textile Raw Material	100.2	100.8	102.7	101.4

表 9.13 固定资产投资价格指数 (2001~2018,以 2000 年价格为 100)
PRICE INDEX OF INVESTMENT IN FIXED ASSETS (2000 = 100)

年 份 Year	固定资产投资价格指数 Price Index of Fixed Asset Investment	建筑安装工程 Building Project Price Index	其中 of which #人工费 Manpower Cost Price Index	材料费 Material Price Index	机械使用费 Machinery Used Price Index	设备、工器具购置 Equipment and Instrument Price Index	其他费用投资 Other Investment Price Index
2001	100.7	102.4	109.0	101.2	99.7	96.5	101.3
2002	101.0	104.3	120.4	101.0	102.5	93.3	101.6
2003	103.4	109.7	125.8	106.6	107.5	91.0	103.0
2004	110.3	121.3	133.0	119.4	116.9	90.5	107.8
2005	111.2	122.4	139.4	118.7	123.4	88.1	111.2
2006	111.3	122.5	146.1	117.0	127.0	85.7	113.4
2007	115.2	128.1	156.8	122.0	130.0	85.2	118.0
2008	124.3	143.6	170.6	139.0	136.4	84.8	124.4
2009	120.6	136.1	181.2	126.6	138.9	81.5	127.1
2010	125.2	144.4	193.7	134.8	142.2	80.4	130.2
2011	133.3	159.7	213.5	150.4	148.0	80.2	133.7
2012	132.5	157.6	230.8	144.1	152.9	79.1	135.8
2013	132.8	157.3	250.2	140.2	158.1	77.9	138.8
2014	133.5	157.8	271.0	137.5	162.5	77.5	140.9
2015	129.5	149.8	286.7	125.8	164.0	77.3	141.7
2016	128.9	148.8	300.5	123.0	165.3	77.0	142.0
2017	137.5	165.0	314.3	139.9	167.9	77.2	143.3
2018	145.2	180.2	328.4	155.6	171.8	77.8	144.7

表 9.14 固定资产投资价格指数 (1995~2018,以上年价格为 100)
PRICE INDEX OF INVESTMENT IN FIXED ASSETS (PRECEDING YEAR = 100)

年 份 Year	固定资产投资价格指数 Price Index of Fixed Asset Investment	建筑安装工程 Building Project Price Index	其中 of which #人工费 Manpower Cost Price Index	材料费 Material Price Index	机械使用费 Machinery Used Price Index	设备、工器具购置 Equipment and Instrument Price Index	其他费用投资 Other Investment Price Index
1995	103.1	101.9	108.7	99.5		104.8	107.0
1996	107.0	108.9	114.2	97.4	118.5	101.7	107.7
1997	100.5	101.4	109.0	98.7	104.5	97.8	100.8
1998	98.4	98.9	96.0	98.3	99.7	96.1	99.6
1999	98.1	97.8	103.4	96.1	100.5	96.9	99.8
2000	100.0	101.5	100.6	101.8	99.8	97.0	99.9
2001	100.7	102.4	109.0	101.2	99.7	96.5	101.3
2002	100.3	101.9	110.5	99.8	102.8	96.7	100.3
2003	102.4	105.2	104.5	105.5	104.9	97.5	101.4
2004	106.7	110.6	105.7	112.0	108.7	99.4	104.7
2005	100.8	100.9	104.8	99.4	105.6	97.4	103.2
2006	100.1	100.1	104.8	98.6	102.9	97.3	102.0
2007	103.5	104.6	107.3	104.3	102.4	99.4	104.1
2008	107.9	112.1	108.8	113.9	104.9	99.5	105.4
2009	97.0	94.8	106.2	91.1	101.8	96.1	102.2
2010	103.8	106.1	106.9	106.5	102.4	98.6	102.4
2011	106.5	110.6	110.2	111.6	104.1	99.7	102.7
2012	99.4	98.7	108.1	95.8	103.3	98.6	101.6
2013	100.2	99.8	108.4	97.3	103.4	98.5	102.2
2014	100.5	100.3	108.3	98.1	102.8	99.5	101.5
2015	97.0	94.9	105.8	91.5	100.9	99.8	100.6
2016	99.6	99.3	104.8	97.8	100.8	99.7	100.2
2017	106.7	110.9	104.6	113.7	101.6	100.2	100.9
2018	105.6	109.2	104.5	111.2	102.3	100.8	101.0

上 / 海 / 统 / 计 / 年 / 鉴

主要统计指标解释

■ 居民消费价格指数

居民消费价格指数是度量一组代表性消费商品及服务项目价格水平随着时间而变动的相对数，反映居民家庭购买的消费品及服务价格水平的变动情况。它是宏观经济分析和决策、价格总水平监测和调控以及国民经济核算的重要指标。其按年度计算的变动率通常被用来作为反映通货膨胀或紧缩程度的指标。

现行的居民消费价格指数按用途分为八个大类，包括食品烟酒、衣着、居住、生活用品和服务、交通和通信、教育文化和娱乐、医疗保健、其他用品和服务。

■ 商品零售价格指数

商品零售价格指数是反映一定时期内城乡商品零售价格变动趋势和程度的相对数。商品零售价格的变动直接影响城乡居民的生活支出和国家的财政收入，影响居民购买力和市场供需的平衡，影响消费与积累的比例关系。因此，该指数可以从一个侧面对上述经济活动进行观察和分析。

■ 工业生产者出厂价格指数

从2011年起工业品出厂价格指数改为工业生产者出厂价格指数，它是反映一定时期内全部工业产品出厂价格总水平的变动趋势和程度的相对数，包括工业企业售给本企业以外所有单位的各种产品和直接售给居民用于生活消费的产品。该指数可以观察出厂价格变动对工业总产值及增加值的影响。

■ 工业生产者购进价格指数

从2011年起原材料、燃料和动力购进价格指数改为工业生产者购进价格指数，它是反映工业企业作为生产投入，从物资交易市场和能源、原材料生产企业购买原材料、燃料和动力产品时，所支付的价格水平变动趋势和程度的统计指标，是扣除工业企业物质消耗成本中的价格变动影响的重要依据。

■ 固定资产投资价格指数

固定资产投资价格指数是反映一定时期内固定资产投资品及项目的价格变动趋势和程度的相对数。固定资产投资额是由建筑安装工程投资完成额、设备工器具购置投资完成额和其他费用投资完成额三部分组成的。编制固定资产投资价格指数应首先分别编制上述三部分投资的价格指数，然后采用加权算术平均法求出固定资产投资价格总指数。

该指数可以准确地反映固定资产投资中涉及的各类投资品和收费项目价格变动趋势和变动幅度，消除按现价计算的固定资产投资指标中的价格变动因素，真实地反映固定资产投资的规模、速度、结构和效益，为国家科学地制定、检查固定资产投资计划并提高宏观调控水平，为完善国民经济核算体系提供科学的、可靠的依据。

SHANGHAI STATISTICAL YEARBOOK

EXPLANATORY NOTES TO MAJOR STATISTICAL INDICATORS

□ Consumer Price Index

The Consumer Price Index is an index that reflects the time-based change of prices of a group of representative consumption commodities and services. It is an important reference factor for macro-economic analysis and strategy, monitoring and adjustment of overall price level and the national economic budgeting. The year-on-year change of the index is often a norm reflecting the inflation or deflation.

The current CPI covers eight categories of goods and services: food; tobacco and liquor; garments; household facilities, articles and repair services; medical and health care and personal items; traffic and telecommunications; education, culture and recreation articles and services and residence.

□ Retail Price Index

Retail Price Index reflects the trend and degree of change in retail prices of commodities during a given period. The change in retail prices of commodities directly affect the living expenditure of urban and rural residents, government revenue, purchasing power of residents and the equilibrium of market supply and demand, and the ratio of consumption to accumulation. Therefore, the retail price index is useful to analyze the changes of the above economic activities.

□ Producer Ex-factory Price Index

Since 2011, Ex-factory Price Index of Industrial Products? has been changed into Producer Ex- factory Price Index. Producer Ex- factory Price Index reflects the trend and degree of changes in general ex- factory prices of all industrial products during a given period, including sales of industrial products by an industrial enterprise to all units outside the enterprise, as well as sales of consumer goods to residents. It can be used to analyze the impact of ex- factory prices on gross output value and value-added of the industrial sector.

□ Producer Purchasing Price Index

Since 2011, Index of Purchasing Prices of Raw Materials, Fuels and Power? has been changed into Producer Purchasing Price Index which reflects changes in the level and degree of prices paid by industrial enterprises when they purchase production input such as raw materials, fuels and power from the market or from other energy or raw materials producing enterprises. This index provides important basis for measuring the material consumption of industrial enterprises after removing influence of price changes.

□ Price Index of Investment in Fixed Assets

Price Index of Investment in Fixed Assets?reflects the trend and degree of changes in prices of investment goods and projects in fixed assets during a given period. The investment in fixed assets consists of three components, namely the investment in construction and installation, the investment in purchases of equipment and instrument, and the investment in other items. Price index of investment in fixed assets is calculated as the weighted arithmetic mean of the price indices of the three components of investment in fixed assets.

Removing the factor of price change in the aggregates of investment at current prices, this indicator shows the changes in the prices of commodities and fees involved in the investment of fixed assets, and can be used to observe the actual size, growth, structure, and efficiency of investment in fixed assets and provides reliable and scientific data for government planning, management, decision- making, and further improving the current national accounting system.

第十篇
CHAPTER 10

人民生活
LIVING STANDARDS

简要说明

第一部分　2015年以来上海居民收支与生活状况调查主要数据(新口径)(见表10.1到表10.17)

一、主要内容

第一部分资料反映2015～2018年上海常住居民收入、消费及其他生活状况。

二、资料来源

上海常住居民生活状况数据来源于国家统计局上海调查总队居民收支与生活状况抽样调查。

三、住户调查对象

上海居民收支与生活状况调查(简称住户调查,下同)对象为"本市常住居民",既包括本地户籍,也包括外地户籍;既包括以家庭形式居住的户,也包括以集体形式居住的户,即在本市常住的外来务工人员也被纳入调查对象。调查区域扩展到全市16个区的城镇、农村地区。全市城镇、农村调查样本量分别扩大到4600户和1400户,合计为6000户。

四、调查内容

调查主要内容包括居民现金和实物收支情况、住户成员及劳动力从业情况、居民家庭食品和能源消费情况、住房和耐用消费拥有情况、家庭经营和生产投资情况、社区基本情况以及其他民生状况等。

五、指标发布的变化

根据国家统计局要求,国家统计局上海调查总队从2015年1季度起,发布城乡一体化住户调查新口径调查数据。主要指标包括:上海居民人均可支配收入、城镇常住居民人均可支配收入、农村常住居民人均可支配收入;上海居民人均消费支出、城镇常住居民人均消费支出、农村常住居民人均消费支出等。

六、数据主要变化情况

根据城乡一体化住户调查改革,2015年起,遵照"统计上的城乡划分标准",新口径城镇常住居民收入、消费等数据覆盖范围在原有基础上扩大,包括城乡结合部,而农村常住居民范围缩小,不再以行政村划分;新口径城镇常住居民"人均可支配收入"指标加入了自有住房折算净租金,扣除了财产性支出和转移性支出等。计算城镇和农村常住居民消费支出时,包括了自有住房折算租金。

第二部分　1980~2014年城镇和农村住户调查主要数据（老口径）（见表10.18到表10.27）

一、主要内容

第二部分资料反映1980～2014年上海市居民生活现状及变化情况，分为城市居民生活和农村居民生活两部分。

二、城镇住户调查资料来源

城镇居民生活状况的数据来源于国家统计局上海调查总队的城镇住户抽样调查。主要内容包括城市居民生活基本情况、收入、生活消费支出、主要消费品消费量等。

三、城镇住户调查方法

上海城镇住户调查以城市常住户为调查对象，2003年及之前，调查样本为500户，2004年至2014年，调查样本增至1000户，分布于黄浦、卢湾、徐汇、长宁、静安、普陀、闸北、虹口、杨浦、闵行、宝山、浦东等12个区。

城镇住户调查采用分层、多阶段与大小成比例(pps)、随机等距等方法抽选调查样本户，采用日记账与问卷调查相结合的方法取得数据。首先，每月向抽中的调查户发放帐本，由调查户采用日记帐方式对本住户及每个成员的收支情况进行记录；然后由调查人员每月在规定的时间将帐本回收并进行审核、编码和录入；最后由国家统计局上海调查总队进行数据汇总得出人均可支配收入等数据资料。另外，家庭和个人基本情况以及部分调查户的收支情况通过问卷的形式取得数据。

四、农村住户调查资料来源

农村居民生活状况的数据来源于国家统计局上海调查总队的住户收支与生活状况调查。主要内容包括农村居民生活基本情况、收入、生活消费支出、主要消费品消费量等。

五、农村住户调查方法

农村住户调查是以农村常住户为调查对象，农村常住户指长期(半年以上)居住在农村范围内的住户。户口不在本地而在本地居住半年及以上的住户也包括在本地农村常住户范围内。按国家统计局住户收支与生活状况调查方案，采用抽样调查方法在全市郊区县抽取约1200户农村居民家庭作为调查样本，分布于浦东、闵行、宝山、嘉定、金山、松江、青浦、奉贤、崇明9个区县。

为保证农村住户调查资料的准确性，住户收支与生活状况调查在95%的概率把握程度下要求抽样误差不得超过±3%。调查数据采用农村居民记账与一次性调查相结合的方法取得，调查户按照国家统计局上海调查总队统一编制的帐本和要求记账，现金收支帐、实物收支帐发生一笔记一笔，由区县调查员每月收取调查户的帐本，录入计算机，通过乡镇、区县、总队多级审核确保调查数据真实可靠。

BRIEF INTRODUCTION

Part 1 Main Data from Survey of Income and Expenditure and Living Conditions of Residents in Shanghai Since 2015 (New Statistical Standard)(Table 10.1 to Table 10.17)

I. Main Contents

The data of first part reflect the income and consumption and other living conditions of residents in Shanghai from 2015 to 2018.

II. Sources of Data

Data on the living conditions of Shanghai residents come from the sample survey on residents revenue and expenditure and living conditions, which is conducted by Survey Office of the National Bureau of Statistics in Shanghai.

III. Objects of Household Survey

The objects of survey on Shanghai residents revenue and expenditure and living conditions (abbreviated as household survey, the same below) are residents in Shanghai with residence registration or non−residence registration, including both households living in the form of family and households living in the form of groups, that is, resident migrant workers in the city are also included in the survey. The survey area is extended to urban and rural areas of 16 districts in the whole city. The survey samples of urban and rural are expanded to 4600 households and 1400 households respectively, which amount to 6000 households.

IV. Contents of the Survey

The main contents of the survey include income and expenditure of residents in cash and in kind, employment situation of household members and labor force, food and energy consumption of households, possession of housing and durable goods consumption, situation of household business and production investment, basic situation of the community and other livelihood of people, etc.

V.Changes of Index Releasing

According to the requirements of the National Bureau of Statistics, Survey Office of the National Bureau of Statistics in Shanghai releases the data of household survey of urban and rural integration according to new statistic standard since the first quarter of 2015. The main indicators include: per capita disposable income of Shanghai residents, per capita disposable income of urban residents, per capita disposable income of rural residents, per capita consumption expenditure of Shanghai residents, per capita consumption expenditure of urban residents, and per capita consumption expenditure of rural residents

VI. Main Changes of Data

According to the household survey reform of urban and rural integration, since 2015,following the Statistical Classification of Urban and Rural Areas, coverage of data of new standard on urban resident income and consumption is expanded on the original basis , including the Urban−Rural Binding Region. But Coverage of rural residents is reduced, and is no longer divided by administrative village. The indicator of Per Capita Disposable Income includes self-ownedhousing converted net rent, and excludes property expenditure and transfer expenditure, etc. The calculation of consumption expenditure of urban and rural residents includes self-owned housing converted net rent.

Part 2 Main Data from Urban and Rural Household Survey from 1980 to 2014 (Old Statistical Standard)(Table 10.18 to Table 10.27)

I. Main Contents

Data in the second part of this chapter reflect the Shanghai people's living conditions and changes from 1980 to 2014, consisting of two parts, on the life of urban and rural households respectively.

II. Sources of Data on the Living Conditions of Urban Residents

Data on the living conditions of urban residents come from the data collected through a sample survey on the urban households conducted by the Survey Office of the National Bureau of Statistics in Shanghai. The main contents of the survey include basic situation of urban residents living, income, consumer spending and the main consumption of consumer goods, etc.

III. Methodology for Urban Household Survey

Data on the survey of urban residents cover long-term residents in urban areas. Shanghai's sample included 500 households before 2003; it increased to 1,000 households between 2004 and 2014, covering 12 districts of Huangpu, Luwan, Xuhui, Changning, Jing'an, Putuo, Zhabei, Hongkou, Yangpu, Minhang, Baoshan and Pudong.

Samples in urban household survey are selected by systematic sampling method schemes, such as stratifying method, multi-stage method and probability proportional to size (PPS) method, and the data are obtained by method of journal combined with questionnaire. Selected households receive account books each month and keep diaries to record income and expenditure of the household and its individual members. Professional inspectors will then collect, encode and audit the data at fixed time each month, deliver them to the Survey Office of the National Bureau of Statistics to calculate data such as the average disposable income per capita. In addition, data of household and personal basic situation as well as the balance of the selected households are obtained through the form of questionnaire.

IV. Sources of Data on the Living of Rural Residents

Data on the living conditions of rural residents come from data collected through the survey on household revenue and expenditure and living condition, which is organized by the Survey Office of the National Bureau of Statistics in Shanghai. The main contents of the survey include the basic condition of rural households, income, consumption expenditure and consumption of major consumer goods.

V. Methodology for Rural Household Survey

Data on the survey of income and expenditure of rural residents cover long-term residents in rural areas. Long-term residents refer to people living within the administered villages for more than half a year. Households without local registered residence are included given they have lived in the area for more than half a year. According to the scheme of the survey on rural household revenue, expenditure and living condition, the sampling approach is used to select about 1,200 rural households as samples through 9 districts and counties of Pudong, Minhang, Baoshan, Jiading, Jinshan, Songjiang, Qingpu, Fengxian, and Chongming.

To guarantee accuracy of the data on the revenue, expenditure and living condition of rural household, it is required that the sampling error should not exceed ±3%, with a confidence probability as 95%. A combination of diaries kept by rural households and the one-time survey is used for collecting data. The households are keeping diaries on unified requirements compiled by the Survey Office of the National Bureau of Statistics in Shanghai. Income and expenditure of cash and real goods are recorded case by case. Data are collected by inspectors from districts and counties and compiled into computers. Inspectors from townships, counties, districts and the headquarters office will audit the data to make them accurate and reliable.

表 10.1 全市居民家庭生活基本情况(2015~2018)
BASIC STATISTICS OF WHOLE CITY HOUSEHOLDS

指　标	Indicators	2015	2016	2017	2018
基本情况(人)	**Basic Statistics(person)**				
户均人口	Population per Household	2.62	2.69	2.69	2.53
户均从业人口	Employees per Household	1.29	1.28	1.25	1.19
平均每一从业人口负担人数(包括从业者本人)	Persons Supported by Each Employee(person)	2.03	2.09	2.16	2.13
家庭收入与支出(元)	**Household Income and Expenditure (yuan)**				
人均可支配收入	Per Capita Disposable Income	49 867	54 305	58 988	64 183
人均消费支出	Per Capita Consumption Expenditure	34 784	37 458	39 792	43 351

表 10.2 城镇常住居民家庭生活基本情况(2015~2018)
BASIC STATISTICS OF URBAN HOUSEHOLDS

指　标	Indicators	2015	2016	2017	2018
基本情况(人)	**Basic Statistics(person)**				
户均人口	Population per Household	2.64	2.69	2.69	2.54
户均从业人口	Employees per Household	1.26	1.25	1.22	1.18
平均每一从业人口负担人数(包括从业者本人)	Persons Supported by Each Employee(person)	2.09	2.14	2.21	2.16
家庭收入与支出(元)	**Household Income and Expenditure (yuan)**				
人均可支配收入	Per Capita Disposable Income	52 962	57 692	62 596	68 034
人均消费支出	Per Capita Consumption Expenditure	36 946	39 857	42 304	46 015

表 10.3 农村常住居民家庭生活基本情况(2015~2018)
BASIC STATISTICS OF RURAL HOUSEHOLDS

指　标	Indicators	2015	2016	2017	2018
基本情况(人)	**Basic Statistics(person)**				
户均人口	Population per Household	2.47	2.69	2.69	2.39
户均从业人口	Employees per Household	1.54	1.54	1.48	1.28
平均每一从业人口负担人数(包括从业者本人)	Persons Supported by Each Employee(person)	1.60	1.75	1.82	1.87
家庭收入与支出(元)	**Household Income and Expenditure (yuan)**				
人均可支配收入	Per Capita Disposable Income	23 205	25 520	27 825	30 375
人均消费支出	Per Capita Consumption Expenditure	16 152	17 071	18 090	19 965

注：2012 年起，国家统计局实施了城乡一体化住户调查改革，统一了城乡居民收入名称、分类和统计标准。2015 年起，发布城乡可比的新口径全市居民人均可支配收入以及分城乡常住居民人均可支配收入。

Note: Since 2012, the National Bureau of Statistics has implemented the integrated household survey reform of urban and rural integration with unifying the urban and rural income name, classification and statistical standards. Since 2015, the per capita disposable income of city′s residents and per capita disposable income of urban and rural residents which can be compared by new statistical coverage have been released.

表 10.4 个人存款(住户存款)年末余额(1997~2018) HOUSEHOLD DEPOSITS AT YEAR-END

年 份 Year	个人存款(住户存款)余额 (亿元) Household Deposits (100 million yuan)	其 中 of which 活期存款 Current Deposits	定期及其他存款 Time Deposits and Other Deposits	人均个人存款余额 (元) Average Deposits (yuan)
1997	2 109.18	265.93	1 843.25	14 165
1998	2 372.94	355.78	2 017.16	15 540
1999	2 597.12	477.30	2 119.82	16 574
2000	2 627.07	542.86	2 084.21	16 331
2001	3 109.50	808.17	2 301.33	19 266
2002	4 915.54	1 312.49	3 603.05	30 249
2003	6 054.60	1 793.73	4 260.87	35 386
2004	6 960.99	2 056.06	4 904.93	39 956
2005	8 432.49	2 360.66	6 071.83	47 416
2006	9 480.28	2 778.31	6 701.97	52 223
2007	9 326.45	3 140.60	6 185.85	50 194
2008	12 083.66	3 528.02	8 555.64	63 987
2009	14 357.65	4 624.53	9 733.13	74 728
2010	16 249.29	5 396.19	10 853.11	70 918
2011	18 920.43	5 925.39	12 995.04	82 168
2012	21 512.01	6 644.11	14 867.90	90 370
2013	23 097.35	7 251.30	15 846.05	95 635
2014	24 057.05	7 409.90	16 647.15	99 177
2015	23 384.73	8 184.76	15 199.97	96 612
2016	25 112.99	9 416.99	15 696.00	103 786
2017	25 763.20	9 560.65	16 202.54	106 533
2018	28 569.24	10 170.61	18 398.63	117 871

注：本表数据由中国人民银行上海总部提供。 1997 年~1999 年，个人存款余额为中资金融机构人民币储蓄存款余额；2000 年~2010 年，个人存款余额为中外资金融机构本外币储蓄存款余额；2011 年~2016 年，个人存款余额含中外资金融机构本外币活期存款余额、定期存款余额、结构性存款余额、保证金存款余额等。

Note: Data in this table are provided by Shanghai Headquarters of the People's Bank of China. From 1997 to 1999, the household deposits refer to RMB savings deposits in domestic funded financial institutions. From 2000 to 2010, the household deposits refer to all personal savings deposits in foreign and domestic funded financial institutions. From 2011 to 2016, the household deposits include current deposits、time deposits、structured deposits、margin deposit for security and so on.

表 10.5　全市居民收支情况(2015~2018)
BASIC STATISTICS OF INCOME AND EXPENDITURE OF RESIDENTS

单位:元

指　标	Indicators	2015	2016	2017	2018
居民人均可支配收入	**Per Capita Disposable Income of Residents**	**49 867**	**54 305**	**58 988**	**64 183**
工资性收入	Wages	30 499	32 718	34 365	37 137
经营净收入	Net Business Income	1 319	1 399	1 533	1 821
财产净收入	Net Property Income	7 173	7 684	9 030	9 666
转移净收入	Net Transferred Income	10 876	12 504	14 060	15 559
居民人均消费支出	**Per Capita Consumption Expenditure of Residents**	**34 784**	**37 458**	**39 792**	**43 351**
食品烟酒	Food, Cigarettes and Liquors	9 272	9 564	10 006	10 728
衣　着	Clothing	1 623	1 734	1 733	2 037
居　住	Residence	11 308	12 264	13 709	14 209
生活用品及服务	Living Goods and Services	1 485	1 755	1 825	2 096
交通通信	Transportation	4 206	4 228	4 058	4 881
教育文化娱乐	Education, Culture and Entertainment	3 718	4 174	4 686	5 049
医疗保健	Medicine and Medical Services	2 268	2 721	2 602	3 070
其他用品及服务	Other Goods and Services	904	1 018	1 173	1 281

表 10.6　全市居民收支比上年名义增长(2015~2018)
GROWTH RATE OF INCOME AND EXPENDITURE OF RESIDENTS ON PRECEDING YEAR

单位:%

指　标	Indicators	2015	2016	2017	2018
居民人均可支配收入	**Per Capita Disposable Income of Residents**	**8.5**	**8.9**	**8.6**	**8.8**
工资性收入	Wages	6.1	7.3	5.0	8.1
经营净收入	Net Business Income	-4.2	6.0	9.6	18.8
财产净收入	Net Property Income	10.3	7.1	17.5	7.0
转移净收入	Net Transferred Income	16.5	15.0	12.4	10.7
居民人均消费支出	**Per Capita Consumption Expenditure of Residents**	**5.2**	**7.7**	**6.2**	**8.9**
食品烟酒	Food, Cigarettes and Liquors	2.9	3.2	4.6	7.2
衣　着	Clothing	0.6	6.9	平	17.5
居　住	Residence	4.8	8.5	11.8	3.6
生活用品及服务	Living Goods and Services	-3.1	18.2	4.0	14.8
交通通信	Transportation and Communication	17.0	0.5	-4.0	20.3
教育文化娱乐	Education, Culture and Entertainment	12.3	12.3	12.2	7.7
医疗保健	Medicine and Medical Services	2.0	19.9	-4.4	18.0
其他用品及服务	Other Goods and Services	-8.4	12.5	15.3	9.2

表 10.7 城镇常住居民收支情况(2015~2018)
BASIC STATISTICS OF INCOME AND EXPENDITURE OF URBAN RESIDENTS

单位:元

指 标	Indicators	2015	2016	2017	2018
居民人均可支配收入	**Per Capita Disposable Income of Residents**	**52 962**	**57 692**	**62 596**	**68 034**
工资性收入	Wages	32 010	34 339	35 995	39 146
经营净收入	Net Business Income	1 303	1 400	1 551	1 829
财产净收入	Net Property Income	7 915	8 487	9 976	10 653
转移净收入	Net Transferred Income	11 734	13 466	15 074	16 406
居民人均消费支出	**Per Capita Consumption Expenditure of Residents**	**36 946**	**39 857**	**42 304**	**46 015**
食品烟酒	Food, Cigarettes and Liquors	9 691	10 015	10 456	11 104
衣 着	Clothing	1 711	1 835	1 827	2 139
居 住	Residence	12 137	13 216	14 749	15 376
生活用品及服务	Living Goods and Services	1 573	1 868	1 928	2 205
交通通信	Transportation	4 457	4 447	4 253	5 108
教育文化娱乐	Education, Culture and Entertainment	4 046	4 534	5 087	5 491
医疗保健	Medicine and Medical Services	2 362	2 840	2 735	3 222
其他用品及服务	Other Goods and Services	969	1 102	1 269	1 370

表 10.8 城镇常住居民收支比上年名义增长(2015~2018)
GROWTH RATE OF INCOME AND EXPENDITURE OF URBAN RESIDENTS ON PRECEDING YEAR

单位:%

指 标	Indicators	2015	2016	2017	2018
居民人均可支配收入	**Per Capita Disposable Income of Residents**	**8.4**	**8.9**	**8.5**	**8.7**
工资性收入	Wages	6.0	7.3	4.8	8.8
经营净收入	Net Business Income	-4.9	7.5	10.8	17.9
财产净收入	Net Property Income	10.3	7.2	17.5	6.8
转移净收入	Net Transferred Income	16.4	14.8	11.9	8.8
居民人均消费支出	**Per Capita Consumption Expenditure of Residents**	**5.0**	**7.9**	**6.1**	**8.8**
食品烟酒	Food, Cigarettes and Liquors	2.7	3.3	4.4	6.2
衣 着	Clothing	0.7	7.2	-0.4	17.1
居 住	Residence	4.4	8.9	11.6	4.3
生活用品及服务	Living Goods and Services	-3.5	18.8	3.2	14.4
交通通信	Transportation and Communication	17.2	-0.2	-4.4	20.1
教育文化娱乐	Education, Culture and Entertainment	12.2	12	12.2	7.9
医疗保健	Medicine and Medical Services	1.5	20.3	-3.7	17.8
其他用品及服务	Other Goods and Services	-8.4	13.7	15.1	8.0

表 10.9 全市居民可支配收入及构成(2015~2018)
DISPOSABLE INCOME AND ITS COMPOSITION OF WHOLE CITY RESIDENTS

指 标	Indicators	2015	2016	2017	2018
可支配收入(元/人)	**Disposable Income(yuan/person)**	**49 867**	**54 305**	**58 988**	**64 183**
工资性收入	Wages	30 499	32 718	34 365	37 137
经营净收入	Net Business Income	1 319	1 399	1 533	1 821
财产净收入	Net Property Income	7 173	7 684	9 030	9 666
转移净收入	Net Transferred Income	10 876	12 504	14 060	15 559
可支配收入构成(%)	**Composition of Disposable Income**	**100.0**	**100.0**	**100.0**	**100.0**
工资性收入	Wages	61.2	60.3	58.3	57.9
经营净收入	Net Business Income	2.6	2.6	2.6	2.8
财产净收入	Net Property Income	14.4	14.1	15.3	15.1
转移净收入	Net Transferred Income	21.8	23.0	23.8	24.2

表 10.10 城镇常住居民可支配收入及构成(2015~2018)
DISPOSABLE INCOME AND ITS COMPOSITION OF URBAN RESIDENTS

指 标	Indicators	2015	2016	2017	2018
可支配收入(元/人)	**Disposable Income(yuan/person)**	**52 962**	**57 692**	**62 596**	**68 034**
工资性收入	Wages	32 010	34 339	35 995	39 146
经营净收入	Net Business Income	1 303	1 400	1 551	1 829
财产净收入	Net Property Income	7 915	8 487	9 976	10 653
转移净收入	Net Transferred Income	11 734	13 466	15 074	16 406
可支配收入构成(%)	**Composition of Disposable Income**	**100.0**	**100.0**	**100.0**	**100.0**
工资性收入	Wages	60.4	59.5	57.5	57.5
经营净收入	Net Business Income	2.5	2.4	2.5	2.7
财产净收入	Net Property Income	14.9	14.7	15.9	15.7
转移净收入	Net Transferred Income	22.2	23.4	24.1	24.1

表 10.11 全市居民消费支出(2015~2018)
CONSUMPTION EXPENDITURE OF WHOLE CITY RESIDENTS

单位:元/人(yuan/person)

指标	Indicators	2015	2016	2017	2018
消费支出	**Consumption Expenditure**	**34 784**	**37 458**	**39 792**	**43 351**
食品烟酒	Food, Cigarettes and Liquors	9 272	9 564	10 006	10 728
#食　品	Food	5 905	6 114	6 238	6 276
在外饮食(不含食堂用餐)	Dining Out(excluding the canteen)	2 191	2 267	2 576	3 207
衣　着	Clothing	1 623	1 734	1 733	2 037
衣　类	Garments	1 270	1 354	1 379	1 665
鞋　类	Shoes	353	380	354	372
居　住	Residence	11 308	12 264	13 709	14 209
#租赁房房租	Rents	829	717	727	1 584
水电燃料及其他	Water, Electricity, Fuel and Others	951	1 001	1 037	1 161
生活用品及服务	Living Goods and Services	1 485	1 755	1 825	2 096
#家用器具	Home Appliances	335	449	442	515
家庭日用杂品	Household Daily Groceries	341	374	370	405
交通通信	Transportation and Communication	4 206	4 228	4 058	4 881
交　通	Transportation	2 913	3 017	2 826	3 669
通　信	Communication	1 293	1 211	1 232	1 212
教育文化娱乐	Education, Culture and Entertainment	3 718	4 174	4 686	5 049
教　育	Education	1 345	1 536	1 677	2 263
文化和娱乐	Culture and Entertainment	2 373	2 638	3 008	2 786
医疗保健	Medicine and Medical Services	2 268	2 721	2 602	3 070
医疗器具及药品	Medical Devices and Drugs	400	459	482	518
医疗服务	Medical Service	1 868	2 262	2 121	2 552
其他用品及服务	Other Goods and Services	904	1 018	1 173	1 281

表 10.12 城镇常住居民消费支出(2015~2018)
CONSUMPTION EXPENDITURE OF URBAN RESIDENTS

单位:元/人(yuan/person)

指 标	Indicators	2015	2016	2017	2018
消费支出	**Consumption Expenditure**	**36 946**	**39 857**	**42 304**	**46 015**
食品烟酒	Food,Cigarettes and Liquors	9 691	10 015	10 456	11 104
#食 品	Food	6 129	6 346	6 465	6 449
在外饮食(不含食堂用餐)	Dining Out(excluding the canteen)	2 387	2 472	2 784	3 428
衣 着	Clothing	1 711	1 835	1 827	2 139
衣 类	Garments	1 343	1 436	1 458	1 754
鞋 类	Shoes	368	399	369	385
居 住	Residence	12 137	13 216	14 749	15 376
#租赁房房租	Rents	870	757	753	1 701
水电燃料及其他	Water,Electricity,Fuel and Others	973	1 029	1 063	1 191
生活用品及服务	Living Goods and Services	1 573	1 868	1 928	2 205
#家用器具	Home Appliances	355	476	458	535
家庭日用杂品	Household Daily Groceries	354	389	386	415
交通通信	Transportation and Communication	4 457	4 447	4 253	5 108
交 通	Transportation	3 113	3 192	2 978	3 850
通 信	Communication	1 344	1 255	1 276	1 258
教育文化娱乐	Education,Culture and Entertainment	4 046	4 534	5 087	5 491
教 育	Education	1 453	1 636	1 789	2 452
文化和娱乐	Culture and Entertainment	2 593	2 898	3 298	3 039
医疗保健	Medicine and Medical Services	2 362	2 840	2 735	3 222
医疗器具及药品	Medical Devices and Drugs	425	485	515	534
医疗服务	Medical Service	1 937	2 355	2 220	2 688
其他用品及服务	Other Goods and Services	969	1 102	1 269	1 370

表 10.13 全市居民消费支出及构成(2015~2018)
CONSUMPTION EXPENDITURE AND ITS COMPOSITION OF WHOLE CITY RESIDENTS

指 标	Indicators	2015	2016	2017	2018
消费支出(元/人)	**Consumption Expenditure(yuan/person)**	**34 784**	**37 458**	**39 792**	**43 351**
食品烟酒	Food, Cigarettes and Liquors	9 272	9 564	10 006	10 728
衣　着	Clothing	1 623	1 734	1 733	2 037
居　住	Residence	11 308	12 264	13 709	14 209
生活用品及服务	Living Goods and Services	1 485	1 755	1 825	2 096
交通通信	Transportation and Communication	4 206	4 228	4 058	4 881
教育文化娱乐	Education, Culture and Entertainment	3 718	4 174	4 686	5 049
医疗保健	Medicine and Medical Services	2 268	2 721	2 602	3 070
其他用品及服务	Other Goods and Services	904	1 018	1 173	1 281
消费支出构成(%)	**Composition of Consumption Expenditure(%)**	**100**	**100.0**	**100**	**100**
食品烟酒	Food, Cigarettes and Liquors	26.6	25.5	25.1	24.7
衣　着	Clothing	4.7	4.6	4.4	4.7
居　住	Residence	32.5	32.7	34.5	32.8
生活用品及服务	Living Goods and Services	4.3	4.7	4.6	4.8
交通通信	Transportation and Communication	12.1	11.3	10.2	11.3
教育文化娱乐	Education, Culture and Entertainment	10.7	11.2	11.8	11.6
医疗保健	Medicine and Medical Services	6.5	7.3	6.5	7.1
其他用品及服务	Other Goods and Services	2.6	2.7	2.9	3.0

注：因指标口径调整，"食品烟酒"占"消费支出"比重与历史数据不可比，表 10.14 同。

Note: Because of the adjustment of statistical coverage, the proportion of "food, cigarettes and liquors" in the "consumption expenditure" cannot be compared with the historical data. Same as table 10.14.

表 10.14 城镇常住居民消费支出及构成(2015~2018)
CONSUMPTION EXPENDITURE AND ITS COMPOSITION OF URBAN RESIDENTS

指标	Indicators	2015	2016	2017	2018
消费支出(元/人)	**Consumption Expenditure(yuan/person)**	**36 946**	**39 857**	**42 304**	**46 015**
食品烟酒	Food,Cigarettes and Liquors	9 691	10 015	10 456	11 104
衣着	Clothing	1 711	1 835	1 827	2 139
居住	Residence	12 137	13 216	14 749	15 376
生活用品及服务	Living Goods and Services	1 573	1 868	1 928	2 205
交通通信	Transportation and Communication	4 457	4 447	4 253	5 108
教育文化娱乐	Education,Culture and Entertainment	4 046	4 534	5 087	5 491
医疗保健	Medicine and Medical Services	2 362	2 840	2 735	3 222
其他用品及服务	Other Goods and Services	969	1 102	1 269	1 370
消费支出构成(%)	**Composition of Consumption Expenditure(%)**	**100.0**	**100.0**	**100.0**	**100.0**
食品烟酒	Food,Cigarettes and Liquors	26.2	25.1	24.7	24.1
衣着	Clothing	4.6	4.6	4.3	4.7
居住	Residence	32.8	33.2	34.9	33.4
生活用品及服务	Living Goods and Services	4.3	4.7	4.6	4.8
交通通信	Transportation and Communication	12.1	11.1	10.0	11.1
教育文化娱乐	Education,Culture and Entertainment	11.0	11.4	12.0	11.9
医疗保健	Medicine and Medical Services	6.4	7.1	6.5	7.0
其他用品及服务	Other Goods and Services	2.6	2.8	3.0	3.0

表 10.15 每百户居民家庭年末耐用消费品拥有量(2015~2018)
DURABLE CONSUMER GOODS OWNED BY EACH HUNDRED HOUSEHOLDS AT YEAR-END

指 标	Indicators	2015	2016	2017	2018
家用汽车(辆)	Family Cars(vehicle)	24	29	31	37
电动助力车(辆)	Electric Booster Vehicles(vehicle)	58	65	67	68
洗衣机(台)	Washing Machine (unit)	89	93	95	93
电冰箱(柜)(台)	Refrigerators or Freezers(unit)	96	99	100	100
微波炉(台)	Microwave Ovens (unit)	84	87	88	85
彩色电视机(台)	Colour Televisions(unit)	174	183	186	173
空 调(台)	Air-conditioner(unit)	181	197	203	200
热水器(台)	Water Heaters(unit)	88	93	95	95
排油烟机(台)	Range Hoods(unit)	74	78	81	81
固定电话(线)	Fixed Telephones(line)	75	73	73	56
移动电话(部)	Mobile Phones(unit)	217	228	230	220
#接入互联网	Of Which: Access to the Internet	153	185	196	194
计算机(台)	Computers(unit)	117	131	131	99
#接入互联网	Of Which: Access to the Internet	111	125	127	95
照相机(架)	Camera(set)	50	48	48	33
健身器材(套)	Health Equipment(set)	6	7	8	8
空气净化器(含新风系统)(台)	Air Purifier(Fresh Air System Included)			6	16
吸尘器(台)	Dust Catcher(unit)			14	33

注：2018 年住户调查进行样本轮换，部分数据可能存在波动。表 10.16 和 10.17 同。
Note: Sample rotation was conducted in household survey in 2018, and some data may fluctuate. Same as table 10.16 and 10.17.

表 10.16 每百户城镇常住居民家庭年末耐用消费品拥有量(2015~2018)
DURABLE CONSUMER GOODS OWNED BY EACH HUNDRED URBAN HOUSEHOLDS AT YEAR-END

指 标	Indicators	2015	2016	2017	2018
家用汽车(辆)	Family Cars(vehicle)	26	30	32	38
电动助力车(辆)	Electric Booster Vehicles(vehicle)	51	56	59	61
洗衣机(台)	Washing Machine (unit)	92	95	96	94
电冰箱(柜)(台)	Refrigerators or Freezers(unit)	97	100	101	100
微波炉(台)	Microwave Ovens (unit)	87	89	90	86
彩色电视机(台)	Colour Televisions(unit)	177	185	188	175
空 调(台)	Air-conditioner(unit)	191	205	210	207
热水器(台)	Water Heaters(unit)	91	95	97	96
排油烟机(台)	Range Hoods(unit)	79	82	85	85
固定电话(线)	Fixed Telephones(line)	77	74	75	56
移动电话(部)	Mobile Phones(unit)	221	230	233	223
#接入互联网	Of Which: Access to the Internet	161	192	203	201
计算机(台)	Computers(unit)	126	141	140	107
#接入互联网	Of Which: Access to the Internet	120	135	136	102
照相机(架)	Camera(set)	55	52	52	36
健身器材(套)	Health Equipment(set)	6	8	9	8
空气净化器(含新风系统)(台)	Air Purifier(Fresh Air System Included)			6	18
吸尘器(台)	Dust Catcher(unit)			15	36

表 10.17 每百户农村常住居民家庭年末耐用消费品拥有量(2015~2018)
DURABLE CONSUMER GOODS OWNED BY EACH HUNDRED RURAL HOUSEHOLDS AT YEAR-END

指 标	Indicators	2015	2016	2017	2018
家用汽车(辆)	Family Cars(vehicle)	14	21	24	28
电动助力车(辆)	Electric Booster Vehicles(vehicle)	121	139	140	129
洗衣机(台)	Washing Machine (unit)	70	81	83	83
电冰箱(柜)(台)	Refrigerators or Freezers(unit)	84	91	93	101
微波炉(台)	Microwave Ovens (unit)	65	73	73	75
彩色电视机(台)	Colour Televisions(unit)	148	166	169	162
空 调(台)	Air-conditioner(unit)	101	129	136	142
热水器(台)	Water Heaters(unit)	66	76	79	85
排油烟机(台)	Range Hoods(unit)	38	44	46	49
固定电话(线)	Fixed Telephones(line)	61	61	60	50
移动电话(部)	Mobile Phones(unit)	187	208	210	197
#接入互联网	Of Which: Access to the Internet	94	126	134	133
计算机(台)	Computers(unit)	47	51	53	37
#接入互联网	Of Which: Access to the Internet	40	47	50	35
照相机(架)	Camera(set)	12	12	14	7
健身器材(套)	Health Equipment(set)	1	2	2	3
空气净化器(含新风系统)(台)	Air Purifier(Fresh Air System Included)			5	2
吸尘器(台)	Dust Catcher(unit)			4	9

表 10.18 主要年份城乡居民家庭人均收入及消费支出
PER CAPITA INCOME AND CONSUMPTION EXPENDITURE OF URBAN AND RURAL HOUSEHOLDS IN MAIN YEARS

年 份 Year	城市居民家庭人均可支配收入（元） Per Capita Disposable Income of Urban Households (yuan)	农村居民家庭人均可支配收入（元） Per Capita Disposable Income of Rural Households (yuan)	城市居民家庭人均消费支出（元） Per Capita Consumption Expenditure of Urban Households (yuan)	农村居民家庭人均消费支出（元） Per Capita Consumption Expenditure of Rural Households (yuan)
1980	637	401	553	323
1985	1 075	806	992	778
1990	2 183	1 665	1 937	1 262
1995	7 172	4 246	5 868	3 368
1996	8 159	4 846	6 763	3 868
1997	8 439	5 277	6 820	4 228
1998	8 773	5 407	6 866	4 207
1999	10 932	5 481	8 248	3 867
2000	11 718	5 565	8 868	4 138
2001	12 883	5 850	9 336	4 753
2002	13 250	6 212	10 464	5 311
2003	14 867	6 658	11 040	5 670
2004	16 683	7 337	12 631	6 329
2005	18 645	8 342	13 773	7 265
2006	20 668	9 213	14 762	8 006
2007	23 623	10 222	17 255	8 845
2008	26 675	11 385	19 398	9 115
2009	28 838	12 324	20 992	9 804
2010	31 838	13 746	23 200	10 225
2011	36 230	15 644	25 102	11 272
2012	40 188	17 401	26 253	12 096
2013	43 851	19 208	28 155	13 425
2014	47 710	21 192	30 520	15 291

表 10.19 城市居民家庭生活基本情况(1980~2014)
BASIC STATISTICS OF URBAN HOUSEHOLDS

年 份 Year	调查户数 (户) Number of Households Surveyed (household)	平均每人 可支配收入 (元) Per Capita Disposable Income (yuan)	平均每人 消费支出 (元) Per Capita Consumption Expenditures (yuan)	可支配收入 比上年增长(%) (按当年价格) Growth Rate of Disposable Income on Preceding Year(%) (at Current Price)	消费支出 比上年增长(%) (按当年价格) Growth Rate of Consumption Expenditure on Preceding Year(%) (at Current Price)	恩格尔 系数(%) Engel Coefficient (%)
1980	500	637	553	32.5	28.8	56.0
1981	500	637	585	平	5.7	56.8
1982	500	659	576	3.5	-1.5	58.9
1983	500	686	615	4.0	6.9	58.5
1984	500	834	726	21.6	18.0	56.5
1985	500	1 075	992	28.9	36.6	52.1
1986	500	1 293	1 170	20.3	18.0	52.7
1987	500	1 437	1 282	11.1	9.6	54.4
1988	500	1 723	1 648	19.9	28.6	52.7
1989	500	1 976	1 812	14.6	9.9	55.8
1990	500	2 183	1 937	10.5	6.9	56.5
1991	500	2 486	2 167	13.9	11.9	56.9
1992	500	3 009	2 509	21.1	15.8	55.9
1993	500	4 277	3 530	42.2	40.7	53.1
1994	500	5 868	4 669	37.2	32.3	53.5
1995	500	7 172	5 868	22.2	25.7	53.4
1996	500	8 159	6 763	13.8	15.3	50.7
1997	500	8 439	6 820	3.4	0.8	51.7
1998	500	8 773	6 866	4.0	0.7	50.6
1999	500	10 932	8 248	24.6	20.1	45.2
2000	500	11 718	8 868	7.2	7.5	44.5
2001	500	12 883	9 336	9.9	5.3	43.4
2002	500	13 250	10 464	11.5	11.4	39.4
2003	500	14 867	11 040	12.2	5.5	37.2
2004	1 000	16 683	12 631	12.2	14.4	36.4
2005	1 000	18 645	13 773	11.8	9.0	35.9
2006	1 000	20 668	14 762	10.8	7.2	35.6
2007	1 000	23 623	17 255	14.3	16.9	35.5
2008	1 000	26 675	19 398	12.9	12.4	36.6
2009	1 000	28 838	20 992	8.1	8.2	35.0
2010	1 000	31 838	23 200	10.4	10.5	33.5
2011	1 000	36 230	25 102	13.8	8.2	35.5
2012	1 000	40 188	26 253	10.9	4.6	36.8
2013	1 000	43 851	28 155	9.1	7.2	34.9
2014	1 000	47 710	30 520	8.8	8.4	35.0

①本表数据为城市居民家庭收支抽样调查资料，由国家统计局上海调查总队提供。
②2002 年起，人均可支配收入不包括出售财物收入和个人交纳的社会保障支出。 其他年份按原口径计算。
③平均每人可支配收入和平均每人消费支出增长按同口径计算的。
❶Data in this table are obtained from the sample survey of urban households and provided by Survey Office of the National Bureau of Statistics in Shanghai.
❷Incomes from selling properties and social security expenditure are excluded from disposable income since 2002.Other years follow the original caliber.
❸Growth of per Capita Disposable Income and growth of per Capita Consumption Expenditures are calculated.

表 10.20　主要年份城市居民家庭人均可支配收入
PER CAPITA DISPOSABLE INCOME OF URBAN HOUSEHOLDS IN MAIN YEARS

单位：元(yuan)

年　份 Year	人均可支配收入 Average per Capita Disposable Income	工资性收入 Salaries	经营净收入 Net Income from Household Business	财产性收入 Property Income	转移性收入 Transferred Income
1980	637	551			86
1985	1 075	794	1		280
1990	2 183	1 548	1	21	613
1991	2 486	1 780		29	677
1992	3 009	2 138	3	44	824
1993	4 277	3 099	4	37	1 137
1994	5 868	4 224	28	54	1 562
1995	7 172	5 002	69	92	2 009
1996	8 159	5 889	87	61	2 122
1997	8 439	5 969	150	69	2 251
1998	8 773	6 004	98	57	2 614
1999	10 932	7 326	156	68	3 382
2000	11 718	7 832	120	65	3 701
2001	12 883	7 975	119	39	4 750
2002	13 250	7 915	436	94	4 805
2003	14 867	10 097	377	130	4 263
2004	16 683	11 422	507	215	4 539
2005	18 645	12 409	798	292	5 146
2006	20 668	13 962	959	300	5 447
2007	23 623	16 598	1 158	369	5 498
2008	26 675	18 909	1 399	369	5 998
2009	28 838	19 811	1 435	474	7 118
2010	31 838	21 745	1 628	511	7 954
2011	36 230	24 454	1 994	633	9 149
2012	40 188	26 752	2 267	576	10 593
2013	43 851	28 518	2 317	788	12 228
2014	47 710	30 629	2 345	846	13 890

表 10.21　主要年份城市居民家庭人均可支配收入与消费支出
PER CAPITA ANNUAL DISPOSABLE INCOME AND CONSUMPTION EXPENDITURES OF URBAN HOUSEHOLDS IN MAIN YEARS

单位：元(yuan)

指　标	Indicators	2000	2005	2010	2014
人均可支配收入	**Per Capita Disposable Income**	**11 718**	**18 645**	**31 838**	**47 710**
低收入户	Low Income	6 840	7 851	14 996	24 317
中低收入户	Medium-low Income	8 815	11 800	21 780	34 120
中间收入户	Medium Income	10 529	15 668	27 484	40 799
中高收入户	Medium-high Income	12 892	21 313	35 120	52 089
高收入户	High Income	19 959	37 722	62 465	93 901
人均消费支出	**Per Capita Consumption Expenditures**	**8 868**	**13 773**	**23 200**	**30 520**
低收入户	Low Income	6 272	7 698	12 555	17 879
中低收入户	Medium-low Income	7 516	9 807	15 970	20 881
中间收入户	Medium Income	8 555	11 524	21 611	27 974
中高收入户	Medium-high Income	9 445	15 024	26 773	35 904
高收入户	High Income	12 763	25 470	40 744	53 734

表 10.22 主要年份城市居民家庭人均消费支出
PER CAPITA CONSUMPTION EXPENDITURES OF URBAN HOUSEHOLDS IN MAIN YEARS

单位:元

年份 Year	消费支出 Total Consumption Expenditures	食品 Food	衣着 Clothing	居住 Residence	家庭设备用品及服务 Household Facilities, Articles and Services	医疗保健 Medicines and Medical Services	交通和通信 Traffic and Communi-cations	教育文化娱乐服务 Education, Culture and Recreation Services	其他商品和服务 Other Commodities and Services
1980	553	310	79	26	50	7	20	49	12
1985	992	517	148	43	131	5	30	91	27
1990	1 937	1 095	208	90	196	11	58	231	48
1995	5 868	3 131	561	401	637	113	321	508	196
1996	6 763	3 429	590	416	614	148	496	827	243
1997	6 820	3 526	552	605	525	197	397	828	190
1998	6 866	3 477	472	674	453	261	406	893	230
1999	8 248	3 731	551	842	772	347	583	1 094	328
2000	8 868	3 947	567	794	683	501	759	1 287	330
2001	9 336	4 056	577	796	579	558	958	1 422	390
2002	10 464	4 120	613	1 189	653	734	1 115	1 668	372
2003	11 040	4 102	751	1 280	792	603	1 259	1 834	419
2004	12 631	4 593	797	1 327	780	762	1 703	2 195	474
2005	13 773	4 940	940	1 412	800	797	1 984	2 273	627
2006	14 762	5 249	1 027	1 436	877	763	2 333	2 432	645
2007	17 255	6 125	1 330	1 412	959	857	3 154	2 654	764
2008	19 398	7 109	1 521	1 646	1 182	755	3 373	2 875	937
2009	20 992	7 345	1 593	1 913	1 365	1 002	3 499	3 139	1 136
2010	23 200	7 777	1 794	2 166	1 800	1 006	4 076	3 363	1 218
2011	25 102	8 906	2 054	2 226	1 826	1 141	3 808	3 746	1 395
2012	26 253	9 656	2 111	1 790	1 906	1 017	4 564	3 724	1 485
2013	28 155	9 823	2 032	2 848	1 706	1 350	4 736	4 122	1 538
2014	30 520	10 677	2 038	3 031	1 779	1 449	4 885	4 931	1 730

表 10.23 主要年份城市居民家庭人均消费支出构成
COMPOSITION OF PER CAPITA CONSUMPTION EXPENDITURES OF URBAN HOUSEHOLDS IN MAIN YEARS

单位:%

年份 Year	消费支出 Total Consumption Expenditures	食品 Food	衣着 Clothing	居住 Residence	家庭设备用品及服务 Household Facilities, Articles and Services	医疗保健 Medicines and Medical Services	交通和通信 Traffic and Communi-cations	教育文化娱乐服务 Education, Culture and Recreation Services	其他商品和服务 Other Commodities and Services
1980	100	56.0	14.3	4.7	9.0	1.3	3.6	8.9	2.2
1985	100	52.1	14.9	4.4	13.2	0.5	3.0	9.2	2.7
1990	100	56.5	10.7	4.7	10.1	0.6	3.0	11.9	2.5
1995	100	53.4	9.6	6.8	10.8	1.9	5.5	8.7	3.3
1996	100	50.7	8.7	6.2	9.1	2.2	7.3	12.2	3.6
1997	100	51.7	8.1	8.9	7.7	2.9	5.8	12.1	2.8
1998	100	50.6	6.9	9.8	6.6	3.8	5.9	13.0	3.4
1999	100	45.2	6.7	10.2	9.3	4.2	7.1	13.3	4.0
2000	100	44.5	6.4	9.0	7.7	5.6	8.6	14.5	3.7
2001	100	43.4	6.2	8.5	6.2	6.0	10.3	15.2	4.2
2002	100	39.4	5.9	11.4	6.2	7.0	10.7	15.9	3.5
2003	100	37.2	6.8	11.6	7.2	5.4	11.4	16.6	3.8
2004	100	36.4	6.3	10.5	6.2	6.0	13.5	17.4	3.7
2005	100	35.9	6.8	10.2	5.8	5.8	14.4	16.5	4.6
2006	100	35.6	6.9	9.7	5.9	5.2	15.8	16.5	4.4
2007	100	35.5	7.7	8.2	5.5	5.0	18.3	15.4	4.4
2008	100	36.6	7.9	8.5	6.1	3.9	17.4	14.8	4.8
2009	100	35.0	7.6	9.1	6.5	4.8	16.7	14.9	5.4
2010	100	33.5	7.7	9.3	7.8	4.3	17.6	14.5	5.3
2011	100	35.5	8.2	8.9	7.3	4.5	15.2	14.9	5.5
2012	100	36.8	8.0	6.8	7.3	3.9	17.4	14.2	5.6
2013	100	34.9	7.2	10.1	6.1	4.8	16.8	14.6	5.5
2014	100	35.0	6.7	9.9	5.8	4.7	16.0	16.2	5.7

表 10.24　农村居民家庭生活基本情况(1990~2014)
BASIC STATISTICS OF RURAL HOUSEHOLDS

年　份 Year	调查户数(户) Number of Households Surveyed (household)	平均每人可支配收入(元) Disposable Income Per Capita (yuan)	平均每人生活消费支出(元) Per Capita Consumption Expenditures (yuan)	平均每人可支配收入指数(以 1990 年为 100) Index of Per Capita Disposable Income (1990=100)	平均每人生活消费支出指数(以 1990 年为 100) Index of Per Capita Consumption Expenditures (1990=100)	平均每人年底居住房屋面积(平方米) Per Capita Living Space Year-end (sq.m)
1990	1 000	1 665	1 262	100.0	100.0	37.08
1991	600	2 003	1 540	120.3	122.0	39.60
1992	600	2 226	1 967	133.7	155.9	42.07
1993	600	2 727	2 200	163.8	174.3	44.22
1994	600	3 437	2 715	206.4	215.1	44.15
1995	600	4 246	3 368	255.0	266.9	43.08
1996	600	4 846	3 868	291.1	306.5	45.47
1997	600	5 277	4 228	316.9	335.0	46.44
1998	600	5 407	4 207	324.7	333.4	47.24
1999	600	5 481	3 867	329.2	306.4	49.00
2000	600	5 565	4 138	334.2	327.9	53.58
2001	600	5 850	4 753	351.4	376.6	54.70
2002	600	6 212	5 311	373.1	420.8	57.08
2003	600	6 658	5 670	399.9	449.3	59.03
2004	600	7 337	6 329	440.7	501.5	59.84
2005	600	8 342	7 265	501.0	575.7	56.56
2006	600	9 213	8 006	553.3	634.4	59.99
2007	600	10 222	8 845	613.9	700.9	61.22
2008	600	11 385	9 115	683.8	722.3	62.30
2009	600	12 324	9 804	740.2	776.9	60.18
2010	600	13 746	10 225	825.6	810.2	59.68
2011	1 200	15 644	11 272	939.6	893.2	58.90
2012	1 200	17 401	12 096	1 045.1	958.5	60.42
2013	1 200	19 208	13 425	1 153.6	1 063.8	58.48
2014	1 200	21 192	15 291	1 272.8	1 211.6	58.92

表 10.25 主要年份农村居民家庭人均可支配收入
PER CAPITA DISPOSABLE INCOME OF RURAL HOUSEHOLDS IN MAIN YEARS

指 标 Indicators	人均可支配收入(元) Per Capita Disposable Income (yuan)	工资性收入 Wages	家庭经营纯收入 Household Business Income	转移性和财产性收入 Property and Transferred Income	比重(以人均可支配收入为100) Proportion Per Capita Disposable Income =100)		
					工资性收入 Wages	家庭经营纯收入 Household Business Income	转移性和财产性收入 Property and Transferred Income
1990	1 665	1 066	539	60	64.0	32.4	3.6
1995	4 246	2 734	1 183	329	64.4	27.9	7.7
2000	5 565	4 310	934	321	77.4	16.8	5.8
2005	8 342	6 364	811	1 167	76.3	9.7	14.0
2006	9 213	6 892	766	1 555	74.8	8.3	16.9
2007	10 222	7 498	754	1 970	73.3	7.4	19.3
2008	11 385	8 182	711	2 492	71.9	6.2	21.9
2009	12 324	8 721	590	3 013	70.8	4.8	24.4
2010	13 746	9 606	589	3 551	69.9	4.3	25.8
2011	15 644	10 493	877	4 274	67.1	5.6	27.3
2012	17 401	11 496	905	5 000	66.1	5.2	28.7
2013	19 208	12 378	920	5 910	64.4	4.8	30.8
2014	21 192	13 430	1 035	6 727	63.4	4.9	31.7

注：2000 年前平均每人可支配收入按纯收入口径计算。 2011 年起，按可比口径计算，全年家庭经营纯收入增长为 22%；“土地征用补偿收入”不再列入财产性收入中。

Note: The per Capita Annual Disposable Income before 2000 refers to the Net Income. Since 2011, according to the calculation with comparable caliber, the growth rate of annual Household Business Income is 22%.Land Requisition Compensation Income is no longer included in the property income.

表 10.26 主要年份农村居民家庭人均可支配收入和人均生活消费支出
PER CAPITA DISPOSABLE INCOME AND LIVING EXPENDITURES FOR CONSUMPTION OF RURAL HOUSEHOLDS IN MAIN YEARS

单位:元(yuan)

年 份 Year	总平均 Average	低收入户 Low Income	中低收入户 Medium-low Income	中间收入户 Medium Income	中高收入户 Medium-high Income	高收入户 High Income
人均可支配收入	**Average per Capita Disposable Income**					
2000	5 565	2 330	3 906	5 264	6 725	10 405
2005	8 342	3 347	5 594	7 612	9 755	15 309
2006	9 213	3 830	6 194	8 412	10 714	16 843
2007	10 222	4 321	7 098	9 442	11 807	18 443
2008	11 385	4 690	8 065	10 487	13 094	20 748
2009	12 324	5 279	8 785	11 184	14 039	22 465
2010	13 746	5 968	10 107	12 929	16 327	24 536
2011	15 644	7 018	11 772	14 568	18 145	27 227
2012	17 401	7 707	13 071	16 490	20 340	29 180
2013	19 208	8 708	14 415	18 152	22 618	31 196
2014	21 192	10 476	16 375	20 693	25 129	32 631
人均生活消费支出	**Average per Capita Consumption Expenditures**					
2000	4 138	2 390	3 387	3 887	5 487	5 880
2005	7 265	4 618	5 690	6 317	7 059	12 975
2006	8 006	4 788	6 001	6 951	8 015	15 058
2007	8 845	4 890	6 077	7 305	9 541	17 317
2008	9 115	5 024	6 280	9 555	10 700	14 517
2009	9 804	5 472	6 266	9 026	12 843	16 035
2010	10 225	5 026	7 881	8 739	15 103	15 187
2011	11 272	6 979	9 881	11 701	11 654	16 531
2012	12 096	7 784	8 813	10 802	13 725	19 773
2013	13 425	8 011	10 048	12 150	15 793	20 775
2014	15 291	9 629	12 208	13 487	17 909	22 645

表 10.27 主要年份农村居民家庭人均生活消费支出
PER CAPITA CONSUMPTION EXPENDITURES OF RURAL HOUSEHOLDS IN MAIN YEARS

单位：元（yuan）

年 份 Year	生活消费支出 Total Consumption Expenditures	食 品 Food	衣 着 Clothing	居 住 Residence	家庭设备用品及服务 Household Facilities, Articles and Services	交通和通 信 Traffic and Communi-cations	文教娱乐用品及服务 Education, Culture and Recreation Articles and Services	医 疗保 健 Medicines and Medical Services	其他商品和服务 Other Commodities and Services
1990	1 262	586	107	272	129	6	59	33	70
1995	3 368	1 491	233	761	284	159	256	73	111
2000	4 138	1 823	201	724	225	279	559	209	118
2001	4 753	1 915	226	890	294	340	673	265	150
2002	5 311	1 872	226	1 392	281	462	661	280	137
2003	5 670	2 004	250	1 437	297	587	676	333	86
2004	6 329	2 191	280	1 446	344	720	806	425	117
2005	7 265	2 676	367	1 323	458	739	936	562	204
2006	8 006	3 024	418	1 658	481	780	920	549	176
2007	8 845	3 259	476	2 097	452	884	857	571	249
2008	9 115	3 732	467	1 806	504	880	850	697	179
2009	9 804	3 639	496	2 103	481	1 212	943	739	191
2010	10 225	3 807	554	2 070	528	1 459	1 012	585	210
2011	11 272	4 517	644	1 806	649	1 309	1 139	909	299
2012	12 096	4 837	704	1 834	646	1 705	1 088	1 029	253
2013	13 425	5 334	771	2 260	694	1 719	964	1 181	502
2014	15 291	6 188	801	2 747	712	1 891	1 069	1 308	575

表 10.28 主要年份农村居民家庭人均生活消费支出构成
COMPOSITION OF PER CAPITA CONSUMER EXPENDITURES OF RURAL HOUSEHOLDS IN MAIN YEARS

单位：%

年 份 Year	生活消费支出 Total Consumption Expenditures	食 品 Food	衣 着 Clothing	居 住 Residence	家庭设备用品及服务 Household Facilities, Articles and Services	交通和通 信 Traffic and Communi-cations	文教娱乐用品及服务 Education, Culture and Recreation Articles and Services	医 疗保 健 Medicines and Medical Services	其他商品和服务 Other Commodities and Services
1990	100	46.4	8.5	21.6	10.2	0.5	4.7	2.6	5.5
1995	100	44.3	6.9	22.6	8.4	4.7	7.6	2.2	3.3
2000	100	44.0	4.9	17.5	5.4	6.7	13.5	5.1	2.9
2001	100	40.3	4.7	18.7	6.2	7.1	14.2	5.6	3.2
2002	100	35.2	4.3	26.2	5.3	8.7	12.4	5.3	2.6
2003	100	35.4	4.4	25.3	5.2	10.4	11.9	5.9	1.5
2004	100	34.6	4.4	22.9	5.4	11.4	12.7	6.7	1.9
2005	100	36.8	5.1	18.2	6.3	10.2	12.9	7.7	2.8
2006	100	37.8	5.2	20.7	6.0	9.7	11.5	6.9	2.2
2007	100	36.8	5.4	23.7	5.1	10.0	9.7	6.5	2.8
2008	100	40.9	5.1	19.8	5.5	9.7	9.3	7.7	2.0
2009	100	37.1	5.1	21.5	4.9	12.4	9.6	7.5	1.9
2010	100	37.2	5.4	20.2	5.2	14.3	9.9	5.7	2.1
2011	100	40.1	5.7	16.0	5.8	11.6	10.1	8.1	2.6
2012	100	40.0	5.8	15.2	5.3	14.1	9.0	8.5	2.1
2013	100	39.7	5.8	16.8	5.2	12.8	7.2	8.8	3.7
2014	100	40.5	5.2	17.9	4.7	12.4	7.0	8.5	3.8

上 / 海 / 统 / 计 / 年 / 鉴

主要统计指标解释

第一部分　2015年以来上海居民收支与生活状况调查主要数据(新口径)(适用表10.1到表10.17)

■ 居民可支配收入(城镇/农村常住居民)

指居民可用于最终消费支出和储蓄的总和,即居民可用于自由支配的收入。既包括现金收入,也包括实物收入。按照收入的来源,可支配收入包含四项,分别为:工资性收入、经营净收入、财产净收入和转移净收入。

■ 居民消费支出(城镇/农村常住居民)

是指居民用于满足家庭日常生活消费需要的全部支出,既包括现金消费支出,也包括实物消费支出。消费支出可划分为食品烟酒、衣着、居住、生活用品及服务、交通通信、教育文化娱乐、医疗保健以及其他用品及服务八大类。

第二部分　1980~2014年城镇和农村住户调查主要数据(老口径)(适用表10.18到表10.28)

■ 城镇居民家庭可支配收入

指居民家庭可用于最终消费支出和其他非义务性支出以及储蓄的总和,即居民家庭可以用来自由支配的收入。它是家庭总收入扣除交纳的所得税、个人交纳的社会保障费以及调查户的记账补贴后的收入。

■ 城镇居民家庭消费支出

指居民家庭用于满足家庭日常生活消费需要的全部支出,包括食品、衣着、居住、家庭设备及用品、交通通信、文教娱乐、医疗保健、其他等八大类。消费支出构成是按照商品或服务的用途进行分类,如果消费支出的目的与用途不一致时,必须按照用途归入相应类内。

■农村居民家庭可支配收入

指农村居民家庭获得的经过初次分配与再分配后的收入。可支配收入可用于住户的最终消费、非义务性支出以及储蓄。

农村居民家庭可支配收入=总收入-家庭经营费用支出-税费支出-生产性固定资产折旧-财产性支出-转移性支出。

■ 农村居民家庭生活消费支出

指农村住户用于物质生活和精神生活方面的支出。包括食品,衣着,居住,家庭设备用品及服务,医疗保健,交通和通信,文化教育娱乐用品及服务,其他商品和服务等消费支出。

SHANGHAI STATISTICAL YEARBOOK

EXPLANATORY NOTES TO MAJOR STATISTICAL INDICATORS

Part I Main Data from Survey of Income and Expenditure and Living Conditions of Residents in Shanghai Since 2015(New Statistical Standard,applicable for table 10.1–10.17)

□ Disposable Income of Residents (urban / rural residents)

Refers to the sum of final consumption expenditure and savings of residents, which can be freely allocated by residents. It includes income in cash and in kind. In accordance with the source of income, disposable income includes four parts: wage income, operating income, net income from property and net transfer income.

□ Consumption Expenditures of Residents (urban / rural resident)

Refers to all the expenses that are used to meet the needs of the daily life of the household, including consumption in cash and in kind. Consumption spending can be divided into eight categories: food, alcohol and tobacco, clothing, housing, daily necessities and services, transportation and communication, education culture and entertainment, health care and other goods and services.

Part II Main Data from Urban and Rural Household Survey from 1980 to 2014(Old Statistical Standard,applicable for table 10.18 to 10.28)

□ Disposable Income of Urban Households

Refers to the actual income at the disposal of members of the households which can be used for final consumption, other non–compulsory expenditure and savings, which is part of the urban households′ income that can be disposed by the urban households themselves. It is the income after deducting personal income tax, social insurance paid by individuals and investigation allowance from the total income of the households. The income from selling properties and borrowing are not included.

□ Consumption Expenditures of Urban Households

Refers to all the expenditure paid by household for consumption in daily life, including 8 categories as follows: food; clothing; housing; household facilities and articles; traffic and communication; culture, education, and recreation; medical and health care; the others. Consumption expenditure is classified according to the use of goods or services. If the purpose and use of consumption expenditure are inconsistent, it should be included in the appropriate class according to the use.

□ Disposable Income of Rural Households

Refers to the actual income at the disposal of rural households after initial distribution and reallocation. Disposal Income can be used for final consumption, non–compulsory expenditure and savings.

Disposal Income of Rural Households=total household income– expenditure for household operations– taxes and fees– depreciation of productive fixed assets– expenses on properties–expenses on transfers.

□ Living Expenditures for Consumption of Rural Households

Refers to expenditures of material and culture life of rural household, including expenses on food, clothing, housing, household appliances and service, medical and health care, traffic and communication items, cultural, education and recreation items and service and other commodities and service.

第十一篇

CHAPTER 11

2019上海统计年鉴 SHANGHAI STATISTICAL YEARBOOK

城市建设

URBAN CONSTRUCTION

简要说明

一、本篇资料的主要内容

本篇资料反映上海市城市建设的规模、速度及综合水平等基本情况，主要内容包括：市政道路、房屋建筑、供水排水、供气、城市绿化等城市建设情况。

二、本篇资料的来源

城市基础设施建设、公共事业和市政建设投资统计资料依据上海市统计局制定的《固定资产投资统计报表制度》收集整理提供。

房屋建筑统计资料由上海市住房和城乡建设管理委员会汇总整理提供。

市政工程部分统计资料和供气统计资料由上海市住房和城乡建设管理委员会、上海市交通委员会汇总整理提供。

供水排水统计资料由上海市水务局汇总整理提供。

城市绿化统计资料由上海市绿化和市容管理局汇总整理提供。

三、本篇资料的统计范围

城市基础设施建设、公共事业和市政建设投资的统计资料执行范围同《固定资产投资篇》的执行范围。房屋建筑、市政工程、供水排水、供气、城市绿化的统计资料范围均是全市范围。

BRIEF INTRODUCTION

I. Main Contents

The data in this chapter reflect the basic conditions of the scale, growth rate, and overall level of urban construction of Shanghai. The main contents include municipal roads, house construction, water supply, drainage, gas supply, and urban afforestation.

II. Sources of data

Data on infrastructure construction, public facilities, urban construction investment are collected, prepared and provided by Shanghai Municipal Statistics Bureau in accordance with the Statistics Reporting Form System on the Fixed Asset Investment, which is stipulated by the Shanghai Municipal Statistics Bureau.

Data on house construction are collected, prepared, and provided by Shanghai Municipal Housing and Urban Rural Construction Management Commission.

Data on urban construction projects and gas supply are collected, prepared, and provided by Shanghai Municipal Housing and Urban and Rural Construction Management Commission and Shanghai Municipal Transportation Commission.

Data on water supply and drainage are collected, prepared, and provided by Shanghai Water Authority.

Data on urban afforestation are collected, prepared, and provided by Shanghai Municipal Afforestation & City Appearance and Environmental Sanitation Administration.

III. Scope and Coverage of Statistics

Coverage of data on urban infrastructure construction, public facilities, and urban construction investment is the same with that in the chapter of Fixed Assets Investment. Data on house construction, urban construction projects, water supply, drainage, gas supply, and urban afforestation cover the whole city.

表 11.1 主要年份城市基础设施投资额
URBAN INFRASTRUCTURE INVESTMENT IN MAIN YEARS

单位:亿元(100 million yuan)

年 份 Year	合 计 Total	其 中 of which						
		电力建设 Power Generation	运输邮电 Transportation, Postal and Telecommunications	其 中 of which		公用设施 Facilities for Public Use	其 中 of which	
				交通运输 Transportation	邮电通信 Postal and Telecommunications		公用事业 Public Utilities	市政建设 Civil Construction
1950~1978	60.08	19.71	23.25	19.41	3.84	17.12	6.85	10.27
1980	9.55	5.31	2.91	2.31	0.60	1.33	0.64	0.69
1985	23.49	3.97	6.75	5.52	1.23	12.77	7.88	4.89
1986	24.78	5.68	8.40	6.56	1.84	10.70	5.67	5.03
1987	32.64	9.31	12.39	10.02	2.37	10.94	5.36	5.58
1988	37.08	14.18	12.35	8.80	3.55	10.55	4.01	6.54
1989	36.09	11.69	9.96	6.16	3.80	14.44	6.84	7.60
1990	47.22	17.53	10.06	7.17	2.90	19.63	10.83	8.80
1991	61.38	19.79	19.07	14.49	4.58	22.52	9.15	13.37
1992	84.35	19.70	21.44	15.01	6.43	43.21	12.58	30.63
1993	167.94	25.77	46.44	31.75	14.69	95.73	37.91	57.82
1994	238.16	41.57	72.68	36.83	35.85	123.91	26.77	97.14
1995	273.78	57.33	79.36	25.94	53.42	137.09	35.03	102.06
1996	378.78	77.61	147.21	69.66	77.55	153.96	48.31	105.65
1997	412.85	80.24	146.10	85.06	61.04	186.51	52.24	134.27
1998	531.38	89.58	181.46	108.79	72.67	260.34	58.37	201.97
1999	501.39	83.05	166.16	102.24	63.92	252.18	64.20	187.98
2000	449.90	64.61	117.52	48.83	68.69	267.77	104.43	163.34
2001	510.78	72.22	168.42	60.72	107.70	270.14	92.25	177.89
2002	583.49	62.14	171.24	63.01	108.23	350.11	148.42	201.69
2003	604.62	66.00	350.35	273.77	76.58	188.28	36.91	151.36
2004	672.58	89.52	371.35	316.96	54.39	211.71	26.92	184.80
2005	885.74	124.22	443.90	385.58	58.32	317.62	41.33	276.28
2006	1 125.54	116.23	703.24	589.52	113.72	306.07	56.23	249.84
2007	1 466.33	163.30	942.03	840.46	101.57	361.01	60.90	300.11
2008	1 733.18	129.53	947.49	838.91	108.59	656.15	112.81	543.34
2009	2 113.45	253.39	1 100.90	978.24	122.66	759.16	135.95	623.21
2010	1 497.46	148.50	866.20	754.66	111.54	482.76	86.58	396.18
2011	1 157.34	118.81	668.52	595.75	72.76	370.01	54.22	315.80
2012	1 038.61	110.06	570.37	473.43	96.94	358.18	56.45	301.74
2013	1 043.31	110.35	550.42	458.70	91.72	382.54	47.57	334.97
2014	1 057.25	134.22	510.42	422.48	87.94	412.61	32.80	379.81
2015	1 425.08	129.36	854.89	759.23	95.67	440.83	66.73	374.10
2016	1 551.87	145.04	990.18	883.81	106.37	416.66	70.90	345.75
2017	1 705.22	137.85	996.10	903.62	92.48	571.27	97.68	473.60

注：本表各项投资额均不包括住宅建设投资。 从 2003 年起，交通运输投资包括公用设施中市内公共交通投资。 2011 年始，固定资产投资统计起点为 500 万元以上(含 500 万元)项目(下表同)。

Note: All items in this table exclude investment in residential housing. Since 2003, public traffic investment, which is belong to facilities for public use has been included in Transportation Investment. Since 2011, statistics of Investment in Fixed Assets only contain the projects with investment of 5 million yuan and above(same as follows).

表 11.2 用于公用事业和市政建设的投资额(1985~2017)
INVESTMENT IN PUBLIC UTILITIES AND CIVIL CONSTRUCTION

单位:亿元(100 million yuan)

年份 Year	公用事业 Public Utilities	其中 of which 自来水 Tap Water	燃气 Gas	市政建设 Civil Construction	其中 of which 园林绿化 Parks and Green Areas	环境卫生 Environmental Sanitation	市政设施 Municipal Facilities	其他 Others
1985	7.88			4.89				
1986	5.67	2.74	1.78	5.03	0.43	0.71	3.84	0.05
1987	5.36	2.53	1.79	5.58	0.30	0.34	4.94	…
1988	4.01	0.72	1.25	6.54	0.24	0.58	5.72	…
1989	6.84	1.52	0.90	7.60	0.01	0.52	7.02	0.05
1990	10.83	1.06	1.81	8.80	0.11	0.37	8.31	0.01
1991	9.15	2.34	2.35	13.37	0.15	0.45	12.77	…
1992	12.58	3.20	3.24	30.63	0.32	0.79	28.45	1.07
1993	37.91	6.90	16.72	57.82	0.52	1.06	56.24	…
1994	26.77	11.49	7.80	97.14	2.42	1.01	93.47	0.24
1995	35.03	13.12	12.97	102.06	4.27	1.26	96.21	0.32
1996	48.31	22.12	14.61	105.65	2.66	1.14	101.80	0.05
1997	52.24	27.08	10.03	134.27	5.11	1.62	127.41	0.13
1998	58.37	14.59	13.15	201.97	9.10	3.35	189.41	0.11
1999	64.20	6.41	9.89	187.98	28.62	2.97	155.73	0.66
2000	104.43	5.35	6.88	163.34	38.76	19.34	102.36	2.88
2001	92.25	5.97	5.83	177.89	32.92	2.97	140.63	1.37
2002	148.42	8.62	6.83	201.69	38.83	1.47	160.64	0.75
2003	36.91	22.89	14.02	151.36	33.85	9.25	107.73	0.53
2004	26.92	16.66	10.26	184.80	16.69	7.01	160.22	0.88
2005	41.33	29.66	11.67	276.28	13.88	15.36	246.58	0.46
2006	56.23	43.79	12.44	249.84	26.41	10.17	213.26	
2007	60.90	50.12	10.78	300.11	34.66	11.26	254.19	
2008	112.81	93.24	19.57	543.34	29.01	20.04	494.29	
2009	135.95	109.79	26.16	623.21	27.96	21.91	573.19	0.15
2010	86.58	61.63	24.95	396.18	35.87	10.80	349.27	0.25
2011	54.22	41.85	12.37	315.80	44.71	23.91	247.15	0.03
2012	56.45	40.75	15.70	301.74	20.99	23.74	256.73	0.26
2013	47.57	24.83	22.74	334.97	27.16	12.52	292.48	2.82
2014	32.80	20.00	12.80	379.81	56.46	9.41	313.94	
2015	66.73	58.63	8.10	374.10	34.84	18.49	320.77	
2016	70.90	58.76	12.14	345.75	29.50	16.37	299.88	
2017	97.68	92.75	4.92	473.60	112.03	20.73	340.83	

表 11.3 主要年份各类房屋构成情况
COMPOSITION OF BUILDING IN MAIN YEARS

单位：万平方米(10 000 sq.m)

指 标	Indicators	2010	2015	2017	2018
总 计	**Total**	**93 591**	**120 390**	**131 908**	**136 882**
居住房屋	Residential Buildings	52 639	63 007	67 281	68 651
花园住宅	Villas	2 064	1 790	1 840	1 852
职工住宅	Staff Dwellings	47 951			
联列住宅	United Columns Residences		1 400	1 565	1 610
公 寓	Apartments	492	58 308	62 453	63 962
新式里弄	Improved Residential Blocks	527	308	303	234
旧式里弄	Old Residential Blocks	1 237	1 190	1 109	982
简 屋	Simple Housings	29	11	11	11
其 他	Others	339			
非居住房屋	Non-Residential Buildings	40 952	57 383	64 626	68 232
工 厂	Plants	18 524	25 103	27 206	28 306
学 校	Schools	3 172	3 366	3 648	3 798
仓库堆栈	Warehouses	1 654	1 868	1 954	2 062
办公建筑	Offices	6 365	7 343	8 461	8 998
商场店铺	Stores	5 497	6 773	7 804	8 158
医 院	Hospitals	754	631	718	760
旅 馆	Hotels	931	1 265	1 421	1 520
影剧院	Theatres and Cinemas	75	65	70	71
其 他	Others	3 979	10 970	13 345	14 558

注：根据市住房保障和房屋管理局提供居住房屋分类的调整，2011 年起公寓数据包含职工住宅数据，2012 年起取消其他分类。
Note: According to the adjustment of residential houses classification provided by Shanghai Municipal Housing Security and Building Administration Bureau, since 2011, the apartment data contains data of the staff housing, and since 2012, other classifications are canceled.

表 11.4 主要年份八层以上房屋情况
BUILDINGS OVER EIGHT STOREYS IN MAIN YEARS

类 别	Types	单 位 Unit	2010	2015	2017	2018
总 计	**Total**	**幢 (building)**	**20 579**	**40 822**	**46 220**	**47 555**
		万平方米 (10 000 sq.m)	21 911	39 652	45 522	47 455
8~10 层	8~10 Storeys	幢 (building)	2 744	5 568	6 588	6 919
		万平方米 (10 000 sq.m)	2 430	3 903	4 789	5 201
11~15 层	11~15 Storeys	幢 (building)	9 672	18 302	20 094	20 436
		万平方米 (10 000 sq.m)	6 320	12 712	14 239	14 653
16~19 层	16~19 Storeys	幢 (building)	4 247	10 046	11 962	12 391
		万平方米 (10 000 sq.m)	4 449	9 640	11 605	12 146
20~29 层	20~29 Storeys	幢 (building)	2 936	5 337	5 906	6 106
		万平方米 (10 000 sq.m)	5 504	8 917	9 987	10 404
30 层以上	Over 30 Storeys	幢 (building)	980	1 569	1 670	1 703
		万平方米 (10 000 sq.m)	3 208	4 481	4 901	5 051

注：本页数据按建筑面积计算。
Note: Data on this page are calculated according to floor space of builings.

表 11.5 各区房屋分布情况 (2018)
DISTRIBUTION OF BUILDINGS IN DIFFERENT DISTRICTS

单位：万平方米(10 000 sq.m)

地 区	District	全部房屋合 计 Total	其 中 of which 居住房屋 Residential	非居住房屋 Non-Residential
总 计	**Total**	**136 882**	**68 651**	**68 232**
浦东新区	Pudong New Area	31 450	16 073	15 377
黄 浦 区	Huangpu	3 779	1 680	2 098
徐 汇 区	Xuhui	6 386	3 543	2 844
长 宁 区	Changning	4 252	2 426	1 825
静 安 区	Jing'an	5 871	3 072	2 799
普 陀 区	Putuo	6 198	3 746	2 452
虹 口 区	Hongkou	3 692	2 183	1 510
杨 浦 区	Yangpu	6 074	3 382	2 692
闵 行 区	Minhang	15 303	8 055	7 248
宝 山 区	Baoshan	10 645	6 154	4 491
嘉 定 区	Jiading	9 887	4 390	5 497
金 山 区	Jinshan	5 292	1 923	3 369
松 江 区	Songjiang	11 124	4 913	6 211
青 浦 区	Qingpu	7 228	2 795	4 433
奉 贤 区	Fengxian	6 945	2 719	4 226
崇 明 区	Chongming	2 756	1 597	1 159

表 11.6 各区各类房屋分布情况(2018)
DISTRIBUTION OF VARIOUS BUILDINGS IN DIFFERENT DISTRICTS

单位：万平方米(10 000 sq.m)

地 区	District	居住房屋 Residential Buildings	其中 of which 花园住宅 Villas	联列住宅 United Columns Residences	公 寓 Apartments
总 计	**Total**	**68 651**	**1 852**	**1 610**	**63 962**
浦东新区	Pudong New Area	16 073	377	278	15 273
黄 浦 区	Huangpu	1 680	8	…	1 394
徐 汇 区	Xuhui	3 542	53	11	3 411
长 宁 区	Changning	2 426	57	1	2 350
静 安 区	Jing'an	3 072	21	4	2 926
普 陀 区	Putuo	3 746	13	23	3 687
虹 口 区	Hongkou	2 183	7	…	2 015
杨 浦 区	Yangpu	3 382	4	18	3 276
闵 行 区	Minhang	8 055	313	183	7 502
宝 山 区	Baoshan	6 154	30	135	5 940
嘉 定 区	Jiading	4 390	94	172	4 100
金 山 区	Jinshan	1 923	18	46	1 821
松 江 区	Songjiang	4 913	395	391	4 078
青 浦 区	Qingpu	2 795	318	217	2 223
奉 贤 区	Fengxian	2 719	99	91	2 495
崇 明 区	Chongming	1 597	45	37	1 472

表 11.6 续表 1 continued

单位：万平方米(10 000 sq.m)

地区	District	其中 of which 新式里弄 Improved Residential Blocks	旧式里弄 Old Residential Blocks	简屋 Simple Housings
总 计	**Total**	**234**	**982**	**11**
浦东新区	Pudong New Area		145	1
黄浦区	Huangpu	75	202	1
徐汇区	Xuhui	29	36	2
长宁区	Changning	17	…	…
静安区	Jing'an	65	56	…
普陀区	Putuo	…	23	…
虹口区	Hongkou	44	113	2
杨浦区	Yangpu		83	1
闵行区	Minhang	3	53	…
宝山区	Baoshan	…	49	…
嘉定区	Jiading		24	…
金山区	Jinshan	…	37	…
松江区	Songjiang	…	49	…
青浦区	Qingpu	…	36	…
奉贤区	Fengxian	1	34	…
崇明区	Chongming	…	41	2

表 11.6 续表2 continued

单位：万平方米(10 000 sq.m)

地 区 District		非居住房屋 Non-Residential Buildings	其中 of which			
			工厂 Plants	学校 Schools	仓库堆栈 Warehouses	办公建筑 Offices
总 计	**Total**	**68 232**	**28 306**	**3 798**	**2 062**	**8 998**
浦东新区	Pudong New Area	15 377	5 842	760	643	1 928
黄 浦 区	Huangpu	2 098	123	109	18	789
徐 汇 区	Xuhui	2 844	533	335	62	798
长 宁 区	Changning	1 825	200	123	31	639
静 安 区	Jing'an	2 799	458	156	50	774
普 陀 区	Putuo	2 452	395	216	174	561
虹 口 区	Hongkou	1 510	152	121	27	485
杨 浦 区	Yangpu	2 692	754	396	76	546
闵 行 区	Minhang	7 248	3 306	455	255	638
宝 山 区	Baoshan	4 491	1 819	218	305	310
嘉 定 区	Jiading	5 497	2 476	221	152	572
金 山 区	Jinshan	3 369	2 248	119	61	165
松 江 区	Songjiang	6 211	4 058	218	53	268
青 浦 区	Qingpu	4 433	2 652	99	59	210
奉 贤 区	Fengxian	4 226	2 826	152	53	218
崇 明 区	Chongming	1 159	467	98	45	94

表 11.6 续表 3 continued

单位：万平方米(10 000 sq.m)

地区 District		其中 of which 商场店铺 Stores	医院 Hospitals	旅馆 Hotels	影剧院 Theatres and Cinemas	其他 Others
总　计	**Total**	**8 158**	**760**	**1 520**	**71**	**14 558**
浦东新区	Pudong New Area	1 708	123	370	5	3 998
黄 浦 区	Huangpu	386	64	147	15	449
徐 汇 区	Xuhui	300	121	91	3	600
长 宁 区	Changning	245	37	114	2	435
静 安 区	Jing'an	408	67	164	8	713
普 陀 区	Putuo	432	38	74	3	560
虹 口 区	Hongkou	268	29	97	6	326
杨 浦 区	Yangpu	305	47	44	3	520
闵 行 区	Minhang	891	63	86	5	1 548
宝 山 区	Baoshan	578	30	40	2	1 187
嘉 定 区	Jiading	707	38	75	8	1 249
金 山 区	Jinshan	398	29	27	1	321
松 江 区	Songjiang	584	24	51	3	952
青 浦 区	Qingpu	469	21	66	3	856
奉 贤 区	Fengxian	368	9	34	3	563
崇 明 区	Chongming	110	20	40	2	283

表 11.7 各区八层以上房屋分布情况 (2018)
DISTRIBUTION OF BUILDINGS OVER EIGHT STOREYS BY DISTRICTS

单位：万平方米(10 000 sq.m)

地 区 District		合 计 Total		8~10 层 8~10 Storeys		11~15 层 11~15 Storeys	
		幢 Building	面 积 Floor Space	幢 Building	面 积 Floor Space	幢 Building	面 积 Floor Space
总 计	**Total**	**47 555**	**47 455**	**6 919**	**5 201**	**20 436**	**14 653**
浦东新区	Pudong New Area	11 098	11 165	1 337	1 100	5 559	4 026
黄 浦 区	Huangpu	1 294	2 400	154	158	170	186
徐 汇 区	Xuhui	2 186	3 117	307	299	602	566
长 宁 区	Changning	1 602	2 180	362	303	440	379
静 安 区	Jing'an	2 305	3 023	326	219	660	509
普 陀 区	Putuo	2 586	3 040	262	176	801	613
虹 口 区	Hongkou	1 443	1 855	215	141	354	256
杨 浦 区	Yangpu	2 165	2 330	307	247	843	690
闵 行 区	Minhang	6 206	5 082	1 077	983	3 742	2 543
宝 山 区	Baoshan	3 972	3 073	561	312	1 969	1 273
嘉 定 区	Jiading	3 615	3 209	404	297	1 215	855
金 山 区	Jinshan	1 275	898	214	127	679	415
松 江 区	Songjiang	3 802	2 791	746	423	1 823	1 220
青 浦 区	Qingpu	1 874	1 557	322	235	731	531
奉 贤 区	Fengxian	1 603	1 393	153	106	599	435
崇 明 区	Chongming	529	341	172	73	249	155

表 11.7 续表 continued

单位：万平方米(10 000 sq.m)

地 区 District		16～19 层 16～19 Storeys		20～29 层 20～29 Storeys		30 层以上 Over 30 Storeys	
		幢 Building	面 积 Floor Space	幢 Building	面 积 Floor Space	幢 Building	面 积 Floor Space
总 计	**Total**	**12 391**	**12 146**	**6 106**	**10 404**	**1 703**	**5 051**
浦东新区	Pudong New Area	2 792	2 790	1 083	1 956	327	1 293
黄 浦 区	Huangpu	254	345	469	957	247	755
徐 汇 区	Xuhui	532	666	554	1 095	191	491
长 宁 区	Changning	283	308	382	714	135	477
静 安 区	Jing'an	435	448	629	1 137	255	710
普 陀 区	Putuo	599	650	719	1 093	205	508
虹 口 区	Hongkou	358	386	363	652	153	419
杨 浦 区	Yangpu	582	611	378	658	55	125
闵 行 区	Minhang	1 128	1 124	235	358	24	75
宝 山 区	Baoshan	1 171	1 089	230	334	41	65
嘉 定 区	Jiading	1 388	1 269	571	729	37	59
金 山 区	Jinshan	335	279	38	61	9	15
松 江 区	Songjiang	1 022	842	203	286	8	19
青 浦 区	Qingpu	717	633	103	156	1	1
奉 贤 区	Fengxian	688	596	148	217	15	39
崇 明 区	Chongming	107	110	1	2		

表 11.8 主要年份市政工程设施情况
CIVIL FACILITIES IN MAIN YEARS

指 标	Indicators	2010	2015	2017	2018
道路长度(公里)	Length of Roads(km)	16 687	18 184	18 546	18 423
道路面积(万平方米)	Area of Roads (10 000 sq.m)	25 607	28 567	29 841	30 281
城市桥梁(座)	Bridges (bridge)	11 849	13 677	14 019	14 146
防洪堤长度(公里)	Length of Floodwalls (km)	1 009	1 159	1 153	1 140
城市排水管道长度(公里)	Length of Sewage Pipelines (km)	11 483	23 339	24 886	27 483
污水处理厂污水处理能力(万吨/日)	Capacity of Sewage Treatment(10 000 tons/day)	684	795	825.7	812.95
城镇污水处理率(%)	Urban Sewage Treatment Rate(%)	81.9	92.8	94.5	95.2

表 11.9 主要年份自来水情况
TAP WATER SUPPLY IN MAIN YEARS

指 标	Indicators	2010	2015	2017	2018
水厂个数(个)	Number of Water Treatment Works (unit)	105	37	36	37
供水能力(万立方米/日)	Water Supply Capacity (10 000 cu.m/day)	1 131	1 137	1 184	1 250
供水管道长度(公里)	Length of Water Supply Mainss (km)	31 182	36 383	37 643	38 414
供水总量(亿立方米)	Total Quantity of Water Supply (100 million cu.m)	30.90	31.22	31.01	30.55
售水总量(亿立方米)	Total Quantity of Water Sales (100 million cu.m)	24.44	24.58	24.52	24.35
工业用水	Industrial Water Consumption	5.80	4.94	4.53	4.33
非工业用水	Comprehensive Domestic Water Consumption	6.02	7.11	7.48	7.66
居民生活用水	Domestic Water Consumption	9.80	9.88	10.50	10.59
其他用水	Others	2.82	2.65	2.01	1.77
人均日居民生活用水量(升)	Per Capita Daily Domestic Water Consumption(liter)	117	112	119	120

表 11.10 用电量(2018)
ELECTRICITY POWER CONSUMPTION

指 标	Indicators	2018
用电量（亿千瓦时）	Power Consumption（100 million kwh）	1 566.66
农、林、牧、渔业	Farming, Forestry, Animal Husbandry and Fishery	6.37
工 业	Industry	780.21
交通运输、仓储和邮政业	Transportation, Warehousing and Post	54.23
批发和零售业	Retail and Wholesale Industries	73.30
住宿和餐饮业	Hoteling and Catering	15.52
金融业	Financial Industry	18.21
房地产业	Real Estate Industry	167.24
公共服务及管理组织	Public Service and Management Organizations	141.42
居民生活	Residents Living Industry	243.55

注：2018 年起，电力公司对用电量指标的行业分类进行了调整。
Note: Since 2018, Power Companies have Adjusted the Industry Classification of Electricity Consumption Indicators.

表 11.11 主要年份电力建设情况
ELECTRICITY POWER CONSTRUCTION IN MAIN YEARS

指 标	Indicators	2001	2010	2017	2018
年末发电设备容量(万千瓦)	Year-end Capacity of Electricity Generating Equipment(10 000 KW)	1 121.09	1 855.38	2 399.67	2 446.88
架空线长度(公里)	Length of Trolly Wire(k.m.)	6 480.72	8 549.50	9 880.37	10 096.89
#220KV	220KV	1 756.74	2 956.08	3 601.04	3 716.88
电缆长度(公里)	Length of Cable(k.m.)	3 633.00	7 846.98	13 626.81	14 323.45
#220KV	220KV	145.00	516.44	721.93	820.07
公用变电容量(万千伏安)	Public Power Transformation Capacity(10 000 KVA)	4 601.08	11 657.19	17 422.64	18 141.59
#220KV-35KV	220KV-35KV	3 716.68	7 827.75	11 393.00	11 946.95

注：本页数据由市电力公司提供。
Note: Data on this page are provided by Shanghai Electric Power Corporation.

表 11.12 主要年份液化石油气、天然气情况
LIQUEFIED PETROLEUM GAS AND NATURAL GAS IN MAIN YEARS

指 标	Indicators	2010	2015	2017	2018
液化石油气	**Liquefied Petroleum Gas (LPG)**				
液化石油气销售总量(万吨)	Sales of LPG (10 000 tons)	40.05	42.41	34.85	31.55
#家庭用量	Household Consumption	23.62	25.23	17.51	17.49
家庭液化石油气用户数(万户)	Household Users (10 000 households)	316.37	335.50	281.47	253.48
天然气	**Natural Gas**				
天然气销售总量(亿立方米)	Sales of Natural Gas (100 million cu.m)	42.66	69.73	77.20	85.44
#家庭用量	Household Consumption	7.79	13.50	15.08	16.13
天然气管线长度(公里)	Length of Natural Gas Pipelines (km)	17 316	28 601	30 387	31 233
家庭天然气用户数 (万户)	Household Users of Natural Gas (10 000 households)	405.89	651.32	700.60	735.60

表 11.13 主要年份公共交通和轮渡情况
PUBLIC TRANSPORTATION AND FERRY IN MAIN YEARS

指 标	Indicators	2010	2015	2017	2018
公共汽电车	**Buses and Trolley Buses**				
公交线路长度(公里)	Length of Public Bus Lines (km)	23 131	24 027	24 161	24 525
公交线路条数(条)	Number of Public Bus Lines (line)	1 165	1 429	1 496	1 543
运营公交车辆数(辆)	Operating Public Transportation Vehicles (vehicle)	17 455	16 531	17 461	17 513
#公共汽车	Buses	17 038	15 056	12 792	10 274
公交客运总量(亿人次)	Passenger Volume of Pubilc Bus (100million person-times)	28.08	25.49	22.01	21.01
出租汽车	**Taxi**				
运营车辆(辆)	Operating Vehicles (vehicle)	50 007	49 586	46 397	41 881
#小客车	Small Passenger Car	49 016	48 840	45 666	41 245
载客车次(万次)	Number of Carryings(10 000 times)	63 306.89	53 974.00	42 173.00	35 422.00
运营里程(亿公里)	Operation Length (100 million km)	64.85	60.85	56.58	51.18
#载客里程	Transport Lengths of Passengers	39.79	39.27	36.13	31.79
运营收入(亿元)	Operation Revenues(100 million yuan)	154.72	166.30	152.49	135.80
运营单位(个)	Operation Unit (unit)	3 301	3 113	3 068	3 067
轮 渡	**Ferry**				
年末轮渡船数(艘)	Year-end Number of Ferry Boats (ship)	42	44	44	41
乘客人数(亿人次)	Passenger Volume (100 million person-times)	0.89	0.53	0.50	0.45

表 11.14 轨道交通、城市快速路、黄浦江大桥和隧道基本情况(2015~2018)
BASIC FACTS OF RAILWAY COMMUNICATION,URBAN EXPRESSWAYS,BRIDGES ACROSS HUANGPU RIVER AND TUNNELS

指 标	Indicators	2015	2016	2017	2018
轨道交通	**Urban Metro**				
运营车辆(节)	Operating Vehicles(car)	3 797	4 025	4 753	5 302
轨道交通线路条数(条)	Number of Operation Lines(line)	15	15	16	17
运营线路长度(公里)	Length of Operation Lines(km)	617.53	617.53	666.40	704.91
运营里程(万列·公里)	Operation Mileage(10 000 vehicle-km)	7 574	8 430	8 648	9 564
客运总量(万人次)	Volume of Passenger Traffic (10 000 person-times)	306 798	340 106	353 769	371 012
年末从业人数(人)	Year-end Number of Staff and Workers (person)	29 315	28 733	28 317	28 601
城市快速路、大桥和隧道	**Urban Expressways, Bridges and Tunnels**				
城市快速路长度(公里)	Length of Urban Expressways(km)	197	200	207	207
越江大桥数(座)	Number of Bridges Across Huangpu River (bridge)	11	11	11	11
越江隧道数(条)	Tunnels Across Huangpu River (tunnel)	14	15	15	15

注：越江大桥、越江隧道是指跨越长江、黄浦江的桥梁和隧道，不含东海大桥。

Note: River-Crossing Bridges and River-Crossing Tunnels refer to the bridges and tunnels which cross the Yangtze River and Huangpu River, and exclude the East China Sea Bridge.

表 11.15 主要年份城市设施水平
LEVEL OF URBAN FACILITIES IN MAIN YEARS

指 标	Indicators	2010	2015	2017	2018
人均日综合生活用水量(升)	Per Capita Daily Consumption of Water for Life (liter)	223	224	229	229
人均日居民生活用水量(升)	Per Capita Daily Consumption of Water (liter)	117	112	119	120
自来水普及率(%)	Percentage of Population with Access to Tap Water (%)	99.99	99.99	99.99	99.99
拥有道路长度(公里/万人)	Per Capita Length of Roads (km/10 000 persons)	7.25	7.53	7.67	7.6
人均拥有道路面积(平方米)	Per Capita Area of Roads (sq.m)	11.12	11.83	12.34	12.49
每万人拥有城市排水管道长度(公里)	Length of Sewage Pipelines Per 10 000 Persons (km)	4.99	8.83	10.29	11.34
每万人拥有公共交通车辆(标台)	Number of Public Transportation Vehicles Per 10 000 Persons (vehicle)	12.46	12.36	13.94	14.53
每万人拥有出租汽车(辆)	Number of Taxi Per 10 000 Persons (vehicle)	21.72	20.53	19.55	17.28
人均公园绿地面积(平方米)	Per Capita Park Green Areas (sq.m)	13.0	7.6	8.1	8.2
每万人拥有公共厕所(座)	Number of Public Lavatories Per 10 000 Persons (unit)	4.27	4.32	4.31	3.56

注：2000 年起，每万人拥有城市排水管道长度由原先的根据户籍人口计算调整为根据常住人口计算；2010 年起，拥有道路长度和人均拥有道路面积由原先的根据户籍人口计算调整为根据常住人口计算；2014 年起，人均公园绿地面积(平方米)由原先的根据非农户籍人口计算调整为根据常住人口计算。

Note: The indicators of Length of Sewage Pipelines Per 10 000 Persons are calculated by resident population since 2000. The indicators of Per Capita Length of Roads and Per Capita Area of Roads are calculated by resident population since 2010.The indicators of Per Capita Park Green Areas are calculated by resident population since 2014.

表 11.16 主要年份城市绿地情况
URBAN GREEN SPACE IN MAIN YEARS

单位:公顷(hectare)

年份 Year	绿地面积 Urban Green Space	其中 of which				
		公园绿地 Public Green Space	生产绿地 Production Green Space	防护绿地 Environmental Protection Green Space	附属绿地 Sub Green Space	其他绿地 Other Green Space
1990	3 570	983	294	37	2 255	
1995	6 561	1 793	309	30	4 429	
2000	12 601	4 812	388	55	7 346	
2005	28 865	12 038	336	2 743	12 464	1 284
2006	30 609	13 307	331	2 869	13 218	884
2007	31 795	13 899	204	2 025	14 784	884
2008	34 256	14 777	189	2 039	16 120	1 131
2009	116 929	15 406	230	1 877	17 376	82 040
2010	120 148	16 053	230	1 936	18 589	83 340
2011	122 283	16 446	213	2 081	19 442	84 102
2012	124 204	16 848	269	2 087	20 084	84 917
2013	124 295	17 142	267	2 089	20 645	84 152
2014	125 741	17 789	417	2 152	23 020	82 363
2015	127 332	18 395	417	2 108	23 711	82 701
2016	131 681	18 957	417	2 203	24 337	85 767
2017	136 327	19 805	335	2 238	24 688	89 262
2018	139 427	20 578	335	2 277	25 125	91 111

注：根据《城市和村镇建设统计报表制度》，2009 年对绿地分类进行了调整。城市绿地由公园绿地、生产绿地、防护绿地、附属绿地和其他绿地五大类构成。

Note：The Categories of Urban Green include Public Green Area, Production Green Area, Protection Green Area, Sub Green Area and Other Green Area, which have been adjusted by the Statistical Reporting Regulation of City and Town Construction since 2009.

表 11.16 续表 continued

年份 Year	公园数（个） Parks (unit)	游园人数（万人次） Visitors to Parks and Zooes (10 000 person-times)	行道树实有数（万株） Roadside Trees (10 000 trees)	新建绿地面积(公顷) Greenlands Newly Created (hectare)	建成区绿化覆盖率（%） Coverage Rate of Urban Green Areas(%)
1990	83	8 474	23	186	12.4
1995	100	9 064	33	516	16.0
2000	122	8 184	57	1 458	22.2
2005	144	13 656	83	2 116	37.0
2006	144	16 652	86	1 691	37.3
2007	146	18 342	69	1 629	37.6
2008	147	22 119	73	1 190	38.0
2009	147	21 671	76	1 096	38.1
2010	148	21 794	81	1 223	38.2
2011	153	20 481	93	1 063	38.2
2012	157	22 231	98	1 038	38.3
2013	158	20 574	99	1 050	38.4
2014	161	22 286	103	1 105	38.4
2015	165	22 208	110	1 190	38.5
2016	217	21 797	113	1 221	38.8
2017	243	26 019	115	1 361	39.1
2018	300	25 743	128	1 307	39.4

表 11.17 各区绿化情况（2018）
URBAN GREEN AREA IN DIFFERENT DISTRICTS

地 区	District	绿地面积（公顷）Urban Green Space (hectare)	其中 of which #公园绿地面积 Park Green Areas	公园数（个）Quantity of Parks (unit)	公园面积（公顷）Park Area (Hectare)	公园游园人数（万人次）Visitors to Parks and Zoos (10 000 person-times)
总 计	**Total**	**139 426.73**	**20 577.89**	**300**	**3 141.21**	**25 742.75**
浦东新区	Pudong New Area	28 760.91	7 129.60	43	767.70	2 276.41
黄 浦 区	Huangpu	282.46	176.45	16	69.54	2 545.20
徐 汇 区	Xuhui	1 394.03	585.69	15	146.27	3 604.90
长 宁 区	Changning	1 113.55	510.34	16	141.04	1 470.73
静 安 区	Jing'an	797.95	313.75	16	116.26	2 637.05
普 陀 区	Putuo	1 416.00	679.32	24	89.57	2 654.15
虹 口 区	Hongkou	426.12	157.95	11	64.83	3 407.99
杨 浦 区	Yangpu	1 444.25	490.57	18	234.48	1 930.44
闵 行 区	Minhang	7 659.75	2 582.49	37	281.52	1 016.32
宝 山 区	Baoshan	7 790.49	2 446.74	27	438.24	1 778.38
嘉 定 区	Jiading	9 936.76	1 423.43	25	154.73	1 353.10
金 山 区	Jinshan	10 017.80	699.90	9	18.79	112.36
松 江 区	Songjiang	11 748.04	1 244.71	17	324.91	510.13
青 浦 区	Qingpu	12 141.00	1 050.67	13	188.38	189.36
奉 贤 区	Fengxian	11 827.87	665.08	10	77.34	192.59
崇 明 区	Chongming	32 669.24	421.20	3	25.61	63.64

上/海/统/计/年/鉴

主要统计指标解释

■ 城市基础设施

城市基础设施包括电力建设、交通运输、邮电通信、公用事业和市政建设等。

■ 道路长度

指道路长度和与道路相通的桥梁、隧道的长度，按车行道中心线计算。

■ 绿地面积

指报告期末用作园林和绿化的各种绿地面积。包括公园绿地、生产绿地、防护绿地、附属绿地和其他绿地面积。

其中，公园绿地：指向公众开放的、以游憩为主要功能，有一定的游憩设施和服务设施，同时兼有健全生态、美化景观、防灾减灾等综合作用的绿化用地。它是城市建设用地、城市绿地系统和城市市政公用设施的重要组成部分。

■ 供水管道长度

指从送水泵至用户水表之间所有管道的长度。不包括新安装尚未使用的管道。

■ 供水总量

指报告期供水企业（单位）供出的全部水量。包括有效供水量和漏损水量。

■ 售水总量

指供水企业收费供应的水量，包括工业用水、非工业用水、居民生活用水、其它用水（如消防用水、工房配套水、排管冲洗水等其他用水）。

■ 天然气销售总量

指报告期内燃气供应企业（单位）售给本区域内各类用户的全部燃气量。包括工业企业生产用气量、家庭用气量、商业用气量、燃气汽车用气量和其他用气量。其中，家庭用气量指城市居民日常生活所耗用的燃气数量。

■ 排水管道长度

指所有排水总管、干管、支管、检查井及连接井进出口等长度之和。

■ 运营公交车辆数

指年末公交企业（单位）用于运营业务的全部车辆数。以企业（单位）固定资产台帐中已投入运营的车辆数为准。

■ 污水日处理能力

指城镇污水处理厂（或处理装置）每昼夜处理污水量的设计能力。

SHANGHAI STATISTICAL YEARBOOK

EXPLANATORY NOTES TO MAJOR STATISTICAL INDICATORS

□ Urban Infrastructure Facilities

Urban Infrastructure Facilities include facilities for power generating, transportation, post and telecommunication, public utilities, development of municipal engineering.

□ Length of Roads

The length of roads refers to the length of roads and of the bridges and tunnels connected to the roads, calculated by the center line of the roads.

□ Green Space

Green Space includes all kinds of gardens and green at the end of reporting period. Park green area, production green area, protection green area, sub green area and other green area are all included.

Park green area refers to green areas open to the public for amusement and rest with the facilities of amusement, rest and services. Its function includes perfecting ecology, beautifying landscape, and preventing and reducing disaster. It is an important part of urban construction land, urban green and municipal public infrastructure in city.

□ Length of Water Supply Pipelines

Length of Water Supply Pipelines refers to the total length of all the pipelines between the water pumps and the user′s water meters, excluding pipelines newly installed but not used yet.

□ Volume of Water Supply

Volume of Water Supply refers to the total volume of water supplied by water-works (units) during the reference period, including both the effective water supply and loss during the water supply.

□ Total amount of Water Sold

The total amount of water sold refers to the amount of water charged by water supply enterprises, including industrial water, non-industrial water, residential water and other water (such as firewater, auxiliary water for industrial buildings, flushing water for drainage pipes, etc.).

□ Total amount of Natural Gas Sales

The total amount of natural gas sales refers to the total amount of gas sold by the internal combustion gas supply enterprises(units) to various users in the region during the reporting period. Including industrial production gas consumption, household gas consumption, commercial gas consumption, gas automobile gas consumption and other gas consumption. Among them, household gas consumption refers to the amount of gas consumed by urban residents in daily life.

□ Production Capacity of Gas

Production Capacity of Gas refers to the comprehensive production capacity of the urban gasworks in gas generation, purification and delivery at the end of the reference period, excluding capacity of the reserved facilities. In general, it is determined by the designed capacity, and when actual production capacity is larger than the designed capacity, the capacity is determined by the actual measurement on the weakest link in the production, purification and delivery.

□ Length of Sewage Pipes

Length of Sewage Pipes refers to the total length of general drainage, trunks, branch and inspection wells, connection wells, inlets and outlets, etc.

□ Number of Operating Public Transportation Vehicles

Number of Operating Public Transportation Vehicles refers to the total number of vehicles under operation by public transport enterprises (units) at the end of the year, based on the records of operational vehicles by the enterprises (units).

□ Daily Disposal Capacity of Urban Sewage

Daily Disposal Capacity of Urban Sewage refers to the designed 24 hour capacity of sewage disposal by the sewage treatment works or urban facilities.

第十二篇

CHAPTER 12

农 业

AGRICULTURE

简要说明

一、本篇资料的主要内容

本篇资料反映本市农业生产和农村经济的基本情况，内容主要包括农林牧渔业产值、农村户数和人口、农作物播种面积、主要农产品产量、农业机械拥有量、农业技术应用等方面的统计资料。

二、本篇资料的统计范围

农业统计范围为上海市，包括闵行区、宝山区、嘉定区、松江区、金山区、青浦区、奉贤区、崇明区和浦东新区（农村）行政区域范围内所有建制乡镇、行政村和涉农街道、居委会辖区内的生产经营单位和农户；上海光明食品（集团）、上海水产（集团）总公司、青东农场、前卫农场、上实现代农业园区以及其他中央属、市属和军委系统的农业生产（经营）活动单位。

1. 种植业:指对各种农作物的种植活动。包括谷物、豆类、薯类、棉花、油料、糖料、麻类、烟叶、蔬菜、园艺作物、水果、坚果、饮料和香料作物、中草药及其他作物的种植。

2. 林业:包括林木的栽培(不包括茶园、桑园和果园的栽培、管理和收获等活动),木材和竹材的采运，林产品的采集。

3. 牧业:包括牲畜饲养和放牧，家禽饲养以及野生动物的捕猎和饲养。

4. 渔业:包括水生动物和海藻类植物的养殖和捕捞。

5. 农林牧渔服务业:指对种植业、林业、牧业、渔业生产活动进行的各种支持性服务。但不包括各种科学技术和专业性技术服务活动。

农村社会经济统计范围包括除城关镇以外所有乡镇的社会经济活动。

三、本篇的资料来源及统计调查方法

主要由国家统计局上海调查总队根据《农村统计报表制度》的有关资料整理提供。

《农村统计报表制度》包括三部分内容：

一是农林牧渔业统计调查。包括农作物播种面积、主要农作物产量、农产量抽样调查等内容，调查方法由统计部门确定。其中，水果、林业、渔业、农业机械和部分畜牧业数据来源为农委相关部门，调查方法由资料来源相关部门确定。

二是农业产值综合统计。包括农业总产值、农林牧渔业中间消耗等内容，调查方法由统计部门确定。

三是农村社会经济基本情况统计。包括乡镇社会经济基本情况、行政村基本情况等内容。上海参照国家统计局《县域社会经济基本情况统计报表制度》充实部分指标进行调查。

BRIEF INTRODUCTION

I. Main Contents

The data in this chapter reflect the basic conditions of agricultural production and rural economy in Shanghai. The main contents include output of agriculture, forestry, animal husbandry and fishery, number of rural households, rural population, sown area of farm crops, output of major agricultural products, agricultural products export, investment in facilities of water conservancy, electricity consumption in rural areas, ownership of agricultural machinery, application and comprehensive development of rural technology.

II. Scope and Coverage of Statistics

Data on agriculture cover the whole Shanghai Municipality including Minhang, Baoshan, Jiading, Songjiang, Jinshan, Qingpu, Fengxian, Chongming districts, and Pudong New Area(rural area). Included in agriculture statistics are production activities in agriculture by rural production units and by rural households; production activities of farms in counties, villages and rural communities; production activities in agriculture undertaken by Shanghai Bright Food (Group), Shanghai Fisheries (Group) Corporation, the Qingdong Farm, the Qianwei Farm, SIIC Modern Agriculture Park and agricultural production units owned by the central government, municipal government and military agencies.

(1) Agriculture: it refers to cultivation of farm crops, including cereals, beans, tuber crops, cotton, oil-bearing crops, sugar crops, hemp, tobacco leaves, vegetables, gardening plants, fruits, nuts, crops for beverages and spices, medicinal herbs and other farm crops.

(2) Forestry: it includes the planting of trees (excluding activities of planting, managing and harvesting of tea, mulberry fields and fruits), cutting and transport of timber and bamboo and collection of forest products.

(3) Animal husbandry: it includes the raising and grazing of domestic animals and poultry, and the hunting and raising of wild animals.

(4) Fishery: it includes cultivation and catching of aquatic animals and seaweed.

(5) Services in support of agriculture, forestry, animal husbandry and fishery: they include supporting services to production activities in agriculture, forestry, animal husbandry and fishery but do not include activities of science and technology and professional services.

Rural social and economic statistics cover social and economic activities in all townships except towns, where county governments are located.

III. Data Sources and Survey Methodology

Data in this chapter are provided by the Survey Office of the National Bureau of Statistics in Shanghai using data from the Statistical Survey System on Rural Areas.

Statistical Survey System on Rural Areas consists of three parts:

First, it includes statistics on agriculture, forestry, animal husbandry and fishery, including agricultural production area, main crop output and sampling survey of agricultural products, whose survey methodologies are determined by the statistics department. Fruit, forestry, fishery, agricultural machinery and part of animal husbandry data are provided by Shanghai Municipal Agriculture Commission, and survey methodologies are determined by relevant providers of the data.

Second, it includes comprehensive statistics on value of agricultural output, including output of agriculture, intermediate consumption of agriculture, forestry, animal husbandry, and fishery, Survey methodologies are determined by the statistics department.

Third, it includes comprehensive statistics on rural areas. The data include basic conditions of social and economic activities at county, township and rural administrations, and municipal agricultural zones. Data are provided according to Statistical Reporting System on the Basic Condition of Social and Economic Activities of Counties with additional standards supplemented by Shanghai authorities.

表 12.1 农业总产值(1978~2018) GROSS OUTPUT VALUE OF AGRICULTURE

单位:亿元(100 million yuan)

年 份 Year	农业总产值 Gross Output Value of Agriculture	其中 ofwhich 种植业 Planting	林 业 Forestry	畜牧业 Husbandry	渔 业 Fishery	农林牧渔服务业 Service Industry for Agriculture
1978	18.26	13.49	0.06	3.67	0.86	
1979	20.41	15.10	0.04	4.22	0.90	
1980	18.90	11.40	0.06	6.27	0.97	
1981	20.33	11.91	0.21	6.38	1.23	
1982	23.97	13.80	0.23	7.81	1.56	
1983	22.68	12.59	0.20	7.80	1.29	
1984	26.59	16.41	0.21	8.06	1.40	
1985	31.38	15.63	0.21	12.25	2.82	
1986	33.76	16.83	0.24	12.75	3.45	
1987	38.84	17.69	0.34	15.48	4.79	
1988	53.07	22.47	0.45	22.18	7.43	
1989	60.63	25.53	0.39	26.41	7.88	
1990	68.16	29.09	0.37	30.25	8.04	
1991	73.65	30.51	0.39	33.38	8.97	
1992	80.01	32.80	0.43	37.19	9.18	
1993	96.20	40.52	0.41	42.95	12.31	
1994	140.24	60.19	0.49	62.04	17.52	
1995	182.47	77.71	0.45	81.48	22.83	
1996	200.95	87.64	0.67	85.46	27.18	
1997	204.41	85.20	0.47	88.37	30.37	
1998	206.75	89.10	0.84	87.27	29.54	
1999	206.90	87.86	0.98	86.35	31.71	
2000	216.50	89.81	1.41	87.35	37.92	
2001	227.61	95.53	3.52	88.43	40.13	
2002	233.57	97.21	7.75	83.48	45.13	
2003	247.29	98.17	13.05	81.13	49.21	5.73
2004	248.89	109.32	13.14	70.77	49.90	5.76
2005	233.39	111.25	11.11	54.34	51.64	5.05
2006	237.01	119.99	10.43	46.29	55.25	5.05
2007	255.98	126.74	10.05	58.00	54.19	7.00
(2007)	(257.76)	(128.17)	(10.06)	(58.07)	(54.46)	(7.00)
2008	282.63	139.29	9.13	68.52	57.48	8.20
2009	287.76	151.00	9.02	64.72	54.54	8.49
2010	296.24	159.98	7.58	65.72	54.25	8.71
2011	328.24	169.82	7.73	83.82	57.14	9.73
2012	337.81	176.80	9.77	79.75	60.84	10.66
2013	342.29	177.93	9.80	79.52	63.35	11.69
2014	343.78	175.46	8.83	81.96	66.02	11.50
2015	327.71	167.86	12.30	80.84	55.67	11.04
2016	300.84	146.58	13.21	80.17	50.31	10.57
2017	292.61	146.40	15.31	61.17	58.39	11.34
2018	289.58	150.09	15.80	48.32	56.21	19.16

①2003 年以前，农业总产值不包括农林牧渔服务业。
②2018 年，根据第三次农业普查结果对 2007 年以后的数据进行了修订，括号内数为 2007 年修订后的数据(后表同)。
❶The Gross Output Value of Agriculture did not include the output value of service industry for planting, forestry, animal husbandry and fishery before 2003.
❷In 2018, the data after 2007 were revised according to the results of the third agricultural census. The figures in brackets are the revised data in 2007 (the same as the table below).

表 12.2 农业总产值指数(以 1978 年为 100，1978~2018)
GROSS OUTPUT VALUE INDEX OF AGRICULTURE (1978=100)

年 份 Year	农业总产值指数 Index of Gross Output Value of Agriculture	其 中 ofwhich				
		种植业 Planting	林 业 Forestry	畜牧业 Animal Husbandry	渔 业 Fishery	农林牧渔服务业 Service Industry for Agriculture
1978	100.0	100.0	100.0	100.0	100.0	
1979	101.4	92.9	121.9	128.1	101.6	
1980	92.1	78.6	152.9	115.8	104.1	
1981	100.0	83.9	144.0	140.2	97.3	
1982	117.4	97.4	161.1	170.1	107.3	
1983	109.9	86.0	116.1	167.3	123.6	
1984	124.5	109.0	98.4	167.5	114.7	
1985	113.0	88.2	107.2	181.4	127.6	
1986	119.7	89.5	134.5	201.2	149.5	
1987	122.5	90.6	138.9	206.7	158.1	
1988	130.3	95.3	166.0	227.0	160.0	
1989	132.0	92.3	134.9	245.6	171.8	
1990	139.5	96.3	139.7	271.2	164.3	
1991	146.2	95.6	153.7	299.0	172.7	
1992	154.7	101.3	144.0	322.9	168.8	
1993	147.9	94.1	129.4	313.8	166.8	
1994	159.4	96.0	130.5	336.7	215.0	
1995	177.0	104.0	125.2	363.0	252.4	
1996	191.6	114.5	168.6	389.1	269.6	
1997	202.5	123.1	133.0	404.3	288.4	
1998	207.3	129.4	185.2	412.1	278.6	
1999	212.6	133.2	258.3	418.0	289.2	
2000	220.9	141.2	414.9	414.6	321.9	
2001	236.5	145.2	629.7	433.7	392.0	
2002	243.6	145.7	1 546.0	416.4	442.6	100.0
2003	246.3	135.3	2 062.4	395.5	544.4	102.6
2004	229.6	144.0	2 070.6	306.5	526.4	103.2
2005	205.5	136.7	1 613.0	221.6	555.4	91.4
2006	206.9	141.1	1 514.6	205.0	587.6	90.3
2007	210.0	142.9	1 458.6	214.2	573.5	121.6
(2007)	(211.6)	(144.5)	(1 460.9)	(214.4)	(576.3)	(121.4)
2008	212.0	149.1	1 188.0	224.1	523.6	134.4
2009	212.5	148.6	1 151.2	239.0	490.9	139.8
2010	204.7	142.6	966.2	242.3	457.0	139.2
2011	205.4	143.2	926.7	256.7	425.4	147.6
2012	207.9	144.1	1 057.7	256.2	434.6	157.4
2013	203.5	138.6	1 092.9	255.7	425.3	168.7
2014	207.3	138.3	1 011.4	269.2	450.7	161.6
2015	196.4	131.0	1 237.8	257.4	407.5	150.3
2016	173.2	113.0	1 345.3	234.7	343.1	137.8
2017	165.8	112.9	1 538.2	178.2	372.2	145.3
2018	162.0	113.6	1 486.5	147.2	346.2	241.5

注：根据国家统计局方法制度规定，从 2006 年起，农业总产值指数按可比价计算，2006 年以前按不变价计算。

Note: According to the regulation of National Bureau of Statistics, since 2006, index of gross output value of agriculture has been calculated by comparable price, and before 2006, it was calculated by constant price.

表 12.3　主要年份农村户数、人口和从业人员
RURAL HOUSEHOLDS, POPULATION AND EMPLOYEES IN MAIN YEARS

指　标	Indicators	2000	2010	2017	2018
户 数(万户)	**Households (10 000 households)**	**115.17**	**114.22**	**100.22**	**95.68**
人 口(万人)	**Population (10 000 persons)**	**360.71**	**305.68**	**253.58**	**241.56**
农村从业人员(万人)	**Rural Employees(10 000 persons)**	**253.45**	**188.70**	**154.83**	**147.26**
第一产业	Primary Industry	81.45	34.06	34.62	33.40
第二产业	Secondary Industry	119.89	109.84	90.52	85.80
第三产业	Tertiary Industry	52.11	44.80	29.69	28.06

注：根据国家统计制度规定，本表中 2010~2012 年第一产业从业人员中包括农林牧渔服务业从业人员；从 2013 年起，农林牧渔服务业从业人员从第一产业中划出，归入第三产业。

Note: According to the provisions of the national statistical system, the first industry employees of 2010−2012 in this table contained the employees in the service industries of farming, forestry, animal husbandry and fishery. Since 2013, employees in the service industries of farming, forestry, animal husbandry and fishery are separated from first industry and merged into third industry.

表 12.4　主要年份农作物总播种面积
TOTAL SOWN AREA OF PLANTING IN MAIN YEARS

年　份 Year	总播种面积 (万公顷) Total Sown Area (10 000 hectare)	粮食作物 Grain Crops		经济作物 Cash Crops	
		播种面积 Sown Area	占总播种面积(%) Percentage (%)	播种面积 Sown Area	占总播种面积(%) Percentage (%)
1990	63.11	41.71	66.1	21.40	33.9
1995	54.22	34.40	63.5	19.82	36.5
1996	57.01	35.38	62.1	21.63	37.9
1997	55.23	36.58	66.2	18.65	33.8
1998	55.64	35.25	63.4	20.39	36.6
1999	55.17	33.50	60.7	21.67	39.3
2000	52.15	25.88	49.6	26.27	50.4
2001	49.09	21.12	43.0	27.97	57.0
2002	47.67	18.77	39.4	28.90	60.6
2003	41.92	14.83	35.4	27.09	64.6
2004	40.44	15.47	38.3	24.97	61.7
2005	40.36	16.61	41.1	23.75	58.9
2006	40.14	16.55	41.2	23.59	58.8
2007	39.07	16.96	43.4	22.11	56.6
(2007)	(40.06)	(17.92)	(44.7)	(22.14)	(55.3)
2008	39.78	18.42	46.3	21.36	53.7
2009	41.72	21.55	51.7	20.17	48.3
2010	41.74	20.12	48.2	21.62	51.8
2011	42.19	20.83	49.4	21.36	50.6
2012	40.33	20.81	51.6	19.52	48.4
2013	39.29	19.05	48.5	20.24	51.5
2014	37.15	18.67	50.3	18.48	49.7
2015	35.17	18.13	51.6	17.04	48.4
2016	30.51	15.85	51.9	14.66	48.1
2017	28.59	13.31	46.6	15.28	53.4
2018	28.53	12.99	45.5	15.54	54.5

表 12.5 主要年份农产品产量
OUTPUT OF MAJOR FARM PRODUCTS IN MAIN YEARS

指 标	Indicators	2000	2010	2017	2018
农产品	**Farm Products**				
粮 食(万吨)(包括大豆)	Grain (10 000 tons) (Including Soybean)	174.00	132.12	99.78	103.74
棉 花(万吨)	Cotton (10 000 tons)	0.12	0.36		0.01
油 料(万吨)	Oil Plants (10 000 tons)	16.37	2.45	0.76	0.71
#油菜籽	Rapeseed	15.71	2.14	0.48	0.54
蔬 菜(万吨)	Vegetables (10 000 tons)	377.00	374.52	281.89	284.73
食用菌(万吨)	Edible Fungus(10 000 tons)		8.75	11.61	9.76
西甜瓜(万吨)	Watermelons and Muskmelons (10 000 tons)	49.88	55.49	19.70	22.20
园林水果(万吨)	Garden Fruits (10 000 tons)	22.54	40.83	24.57	29.54
#生 梨	Pear	1.74	3.82	3.18	3.80
柑 橘	Citrus Fruits	10.18	18.88	9.38	10.75
畜禽产品	**Livestock and Poultry**				
生猪出栏量(万头)	Quantity of Sold Hogs(10 000 heads)	471.46	272.92	189.67	148.86
生猪年末圈存量(万头)	Hogs In Pens By Year-end (10 000 heads)	241.60	175.00	111.24	96.48
奶牛年末头数(万头)	Cows In Pens By Year-end (10 000 heads)	5.83	6.97	6.50	5.58
羊年末头数(万头)	Sheep In Pens By Year-end (10 000 heads)	55.44	19.46	19.56	13.72
猪 肉(万吨)	Pork (10 000 tons)	25.96	18.34	14.57	11.27
牛羊肉(万吨)	Beef and Mutton (10 000 tons)	0.79	0.43	0.48	0.28
家禽出栏量(万羽)	Quantity of Poultry Sold Birds (10 000 fowls)	17 213	3 994	1 273	984
生牛奶(万吨)	Raw Milk (10 000 tons)	25.95	25.08	36.37	33.44
禽 蛋(万吨)	Poultry Eggs (10 000 tons)	16.64	6.01	3.38	3.16
水产品	**Aquatic Products**	**28.87**	**27.28**	**29.54**	**30.85**
海水产品(万吨)	Seawater Aquatic Products (10 000 tons)	12.23	12.15	14.52	16.84
淡水产品(万吨)	Freshwater Aquatic Products (10 000 tons)	16.64	15.13	15.02	14.01

表 12.6 农牧业特色种养产品产量(2017~2018)
OUTPUT OF SPECIAL PRODUCTS IN FARMING AND ANIMAL HUSBANDRY

指 标	Indicators	2017	2018	指 标	Indicators	2017	2018
桃(万吨)	Peach (10 000 tons)	4.92	7.46	野 鸡(万只)	Pheasant(10 000 fowls)	5.10	21.03
葡 萄(万吨)	Grape (10 000 tons)	6.36	6.57	野 鸭(万只)	Mallard(10 000 fowls)	50.27	42.21
草 莓(万吨)	Strawberry (10 000 tons)	2.12	2.58	肉 鸽(万只)	Meat Dove(10 000 fowls)	629	691
枣(吨)	Date(ton)	269	456	鳖(吨)	Soft-shelled Turtle(ton)	460	279
弥猴桃(吨)	Kiwi (ton)	1 448	1 484	中华绒毛蟹(万吨)	Chinese Hairy Crab(10 000 tons)	0.94	0.74

表 12.7　主要农副产品产量与建国以来最高年产量的比较 (2018)
OUTPUT OF MAJOR FARM AND SIDELINE PRODUCTS IN COMPARISON WITH THE PEAK YEAR SINCE 1949

指　标	Indicators	2018	建国以来最高年 Peak Year Since 1949		2018 年为建国以来最高年份(%) 2017/Peak Year Since 1949
			年　份 Year	产　量 Output	
农产品	Farm products				
粮　食(万吨)	Grain (10 000 tons)	103.74	1978	260.88	39.80
油菜籽(万吨)	Rapeseed (10 000 tons)	0.54	1992	21.84	2.47
蔬　菜(万吨)	Vegetables (10 000 tons)	284.73	2002	476.60	59.74
西甜瓜(万吨)	Watermelons and Muskmelons (10 000 tons)	22.20	2003	76.49	29.02
园林水果(万吨)	Garden Fruits (10 000 tons)	29.54	2008	44.34	66.62
畜禽产品	Animal Husbandry Products				
猪年末圈存数 (万头)	Quantity of Hogs in Pens (year-end) (10 000 heads)	96.48	1978	365.74	26.38
猪　肉 (万吨)	Pork (10 000 tons)	11.27	2001	26.40	42.69
奶牛年末头数 (万头)	Quantity of Milk Cow (year-end) (10 000 heads)	5.58	2015	8.60	64.88
生牛奶 (万吨)	Raw Milk (10 000 tons)	33.44	2015	37.06	90.23
家禽出栏量(万只)	Quantity of Poultry Sold(10 000 fowls)	984	1997	17 851	5.51
禽　蛋 (万吨)	Poultry Eggs (10 000 tons)	3.16	2001	16.87	18.73
水产品	Aquatic Products				
海水产品(万吨)	Seawater Aquatic Products (10 000 tons)	16.84	1989	19.63	85.79
淡水产品(万吨)	Freshwater Aquatic Products (10 000 tons)	14.01	2003	22.13	63.31

注：建国以来最高年年份和产量均是指 2017 及以前的年份和产量，不包括 2018 年在内。
Note: Peak year and output of peak year since 1949 refer to the years before 2017, excluding 2018.

表 12.8　主要年份农业商品产值和商品率
OUTPUT VALUE OF AGRICULTURAL COMMODITY AND COMMODITY RATE IN MAIN YEARS

	指　标 Indicators	2000	2010	2017	2018
农业商品产值(亿元)	**Output Value of Agricultural Commodity (100 million yuan)**	**179.79**	**236.15**	**219.36**	**248.58**
#种植业	Planting	61.84	120.22	120.67	129.95
#粮食作物	Grain Crops	10.15	16.43	19.51	23.37
畜牧业	Animal Husbandry	80.75	58.01	36.68	44.71
#生　猪	Hogs	29.82	30.38	18.49	20.54
家　禽	Poultry	33.41	8.95	2.83	2.33
禽　蛋	Eggs	7.94	5.10	2.40	2.97
渔　业	Fishery	36.53	50.42	50.84	54.72
#淡水产品	Freshwater Aquatic Products	25.14	36.62	30.00	30.71
农业商品率(%)	**Agricultural Commodity Rate (%)**	**83.0**	**82.3**	**83.9**	**85.8**
#种植业	Planting	68.8	77.4	85.5	86.6
#粮食作物	Grain Crops	45.4	53.8	74.9	81.01
畜牧业	Animal Husbandry	92.4	92.2	89.8	92.5
#生　猪	Hogs	95.8	94.7	91.9	93.9
家　禽	Poultry	91.9	86.5	84.0	83.1
禽　蛋	Poultry Eggs	82.3	93.3	95.8	96.2
渔　业	Fishery	96.3	95.8	95.4	97.3
#淡水产品	Freshwater Aquatic Products	95.9	95.0	93.1	96.1

注：根据国家统计局方法制度规定，从2018年起农业商品产值包括上海市光明(集团)有限公司所属的外地农场。
Note: According to the method system of the National Bureau of Statistics, the output value of agricultural commodities includes the non-local farms of Shanghai Guangming (Group) Co., Ltd since 2018.

表 12.9　农民专业合作社组织情况(2015~2018)
ORGANIZATION OF FARMER PROFESSIONAL COOPERATIVES

	指　标 Indicators	2015	2016	2017	2018
农民专业合作社总数(个)	**Total Number of Farmer Professional Cooperatives (unit)**	**3 216**	**3 202**	**2 813**	**2 865**
种植业	Planting	2 246	2 258	1 963	1 996
畜牧业	Animal Husbandry	176	145	123	119
渔　业	Fishery	380	353	332	347
林　业	Forestry	82	103	93	94
服务业	Service	194	202	168	170
手工业	Handicraft		4	3	3
其　他	Others	138	137	131	136
成员总数(人)	Total Members(person)	64 561	64 421	62 966	62 686
带动非成员农户数(户)	Affected Non-member Peasant Households(household)	122 809	122 848	144 200	146 693

表12.10　主要年份农业机械拥有量
POSSESSION OF AGRICULTURAL MACHINERY IN MAIN YEARS

机械名称	Name of Machinery	2000	2010	2017	2018
农业机械总动力（万千瓦）	**Total Power of Agricultural Machinery (10 000 kw)**	**142.50**	**104.15**	**121.84**	**119.77**
耕作机械动力合计（万千瓦）	Total Power of Farming Machinery (10 000 kw)	37.60	29.54	38.56	40.29
#大、中型拖拉机（台）	Large and Medium Tractors (set)	7 844	5 796	7 728	7 466
（万千瓦）	(10 000 kw)	29.30	24.21	36.36	37.36
小型拖拉机（台）	Small Tractors (set)	9 253	5 788	2 317	2 554
（万千瓦）	(10 000 kw)	8.30	5.34	2.21	2.93
排灌机械动力合计（万千瓦）	Total Power of Drainage and Irrigation Machinery (10 000 kw)	25.92	21.80	25.17	25.80
收获机械动力合计（万千瓦）	Total Power of Harvest Machinery (10 000 kw)	33.30	12.19	16.26	13.55
#联合收割机（台）	Combined Harvesters (set)	4 991	2 230	2 240	2 177
（万千瓦）	(10 000 kw)	2.70	8.52	12.80	12.61
机动植保机械动力合计（万千瓦）	Total Power of Plant Protecting Machine (10 000 kw)	3.07	5.34	5.47	5.59
#机动喷雾器（万台）	Motorized Nebulizers (10 000 sets)	2.07	2.11	2.13	2.04
（万千瓦）	(10 000 kw)	3.07	4.72	5.08	5.06
渔业机械动力合计（万千瓦）	Total Power of Fishery Machinery (10 000 kw)	23.40	23.23	24.25	22.61
#机动渔船（艘）	Motorized Fishing Boats (ship)	2 905	1 788	871	856
（万千瓦）	(10 000 kw)	20.50	18.74	17.19	16.21
其他农业机械动力合计（万千瓦）	Total Power of Other Agricultural Machine (10 000 kw)	11.13	11.05	12.13	11.93

注：本表农业机械化统计范围未包括上海光明食品（集团）有限公司所属的域外农场（下表同）。
Note: The statistical scope of Agricultural Mechanization in this table does not include the farms outside Shanghai territory of Shanghai Guangming Food (Group) Co., Ltd.

表 12.11 主要年份农业技术应用和综合开发情况
TECHNOLOGY APPLICATIONS AND INTEGRATIVE EXPLOITATION IN AGRICULTURE IN MAIN YEARS

指标	Indicators	2000	2010	2017	2018
机耕面积（万公顷）	Areas of Motorized Cultivation（10 000 hectares）	23.46	39.47	28.07	28.53
机电排灌总控制面积（万公顷）	Total Area with Motorized Drainage and Irrigation Facilities（10 000 hectares）	28.59	17.61	18.82	18.82
粮食机种面积（万公顷）	Areas of Motorized Planting（10 000 hectares）	6.08	5.30	7.71	8.56
占粮食播种面积（%）	Percentage in Total Planting Area of Grain（%）	23.5	29.6	65.0	80.1
粮食机收面积（万公顷）	Areas of Motorized Harvesting（10 000 hectares）	16.42	16.57	11.82	10.49
占粮食收获面积（%）	Percentage in Total Harvesting Area of Grain（%）	63.4	92.5	99.6	98.1
机械植保面积（万公顷）	Areas of Mechancial Protecting（10 000 hectares）	41.10	30.41	26.95	27.39
化肥施用量（实物量）（万吨）	Chemical Fertilizer Consumption（real）（10 000 tons）	82.54	47.05	29.79	24.92
化肥施用量（折纯量）（万吨）	Chemical Fertilizer Consumption（convert to pure amount）（10 000 tons）	19.33	12.76	9.88	8.37
农药施用量(万吨）	Farm Pesticides Consumption（10 000 tons）	1.10	0.76	0.37	0.32
农用塑料薄膜使用量（万吨）	Agricultural Plastic Film Consumption（10 000 tons）	2.13	2.11	1.57	1.48
地膜覆盖面积（万公顷）	Areas Covered by Plastic Film（10 000 hectares）	2.05	2.62	1.66	1.40

表 12.12　域外市属农场农业生产情况(2015~2018)
AGRICULTURAL PRODUCTION OF EXTERNAL MUNICIPAL FARM

指　标	Indicators	2015	2016	2017	2018
农业总产值(亿元)	**Gross Output Value of Agriculture(100 million yuan)**	**25.09**	**32.36**	**31.02**	**31.52**
#种植业	Planting	5.82	6.16	5.22	6.29
林　业	Forestry	0.15	0.06	0.37	0.11
牧　业	Animal Husbandry	15.23	21.06	20.31	18.92
渔　业	Fishery	3.89	5.08	5.12	4.90
主要农产品产量	Output of Major Farm Products				
粮　食(万吨)	Grain(10 000 tons)	17.87	16.34	14.84	16.27
夏　粮	Summer Grain Crops	6.77	6.06	4.98	6.32
秋　粮	Autumn Grain Crops	11.10	10.28	9.86	9.95
油菜籽(吨)	Rapeseed(ton)	4 103	1 186	761	1 433
蔬　菜(吨)	Vegetables(ton)	155	168		4 761
园林水果(吨)	Fruits(ton)	604	157	200	207.00
西　瓜(吨)	Watermelon(ton)	7 298	32 413	9 020	33 339
茶　叶(吨)	Tea-leaves(ton)	2.43	0.80	2.21	2.50
生猪出栏(万头)	Quantity of Sold Hogs(10 000 heads)	63.27	79.51	77.95	72.61
生牛奶(万吨)	Raw Milk(10 000 tons)	5.97	10.12	15.07	16.23
水产品(万吨)	Aquatic Products(10 000 tons)	3.23	3.65	3.80	4.42

注：域外市属农场是指上海光明食品(集团)有限公司所属的外地农场。
Note: External municipal farm refers to the nonlocal farms owned to Shanghai bright food (Group) Co., Ltd.

上/海/统/计/年/鉴

主要统计指标解释

■ 农村从业人员

指乡村人口中16岁以上实际参加生产经营活动并取得实物或货币收入的人员，既包括劳动年龄内实际参加劳动人员，也包括超过劳动年龄但实际参加劳动的人员，但不包括户口在家的在外学生、现役军人和丧失劳动能力的人，也不包括待业人员和家务劳动者。劳动者年龄为16岁以上。

■ 农业总产值

农业总产值是以货币表现的农、林、牧、渔业全部产品的总量和对农林牧渔生产活动进行的各种支持性服务活动的价值。它反映一定时期内农业生产的总规模和总成果。

农、林、牧、渔业的统计范围是：

(1) 种植业　包括谷物、豆类、薯类、棉、油料、糖料、麻类、烟叶、蔬菜、药材、瓜类和其他农作物的种植，以及茶园、桑园、果园的生产经营。

(2) 林业　包括林木的栽培(不包括茶园、桑园和果园的栽培、管理和收获等活动)、林产品的采集和村及村以下合作经济组织和农户的竹木采伐。

(3) 牧业　包括除渔业养殖以外的一切动物饲养和放牧，以及野生动物的捕猎和饲养。

(4) 渔业　包括水生动物和海藻类植物的养殖和捕捞。

(5) 农林牧渔服务业　包括农林牧渔业生产活动进行的各种支持性服务活动。但不包括各种科学技术和专业技术服务活动。

农业总产值的计算方法通常是按农林牧渔业产品及其副产品的产量分别乘以各自单位产品价格求得，少数生产周期较长、当年没有产品或产品产量不易统计的，则采用间接方法匡算其产值，然后将四业产品产值和服务业产值相加即为农业总产值。

1957年以前的农业总产值中包括了厩肥和农民自给性手工业(如农民自制衣服、鞋、袜，自己从事粮食初步加工等)。1958年及以后的农业总产值，林业中增加了村及村以下竹木采伐产值；牧业中取消了厩肥产值；副业中取消了农民自给性手工业产值，增加了村及村以下办的工业产值；渔业中增加了海洋捕捞水产品产值。1980年及以后的农业总产值，在副业中增加了农民家庭兼营工业商品部分的产值。从1984年起村及村以下办工业产值划归工业。从1993年起，取消副业。将野生动物的捕猎划入牧业，野生植物采集和农民家庭兼营商品性工业划归农业。从2003年起，农业总产值中包括了农林牧渔服务业产值。

■ 农业机械总动力

指用于农、林、牧、渔业生产的各种动力机械的动力总和。动力机械包括耕作、排灌、种植、植物保护、收获、农产品加工、运输、畜牧、渔业、农田水利等各种机械。不包括专门用于乡办工业、基本建设、非农业运输、科学试验和教学等非农业生产方面用的动力机械与作业机械的数量。

■ 农作物播种面积

指报告期内收获农产品的作物的实际播种或移植有农作物的面积。凡是实际种植农作物的面积，不论种植在耕地上还是种植在非耕地上，均包括在农作物播种面积中。在播种季节基本结束后，因遭灾而重新改种和补种的农作物面积，也包括在内。

■ 粮食产量

指全社会的产量。包括国有经济经营的、集体统一经营的和农民家庭经营的粮食产量，还包括工矿企业办的农场和其他生产单位的产量。粮食除包括稻谷、小麦、玉米、高粱、谷子及其他杂粮外，还包括薯类和豆类。其产量计算方法，豆类按去豆荚后的干豆计算；薯类(包括甘薯和马铃薯，不包括芋头和木薯)1963年以前按每4公斤鲜薯折1公斤粮食计算，从1964年开始改为按5公斤鲜薯折1公斤粮食计算。城市郊区作为蔬菜的薯类(如马铃薯等)按鲜品计算，并且不作粮食统计。其他粮食一律按脱粒后的原粮计算。1989年以前粮食产量数据主要靠全面报表取得，1989年开始使用抽样调查数据。

■ 棉花产量

指全社会的产量。包括春播棉和夏播棉。产量按皮棉计算。3公斤籽棉折1公斤皮棉，不包括木棉。

■ 油料产量

指全部油料作物的生产量。包括花生、油菜籽、芝麻、向日葵籽、胡麻籽(亚麻籽)和其他油料。不包括大

主要统计指标解释

豆、木本油料和野生油料。花生以带壳干花生计算。

■ 水产品产量

指人工养殖的水产品和天然生长的水产品的捕捞量。包括海水的鱼类、虾蟹类、贝类和藻类以及内陆水域的鱼类、虾蟹类和贝类，不包括淡水生植物。水产品产量是通过各级水产和统计部门逐级上报取得数据。1995年及以前，贝类中牡蛎按鲜肉计算；蚶、蛤、蛙按5斤鲜品折1斤计算。1996年以后则统一按鲜品计算。

■ 猪、牛、羊肉产量

指当年出栏并已屠宰、除去头蹄下水后带骨肉(即胴体重)的重量。包括全社会范围内的产量。1996年前为各级逐级上报数据。1996年第一次农业普查以后，由于畜牧业产品年报数据与普查数据之间存在一定的差距，国家统计局农调总队对畜牧业年报数据与普查数据进行衔接。上海仍使用各级统计部门逐级上报数据。

SHANGHAI STATISTICAL YEARBOOK

EXPLANATORY NOTES TO MAJOR STATISTICAL INDICATORS

□ Employees in Rural Areas

Employees in Rural Areas refers to people in rural areas who are older than 16 years and engaged in production and business activities that generate incomes in cash or in practicality. It includes all working laborers, no matter whether they are within the working age or not, whereas students studying outside but with their registered residence at home, active serviceman, people who lost their ability to work, unemployed people, and those engaged in housework are not included. The working age is defined as older than 16 years.

□ Gross Output Value of Agriculture

Gross Output Value of Agriculture refers to the total volume of products of farming, forestry, animal husbandry and fishery expressed in the monetary terms and output value of all kinds of service activities that support farming, forestry, animal husbandry and fishery production. It reflects the overall scale and achievements of agricultural production during a given period of time.

The scope of statistics on farming, forestry, animal husbandry, and fishery are as follows:

(1) Farming includes cultivation of grain crops, legume crops, tuber–crops, cotton, oil–bearing crops, sugar crops, bastfiber plants, tobacco, vegetables, medicinal herbs, melon crops, and cultivation and management of tea plantations, mulberry fields and orchards.

(2) Forestry refers to planting trees of various kinds (excluding tea plantations, mulberry fields and orchards), collection of forestry products and cutting and felling of bamboo and trees by villages and other cooperative organizations under village level.

(3) Animal husbandry refers to raising and grazing of all kinds of farm animals except fishing and aquatic cultivating, and hunting and rising of wild animals.

(4) Fishery refers to cultivation and catching of fish and other aquatic products and cultivation and collection of seaweed and other aquatic plants.

(5) Service Industry for Farming, Forestry, Animal Husbandry and Fishery refers to all kinds of service activities that support farming, forestry, animal husbandry and fishery production, whereas activities of science, technology and professional service are not included.

Gross output value of agriculture is obtained by first multiplying the output of products or by–products by their unit price. For a small number of products, annual output of which is not available or difficult to get due to the long production/growing process involved, the output value will be estimated through an indirect approach. The sum of output value of all products of farming, forestry, animal husbandry and fishery and output value of service activities will then and together to form gross output value of agriculture.

Before 1957, China′s gross agricultural output value included the value of barnyard manure and handicraft products for self– consumption (clothes, shoes, stockings, and initial grain processing under–taken by peasants). After 1958, the output value of cutting and felling of bamboo and trees by villages and other cooperative organizations under villages have been included in forestry; value of barnyard manure has been excluded from animal husbandry; the value of self– consumed handicrafts has been excluded from sideline occupations, while output value of industries run by villages and cooperative organizations under village level has been included in sideline occupations and output value of fish catches by motor fishing boats has been added to fishery. Since 1980, the output value of handicraft products made for sale by farmer households has been added to sideline occupations. From 1984, industries run by villages and cooperative organizations under village level have been included in the sector of industry. After 1993, the category of sideline occupations has been canceled and hunting of wild animals has been classified into husbandry, and harvesting of wild vegetation and commodity industry run by rural households have been grouped into the category of agriculture. Since 2003, the output value of service industry for farming, forestry, animal husbandry and fishery is included in the gross output value of agriculture.

□ Total Power of Agricultural Machinery

Total Power of Agricultural Machinery refers to the total mechanical power of machinery used in farming, forestry animal husbandry and fishery, including machines used for ploughing, irrigation and drainage, crop growing, plant protection, harvesting, farm product processing, transport, stock breeding, fishery

EXPLANATORY NOTES TO MAJOR STATISTICAL INDICATORS

and water conservancy. Machinery employed for non-agricultural purposes such as township industry, capital construction, non-agricultural transport, scientific experiments and for teaching is excluded.

□ Sown Area of Planting

Sown Area of Planting refers to area of land sown or transplanted with crops that have been harvested during report period, regardless of being in cultivated area or non-cultivated area. Area of land re-sown due to natural disasters is also included.

□ Grain Output

Grain Output refers to the total output in the whole country including grains produced by state farms, collective units, rural households, as well as by farms affiliated to industrial and mining enterprises and other production units. Grain includes rice, wheat, corn, sorghum, millet and other miscellaneous grains as well as tubers and bean. Output of beans refers to dry beans without pods. The output of tubers (sweet potatoes and potatoes, not including taros and cassava) was converted into that of grain at the ratio 4:1, i.e. 4 kilograms of fresh tubers was equivalent to 1 kilogram of grain up to 1963. Since 1964 the ratio for conversion has been 5:1. Tubers supplied as vegetables (such as potatoes) in cities and suburbs are calculated as fresh vegetables and their output is not included in the output of grain. Output of all other grains refers to husked grain. Data on grain production before 1989 were obtained through Comprehensive Statistical Reporting System. Since 1989, data from sample surveys are used.

□ Cotton Output

Cotton Output refers to the cotton production in the whole country including cotton sown in spring and in autumn. Output is measured as the weight of ginned cotton. Three kilograms of seed-cotton are equivalent to 1 kilogram of ginned cotton, excluding ceiba.

□ Output of Oil-bearing Crops

Output of Oil-bearing Crops refers to the total production of oil-bearing crops of various kinds, including peanuts, (dry, in shell) rapeseeds, sesame, sunflower seeds, flax seeds, and other oil- bearing crops. Soybeans, oil- bearing woody plants, and wild oil-bearing crops are not included.

□ Output of Aquatic Products

Output of Aquatic Products refers to catches of both artificially cultured and naturally grown aquatic products, including fish, shrimps, crabs and shellfish in sea and inland water as well as seaweed. Freshwater plants are not included. Data on output of aquatic products are reported by aquatic product and statistical agencies level by level. Before 1995, among the shellfish, the oyster was counted as fresh meat; 5 kilograms of ark shell, clams and frogs are equivalent to 1 kilogram of fresh aquatic products; they are all counted as fresh aquatic products since 1996.

□ Output of Pork, Beef, and Mutton

Output of Pork, Beef, and Mutton refers to the meat of slaughtered hogs, cattle, sheep and goats with head, feet, and offal taken away. Data refers to the production of the whole country. The first agriculture census of China in 1996 revealed some discrepancy between the production of animal products from the annual reports and that from the census. Efforts were made by the Rural Socio-economic Survey Organization of NBS to adjust the output value of animal husbandry to make the figures from the annual reports consistent with the census data. Data of Shanghai are still reported by statistical agencies level by level.

第十三篇

CHAPTER 13

2019上海统计年鉴 SHANGHAI STATISTICAL YEARBOOK

工　业

INDUSTRY

简要说明

一、本章资料的主要内容

本篇资料反映上海市工业经济方面的基本情况，主要内容包括：

1.上海工业经济概况。规模以上工业企业主要经济指标，以及按地区、隶属关系、企业登记注册类型、企业规模和工业行业大类分组的主要经济指标；按隶属关系、企业规模分组和国有控股的主要经济效益指标。

2.国有控股主要经济指标及其占全市比重。

3.六个重点工业行业主要经济指标。

4.高技术产业（制造业）主要经济指标。

5.都市型工业按企业规模、登记注册类型和行业分组的主要经济指标。

6.历年主要工业产品产量及2018年主要工业产品产、销量。

7.大中小型工业企业按隶属关系、工业总产值、行业分组的主要经济指标。

8.国家级、市级工业园区主要经济指标。

二、本篇资料的统计范围

本篇资料除表13.1为全市工业企业以外，其余工业数据的统计范围如下：1998年至2006年为全部国有和年主营业务收入500万元及以上的非国有工业企业；2007至2010年为年主营业务收入500万元及以上的工业企业（即规模以上工业企业）；从2011年开始，为年主营业务收入2000万元及以上的工业企业（即规模以上工业企业）。

本篇资料中工业行业分类按2017年《国民经济行业分类（2017版）》标准划分；企业大中小微型划分按《统计上大中小微型企业划分办法（2017）》标准执行。

本篇资料中税金总额包含的应交增值税指标从2015年年报起，负数不做替零处理。

三、本篇的资料来源和统计调查方法

本篇工业企业统计数据1978-2017年根据工业统计年度报表整理汇总，2018年根据2018年工业统计定报报表中有关资料整理汇总。

BRIEF INTRODUCTION

I. Major Contents

The Data in this chapter reflect the basic conditions of the industrial sector in Shanghai. Major contents include:

(1) Basic conditions of industrial sectors in Shanghai; major economic indicators of industrial enterprises above designated sizes; as well as major economic indicators classified by regions, by subordination, by types of registration, by size of enterprise, and by branch of industry; and major economic efficiency indicators classified by subordination, by sizes of enterprise, and on state-controlled industrial enterprises.

(2) Major economic indicators of state-controlled industrial enterprises and their proportions of the city's total.

(3) Major economic indicators of six key industrial sectors.

(4) Major economic indicators of high technology industries (manufacturing).

(5) Major economic indicators of urban industries classified by sizes of enterprise, by type of registration, and by industrial sectors.

(6) Output of major industrial products in recent years, as well as output and sales of major industrial products in 2018.

(7)Major economic indicators of large-, medium-, and small-size industrial enterprises classified by subordination, by gross output value of industry.

(8) Major economic indicators of municipal and national industrial zones.

II. Scope and Coverage of Statistics

Except for table 13.1, which covers all industrial enterprises in the city, the scopes of industrial statistics were all state-owned industrial enterprises and non-state-owned industrial enterprises whose annual revenue from principal business was more than 5 million yuan from 1998 to 2006. For 2007 to 2010, the scopes of industrial statistics were all industrial enterprises whose annual revenue from principal business was more than 5 million yuan, (i.e., the industrial enterprises above designated size). Since 2011, the scope is adjusted to all industrial enterprises whose annual revenue from principal business was more than 20 million yuan (i.e. industrial enterprises above designated size).

Branches of industry in this chapter are based on the 2017's National Industrial Classification of all Economic Activities, and data by size of enterprise are based on 2017 Standards of Enterprises by Size.

In this chapter, the negative numbers of value added tax payable included in the total amount of tax needn't do zero treatment since annual report of 2015.

Ⅲ.Sources of Data and Methodology of Survey

The data of industrial enterprises statistics from 1978-2017 in this Chapter are collected mainly from the relevant data in the annual industrial statistics reporting forms while the data of 2018 are collected from the relevant data in the periodic industrial statistics reporting forms.

表 13.1 工业总产值及指数 (1978~2018)
GROSS OUTPUT VALUE OF INDUSTRY AND INDEX

年 份 Year	工业总产值 (亿元) Gross Output Value of Industry (100 million yuan)	工业总产值指数 (以 1978 年为 100) Indices of Gross Output Value of Industry (1978=100)	年 份 Year	工业总产值 (亿元) Gross Output Value of Industry (100 million yuan)	工业总产值指数 (以 1978 年为 100) Indices of Gross Output Value of Industry (1978=100)
1978	514.01	100.0	1998	5 763.67	728.5
1979	556.30	108.6	1999	6 213.24	805.1
1980	598.75	115.7	2000	7 022.98	913.7
1981	620.12	120.0	2001	7 806.18	1 063.8
1982	634.65	125.6	2002	8 730.00	1 219.1
1983	663.53	134.4	2003	11 708.49	1 601.9
1984	728.12	147.7	2004	14 595.29	1 927.1
1985	862.73	167.7	2005	16 876.78	2 195.0
1986	952.21	177.0	2006	19 631.23	2 500.1
1987	1 073.84	188.9	2007	23 108.63	2 892.6
1988	1 304.66	208.8	2008	25 968.38	3 126.9
1989	1 524.67	215.0	2009	24 888.08	3 227.0
1990	1 642.75	223.6	2010	31 038.57	3 966.0
1991	1 947.18	255.2	2011	33 834.44	4 227.8
1992	2 429.96	306.7	2012	33 186.41	4 215.1
1993	3 327.04	368.2	2013	33 899.38	4 396.3
1994	4 255.19	435.3	2014	34 071.19	4 466.7
1995	5 349.53	510.9	2015	33 211.57	4 444.3
(1995)	(4 547.47)		2016	33 079.72	4 475.4
1996	5 126.22	590.1	2017	36 094.36	4 766.3
1997	5 649.93	675.7	2018	36 451.84	4 828.3

注：从 1996 年开始，工业总产值按新规定计算，括号内数为 1995 年新规定数(以下同)。
Note: Since 1996, new regulations have been adopted in calculating total industrial gross output value of industry. The figures of 1995 in brackets are calculated in line with the new regulations(same as follows).

表 13.2 各区工业企业主要指标（2018）
MAJOR INDICATIORS OF INDUSTRIAL ENTERPRISES IN DISTRICTS

单位：亿元（100 million yuan）

地 区	District	工业总产值 Gross Output Value of Industry	年末资产总计 Total Assets (year-end)	主营业务收入 Prime Operating Revenue	利润总额 Total Pre-tax Profits
总 计	**Total**	**34 841.84**	**43 885.51**	**38 886.41**	**3 350.44**
#浦东新区	Pudong New Area	10 307.67	14 969.32	12 083.40	1 027.97
黄 浦 区	Huangpu	43.28	95.87	98.51	3.95
徐 汇 区	Xuhui	574.37	496.95	715.43	47.37
长 宁 区	Changning	121.04	151.78	120.83	6.47
静 安 区	Jing'an	90.68	148.16	86.12	6.36
普 陀 区	Putuo	146.39	290.61	200.37	20.53
虹 口 区	Hongkou	48.21	107.47	56.85	3.01
杨 浦 区	Yangpu	1 161.30	1 992.64	1 175.63	253.02
闵 行 区	Minhang	3 367.19	4 210.37	3 744.38	286.87
宝 山 区	Baoshan	2 039.88	3 800.23	2 636.48	222.65
嘉 定 区	Jiading	6 054.66	4 930.45	6 389.94	656.39
金 山 区	Jinshan	2 072.56	2 077.56	2 117.99	129.93
松 江 区	Songjiang	3 766.13	3 341.50	3 968.56	160.86
青 浦 区	Qingpu	1 537.31	1 865.92	1 698.20	85.01
奉 贤 区	Fengxian	1 724.02	2 160.79	1 835.45	148.35
崇 明 区	Chongming	372.65	854.42	364.70	16.65

表 13.3 规模以上工业企业主要指标(2018)
MAJOR INDICATORS OF INDUSTRIAL ENTERPRISES ABOVE THE SET SCALE

类 别	Types	工业总产值 Gross Output Value of Industry
总 计	**Total**	**34 841.84**
按隶属关系分	**Grouped by Subordination**	
中央工业	Central Government	5 928.59
地方工业	Local Government	28 913.26
按登记注册类型分	**Grouped by Registration Categories**	
内 资	Domestic Funded	13 429.87
#国 有	State-owned	40.39
集 体	Collective-owned	15.86
有限责任公司	Companies with Limited Liabilities	6 746.42
股份有限公司	Share-holding Companies with Limited Liabilities	2 371.38
私 营	Private	4 224.69
港澳台商投资	Hong Kong, Macao and Taiwan Funded	4 929.59
#与港澳台商合资经营	Joint-venture	1 022.61
港澳台商独资	Sole Funded	2 824.59
港澳台商投资股份有限公司	Share-holding Companies Ltd.	998.82
外商投资	Foreign Funded	16 482.37
#中外合资经营	Joint-venture	7 379.46
外资企业	Sole Funded	8 290.21
外商投资股份有限公司	Share-holding Companies Ltd.	509.46
按企业规模分	**Grouped by Size of Enterprises**	
大 型	Large	18 448.12
中 型	Medium	7 141.08
小 型	Small	9 252.64
按工业行业分	**Grouped by Sectors**	
采矿业	**Mining Industry**	**6.72**
石油和天然气开采业	Petroleum and Natural Gas Exploiting	6.72
制造业	**Manufacture Industry**	**33 228.61**
农副食品加工业	Farm and Sideline Products Processing	296.49
食品制造业	Food Manufacturing	643.46
酒、饮料和精制茶制造业	Wine, Beverage and Refined Tea Manufacturing	98.73
烟草制品业	Tabacco Manufacturing	926.10

单位:亿元(100 million yuan)

年末资产总计 Total Assets (year-end)	流动资产合计 Current Assets	年末负债合计 Total Liabilities (year-end)
43 885.51	**25 586.81**	**20 933.70**
10 801.48	4 717.67	4 552.85
33 084.03	20 869.14	16 380.84
24 935.70	13 051.13	10 893.46
95.17	57.31	48.44
26.65	21.99	11.24
12 090.65	6 246.16	5 631.48
7 250.32	2 930.13	2 379.83
5 449.05	3 776.44	2 811.76
4 531.41	2 890.93	2 203.30
1 434.40	940.84	782.30
2 161.56	1 459.86	1 136.93
852.09	427.51	233.02
14 418.40	9 644.75	7 836.94
5 687.84	3 645.77	3 324.64
7 135.73	5 086.13	3 624.91
1 316.93	691.70	771.78
24 187.39	12 563.03	11 189.55
8 686.65	5 597.57	4 224.59
11 011.47	7 426.22	5 519.56
35.36	**26.88**	**7.34**
35.36	26.88	7.34
39 632.05	**24 869.79**	**19 272.56**
311.61	205.55	152.79
720.49	444.68	355.75
166.94	106.49	88.15
1 428.85	1 067.72	170.95

表 13.3 续表 1 continued

类别	Types	工业总产值 Gross Output Value of Industry
纺织业	Textile	181.35
纺织服装、服饰业	Textiles and Clothing Industry	313.72
皮革、毛皮、羽毛及其制品和制鞋业	Leather, Fur, Wool Products and Shoes Manufacturing	170.92
木材加工和木、竹、藤、棕、草制品业	Timber Processing and Timber, Bamboo, Rattan, Coir and Straw Products Manufacturing	48.72
家具制造业	Furniture Manufacturing	327.23
造纸和纸制品业	Paper-making and Paper Products Manufacturing	235.14
印刷和记录媒介复制业	Printing and Record Duplicating	191.28
文教、工美、体育和娱乐用品制造业	Culture, Education, Industrial Arts, Sports and Entertainment Goods Manufacturing	399.83
石油、煤炭及其他燃料加工业	Oil, Coal and Other Fuel Processing	1 369.41
化学原料和化学制品制造业	Raw Chemical Materials and Chemical Products Manufacturing	3 017.19
医药制造业	Medicine Manufacturing	844.37
化学纤维制造业	Chemical Fiber Manufacturing	23.99
橡胶和塑料制品业	Rubber and Plastic Products Manufacturing	888.13
非金属矿物制品业	Non-metallic Mineral Products Manufacturing	600.42
黑色金属冶炼和压延加工业	Ferrous Metal Smelting and Rolling Processing Industry	1 233.42
有色金属冶炼和压延加工业	Nonferrous Metal Smelting and Rolling Processing Industry	362.59
金属制品业	Metal Products Manufacturing	974.25
通用设备制造业	General Equipment Manufacturing	2 888.06
专用设备制造业	Special Purpose Equipment Manufacturing	1 254.03
汽车制造业	The Automotive Manufacturing	6 832.07
铁路、船舶、航空航天和其他运输设备制造业	The Railroad, Marine, Aerospace and Other Transportation Equipment Manufacturing	707.90
电气机械和器材制造业	Electric Machinery Equipments and Manufacturing	2 239.74
计算机、通信和其他电子设备制造业	Computer, Communications and Other Electronic Equipment Manufacturing	5 467.58
仪器仪表制造业	Instrumentation Manufacturing	414.14
其他制造业	Other Manufacturing	46.81
废弃资源综合利用业	Comprehensive Utilization of Waste Resources	37.71
金属制品、机械和设备修理业	Metal Products, Machinery and Equipment Repair Industry	193.84
电力、热力、燃气及水生产和供应业	**Electricity, Heat, Gas and Water Production and Supply Industry**	**1 606.50**
电力、热力生产和供应业	Production and Supply of Electricity and Thermal Power	1 199.20
燃气生产和供应业	Production and Supply of Gas	334.42
水的生产和供应业	Production and Supply of Water	72.88

单位:亿元(100 million yuan)

年末资产总计 Total Assets (year-end)	流动资产合计 Current Assets	年末负债合计 Total Liabilities (year-end)
167.29	126.12	70.78
304.59	233.65	167.03
256.21	227.90	63.03
60.68	39.11	28.40
334.41	241.28	199.80
275.56	178.64	118.86
244.75	149.84	93.78
278.39	214.24	142.59
809.14	396.84	315.04
3 015.83	1 835.96	1 215.60
1 475.37	824.23	519.27
39.63	29.74	22.91
1 065.53	657.88	441.59
825.52	626.58	483.61
2 722.24	1 102.07	999.85
253.16	186.43	139.11
1 121.73	790.18	605.75
4 102.26	2 870.29	2 397.42
1 937.10	1 399.60	1 000.83
7 849.76	4 188.60	3 662.67
1 770.60	1 168.14	1 447.72
2 454.67	1 828.60	1 268.91
4 861.82	3 170.10	2 736.14
423.85	352.87	173.14
64.36	41.86	26.48
48.20	25.67	26.46
241.50	138.93	138.15
4 218.10	**690.15**	**1 653.80**
2 845.64	378.50	1 112.82
450.13	191.54	225.03
922.33	120.10	315.95

表 13.3 续表 2 continued

	类 别 Types	年末所有者权益 Owners' Equity (year-end)
总 计	**Total**	**22 951.81**
按隶属关系分	**Grouped by Subordination**	
中央工业	Central Government	6 248.63
地方工业	Local Government	16 703.18
按登记注册类型分	**Grouped by Registration Categories**	
内 资	Domestic Funded	14 042.25
#国 有	State-owned	46.74
集 体	Collective-owned	15.41
有限责任公司	Companies with Limited Liabilities	6 459.17
股份有限公司	Share-holding Companies with Limited Liabilities	4 870.49
私 营	Private	2 637.30
港澳台商投资	Hong Kong, Macao and Taiwan Funded	2 328.10
#与港澳台商合资经营	Joint-venture	652.10
港澳台商独资	Sole Funded	1 024.63
港澳台商投资股份有限公司	Share-holding Companies Ltd.	619.08
外商投资	Foreign Funded	6 581.46
#中外合资经营	Joint-venture	2 363.20
外资企业	Sole Funded	3 510.81
外商投资股份有限公司	Share-holding Companies Ltd.	545.14
按企业规模分	**Grouped by Size of Enterprises**	
大 型	Large	12 997.84
中 型	Medium	4 462.06
小 型	Small	5 491.91
按工业行业分	**Grouped by Sectors**	
采矿业	**Mining Industry**	**28.02**
石油和天然气开采业	Petroleum and Natural Gas Exploiting	28.02
制造业	**Manufacture Industry**	**20 359.49**
农副食品加工业	Farm and Sideline Products Processing	158.82
食品制造业	Food Manufacturing	364.73
酒、饮料和精制茶制造业	Wine, Beverage and Refined Tea Manufacturing	78.79
烟草制品业	Tabacco Manufacturing	1 257.90

单位：亿元(100 million yuan)

主营业务收入 Prime Operating Revenue	利润总额 Total Pre-tax Profits	税金总额 Total Tax and Duties	成本费用总额 Total Cost and Expenses
38 886.41	**3 350.44**	**1 972.63**	**35 552.67**
6 530.37	630.75	1 077.39	5 304.12
32 356.05	2 719.69	895.24	30 248.55
15 564.56	1 430.14	1 187.90	14 214.45
41.94	1.06	-1.13	41.07
18.96	1.35	0.96	18.25
7 504.56	548.29	900.57	6 527.06
3 440.40	598.95	163.27	3 294.84
4 526.91	279.56	123.24	4 301.63
5 179.58	326.86	202.42	4 775.23
1 197.43	118.09	24.63	1 114.61
2 880.96	142.59	28.43	2 749.13
1 004.65	63.76	147.03	818.17
18 142.27	1 593.44	582.32	16 562.99
8 306.11	911.29	422.79	7 337.50
8 937.42	626.43	150.25	8 362.12
575.61	35.69	1.65	560.29
20 859.30	2 081.19	1 547.05	18 572.63
7 974.27	589.46	194.11	7 480.79
10 052.84	679.79	231.48	9 499.26
6.65	**1.35**	**1.08**	**5.19**
6.65	1.35	1.08	5.19
37 142.95	**3 273.29**	**1 914.93**	**33 836.32**
382.14	15.68	4.80	368.88
733.34	68.25	33.54	674.64
145.11	4.82	9.61	137.83
931.73	232.02	721.60	142.58

表 13.3 续表 3 continued

类 别	Types	年末所有者权益 Owners' Equity (year-end)
纺织业	Textile	96.51
纺织服装、服饰业	Textiles and Clothing Industry	137.57
皮革、毛皮、羽毛及其制品和制鞋业	Leather, Fur, Wool Products and Shoes Manufacturing	193.18
木材加工和木、竹、藤、棕、草制品业	Timber Processing and Timber, Bamboo, Rattan, Coir and Straw Products Manufacturing	32.28
家具制造业	Furniture Manufacturing	134.61
造纸和纸制品业	Paper-making and Paper Products Manufacturing	156.70
印刷和记录媒介复制业	Printing and Record Duplicating	150.97
文教、工美、体育和娱乐用品制造业	Culture, Education, Industrial Arts, Sports and Entertainment Goods Manufacturing	135.80
石油、煤炭及其他燃料加工业	Oil, Coal and Other Fuel Processing	494.09
化学原料和化学制品制造业	Raw Chemical Materials and Chemical Products Manufacturing	1 800.23
医药制造业	Medicine Manufacturing	956.10
化学纤维制造业	Chemical Fiber Manufacturing	16.72
橡胶和塑料制品业	Rubber and Plastic Products Manufacturing	623.94
非金属矿物制品业	Non-metallic Mineral Products Manufacturing	341.91
黑色金属冶炼和压延加工业	Ferrous Metal Smelting and Rolling Processing Industry	1 722.40
有色金属冶炼和压延加工业	Nonferrous Metal Smelting and Rolling Processing Industry	114.05
金属制品业	Metal Products Manufacturing	515.98
通用设备制造业	General Equipment Manufacturing	1 704.84
专用设备制造业	Special Purpose Equipment Manufacturing	936.27
汽车制造业	The Automotive Manufacturing	4 187.09
铁路、船舶、航空航天和其他运输设备制造业	The Railroad, Marine, Aerospace and Other Transportation Equipment Manufacturing	322.88
电气机械和器材制造业	Electric Machinery Equipments and Manufacturing	1 185.77
计算机、通信和其他电子设备制造业	Computer, Communications and Other Electronic Equipment Manufacturing	2 125.67
仪器仪表制造业	Instrumentation Manufacturing	250.71
其他制造业	Other Manufacturing	37.89
废弃资源综合利用业	Comprehensive Utilization of Waste Resources	21.74
金属制品、机械和设备修理业	Metal Products, Machinery and Equipment Repair Industry	103.36
电力、热力、燃气及水生产和供应业	**Electricity, Heat, Gas and Water Production and Supply Industry**	**2 564.30**
电力、热力生产和供应业	Production and Supply of Electricity and Thermal Power	1 732.82
燃气生产和供应业	Production and Supply of Gas	225.10
水的生产和供应业	Production and Supply of Water	606.38

单位：亿元(100 million yuan)

主营业务收入 Prime Operating Revenue	利润总额 Total Pre-tax Profits	税金总额 Total Pre-tax and Duties	成本费用总额 Total Cost and Expenses
204.61	9.75	3.96	195.75
363.44	6.75	5.54	365.79
177.22	10.63	3.64	166.65
53.56	2.07	2.07	51.25
337.36	39.80	8.51	318.72
293.57	13.04	9.47	281.38
200.67	16.47	7.93	189.25
575.60	35.14	6.24	551.02
1 378.78	108.50	242.75	1 103.68
3 360.83	420.56	91.66	2 966.50
846.58	110.34	50.44	743.92
24.89	0.44	0.45	26.09
954.64	63.47	22.69	900.59
679.76	52.12	19.61	640.54
1 731.79	163.61	30.48	1 635.07
392.41	14.50	2.69	378.84
1 081.97	55.43	29.55	1 039.85
3 151.51	210.41	72.46	2 959.01
1 343.35	121.47	28.68	1 242.18
8 334.23	1 077.68	410.80	7 604.75
683.98	12.85	15.69	694.41
2 394.83	183.33	49.49	2 240.17
5 675.34	152.39	11.05	5 574.65
432.86	52.16	9.37	388.26
52.60	5.32	2.15	47.65
38.94	7.19	1.90	34.25
185.34	7.10	6.10	172.16
1 736.81	**75.80**	**56.62**	**1 711.17**
1 234.98	49.55	50.38	1 211.26
401.97	14.96	2.19	400.60
99.85	11.30	4.04	99.30

表 13.4 工业企业销售产值(2018)
SALES VALUE OF INDUSTRIAL ENTERPRISES

单位:亿元(100 million yuan)

类 别	Types	工业销售产值 Sales Value of Industry	其中 of which #出口交货值 Delivery Value of Industrial Exports
总 计	**Total**	**34 783.89**	**7 739.27**
按隶属关系分	**Grouped by Subordination**		
中央工业	Central Government	5 928.32	592.71
地方工业	Local Government	28 855.58	7 146.55
按登记注册类型分	**Grouped by Registration Categories**		
内 资	Domestic Funded	13 442.49	1 143.79
#国 有	State-owned	40.54	0.04
集 体	Collective-owned	16.10	1.09
有限责任公司	Companies with Limited Liabilities	6 769.26	542.23
股份有限公司	Share-holding Companies with Limited Liabilities	2 376.04	215.93
私 营	Private	4 209.28	383.47
港澳台商投资	Hong Kong, Macao and Taiwan Funded	4 896.14	2 262.17
#与港澳台商合资经营	Joint-venture	1 021.94	204.04
港澳台商独资	Sole Funded	2 794.62	1 862.10
港澳台商投资股份有限公司	Share-holding Companies Ltd.	996.65	176.21
外商投资	Foreign Funded	16 445.26	4 333.31
#中外合资经营	Joint-venture	7 375.34	550.21
外资企业	Sole Funded	8 252.37	3 550.73
外商投资股份有限公司	Share-holding Companies Ltd.	513.14	171.80
按企业规模分	**Grouped by Size of Enterprises**		
大 型	Large	18 433.44	5 147.09
中 型	Medium	7 151.02	1 380.72
小 型	Small	9 199.44	1 211.45
按工业行业分	**Grouped by Sectors**		
采矿业	**Mining Industry**	**6.65**	
石油和天然气开采业	Petroleum and Natural Gas Exploiting	6.65	
制造业	**Manufacture Industry**	**33 175.72**	**7 739.27**
农副食品加工业	Farm and Sideline Products Processing	298.95	12.76
食品制造业	Food Manufacturing	645.78	33.43
酒、饮料和精制茶制造业	Wine, Beverage and Refined Tea Manufacturing	99.96	4.99
烟草制品业	Tabacco Manufacturing	932.48	11.00

表 13.4 续表 continued

单位:亿元(100 million yuan)

类　别	Types	工业销售产值 Sales Value of Industry	其　中 of which #出口交货值 Delivery Value of Industry Exports
纺织业	Textile	180.21	41.28
纺织服装、服饰业	Textiles and Clothing Industry	312.18	78.03
皮革、毛皮、羽毛及其制品和制鞋业	Leather, Fur, Wool Products and Shoes Manufacturing	173.93	31.72
木材加工和木、竹、藤、棕、草制品业	Timber Processing and Timber, Bamboo, Rattan, Coir and Straw Products Manufacturing	49.03	6.09
家具制造业	Furniture Manufacturing	330.40	58.51
造纸和纸制品业	Paper-making and Paper Products Manufacturing	246.05	16.79
印刷和记录媒介复制业	Printing and Record Duplicating	190.04	23.37
文教、工美、体育和娱乐用品制造业	Culture, Education, Industrial Arts, Sports and Entertainment Goods Manufacturing	408.26	53.66
石油、煤炭及其他燃料加工业	Oil, Coal and Other Fuel Processing	1 363.41	99.99
化学原料和化学制品制造业	Raw Chemical Materials and Chemical Products Manufacturing	3 019.57	316.43
医药制造业	Medicine Manufacturing	818.74	74.32
化学纤维制造业	Chemical Fiber Manufacturing	24.47	9.07
橡胶和塑料制品业	Rubber and Plastic Products Manufacturing	880.02	171.81
非金属矿物制品业	Non-metallic Mineral Products Manufacturing	606.43	74.91
黑色金属冶炼和压延加工业	Ferrous Metal Smelting and Rolling Processing Industry	1 230.94	117.20
有色金属冶炼和压延加工业	Nonferrous Metal Smelting and Rolling Processing Industry	359.39	58.89
金属制品业	Metal Products Manufacturing	984.45	250.74
通用设备制造业	General Equipment Manufacturing	2 883.16	577.88
专用设备制造业	Special Purpose Equipment Manufacturing	1 238.12	290.10
汽车制造业	The Automotive Manufacturing	6 834.89	237.70
铁路、船舶、航空航天和其他运输设备制造业	The Railroad, Marine, Aerospace and Other Transportation Equipment Manufacturing	718.80	263.44
电气机械和器材制造业	Electric Machinery Equipments and Manufacturing	2 263.70	455.74
计算机、通信和其他电子设备制造业	Computer, Communications and Other Electronic Equipment Manufacturing	5 394.77	4 179.63
仪器仪表制造业	Instrumentation Manufacturing	411.42	131.69
其他制造业	Other Manufacturing	46.34	6.68
废弃资源综合利用业	Comprehensive Utilization of Waste Resources	37.62	0.01
金属制品、机械和设备修理业	Metal Products, Machinery and Equipment Repair Industry	192.22	51.40
电力、热力、燃气及水生产和供应业	**Electricity, Heat, Gas and Water Production and Supply Industry**	**1 601.52**	
电力、热力生产和供应业	Production and Supply of Electricity and Thermal Power	1 200.04	
燃气生产和供应业	Production and Supply of Gas	334.19	
水的生产和供应业	Production and Supply of Water	67.29	

表 13.5 工业企业经济效益指标（2018）
ECONOMIC EFFICIENCY INDICATORS OF INDUSTRIAL ENTERPRISES

类 别	Types	总资产贡献率(%) Total Assets Contribution Ratio (%)	资产保值增值率(%) Ratio of Capital Hold and Rise (%)	资 产 负债率(%) Asset-debt Ratio (%)
总 计	**Total**	**12.52**	**105.47**	**47.70**
#国有控股企业	Enterprises with the State Holding Major Shares	15.66	104.86	44.77
按隶属关系分	**Grouped by Subordination**			
中央工业	Central Government	16.20	103.97	42.15
地方工业	Local Government	11.32	106.04	49.51
按企业规模分	**Grouped by Size of Enterprise**			
大 型	Large	15.23	106.00	46.26
中 型	Medium	9.55	103.98	48.63
小 型	Small	8.91	105.44	50.13

表 13.5 续表 continued

类 别	Types	流动资产周转次数(次) Turnover of Current Assets (time)	成本费用利润率(%) Ratio of pre-tax Profits to Cost and Expenses(%)	工业产品销售率(%) Sales Rate of Industrial Products(%)
总 计	**Total**	**1.54**	**9.43**	**99.83**
#国有控股企业	Enterprises with the State Holding Major Shares	1.61	12.60	99.95
按隶属关系分	**Grouped by Subordination**			
中央工业	Central Government	1.39	11.89	100.00
地方工业	Local Government	1.61	8.99	99.80
按企业规模分	**Grouped by Size of Enterprise**			
大 型	Large	1.70	11.21	99.92
中 型	Medium	1.48	7.88	100.14
小 型	Small	1.40	7.16	99.43

表 13.6　国有控股企业主要指标占全市比重（2018）
PROPORTION OF THE MAJOR INDICATORS OF ENTERPRISES WITH THE STATE HOLDING MAJOR SHARES

指　标	Indicators	合　计 Total	国有控股企业 Enterprises with the State Holding Major Shares	占全市比重(%) Proportion of City(%)
工业总产值(亿元)	Gross Output Value of Industry (100 million yuan)	34 841.84	13 588.42	39.0
年末资产总计(亿元)	Total Assets (year-end) (100 million yuan)	43 885.51	21 305.00	48.5
流动资产合计(亿元)	Current Assets(100 million yuan)	25 586.81	10 022.59	39.2
年末负债合计(亿元)	Total Liabilities (year-end) (100 million yuan)	20 933.70	9 539.23	45.6
年末所有者权益(亿元)	Owners Equity (year-end) (100 million yuan)	22 951.81	11 765.77	51.3
主营业务收入(亿元)	Prime Operating Revenue(100 million yuan)	38 886.41	16 069.93	41.3
主营业务税金及附加(亿元)	Product Sales Tax and Addition (100 million yuan)	1 071.30	1 009.04	94.2
利润总额(亿元)	Total Pre-Tax Profits (100 million yuan)	3 350.44	1 777.40	53.0
税金总额(亿元)	Total Tax and Duty (100 million yuan)	1 972.63	1 528.90	77.5
亏损企业亏损额(亿元)	Total Losses Made by Enterprises-in-red (100 million yuan)	246.71	68.77	27.9

表 13.7 六个重点工业行业主要指标(2018) MAJOR INDICATORS OF SIX KEY INDUSTRIES ABOVE THE SET SCALE

单位:亿元(100 million yuan)

行 业	Sectors	工业总产值 Gross Output Value of Industry	工业销售产值 Sales Value of Industry
总 计	**Total**	**23 870.77**	**23 780.30**
电子信息产品制造业	Electronic Information Product Manufacturing	6 450.23	6 383.08
汽车制造业	Automobile Manufacturing	6 832.07	6 834.89
石油化工及精细化工制造业	Petrochemical and Fine Chemical Products Manufacturing	4 006.76	4 002.74
精品钢材制造业	Fine Steel Manufacturing	1 233.42	1 230.94
成套设备制造业	Equipment Complex Manufacturing	4 171.70	4 182.67
生物医药制造业	Bio-medicine Manufacturing	1 176.60	1 145.98
六个重点工业行业占全市比重(%)	Percentage of the Six Key Industries in Shanghai (%)	68.5	68.4

表 13.7 续表 1 continued

单位:亿元(100 million yuan)

行 业	Sectors	年末资产总计 Total Assets (year-end)	主营业务收入 Prime Operating Revenue
总 计	**Total**	**28 919.20**	**26 741.49**
电子信息产品制造业	Electronic Information Product Manufacturing	5 889.92	6 730.13
汽车制造业	Automobile Manufacturing	7 849.76	8 334.23
石油化工及精细化工制造业	Petrochemical and Fine Chemical Products Manufacturing	3 426.81	4 314.73
精品钢材制造业	Fine Steel Manufacturing	2 722.24	1 731.79
成套设备制造业	Equipment Complex Manufacturing	7 037.46	4 432.34
生物医药制造业	Bio-medicine Manufacturing	1 993.01	1 198.27
六个重点工业行业占全市比重(%)	Percentage of the Six Key Industries in Shanghai (%)	65.9	68.8

表 13.7 续表 2 continued

单位:亿元(100 million yuan)

行　业	Sectors	利润总额 Total Pre-tax Profits	税金总额 Total Tax and Duties
总　计	**Total**	**2 369.23**	**954.77**
电子信息产品制造业	Electronic Information Product Manufacturing	236.43	30.54
汽车制造业	Automobile Manufacturing	1 077.68	410.80
石油化工及精细化工制造业	Petrochemical and Fine Chemical Products Manufacturing	469.41	320.35
精品钢材制造业	Fine Steel Manufacturing	163.61	30.48
成套设备制造业	Equipment Complex Manufacturing	264.74	102.44
生物医药制造业	Bio-medicine Manufacturing	157.35	60.16
六个重点工业行业占全市比重(%)	Percentage of the Six Key Industries in Shanghai (%)	70.7	48.4

表 13.8 高技术产业(制造业)主要指标 (2018)
MAIN FACT ABOUT HIGH TECHNOLOGY INDUSTRY

单位:亿元(100 million yuan)

行　业	Sectors	工业总产值 Gross Output Value of Industry	工业销售产值 Sales Value of Industry
总　计	**Total**	**7 289.10**	**7194.40**
占全市比重 (%)	**Proportion (%)**	**20.9**	**20.7**
按技术领域分	**Grouped by Technology Areas**		
医药制造业	Medical and Pharmaceutical Product	844.37	818.74
航空航天器及设备制造业	Aviation, Aircraft and Equipments Manufaturing	255.00	257.00
电子及通信设备制造业	Electron and Communicate Equipments	3 786.06	3 757.99
计算机及办公设备制造业	Electronic Computers and Office Equipments	1 828.13	1 789.98
医疗仪器设备及仪器仪表制造业	Medical Treatment Instrument and Meter	560.39	555.63
信息化学品制造业	Information Chemical Product	15.16	15.05

表 13.8 续表 1 continued

单位:亿元(100 million yuan)

行业	Sectors	年末资产总计 Total Assets (year-end)	主营业务收入 Prime Operating Revenue
总 计	**Total**	**7 672.16**	**7 513.97**
占全市比重(%)	**Proportion (%)**	**17.5**	**19.3**
按技术领域分	**Grouped by Technology Areas**		
医药制造业	Medical and Pharmaceutical Product	1 475.37	846.58
航空航天器及设备制造业	Aviation, Aircraft and Equipments Manufaturing	418.86	224.94
电子及通信设备制造业	Electron and Communicate Equipments	4 105.87	3 908.58
计算机及办公设备制造业	Electronic Computers and Office Equipments	971.64	1 932.23
医疗仪器设备及仪器仪表制造业	Medical Treatment Instrument and Meter	688.34	586.62
信息化学品制造业	Information Chemical Product	12.08	15.01

表 13.8 续表 2 continued

单位:亿元(100 million yuan)

行业	Sectors	利润总额 Total Pre-tax Profits	税金总额 Total Tax and Duties
总 计	**Total**	**367.62**	**84.02**
占全市比重(%)	**Proportion (%)**	**11.0**	**4.3**
按技术领域分	**Grouped by Technology Areas**		
医药制造业	Medical and Pharmaceutical Product	110.34	50.44
航空航天器及设备制造业	Aviation, Aircraft and Equipments Manufaturing	8.37	4.68
电子及通信设备制造业	Electron and Communicate Equipments	159.30	10.48
计算机及办公设备制造业	Electronic Computers and Office Equipments	7.38	2.69
医疗仪器设备及仪器仪表制造业	Medical Treatment Instrument and Meter	80.22	15.67
信息化学品制造业	Information Chemical Product	2.01	0.06

表 13.9 都市型工业主要指标（2018）
MAIN INDICATORS OF URBAN INDUSTRIES

单位：亿元（100 million yuan）

类　别	Types	工业总产值 Gross Output Value of Industry	工业销售产值 Sales Value of Industry	年末资产总计 Total Assets (year-end)
总　计	**Total**	**3 607.63**	**3 624.86**	**3 901.84**
按企业规模分	**Grouped by Size of Enterprises**			
大　型	Large	1 026.80	1 025.73	1 122.11
中　型	Medium	1 148.77	1 162.49	1 153.79
小　型	Small	1 432.06	1 436.63	1 625.95
按登记注册类型分	**Grouped by Registration Categories**			
内　资	Domestic Funded	1 520.83	1 538.20	1 707.87
#国　有	State-owned	3.59	3.55	6.69
集　体	Collective-owned	2.28	2.34	5.46
有限责任公司	Companies with Limited Liabilities	595.47	608.27	491.50
股份有限公司	Share-holding Companies with Limited Liabilities	230.71	231.85	368.98
私　营	Private	686.98	690.07	832.63
港澳台商投资	Hong Kong, Macao and Taiwan Funded	688.25	688.24	801.55
#与港澳台商合资经营	Joint-venture	215.59	216.95	243.70
港澳台商独资	Sole Funded	342.24	341.23	387.25
外商投资	Foreign Funded	1 398.55	1 398.41	1 392.42
#中外合资经营	Joint-venture	301.53	298.93	256.98
外资企业	Sole Funded	963.56	964.63	973.54
按行业分	**Grouped by Sectors**			
服装服饰业	Garment and Trappings	321.84	322.92	337.35
食品加工制造业	Food Processing	982.00	989.11	1 143.08
包装、印刷业	Packaging and Printing	286.48	286.04	354.43
室内装饰用品制造业	Indoor Decoration Materials and Equipments Manufacturing	741.42	746.12	716.06
化妆品及清洁洗涤用品制造业	Cosmetics and Cleaning Manufacturing	412.46	409.76	573.70
工艺美术品、旅游用品制造业	Art Crafts and Tourism Equipments Manufacturing	455.74	462.86	379.22
小型电子信息产品制造业	Small Electronic Information Products Manufacturing	407.69	408.05	397.98

表 13.9 续表 1 continued

单位:亿元(100 million yuan)

类　别	Types	主营业务收入 Prime Operating Revenue	利润总额 Total Pre-tax Profits	税金总额 Total Tax and Duties
总　计	**Total**	**4 219.03**	**309.45**	**109.33**
按企业规模分	**Grouped by Size of Enterprises**			
大　型	Large	1 200.41	122.28	30.15
中　型	Medium	1 388.27	102.61	42.71
小　型	Small	1 630.35	84.56	36.46
按登记注册类型分	**Grouped by Registration Categories**			
内　资	Domestic Funded	1 831.06	112.43	46.75
#国　有	State-owned	3.56	0.07	0.20
集　体	Collective-owned	5.23	0.64	0.35
有限责任公司	Companies with Limited Liabilities	801.04	45.29	16.84
股份有限公司	Share-holding Companies with Limited Liabilities	295.78	25.21	8.59
私　营	Private	723.14	41.20	20.76
港澳台商投资	Hong Kong, Macao and Taiwan Funded	752.42	58.22	18.01
#与港澳台商合资经营	Joint-venture	221.22	35.65	5.09
港澳台商独资	Sole Funded	390.40	14.33	12.03
外商投资	Foreign Funded	1 635.55	138.81	44.56
#中外合资经营	Joint-venture	331.00	18.44	6.90
外资企业	Sole Funded	1 163.10	112.14	33.55
按行业分	**Grouped by Sectors**			
服装服饰业	Garment and Trappings	380.99	9.10	5.93
食品加工制造业	Food Processing	1 196.81	84.17	46.08
包装、印刷业	Packaging and Printing	305.99	21.77	10.87
室内装饰用品制造业	Indoor Decoration Materials and Equipments Manufacturing	772.61	64.29	16.88
化妆品及清洁洗涤用品制造业	Cosmetics and Cleaning Manufacturing	497.36	60.35	16.70
工艺美术品、旅游用品制造业	Art Crafts and Tourism Equipments Manufacturing	641.10	42.07	9.00
小型电子信息产品制造业	Small Electronic Information Products Manufacturing	424.15	27.71	3.88

表 13.10　主要年份工业产品产量
OUTPUT OF INDUSTRIAL PRODUCTS IN MAIN YEARS

年　份 Year	精制食用植物油 （万吨） Refined Vegetable Oil （10 000 tons）	啤　酒 （亿升） Beer （100 million litres）	服　装 （亿件） Garments （100 million cases）	机制纸及纸板（万吨） Machine-Made Paper and Paperboards （10 000 tons）
1978	7.32		0.73	27.34
1980	6.77		1.19	29.57
1985	11.13		2.33	41.29
1990	13.42		2.43	46.49
1995	39.94		6.30	39.97
2000	11.55	3.04	4.45	43.54
2001	10.32	3.33	4.35	41.35
2002	9.65	3.62	4.84	42.61
2003	8.64	3.99	4.91	44.40
2004	3.51	5.92	4.63	35.96
2005	45.11	7.05	6.72	35.73
2006	72.86	7.17	6.73	85.87
2007	85.24	7.30	6.60	83.76
2008	96.88	7.27	6.10	80.46
2009	92.27	6.74	3.91	71.03
2010	85.31	6.54	5.72	86.94
2011	84.56	5.09	5.06	87.28
2012	101.70	5.95	5.04	91.46
2013	104.24	4.92	4.78	85.30
2014	109.85	6.11	5.00	92.14
2015	111.45	6.11	4.49	65.79
2016	98.76	6.08	4.04	62.08
2017	90.91	5.64	4.00	46.25
2018	83.10	5.00	3.38	16.79

表 13.10 续表 1 continued

年　份 Year	硫酸（折 100%） （万吨） Sulfuric （100% Pure） （10 000 tons）	乙　烯 （万吨） Ethylene （10 000 tons）	化学药品原药 （万吨） Raw Chemicals （10 000 tons）	化学纤维 （万吨） Chemical Fibers （10 000 tons）
1978	34.49	12.69	0.69	11.59
1980	38.76	13.59	0.62	15.15
1985	35.22	14.02	0.59	22.49
1990	40.04	21.95	1.51	25.74
1995	31.03	40.83	3.47	37.83
2000	34.22	59.05	1.98	47.15
2001	36.15	63.10	1.76	45.46
2002	30.41	80.00	1.24	51.67
2003	31.41	94.83	0.77	54.17
2004	33.67	95.60	1.34	48.45
2005	33.32	160.44	1.27	49.78
2006	30.37	193.83	1.34	50.60
2007	30.46	187.24	1.65	51.48
2008	26.06	182.03	1.74	43.00
2009	27.02	180.30	2.57	37.91
2010	28.66	226.72	2.80	49.00
2011	27.98	197.53	2.61	51.34
2012	18.15	195.57	2.71	48.24
2013	19.47	212.00	2.90	47.76
2014	18.10	188.53	3.31	45.35
2015	19.38	210.76	4.33	45.85
2016	17.32	209.32	5.00	43.34
2017	19.02	201.20	3.89	43.44
2018	15.92	172.88	3.55	39.70

表 13.10 续表 2 continued

年 份 Year	橡胶轮胎外胎 (万条) Rubber Tires (10 000 tires)	水 泥 (万吨) Cement (10 000 tons)	生 铁 (万吨) Pig Iron (10 000 tons)	粗 钢 (万吨) Steel (10 000 tons)
1978	149.59	139.47	149.86	476.52
1980	174.85	161.28	171.12	521.61
1985	219.00	219.31	215.37	570.16
1990	318.78	230.30	526.90	914.62
1995	639.09	433.22	1 048.38	1 454.11
2000	830.66	311.69	1 473.00	1 778.70
2001	545.97	334.75	1 468.91	1 874.71
2002	704.80	351.58	1 276.12	1 719.42
2003	846.92	568.24	1 300.24	1 726.65
2004	927.17	665.01	1 356.47	1 823.65
2005	932.27	719.97	1 582.89	1 927.96
2006	1 055.47	818.28	1 639.13	1 902.82
2007	932.54	786.24	1 790.00	2 081.58
2008	866.65	765.46	1 735.87	1 992.09
2009	849.07	754.19	1 787.48	2 032.24
2010	915.22	670.80	1 901.39	2 214.27
2011	908.26	805.56	1 947.48	2 225.48
2012	1 004.37	794.71	1 800.44	1 970.91
2013	1 079.57	750.31	1 637.58	1 811.08
2014	1 045.49	685.97	1 643.29	1 774.55
2015	971.00	433.59	1 686.66	1 783.77
2016	894.75	418.42	1 587.21	1 709.14
2017	806.03	415.73	1 447.72	1 607.70
2018	649.37	409.08	1 476.75	1 630.10

表 13.10 续表 3 continued

年 份 Year	成品钢材 (万吨) Rolled-Steel Products (10 000 tons)	汽 车 (万辆) Motor Vehicles (10 000 vehicles)	其 中 of which #轿 车 Cars	发电机组(发电设备) (万千瓦) Generator Set (Power Generating Equipments) (10 000 kw)
1978	360.08	1.04	0.26	109.80
1980	412.63	1.47	0.53	58.20
1985	451.18	1.22	0.86	133.00
1990	609.59	2.81	2.46	210.20
1995	1 185.89	16.27	16.07	496.50
2000	1 544.46	25.29	25.15	179.00
2001	1 641.11	29.00	28.88	336.20
2002	1 626.98	39.19	39.05	461.90
2003	1 710.80	59.58	58.84	1 013.70
2004	1 818.41	55.96	54.99	1 520.30
2005	1 964.16	48.45	48.09	2 138.05
2006	2 129.78	65.28	64.47	2 944.71
2007	2 144.16	82.12	81.15	2 845.59
2008	2 074.95	80.65	80.00	2 831.10
2009	2 181.37	125.03	122.46	2 440.70
2010	2 475.95	169.89	159.77	2 555.60
2011	2 482.81	191.57	174.20	2 889.59
2012	2 340.76	202.43	180.68	2 886.30
2013	2 322.76	226.89	201.03	2 538.84
2014	2 309.14	247.45	214.22	3 632.46
2015	2 202.72	242.97	203.91	2 080.69
2016	2 080.14	260.77	207.39	2 561.00
2017	2 056.04	291.32	195.94	3 458.46
2018	1 983.32	297.76	194.77	3 235.62

表 13.10 续表 4 continued

年 份 Year	家用电冰箱 (万台) Household Refrigerators (10 000 units)	房间空气调节器 (万台) Household Airconditioners (10 000 units)	家用洗衣机 (万台) Household Washing Machines (10 000 units)	家用燃气热水器 (万台) Gas Water Heaters (10 000 units)
1980	0.42	0.10	0.81	
1985	20.49	0.74	113.85	
1990	53.36	1.83	101.29	
1995	128.72	62.46	144.80	34.45
2000	43.12	186.08	62.11	32.27
2001	43.44	223.57	70.79	27.86
2002	35.97	217.57	95.92	36.32
2003	34.46	239.72	134.27	37.24
2004	33.14	399.16	165.67	51.86
2005	42.68	358.57	183.26	65.64
2006	101.08	410.60	288.74	69.89
2007	100.66	395.21	289.68	80.46
2008	123.21	387.12	234.63	67.89
2009	189.15	317.78	207.79	59.35
2010	218.55	400.41	216.57	103.70
2011	185.19	619.91	218.96	104.44
2012	151.63	584.10	197.12	106.49
2013	153.93	410.00	184.23	126.22
2014	153.98	403.53	181.93	171.47
2015	148.18	327.33	160.27	173.62
2016	56.38	349.00	163.21	185.88
2017	54.74	389.74	148.76	200.58
2018	46.08	382.84	140.07	178.93

表 13.10 续表 5 continued

年 份 Year	微型计算机设备(万部) Personal Computers (10 000 units)	彩色电视机 (万台) Color TV Set (10 000 units)	集成电路 (万块) Semi-conduct IC (10 000 units)	发电量 (亿千瓦时) Electric Power Generation (100 million kwh)
1978		0.24		199.32
1980		0.55		206.41
1985		71.75		256.25
1990	0.77	81.48	1 167	284.10
1995	4.07	111.77	15 290	403.42
2000	42.04	147.97	239 330	553.09
2001	47.13	108.30	225 315	572.86
2002	75.25	137.02	339 494	608.92
2003	734.68	158.15	397 313	684.99
2004	996.09	135.08	548 727	766.15
2005	2 176.17	145.46	677 003	728.74
2006	2 670.09	251.67	640 483	710.96
2007	4 478.78	158.37	891 138	737.80
2008	5 767.97	185.78	830 487	773.54
2009	7 320.15	195.51	722 883	778.20
2010	9 388.44	254.03	1 134 629	876.19
2011	10 162.53	224.63	1 663 143	946.96
2012	9 804.83	142.87	1 602 978	886.19
2013	8 101.30	99.38	1 613 762	959.51
2014	6 295.42	155.28	2 233 261	792.30
2015	3 651.98	135.39	2 173 552	792.70
2016	3 083.95	115.41	2 380 730	872.29
2017	2 487.32	136.12	2 331 854	830.26
2018	1 448.81	144.38	2 334 807	824.66

表 13.11　主要工业产品生产、销售总量（2018）
OUTPUT AND SALES OF MAIN INDUSTRIAL PRODUCTS

产品名称	Product	单　位 Unit	生产量 Output	销售量 Sales
糖　果	Candy	万吨（10 000 tons）	13.40	13.39
乳制品	Dairy Product	万吨（10 000 tons）	44.64	44.82
饮　料	Beverage	万吨（10 000 tons）	257.08	255.81
啤　酒	Beer	亿升（100 million liters）	5.00	5.00
卷　烟	Cigarettes	亿支(100 million pieces)	892.70	901.78
纱	Yarn	万吨（10 000 tons）	2.09	2.05
布	Cloth	亿米（100 million m）	0.83	0.45
服　装	Garments	亿件（100 million cases）	3.38	3.34
皮革鞋靴	Leather Shoes	亿万双（100 million pairs）	0.04	0.04
实木木地板	Solid Wood Flooring	万平方米(10 000 sq.m)	104.65	106.50
复合木地板	Flooring	万平方米(10 000 sq.m)	2 171.95	2 194.87
机制纸及纸版	Paperboard	万吨（10 000 tons）	16.79	10.05
汽　油	Gasoline	万吨（10 000 tons）	528.43	532.89
柴　油	Diesel Oil	万吨（10 000 tons）	637.01	636.81
焦　炭	Coke	万吨（10 000 tons）	544.91	170.49
硫　酸(折 100%)	Sulphuric Acid（100% pure）	万吨（10 000 tons）	15.92	13.79
烧　碱(折 100%)	Caustic Soda（100% pure）	万吨（10 000 tons）	71.13	66.59
化学农药原药	Chemical Pesticides	万吨（10 000 tons）	1.06	1.05
化学纤维	Chemical Fibers	万吨（10 000 tons）	39.70	42.60
乙　烯	Ethylene	万吨（10 000 tons）	172.88	23.81
合成橡胶	Synthetic Rubber	万吨（10 000 tons）	9.50	6.56
合成洗涤剂	Synthetic Detergents	万吨（10 000 tons）	49.68	49.57
轮胎外胎	Tires	万条（10 000 tires）	649.37	652.69
涂　料	Coating	万吨（10 000 tons）	200.10	185.00
水　泥	Cement	万吨（10 000 tons）	409.08	406.73
铜　材	Copper Materials	万吨（10 000 tons）	29.93	29.84
生　铁	Pig Iron	万吨（10 000 tons）	1 476.75	0.99
粗　钢	Steel	万吨（10 000 tons）	1 630.09	32.48

表 13.11 续表 continued

产品名称	Product	单　位 Unit	生产量 Output	销售量 Sales
成品钢材	Rolled-steel Products	万吨（10 000 tons）	1 983.32	1 976.78
金属切削机床	Metal-cutting Machines	台(unit)	5 990	5 912
#数控金属切削机床	Digital Machine Tools	台(unit)	2 383	2 383
金属集装箱	Metal Container	万立方米（10 000 cu.m）	864.24	861.86
发动机	Engines	万千瓦（10 000 kw）	38 679.61	22 141.69
汽　车	Motor Vehicles	万辆（10 000 vehicles）	297.76	297.47
#轿　车	Cars	万辆（10 000 vehicles）	194.77	194.74
摩托车	Motorcycles	万辆（10 000 vehicles）	72.07	73.88
两轮脚踏自行车	Bicycles	万辆（10 000 vehicles）	139.66	141.46
民用钢质船舶	Civil Steel Ships	万载重吨（10 000 syn-tons）	585.74	585.74
发电机组(发电设备)	Generator Set (Power Generating Equipments)	万千瓦（10 000 kw）	3 235.62	3 072.63
电力电缆	Electric Cable	万公里（10 000 km）	167.47	153.68
家用洗衣机	Household Washing Machines	万台（10 000 units）	140.07	139.49
家用电冰箱	Household Refrigerators	万台（10 000 units）	46.08	46.58
房间空气调节器	Household Air-conditioners	万台（10 000 units）	382.84	382.11
家用吸排油烟机	Range Hoods	万台（10 000 units）	9.31	9.55
微波炉	Microwave Oven	万台（10 000 units）	260.83	260.70
电饭锅	Electric Rice Cookers	万个（10 000 units）	13.51	13.51
家用吸尘器	Vacuum Cleaners	万台（10 000 units）	59.85	63.08
家用燃气热水器	Gas Water Heaters	万台（10 000 units）	178.93	183.16
程控交换机	Program-controlled Exchanges	万线（10 000 lines）	27.70	27.70
集成电路	Integrated Circuits	亿块（100 million units）	233.48	230.68
集成电路圆片	Wafer	万片（10 000 units）	597.25	595.60
微型计算机设备	Personal Computers	万台（10 000 units）	1 448.81	1 468.96
移动通信手持机(手机)	Mobile Phone	万台（10 000 units）	4 729.04	4 751.84
彩色电视机	Color Television Sets	万台（10 000 units）	144.38	144.31
光学仪器	Optical Instruments	万台（10 000 units）	49.36	51.70

表 13.12 大型工业企业主要指标(2018)
MAJOR INDICATORS OF LARGE SIZED INDUSTRIAL ENTERPRISES

类别	Types	工业总产值 Gross Output Value of Industry	工业销售产值 Sales Valueof Industry Products
总 计	**Total**	**18 448.12**	**18 433.44**
按隶属关系分	**Grouped by Subordination**		
中央工业	Central Government	5 172.85	5 191.46
地方工业	Local Government	13 275.26	13 241.97
按工业总产值分	**Grouped by Gross Output Value of Industry**		
10 亿元及以上	1000 million yuan and above	18 064.95	18 048.04
5~9.99 亿元	500~999 million yuan	338.88	340.70
5 亿元以下	Below 500 million yuan	44.28	44.70
按工业行业分	**Grouped by Sectors**		
制造业	**Manufacture Industry**	**17 524.98**	**17 510.31**
农副食品加工业	Farm and Sideline Products Processing	25.19	25.06
食品制造业	Food Manufacturing	213.40	215.86
酒、饮料和精制茶制造业	Wine, Beverage and Refined Tea Manufacturing	32.69	32.48
烟草制品业	Tabacco Manufacturing	926.10	932.48
纺织业	Textile	32.43	31.61
纺织服装、服饰业	Textiles and Clothing Industry	81.37	82.69
皮革、毛皮、羽毛及其制品和制鞋业	Leather, Fur, Wool Products and Shoes Manufacturing	124.91	127.15
家具制造业	Furniture Manufacturing	117.31	119.63
印刷和记录媒介复制业	Printing and Record Duplicating	32.14	31.99
文教、工美、体育和娱乐用品制造业	Culture, Education, Industrial Arts, Sports and Entertainment Goods Manufacturing	62.23	62.45
石油、煤炭及其他燃料加工业	Oil, Coal and Other Fuel Processing	1 267.08	1 268.79

单位：亿元（100 million yuan）

年末资产总计 TotalAssets （year-end）	年末负债合计 Total Liabilities （year-end）	主营业务收入 Prime Operating Revenue	利润总额 Total Pre-tax Profits	税金总额 Total Tax and Duties	成本费用总额 Total Costs and Expenses
24 187.39	**11 189.55**	**20 859.30**	**2 081.19**	**1 547.05**	**18 572.63**
9 302.07	3 785.38	5 676.48	576.79	1 053.07	4 472.15
14 885.31	7 404.17	15 182.82	1 504.40	493.98	14 100.48
23 213.01	10 634.27	20 335.41	2 050.23	1 540.60	18 066.68
811.99	463.39	368.83	7.58	3.13	372.99
162.39	91.89	155.06	23.37	3.31	132.96
21 579.14	**10 379.12**	**19 884.91**	**2 067.86**	**1 506.26**	**17 612.88**
22.74	11.67	23.29	1.63	0.91	22.09
225.55	134.59	299.49	14.37	10.51	288.37
39.25	20.30	43.20	2.07	2.07	40.84
1 428.85	170.95	931.73	232.02	721.60	142.58
30.45	7.89	31.76	2.88	0.15	29.03
112.86	58.89	83.89	1.27	1.48	87.24
206.83	32.93	127.72	10.05	2.66	117.57
	75.21	119.53	24.44	3.35	112.50
34.83	4.81	32.30	6.21	1.74	27.54
75.21	25.81	70.16	9.80	0.39	61.15
755.76	284.60	1 264.35	101.70	239.44	996.51

表 13.12 续表 continued

	类　别 Types	工业总产值 Gross Output Value of Industry	工业销售产值 Sales Value of Industry Products
化学原料和化学制品制造业	Raw Chemical Materials and Chemical Products Manufacturing	887.52	890.63
医药制造业	Medicine Manufacturing	271.81	259.71
橡胶和塑料制品业	Rubber and Plastic Products Manufacturing	126.46	123.96
非金属矿物制品业	Non-metallic Mineral Products Manufacturing	96.42	102.73
黑色金属冶炼和压延加工业	Ferrous Metal Smelting and Rolling Processing Industry	934.40	933.48
有色金属冶炼和压延加工业	Nonferrous Metal Smelting and Rolling Processing Industry	35.35	35.63
金属制品业	Metal Products Manufacturing	117.51	119.32
通用设备制造业	General Equipment Manufacturing	1 062.57	1 070.52
专用设备制造业	Special Purpose Equipment Manufacturing	278.95	273.05
汽车制造业	The Automotive Manufacturing	4 909.08	4 913.56
铁路、船舶、航空航天和其他运输设备制造业	The Railroad, Marine, Aerospace and Other Transportation Equipment Manufacturing	584.50	597.63
电气机械和器材制造业	Electric Machinery Equipments and Manufacturing	771.92	785.94
计算机、通信和其他电子设备制造业	Computer, Communications and Other Electronic Equipment Manufacturing	4 328.31	4 269.25
仪器仪表制造业	Instrumentation Manufacturing	68.99	68.81
其他制造业	Other Manufacturing	20.72	20.72
金属制品、机械和设备修理业	Metal Products, Machinery and Equipment Repair Industry	115.60	115.18
电力、热力、燃气及水生产和供应业	**Electricity, Heat, Gas and Water Production and Supply Industry**	**923.13**	**923.13**
电力、热力生产和供应业	Production and Supply of Electricity and Thermal Power	879.31	879.31
燃气生产和供应业	Production and Supply of Gas	16.47	16.47
水的生产和供应业	Production and Supply of Water	27.34	27.34

单位：亿元（100 million yuan）

年末资产总计 Total Assets (year-end)	年末负债合计 Total Liabilities (year-end)	主营业务收入 Prime Operating Revenue	利润总额 Total Pre-tax Profits	税金总额 Total Tax and Duties	成本费用总额 Total Costs and Expenses
914.39	310.76	1 088.69	190.55	33.91	901.73
328.94	137.42	269.58	25.63	15.31	257.23
162.93	50.73	121.64	16.16	5.13	107.95
169.58	115.63	112.16	15.04	2.70	102.99
2 528.89	911.27	1 384.20	152.07	25.63	1 299.11
35.87	23.07	35.22	1.61		33.52
134.34	69.82	137.68	9.81	6.90	129.19
1 913.67	1 325.18	1 201.21	63.44	23.03	1 139.40
428.41	211.58	286.78	37.09	7.54	253.52
5 998.03	2 627.62	6 299.67	965.46	365.74	5 666.80
1 580.29	1 338.07	561.29	4.62	12.42	577.16
709.88	409.81	827.48	82.07	18.88	758.03
3 411.56	1 922.55	4 332.73	88.39	-1.30	4 275.98
41.49	16.06	69.09	4.61	-0.03	66.07
20.77	3.74	20.39	2.73	1.41	17.98
143.34	8.16	109.70	2.15	4.70	100.82
2 608.25	**810.43**	**974.38**	**13.33**	**40.79**	**959.74**
1 876.49	569.31	879.31	12.55	36.93	864.27
91.85	68.35	47.38	-1.40	1.50	49.40
639.91	172.77	47.69	2.18	2.36	46.07

表 13.13 中型工业企业主要指标（2018）
MAJOR INDICATORS OF MEDIUM SIZED INDUSTRIAL ENTERPRISES

类 别	Types	工业总产值 Gross Output Value of Industry	工业销售产值 Sales Valueof Industry Products
总 计	**Total**	**7 141.08**	**7 151.02**
按隶属关系分	**Grouped by Subordination**		
中央工业	Central Government	464.84	453.25
地方工业	Local Government	6 676.24	6 697.77
按工业总产值分	**Grouped by Gross Output Value of Industry**		
10 亿元及以上	1 billion yuan and above	3 881.74	3 874.49
5～9.99 亿元	500～999 million yuan	1 613.82	1 611.02
1～4.99 亿元	100～499 million yuan	1 590.49	1 604.46
5000～9999 万元	50～99.99 million yuan	44.99	50.20
5000 万元以下	Below 50 million yuan	10.05	10.85
按工业行业分	**Grouped by Sectors**		
制造业	**Manufacture Industry**	**7 025.75**	**7 037.59**
农副食品加工业	Farm and Sideline Products Processing	87.42	87.20
食品制造业	Food Manufacturing	253.30	249.38
酒、饮料和精制茶制造业	Wine, Beverage and Refined Tea Manufacturing	34.01	33.95
纺织业	Textile	53.94	54.63
纺织服装、服饰业	Textiles and Clothing Industry	89.92	87.74
皮革、毛皮、羽毛及其制品和制鞋业	Leather, Fur, Wool Products and Shoes Manufacturing	13.23	14.02
木材加工和木、竹、藤、棕、草制品业	Timber Processing and Timber, Bamboo,Rattan, Coir and Straw Products Manufacturing	18.20	18.25
家具制造业	Furniture Manufacturing	91.60	92.11
造纸和纸制品业	Paper-making and Paper Products Manufacturing	58.90	68.33
印刷和记录媒介复制业	Printing and Record Duplicating	58.67	58.52

单位:亿元(100 million yuan)

年末资产总计 Total Assets (year-end)	年末负债合计 Total Liabilities (year-end)	主营业务收入 Prime Operating Revenue	利润总额 Total Pre-tax Profits	税金总额 Total Tax and Duties	成本费用总额 Total Costs and Expenses
8 686.65	**4 224.59**	**7 974.27**	**589.46**	**194.11**	**7 480.79**
1 023.91	520.52	494.83	25.84	14.06	494.28
7 662.74	3 704.07	7 479.44	563.62	180.05	6 986.51
3 972.34	2 042.63	4 316.81	317.27	92.78	4 026.02
1 981.14	890.95	1 738.48	172.99	44.31	1 585.56
2 461.23	1 123.97	1 788.93	94.46	52.64	1 730.73
146.14	89.91	75.13	2.03	2.59	77.93
125.81	77.13	54.92	2.70	1.79	60.54
8 006.17	**3 789.44**	**7 824.26**	**578.14**	**190.32**	**7 303.86**
127.73	57.19	116.14	6.46	1.54	111.68
258.19	98.03	240.70	40.80	16.90	204.58
58.60	28.58	64.49	2.53	5.08	60.91
47.67	20.51	66.39	4.31	1.92	62.57
69.56	33.57	89.99	1.26	1.57	90.04
19.71	11.29	14.60	-0.09	0.23	14.64
25.47	10.32	18.38	1.46	0.90	16.66
79.89	46.31	93.89	7.58	2.37	87.83
100.40	34.32	98.76	3.43	4.80	91.93
83.58	28.90	65.32	5.53	2.96	61.69

表 13.13 续表 continued

类 别	Types	工业总产值 Gross Output Value of Industry	工业销售产值 Sales Value of Industry Products
文教、工美、体育和娱乐用品制造业	Culture, Education, Industrial Arts, Sports and Entertainment Goods Manufacturing	251.76	261.01
石油、煤炭及其他燃料加工业	Oil, Coal and Other Fuel Processing	26.12	26.12
化学原料和化学制品制造业	Raw Chemical Materials and Chemical Products Manufacturing	580.96	586.73
医药制造业	Medicine Manufacturing	303.31	298.29
化学纤维制造业	Chemical Fiber Manufacturing	261.00	259.19
橡胶和塑料制品业	Rubber and Plastic Products Manufacturing	151.90	151.63
非金属矿物制品业	Non-metallic Mineral Products Manufacturing	203.63	201.31
黑色金属冶炼和压延加工业	Ferrous Metal Smelting and Rolling Processing Industry	122.58	120.57
有色金属冶炼和压延加工业	Nonferrous Metal Smelting and Rolling Processing Industry	296.68	305.32
金属制品业	Metal Products Manufacturing	796.31	795.38
通用设备制造业	General Equipment Manufacturing	410.18	406.45
专用设备制造业	Special Purpose Equipment Manufacturing	1 144.65	1 149.93
汽车制造业	The Automotive Manufacturing	32.53	33.01
铁路、船舶、航空航天和其他运输设备制造业	The Railroad, Marine, Aerospace and Other Transportation Equipment Manufacturing	756.69	761.36
电气机械和器材制造业	Electric Machinery Equipments and Manufacturing	686.63	676.88
计算机、通信和其他电子设备制造业	Computer, Communications and Other Electronic Equipment Manufacturing	175.34	175.64
仪器仪表制造业	Instrumentation Manufacturing	9.32	9.00
其他制造业	Other Manufacturing	4.65	4.65
金属制品、机械和设备修理业	Metal Products, Machinery and Equipment Repair Industry	52.33	51.01
电力、热力、燃气及水生产和供应业	**Electricity, Heat, Gas and Water Production and Supply Industry**	**115.33**	**113.43**
电力、热力生产和供应业	Production and Supply of Electricity and Thermal Power	80.46	80.46
燃气生产和供应业	Production and Supply of Gas	10.37	10.37
水的生产和供应业	Production and Supply of Water	24.50	22.60

单位：亿元(100 million yuan)

年末资产总计 Total Assets (year-end)	年末负债合计 Total Liabilities (year-end)	主营业务收入 Prime Operating Revenue	利润总额 Total Pre-tax Profits	税金总额 Total Tax and Duties	成本费用总额 Total Costs and Expenses
123.11	75.84	413.84	20.21	4.26	400.31
14.94	9.15	25.37	2.76	1.08	22.35
593.17	256.10	617.18	51.10	16.70	574.65
672.40	206.23	306.79	39.17	20.59	256.13
314.38	105.48	305.80	23.40	6.01	284.85
188.70	99.77	179.20	15.38	4.98	164.67
94.15	26.03	205.52	10.13	3.06	195.26
76.68	33.81	122.00	7.71	0.96	114.95
339.30	181.82	320.85	18.45	7.04	305.14
912.38	438.04	857.18	71.55	21.70	793.09
617.02	340.49	446.54	34.57	7.92	414.91
1 124.92	600.03	1 225.43	73.48	28.66	1 160.33
57.10	34.21	32.67	3.33	1.01	30.85
842.52	399.45	807.71	64.38	15.58	747.06
873.63	476.02	838.08	36.21	6.91	814.05
205.17	84.72	188.06	29.84	4.17	161.81
11.67	4.47	9.00	0.22	0.26	8.99
7.28	4.05	4.66	2.12	0.54	2.89
66.85	44.70	49.72	0.83	0.61	49.05
680.49	**435.15**	**150.01**	**11.32**	**3.79**	**176.92**
479.16	304.14	110.56	8.48	2.44	127.60
45.88	40.63	10.42	0.01	0.13	14.43
155.44	90.38	29.03	2.83	1.22	34.89

表 13.14 小型工业企业主要指标(2018)
MAJOR INDICATORS OF SMALL SIZED INDUSTRIAL ENTERPRISES

类别	Types	工业总产值 Gross Output Value of Industry	工业销售产值 Sales Value of Industry Products
总　计	**Total**	**9 252.64**	**9 199.44**
按隶属关系分	**Grouped by Subordination**		
中央工业	Central Government	290.89	283.60
地方工业	Local Government	8 961.75	8 915.84
按工业总产值分	**Grouped by Gross Output Value of Industry**		
5 亿元及以上	500 million yuan and above	3 241.67	3 204.64
1~4.99 亿元	100~499 million yuan	3 932.91	3 903.47
5000~9999 万元	50~99.99 million yuan	1 306.93	1 304.74
5000 万元以下	Below 50 million yuan	771.13	786.59
按工业行业分	**Grouped by Sectors**		
采矿业	**Mining Industry**	**6.72**	**6.65**
石油和天然气开采业	Petroleum and Natural Gas Exploiting	6.72	6.65
制造业	**Manufacture Industry**	**8 677.88**	**8 627.83**
农副食品加工业	Farm and Sideline Products Processing	183.88	186.70
食品制造业	Food Manufacturing	176.76	180.53
酒、饮料和精制茶制造业	Wine, Beverage and Refined Tea Manufacturing	32.03	33.54
纺织业	Textile	94.98	93.97
纺织服装、服饰业	Textiles and Clothing Industry	142.43	141.75
皮革、毛皮、羽毛及其制品和制鞋业	Leather, Fur, Wool Products and Shoes Manufacturing	32.77	32.75
木材加工和木、竹、藤、棕、草制品业	Timber Processing and Timber, Bamboo, Rattan, Coir and Straw Products Manufacturing	30.52	30.78
家具制造业	Furniture Manufacturing	118.32	118.66
造纸和纸制品业	Paper-making and Paper Products Manufacturing	176.25	177.72
印刷和记录媒介复制业	Printing and Record Duplicating	100.46	99.54

单位:亿元(100 million yuan)

年末资产总计 Total Assets (year-end)	年末负债合计 Total Liabilities (year-end)	主营业务收入 Prime Operation Revenue	利润总额 Total Pre-tax Profits	税金总额 Total Tax and Duties	成本费用总额 Total Costs and Expenses
11 011.47	**5 519.56**	**10 052.84**	**679.79**	**231.48**	**9 499.26**
475.49	246.96	359.05	28.12	10.26	337.70
10 535.98	5 272.60	9 693.79	651.67	221.22	9 161.56
2 858.60	1 482.06	3 514.68	296.99	63.90	3 241.89
4 845.90	2 335.20	4 159.31	311.51	95.21	3 911.98
1 665.78	848.82	1 422.04	60.89	41.35	1 379.41
1 641.18	853.49	956.82	10.41	31.02	965.98
35.36	**7.34**	**6.65**	**1.35**	**1.08**	**5.19**
35.36	7.34	6.65	1.35	1.08	5.19
10 046.74	**5 104.01**	**9 433.77**	**627.29**	**218.35**	**8 919.57**
161.15	83.93	242.71	7.60	2.35	235.10
236.75	123.14	193.15	13.08	6.14	181.69
69.09	39.27	37.42	0.23	2.46	36.08
89.16	42.38	106.46	2.56	1.88	104.16
122.18	74.57	189.56	4.22	2.50	188.51
29.68	18.81	34.89	0.67	0.76	34.45
35.20	18.08	35.18	0.60	1.17	34.59
130.07	78.28	123.95	7.78	2.79	118.39
175.16	84.54	194.81	9.61	4.68	189.45
126.34	60.07	103.05	4.73	3.23	100.02

表 13.14 续表 continued

类 别 Types		工业总产值 Gross Output Value of Industry	工业销售产值 Sales Value of Industry Products
文教、工美、体育和娱乐用品制造业	Culture, Education, Industrial Arts, Sports and Entertainment Goods Manufacturing	85.84	84.80
石油、煤炭及其他燃料加工业	Oil, Coal and Other Fuel Processing	76.21	68.50
化学原料和化学制品制造业	Raw Chemical Materials and Chemical Products Manufacturing	1 548.71	1 542.21
医药制造业	Medicine Manufacturing	269.25	260.74
化学纤维制造业	Chemical Fiber Manufacturing	23.99	24.47
橡胶和塑料制品业	Rubber and Plastic Products Manufacturing	500.66	496.87
非金属矿物制品业	Non-metallic Mineral Products Manufacturing	352.11	352.07
黑色金属冶炼和压延加工业	Ferrous Metal Smelting and Rolling Processing Industry	95.39	96.15
有色金属冶炼和压延加工业	Nonferrous Metal Smelting and Rolling Processing Industry	204.65	203.20
金属制品业	Metal Products Manufacturing	560.06	559.81
通用设备制造业	General Equipment Manufacturing	1 029.18	1 017.27
专用设备制造业	Special Purpose Equipment Manufacturing	564.90	558.62
汽车制造业	The Automotive Manufacturing	778.34	771.40
铁路、船舶、航空航天和其他运输设备制造业	The Railroad, Marine, Aerospace and Other Transportation Equipment Manufacturing	90.86	88.16
电气机械和器材制造业	Electric Machinery Equipments and Manufacturing	711.13	716.40
计算机、通信和其他电子设备制造业	Computer, Communications and Other Electronic Equipment Manufacturing	452.64	448.63
仪器仪表制造业	Instrumentation Manufacturing	169.81	166.97
其他制造业	Other Manufacturing	16.77	16.62
废弃资源综合利用业	Comprehensive Utilization of Waste Resources	33.06	32.98
金属制品、机械和设备修理业	Metal Products, Machinery and Equipment Repair Industry	25.91	26.02
电力、热力、燃气及水生产和供应业	**Electricity, Heat, Gas and Water Production and Supply Industry**	**568.04**	**564.96**
电力、热力生产和供应业	Production and Supply of Electricity and Thermal Power	239.43	240.27
燃气生产和供应业	Production and Supply of Gas	307.57	307.34
水的生产和供应业	Production and Supply of Water	21.04	17.35

单位:亿元(100 million yuan)

年末资产总计 Total Assets (year-end)	年末负债合计 Total Liabilities (year-end)	主营业务收入 Prime Operation Revenue	利润总额 Total Pre-tax Profits	税金总额 Total Tax and Duties	成本费用总额 Total Costs and Expenses
80.08	40.93	91.60	5.12	1.59	89.56
38.43	21.30	89.06	4.04	2.22	84.82
1 508.27	648.74	1 654.96	178.90	41.04	1 490.12
474.04	175.62	270.20	45.54	14.54	230.56
39.63	22.91	24.89	0.44	0.45	26.09
588.22	285.38	527.20	23.91	11.55	507.78
467.23	268.20	388.40	21.70	11.93	372.88
99.21	62.55	142.07	1.41	1.79	140.70
140.61	82.23	235.19	5.18	1.74	230.37
648.09	354.10	623.44	27.16	15.61	605.53
1 276.22	634.21	1 093.12	75.42	27.73	1 026.52
891.67	448.76	610.03	49.81	13.23	573.76
726.81	435.02	809.14	38.74	16.39	777.62
133.21	75.44	90.03	4.91	2.26	86.41
902.27	459.65	759.64	36.88	15.03	735.07
576.63	337.57	504.53	7.79	5.44	484.62
177.18	72.36	175.70	17.70	5.23	160.37
31.92	18.27	23.21	2.38	0.49	20.69
40.92	22.41	34.28	5.07	1.37	31.37
31.32	15.28	25.92	4.11	0.78	22.29
929.37	**408.21**	**612.41**	**51.16**	**12.04**	**74.50**
489.99	239.37	245.11	28.51	11.02	219.39
312.40	116.05	344.18	16.35	0.57	336.77
126.98	52.80	23.13	6.29	0.46	18.34

表 13.15 国家级、市级工业园区主要经济指标(2018)
MAJOR ECONOMIC INDICATORS OF MUNICIPAL AND NATIONAL INDUSTRIAL ZONE

指 标	Indicators	国家级开发区 National Level Develop Zone	其中 of which	
			上海张江高新技术产业开发区 Zhangjiang High and New Technical Industrial Development Zone	中国(上海)自由贸易试验区 China(Shanghai) Pilot Free Trade Zone
工业总产值	Gross Output Value of Industry	10 821.01	1 424.62	536.69
出口交货值	Delivery Value of Industry Exports	3 482.88	428.42	202.88
年末资产总计	Total Assets (year-end)	14 030.63	4 387.42	593.55
流动资产合计	Total Current Assets	7 354.49	1 880.22	499.32
年末负债合计	Total Liabilities (year-end)	6 098.72	1 297.78	369.03
年末所有者权益	Owners' Equity (year-end)	7 931.91	3 089.65	224.52
主营业务收入	Prime Operating Revenue	12 643.62	1 856.30	703.67
利润总额	Total Pre-tax Profits	1 203.78	408.27	34.02
税金总额	Total Tax and Duties	312.91	43.96	4.08
亏损企业亏损额	Total Losses Made by Enterprises-in-red	42.09	4.54	3.55

表 13.15 续表 1 continued

指 标	Indicators	其中 of which		
		松江出口加工区 Songjiang Export Processing Zone	青浦出口加工区 Qingpu Export Processing Zone	上海化学工业经济技术开发区 Chemical Industry Economic and Technological Development Zone
工业总产值	Gross Output Value of Industry	1 465.48	68.16	1 160.54
出口交货值	Delivery Value of Industry Exports	1 420.95	65.76	126.10
年末资产总计	Total Assets (year-end)	592.47	69.09	1 068.51
流动资产合计	Total Current Assets	511.98	48.49	503.93
年末负债合计	Total Liabilities (year-end)	451.89	45.86	436.33
年末所有者权益	Owners' Equity (year-end)	140.58	23.23	632.18
主营业务收入	Prime Operating Revenue	1 415.85	67.86	1 258.57
利润总额	Total Pre-tax Profits	6.05	4.27	248.97
税金总额	Total Tax and Duties	0.36	0.01	41.53
亏损企业亏损额	Total Losses Made by Enterprises-in-red	0.95		3.78

单位：亿元(100 million yuan)

其 中 of which							
虹桥经济技术开发区 Hongqiao Economic and Technological Development Zone	闵行经济技术开发区 Minhang Hi-tec Park	漕河泾综合保税区 Caohejing Comprehensive Bonded Zone	上海紫竹高新技术产业开发区 Zizhu High and New Technical Industrial Development Zone	嘉定出口加工区 Jiading Export Processing Zone	陆家嘴金融贸易区 Lujiazui Financial Trade Zone	金桥经济技术开发区 Jinqiao Economic and Technological Development Zone	金桥经济技术开发区南区 Jinqiao Economic and Technological Development Zone South Area
1.25	538.00	374.34	163.05	7.13	1 001.29	2 126.27	341.80
0.32	73.59	280.17	30.37	8.54	5.42	242.60	138.51
3.01	585.58	175.40	318.84	10.32	2 158.50	1 972.32	236.44
1.71	478.83	152.97	237.38	8.93	379.36	1 225.90	194.14
1.22	376.74	132.74	184.00	4.17	764.84	1 087.20	123.28
1.78	208.84	42.66	134.85	6.14	1 393.66	885.13	113.15
1.18	620.66	374.31	178.41	9.40	1 125.60	2 911.85	336.91
-0.15	53.72	3.00	28.57	-0.08	25.76	254.01	21.50
0.04	17.41	0.03	10.46		41.76	115.04	3.45
0.15	2.72	1.96		0.08	0.02	7.75	0.86

单位：亿元(100 million yuan)

其 中 of which			市级开发区 Municipal Level Development Zone	其 中 of which		
奉贤综合保税区 Fengxian Comprehensive Bonded Zone	漕河泾开发区浦江高科技园 Pujiang Hi-Tech Park of Caohejing Development Zone	上海松江经济技术开发区 Songjiang Economic and Technological Development Zone		上海新杨工业园区 Xinyang Industrial Psrk	上海未来岛高新技术产业园区 Weilai Island High and New Technical Industrial Park	上海市市北高新技术服务园区 Shibei Hi-Tech Park
51.47	103.45	1 457.47	8 444.76	11.81	35.27	7.46
49.01	33.50	376.74	1 445.85	0.01	3.54	2.35
40.96	113.83	1 704.41	10 006.92	43.81	34.25	13.06
37.98	70.66	1 122.71	6 618.24	20.23	26.27	11.62
22.70	61.96	738.98	4 975.80	14.66	15.43	5.09
18.26	51.87	965.43	5 031.12	29.15	18.82	7.96
58.92	110.11	1 614.00	9 196.55	18.53	36.50	8.19
4.57	8.56	102.72	694.25	2.98	5.68	0.08
0.03	2.91	31.86	212.61	0.76	1.85	0.26
0.11	0.96	14.67	100.11	0.01	0.10	0.33

表 13.15 续表 2 continued

指 标	Indicators	其 中 of which 上海市莘庄工业园区 Xinzhuang Industrial Paek	上海宝山工业园区 Haibaoshan Industrial Park	上海月杨工业园区 Yueyang Industrial Park
工业总产值	Gross Output Value of Industry	1 125.29	411.67	259.37
出口交货值	Delivery Value of Industry Exports	272.59	89.14	14.23
年末资产总计	Total Assets (year-end)	1 477.38	626.68	294.73
流动资产合计	Total Current Assets	1 055.52	394.42	215.03
年末负债合计	Total Liabilities (year-end)	777.59	329.11	158.02
年末所有者权益	Owners' Equity (year-end)	699.78	297.58	136.71
主营业务收入	Prime Operating Revenue	1 228.39	487.42	313.31
利润总额	Total Pre-tax Profits	113.06	28.28	19.66
税金总额	Total Tax and Duties	33.38	12.58	8.54
亏损企业亏损额	Total Losses Made by Enterprises-in-red	6.95	7.07	0.58

表 13.15 续表 3 continued

指 标	Indicators	其 中 of which 上海松江经济开发区 Songjiang Economic Development Zone	上海青浦工业园区 Qingpu Industrial Park	上海西郊工业园区 Xijiao Economic Development Zone
工业总产值	Gross Output Value of Industry	148.35	888.31	212.63
出口交货值	Delivery Value of Industry Exports	28.98	201.96	56.93
年末资产总计	Total Assets (year-end)	165.51	1 073.56	262.87
流动资产合计	Total Current Assets	120.91	755.66	168.91
年末负债合计	Total Liabilities (year-end)	79.52	492.06	125.00
年末所有者权益	Owners' Equity (year-end)	85.99	581.50	137.87
主营业务收入	Prime Operating Revenue	157.32	986.74	230.64
利润总额	Total Pre-tax Profits	8.23	54.53	8.21
税金总额	Total Tax and Duties	3.97	30.44	2.86
亏损企业亏损额	Total Losses Made by Enterprises-in-red	1.05	24.89	1.96

单位：亿元(100 million yuan)

其　中　of which						
上海嘉定工业园区 Jiading Industrial Park	上海嘉定汽车产业园区 Jiading Automobile Industrial Park	上海浦东空港工业园区 Pudong Konggang Industrial Park	上海浦东合庆工业园区 Pudong Heqing Industrial Park	上海朱泾工业园区 Zhujing Industrial Park	上海枫泾工业园区 Fengjing Industrial Park	上海金山工业园区 Jinshan Industrial Park
1 601.11	1 008.04	210.61	142.17	55.74	141.42	764.24
267.75	63.02	61.44	50.60	12.83	7.85	109.99
1 674.04	770.44	265.36	183.30	75.14	199.93	1 039.66
1 156.93	551.66	171.74	118.44	46.26	143.36	530.42
876.40	445.54	116.46	82.21	53.88	98.93	478.42
797.64	324.90	148.91	101.09	21.26	101.00	561.24
1 751.20	1 053.29	228.64	153.90	64.47	136.63	808.47
129.38	90.37	20.95	11.80	1.29	8.64	41.55
40.28	21.13	2.85	1.27	1.35	3.57	9.34
6.75	2.03	2.97	0.21	0.75	1.84	17.33

单位：亿元(100 million yuan)

其　中　of which						
上海浦东康桥工业园区 Pudong Kangqiao Industial Park	上海南汇工业园区 Nanhui Industrial Park	上海奉城工业园区 Fengcheng Industrial Park	上海星火工业园区 Xinghuo Industrial Park	上海奉贤经济开发区 Fengxian Economic Development Zone	上海崇明工业园区 Congming Industrial Park	上海富盛经济开发区 Fusheng Economic Development Zone
512.18	145.64	63.24	213.10	456.79	16.79	13.53
43.00	28.56	6.62	34.95	77.46	0.47	11.59
545.89	190.58	60.75	225.64	719.84	22.20	42.29
385.11	125.76	39.01	127.24	428.54	14.81	10.39
265.83	109.84	32.13	83.97	289.79	11.92	33.99
280.05	80.75	28.62	141.67	430.04	10.27	8.30
545.37	153.11	62.42	220.21	521.62	16.54	13.66
69.87	12.00	2.33	12.38	51.97	0.72	0.24
18.06	2.67	1.18	3.12	12.67	0.44	0.04
2.40	0.84	0.49	1.20	20.27	0.09	

上/海/统/计/年/鉴

主要统计指标解释

■工　业

指从事自然资源的开采，对采掘品和农产品进行加工和再加工的物质生产部门。具体包括：(1)对自然资源的开采，如采矿、晒盐等(但不包括禽兽捕猎和水产捕捞)；(2)对农副产品的加工、再加工，如粮油加工、食品加工、缫丝、纺织、制革等；(3)对采掘品的加工、再加工，如炼铁、炼钢、化工生产、石油加工、机器制造、木材加工等，以及电力、自来水、燃气的生产和供应等；(4)对工业品的修理、翻新，如机器设备的修理、交通运输工具(不包括汽车)的修理等。

工业统计调查单位为独立核算法人工业企业。

独立核算法人工业企业指从事工业生产经营活动的单位。独立核算法人工业企业应同时具备以下条件：①依法成立，有自己的名称、组织机构和场所，能够承担民事责任；②独立拥有和使用资产，承担负债，有权与其他单位签订合同；③独立核算盈亏，并能够编制资产负债表。

■工业总产值

(1)定义：工业总产值是以货币形式表现的，工业企业在一定时期内生产的工业最终产品或提供工业性劳务活动的总价值量。它反映一定时间内工业生产的总规模和总水平。

(2)计算原则：

工业生产的原则，即凡是企业在报告期生产的经检验合格的产品，不管是否在报告期销售，均包括在内。

最终产品的原则，即凡是计入工业总产值的产品，必须是本企业生产的经检验合格的，不需要再进行任何加工的最终产品。如果企业有中间产品(半成品)对外销售，则对外销售的中间产品应视为企业的最终产品。

工厂法原则，即工业总产值是以工业企业作为基本计算(核算)单位，即按企业的最终产品计算工业总产值。按这种方法计算的工业总产值，不允许同一产品价值在企业内部重复计算，不能把企业内部各个车间(分厂)生产的成果相加，但允许企业间的重复计算。

(3)内容及计算方法：

1995年全国工业普查对工业总产值(原规定)的内容及计算原则和方法做了某些修订，修订后的工业总产值(新规定)包括三项内容：即本期生产成品价值、对外加工费收入、在制品半成品期末期初差额价值三部分。

本期生产成品价值：指企业本期生产，并在报告期内不再进行加工，经检验、包装入库的全部工业成品(半产品)价值合计，包括企业生产的自制设备及提供给本企业在建工程、其他非工业部门和福利部门等单位使用的成品价值。本期生产成品价值为按自备原材料生产的产品的数量乘以本期不含增值税(销项税额)的产品实际销售平均单价计算；会计核算中按成本价格转帐的自制设备和自产自用的成品，按成本价格计算生产成品价值。生产成品价值中不包括用定货者来料加工的成品(半产品)价值。

对外加工费收入：指企业在报告期内完成的对外承接的工业品加工(包括用定货者来料加工产品)的加工费收入和对外工业修理作业所取得的加工费收入。对外加工费收入按不含增值税(销项税额)的价格计算，可根据会计“产品销售收入”科目的有关资料取得。

对于本企业对内非工业部门提供的加工修理、设备安装的劳务收入，如果企业会计核算基础较好，能取得这部分资料，而且这部分价值所占比重较大，应包括在对外加工费收入中。

自制半成品在制品期末期初差额价值：指企业报告期在制品期末减期初的差额价值，本指标一般可以从会计核算资料中取得。如果会计产品成本核算中不计算半成品、在制品的成本，则总产值中也不包括这部分价值，反之则包括。

(4)工业总产值统计范围变化和计算方法修订情况：

1984年以前工业总产值不包括村办工业，村办工业总产值划归农业。1984年以后工业总产值包括村办工业。

1995年工业普查对工业总产值计算方法做了修订，即从1995年始按新修订(新规定)方法计算工业总产值。新规定与原规定的区别如下：

全价与加工费的计算原则不同：新规定为凡自备原材料，不论其生产繁简程度如何，一律按全价计算工业总产值；凡来料加工，允许按加工费计算工业总产值。原规定则视生产加工的繁简程度不同，规定哪些行业按全价，哪些行业按加工费计算工业总产值。

自制半成品、在产品期末期初差额价值的计算原则不同：新规定要求，凡会计产品成本核算时计算了成本的

主要统计指标解释

差额价值，总产值中就应包括，否则可不包括；原规定则按生产周期六个月的界限区分，凡生产周期六个月以上的企业，总产值计算中应包括这部分差额价值，否则可不包括。

计算价格不同：新规定按不含增值税(销项税额)的价格计算；原规定则按含增值税(销项税额)的价格计算。

■ 工业大、中、小、微型企业

大中小微型企业划分标准执行《统计上大中小微型企业划分办法(2017)》。即对于工业企业来说，大型企业必须同时达到从业人员≥1000人、营业收入≥40000万元；中型企业必须同时达到1000人>从业人员≥300人、40000万元>主营业务收入≥2000万元；小型企业必须同时达到300人>从业人员≥20人、2000万元>主营业务收入≥300万元；其余的均为微型企业。(大型、中型和小型企业须同时满足所列指标的下限，否则下滑一档。)

■ 资产总计

指企业过去的交易或者事项形成的、由企业拥有或者控制的、预期会给企业带来经济利益的资源。资产一般按流动性(资产的变现或耗用时间长短)分为流动资产和非流动资产。其中流动资产可分为货币资金、交易性金融资产、应收票据、应收账款、预付款项、其他应收款、存货等；非流动资产可分为长期股权投资、固定资产、无形资产及其他非流动资产等。

■ 流动资产

资产满足以下条件之一应归为流动资产：(1)预计在一个正常营业周期中变现、出售或耗用，主要包括存货、应收账款等；(2)主要为交易目的而持有；(3)预计在资产负债表日起一年内(含一年)变现；(4)自资产负债日起一年内，交换其他资产或清偿负债的能力不受限制的现金或现金等价物。包括货币资金、应收票据、应收账款、存货等项目。

■ 负债合计

指企业过去的交易或者事项形成的，预期会导致经济利益流出企业的现时义务。负债一般按偿还期长短分为流动负债和非流动负债。

■ 所有者权益

指企业投资人对企业净资产的所有权。企业净资产等于企业全部资产减去全部负债后的余额，包括企业投资人对企业的最初投入的实际到位的资产及资本公积金、盈余公积金和未分配利润。所有者权益合计数小于零，表示企业资不抵债。

■ 总资产贡献率

反映企业全部资产的获利能力，是企业经营业绩和管理水平的集中体现，是评价和考核企业盈利能力的核心指标。计算公式为：

总资产贡献率(%)=(利润总额+税金总额+利息净支出)/平均资产总额×100%

公式中：税金总额为主营业务税金及附加与应交增值税之和；平均资产总额为期初期末资产之和的算术平均值。

■ 资产负债率

该指标既反映企业经营风险的大小，也反映企业利用债权人提供的资金从事经营活动的能力。计算公式为：

资产负债率(%)=负债合计/资产总计×100%

资产与负债均为报告期期末数。

■ 流动资产周转次数

指一定时期内流动资产完成的周转次数，反映投入工业企业流动资金的周转速度。计算公式为：

流动资产周转次数=主营业务收入/平均流动资产

公式中：平均流动资产为期初和期末的流动资产之和的算术平均值。

■ 成本费用利润率

反映企业投入的生产成本及费用的经济效益，同时也反映企业降低成本所取得的经济效益。计算公式为：

成本费用利润率(%)=利润总额/成本费用总额×100%

公式中：成本费用总额为主营业务成本、销售费用、管理费用、财务费用之和。

■ 产品销售率

该指标反映工业产品已实现销售的程度，是分析工业产销衔接情况、研究工业产品满足社会需求的指标。计算公式为：

产品销售率(%)=工业销售产值/工业总产值(现价)×100%

主要统计指标解释

■ 资本保值增值率

该指标反映企业净资产的变动状况，是企业发展能力的集中体现。计算公式为：

资本保值增值率(%)=报告期期末所有者权益/上年同期期末所有者权益×100%

所有者权益等于资产总计减负债合计。

SHANGHAI STATISTICAL YEARBOOK

EXPLANATORY NOTES TO MAJOR STATISTICAL INDICATORS

□ Industry

Industry refers to the material production sector which is engaged in extraction of natural resources and processing and reprocessing of minerals and agricultural products, including (1) extraction of natural resources, such as mining, salt production (but not including hunting and fishing); (2) processing and reprocessing of farm and sideline produces, such as rice husking, flour milling, wine making, oil pressing, silk reeling, spinning and weaving, and leather making; (3) manufacture of industrial products, such as steel making, iron smelting, chemicals manufacturing, petroleum processing, machine building, timber processing; water and gas production and electricity generation and supply; (4)repairing of industrial products such as the repairing of machinery and means of transport (cars are not included).

Units of industrial statistics survey corporate industrial enterprises with independent accounting system.

Corporate industrial enterprises with independent accounting system refer to enterprises engaging in industrial production activities, which meet the following requirements: ①They are established legally, having their own names, organizations, location, able to take civil liability; ②They possess and use their assets independently, assume liabilities, and are entitled to sign contracts with other units; ③They are financially independent and compile their own balance sheets.

□ Gross Output Value of Industry

(1) Definition: Gross industrial output value is the total volume of final industrial products produced and industrial services provided during a given period. It reflects the total achievements and overall scale of industrial production during a given period.

(2) Principles for calculation:

Statistics on industrial production follow the principle that all products produced by the enterprises and accepted during the reference period are to be included no matter whether they are sold or not during the reference period.

Determination of final products follow the principle that all products that are included in the calculation of grow industrial output value are the final products of the enterprise which have been accepted through quality check and require no further processing. If an enterprise has intermediate (semi-finished) products to sell, these intermediate products are considered as the final products of the enterprise.

Gross industrial output value is calculated following the principle of factory approach, i.e. industrial enterprise is used as the basic accounting unit in calculating the gross industrial output value. By this approach, value of the same product is not to be double counted, and the output value of different workshops (branch factories) should not be added. However, this approach does not exclude the possibility of double counting between enterprises.

(3) Content and calculation method:

The old definition of gross industrial output value was modified during the national industrial census in 1995. The revised (new) definition of gross industrial output value consists of 3 components: value of the finished products during the reference period, income from external processing, and value of change in semi-finished products at the end and at the beginning of the reference period.

Value of the finished products during the reference period: refers to the value of all finished (semi-finished) industrial products that are produced during the reference period without the need for further processing, checked for acceptance, packed and put into the warehouse of the enterprise, including the value of own-produced equipment and the value of products provided to the projects under construction of the enterprise, and to other non-industrial or welfare units. Value of finished products during the reference period is calculated by the quantity of products produced using own materials multiplied by the average unit prices at which products are sold (excluding value-added tax). Own-produced equipment and products produced for own use are value at cost prices as in the case of enterprise accounting. Value of finished products does not include the value of finished products (semi-finished products) that are produced using the materials from the clients who make the orders.

Income from external processing: refers to income from contracted external processing of industrial products (including processing of industrial products using materials from the clients), and the income from industrial repairing work provided to

EXPLANATORY NOTES TO MAJOR STATISTICAL INDICATORS

other units. Income from external processing is calculated using information from the item "products sales income" in the enterprise accounting at the prices excluding value-added tax.

For income from services such as processing, repairing and installation of equipment provided to non-industrial units within the enterprise, if the accounting work of the enterprise is good enough to separate it from other records, and the share of such services is significant, it should also be included in the income from external processing.

Value of change in semi-finished products at the end and at the beginning of the reference period: refers to the value of change in semi-finished products at the end and at the beginning of the reference period, which generally can be obtained from accounting records of enterprises. If the enterprise accounting excludes the cost of semi-finished products, then it should not be included in the gross industrial output value, and vice versa.

(4) Changes in the coverage and method of calculation of gross industrial output value

Prior to 1984, the value of rural industry run by villages was classified into agriculture instead of industry. Since 1984, it has been included in the gross industrial output value.

Method of calculation for the gross industrial output value was modified in the industrial census in 1995. The difference in the new method as compared with the old one is outlined below:

Principle in using full value vs. processing fee: The new method stipulates that all products produced using own materials are to be calculated with full value in reporting the gross industrial output value irrespective of sophistication of production, and for external processing, it allows calculation using processing fee. In the old method, however, the use of full value or processing fee was determined by the degree of sophistication of production in different branches of industries.

Principle in determining the value of change in semi-finished products: The new method requires that value of the change in semi-finished products should be included in the gross industrial output value if it is included in the accounting record of the enterprise, otherwise it should not be included. By the old method, it is determined by the type of enterprises in terms of production cycle. If the production cycle is over 6 months, the value of change in semi-finished products is included in the gross industrial output value, otherwise it is excluded.

Difference in prices: The new method uses prices excluding value-added tax in the calculation of gross industrial output value, while the old method used prices including value-added tax.

□ Large, Medium, Small and Micro Industrial Enterprises

Large, Medium, Small and Micro Industrial Enterprises division criteria is in accordance with the Method for the Division of Large, Medium, Small and Micro Enterprises in Statistics (2017). Under the new classification criteria, an industrial enterprise could be entitled Large Enterprise only when it has more than 1000 employees, its main operating revenue exceeds 400 million yuan, simultaneously. An enterprise could be entitled Medium Enterprise only when its employee number ranges from 300 to 1000, its main operating revenue ranges from 20 million and 400 million yuan, simultaneously. An enterprise could be entitled Small Enterprise only when its employee number ranges from 20 to 300, its main operating revenue ranges from 3 million and 200 million yuan, simultaneously. All other enterprises should be entitled Micro Enterprise. (Large, Medium and Small Enterprises need to meet the lower limit of the listed indicators simultaneously, otherwise,they will be next ranked.)

□ Total Assets

Total Assets refer to economic resources which are gained from past transactions or events by enterprise, owned or controlled by enterprise, and are expected to bring economic benefits to enterprise. According to liquidity(length of time that assets are realized of consumed), assets are generally divided into current assets and non current assets. Current assets can by divided into monetary funds, financial trading assets, notes receivable, accounts receivable, prepayments, other receivables and inventories, etc. Non current assets can be divided into longterm equity investments, fixed assets, intangible assets and other non current assets, etc.

□ Current Assets

Assets which meet one of the following conditions can be classed as current assets: (1)expected to be realized, sold or consumed in a normal operating cycle; (2)held for trading purposes; (3)expected to be realized within one year(including one year) from the balance sheet; (4)cash or cash equivalents of which the ability to exchange other assets or to repay debts is not restricted within one year from the date of balance sheet. Current Assets

EXPLANATORY NOTES TO MAJOR STATISTICAL INDICATORS

include monetary funds, notes receivable, accounts receivable, inventory and other projects.

□ Total Liabilities

Total Liabilities refer to the current obligations which are created from business transactions or events in the past and expected to result in an outflow of economic benefits from the enterprise. Liabilities are generally divided into current liabilities and non current liabilities according to the length of repayment period.

□ Creditors' Equity

Creditors´ Equity refers to investors ownership of net assets of the enterprise, which is equal to the total assets of the enterprise minus its total liabilities, including the primary input actually received at the enterprise from investors, capital accumulation fund, surplus accumulation fund and undistributed profit. When the total of creditors' equity is less than zero, that indicates the liability of the enterprise is larger that its assets.

□ Ratio of Profits, Taxes and Interests to Average Assets

Ratio of Profits, Taxes and Interests to Average Assets reflects the profit-making capability of all assets of the enterprise and is a key indicator manifesting the performance and management and evaluating the profit-making potential of the enterprise. It is calculated as follows:

Ratio of Profits, Taxes and Interests to Average Assets (%) = [(total profits + total taxes +net interest payment) / average assets]×100%

In the above formula, total taxes is the sum of tax and extra charges of prime operating and value-added tax payable; and average assets is the arithmetic mean of the sum of beginning assets and ending assets.

□ Ratio of Debts to Assets

Ratio of Debts to Assets reflect both the operation risk and the capability of the enterprise in making use of the capital from the creditors. It is calculated as follows:

Ratio of Debts to Assets (%) = (total debts / total assets)× 100%

Both assets and debts are figures at the end of the reference period.

□ Turnover of Working Capital

Turnover of Working Capital refers to the number of times of turnover of working capital in a given period of time, which reflects the speed of the turnover of working capital of industrial enterprises, and is calculated as follows:

Turnover of Working Capital=(prime operating revenue) / (average working capital)

In the above formula, average working capital refers to the arithmetic mean of the sum of working capital at the beginning and at the end of the reference period.

□ Ratio of Profits to Total Industrial Costs

Ratio of Profits to Total Industrial Costs refers to the ratio of profits realized in a given period to the total costs in the same period, which reflects the economic efficiency of input cost and is calculated as follows:

Ratio of Profits to Total Industrial Cost(%)=(total profits/ total costs)×100%

Total costs in the above formula is the sum of prime operating costs, marketing cost, management cost and financial cost.

□ Ratio of Sales to Gross Output Value

Ratio of Sales to Gross Output Value reflects the degree at which industrial products are sold. It helps to analyze the linkage between production and sales and the extent of the needs of the society that has been met by the supply of industrial products. It is calculated as follows:

Ratio of Sales to Gross Output Value(%)=(industrial sales / gross industrial output value at current prices) ×100%

□ Capital Maintenance and Appreciation Rate

Capital Maintenance and Appreciation Rate reflects the changes of an enterprise´s net assets. It epitomizes the growth capability of an enterprise. Its calculating formula is:

Capital Maintenance and Appreciation Rate(%)=(ownership equity at the end of the reporting period/ownership equity at the same period of the previous year)×100%.

Ownership equity is the result of total assets minus total liabilities.

第十四篇

CHAPTER 14

2019上海统计年鉴 SHANGHAI STATISTICAL YEARBOOK

建筑业

CONSTRUCTION

简要说明

一、本章资料的主要内容

本篇资料反映上海市建筑业概况和发展情况。包括建筑业企业基本情况和生产经营情况。主要指标有企业个数、从业人员数、建筑业签订的合同额、建筑业总产值、房屋建筑面积和劳动生产率指标等。此外，还包括本市各区主要建筑业指标完成情况。

二、本篇资料的统计范围

根据建筑业发展的实际情况，建筑业统计范围从2002年年报起由原具有建筑业资质等级四级及四级以上的独立核算的建筑业企业调整为具有建筑业资质的独立核算建筑业企业。

三、本篇的资料来源及统计调查方法

本篇建筑业企业统计数据是根据国家统计局制定的《建筑业统计报表制度》整理汇总的。建筑业统计报表是上海市统计局根据企业实际情况采取全面调查的方法布置、收集，由各资质内建筑业企业通过联网直报上报的全面报表。

BRIEF INTRODUCTION

I. Main Contents

Data in this chapter show a general situation and development of the construction industry in Shanghai. They cover the situation of production and management of the construction enterprises, including the number of enterprises; number of employed persons; construction contracts signed; gross output value of construction industry; floor space of buildings under construction and labor productivity etc. They also cover the performance of main construction indicators in districts.

II. Scope of Statistics

In view of the development of the construction industry, since 2002, the scope of construction statistics has been adjusted to include all the construction enterprises of various types of ownership with qualification certificates and independent accounting systems, replacing the previous criteria that required construction enterprises of various types of ownership to have qualification certificates at or above Class 4 with independent accounting systems.

III. Sources of Data and Methods of Survey

Data on construction enterprises are collected in accordance with the Reporting Form System of Construction Statistics stipulated by the NBS. The annual reporting forms on construction statistics are designed by the Shanghai Municipal Statistics Bureau in accordance with local situations for comprehensive collection by the qualified construction enterprises through the comprehensive network straight report.

表 14.1　建筑业主要指标(1978~2018)
MAJOR INDICATORS OF CONSTRUCTION INDUSTRY

年　份 Year	年末从业人员 (万人) Year-end Employees (10 000 persons)	总产值 (亿元) Output Value (100 million yuan)	房屋竣工面积 (万平方米) Floor Space of Building Completed (10 000 sq.m)	人均房屋竣工面积 (平方米/人) Area of Completed Building Per Employee(sq.m/person)	全员劳动生产率 (按总产值计算) (元/人) Overall Labor Productivity (In Term of Output Value) (yuan/person)
1978	10.07	5.55	234.03	26.32	6 005
1979	23.35	13.98	564.62	26.10	6 226
1980	27.27	17.07	607.91	24.13	6 513
1981	30.21	18.03	649.93	22.28	5 941
1982	30.73	21.56	684.61	22.90	6 928
1983	33.35	24.64	736.34	22.46	7 189
1984	32.94	30.62	799.40	23.10	8 402
1985	33.35	36.73	819.24	23.78	10 070
1986	35.53	49.91	867.08	22.87	12 147
1987	35.83	59.45	872.25	22.66	14 455
1988	36.70	68.83	836.73	21.26	16 251
1989	34.43	74.75	758.34	19.70	18 053
1990	34.01	75.62	747.88	20.01	18 569
1991	34.62	84.30	775.63	20.14	21 022
1992	36.33	117.68	860.49	19.92	26 221
1993	36.90	193.00	1 144.16	26.10	44 020
1994	39.95	309.68	1 557.87	29.33	58 305
1995	41.10	391.42	1 485.87	25.44	67 023
1996	36.19	450.41	1 514.58	26.95	80 161
1997	37.40	564.37	1 777.41	29.60	93 995
1998	40.88	593.11	1 913.55	33.08	102 531
1999	39.01	573.06	1 950.76	33.86	99 473
2000	35.91	631.64	1 909.11	33.02	109 244
2001	35.52	730.33	2 434.73	39.55	118 641
2002	41.97	822.27	2 596.95	42.23	133 698
2003	50.52	1 195.80	3 609.20	71.44	153 910
2004	74.26	1 724.40	4 672.53	62.92	168 719
2005	72.23	1 889.25	5 648.85	78.21	182 299
2006	73.44	2 285.38	6 506.41	88.59	208 368
2007	69.33	2 524.18	6 090.22	87.84	228 710
2008	80.79	3 245.77	5 723.90	70.85	293 520
2009	88.88	3 830.53	5 719.93	64.36	312 360
2010	96.09	4 300.19	6 217.15	64.70	344 720
2011	96.86	4 586.28	5 984.74	61.79	359 232
2012	88.08	4 843.44	6 476.07	73.52	451 564
2013	81.54	5 102.84	6 274.25	76.95	417 313
2014	77.65	5 499.94	7 580.77	97.63	416 002
2015	69.19	5 652.47	7 258.69	104.91	445 768
2016	65.45	6 046.19	7 481.15	114.30	477 994
2017	60.07	6 426.42	8 066.54	134.29	531 442
2018	58.28	7 112.32	7 886.31	135.36	577 007

表 14.2　建筑业主要指标（2018）
MAJOR INDICATORS OF CONSTRUCTION INDUSTRY

类　别	Types	企业数（个）Quantity of Enterprises (unit)	年末从业人员（万人）Year-end Employees (10 000 persons)	竣工产值（亿元）Output Value of Construction Completed (100 million yuan)
总　计	**Total**	**2 779**	**58.28**	**3 601.50**
按登记注册类型分	**By Registration Categories**			
内　资	Domestic Funded	2 670	56.70	3 532.76
#国　有	State-owned	9	0.07	5.68
集　体	Collective Owned	20	0.85	12.84
股份合作	Stock-holding Cooperative	13	0.05	4.58
联　营	Joint Owned	3	0.04	1.46
有限责任公司	Limited Liability Companies	607	21.46	2 203.79
股份有限公司	Stock-holding Companies Ltd.	48	3.13	242.50
私　营	Private	1 970	31.10	1 061.91
港澳台商投资	Hong Kong, Macao and Taiwan Funded	58	0.62	24.31
外商投资	Foreign Funded	51	0.96	44.43
按行业分	**By Sectors**			
房屋建筑业	Housing Construction Industry	790	31.47	2 254.58
土木工程建筑业	Civil Engineering Industry	607	11.45	662.62
建筑安装业	Construction and Installation Industry	671	7.42	327.90
建筑装饰和其他建筑业	Construction and Decoration Industry and Other Construction Industry	711	7.94	356.40
按资质标准分	**By Qualification Standard**			
施工总承包	Chief Construction Contract	1 380	45.03	3 049.36
专业承包	Professional Contract	1 399	13.25	552.14

表 14.2 续表 1 continued

类 别	Types	总产值（亿元）Output Value (100 million yuan)	其 中 of which	
			#建筑工程 Construction	安装工程 Installation
总 计	**Total**	**7 112.32**	**5 987.24**	**959.49**
按登记注册类型分	**By Registration Categories**			
内 资	Domestic Funded	6 937.08	5 898.60	886.95
#国 有	State-owned	6.46	6.40	
集 体	Collective Owned	17.15	12.23	4.75
股份合作	Stock-holding Cooperative	5.12	4.64	0.41
联 营	Joint Owned	1.46	1.46	
有限责任公司	Limited Liability Companies	4 750.50	4 125.42	520.72
股份有限公司	Stock-holding Companies Ltd.	376.39	305.52	69.04
私 营	Private	1 780.00	1 442.93	292.04
港澳台商投资	Hong Kong, Macao and Taiwan Funded	78.13	30.15	40.69
外商投资	Foreign Funded	97.10	58.49	31.84
按行业分	**By Sectors**			
房屋建筑业	Housing Construction Industry	3 850.17	3 517.91	225.91
土木工程建筑业	Civil Engineering Industry	1 937.64	1 732.77	179.31
建筑安装业	Construction and Installation Industry	634.40	104.55	503.96
建筑装饰和其他建筑业	Construction and Decoration Industry and Other Construction Industry	690.10	632.01	50.31
按资质标准分	**By Qualification Standard**			
施工总承包	Chief Construction Contract	5 956.52	5 209.99	604.19
专业承包	Professional Contract	1 155.80	777.25	355.30

表 14.2 续表 2 continued

类别	Types	房屋建筑面积(万平方米) Floor Space of Buildings (10 000 sq.m) 施工面积 Under Construction	竣工面积 Completed
总计	**Total**	**47 436.20**	**7 886.31**
按登记注册类型分	**By Registration Categories**		
内资	Domestic Funded	47 251.11	7 832.00
#国有	State-owned	4.98	
集体	Collective Owned	76.65	45.17
股份合作	Stock-holding Cooperative		
联营	Joint Owned	8.38	6.18
有限责任公司	Limited Liability Companies	35 844.85	5 075.60
股份有限公司	Stock-holding Companies Ltd.	3 812.88	631.03
私营	Private	7 503.38	2 074.03
港澳台商投资	Hong Kong, Macao and Taiwan Funded	51.38	
外商投资	Foreign Funded	133.70	54.31
按行业分	**By Sectors**		
房屋建筑业	Housing Construction Industry	46 397.78	7 665.99
土木工程建筑业	Civil Engineering Industry	956.90	166.48
建筑安装业	Construction and Installation Industry	49.83	22.34
建筑装饰和其他建筑业	Construction and Decoration Industry and Other Construction Industry	31.68	31.51
按资质标准分	**By Qualification Standard**		
施工总承包	Chief Construction Contract	47 112.95	7 744.46
专业承包	Professional Contract	323.25	141.85

表 14.3 各区建筑业主要指标(2018)
MAIN CONSTRUCTION INDICATORS OF DISTRICTS

地 区	District	企业数(个) Quantity of Enterprises (unit)	年末从业人员(万人) Year-end Employees (10 000 persons)	总产值(亿元) Output Value (100 million yuan)
总 计	**Total**	**2 779**	**58.28**	**7 112.32**
浦东新区	Pudong New Area	523	11.98	1 863.92
黄 浦 区	Huangpu	128	2.33	245.16
徐 汇 区	Xuhui	182	4.73	724.68
长 宁 区	Changning	136	2.33	317.13
静 安 区	Jing'an	165	6.12	787.80
普 陀 区	Putuo	182	3.94	455.47
虹 口 区	Hongkou	120	2.81	468.88
杨 浦 区	Yangpu	195	3.11	267.25
闵 行 区	Minhang	189	3.88	504.53
宝 山 区	Baoshan	222	5.81	773.86
嘉 定 区	Jiading	167	2.17	153.83
金 山 区	Jinshan	120	1.85	104.22
松 江 区	Songjiang	150	2.66	154.97
青 浦 区	Qingpu	66	1.32	108.18
奉 贤 区	Fengxian	172	2.69	145.49
崇 明 区	Chongming	62	0.57	36.93

表 14.3 续表 Continued

地 区	District	房屋施工面积（万平方米）Floor Space of Buildings Under Construction (10 000 sq.m)	房屋竣工面积（万平方米）Floor Space of Buildings Completed (10 000 sq.m)	其中 of which #住宅房屋 Residence
总 计	**Total**	**47 436.20**	**7 886.31**	**4 274.48**
浦东新区	Pudong New Area	16 185.96	2 255.10	880.35
黄 浦 区	Huangpu	326.33	74.90	46.09
徐 汇 区	Xuhui	807.51	161.05	39.18
长 宁 区	Changning	3 781.55	637.19	451.05
静 安 区	Jing′an	2 094.50	386.78	302.83
普 陀 区	Putuo	3 701.12	777.39	621.72
虹 口 区	Hongkou	3 274.07	793.66	553.56
杨 浦 区	Yangpu	554.60	139.63	84.21
闵 行 区	Minhang	7 413.60	871.67	528.47
宝 山 区	Baoshan	6 144.96	915.75	280.34
嘉 定 区	Jiading	981.66	392.53	332.77
金 山 区	Jinshan	248.99	63.59	37.48
松 江 区	Songjiang	603.01	184.34	52.87
青 浦 区	Qingpu	228.89	84.81	28.06
奉 贤 区	Fengxian	1 024.06	123.84	35.50
崇 明 区	Chongming	65.38	24.08	

表 14.4 建筑业主要财务指标(2018)
MAJOR ACCOUNTING INDICATORS OF CONSTRUCTION ENTERPRISES

指 标	Indicators	合 计 Total	内 资 Domestic Investment
施工企业单位数（个）	Quantity of Construction Enterprises (unit)	2 779	2 670
固定资产原价（亿元）	Fixed Assets (Original Value) (100 million yuan)	814.38	791.00
固定资产净值（亿元）	Fixed Assets (Net Value) (100 million yuan)	383.44	367.81
总产值（亿元）	Output Value(100 million yuan)	7 112.32	6 937.08
资产合计（亿元）	Assets at Year-end (100 million yuan)	11 093.00	10 803.30
# 流动资产	Current Assets	9 174.36	8 921.18
无形资产	Intangible Assets	44.82	44.61
负债合计（亿元）	Total Liabilities at Year-end (100 million yuan)	8 575.39	8 377.76
流动负债	Current Liabilities	7 967.35	7 808.94
非流动负债	Non-current Liabilities	276.24	266.02
所有者权益（亿元）	Total Owners Equity (100 million yuan)	2 517.66	2 425.59
企业总收入（亿元）	Total Revenue of Enterprises (100 million yuan)	9 131.61	8 861.92
主营业务收入	Prime Operating Revenue	9 069.19	8 802.94
其他业务收入	Other Revenue	62.43	58.98
房屋施工面积（万平方米）	Floor Space of Building Under Construction (10 000 sq.m)	47 436.20	47 251.11
房屋竣工面积（万平方米）	Floor Space of Building Completed (10 000 sq.m)	7 886.31	7 832.00
利润总额（亿元）	Total Profits (100 million yuan)	227.01	212.91
全员劳动生产率（元/人）（按总产值计算）	Overall Labor Productivity (yuan/person) (In Term of Output Value)	577 007	587 031
房屋建筑面积竣工率（%）	Rate of Buiding Completed (%)	16.6	16.6
产值利润率（%）	Ratio of Profit/Gross Output Value (%)	3.2	3.1

其中 of which					
#国有 State-owned	集体 Collective Owned	股份合作 Stock-holding Cooperation	联营 Joint Owned	有限责任公司 Companies With Limited Liabilition	股份有限公司 Stock-holding Companies Liabilities
9	20	13	3	607	48
0.48	1.48	0.43	0.14	548.46	28.50
0.23	0.72	0.19	0.10	249.46	11.50
6.46	17.15	5.12	1.46	4 750.50	376.39
20.36	15.20	4.12	1.11	7 691.96	530.81
18.34	13.98	3.85	1.01	6 185.84	473.19
1.02	0.01	0.04		31.80	1.72
17.15	9.11	2.72	0.19	6 199.64	419.26
16.78	9.03	2.69	0.01	5 830.46	375.64
0.38	0.02		0.10	196.47	2.83
3.20	6.09	1.40	0.92	1 492.32	111.54
12.61	32.16	5.99	2.17	6 146.51	540.65
12.55	32.08	5.74	2.17	6 120.80	534.59
0.06	0.08	0.24		25.71	6.06
4.98	76.65		8.38	35 844.85	3 812.88
0.00	45.17		6.18	5 075.60	631.03
0.15	0.21	0.12	0.04	157.26	12.24
305 206	176 469	527 702	245 921	751 757	430 696
	58.9		73.8	14.2	16.5
2.3	1.2	2.3	2.5	3.3	3.3

表 14.4 续表 Continued

指标	Indicators	其中 of which 私营 Private	港澳台商投资 Hong Kong, Macao and Taiwan Funded	外商投资 Foreign Funded
施工企业单位数（个）	Quantity of Construction Enterprises (unit)	1 970	58	51
固定资产原价（亿元）	Fixed Assets (Original Value) (100 million yuan)	211.52	19.98	3.40
固定资产净值（亿元）	Fixed Assets (Net Value) (100 million yuan)	105.61	14.73	0.91
总产值（亿元）	Output Value(100 million yuan)	1 780.00	78.13	97.10
资产合计（亿元）	Assets at Year-end (100 million yuan)	2 539.74	164.29	125.42
#流动资产	Current Assets	2 224.96	138.86	114.32
无形资产	Intangible Assets	10.02	0.10	0.10
负债合计（亿元）	Total Liabilities at Year-end (100 million yuan)	1 729.69	110.41	87.22
流动负债	Current Liabilities	1 574.33	99.23	59.18
非流动负债	Non-current Liabilities	66.23	10.09	0.13
所有者权益（亿元）	Total Owners Equity (100 million yuan)	810.10	53.88	38.20
企业总收入（亿元）	Total Revenue of Enterprises (100 million yuan)	2 121.83	98.49	171.21
主营业务收入	Prime Operating Revenue	2 095.01	96.16	170.09
其他业务收入	Other Revenue	26.82	2.33	1.12
房屋施工面积（万平方米）	Floor Space of Building Under Construction (10 000 sq.m)	7 503.38	51.38	133.70
房屋竣工面积（万平方米）	Floor Space of Building Completed (10 000 sq.m)	2 074.03		54.31
利润总额（亿元）	Total Profits (100 million yuan)	42.89	3.97	10.13
全员劳动生产率（元/人）（按总产值计算）	Overall Labor Productivity (yuan/person) (In Term of Output Value)	396 426	608 495	255 128
房屋建筑面积竣工率（%）	Rate of Buiding Completed (%)	27.6		40.6
产值利润率（%）	Ratio of Profit/Gross Output Value (%)	2.4	5.1	10.4

表 14.5 建筑业签订合同情况(2018)
SITUATION OF CONSTRUCTION CONTRACTS

单位:亿元(100 million yuan)

类 别	Types	签订合同额 Signed Contract Value	上年结转合同额 Value from Contracts Signed Last Year	本年新签合同额 Value from New Contracts Signed This Year
总 计	**Total**	**22 881.78**	**11 210.94**	**11 670.83**
按经济类型分	**Grouped by Registration Categories**			
内 资	Domestic Funded	22 393.20	10 995.80	11 397.40
#国 有	State-owned	16.75	1.98	14.77
集 体	Collective Owned	30.41	9.84	20.57
股份合作	Stock-holding Cooperation	5.48	0.31	5.17
联 营	Joint Owned	2.23	1.29	0.94
有限责任公司	Limited Liability Companies	17 394.36	8 638.64	8 755.72
股份有限公司	Stock-holding Companies Ltd.	1 837.26	1 029.05	808.21
私 营	Private	3 106.72	1 314.68	1 792.03
港澳台商投资	Hong Kong, Macao and Taiwan Funded	213.50	70.22	143.29
外商投资	Foreign Funded	275.07	144.93	130.14
按隶属关系分	**Grouped by Subordination**			
#中央属	Central Government	10 181.95	5 006.14	5 175.80
地方属	Local Government	6 273.54	3 240.72	3 032.82
其他属	Others	6 426.29	2 964.08	3 462.21
按资质等级分	**Grouped by Quarlification Level**			
#特 级	Special Grade	13 382.16	6 718.55	6 663.61
一 级	First Grade	6 744.84	3 309.98	3 434.86
二 级	Second Grade	1 777.80	773.38	1 004.43
三 级	Third Grade	959.06	402.00	557.06
按行业类别分	**Grouped by Sector**			
房屋建筑业	Housing Construction Industry	13 550.68	6 542.18	7 008.50
土木工程建筑业	Civil Engineering Industry	6 892.20	3 729.93	3 162.27
建筑安装业	Construction and Installation Industry	1 411.81	597.94	813.87
建筑装饰和其他建筑业	Construction and Decoration Industry and Other Construction Industry	1 027.08	340.89	686.19
按资质标准分	**Grouped by Qualification**			
施工总承包	Chief Construction Contract	21 131.41	10 586.65	10 544.76
专业承包	Professional Contract	1 750.36	624.29	1 126.07

表 14.6 建筑业承包工程完成情况(2018)
COMPLETION OF CONTRACTED PROJECTS BY CONSTRUCTION ENTERPRISES

单位:亿元(100 million yuan)

类别	Types	直接从建设单位承揽工程完成产值 Completed Output Value of Projects Contracted Directly from Investors	其中 of Which		从建设单位外承揽工程完成产值 Completed Output Value of Projects Contracted from Non-investors
			自行完成施工产值 Own-completed Output Value	分包出去工程的产值 Output Value of Out-sourced Projects	
总计	**Total**	**7 376.32**	**6 372.91**	**1 003.41**	**739.40**
按经济类型分	**Grouped by Registration Categories**				
内资	Domestic Funded	7 141.85	6 219.24	922.61	717.84
#国有	State-owned	9.98	5.95	4.03	0.50
集体	Collective Owned	16.68	16.37	0.31	0.78
股份合作	Stock-holding Cooperation	4.98	4.83	0.14	0.29
联营	Joint Owned	1.97	1.46	0.51	
有限责任公司	Limited Liability Companies	4 972.95	4 322.60	650.35	427.91
股份有限公司	Stock-holding Companies Ltd.	471.79	273.89	197.91	102.50
私营	Private	1 663.50	1 594.14	69.36	185.86
港澳台商投资	Hong Kong, Macao and Taiwan Funded	81.09	71.70	9.39	6.43
外商投资	Foreign Funded	153.37	81.97	71.40	15.13
按隶属关系分	**Grouped by Subordination**				
#中央属	Central Government	2 673.46	2 593.04	80.42	75.60
地方属	Local Government	1 882.19	1 211.89	670.29	252.95
其他属	Others	2 820.68	2 567.98	252.70	410.84
按资质等级分	**Grouped by Quarlification Level**				
#特级	Special Grade	3 162.87	2 578.18	584.69	203.38
一级	First Grade	2 788.79	2 517.16	271.63	388.96
二级	Second Grade	945.77	854.52	91.26	99.53
三级	Third Grade	466.00	410.30	55.70	45.16
按行业类别分	**Grouped by Sector**				
房屋建筑业	Housing Construction Industry	4 066.88	3 381.12	685.76	469.05
土木工程建筑业	Civil Engineering Industry	2 043.19	1 851.35	191.83	86.28
建筑安装业	Construction and Installation Industry	674.25	566.44	107.81	67.96
建筑装饰和其他建筑业	Construction and Decoration Industry and Other Construction Industry	592.00	574.00	18.00	116.10
按资质标准分	**Grouped by Qualification**				
施工总承包	Chief Construction Contract	6 398.51	5 431.28	967.23	525.24
专业承包	Professional Contract	977.81	941.64	36.18	214.16

上 / 海 / 统 / 计 / 年 / 鉴

主要统计指标解释

■ 建筑业总产值

建筑业总产值是以货币表现的建筑业企业在一定时期内生产的建筑业产品和服务的总和。建筑业总产值包括:

(1)建筑工程产值: 指列入建筑工程预算内的各种工程价值。

(2)安装工程产值: 指设备安装工程价值,不包括被安装设备本身价值。

(3)其他产值:建筑业总产值中除建筑工程、安装工程以外的产值。包括房屋构筑物修理产值、非标准设备制造产值、总包企业向分包企业收取的管理费以及不能明确划分的施工活动所完成的产值。

a.房屋构筑物修理产值:指房屋和构筑物修理所完成的产值,但不包括被修理房屋、构筑物本身价值和生产设备的修理产值。

b.非标准设备制造产值:指加工制造没有定型的非标准生产设备的加工费和原材料价值(如化工厂、炼油厂用的各种罐、槽,矿井生产统一使用的各种漏斗、三角槽、阀门等)以及附属加工厂为本企业承建工程制作的非标准设备的价值。

■ 按建筑业总产值计算的全员劳动生产率

即平均每个从事建筑业生产活动的人员的建筑业总产值,计算公式为:

按建筑业总产值计算的全员劳动生产率=建筑业总产值/计算建筑业劳动生产率的平均人数

计算建筑业劳动生产率的平均人数指建筑业企业报告期实际拥有的、与建筑施工活动有关的人员的平均人数,包括参加本企业建筑施工活动的非本企业人员,但不包括企业内部社会服务性机构的人员以及由本企业支付工资但所从事的工作与本企业生产基本无关的人员。

■ 房屋建筑面积

指房屋全部平面面积的总和。它从房屋的外墙线算起,包括可供使用的有效面积和墙柱等结构占用面积。多层房屋按各层(包括地下室)面积总和计算。旧房加层或改造,只计算增加的建筑面积;旧房拆除重建,计算其全部面积;临时房屋不计算建筑面积。

■ 房屋施工面积

指报告期内施工的全部房屋建筑面积,包括本期新开工的房屋面积、上期跨入本期继续施工的房屋面积、上期停缓建在本期恢复施工的房屋面积、本期竣工的房屋面积及本期施工后又停缓建的房屋面积。

■ 房屋竣工面积

指在报告期内房屋建筑按照设计要求已全部完工,达到了使用条件,经检查验收鉴定合格,正式移交使用单位的房屋建筑面积。

SHANGHAI STATISTICAL YEARBOOK

EXPLANATORY NOTES TO MAJOR STATISTICAL INDICATORS

□ Gross Output Value of Construction

Gross Output Value of Construction refers to total of construction products and services, expressed in money terms, produced of rendered by construction and installation enterprises during a given period of time. It includes:

(1) Output value of construction projects: the value of projects covered by the project budgets;

(2) Output value of installation projects: the value of the installation of equipments, (excluding the value of the equipment to be installed);

(3) Other output values: the output value of construction industry apart from that of construction projects and installation projects. It includes: output value of repair of buildings and structures; output value of non-standard equipment manufacturing; overhead expenses received by contracted enterprises from the sub-contracted enterprises and the complete output value of construction activities for which there is no clear definition.

a. Output value of repair of buildings and structures: the value created through the repair of buildings and structures. It doesn't include the value of buildings or structures being repaired and the value of the repair of production equipment;

b. Output value of manufactured non-standard equipment: the value of non-standard production equipment, including raw materials and manufacturing cost, made for the project (i.e., chemical plant; kettles or tanks used by refineries; various fillers, triangle tanks, valves used by mines). It also includes the output value of equipment manufactured by subsidiary workshops.

□ All-personnel Labor Productivity Calculated by Gross Output Value of Construction Industry

All-personnel labor productivity calculated by gross output value of construction industry refers to the average gross output value of construction industry by every personnel engaged in production activities in the construction industry.

All-personnel labor Productivity Calculated by Gross Output Value of Construction Industry = Gross Output Value of Construction Industry / Average Number of Construction Industry

Average Number of Construction Industry refers to average number of persons that construction enterprises actually have and related to construction activities, includes those engaged in the construction activities of the enterprises but belong to other enterprises, and excludes those work for the social service institutions inside the enterprise and those paid by the enterprise but whose work has nothing to do with the construction.

□ Floor Space of Buildings

Floor Space of Buildings under Construction refers to total floor space of the horizontal section of outer walls above the plinth of the building, including the effective area and the area occupied by the structure. Multi- storey building refers to the sum of each storey, including the basement. The old buildings with storey added or rebuild only calculate the floor space added. The old buildings after dismantling and reconstruction calculate the total floor space. The tabernacle calculates no floor space.

□ Floor Space of Buildings Under Construction

Floor Space of Buildings under Construction refers to floor space of buildings under construction during the reference period, including newly started buildings, buildings started earlier and continued during the reference period, and buildings suspended earlier but restarted during the reference period, buildings completed during the reference period, and buildings under construction and then suspended during the reference period.

□ Floor Space of Buildings Completed

Floor Space of Buildings Completed refers to the floor space of buildings that are completed in the reference period in accordance with the requirements of the design, up to the standard for putting them into use, and have been checked and accepted by concerned departments as qualified ones.

第十五篇

CHAPTER 15

服务业

SERVICE

简要说明

一、本篇资料的主要内容

本篇资料反映上海服务业经济概况。包括规模以上服务业企业主要经济指标,以及按隶属关系、企业登记注册类型、地区和服务业行业大类分组的主要经济指标。

二、本篇资料的统计范围

本篇资料统计范围为达到规模以上服务业统计标准的服务业企业。包括交通运输、仓储和邮政业,信息传输、软件和信息技术服务业,租赁和商务服务业,科学研究和技术服务业,水利、环境和公共设施管理业,居民服务、修理和其他服务业,教育,卫生和社会工作,文化、体育和娱乐业,公共管理、社会保障和社会组织;以及物业管理、房地产中介服务、房地产租赁经营和其他房地产业等国民经济行业。

三、本篇的资料来源及统计调查方法

本篇服务业企业统计数据根据国家统计局制定的《服务业统计报表制度》整理汇总得到。

BRIEF INTRODUCTION

I. Main Contents

This data reflects the general situation of Shanghai´s service industry economy. It includes the main economic indicators of service enterprises above Designated Size, and the main economic indicators grouped by affiliation, enterprise registration type, region and service industry.

II. Statistical Scope

The statistical scope of the data in this article is service enterprises that have reached the statistical standard of service industry above designated size. Including national economic industries of transportation, warehousing and postal services, information transmission, software and information technology services, leasing and business services, scientific research and technology services, water conservancy, environment and public facilities management, residential services, repair and other services, education, health and social work, culture, sports and entertainment, public management, social security and social organizations; and Property management, real estate intermediary services, real estate leasing and other real estate industries.

III. Data Sources and Statistical Investigation Methods

The statistical data of service industry enterprises in this part are collected according to the service industry statistical report system formulated by the National Bureau of statistics.

表 15.1 主要年份规模以上服务业企业主要指标
MAIN INDICATORS OF SERVICE ENTERPRISES ABOVE DESIGNATED SIZE IN MAIN YEARS

单位：亿元（100 million yuan）

年 份 Year	营业收入 Operating Revenue	利润总额 Total Pre-tax Profits	税金总额 Total Tax and Duties	资产总计 Total Assets
2013	15 830.94	1 600.94	396.35	42 072.36
2014	18 323.06	1 950.83	468.47	52 541.82
2015	19 557.92	2 600.23	484.54	60 384.33
2016	21 535.69	2 884.45	639.26	70 212.45
2017	24 412.78	2 639.98	717.93	69 957.57
2018	27 648.25	2 705.66	667.59	82 643.06

表 15.2 分类型服务业企业主要指标（2018）
MAIN INDICATORS OF SERVICE ENTERPRISES CLASSIFIED BY TYPES

单位：亿元（100 million yuan）

地 区	District	营业收入 Operating Revenue	利润总额 Total Pre-tax Profits	税金总额 Total Tax and Duties	资产总计 Total Assets
总 计	**Total**	**27 648.25**	**2 705.66**	**667.59**	**82 643.06**
按隶属关系分	Grouped by Subordination				
中 央	Central Government	4 741.57	364.63	116.07	17 119.52
地 方	Local Government	22 906.68	2 341.03	551.52	65 523.55
按登记注册类型分	Grouped by Registration Categories				
内 资	Domestic Funded	19 982.00	1 735.04	488.77	65 721.10
#国 有	State-owned	1 925.33	78.76	81.11	7 883.42
集 体	Collective-owned	49.14	7.67	2.29	316.49
有限责任公司	Companies with Limited Liabilities	7 158.60	435.19	175.50	18 768.15
股份有限公司	Share-holding Companies with Limited Liabilities	2 688.14	553.04	48.69	12 599.77
私 营	Private	5 787.63	264.06	137.39	7 757.99
港澳台商投资	Hong Kong, Macao and Taiwan Funded	3 789.35	392.90	74.18	7 654.20
外商投资	Foreign Funded	3 876.90	577.73	104.64	9 267.76

表 15.3 各区服务业企业主要指标(2018)
MAJOR INDICATIORS OF INDUSTRIAL ENTERPRISES IN DISTRICTS

单位:亿元(100 million yuan)

地 区	District	营业收入 Operating Revenue	利润总额 Total Pre-tax Profits	税金总额 Total Tax and Duties	资产总计 Total Assets
总 计	**Total**	**27 648.25**	**2 705.66**	**667.59**	**82 643.06**
黄 浦 区	Huangpu	2 227.81	246.53	46.53	10 026.08
徐 汇 区	Xuhui	2 751.06	319.46	73.16	11 747.23
长 宁 区	Changning	3 364.35	254.23	70.14	8 406.49
静 安 区	Jing'an	3 312.00	258.34	137.61	11 662.38
普 陀 区	Putuo	875.45	56.41	24.14	2 516.93
虹 口 区	Hongkou	3 118.83	205.13	19.86	3 761.35
杨 浦 区	Yangpu	899.88	49.99	23.46	1 417.20
闵 行 区	Minhang	1 319.62	197.16	31.90	5 743.11
宝 山 区	Baoshan	606.49	36.99	21.70	1 440.51
嘉 定 区	Jiading	773.62	12.84	13.19	1 342.51
浦东新区	Pudong New Area	6 616.06	870.61	175.41	20 790.26
金 山 区	Jinshan	115.04	12.39	2.43	404.34
松 江 区	Songjiang	313.20	23.34	11.51	917.90
青 浦 区	Qingpu	1 155.10	129.50	12.26	1 591.09
奉 贤 区	Fengxian	125.93	25.88	2.71	685.36
崇 明 区	Chongming	73.83	6.86	1.59	190.34

表 15.4 分行业规模以上服务业企业主要指标(2018)
MAIN INDICATORS OF SERVICE ENTERPRISES ABOVE DESIGNATED SIZE BY SECTORS

单位:亿元(100 million yuan)

类 别	Types	营业收入 Operating Revenue	利润总额 Total Pre-tax Profits	税金总额 Total Tax and Duties	资产总计 Total Assets
总 计	**Total**	**27 648.25**	**2 705.66**	**667.59**	**82 643.06**
#交通运输、仓储和邮政业	**Transportation, Warehousing and Postal Service Industry**	**9 300.54**	**559.43**	**147.16**	**20 393.65**
铁路运输业	Railway Transportation	1 183.26	32.17	72.49	5 814.01
道路运输业	Road Transportation	988.70	-0.27	20.94	4 462.67
水上运输业	Water Transportation	1 482.44	216.36	13.72	3 837.48
航空运输业	Air Transportation	1 372.97	120.50	21.73	3 646.24
管道运输业	Pipeline Transportation	227.21	9.28	1.12	172.69
多式联运和运输代理业	Multimodal Transport and Ttransport Agency	2 716.09	75.01	7.72	1 211.82
装卸搬运和仓储业	Handling and Warehousing	374.68	33.78	6.64	589.61
邮政业	Postal	955.20	72.60	2.80	659.13
信息传输、软件和信息技术服务业	**Information Transmission, Software and Information Technology Service Industry**	**5 104.67**	**473.13**	**162.62**	**9 474.55**
电信、广播电视和卫星传输服务	Telecommunications, Radio, Television and Satellite Transmission Service	806.16	130.85	23.17	1 484.32
互联网和相关服务	Internet and Related Services Service	578.98	105.10	21.36	1 517.70
软件和信息技术服务业	Software and Information Technology Service	3 719.53	237.19	118.09	6 472.52
房地产业(除房地产开发经营外)	**Real Estate Industry (Except for Real Estate Development and Operation)**	**728.51**	**67.13**	**40.95**	**2 831.25**
租赁和商务服务业	**Leasing and Business Service Industry**	**8 778.80**	**1 311.88**	**193.56**	**39 855.31**
租赁业	Leasing	208.02	10.39	8.30	1 571.60
商务服务业	Business Service	8 570.78	1 301.50	185.26	38 283.72
科学研究和技术服务业	**Scientific Research and Technical Service Industry**	**2 330.51**	**168.19**	**72.55**	**4 054.60**
研究和试验发展	Research and Experimental Development	517.91	72.87	12.95	1 169.20
专业技术服务业	Professional technical Service	1 458.92	126.34	49.79	2 167.15
科技推广和应用服务业	Science and Technology Promotion and Application Service	353.69	-31.02	9.81	718.26

表 15.4 续表 continued

单位:亿元(100 million yuan)

类别	Types	营业收入 Operating Revenue	利润总额 Total Pre-tax Profits	税金总额 Total Tax and Duties	资产总计 Total Assets
水利、环境和公共设施管理业	**Water Conservancy, Environment and Public Facilities Management Industry**	**402.86**	**38.00**	**24.60**	**3 270.07**
水利管理业	Water Conservancy Management	7.03	1.24	0.16	64.44
生态保护和环境治理业	Ecological Protection and Environmental Governance	49.38	8.27	2.79	136.21
公共设施管理业	Public Facilities Management	304.35	19.49	20.37	1 288.50
土地管理业	Land Management	42.10	9.00	1.29	1 780.92
居民服务、修理和其他服务业	**Residential Services, Repairs and Other Service Industries**	**298.72**	**36.22**	**9.50**	**399.29**
居民服务业	Resident Service	131.83	23.14	2.49	197.17
机动车、电子产品和日用品修理业	Automobile, Electronic Products and Daily Necessities Repair Industry	96.90	9.14	4.26	143.91
其他服务业	Other Services	69.99	3.95	2.74	58.21
教　育	**Education**	**129.02**	**5.34**	**4.38**	**246.45**
卫生和社会工作	**Health and Social Work**	**154.97**	**5.87**	**0.24**	**199.69**
卫　生	Health	150.42	5.26	0.19	179.16
社会工作	Social Work	4.55	0.61	0.04	20.53
文化、体育和娱乐业	**Culture, Sports and Entertainment**	**419.66**	**40.46**	**12.03**	**1 918.20**
新闻和出版业	Press and publishing	65.81	8.83	2.61	334.13
广播、电视、电影和影视录音制作业	Radio, Television, Film and Television Recording and Production Industry	177.62	36.50	4.60	1 032.89
文化艺术业	Culture and Art Industry	12.70	2.56	0.51	32.82
体　育	Sports	81.78	−2.33	3.13	139.30
娱乐业	Entertainment	81.75	−5.09	1.19	379.05

上/海/统/计/年/鉴

主要统计指标解释

营业收入

指企业经营主要业务和其他业务所确认的收入总额。营业收入包括“主营业务收入”和“其他业务收入”。

利润总额

指企业在一定会计期间的经营成果，是生产经营过程中各种收入扣除各种耗费后的盈余，反映企业在报告期内实现的盈亏总额。利润总额为营业利润加上营业外收入，减去营业外支出后的金额。

营业利润

指企业从事生产经营活动所取得的利润。执行《企业会计准则》或《小企业会计准则》的企业，营业利润为营业收入减去营业成本、税金及附加、销售费用、管理费用、财务费用、研发费用、资产减值损失、信用减值损失，再加上公允价值变动收益、资产处置收益、投资收益、净敞口套期收益和其他收益。执行其他企业会计制度的企业，营业利润为营业收入减去营业成本、税金及附加，加上其他业务利润后，再减去销售费用、管理费用、财务费用、研发费用后的金额，应符合以下逻辑关系：营业利润等于营业收入减去营业成本、税金及附加、销售费用、管理费用、财务费用、研发费用。

营业外收入

指企业发生的除营业利润以外的收益，主要包括与企业日常活动无关的政府补助、盘盈利得、捐赠利得等。

营业外支出

指企业发生的除营业利润以外的支出，主要包括公益性捐赠支出、非常损失、盘亏损失、非流动资产毁损报废损失等。

税金合计

税金是指企业发生的除企业所得税和允许抵扣的增值税以外的各项税金及其附加。税金合计=税金及附加+应交增值税。

税金及附加

指企业因从事生产经营活动按税法规定应缴纳的消费税、城市维护建设税、资源税、教育费附加及房产税、土地使用税、车船使用税、印花税等相关税费。

应交增值税

指按照税法规定，以销售货物、服务、无形资产、不动产或提供加工、修理修配劳务的增值额和货物进口金额为计税依据而课征的一种流转税。按照权责发生制核算本期应负担的增值税额。

资产总计

指企业过去的交易或者事项形成的、由企业拥有或者控制的、预期会给企业带来经济利益的资源。资产一般按流动性(资产的变现或耗用时间长短)分为流动资产和非流动资产。其中流动资产可分为货币资金、交易性金融资产、应收票据、应收账款、预付款项、其他应收款、存货等；非流动资产可分为长期股权投资、固定资产、无形资产及其他非流动资产等。包括企业拥有的土地、办公楼、厂房、机器、运输工具、存货等实物资产和现金、存款、应收账款和预付账款等金融资产。

SHANGHAI STATISTICAL YEARBOOK

EXPLANATORY NOTES TO MAJOR STATISTICAL INDICATORS

□ Operating Income

Operating income refers to the total amount of revenue recognized by the main business and other businesses of the enterprise. Operating Income includes "Prime Operating Income" and "Other Operating Income".

□ Total Profit

Total Profit refers to the operating results of an enterprise in a certain accounting period. It is the surplus of various incomes after deducting various expenses in the process of production and operation, reflecting the total profit and loss realized by the enterprise in the reporting period. The Total Profit is the operating profit plus non operating income minus non operating expenditure.

□ Operating Profit

Operating Profit refers to the profit obtained by an enterprise from its production and operation activities. For enterprises implementing the Accounting Standards for Business Enterprises or the Accounting Standards for Small Enterprises, the operating profit is the operating income minus operating costs, taxes and surcharges, sales expenses, management expenses, financial expenses, research and development expenses, asset impairment losses, credit impairment losses, plus the income from changes in fair value, asset disposal income, investment income, net exposure hedging income and other income. For enterprises implementing other enterprise accounting systems, the operating profit is the amount of operating revenue minus operating cost, tax and surcharges, plus other operating profit, plus sales expense, management expense, financial expense and R & D expense, which should conform to the following logical relationship: operating profit equals to operating revenue minus operating cost, tax and surcharges, sales expense, management expense Financial expenses and R & D expenses.

□ Non Operating Income

Non Operating Income refers to the income other than operating profit of an enterprise, mainly including government subsidy, inventory profit, donation profit, etc. unrelated to the daily activities of an enterprise.

□ Non Operating Expenses

Non Operating Expenses refers to expenditure other than operating profit incurred by an enterprise, mainly including public welfare donation expenditure, extraordinary loss, inventory loss, non current assets damage and scrap loss, etc.

□ Total Tax

Total Tax refers to all taxes and surcharges except enterprise income tax and value-added tax that can be deducted. Total tax = tax and surtax + VAT payable.

□ Taxes and Surcharges

Taxes and Surcharges refers to the consumption tax, urban maintenance and construction tax, resource tax, education surtax, real estate tax, land use tax, vehicle and ship use tax, stamp tax and other related taxes that an enterprise shall pay due to its production and operation activities in accordance with the tax law.

□ VAT Payable

VAT Payable refers to a kind of turnover tax levied on the basis of the value-added value of goods, services, intangible assets, real estate or the provision of processing, repair and replacement services and the import amount of goods in accordance with the tax law. The VAT payable in the current period shall be accounted for on the accrual basis.

□ Total Assets

Total Assets refers to the resources formed by the past transactions or events of the enterprise, owned or controlled by the enterprise and expected to bring economic benefits to the enterprise. Assets are generally divided into current assets and non current assets according to liquidity (the time of realization or consumption of assets). Among them, current assets can be divided into monetary capital, trading financial assets, notes receivable, accounts receivable, prepayment, other receivables, inventory, etc.; non current assets can be divided into long-term equity investment, fixed assets, intangible assets and other non current assets, etc. It includes physical assets such as land, office building, factory building, machinery, means of transport, inventory and financial assets such as cash, deposit, accounts receivable and prepayment owned by the enterprise.

第十六篇

CHAPTER 16

2019上海统计年鉴 SHANGHAI STATISTICAL YEARBOOK

交通运输、邮政和信息传输

TRANSPORTATION, POSTS AND INFORMATION TRANSMISSION

简要说明

一、本章资料的主要内容

本篇资料反映上海市交通运输、仓储和邮政业及信息传输业发展的基本状况。

交通运输、仓储和邮政业资料主要包括:运输线路长度、旅客发送量、旅客周转量、货物运输量、货物周转量、港口码头情况、港口货物吞吐量、集装箱吞吐量、邮轮经济、经营性停车场、民用车辆拥有量、邮政业务主要指标等内容。

信息传输业资料主要包括:电信业务开展情况、邮电通信水平、信息化基础设施情况、信息服务业经营情况等方面资料。

二、本篇资料的统计范围和统计方式

1. 铁路资料:包括国家铁路(含控股合资)、地方铁路和非控股合资铁路运营情况,不含军用铁路及由厂矿企事业单位自建的铁路专用线和专用铁道。

2.公路、水路、港口资料:(1)公路、水路运输量统计包括全面调查和非全面调查两种方式,统计范围为在上海市交通运输主管部门登记注册的从事公路、水路客、货运输的营业性的车辆和船舶所完成的运输量;(2)港口统计采用全面调查方式,统计范围为上海市全部沿海港口和内河港口。

3.民用车辆拥有量资料:民用车辆拥有量由民用汽车拥有量和民用拖拉机拥有量组成。

4.民航运输资料:统计范围为在上海市注册从事民用航空运输飞行和通用飞行的航空运输企业和定期航班通航机场,不包括在上海市从事运输飞行的外省市和外国航空公司。

5.邮电业务量按业务种类分为邮政业务量和电信业务量:邮政业务量统计范围是上海市邮政业企业和取得快递业务经营许可的快递企业及其备案分支机构;邮政业基础设施资料统计范围是上海市境内提供国家邮政服务的机构和设施。

三、本篇的资料来源

本篇资料中的交通运输、仓储和邮政业资料由上海市统计局服务业统计处负责整理、编辑。有关交通运输资料分别来源于中国铁路上海局集团有限公司、上海市交通委员会、上海机场(集团)有限公司、上海市公安局车辆管理所、上海市农业机械化管理办公室、上海市邮政公司、上海市邮政管理局。

本篇资料中的信息服务业资料由上海市统计局服务业统计处负责采集、整理和编辑。相关电信业务资料由上海市通信管理局提供,信息化基础设施等方面资料由上海市经济和信息化委员会提供。

BRIEF INTRODUCTION

I. Main Contents

Data in this chapter reflect the basic conditions of transportation, warehousing, postal services and telecommunications industries in Shanghai.

Data on the transportation, warehousing and postal services industries cover mainly the length of the traffic lines, passenger departing volume, turnover volume of passenger traffic, freight traffic volume, turnover volume of freight traffic, conditions of ports, port freight throughput, container throughput, yacht economy, parking lots operation, civil motor vehicles, and postal services.

Data on the telecommunications industry cover mainly conditions of telecommunications services, telecommunications level, infrastructure of informatization, and operation of information service industry.

II. Scope and Methodology of Statistics

(1)Data on railway transportation: They include the operation and management of the national (including state-controlled joint ventures), local and non state-controlled joint-venture railways but exclude railways for military purpose, lines built by industrial and mining enterprises and special railways.

(2) Data on highways, waterways and ports: (a) Data on highway and waterway transportation are collected through both comprehensive reporting system and non-comprehensive reporting system. The statistical scope encompasses all the vehicles and ships registered with the transportation authorities in Shanghai and engaged in highway or waterway freight or passenger transportation business. (b) Data on ports are collected through comprehensive reporting system. The statistical scope encompasses all ports along the sea and the rivers.

(3)Data on civil motor vehicles: They include the numbers of civil automobiles and tractors.

(4)Data on civil aviation transportation: The targets of statistical collection are enterprises registered in Shanghai forengagement in civil aviation transportation flights and flights for general purposes and general aviation airports with scheduled flights. They exclude foreign companies and companies registered in other provinces and cities, which operate flights within the Shanghai territory.

(5)By types of business, the business volumes of postal and telecommunications sectors are divided into those of postal services and telecommunication services: Data on postal businesses include postal enterprises and express delivery companies and its filing branches with express business license. Data on postal infrastructure include institutions and facilities in Shanghai that provide state postal services.

III. Sources of Data

Data on transportation, warehousing and postal services in this chapter are collected, processed and compiled by the Department of Service Industry, Shanghai Municipal Statistics Bureau. Data on transportation are from China Railway Shanghai Group Co., Ltd, Shanghai Municipal Transportation Commission, Shanghai Airport Group, Shanghai City Public Security Bureau vehicle management, Shanghai Civil Agricultural Mechanization Management Office, Shanghai Post Corporation and Shanghai Municipal Postal Administration.

Data on information Service Industry in this chapter are collected, processed and complied by Department of

Serice Industry, Shanghai Municipal Statistics Bureau. Data on telecommunication businesses are provided by Shanghai Communications Administration. Data on infrastructure of informatization are provided by Shanghai Municipal Economic and Informatization Commission.

表 16.1 主要年份运输线路长度
LENGTHS OF TRAFFIC LINES IN MAIN YEARS

指 标	Indicators	2000	2010	2017	2018
铁路运输	**Railway**				
营业里程(公里)	Operation Mileage (km)	257	414	465	466
正线延展里程(公里)	Mainline Railway Length Extended (km)	397	697	836	834
公路运输	**Highway**				
通车里程(公里)	Operation Mileage(km)	5 970	11 974	13 322	13 106
#高速公路	High Speed Highways	98	775	829	836
内河航道	**Navigable Inland Waterways**				
航道里程(公里)	Length of Navigable Inland Waterways (km)	2 100	2 110	2 023	1 973

表 16.2 主要年份交通运输主要指标
MAJOR INDICATORS OF TRANSPORTATION IN MAIN YEARS

指 标	Indicators	2000	2010	2017	2018
公路运输	**Highway Transportation**				
营运汽车拥有量(辆)	Operating Vehicles (vehicle)	155 860	185 531	255 653	259 163
载客汽车	Passenger Vehicles	30 757	20 386	43 337	43 259
载货汽车	Freight Trucks	125 103	165 145	212 316	215 904
载客汽车客位数(客位)	Seat of Passenger Vehicles(seat)	309 834	523 564	650 635	655 219
载货汽车吨位数(万吨)	Tonnage of Freight Trucks(10 000 tons)	48.36	132.59	257.70	289.02
港 口	**Harbor**				
船舶平均在港停泊时间(天)	Average Days of Vessel Berthed at Harbor (day)	0.90	0.40	0.51	0.52
机 场	**Aviation**				
起降航班数(万架次)	Aircraft Movements(10 000 sortie-times)		55.11	76.04	77.16
进出港旅客人次(万人次)	Passenger Turnover(10 000 person-times)		7 187.74	11 188.52	11 763.43
#国内航线	Domestic Flight		5 106.96	7 394.18	7 665.00
国际及地区航线	International and Regional Flight		2 080.78	3 794.34	4 098.43

表 16.3 主要年份旅客发送量
PASSENGER DEPARTING IN MAIN YEARS

单位:万人次(10 000 person-times)

年 份 Year	旅客发送量 Passenger Departures	其 中 of which 铁 路 Railway	公 路 Highway	港 口 Harbor	民用航空 Civil Aviation
1990	3 835	2 476	605	555	199
1995	5 265	2 929	1 257	512	567
2000	6 893	2 980	2 482	539	892
2001	6 324	3 231	1 508	543	1 042
2002	7 326	3 518	2 046	526	1 236
2003	7 212	3 391	2 052	528	1 241
2004	8 968	4 076	2 465	621	1 806
2005	9 487	4 313	2 468	626	2 080
2006	9 619	4 458	2 784	68	2 309
2007	10 371	4 795	2 872	95	2 609
2008	10 927	5 343	2 934	89	2 565
2009	11 136	5 161	2 995	90	2 890
2010	13 456	6 095	3 634	85	3 642
2011	13 519	6 198	3 477	78	3 766
2012	14 547	6 758	3 748	66	3 974
2013	15 933	7 972	3 720	68	4 173
2014	17 560	9 194	3 754	90	4 522
2015	18 571	9 692	3 766	113	5 000
2016	19 564	10 609	3 402	172	5 381
2017	20 855	11 617	3 419	176	5 644
2018	21 497	12 267	3 151	158	5 921

①2000 年前旅客发送量是专业运输部门的数字，2001 年开始改为跨省市旅客运输的行业统计数字。
②港口旅客发送量从 2006 年起口径不包含海港到内河部分。
❶The passenger departures volume before 2000 is based on the figures for special traffic departments and the volume since 2001 is based on the figures for the inter-provincial passenger transport industries.
❷The Volume of Passenger Departures excludes those from seaports to freshwater since 2006.

表 16.4 主要年份旅客周转量
TURNOVER VOLUME OF PASSENGER TRAFFIC IN MAIN YEARS

单位:亿人 · 公里 (100 million persons · km)

年 份 Year	旅客周转量 Turnover Volume of Passenger Traffic	其 中 of which 铁 路 Railway	公 路 Highway	水 运 Waterway	民用航空 Civil Aviation
1990	113.94	26.85	8.42	40.84	37.84
1995	170.98	34.18	8.23	31.71	96.86
2000	234.72	35.40	16.44	6.77	176.11
2001	286.93	37.81	42.31	5.48	201.30
2002	332.12	39.48	50.43	4.41	237.80
2003	353.62	38.10	58.00	4.65	252.88
2004	599.62	46.35	72.09	4.49	476.70
2005	663.93	48.86	75.06	4.52	535.48
2006	742.87	51.23	86.85	4.52	600.28
2007	883.25	51.34	94.02	6.10	731.79
2008	869.07	53.22	94.07	6.73	715.09
2009	1 002.59	51.12	99.57	6.38	845.52
2010	1 214.25	60.16	115.44	3.69	1 034.96
2011	1 307.56	63.11	106.74	1.02	1 136.69
2012	1 223.05	68.38	112.72	0.99	1 040.97
2013	1 343.73	75.26	108.71	0.82	1 158.95
2014	1 427.10	84.46	124.34	1.04	1 217.26
2015	1 661.03	88.95	125.45	0.81	1 445.81
2016	1 903.39	98.73	114.98	0.71	1 688.97
2017	2 130.55	107.34	116.67	0.78	1 905.75
2018	2 325.82	112.09	105.81	0.79	2 107.12

表 16.5 主要年份货物运输量
FREIGHT TRAFFIC VOLUME IN MAIN YEARS

单位:万吨(10 000 tons)

年 份 Year	货物运输量 Freight Traffic Volume	其 中 of which				
		铁 路 Railway	公 路 Highway	水 运 Waterway	其 中 of which #远洋运输 Ocean Shipping	民用航空 Civil Aviation
1990	22 848	1 257	8 714	12 864	2 246	13
1995	22 531	1 376	6 273	14 845	2 778	37
2000	47 954	1 055	28 369	18 442	7 022	88
2005	68 741	1 278	32 684	34 557	10 091	222
2006	72 617	1 223	33 799	37 342	11 766	253
2007	78 108	1 143	35 634	41 041	12 575	290
2008	84 347	1 012	40 328	42 729	12 197	305
2009	76 967	941	37 745	37 983	11 916	298
2010	81 023	959	40 890	38 803	15 172	371
2011	93 318	888	42 685	49 389	16 044	356
2012	94 376	825	42 911	50 302	17 491	338
2013	91 535	694	43 809	46 697	15 255	335
2014	90 341	549	42 848	46 583	16 541	361
2015	91 239	471	40 627	49 770	18 145	371
2016	88 689	461	39 055	48 787	18 912	387
2017	97 257	472	39 743	56 619	23 871	423
2018	107 387	468	39 595	66 906	28 213	418

①2005 年起，民航货物吞吐量不包括旅客行李。
②2008 年，公路货运量为交通部公路运输专项调查数据。
❶The Freight Traffic Volume of Civil Aviation in 2005 doesn't include the freight transportation volume.
❷The Highway Freight Traffic Volume of 2008 refers to the result of highway transportation special investigation hold by Ministry of Communications.

表 16.6 主要年份货物周转量
TURNOVER VOLUME OF FREIGHT TRAFFIC IN MAIN YEARS

单位:亿吨·公里(100 million tons·km)

年 份 Year	货物周转量 Turnover Volume of Freight Traffic	其 中 of which				
		铁 路 Railway	公 路 Highway	水 运 Waterway	其 中 of which #远洋运输 Ocean Shipping	民用航空 Civil Aviation
1990	3 359	111	11	3 236	1 957	1
1995	4 187	143	9	4 030	2 259	5
2000	6 620	122	56	6 430	5 285	12
2005	12 132	47	73	11 986	9 285	27
2006	13 837	55	80	13 683	10 817	19
2007	15 949	35	85	15 789	12 039	40
2008	16 031	29	253	15 712	11 529	37
2009	14 436	25	244	14 118	10 596	49
2010	16 173	26	266	15 818	14 535	63
2011	20 367	21	284	20 005	15 654	57
2012	20 427	18	288	20 067	16 086	54
2013	17 868	14	299	17 497	13 562	57
2014	18 691	12	301	18 320	14 487	57
2015	19 553	11	290	19 196	15 150	57
2016	19 376	10	282	19 026	15 473	58
2017	25 058	10	298	24 691	20 276	60
2018	23 258	10	299	27 991	23 019	62

①2004 年起，上海铁路分局改为上海铁路局，货物周转量数据有所调整。
②2006 年民航货物周转量未包括中国货运航空公司的数据。
③2008 年，公路货物周转量为交通部公路运输专项调查数据。
❶Since 2004, Shanghai Railway Branch Bureau has been change into Shanghai Railway Bureau ,the Turnover Volume of Freight has been adjusted accordingly.
❷In 2006,the date of China Cargo Airlines wasn't included in the Turnover Volume of Freight of Aviation .
❸The Highway Freight Turnover Volume of 2008 refers to the result of highway transportation special investigation hold by Ministry of Communications.

表 16.7　主要年份港口码头情况
PORTS IN MAIN YEARS

年　份 Year	沿海码头长度（万米） Length of Harbor (10 000 m)	沿海泊位（个） Berths (unit)	其中 of which #生产用万吨级 10 000 Tons for Production	其中 of which #集装箱泊位 Container Berths
1990	1.77	122	64	7
1995	1.90	140	68	12
2000	7.64	1 098	111	18
2005	8.95	1 181	124	28
2006	9.16	1 140	131	32
2007	10.15	1 155	133	37
2008	11.49	1 203	137	42
2009	11.68	1 145	153	38
2010	11.92	1 218	157	45
2011	11.97	1 226	160	43
2012	12.29	1 245	162	43
2013	12.40	1 253	170	43
2014	12.60	1 282	170	42
2015	12.69	1 300	174	42
2016	10.92	1 152	172	42
2017	10.61	1 078	172	42
2018	14.92	1 978	181	51

注：1997 年以前，沿海码头长度、沿海泊位为原港务局数据，从 1998 年后，为全港数据。
Note: Before 1997, the figures of length of harbor and berths were from the ports belonged to Port Administration Bureau, and after 1998, data have been collected from all types of ports.

表 16.8　主要年份港口货物吞吐量
PORT FREIGHT THROUGHPUT IN MAIN YEARS

单位：万吨（10 000 tons）

年　份 Year	港口货物吞吐量 Port freight Throughput	其中 of which 内贸 Internal Trade	其中 of which 外贸 Foreign Trade	进　港 Entry	其中 of which 内贸 Internal Trade	其中 of which 外贸 Foreign Trade	出　港 Departure	其中 of which 内贸 Internal Trade	其中 of which 外贸 Foreign Trade
1990	13 959	11 366	2 593	9 461	7 592	1 869	4 498	3 774	724
1995	16 567	12 481	4 086	12 097	9 492	2 605	4 470	2 989	1 481
2000	20 440	12 807	7 633	13 791	9 242	4 549	6 649	3 565	3 084
2005	44 317	25 825	18 492	27 539	17 441	10 098	16 778	8 384	8 394
2006	53 748	32 480	21 268	34 600	23 613	10 987	19 148	8 867	10 281
2007	56 144	30 574	25 570	35 479	22 619	12 860	20 665	7 956	12 709
2008	58 170	30 793	27 377	36 481	22 782	13 699	21 689	8 012	13 677
2009	59 205	33 394	25 811	39 000	24 920	14 080	20 205	8 474	11 731
2010	65 339	35 114	30 225	41 549	25 083	16 466	23 791	10 032	13 759
2011	72 758	38 980	33 778	45 525	27 173	18 352	27 233	11 807	15 426
2012	73 559	37 734	35 825	45 151	25 233	19 918	28 408	12 501	15 907
2013	77 575	39 869	37 706	46 978	25 657	21 321	30 597	14 213	16 384
2014	75 529	37 297	38 232	44 663	23 654	21 009	30 866	13 643	17 223
2015	71 740	33 943	37 797	41 907	21 447	20 460	29 833	12 495	17 337
2016	70 177	32 164	38 012	40 295	20 039	20 256	29 882	12 126	17 756
2017	75 051	34 008	41 043	43 315	21 182	22 133	31 736	12 826	18 910
2018	73 048	32 842	40 206	41 931	21 445	20 486	31 117	11 397	19 720

表 16.9 主要年份国际集装箱吞吐量(按进出港分)
INTERNATIONAL CONTAINERS AND CARGO THROUGHPUT OF FOREIGN TRADE IN MAIN YEARS

年 份 Year	国际标准集装箱吞吐量重量(万吨) Weight of International Containers (10 000 tons)	国际标准集装箱吞吐量(万 TEU) International Containers (10 000 TEU)	其 中 of which 进 港 Entry	 出 港 Degarture
1990	446	45.6	22.4	23.2
1995	1 389	152.6	69.3	83.3
1996	1 785	197.1	92.4	104.7
1997	2 304	252.8	114.7	138.1
1998	2 766	306.6	141.1	165.5
1999	3 949	421.6	196.7	224.9
2000	5 170	561.2	266.1	295.1
2005	16 250	1 808.4	887.2	921.3
2006	19 595	2 171.9	1 064.4	1 107.5
2007	23 850	2 615.2	1 276.3	1 338.9
2008	25 992	2 800.6	1 397.8	1 402.8
2009	24 619	2 500.2	1 222.9	1 277.3
2010	27 992	2 906.9	1 436.1	1 470.8
2011	31 220	3 173.9	1 555.1	1 618.9
2012	32 480	3 252.9	1 605.1	1 647.9
2013	34 243	3 361.7	1 652.2	1 709.5
2014	35 335	3 528.5	1 732.3	1 796.2
2015	35 850	3 653.7	1 818.7	1 835.0
2016	36 736	3 713.3	1 825.2	1 888.1
2017	39 759	4 023.3	1 980.3	2 043.0
2018	41 126	4 201.0	2 064.6	2 136.4

注：TEU 是“折合 20 英尺标准箱”英文缩写语。
Note: TEU is the abbreviation, which refers to 20-feet equivalent unit.

表 16.10 邮轮经济发展情况(2015~2018)
CRUISE ECONOMIC DEVELOPMENT

指 标	Indicators	2015	2016	2017	2018
邮轮靠泊次数(次)	Cruise Berthing Times (time)	341	509	512	406
#以上海为母港靠泊次数	Homeport in Shanghai	317	482	482	378
邮轮旅客吞吐量(万人)	Cruise Passenger Throughput (10 000 persons)	164.26	289.38	297.29	275.29
#以上海为母港吞吐量	Homeport in Shanghai	159.53	282.90	290.82	268.96

表 16.11 经营性停车场(库)营运情况(2015~2018) STATISTICS OF PARKING LOTS (GARAGES) OPERATION

指 标	Indicators	2015	2016	2017	2018
计时停放(万辆次)	Time Parking (10 000 vehicletimes)	16 969.32	18 117.03	26 744.27	33 600.63
包月停放(万辆次)	Monthly Parking (10 000 vehicletimes)	6 237.96	6 372.81	6 702.37	8 083.70
车辆停放车次合计(万辆次)	Quantity of Parking Times (10 000 vehicletimes)	27 715.88	29 295.56	40 218.02	49 318.26
经营车辆停放收入(亿元)	Revenue of Parking Lots (100 million yuan)	23.17	23.39	30.26	35.64

表 16.12 民用车辆拥有量 (2015~2018) CIVIL MOTOR VEHICLES

单位:万辆(10 000 vehicles)

指 标	Indicators	2015	2016	2017	2018
总 计	**Total**	**332.35**	**359.48**	**392.36**	**423.13**
#汽 车	Civil Automobile	282.32	322.94	361.02	393.42
载客汽车	Passenger Vehicles	256.26	293.85	328.17	358.37
#轿 车	Cars	187.28	206.91	196.14	235.85
载货汽车	Freight Trucks	19.49	21.86	30.81	32.87
其他汽车	Other Automobile	6.57	7.23	2.04	2.18
摩托车	Motorcycle	42.90	29.10	22.80	20.57
拖拉机	Tractors	1.05	1.05	1.00	1.00

①本表不包括军用车辆和码头、机场等专用特种车辆。
②从 2012 年起，民用车辆拥有量的数据不含强制报废量(下表同)。
❶This table doesn't include the quantity of military vehicles and special vehicles for port and airport.
❷Since 2012, the civil vehicle ownership data does not contain mandatory retirement amount (the same as the following table).

表 16.13 个人民用车辆拥有量 (2015~2018) INDIVIDUAL CIVIL MOTOR VEHICLES

单位:万辆(10 000 vehicles)

指 标	Indicators	2015	2016	2017	2018
总 计	**Total**	**250.51**	**271.01**	**296.53**	**322.14**
#汽 车	Civil Automobile	208.71	242.71	274.41	302.17
载客汽车	Passenger Vehicles	208.22	242.06	273.63	301.26
#轿 车	Cars	161.98	181.19	196.14	209.53
载货汽车	Freight Trucks	0.25	0.40	0.53	0.65
其它汽车	Other Automobile	0.24	0.25	0.25	0.25
摩托车	Motorcycle	41.74	28.26	22.09	19.94

表 16.14 现代航运服务业营业收入(2017-2018)
OPERATING INCOME OF MODERN SHIPPING SERVICE INDUSTRY

单位:亿元(100 million yuan)

指标	Indicators	2017	2018
现代航运服务业营业收入	**Operating Income of Modern Shipping Service Industry**	**9 102.54**	**10 266.35**
交通运输	Transportation	4 249.69	6 770.73
铁路运输	Railway Transportation	970.82	1 183.26
道路运输	Highway Transportation	695.81	732.06
水上运输	Waterway Transportation	1 401.34	1 482.44
航空运输	Civil Aviation Transportation	1 181.73	1 372.87
装卸搬运和运输代理	Handling and Ttransportation Agency	2 578.02	2 715.41
仓　储	Warehousing	340.82	374.65
快　递	Express delivery	655.48	896.96
金　融	Financial	484.24	498.55
租赁和商业服务	Leasing and Commercial Services	543.05	719.27
科学研究和技术服务	Scientific Research and Technical Services	238.17	276.71
教　育	Education	13.06	14.07

表 16.15 邮政主要指标(2015~2018)
MAIN INDICATORS OF POST

指标	Indicators	2015	2016	2017	2018
邮电局、所(个)	Post Office (unit)	537	538	538	536
报刊图书销售点(个)	Publications Sales Outlet (unit)	1 428	758	470	26
邮政信筒信箱(个)	Mail Boxe (unit)	2 997	3 075	3 025	3 013
集邮品销售点(个)	Stamps Sales Outlet (unit)	220	281	266	254
邮政储蓄网点(个)	Postal Savings Office (unit)	378	380	380	380
邮路条数(条)	Number of Mail Route (route)	496	487	277	281
邮路总长度(万公里)	Total Length of Mail Routes (10 000 km)	6.01	5.75	4.72	5.29
农村投递路线总长度(万公里)	Length of Rural Delivery Routes (10 000 km)	0.11	0.21	0.19	0.16

注：由于邮政速递物流公司成立，邮政公司的部分基础设施被拨出。
Note: The part of post infrastructure are transferred from Shanghai Post Corporation to newly established Shanghai Post Express and Logistics Corporation.

表 16.16 主要年份邮政业务主要指标
MAJOR INDICATORS OF POSTAL BUSINESS IN MAIN YEARS

指 标	Indicators	2000	2010	2017	2018
邮政业务总量(亿元)	Volume of Postal Business (100 million yuan)	22.40	49.48	711.87	820.62
函 件(亿件)	Mails (100 million units)	4.61	11.66	6.74	5.74
国内特快专递(万件)	Domestic Express Mails (10 000 pieces)	709.90	25 708.85	301 583.63	335 366.71
国际及港澳台特快专递(万件)	International and Hong Kong 、Macao and Taiwan Express Mails (10 000 pieces)	52.10	3 088.01	9 920.07	13 282.10
邮政储蓄期末余额(亿元)	Postal Saving Deposit Balance (100 million yuan)	153.50	545.64	920.30	1 018.40
报纸、杂志累计订销数(亿份)	Total Copies of Newspapers and Magazines Subscribed and Sold (100 million pieces)	11.30	11.99	8.33	7.73
集邮业务(万枚)	Stamp Collection Business (10 000 stamps)	9 467	5 156	6 763	5 219

注：2012 年起，"邮政业务总量"包括国家邮政业务总量和非国家邮政业务总量。
Note: Since 2012, Volume of Postal Business contains volume of national postal business and volume of non-national postal-business.

表 16.17 规模以上信息服务业情况(2018)
STATISTICS OF INFORMATION SERVICE INDUSTRY ABOVE DESIGNATED SIZE

类 别	Types	营业收入(亿元) Operating Revenues (100 million yuan)	期末从业人员数(万人) Number of Employees at the End of Term (10 000 persons)
总 计	Total	**5 344.62**	**38.06**
电子信息传输服务	Electronic Information Transmission Service	1 385.14	7.72
电 信	Telecom	731.77	3.45
互联网信息服务	Internet Information Service	578.98	3.67
广播电视传输服务	Radio and Television Transmission Service	73.91	0.60
卫星传输服务	Satellite Transmission Service	0.47	0.01
计算机服务和软件业	Computer Service And Software Industry	3 715.88	28.66
计算机服务	Computer Service	1 323.86	11.18
软件服务	Software Service	2 392.02	17.48
其他信息相关服务	Other Information Related Service	243.60	1.68
广播、电视、电影和音像业	Radio, Television, Film and Video Industry	177.62	1.04
新闻出版业	Press and Publishing Industry	65.81	0.63
图书馆与档案馆	Library and Archives	0.17	0.01

表 16.18 主要年份电信业务主要指标
MAJOR INDICATORS OF TELECOM BUSINESS IN MAIN YEARS

指标	Indicators	2010	2015	2017	2018
电信业务总量(亿元)	Volume of Telecom Business (100 million yuan)	373.00	778.80	693.79	1 436.34
电信业务收入(亿元)	Income of Telecom Business (100 million yuan)	440.49	535.68	582.18	585.50
年末固定电话用户(万户)	Year-end Installed Telephones (10 000 households)	931.80	797.29	690.95	663.19
#住宅电话	Household Phones Installed	574.52	461.52	389.07	360.90
移动电话用户(万户)	Mobile Phone Subscribers Users (10 000 households)	2 361.55	3 132.41	3 298.71	3 722.28
#3G及4G移动电话用户	3G and 4G Mobile Phone Users	199.90	2 042.00	2 807.31	3 626.98
#4G移动电话用户	4G Mobile Phone Users		1 219.90	2 387.81	3 265.20
长途通话时长(亿分钟)	Long-distance Call Lasting Time (100 million minutes)	205.77	243.95	169.29	163.61
固定电话长途通话时长	Installed Telephone Domestic Long-distance Call Lasting Time	38.84	39.83	34.69	30.68
国内长途电话通话时长	Domestic Trunk Calls	36.67	37.82	33.44	29.65
国际及港澳台电话通话时长	Overseas Calls	2.17	2.01	1.25	1.03
移动电话长途通话时长	Mobile Telephone Long-distance Call Lasting Time	37.37	204.12	134.60	132.93
国内长途电话通话时长	Domestic Trunk Calls	36.00	202.25	133.31	131.22
国际及港澳台电话通话时长	Overseas Calls	1.37	1.87	1.29	1.71
固定电话通话时长(亿分钟)	Installed Telephone Call Lasting Time(100 million minutes)	340.05	193.36	142.21	115.54
移动电话通话时长(亿分钟)	Mobile Calls (100 million minutes)	1 011.00	1 238.20	1 068.56	998.41
移动短信业务量(亿条)	Volume of Mobile Short Messages (100 million pieces)	396.00	211.86	236.74	528.99
局用交换机容量(含接入网设备容量)(万门)	Capacity of Office Telephone Exchanges (Including Access Network Capacity) (10 000 units)	1 338.61	1 200.47	550.70	480.10
移动电话交换机容量(万户)	Mobile Phone Exchange Capacity (10 000 households)	3 995	4 424	5 044	6 548
固定互联网宽带接入用户(万户)	Fixed Broadband Internet Access Users (10 000 households)	545.00	568.76	681.33	772.92
移动互联网用户(万户)	Mobile Internet Users (10 000 households)	1 355.00	2 569.29	3 393.14	3 032.00
移动互联网接入流量(万G)	Mobile Internet Access Traffic (10 000G)	1 153.70	10 818.80	48 162.73	134 846.76

①2010年起，固定互联网宽带接入用户的统计口径从基础电信企业的用户调整为所有宽带驻地网企业的用户。
②电信业务总量是指以货币形式表示的电信企业为社会提供的各类电信服务的总数量。包括固定话音业务总量、固定数据及互联网业务总量、固定增值及其他业务总量、移动话音业务总量、移动数据及互联网业务总量、移动增值及其他业务总量。
③2016年起电信业务总量调整为按照2015年不变单价计算。
❶The Indicator "Fixed Broadband Internet Access Users" was calculated by all local business users since 2010.
❷Volume of Telecom Business refers to the total number of telecommunication services provided by telecommunication enterprises for the society in the form of money, including the total volume of fixed voice services, fixed data and total Internet services, fixed value-added and other services, mobile voice services, mobile data and Internet services, mobile value-added and other services.
❸The total amount of telecom business of 2016 and 2017 was calculated according to the costant unit price of 2015.

表 16.19 主要年份邮电通信水平
POSTAL AND TELECOM LEVEL IN MAIN YEARS

指 标	Indicators	2010	2015	2017	2018
固定电话普及率（%）	Popularity Rate of Telephone Line（%）	48.5	33.0	28.6	27.4
住宅电话普及率（%）	Popularity Rate of Household Telephone（%）	110.6	86.0	71.2	65.4
移动电话普及率(%)	Popularity Rate of Mobile Telephone（%）	122.9	129.7	136.4	153.6
平均每一邮政局所服务面积（平方公里）	Average Area Served by One Post Office（sq.km）	10.69	11.81	11.79	11.83
平均每一邮政局所服务人口(万人)	Average Population Served by Every Post Office（10 000 persons）	3.86	4.50	4.50	4.52
人均每年发函件数(件)	Average Number of Letters Mailed（piece）	50.89	37.56	34.14	23.68
人均每年购报刊数(份)	Average Number of Newspaper and Magazine Purchased（piece）	50.50	40.46	37.41	31.89

注：固定电话普及率及移动电话普及率为根据第六次人口普查调整后的数据。
Note: Data of Popularity Rate of Telephone Line and Popularity Rate of Mobile Telephone have been adjusted according to the sixth census.

表 16.20 主要年份信息化基础设施情况
INFRASTRUCTURE OF INFORMATIZATION IN MAIN YEARS

指 标	Indicators	2010	2015	2017	2018
信息通信管线长度(沟公里)	Length of Information Communication Pielines（channel km）	5 821	9 975	10 741	10 967
家庭宽带接入用户(万户)	Household Users of Broadband Access(10 000 households)	440	620	745	804
IPTV 用户(万户)	IPTV Users（10 000 households）	130	177	317	398
有线数字电视用户(万户)	Digital Cable TV Users（10 000 households）	220	662	706	715

注：2013 年起，家庭宽带接入用户的统计口径从基础电信企业的用户调整为所有宽带驻地网企业的用户。
Note: Househole Users of Broadband Acess was calculated by all local business users since 2013.

上 / 海 / 统 / 计 / 年 / 鉴

主要统计指标解释

■ 铁路运营里程

铁路运营里程又称营业长度(包括正式营业和临时营业里程),指办理客货运输业务的铁路正线总长度。凡是全线或部分建成双线及以上的线路,以第一线的实际长度计算;复线、站线、段管线、岔线和特殊用途线以及不计算运费的联络线都不计算营业里程。铁路营业里程是反映铁路运输业基础设施发展水平的重要指标,也是计算客货周转量、运输密度和机车车辆运用效率等指标的基础资料。

■ 内河航道里程

内河航道里程也称内河通航里程,指在一定时期内,能通航运输船舶及排筏的天然河流、湖泊水库、运河及通航渠道的长度。包括全年季节性通航累计三个月以上的航道,不包括仅供零散流放竹、木排的河道。该指标可以反映内河水运网的规模、水平和发展情况。

■ 货物(旅客)周转量

指在一定时期内,由各种运输工具运送的货物(旅客)数量与其相应运输距离的乘积之总和,是反映运输业生产总成果的重要指标,也是编制和检查运输生产计划,计算运输效益、劳动生产率以及核算运输单位成本的主要基础资料。通常以吨公里和人公里为计算单位。计算货物周转量通常按发出站与到达站之间的最短距离,也就是计费距离计算。

■ 货(客)运量

指在一定时期内,各种运输工具实际运送的货物(旅客)数量。它是反映运输业为国民经济和人民生活服务的数量指标,也是制定和检查运输生产计划、研究运输发展规模和速度的重要指标。货运按吨计算,客运按人计算。货物不论运输距离长短、货物类别,均按实际重量统计。旅客不论行程远近或票价多少,均按一人一次客运量统计;半价票、小孩票也按一人统计。

■ 港口货物吞吐量

指经由水路进出港区范围,并经过装卸的货物数量。按货物流向分为进港吞吐量和出港吞吐量,按货物贸易性质分为内贸和外贸吞吐量。按货物的类别分,可根据现行的交通行业标准《运输货物分类和代码》分类。

■ 国际标准集装箱吞吐量

凡经过水运进出港区范围,并经过装卸的集装箱箱数和重量(含集装箱自重),通常是按进港和出港分别统计。

TEU是“折合20英尺标准箱”的英文缩写。它是指各种尺寸的国际标准集装箱的自然箱数,按各自的换算比例,折算为20英尺标准箱的换算箱数。其换算比例为:40英尺箱 1∶2;35英尺箱 1∶1.75;20英尺箱 1∶1;10英尺箱 1∶0.5。

■ 民用车辆拥有量

指报告期末,在公安交通管理部门按照《机动车注册登记工作规范》,已注册登记领有民用车辆牌照的全部汽车数量。汽车拥有量统计的主要分类:根据汽车结构分为载客汽车、载货汽车及其他汽车;根据汽车所有者不同分为个人(私人)汽车、单位汽车;根据汽车的使用性质分为营运汽车、非营运汽车和特种汽车;根据汽车大小规格不同载客汽车分为大型、中型、小型和微型,载货汽车分为重型、中型、轻型和微型。

■ 邮政业务总量

指以货币表现的邮政部门用于邮政服务的总数量。它综合反映了一定时期邮政工作的总成果,是研究邮政业务量构成和发展趋势的重要指标。它用各种邮政分类业务量,如函件件数、电报份数、订销报刊累计份数等,分别乘以相应的平均单位(不变价),加总后再加上其他业务收入求得。

■ 住宅电话用户

指安装在居民住宅或农民家里并按照住宅电话用户登记注册和收费的电话用户。包括私人付费、单位付费和按规定免费安装的住宅电话用户。

主要统计指标解释

■ 移动电话用户

指通过移动电话交换机进入移动电话网、占用移动电话号码的电话用户。用户数量以报告期末在移动电话营业部门实际办理登记手续进入移动电话网的户数进行计算，一部移动电话统计为一户。

■ 局用交换机容量

指安装在电信企业用于接续本地固定电话的电话交换机容量。

■ 电信业务总量

是指以货币形式表示的电信企业为社会提供的各类电信服务的总数量。包括固定话音业务总量、固定数据及互联网业务总量、固定增值及其他业务总量、移动话音业务总量、移动数据及互联网业务总量、移动增值及其他业务总量。

SHANGHAI STATISTICAL YEARBOOK

EXPLANATORY NOTES TO MAJOR STATISTICAL INDICATORS

□ Operation Mileage of Railways

Operation Mileage of Railways refers to the total length of the trunk line under passenger and freight transportation (including both full operation and temporary operation). The calculation is based on the actual length of the first line even if this line has a full or partial double track or more tracks, excluding double tracks, station sidings, tracks under the charge of stations, branch lines, special-purpose lines and the non-payable connecting lines. The length of railways in operation is an important indicator to show the development of the infrastructure for the railway transport, and also the essential data to calculate volume of passenger freight transport, traffic density and utilization efficiency of the locomotives and carriages.

□ Length of Navigable Inland Waterways

Length of Navigable Inland Waterways it is an indicator reflecting the size and development of inland water network, it refers to the length of the natural rivers, lakes, reservoirs, canals, and ditches open to navigation during a given period, which enables the transport by ships and rafts. It includes the channels open to navigation for over an accumulative 3 months in a year, yet this does not include the river courses, which are only used to float odd logs and bamboo rafts. This indicator can reflect the scale, level and development situation of the inland waterway network.

□ Freight (Passenger) Turnover Volume

Freight (Passenger) Turnover Volume refers to the total of the product of the physical volume of transported cargo (passenger) by the transport distance, usually using ton/kilometer and person/kilometer as calculating units. Normally, the shortest distance between the departure point and the destination is the basis to calculate the freight turnover volume, that is to say, the payable distance. This is an important indicator to show the total results of the transport industry, to prepare and examine the transport plan and to measure the efficiency, the labor productivity and the unit cost of transport.

□ Freight (Passenger) Traffic

Freight (Passenger) Traffic refers to the volume of freight (passenger) transported with various means. The freight (passenger) traffic provides a quantitative measure to show how the transport industry serves the national economy and people, and is also an important indicator for planning the transport industry and for studying the development scale and speed of the transport industry. Freight transport is calculated in tons and passenger traffic is calculated in the number of persons. Despite the type of freight and travelling distance, the freight transport is calculated in the actual weight of the goods: and despite the travelling distance and ticket price, the passenger traffic is calculated by the principle that one person can be counted only once in one travel. The passenger who travels with a half price ticket or a child ticket is also calculated as one person.

□ Volume of Freight Handled in Ports

Volume of Freight Handled in Ports refers to the volume of cargo passing in and out of the harbour area of the major coastal ports and having been loaded and unloaded. The volume of freight handled may be classified by direction of flow as freight for import and freight for export, or by nature of cargo as freight for domestic trade and freight for foreign trade. The volume of freight handled maybe classified by the classification of cargo, or the current transport standard of The Classification and Code of Cargo Type.

□ International Container Throughput Capacity

International Container Throughput Capacity refers to number and weight of containers which are loaded or unloaded within port area via water carriage. It is often calculated by entering and leaving port, respectively. TEU was the abbreviation of twenty foot equivalent unit, which refers to converted number of all kinds of containers. The conversion method is based on respective conversion ratio and the number of all kinds of container is converted to the standard number of twenty foot equivalent unit. The conversion ratio is: 40 feet container 1∶2, 35 feet container 1∶1.75, 20 feet container 1∶1, 10 feet container 1∶0.5.

□ Individual Civil Motor Vehicles

Individual Civil Motor Vehicles refers to the total numbers of vehicles that are registered and received vehicles′ license

EXPLANATORY NOTES TO MAJOR STATISTICAL INDICATORS

tags according to the Work Standard for Motor Vehicles Registration formulated by transport management office under department of public security at the end of reference period. They are divided into following categories according to the structure of motor vehicles: passenger vehicles, trucks and others; and private vehicles and vehicles for units use according to ownerships; working vehicles, non-working vehicles and special motor vehicles according to kind of usage; large passenger vehicles, medium passenger vehicles and small passenger vehicles, heavy trucks, light-heavy trucks and light trucks according to sizes of vehicles.

□ Volume of Post Business

Volume of Post Business refers to the total amount of post services provided by the post department, which reflects the total achievements by the post departments during a given period of time in a comprehensive way, and is an important indicator to study the composition and development of the post business. It is arrived by first multiplying the business volume of different types, such as number of letters, telegrams and accumulated number of newspaper and journals subscribed and sold, etc. by their respective average unit price (fixed price) and then adding these products together, plus the income from other business revenues.

□ Household Telephone Subscribers

Household Telephone Subscribers refer to telephone sets installed in the dwelling units of urban or rural residents, and registered as residence subscribers for payment, including 3 types of payment for the service: private payment, public payment and free service.

□ Mobile Phone Subscribers

Mobile Phone Subscribers refer to the persons who own mobile telephone numbers and are connected with the mobile telephone communication network through the mobile telephone switchboards. The number of subscribers is calculated by the subscribers who have completed registration at mobile communication business centers and entered into the mobile telephone network. One mobile telephone is taken as a user.

□ Capacity of Office Telephone Exchanges

Capacity of Office Telephone Exchanges refers to the capacity of telephone exchanges installed in the office of telecommunication service providers for communication between fixed telephones.

□ Total Amount of Telecommunication Services

Total Amount of Telecommunication Services refers to the total amount of various types of telecommunications services in the form of money provided by telecommunications companies for society. It includes the total amount of fixed voice services, fixed data and Internet services, fixed value-added business and other services, mobile voice services, mobile data and internet services, mobile value-added business and other services.

第十七篇
CHAPTER 17

批发、零售和住宿、餐饮
WHOLESALE AND RETAIL, HOTELS AND CATERING SERVICES

简要说明

一、本章资料的主要内容

本篇资料主要反映上海市批发和零售业、住宿和餐饮业的发展与经营状况，同时反映国内商品流通、商品消费、市场运行态势。主要内容包括：限额以上批发和零售业产业活动单位和从业人员、商品流转情况、财务状况；限额以上住宿餐饮业产业活动单位和从业人员、经营状况、财务状况；连锁经营情况；商品交易市场成交情况；社会消费品零售总额；商品销售总额等。

二、本篇资料的统计范围

批发和零售业、住宿和餐饮业的法人企业、产业活动单位、个体户，零售业、住宿和餐饮业连锁集团，商品交易市场。

三、本篇的资料来源

本篇资料是根据《批发和零售业统计报表制度》、《住宿和餐饮业统计报表制度》进行搜集和加工整理而得。

四、本篇的统计调查方法

本篇资料中限额以上批发和零售业、住宿和餐饮业法人企业、个体户、其他行业附营的限额以上批发和零售业、住宿和餐饮业产业活动单位资料，以及零售业、住宿和餐饮业连锁集团，商品交易市场采用全面调查的方法；限额以下企业及个体户等资料采用抽样调查方法推算。

BRIEF INTRODUCTION

I. Main Contents

Data in this chapter reflect the development and operation of Shanghai's wholesale and retail trade, hotels and catering service. Data also reflect domestic commodity circulation, consumption, and market operation. Main contents include the basic conditions, employment, circulation of commodities, and financial status of wholesale and retail trades above the set scale; basic conditions, employment, business situation, and financial status of hotels and catering services above the set scale; chain business conditions, transactions of commodities market, retail sales of main consumer goods, and total sales of consumer goods.

II. Scope of Statistics

Included in this chapter are the registered enterprises and self-employed individuals of wholesale and retail trade, hotels and catering service; chain enterprises in retail, hotels, and catering businesses; and commodities markets.

III. Sources of Data

Data in this chapter are collected and processed in accordance with The Statistical Reporting Form System on Wholesale and Retail Trades and The Statistical Reporting Form System on Hotel and Catering.

IV. Survey Methodology

Data on basic conditions for all corporate enterprises and self-employed individuals above the set scale of wholesale and retail trades, hotel, and catering businesses; affiliating establishments above the set scale of other industries involved in the wholesale and retail trades, hotels and catering businesses; chain enterprises of wholesale and retail trades; and commodities markets data are collected through comprehensive reporting system. Data on enterprises and self-employed individuals below the set scale are collected by sample surveys.

表 17.1 批发和零售业、住宿和餐饮业从业人员(1978~2018)
EMPLOYEES OF WHOLESALE AND RETAIL, HOTELS AND CATERING SERVICES

年 份 Year	从业人员 (万人) Employees (10 000 persons)	其 中 of which				
		批发零售贸易业 Wholesale and Retail	其 中 of which		餐饮业 Catering	住宿业 Hotels
			批发业 Wholesale	零售业 Retail		
1978	39.62	30.70	5.46	25.24	5.57	
1979	44.70	32.94	7.87	25.07	5.82	
1980	45.78	33.94	7.91	26.03	5.66	
1981	48.47	35.31	8.41	26.90	6.25	
1982	50.24	36.70	9.05	27.65	6.51	
1983	51.30	37.64	8.86	28.78	6.51	
1984	55.24	40.57	8.81	31.76	6.86	
1985	62.64	45.41	8.99	36.42	7.66	
1986	63.76	44.98	8.96	36.02	7.97	
1987	66.13	45.98	8.85	37.13	8.18	
1988	72.80	50.89	9.42	41.47	8.67	
1989	77.31	52.20	9.67	42.53	9.35	
1990	74.75	50.48	8.19	42.29	9.33	
1991	75.41	52.47	8.53	43.94	10.71	
1992	87.27	63.71	13.74	49.97	10.98	
1993	109.98	98.44	29.68	68.76	11.54	
1994	88.51	77.49	27.58	49.91	11.02	
1995	111.24	94.78	34.31	60.47	16.46	
1996	145.67	122.21	50.79	71.42	23.46	
1997	149.97	125.64	53.68	71.96	24.33	
1998	150.96	126.56	53.67	72.89	24.40	
1999	153.90	128.18	53.93	74.25	25.72	
2000	154.32	128.41	53.79	74.62	25.91	
2001	165.68	138.73	56.33	82.40	26.95	
2002	179.34	152.19	65.40	86.79	27.15	
2003	174.93	147.91	59.31	88.60	27.02	
2004	181.25	156.21	74.77	81.44	25.04	
2005	195.92	169.60	84.71	84.89	26.32	
2006	203.51	174.49	86.32	88.17	29.02	
2007	204.46	175.50	86.23	89.27	28.96	
2008	202.84	172.72	87.98	84.74	30.12	
2009	205.49	175.32	90.36	84.96	30.17	
2010	207.94	176.69	91.58	85.21	31.25	
2011	215.57	184.61	96.96	87.65	30.96	
2012	226.70	194.28	104.33	89.95	32.42	
2013	230.26	194.91	106.98	87.93	35.35	
2014	286.99	235.52				51.47
2015	290.22	238.31				51.91
2016	291.28	239.06				52.22
2017	295.65	240.39				55.26
2018	304.81	243.92				60.89

注：本表从业人员是指本行业的全部从业人员，包含个体户及非正规就业等。 由于统计制度方法调整，2014 年起本表从业人员由批发零售业、住餐餐饮业两部分组成。

Note: Employees in this table refer to all the employees in the sector, including self-employed and informal employees. Because of the adjustment of statistical method for statistics, since 2014, employees in this table include the employees in the sector of whole and retail, commodation and catering.

表 17.2 限额以上批发业产业活动单位和从业人员(2018)
QUANTITY OF BUSINESS UNITS AND EMPLOYEES OF WHOLESALE ABOVE THE SET SCALE

类 别	Types	法人企业（个） Quantity of Corporations (unit)	产业活动单位数（个） Quantity of Business Units (unit)	从业人员（人） Quantity of Employees (person)
总 计	**Total**	**5 158**	**12 223**	**506 351**
按登记注册类型分	**Grouped by Registration Categories**			
内 资	Domestic Enterprises	3 415	5 829	193 479
#国 有	State-owned	28	51	1 576
集 体	Collective-owned	4	7	129
股份合作	Share Holding Cooperative Enterprises	2	2	51
联 营	Joint-Owned Enterprises	2	2	237
有限责任公司	Companies with Limited Liabilities	1 040	2 401	82 047
股份有限公司	Share Holding Companies with Limited Liabilities	96	221	23 492
私 营	Private	2 243	3 145	85 947
港澳台商投资	Hong Kong, Macao and Taiwan Funded	562	2 929	109 438
外商投资	Foreign Funded	1 181	3 465	203 434
按行业分	**Grouped By Sectors**			
农、林、牧产品批发	Agriculture, Forestry and Animal Husbandry Products	77	108	2 660
食品、饮料及烟草制品批发	Food, Beverage and Tabacco	437	1 453	67 761
#米、面制品及食用油批发	Rice, Flour and Cooking Oil	75	125	17 679
烟草制品批发	Tabacco	24	287	5 125
纺织、服装及日用品批发	Textile Products, Garments and Commodity	709	3 743	137 406
#米、服装批发	Garments	198	1 594	50 173
文化、体育用品及器材批发	Culture & Sports Articles and Equipments	177	486	16 478
医药及医疗器材批发	Medicines and Special Appliances of Medicines	267	560	63 748
矿产品、建材及化工产品批发	Mineral Products, Materials of Construction and Chemical Products	1 943	2 945	67 560
#米、煤炭及制品批发	Coal	48	53	1 158
石油及制品批发	Petroleum	193	620	9 333
金属及金属矿批发	Metal Products and Metal Minerals	787	939	18 329
建材批发	Building Materials	128	166	6 092
机械设备、五金产品及电子产品批发	Mechinery Equipments, Hardwares, Electric Appliances and Eletronic Products	1 339	2 591	139 439
#汽车及零配件批发	Automobiles and Spare Parts	195	310	24 247
电气设备批发	Electrical Equipment	90	176	8 026
计算机、软件及辅助设备批发	Computers, Softwares and Accessorial Equipments	116	238	13 085
贸易经纪与代理	Trade Broker and Agent	90	130	2 945
其他批发	Others	119	207	8 354

表 17.3 限额以上零售业产业活动单位和从业人员(2018)
QUANTITY OF BUSINESS UNITS AND EMPLOYEES OF RETAIL ABOVE THE SET SCALE

类 别	Types	法人企业(个) Quantity of Corporations (unit)	产业活动单位数(个) Quantity of Business Units (unit)	从业人员(人) Quantity of Employees (person)
总 计	**Total**	**1 924**	**20 176**	**365 852**
按登记注册类型分	**Grouped by Registration Categories**			
内 资	Domestic Funded	1 623	12 200	169 957
#国 有	State-owned	32	80	1 620
集 体	Collective-owned	14	109	949
股份合作	Share Holding Cooperative Enterprises	10	58	196
联 营	Joint-Owned Enterprises	18	19	291
有限责任公司	Companies with Limited Liabilities	677	6 290	84 973
股份有限公司	Share Holding Companies with Limited Liabilities	54	412	10 383
私 营	Private	818	5 232	71 545
港澳台商投资	Hong Kong, Macao and Taiwan Funded	175	3 694	91 172
外商投资	Foreign Funded	126	4 282	104 723
按行业分	**Grouped By Sectors**			
综合零售	Comprehensive Retail Sale	225	5 328	85 716
#百货零售	Articles For Daily Use	101	193	15 982
超级市场零售	Retail Sale of Supermarket	93	978	55 437
食品、饮料及烟草制品专门零售	Food, Beverage and Tabacco	124	2 929	22 627
纺织、服装及日用品专门零售	Textile, Garments and Articles for Daily Use	304	7 354	152 874
#服装零售	Garments	188	5 451	118 223
文化、体育用品及器材专门零售	Culture & Sports Articles and Equipments	114	897	17 277
#体育用品及器材零售	Sporting Goods and Equipment	8	81	2 650
图书、报刊零售	Books, Newspapers and Periodicals	16	199	4 347
医药及医疗器材专门零售	Medicines and Special Appliances of Medicines	123	1 655	12 976
#西药零售	Western Medicine	88	1 449	10 693
中药零售	Chinese Medicine	17	148	1 820
汽车、摩托车、零配件和燃料及其他动力设备零售	Automobiles, Motocycles, Spare Parts and Fuels and other Power Equipments	721	1 045	43 659
#汽车新车零售	New Automobiles	504	585	35 145
家用电器及电子产品专门零售	Household Electrical Appliances and Electronic Products	103	490	10 999
#家用视听设备零售	Home Audio-visual Equipment	4	28	539
日用家电零售	Household Appliances	35	160	3 633
计算机、软件及辅助设备零售	Computers, Softwares and Accessorial Equipments	33	105	2 878
通信设备零售	Telecommunication Appliances	13	165	3 549
五金、家具及室内装饰材料专门零售	Hardwares, Furnitures and Materials of Decoration	78	156	5 336
货摊、无店铺及其他零售业	Stall, Non-store and Other Retailing	132	322	14 388
#互联网零售	Internet	98	145	12 249
邮购及电视、电话零售	Mail Order and TV, Telephone Sales	4	4	598

表 17.4 社会消费品零售总额(1978~2018)
TOTAL RETAIL SALES OF CONSUMER GOODS

单位:亿元(100 million yuan)

年 份 Year	社会消费品零售总额 Total Retail Sales of Consumer Goods	按商品用途分 by Use			
		食品类 Foods	衣着类 Clothing	用品类 Articles	燃料类 Fuels
1978	54.10	26.51	11.60	15.16	0.83
1979	68.28	30.05	16.07	21.28	0.88
1980	80.43	34.30	19.75	25.44	0.94
1981	88.73	38.78	21.27	27.73	0.95
1982	89.80	40.72	19.57	28.52	0.99
1983	100.68	44.20	22.31	33.18	0.99
1984	123.72	50.18	27.71	44.81	1.02
1985	173.39	64.08	35.51	72.70	1.10
1986	196.84	76.99	39.38	79.31	1.16
1987	225.25	91.01	42.52	90.41	1.31
1988	295.83	119.36	53.66	121.17	1.64
1989	331.38	140.03	51.95	137.70	1.70
1990	333.86	142.15	52.33	137.23	2.15
1991	382.06	162.82	52.91	163.30	3.03
1992	464.82	190.70	67.04	202.83	4.25
1993	675.92	259.93	101.30	309.26	5.43
1994	834.76	325.44	123.89	378.86	6.57
1995	1 050.96	407.44	153.74	481.96	7.82
1996	1 258.00	490.97	178.80	579.12	9.11
1997	1 435.38	564.62	200.62	659.61	10.53
1998	1 593.27	640.84	212.85	728.22	11.36
1999	1 722.33	694.03	228.18	787.62	12.50
2000	1 865.28	743.31	248.94	858.33	14.70
2001	2 016.37	802.53	266.31	931.02	16.51
2002	2 203.89	874.76	289.43	1 021.84	17.85
2003	2 404.45	939.29	309.70	1 135.27	20.19
2004	2 656.91	1 043.26	341.28	1 247.39	24.98
2005	2 979.50	1 026.70	335.30	1 563.15	54.35
2006	3 375.20	1 119.77	379.83	1 770.75	104.85
2007	3 873.30	1 204.70	435.88	2 032.07	200.65
2008	4 577.23	1 383.63	515.09	2 401.39	277.12
2009	5 213.11	1 408.84	715.94	2 689.51	398.82
2010	6 186.58	1 602.90	843.81	3 210.30	529.57
2011	7 185.83	1 782.84	935.01	3 831.11	636.87
2012	7 840.40	1 844.96	1 060.76	4 261.50	673.18
2013	8 556.96	1 962.39	1 147.71	4 752.34	694.52
2014	9 303.49	2 065.56	1 313.05	5 210.09	714.79
2015	10 131.50	2 248.70	1 531.97	5 769.28	581.55
2016	10 946.57	2 256.20	1 565.91	6 529.34	595.12
2017	11 745.96	2 439.32	1 808.42	6 854.65	643.57
2018	12 668.69	2 572.48	2 087.25	7 277.27	731.69

注：2005 年起社会消费品零售总额及分组依相应年份经普数据，按国家统计局规定进行了修订。
Note: The Total Value of Retail Sales of Cosumer Goods are from Economic Census, and have been revised according to the regulations of NBS since 2005.

表 17.4 续表 1 continued

单位:亿元(100 million yuan)

年 份 Year	按经济类型分 by Type of Ownership				
	国有经济 State-owned	集体经济 Collective-owned	私营经济 Private-owned	个 体 Individual	其 他 Others
1978	39.50	14.41		0.19	
1979	46.47	21.32		0.20	0.29
1980	54.01	25.31		0.24	0.87
1981	56.57	30.28	0.04	0.29	1.55
1982	56.48	31.39	0.03	0.32	1.58
1983	63.17	34.55	0.02	0.70	2.24
1984	75.63	43.80	0.02	1.68	2.59
1985	102.59	59.49	0.18	6.42	4.71
1986	111.73	69.06	0.67	8.47	6.91
1987	123.05	80.38	0.88	11.46	9.48
1988	161.65	103.84	1.72	14.56	14.06
1989	176.07	119.97	1.76	16.16	17.42
1990	179.37	115.59	2.05	16.17	20.68
1991	200.25	135.30	2.72	18.70	25.09
1992	247.68	157.56	5.75	22.88	30.95
1993	250.97	202.05	0.51	41.45	180.94
1994	249.27	198.56	0.64	65.00	321.29
1995	247.10	193.03	0.86	76.44	533.54
1996	238.54	183.50	30.10	92.64	713.22
1997	225.35	173.85	21.83	114.88	899.47
1998	210.92	161.70	59.48	126.94	1 034.23
1999	180.33	141.83	62.77	141.16	1 196.24
2000	150.09	118.26	496.86	153.57	946.50
2001	135.69	105.90	596.21	172.66	1 005.91
2002	131.91	102.19	699.75	190.66	1 079.38
2003	133.36	102.68	803.74	208.45	1 156.22
2004	134.44	102.78	935.44	233.01	1 251.24
2005	157.98	51.63	814.31	443.31	1 512.28
2006	178.96	58.48	922.46	502.18	1 713.12
2007	205.37	67.11	1 058.59	576.29	1 965.93
2008	242.69	79.31	1 250.98	681.03	2 323.22
2009	389.15	28.97	1 267.85	731.77	2 795.37
2010	450.57	32.69	1 521.58	868.42	3 313.32
2011	442.79	35.51	1 652.05	1 008.69	4 046.79
2012	471.36	45.85	1 749.08	1 100.57	4 473.54
2013	470.28	38.82	1 745.91	1 201.15	5 100.80
2014	504.34	37.24	1 869.29	1 305.94	5 586.68
2015	542.82	35.01	2 028.24	1 388.59	6 136.83
2016	527.36	34.21	2 078.70	1 524.85	6 781.45
2017	558.00	33.17	2 201.27	1 651.52	7 302.00
2018	536.50	32.39	2 351.87	1 773.30	7 974.63

注：1997 年以前私营经济为合营。
Note: The figures of Private Owned before 1997 refer to these of Joint Owned.

表 17.4 续表 2 continued

单位:亿元(100 million yuan)

年 份 Year	社会消费品零售总额 Total Retail Sales of Consumer Goods	按行业分 by Sectors			
		批发零售贸易业 Wholesale and Retail Trade	住宿餐饮业 Hotels and Catering Trade	制造业 Manufacturing	其他行业 Others
1978	54.10	47.55	2.39	1.65	2.51
1979	68.28	59.02	2.82	2.54	3.90
1980	80.43	70.28	3.41	4.24	2.50
1981	88.73	77.53	3.68	4.61	2.91
1982	89.80	77.31	3.76	5.44	3.29
1983	100.68	84.93	4.26	7.72	3.77
1984	123.72	103.27	4.90	10.60	4.95
1985	173.39	150.03	7.58	8.41	7.37
1986	196.84	170.12	9.54	8.79	8.39
1987	225.25	193.50	11.09	10.47	10.19
1988	295.83	254.99	14.48	11.90	14.46
1989	331.38	265.87	15.66	16.84	33.01
1990	333.86	265.67	17.08	15.15	35.96
1991	382.06	300.26	20.91	17.70	43.19
1992	464.82	362.03	25.92	20.25	56.62
1993	675.92	559.56	35.47	29.24	51.65
1994	834.76	684.81	42.74	32.75	74.46
1995	1 050.96	864.01	52.61	38.05	96.29
1996	1 258.00	1 032.78	78.50	39.84	106.88
1997	1 435.38	1 173.94	93.49	44.38	123.57
1998	1 593.27	1 298.40	96.58	45.41	152.88
1999	1 722.33	1 391.08	114.93	47.22	169.10
2000	1 865.28	1 493.13	134.12	49.16	188.87
2001	2 016.37	1 619.13	148.88	50.78	197.58
2002	2 203.89	1 756.77	193.68	52.66	200.78
2003	2 404.45	1 920.20	225.83	53.87	204.55
2004	2 656.91	2 108.59	279.44	56.29	212.59
2005	2 979.50	2 637.29	342.21		
2006	3 375.20	2 987.54	387.66		
2007	3 873.30	3 428.43	444.87		
2008	4 577.23	4 051.51	525.72		
2009	5 213.11	4 610.76	602.35		
2010	6 186.58	5 494.69	691.89		
2011	7 185.83	6 446.61	739.22		
2012	7 840.40	7 039.16	801.24		
2013	8 556.96	7 714.96	842.00		
2014	9 303.49	8 414.81	888.68		
2015	10 131.50	9 116.93	1 014.57		
2016	10 946.57	9 874.15	1 072.42		
2017	11 745.96	10 596.67	1 149.29		
2018	12 668.69	11 471.62	1 197.07		

表 17.5 商品交易市场成交情况(2018)
DEALS IN MERCHANDISE EXCHANGE MARKET

分 类	Types	年末出租摊位数(个) Quantity of Year-end Booth Lent (unit)	成交额(亿元) Transaction Volume (100 million yuan)
总 计	**Total**	**119 119**	**9 663.79**
# 粮油、食品类	Grain and Oil, Foodstuff	55 577	1 074.21
饮料类	Beverage	2 378	13.13
烟酒类	Tobacco and Liquor	798	3.89
服装、鞋帽、针纺织品类	Garments, Shoes and Hats, Textile Products	19 592	74.21
化妆品类	Cosmetics	422	1.03
金银珠宝类	Jewelry	344	1.19
日用品类	Articles for Daily Use	3 093	261.80
五金、电料类	Hardware and Electrical Appliances	4 212	43.81
体育、娱乐用品类	Recreation and Sports Articles	325	3.94
书报杂志类	Books, Newspapers and Magazines	33	0.39
电子出版物及音像制品类	Electronic Publications and Audio-video Products	84	0.22
家用电器和音像器材类	Household Appliances and Audio-video Equipments	562	2.25
中西药品类	Medicines	222	1.91
文化办公用品类	Culture and Office Articles	875	6.53
家具类	Furnitures	2 379	17.50
通讯器材类	Telecommunication Appliances	1 724	4.17
木材及制品类	Woods and Woods Product	1 082	58.07
石油及制品类	Oil and Oil Product	408	1 080.01
化工材料及制品类	Chemical Material and Chemical Product	235	66.72
金属材料类	Mental and Mental Product	2 048	6 348.90
建筑及装潢材料类	Construct and Decorate Material	8 611	150.99
机电产品及设备类	Mechanical and Electrical Product and Equipments	775	16.82
汽车类	Automobile	3 309	370.12

表 17.6 主要年份批发零售业销售、库存总额
PURCHASE, SALES AND INVENTORY OF WHOLESALE AND RETAIL IN MAIN YEARS

单位:亿元(100 million yuan)

指 标	Indicators	2000	2010	2015	2017	2018
商品销售总额	**Sales of Commodities**	**7 474.81**	**48 659.55**	**93 406.57**	**113 133.19**	**119 461.28**
零 售	Retail	1 723.31	5 090.26	9 045.17	10 739.01	11 513.86
批 发	Wholesale	5 751.50	43 569.29	84 361.40	102 394.18	107 947.42
年末库存总额	**Year-end Inventory**	**262.50**	**1 913.49**	**4 367.59**	**6 009.24**	**6 948.70**

表 17.7 批发零售业商品销售、库存总额(2018)
PURCHASE, SALES AND INVENTORY OF WHOLESALE AND RETAIL

单位:亿元(100 million yuan)

类 别	Types	商品销售总额 Sales of Commodities	商品库存总额 Year-end Inventory
总 计	**Total**	**119 461.28**	**6 948.70**
限额以上单位	Above the Set Scale	100 517.01	6 699.07
限额以下单位	Below the Set Scale	18 944.27	249.63

表 17.8 住宿餐饮业营业额(2018)
TURNOVER OF HOTELS AND CATERING SERVICES

单位:亿元(100 million yuan)

类 别	Types	总 计 Total	其 中 of which	
			限额以上单位 Above the set scale	限额以下单位 Below the Set Scale
营业额	**Turnover**	**1 487.61**	**1 076.16**	**411.45**
客房收入	Room Revenue	262.88	177.32	85.56
餐费收入	Catering Service Revenue	1 118.73	815.56	303.17
商品销售额	Commodity Sales	30.06	19.18	10.88
其他收入	Other Revenue	75.94	64.10	11.84

表 17.9 汽车交易情况(2015~2018)
DISTRIBUTION OF AUTOMOBILE

单位:万辆(10 000 vehicles)

指标	Indicators	2015	2016	2017	2018
小型客车(本市上牌量)	Small Passenger Cars (Number of New Car Licences)	32.57	42.66	39.58	40.68
#国产轿车	Domestic Cars	19.66	23.21	18.98	20.03
进口小型客车(含轿车)	Small Passerger Cars Imported (including cars)	5.29	6.59	6.52	6.19
二手车交易量	Dealing Number of Secondhand Cars	39.38	45.00	46.20	48.61
#轿　车	Saloon Cars	26.09	30.37	29.76	31.07

表 17.10 限额以上零售企业主要业态零售额(2015~2018)
RETAIL SALES OF MAJOR PATTERNS OF RETAIL ENTERPRISES ABOVE THE SET SCALE

单位:亿元(100 million yuan)

指标	Indicators	2015	2016	2017	2018
有店铺零售	**Store-based Retailing**				
便利店	Convenience Store	126.47	140.25	159.17	161.41
超　市	Supermarket	38.21	39.59	52.51	88.04
大型超市	Hypemarket	560.77	549.45	537.56	493.33
仓储会员店	Warehouse Club	214.79	223.79	227.41	235.83
百货店	Department Store	606.21	592.50	619.79	640.02
专业店	Speciality Store	1 069.75	991.70	1 032.40	1 026.44
专卖店	Franchiesd Store	1 860.84	2 192.29	2 478.05	2 840.06
无店铺零售	**Non-store retailing**				
电视购物	Television Shopping	83.44	75.39	76.46	78.52
网上商店	Online Store	750.21	870.23	1 014.39	1 083.95

表 17.11 限额以上零售业商品购、销、存总额(2018)
PURCHASE, SALES AND INVENTORY OF RETAIL ABOVE THE SET SCALE

单位:亿元(100 million yuan)

类别	Types	商品购进总额 Purchase of Commodities	商品销售总额 Sales of Commodities	商品库存总额 Year-end Inventory
总计	**Total**	**6 372.37**	**8 155.23**	**890.07**
按登记注册类型分	**Grouped by Type of Registration**			
内资	Domestic Funded	4 169.80	4 837.04	455.65
#国有	State-Owned Enterprises	21.11	26.75	5.90
集体	Collective-Owned Enterprises	5.46	7.34	1.04
股份合作	Share Holding Cooperative Enterprises	2.57	3.14	0.08
联营	Joint-Owned Enterprises	12.65	15.17	0.13
有限责任公司	Companies with Limited Liabilities	2 244.33	2 489.33	200.59
股份有限公司	Share Holding Companies with Limited Liabilities	431.79	490.10	73.80
私营	Private Enterprises	1 451.89	1 805.20	174.12
港澳台商投资	Hong Kong, Macao and Taiwan Funded	1 154.86	1 655.37	242.64
外商投资	Foreign Funded Enterprises	1 047.71	1 662.82	191.78
按行业分	**Grouped by Sector**			
#综合零售	Comprehensive Retail Sale	1 032.11	1 372.56	123.17
食品、饮料及烟草制品专门零售	Food, Beverage and Tabacco	105.41	152.37	9.62
纺织、服装及日用品专门零售	Textile Products, Gaments and Commodity	1 161.23	1 957.51	348.37
文化、体育用品及器材专门零售	Culture & Sports Articles and Equipments	207.45	309.71	76.34
医药及医疗器材专门零售	Medicines and Special Appliances of Medicines	223.34	279.80	19.46
汽车、摩托车、零配件和燃料及其他动力销售	Automobiles, Motocycles, Spare Parts and Fuels and other Power Equipments	1 963.54	2 073.43	240.49
家用电器及电子产品专门零售	Household Electrical Appliances and Electronic Products	352.88	499.28	22.10
五金、家具及室内装饰材料专门零售	Hardwares, Furnitures and Materials of Decoration	56.20	99.17	9.01

表 17.12 限额以上批发业商品购、销、存总额(2018)
PURCHASE, SALES AND INVENTORY OF WHOLESALE ABOVE THE SET SCALE

单位:亿元(100 million yuan)

类 别	Types	商品购进总 额 Purchase of Commodities	商品销售总 额 Sales of Commodities	商品库存总 额 Year-end Inventory
总 计	**Total**	**83 679.75**	**92 361.77**	**5 809.00**
按登记注册类型分	**Grouped by Type of Registration**			
内 资	Domestic Funded	51 595.91	53 774.36	2 918.24
#国 有	State-Owned Enterprises	221.97	233.74	13.41
集 体	Collective-Owned Enterprises	3.04	3.47	0.79
股份合作	Share Holding Cooperative Enterprises	2.25	2.40	0.08
联 营	Joint-Owned Enterprises	3.28	3.04	2.11
有限责任公司	Companies with Limited Liabilities	30 024.97	31 056.65	1 220.70
股份有限公司	Share Holding Companies with Limited Liabilities	2 081.75	2 308.23	797.72
私 营	Private Enterprises	19 258.65	20 166.83	883.43
港澳台商投资	Hong Kong, Macao and Taiwan Funded Enterprises	7 697.49	9 320.66	868.49
外商投资	Foreign Funded Enterprises	24 386.35	29 266.75	2 022.27
按行业分	**Grouped by Sector**			
农、林、牧产品批发	Agriculture, Forestry and Animal Husbandry products	791.49	832.04	71.74
食品、饮料及烟草制品批发	Food, Beverage and Tabacco	4 664.63	5 555.05	400.92
#米、面制品及食用油批发	Rice, Flour and Cooking Oil	1 669.92	1 829.30	142.33
烟草制品批发	Tabacco	578.15	700.46	18.63

表 17.12 续表 continued

单位：亿元（100 million yuan）

类 别	Types	商品购进总额 Purchase of Commodities	商品销售总额 Sales of Commodities	商品库存总额 Year-end Inventory
纺织、服装及家庭用品批发	Textile, Clothing and Household Goods	4 230.37	6 089.27	1 377.55
#服装批发	Garments	1 027.95	1 486.39	277.93
文化、体育用品及器材批发	Culture & Sports Articles and Equipments	2 210.37	1 649.65	182.82
医药及医疗器材批发	Medicines and Special Appliances of Medicines	2 608.44	3 401.73	454.69
矿产品、建材及化工产品批发	Mineral Products, Materials of Construction and Chemical Products	47 868.12	50 468.15	1 649.97
#煤炭及制品批发	Coal	1 714.92	1 777.97	13.87
石油及制品批发	Petroleum	8 099.56	8 450.56	134.90
金属及金属矿批发	Metal Products and Metal Minerals	30 821.71	32 066.94	1 094.30
建材批发	Building Materials	659.70	725.80	38.08
化肥批发	Chemical Fertilizer	48.35	51.65	1.82
机械设备、五金产品及电子产品批发	Mechinery Equipments, Hardwares, Electric Appliances and Eletronic Products	20 481.72	23 331.17	1 585.26
#汽车及零配件批发	Automobiles and Spare Parts	8 861.19	10 026.04	783.45
电气设备批发	Electrical Equipment	305.50	416.39	37.61
计算机、软件及辅助设备批发	Computers, Softwares and Accessorial Equipments	1 507.64	1 665.55	137.25
贸易经纪与代理	Trade Broker and Agent	359.65	427.75	22.95
其他批发业	Others	464.96	606.96	63.10

表 17.13 限额以上批发零售业主要商品分类销售额(2018)
TOTAL SALES OF ENTERPRISES ABOVE THE SET SCALE IN WHOLESALE AND RETAIL BY CATEGORY OF MAIN COMMODITIES

单位:亿元(100 million yuan)

类 别	Types	合 计 Total	批发额 Wholesale	零售额 Retail
粮油、食品类	Grain and Oil, and Food	4 639.00	3 872.30	766.70
#粮油类	Grain and Oil	2 098.02	1 892.08	205.94
肉禽蛋类	Meat,Poultry and Eggs	384.50	298.39	86.11
水产品类	Aquatic Products	105.19	74.28	30.91
蔬菜类	Vegetables	107.83	81.22	26.61
干鲜果品类	Dry and Fresh Fruits	341.35	254.90	86.45
饮料类	Beverages	312.25	261.18	51.07
烟酒类	Tobacco and Liquor	1 392.57	1 173.13	219.44
#烟 类	Tobacco	778.13	668.28	109.85
酒 类	Liquor	613.46	504.53	108.93
服装、鞋帽、针纺织品类	Clothing,Shoes,Hats and Textiles	4 272.74	2 404.25	1 868.49
#服装类	Clothing	2 742.11	1 289.46	1 452.65
鞋帽类	Shoes and Hat	789.86	433.12	356.74
针、纺织品类	Knitwear and Textiles	740.77	681.66	59.11
化妆品类	Cosmetics	1 246.88	830.98	415.90
金银珠宝类	Gold,Silver and Jewelry	911.66	680.36	231.30
日用品类	Articles for Daily Use	2 234.91	1 776.38	458.53
五金、电料类	Hardware and Electrical Materials	767.25	750.22	17.03
体育、娱乐用品类	Sports and Recreation Articles	277.68	231.39	46.29
#照相器材类	Photographic Equipment	42.65	36.54	6.11
书报杂志类	Newspapers and Magazines	57.51	28.91	28.60
电子出版物及音像制品类	E-journal and Video Products	1.79	0.91	0.88
家用电器和音像器材类	Household Appliances and Video Appliances	977.32	464.90	512.42
中西药品类	Traditional Chinese and Western Medicines	1 773.09	1 340.79	432.30
#西药类	Western Medicines	1 433.33	1 067.01	366.32
中草药及中成药类	Traditional Chinese Medicines	155.66	99.96	55.70
文化办公用品类	Cultural and Official Goods	2 315.48	2 040.74	274.74
#计算机及其配套产品	Computer and Its Supporting Products	394.11	342.04	52.07
家具类	Furniture	323.05	241.97	81.08
通讯器材类	Communication Appliances	3 032.46	2 633.43	399.03
煤炭及制品类	Coal and Related Product	1 854.56	1 854.48	0.08
木材及制品类	Lumber and Related Product	331.80	331.80	
石油及制品类	Oil and Related Product	8 396.92	7 798.44	598.48
化工材料及制品类	Chemical Material and Related Product	6 986.83	6 986.83	
#化肥类	Fertilizer	247.40	247.40	
金属材料类	Metal Material	30 984.30	30 984.30	
建筑及装潢材料类	Building and Decoration Materials	389.70	352.87	36.83
机电产品及设备类	Mechanical and Electrical Products	6 032.87	6 022.52	10.35
#农机类	Agriculture Machinery	50.99	50.99	
汽车类	Automobile	11 262.04	9 686.51	1 575.53
种子饲料类	Seed and Feedstuff	226.95	226.95	
棉麻类	Cotton and Hemp	94.23	94.21	0.02
其他类	Others	4 877.62	4 746.91	130.71

表 17.14 主要年份限额以上批发零售业主要财务指标
MAIN ACCOUNTING INDICATORS OF WHOLESALE AND RETAIL SALES ABOVE THE SET SCALE IN MAIN YEARS

单位:亿元(100 million yuan)

指 标	Indicators	2005	2010	2015	2017	2018
流动资产	Current Assets	2 929.27	7 608.03	18 831.64	25 147.91	26 580.96
#存 货	Inventory	722.78	1 655.36	4 484.58	4 591.24	5 248.68
固定资产原价	Fixed Assets Original Value	546.78	790.06	1 595.54	1 798.39	1 888.91
累计折旧	Accumulative Depreciation	169.94	291.58	700.05	841.51	893.66
#本年折旧	Depreciation	31.20	55.82	131.06	111.12	112.56
资产总计	Total Assets	3 926.22	9 608.53	23 843.32	32 023.04	33 231.91
负债合计	Total Liabilities	2 727.25	6 710.76	17 274.47	22 726.53	23 382.30
所有者权益合计	Total Owner's Equities	1 198.97	2 897.78	6 568.87	9 297.24	9 857.75
实收资本	Paid-up Capital	862.49	1 464.26	4 098.65	4 910.93	5 525.51
#国家资本	State Capital	132.19	379.67	516.03	783.95	893.89
港澳台资本	Hong Kong, Macao and Taiwan Capital	38.17	137.69	518.11	661.11	723.49
外商资本	Foreign Capital	242.71	376.04	798.17	1 109.56	1 125.59
主营业务收入	Prime Operating Revenues	11 236.19	26 372.58	62 098.50	83 190.48	87 778.98
主营业务成本	Operating Costs	9 874.12	24 300.03	57 228.78	76 638.97	80 545.63
主营业务税金及附加	Sales Taxes and Extra Charges	10.10	40.73	111.30	146.36	148.05
销售费用	Selling Expenses	501.98	1 135.41	2 966.65	3 712.62	4 183.58
管理费用	Management Expenses	243.12	475.41	1 131.59	1 354.41	1 549.84
财务费用	Financial Expenses	24.09	47.93	220.05	165.07	237.97
营业利润	Operating Profits	248.71	535.95	876.70	1 657.51	1 732.88
利润总额	Total Profits	223.35	640.19	1 011.58	1 773.72	1 860.60
主营业务应付工资总额	Total Payable Salaries Involved in Major Business	130.25	258.66	1 001.40	1 254.29	1 376.82
主营业务应付福利费总额	Total Payable Welfare Involved in Major Business	21.89	17.63			

表 17.15 主要年份限额以上餐饮业主要财务指标
MAIN FINANCIAL INDICATORS OF CATERING SECTOR ABOVE THE SET SCALE IN MAIN YEARS

单位:亿元(100 million yuan)

指 标	Indicators	2005	2010	2015	2017	2018
流动资产	Current Assets	43.60	114.24	226.17	274.54	278.39
#存 货	Inventory	5.10	8.28	23.63	22.89	14.91
固定资产原价	Fixed Assets Original Value	44.76	81.97	126.78	126.55	147.89
累计折旧	Accumulative Depreciation	15.65	31.64	56.34	59.25	78.89
#本年折旧	Depreciation	3.83	6.63	8.85	10.27	11.72
资产总计	Total Assets	94.49	214.43	403.13	448.04	451.89
负债合计	Total Liabilities	64.13	156.19	305.59	345.48	324.53
所有者权益合计	Total Owner's Equities	30.36	58.25	97.54	102.55	127.48
实收资本	Paid-up Capital	31.05	62.42	152.31	135.36	194.43
#国家资本	State Capital	0.78	5.28	8.14	5.84	5.39
港澳台资本	Hong Kong, Macao and Taiwan Capital	6.95	13.36	27.97	34.14	31.47
外商资本	Foreign Capital	6.66	17.62	33.53	29.31	34.82
主营业务收入	Prime Operating Revenues	157.66	335.96	612.14	669.85	714.26
主营业务成本	Operating Costs	72.03	145.44	262.62	288.29	313.76
主营业务税金及附加	Sales Taxes and Extra Charges	8.14	17.34	32.79	1.40	1.14
销售费用	Selling Expenses	53.86	123.32	236.70	271.23	292.73
管理费用	Management Expenses	19.42	37.25	68.57	77.93	82.42
财务费用	Financial Expenses	1.15	3.47	6.16	3.07	3.61
营业利润	Operating Profits	5.49	10.96	10.41	35.07	28.88
利润总额	Total Profits	5.49	15.12	13.23	39.11	28.63
主营业务应付工资总额	Total Payable Salaries Involved in Major Business	17.54	41.08	105.86	125.39	135.11
主营业务应付福利费总额	Total Payable Welfare Involved in Major Business	2.26	2.51			

表 17.16 主要年份限额以上连锁批发和零售业、住宿和餐饮业经营情况
BASIC STATISTICS OF CHAIN RETAIL, HOTELS AND CATERING SERVICES ABOVE THE SET SCALE IN MAIN YEARS

指 标	Indicators	2005	2010	2015	2017	2018
门店总数(个)	Quantity of Stores(unit)	15 775	20 977	21 503	21 140	22 066
营业面积(万平方米)	Operational Area(10000 sq.m)	809.16	938.35	1 178.87	1 192.33	1 224.74
从业人数(万人)	Number of Persons Employed(10000 person)	24.47	36.68	34.20	30.26	32.19
批发和零售业商品购进总额(亿元)	Purchase of Commodities(100 million yuan)	1 222.94	2 249.57	2 275.62	2 694.00	2 920.65
批发和零售业商品销售总额(亿元)	Sales of Commodities (100 million yuan)	1 815.32	3 071.67	3 361.41	3 198.41	3 567.14
#零售额	Retail Sales	1 201.03	2 241.97	2 581.26	2 545.54	2 767.01
住宿和餐饮业营业收入(亿元)	Total Operating Revenue (100 million yuan)	35.69	106.81	191.44	246.80	258.71

表 17.17　限额以上住宿和餐饮业经营情况(2018)
OPERATING CONDITIONS OF HOTELS AND CATERING INDUSTRY ABOVE THE SET SCALE

单位:亿元(100 million yuan)

类　别	Types	营业额 Turnover	其中 of which: 客房收入 Room Revenue	餐费收入 Catering Service Revenue	商品销售额 Commodity Sales	其他收入 Other Revenue
总　计	**Total**	**1 076.16**	**177.32**	**815.56**	**19.18**	**64.10**
住宿业	**Accommodation**	**301.42**	**170.73**	**71.85**	**6.80**	**52.04**
按登记注册类型分	**Grouped by Type of Registration**					
内资企业	Domestic Funded Enterprises	222.43	132.61	52.50	3.15	34.17
国有企业	State-Owned Enterprises	16.62	5.98	5.01	0.41	5.22
集体企业	Collective-Owned Enterprises	1.67	0.48	1.08		0.11
联营企业	Joint-Owned Enterprises	0.12	0.04	0.05		0.03
有限责任公司	Companies with Limited Liabilities	123.94	66.01	32.63	2.44	22.86
股份有限公司	Share Holding Companies with Limited Liabilities	6.07	3.75	1.77	0.03	0.52
私营企业	Private Enterprises	73.38	55.94	11.88	0.27	5.29
其他企业	Others	0.63	0.41	0.08		0.14
港、澳、台商投资企业	Hong Kong, Macao and Taiwan Funded Enterprises	47.45	22.27	12.73	0.15	12.30
外商投资企业	Foreign Funded Enterprises	31.54	15.85	6.62	3.50	5.57
按星级分组	**Grouped by Star Level**					
五　星	Five-Star	121.25	55.79	39.14	2.42	23.90
四　星	Four-Star	35.76	19.50	10.15	0.44	5.67
三　星	Three-Star	13.75	7.55	2.59	0.09	3.52
二　星	Two-Star	1.95	1.22	0.35	0.01	0.37
一　星	One-Star	0.01	0.01			
其　他	Others	128.70	86.66	19.62	3.84	18.58
餐饮业	**Catering**	**774.74**	**6.59**	**743.71**	**12.38**	**12.06**
按登记注册类型分	**Grouped by Type of Registration**					
内资企业	Domestic Funded Enterprises	340.12	6.39	319.67	6.93	7.13
国有企业	State-Owned Enterprises	3.68	0.26	2.83	0.11	0.48
集体企业	Collective-Owned Enterprises	2.98	0.03	2.89		0.06
股份合作企业	Share Holding Cooperative Enterprises	0.87	0.01	0.74		0.12
联营企业	Joint-Owned Enterprises	0.09		0.09		
有限责任公司	Companies with Limited Liabilities	72.35	1.67	67.25	0.90	2.53
股份有限公司	Share Holding Companies with Limited Liabilities	15.24		11.17	4.07	
私营企业	Private Enterprises	243.10	4.31	233.14	1.79	3.86
其他企业	Others	1.81	0.11	1.56	0.06	0.08
港、澳、台商投资企业	Hong Kong, Macao and Taiwan Funded Enterprises	244.09	0.04	239.48	2.35	2.22
外商投资企业	Foreign Funded Enterprises	190.53	0.16	184.56	3.10	2.71
按餐饮行业小类分组	**Grouped by Catering Categories**					
正餐服务	Restaurant	472.25	6.43	451.10	8.96	5.76
快餐服务	Fast Food	132.97	0.16	128.48	1.45	2.88
饮料及冷饮服务	Beverages and Cold Drinks	118.45		116.73	0.36	1.36
茶馆服务	Teahouse	0.22		0.22		
咖啡馆服务	Café	103.22		101.79	0.14	1.29
酒吧服务	Bar	0.20		0.20		
其他饮料及冷饮服务	Others	14.81		14.52	0.22	0.07
餐饮配送及外卖送餐服务	Food and Beverage Distribution and Delivery Service of Takeout Food	30.86		28.37	0.53	1.96
餐饮配送服务	Food and Beverage Distribution	28.97		28.35	0.53	0.09
外卖送餐服务	Delivery Service of Takeout Food	1.89		0.02		1.87
其他餐饮业	Others	20.21		19.03	1.08	0.10
小吃服务	Refreshment	11.14		10.19	0.92	0.03
其他未列明餐饮业	Others	9.07		8.84	0.16	0.07

表 17.18　限额以上住宿餐饮业主要财务指标(2018)
MAIN FINANCIAL INDICATORS OF HOTELS AND CATERING ENTERPRISES ABOVE THE SET SCALE

类　别	Types	流动资产 Current Assets	固定资产原价 Fixed Assets Original Value	资产总计 Total Assets
总　计	**Total**	**647.35**	**732.57**	**1 351.55**
按登记注册类型分	**Grouped by Type of Registration**			
住宿业	**Accommodation**	**368.96**	**584.68**	**899.66**
内　资	Domestic Enterprises	231.11	364.26	574.23
#国　有	State-Owned Enterprises	24.68	46.88	71.32
集　体	Collective-Owned Enterprises	1.22	4.15	3.32
联　营	Joint-Owned Enterprises	0.03	0.91	0.66
有限责任公司	Companies with Limited Liabilities	132.56	258.20	376.75
股份有限公司	Share Holding Companies with Limited Liabilities	3.12	11.47	11.68
私　营	Private Enterprises	69.00	40.90	109.70
其　他	Others	0.50	1.75	0.80
港澳台商投资	Hong Kong, Macao and Taiwan Funded	100.71	141.77	228.39
外商投资	Foreign Funded Enterprises	37.14	78.65	97.04
餐饮业	**Catering**	**278.39**	**147.89**	**451.89**
内　资	Domestic Enterprises	163.17	64.30	242.06
国　有	State-Owned Enterprises	1.51	0.47	1.88
集　体	Collective-Owned Enterprises	1.58	0.60	2.14
股份合作	Share Holding Cooperative Enterprises	0.58	0.18	0.73
联　营	Joint-Owned Enterprises	0.01	0.22	0.20
有限责任公司	Responsibility Co.Ltd.	32.18	13.41	48.42
股份有限公司	Share Holding Co.Ltd.	12.73	1.05	21.66
私　营	Private Enterprises	113.78	47.70	165.82
其　他	Others	0.80	0.67	1.21
港澳台商投资	Hong Kong, Macao and Taiwan Funded	62.24	39.01	108.73
外商投资	Foreign Funded Enterprises	52.98	44.58	101.10

单位:亿元(100 million yuan)

负债合计 Total Liabilities	所有者权益合计 Total Owner's Equity	实收资本 Paid-up Capital	主营业务收入 Prime Operating Revenues	主营业务成本 Prime Operating Costs	利润总额 Total Profits
826.81	**525.37**	**880.89**	**1 001.47**	**401.89**	**48.55**
502.28	**397.89**	**686.46**	**287.21**	**88.13**	**19.92**
345.03	229.72	551.46	211.43	57.85	11.08
19.85	51.47	16.40	15.41	3.11	1.66
1.51	1.81	0.32	1.62	0.63	0.03
0.98	-0.32	0.10	0.11	0.04	-0.01
222.98	154.29	143.88	117.34	32.65	7.76
5.58	6.10	7.16	5.68	2.07	-0.45
93.49	16.21	383.53	70.66	19.13	2.02
0.64	0.16	0.07	0.61	0.22	0.07
109.27	119.12	72.02	44.78	18.03	8.36
47.98	49.05	62.98	31.00	12.25	0.48
324.53	**127.48**	**194.43**	**714.26**	**313.76**	**28.63**
188.02	54.15	103.60	312.60	157.80	8.02
0.82	1.07	0.50	3.43	2.18	0.14
1.24	0.89	0.13	2.78	1.29	0.27
0.46	0.27	0.05	0.71	0.35	0.04
0.05	0.15	0.15	0.08	0.05	0.00
35.60	12.81	12.12	66.86	28.98	3.62
12.16	9.50	2.45	8.22	4.28	1.26
136.85	29.09	88.05	228.80	119.65	2.64
0.84	0.37	0.15	1.72	1.02	0.05
72.78	35.95	45.70	178.42	71.51	4.76
63.73	37.38	45.13	223.24	84.45	15.85

表 17.18 续表 continued

类别	Types	流动资产 Current Assets	固定资产原价 Fixed Assets Original Value	资产总计 Total Assets
按行业分	**Grouped by Sector**			
住宿业	**Accommodation**	**368.96**	**584.68**	**899.66**
旅游饭店	Tiyrust Hotel	299.77	528.35	772.31
一般旅馆	Fonda	66.25	54.08	122.72
经济型连锁酒店	Economic Chain Hotel	23.58	9.81	33.23
其他一般旅馆	Other Fonda	42.67	44.27	89.49
民宿服务	Homestay	0.08		0.17
其他住宿业	Others	2.86	2.25	4.46
餐饮业	**Catering**	**278.39**	**147.89**	**451.89**
正餐服务	Restaurant	195.65	103.49	314.42
快餐服务	Fast Food	34.62	22.30	61.46
饮料及冷饮服务	Beverages and Cold Drinks	30.59	18.22	55.29
茶馆服务	Teahouse	0.04	0.02	0.04
咖啡馆服务	Café	22.87	15.03	43.42
酒吧服务	Bar	0.06	0.03	0.19
其他饮料及冷饮服务	Others	7.62	3.14	11.64
餐饮配送及外卖送餐服务	Food and Beverage Distribution and Delivery Service of Takeout Food	10.17	2.46	12.23
餐饮配送服务	Food and Beverage Distribution	10.11	2.46	12.17
外卖送餐服务	Delivery Service of Takeout Food	0.06		0.06
其他餐饮业	Others	7.36	1.42	8.49
小吃服务	Refreshment	4.36	1.17	5.32
其他未列明餐饮业	Others	3.00	0.25	3.17

单位:亿元(100 million yuan)

负债合计 Total Liabilities	所有者权益合计 Total Owner's Equity	实收资本 Paid-up Capital	主营业务收入 Prime Operating Revenues	主营业务成本 Prime Operating Costs	利润总额 Total Profits
502.28	**397.89**	**686.46**	**287.21**	**88.13**	**19.92**
408.63	364.20	639.71	214.30	66.29	15.51
88.35	34.37	45.42	70.56	20.94	4.53
22.51	10.72	14.80	24.18	7.02	2.79
65.84	23.65	30.62	46.38	13.92	1.74
0.18	-0.01	0.05	0.22	0.18	0.01
5.12	-0.67	1.28	2.13	0.72	-0.13
324.53	**127.48**	**194.43**	**714.26**	**313.76**	**28.63**
239.04	75.49	129.54	438.56	199.66	6.51
35.49	25.96	33.26	124.86	55.61	7.19
35.12	20.17	12.29	103.51	26.86	15.01
0.04	0.01	0.03	0.22	0.10	
28.20	15.21	10.66	89.04	22.54	14.78
0.40	-0.21	0.04	0.19	0.12	-0.08
6.48	5.16	1.56	14.06	4.10	0.31
7.65	4.58	13.73	28.57	22.92	0.67
7.60	4.56	13.72	26.79	21.29	0.66
0.05	0.02	0.01	1.78	1.63	0.01
7.23	1.28	5.61	18.76	8.71	-0.75
4.50	0.83	4.72	10.19	4.18	-0.86
2.73	0.45	0.89	8.57	4.53	0.11

表 17.19 限额以上批发零售业主要财务指标(2018)
MAIN FINANCIAL INDICATORS OF WHOLESALE AND RETAIL ENTERPRISES ABOVE THE SET SCALE

类别	Types	流动资产 Current Assets	固定资产原价 Fixed Assets Original Value	资产总计 Total Assets
总计	**Total**	**26 580.96**	**1 888.91**	**33 231.91**
按登记注册类型分	**Grouped by Type of Registration**			
批发贸易业	**Wholesale Trade**	**23 728.75**	**1 170.89**	**29 454.26**
内资	Domestic Funded Enterprises	11 941.90	580.58	15 431.79
#国有	State-Owned Enterprises	66.08	16.18	101.25
集体	Collective-Owned Enterprises	2.79	0.23	2.95
股份合作	Share Holding Cooperative Enterprises	0.90	0.11	0.94
联营	Joint-Owned Enterprises	12.37	0.08	12.41
有限责任公司	Companies with Limited Liabilities	6 315.57	319.82	8 250.89
股份有限公司	Share Holding Companies with Limited Liabilities	902.94	65.08	1 478.62
私营	Private Enterprises	4 641.25	179.08	5 584.73
港澳台商投资	Hong Kong, Macao and Taiwan Funded Enterprises	3 496.97	181.95	4 280.81
外商投资	Foreign Funded Enterprises	8 289.88	408.36	9 741.66
零售贸易业	**Retail Trade**	**2 852.21**	**718.02**	**3 777.65**
内资	Domestic Funded Enterprises	1 550.44	367.63	2 104.61
#国有	State-Owned Enterprises	15.70	3.73	18.12
集体	Collective-Owned Enterprises	7.39	1.27	8.69
股份合作	Share Holding Cooperative Enterprises	1.56	0.19	1.69
联营	Joint-Owned Enterprises	2.40	0.71	2.90
有限责任公司	Responsibility Co.Ltd.	671.74	239.44	998.70
股份有限公司	Share Holding Co.Ltd.	221.02	61.74	324.19
私营	Private Enterprises	630.63	60.55	750.32
港澳台商投资	Hong Kong, Macao and Taiwan Funded Enterprises	686.25	146.15	859.28
外商投资	Foreign Funded Enterprises	615.52	204.24	813.76

单位:亿元(100 million yuan)

负债合计 Total Liabilities	所有者权益合计 Total Owner's Equity	实收资本 Paid-up Capital	主营业务收入 Prime Operating Revenues	主营业务成本 Prime Operating Costs	利润总额 Total Profits
23 382.30	**9 857.75**	**5 525.51**	**87 778.98**	**80 545.63**	**1 860.60**
20 677.57	**8 776.88**	**4 441.61**	**80 607.45**	**74 842.60**	**1 683.85**
11 174.88	4 256.91	2 781.74	46 506.92	45 275.31	464.88
52.48	48.77	19.56	204.38	195.07	5.26
2.26	0.69	0.17	3.02	2.58	0.12
0.30	0.64	0.60	2.10	1.98	0.01
11.17	1.24	1.02	2.66	2.50	-0.40
5 968.74	2 282.15	1 553.35	26 665.39	25 966.34	268.71
753.00	725.62	247.24	2 015.33	1 907.25	76.86
4 386.93	1 197.80	959.80	17 614.04	17 199.59	114.32
2 745.02	1 535.79	598.80	8 100.60	6 948.86	319.09
6 757.67	2 984.18	1 061.07	25 999.93	22 618.43	899.88
2 704.73	**1 080.87**	**1 083.90**	**7 171.53**	**5 703.03**	**176.75**
1 584.37	528.19	709.20	4 224.77	3 749.39	36.87
9.35	8.77	1.50	23.01	18.52	1.55
2.68	6.02	0.61	6.56	5.18	0.60
0.75	0.94	0.16	2.75	2.36	0.18
0.78	2.12	0.27	13.39	12.29	0.55
756.82	241.88	419.90	2 164.01	1 937.87	12.40
158.19	166.00	30.37	430.84	387.30	19.46
655.80	102.46	256.39	1 584.21	1 385.87	2.13
578.14	281.14	175.24	1 440.73	973.79	55.18
542.22	271.54	199.46	1 506.03	979.85	84.70

上/海/统/计/年/鉴

主要统计指标解释

■ 社会消费品零售总额

指批发和零售业、餐饮业、新闻出版业、邮政业和其他服务业等，售予城乡居民用于生活消费的商品和社会集团用于公共消费的商品之总量。社会消费品零售总额包括：

一、批发和零售业企业(单位)：

1.售予城乡居民的各种生活消费品。

2.售予入境旅游的外国人、华侨、港澳台同胞的各类商品。

3.售予行政事业单位、社会团体、军队和武警等机构的商品，以及以零售方式售予各类企业的商品。具体包括：用于非生产和社会交往的办公用品，如通讯设备、计算器具和设备、电讯网络设备、文印设备、音像视听器材和设备、纸张、本册、文具及装订文印材料、家具、日用电器、针纺织品、清洁卫生用品、文体用品、奖品、纪念品、礼品等；供内部人员乘坐的交通工具和燃料；用于办公设施修缮的各类配件、材料、工具等；用于取暖和防暑降温的设备、燃料、材料及食品等；专用于教学的用品和设备；非营利医疗机构的中、西药品、中药材和医疗设备器材；非专用的劳动保护用品；不对外营业的内部食堂用的餐具、炊具、设备、清洁卫生工具和食品、燃料等；军队、武警用于其人员生活的衣着品和个人用品；其他各类非生产性设备和用品。

二、餐饮业出售的主食、菜肴、烟酒饮料和其他商品。

三、新闻出版业、邮政业售予城乡居民、企事业单位、军队和武警等机构的书报杂志、音像制品、邮品等。

四、其他服务业出售的食品、烟酒饮料、服装鞋帽、日常生活用品、医药保健用品、艺术品、工艺美术品、玩具、殡葬用品以及其他消费品。

■ 商品购进总额

指从本企业(单位)以外的单位和个人购进(包括从境外直接进口)作为转卖或加工后转卖的商品总额。它反映批发零售贸易业从国内、国外市场上购进商品的总量。商品购进总额包括：(1)从工农业生产者购进的商品；(2)从出版社、报社的出版发行部门购进的图书、杂志和报纸；(3)从各种登记注册类型的批发零售贸易企业(单位)购进的商品；(4)从其他单位购进的商品，如从机关、团体、企业等单位购进的剩余物资，从餐饮业、服务业购进的商品，从海关、市场管理部门购进的缉私和没收的商品，从居民手中收购的废旧商品等；(5)从国(境)外直接进口的商品。不包括企业(单位)为自身经营用和未通过买卖行为而收入的商品以及销售退回、商品升溢等。

■ 商品销售总额

指对本企业以外的单位和个人出售(包括对国(境)外直接出口)的商品。这个指标反映批发零售贸易业在上海市场以及上海以外市场上销售商品的总量。商品销售总额包括：(1)售给城乡居民和社会集团消费用的商品；(2)售给工业、农业、建筑业、运输邮电业、批发零售贸易业、餐饮业、服务业等作为生产、经营使用的商品；(3)售给批发零售贸易业作为转卖或加工后转卖的商品；(4)对国(境)外直接出口的商品。不包括：出售本企业自用的废旧包装用品，未通过买卖行为付出的商品，经本单位介绍，由买卖双方直接结算，本单位只收取手续费的业务，购货退出的商品以及商品损耗和损失等。

■ 主营业务收入

指企业在销售商品、提供劳务等日常活动中所产生的收入总额。

■ 主营业务成本

指企业已销商品应负担的进货原价和商品进价成本。

SHANGHAI STATISTICAL YEARBOOK

EXPLANATORY NOTES TO MAJOR STATISTICAL INDICATORS

□ Total Retail Sales of Consumer Goods

Total Retail Sales of Consumer Goods refer to the sum of retail sales of commodities sold by wholesale, retail, catering, publishing, post and telecommunications and other service industries to urban and rural households for private consumption and to social institutions for public consumption. Retail sales of consumer goods include:

Sales by wholesale and retail units:

of consumer goods sold to urban and rural households.

of commodities sold to foreigners, overseas Chinese and Chinese compatriots from Hong Kong, Macau and Taiwan visiting in China.

of commodities sold to government agencies, institutions, social organizations, military and armed police units, and commodities sold to enterprises in the form of retail sales. More specifically, they include: office facilities and articles for non-production purposes such as communications equipment, computing equipment and instruments, TV and network equipment, printing and copying equipment, audio-visual equipment and instruments, paper, notebooks, stationeries, furniture, electric appliances, knitwear, sanitation and cleaning articles, cultural and sport articles, articles for prizes, souvenirs, etc.; transport vehicles and fuels for employees; materials, spare parts and tools for the maintenance of office facilities; equipment, fuels, materials and food for winter heating or summer cooling purposes; articles and equipment for teaching purpose; Chinese and western medicines and medical equipment and facilities purchased by non profit-making medical institutes; non-specialized work safety articles; cooking utensils, tableware, equipment, cleaning articles, food and fuels purchased by internal cafeterias; clothes and personal articles purchased by military or armed police units for their officials and soldiers; and other equipment and articles for non-production purposes.

Sales of stable food, cooked dishes, beverages, tobaccos and other articles by catering units.

Sales of books, newspapers, magazines, audio-visual products and post products by publishing, post and telecommunications departments to urban and rural households and to enterprises, institutions, military and armed police units.

Sales of food, beverages, tobaccos, clothing, hats, footwear, articles for daily use, medicines, medical and health articles, work of art, handicrafts, toys, funeral articles and other articles by other service industries.

□ Total Purchase of Commodities

Purchase, Sales and Stock of Commodities by Wholesale and Retail Trades refer to the total volume of commodities purchased, total volume of sales and exports, and the stock of commodities by wholesale and retail enterprises (establishments) of different status of registration from domestic and overseas markets. This indictor reflects the relationship among purchase, sales and stock of commodities in the circulation of goods and reveals the existing problems.

□ Total Sales of Commodities

Total Sales of Commodities refer to the selling of commodities to other establishments and individuals (including direct export). Reflecting the total value of sales of commodities at Shanghai markets and out-of-Shanghai markets, this indicator includes: (1) commodities sold to urban and rural households and institutions for their consumption; (2) commodities sold to establishments in industry, agriculture, construction, transportation, post and telecommunications, wholesale and retail trade, catering and service trade and public utility for their production and operation; (3) commodities sold to wholesale and retail establishments for re-selling, with or without further processing; and (4) commodities for direct export to other countries. Excluded are selling of waste packaging materials used by enterprises themselves commodities transferred without buying or selling procedures, commission income from brokerage in transactions whose settlement is directly handled by buyers and sellers, rejected commodities in the purchase, loss in commodities, etc.

□ Prime Operating Revenue

Prime Operating Revenue refers to the earnings a corporation receives in daily activity such as selling goods and offering labor service.

EXPLANATORY NOTES TO MAJOR STATISTICAL INDICATORS

□ Operating Cost

Operating Cost refers to the cost a corporation paid to buy and deliver the commodities.

第十八篇

CHAPTER 18

金融业

FINANCE

简要说明

本篇反映上海市金融业发展情况。由以下四部分组成：一是保费收支情况，数据由中国银行保险监督管理委员会上海监管局提供；二是金融机构存贷款余额及利率调整情况，数据由中国人民银行上海总部和上海公积金管理中心提供；三是金融市场运行情况，数据由上海证券交易所、上海期货交易所、中国金融期货交易所、全国银行间同业拆借中心和上海黄金交易所提供。

BRIEF INTRODUCTION

Data in this chapter reflect the development of Shanghai´s financial industries. The data consit of four parts: (1)Premium of primary insurance and payment. Data are provided by the China Banking and Insurance Regulatory Commission Shanghai Bureau. (2)The situations regarding the changes of deposit and loan balance, and adjustment of interest rates. Data are provided by the Shanghai Headquarters of People´s Bank of China and the Shanghai Provident Fund Administration Center. (3)Data on the activities of financial institutions. Data are provided by the Shanghai Stock Exchange, the Shanghai Futures Exchange, the China Financial Futures Exchange, the National Interbank Funding Center, and the Shanghai Gold Exchange.

表 18.1 原保险保费收入和赔付支出(1978~2018)
PREMIUM OF PRIMARY INSURANCE AND PAYMENT

单位:亿元(100 million yuan)

年 份 Year	原保险保费收入 Premium of Primary Insurance	其中 of which 人身保险 Liability Insurance	其中 of which 财产保险 Property Insurance	原保险赔付支出 Payment of Primary Insurance	其中 of which 人身保险 Liability Insurance	其中 of which 财产保险 Property Insurance
1978	0.17			0.17		
1979	0.16			0.07		
1980	0.70			0.13		
1981	0.95			0.32		
1982	1.11			0.21		
1983	1.33			0.45		
1984	1.76			0.36		
1985	2.27			0.54		
1986	3.04			0.68		
1987	4.03			0.92		
1988	5.38			1.55		
1989	7.37			1.89		
1990	8.99			2.22		
1991	11.16			4.47		
1992	18.20			4.23		
1993	25.91			5.89		
1994	39.48			11.91		
1995	44.04	17.08	26.96	12.75		
1996	58.10	28.64	29.46	15.00		
1997	87.72	58.13	29.59	19.10		
1998	102.92	70.50	32.42	28.67		
1999	115.28	81.53	33.75	39.46		
2000	127.23	92.14	35.09	36.44	20.56	15.88
2001	180.25	140.30	39.95	38.82	19.61	19.21
2002	237.61	193.30	44.31	49.97	28.38	21.59
2003	289.93	232.50	57.43	61.97	34.87	27.10
2004	307.11	231.30	75.81	70.86	36.79	34.07
2005	333.62	245.76	87.86	87.46	40.20	47.26
2006	407.04	305.72	101.33	91.31	46.14	45.17
2007	482.64	363.22	119.43	139.82	86.79	53.03
2008	600.06	468.27	131.79	184.09	104.57	79.52
2009	665.03	513.22	151.81	176.74	98.24	78.50
2010	883.86	686.68	197.18	194.54	110.28	84.26
2011	753.11	519.71	233.39	260.71	156.39	104.32
2012	820.64	564.26	256.38	255.79	117.16	138.63
2013	821.43	536.18	285.25	301.95	139.62	162.33
2014	986.75	666.39	320.36	378.66	201.42	177.24
2015	1 125.16	769.77	355.40	473.59	282.22	191.38
2016	1 529.26	1 158.11	371.15	528.77	306.22	222.55
2017	1 587.10	1 158.49	428.61	548.93	315.11	233.81
2018	1 405.79	920.70	485.09	581.56	309.93	271.62

注：2010 年原保险保费收入为按财产险公司和寿险公司分类。
Note: Data of Premium of Primary Insurance of 2010 are classified by Property Insurance Company and Liability Insurance Company.

表 18.2 中外资金融机构存贷款年末余额(2016~2018)
DEPOSIT AND LOAN BALANCE OF FINANCIAL INSTITUTIONS AT YEAR-END

单位:亿元(100 million yuan)

指 标	Indicators	2016	2017	2018
中外资金融机构存款余额	**Saving Deposit Balance of Financial Institutions**	**110 510.96**	**112 461.74**	**121 112.33**
中资金融机构	Chinese Financial Institutions	103 141.88	104 835.41	113 253.04
人民币	RMB	97 331.22	99 021.73	106 330.95
外汇(折人民币)	Foreign Currencies(Converting into RMB)	5 810.66	5 813.68	6 922.09
外资金融机构	Foreign-funded Financial Institutions	7 425.59	7 721.40	7 897.53
外汇(折人民币)	Foreign Currencies (Converting into RMB)	1 559.16	1 581.36	1 578.08
人民币	RMB	5 866.43	6 140.04	6 319.45
中外资金融机构贷款余额	**Loan Balance of Financial Institutions**	**59 982.25**	**67 182.01**	**73 272.35**
中资金融机构	Chinese Financial Institutions	55 423.56	62 558.49	68 647.61
人民币	RMB	50 931.26	57 992.21	64 139.82
外汇(折人民币)	Foreign Currencies (Converting into RMB)	4 492.30	4 566.28	4 507.79
外资金融机构	Foreign-funded Financial Institutions	5 479.69	5 998.44	5 928.86
外汇(折人民币)	Foreign Currencies (Converting into RMB)	1 714.50	1 732.64	1 504.43
人民币	RMB	3 765.19	4 265.80	4 424.43

注：自 2015 年起，中资和外资金融机构存贷款统计口径有所不同，外资金融机构各项存贷款包含对银行业非存款类金融机构的存放和拆放款项。
Note: Since 2015, the diposits and loan balance of foreign-funded financial institutions include the deposits and borrowings with non deposit financial institutions in the banking industry.

表 18.3 中外资金融机构存款年末余额(2018)
DEPOSITS OF FINANCIAL INSTITUTIONS AT YEAR-END

单位:亿元(100 million yuan)

指 标	Indicators	2018	比 2018 年初增加 Increase from the Beginning of 2018
中外资金融机构本外币各项存款余额	**All Deposits of Chinese and Foreign-funded Financial Institutions**	**121 112.33**	**8 654.40**
境内存款	Domestic Deposits	115 189.33	7 760.04
住户存款	Household Deposits	28 569.24	2 803.68
活期存款	Current Deposits	10 170.61	607.60
定期及其他存款	Time Deposits and Other Deposits	18 398.63	2 196.08
非金融企业存款	Non Financial Enterprise Deposits	53 643.49	4 291.70
活期存款	Current Deposits	15 968.56	-577.58
定期及其他存款	Time Deposits and Other Deposits	37 674.94	4 869.28
广义政府存款	General Government Deposits	15 880.38	769.41
财政性存款	Fiscal Deposits	2 506.38	-423.06
机关团体存款	Deposits of Non-profit Institutions	13 374.00	1 192.47
非银行业金融机构存款	Deposits of Non Banking Financial Institutions	17 096.22	-104.75
境外存款	Foreign Deposits	5 923.00	894.36

注：自 2015 年起，各项存款包括非银行业金融机构存款。
Note: Since year 2015, deposits has included deposits of non banking financial institutions.

表 18.4 中外资金融机构贷款年末余额(2018)
LOAN BALANCE OF FINANCIAL INSTITUTIONS AT YEAR-END

单位:亿元(100 million yuan)

指标	Indicators	2018	比2018年初增加 Increase from the Beginning of 2018
中外资金融机构本外币各项贷款余额	**All Loans of Chinese and Foreign-funded Financial Institutions**	**73 272.35**	**5 736.67**
境内贷款	Domestic Loans	69 290.97	5 618.26
住户贷款	Household Loans	22 274.95	2 545.75
短期贷款	Short-term Loans	2 437.90	760.97
中长期贷款	Mid and Long-term Loans	19 837.05	1 784.78
非金融企业及机关团体贷款	Loans of Non Financial Enterprise and Non-profit Institutions	46 673.17	3 016.37
#短期贷款	Short-term Loans	15 477.06	63.31
中长期贷款	Mid and Long-term Loans	23 505.43	1 601.37
票据融资	Notes Finacing	3 570.16	1 112.49
非银行业金融机构贷款	Loans of Non Banking Financial Institutions	342.84	56.14
境外贷款	Foreign Loans	3 981.39	118.41

表 18.5 个人消费贷款及公积金贷款年末余额(2016~2018)
PERSONAL CONSUMPTION LOAN AND ACCUMULATION FUND LOAN AT YEAR-END

指标	Indicators	2016	2017	2018
中外资金融机构人民币个人消费贷款余额(亿元)	**Personal Consumption Loan of Chinese and Foreign-funded Financial Institutions**	**15 038.05**	**18 159.18**	**19 962.69**
#个人住房贷款	Housing Mortgage Loan	11 141.86	12 720.89	13 314.01
汽车消费贷款	Car Consumption Loan	2 596.32	3 633.34	4 139.05
个人住房贷款占金融机构人民币个人消费贷款额比重(%)	**Housing Mortgage Loan Percentage of Personal Consumption Loan**	**74.1**	**70.1**	**66.7**
公积金贷款余额(亿元)	**Accumulation Fund Loan(100 million yuan)**	**3 257.77**	**3 531.01**	**3 921.96**

表 18.6 金融机构人民币存款基准利率(1990~2018)
BENCHMARK INTEREST RATE OF RMB DEPOSIT FOR FINANCIAL INSTITUTIONS

单位:年利率%(annual interest rate)

调整时间 Adjust Time	活 期 Checking Deposit	定 期 fixed deposit					
		3个月 3 Months	6个月 6 Months	1年 1 Year	2年 2 Years	3年 3 Years	5年 5 Years
1990.04.15	2.88	6.30	7.74	10.08	10.98	11.88	13.68
1990.08.21	2.16	4.32	6.48	8.64	9.36	10.08	11.52
1991.04.21	1.80	3.24	5.40	7.56	7.92	8.28	9.00
1993.05.15	2.16	4.86	7.20	9.18	9.90	10.80	12.06
1993.07.11	3.15	6.66	9.00	10.98	11.70	12.24	13.86
1996.05.01	2.97	4.86	7.20	9.18	9.90	10.80	12.06
1996.08.23	1.98	3.33	5.40	7.47	7.92	8.28	9.00
1997.10.23	1.71	2.88	4.14	5.67	5.94	6.21	6.66
1998.03.25	1.71	2.88	4.14	5.22	5.58	6.21	6.66
1998.07.01	1.44	2.79	3.96	4.77	4.86	4.95	5.22
1998.12.07	1.44	2.79	3.33	3.78	3.96	4.14	4.50
1999.06.10	0.99	1.98	2.16	2.25	2.43	2.70	2.88
2002.02.21	0.72	1.71	1.89	1.98	2.25	2.52	2.79
2004.10.29	0.72	1.71	2.07	2.25	2.70	3.24	3.60
2006.08.19	0.72	1.80	2.25	2.52	3.06	3.69	4.14
2007.03.18	0.72	1.98	2.43	2.79	3.33	3.96	4.41
2007.05.19	0.72	2.07	2.61	3.06	3.69	4.41	4.95
2007.07.21	0.81	2.34	2.88	3.33	3.96	4.68	5.22
2007.08.22	0.81	2.61	3.15	3.60	4.23	4.95	5.49
2007.09.15	0.81	2.88	3.42	3.87	4.50	5.22	5.76
2007.12.21	0.72	3.33	3.78	4.14	4.68	5.40	5.85
2008.10.09	0.72	3.15	3.51	3.87	4.41	5.13	5.58
2008.10.30	0.72	2.88	3.24	3.60	4.14	4.77	5.13
2008.11.27	0.36	1.98	2.25	2.52	3.06	3.60	3.87
2008.12.23	0.36	1.71	1.98	2.25	2.79	3.33	3.60
2010.10.20	0.36	1.91	2.20	2.50	3.25	3.85	4.20
2010.12.26	0.36	2.25	2.50	2.75	3.55	4.15	4.55
2011.02.09	0.40	2.60	2.80	3.00	3.90	4.50	5.00
2011.04.06	0.50	2.85	3.05	3.25	4.15	4.75	5.25
2011.07.07	0.50	3.10	3.30	3.50	4.40	5.00	5.50
2012.06.08	0.40	2.85	3.05	3.25	4.10	4.65	5.10
2012.07.06	0.35	2.60	2.80	3.00	3.75	4.25	4.75
2014.11.22	0.35	2.35	2.55	2.75	3.35	4.00	–
2015.03.01	0.35	2.10	2.30	2.50	3.10	3.75	–
2015.05.11	0.35	1.85	2.05	2.25	2.85	3.50	–
2015.06.28	0.35	1.60	1.80	2.00	2.60	3.25	–
2015.08.26	0.35	1.35	1.55	1.75	2.35	3.00	–
2015.10.24	0.35	1.10	1.30	1.50	2.10	2.75	–

注：本表数据摘自中国人民银行网站。 自 2014 年 11 月 22 日起，人民银行不再公布金融机构人民币五年期定期存款基准利率。
Note: Data in the table are from the web of People's Bank of China . Since 22 November, 2014, People's Bank of China has stopped announcing five-year benchmark interest rate of RMB deposit .

表 18.7　金融机构人民币贷款基准利率(1991～2018)
BENCHMARK INTEREST RATE OF RMB LOAN FOR FINANCIAL INSTITUTIONS

单位:年利率%(annual interest rate)

调整时间 Adjust Time	6 个月 6 Months	1 年 1 Year	1～3 年(含) 1～3 Years	3～5 年(含) 3～5 Years	5 年以上 Above 5 Years
1991.04.21	8.10	8.64	9.00	9.54	9.72
1993.05.15	8.82	9.36	10.80	12.06	12.24
1993.07.11	9.00	10.98	12.24	13.86	14.04
1995.01.01	9.00	10.98	12.96	14.58	14.76
1995.07.01	10.08	12.06	13.50	15.12	15.30
1996.05.01	9.72	10.98	13.14	14.94	15.12
1996.08.23	9.18	10.08	10.98	11.70	12.42
1997.10.23	7.65	8.64	9.36	9.90	10.53
1998.03.25	7.02	7.92	9.00	9.72	10.35
1998.07.01	6.57	6.93	7.11	7.65	8.01
1998.12.07	6.12	6.39	6.66	7.20	7.56
1999.06.10	5.58	5.85	5.94	6.03	6.21
2002.02.21	5.04	5.31	5.49	5.58	5.76
2004.10.29	5.22	5.58	5.76	5.85	6.12
2006.04.28	5.40	5.85	6.03	6.12	6.39
2006.08.19	5.58	6.12	6.30	6.48	6.84
2007.03.18	5.67	6.39	6.57	6.75	7.11
2007.05.19	5.85	6.57	6.75	6.93	7.20
2007.07.21	6.03	6.84	7.02	7.20	7.38
2007.08.22	6.21	7.02	7.20	7.38	7.56
2007.09.15	6.48	7.29	7.47	7.65	7.83
2007.12.21	6.57	7.47	7.56	7.74	7.83
2008.09.13	6.21	7.20	7.29	7.56	7.74
2008.10.09	6.12	6.93	7.02	7.29	7.47
2008.10.30	6.03	6.66	6.75	7.02	7.20
2008.11.27	5.04	5.58	5.67	5.94	6.12
2008.12.23	4.86	5.31	5.40	5.76	5.94
2010.10.20	5.10	5.56	5.60	5.96	6.14
2010.12.26	5.35	5.81	5.85	6.22	6.40
2011.02.09	5.60	6.06	6.10	6.45	6.60
2011.04.06	5.85	6.31	6.40	6.65	6.80
2011.07.07	6.10	6.56	6.65	6.90	7.05
2012.06.08	5.85	6.31	6.40	6.65	6.80
2012.07.06	5.60	6.00	6.15	6.40	6.55
2014.11.22	5.60		6.00		6.15
2015.03.01	5.35		5.75		5.90
2015.05.11	5.10		5.50		5.65
2015.06.28	4.85		5.25		5.40
2015.08.26	4.60		5.00		5.15
2015.10.24	4.35		4.75		4.90

注：本表数据摘自中国人民银行网站。 自 2014 年 11 月 22 日起，金融机构人民币贷款基准利率期限档次简并为一年以内(含一年)、一至五年(含五年)和五年以上三个档次。

Note：Data in the table are from the web of People′s Bank of China . Since 22 November, 2014, period of benchmark lending rates has been adjusted into three grades：within one year (including one year), one to five years (including five years), and more than five years.

表 18.8 主要金融市场成交额(2016~2018)
TURNOVER OF MAIN FANANCIAL MARKET

单位:亿元(100 million yuan)

指 标	Indicators	2016	2017	2018
上海证券交易所成交额	Turnover of Shanghai Stock Exchange	2 838 724.47	3 063 862.43	2 646 248.80
上海期货交易所成交额	Turnover of Shanghai Future Exchange	849 774.90	899 310.35	815 417.14
中国金融期货交易所成交额	Turnover of China Financial Futures Exchange	182 191.10	245 921.99	261 222.97
银行间市场成交额	Turnover of Interbank Market	9 601 511.38	9 977 729.01	12 628 336.81
上海黄金交易所成交额	Turnover of Shanghai Gold Exchange	174 413.43	97 608.46	106 587.70

注：银行间市场成交额包括银行间本币市场和外汇市场成交额。本表数据中 2016 年上海黄金交易所成交额按双向计算，其他成交额数据均按单向计算。

Note: The turnover of Interbank Market has included turnover of Interbank RMB market and turnover of foreign exchange trading market. The turnover data in the table are calculated by buy or sell, except Shanghai Gold Exchange turnover of year 2016 are calculated by buy and sell.

表 18.9 上海证券交易所上市公司股本结构(2016~2018)
CAPITAL STOCK STRUCTURE OF PUBLIC COMPANIES IN SHANGHAI STOCK EXCHANGE

单位:亿元(100 million yuan)

指 标	Indicators	2016	2017	2018
发行总股本	**Total**	**39 662.91**	**42 323.96**	**45 018.37**
尚未流通股份	Non-circulation Shares	3 335.51	4 168.90	4 211.72
国家拥有股份	State Shares	1 254.59	879.84	144.67
境内法人持有股份	Domestic Sponsoring Corporate Shares	872.40	504.86	102.70
外资法人持有股份	Foreign Corporate Shares	95.08	38.37	2.40
个人发起人股	Personal Sponsor Shares	208.64	108.55	26.36
募集法人股	Raised Corporate	1.04	1.04	0.18
机构配售	Agencies placing	33.58	18.99	9.97
其 他	Others	870.19	2 617.24	3 925.44
已流通股份	Circulation Shares	36 327.40	38 155.06	40 806.65
境内上市的人民币普通股	A Shares	29 218.30	30 963.17	33 337.72
境内上市外资股	B Shares	153.95	156.28	159.52
境外上市外资股	H Shares	6 955.15	7 035.61	7 309.41

表 18.10 上海证券交易所市场概况(2016~2018)
SHANGHAI STOCK EXCHANGE MARKET

指 标	Indicators	2016	2017	2018
上市公司数(个)	Quantity of Public Company (unit)	1 182	1 396	1 450
上市证券数(个)	Quantity of Negotiable Securities(unit)	9 647	12 219	14 069
上市股票数(个)	Quantity of Listed Stock(unit)	1 226	1 440	1 494
股票发行股数(亿股)	Shares of Stocks Issued (100 million shares)	32 707.76	35 288.35	37 708.96
A 股	A Shares	32 553.81	35 132.07	37 549.44
B 股	B Shares	153.95	156.28	159.52
股票市价总值(亿元)	Aggregate Value of Stocks in Market Price (100 million yuan)	284 607.63	331 324.82	269 515.02
A 股	A Shares	283 555.04	330 327.36	268 690.84
B 股	B Shares	1 052.59	997.46	824.18
流通股数(亿股)	Shares in Circulation (100 million shares)	29 372.25	31 119.45	33 497.24
A 股	A Shares	29 218.30	30 963.17	33 337.72
B 股	B Shares	153.95	156.28	159.52
流通市值(亿元)	Value in Circulation (100 million yuan)	240 006.24	281 365.68	232 698.75
A 股	A Shares	238 953.65	280 368.22	231 874.57
B 股	B Shares	1 052.59	997.46	824.18
市场筹资额(亿元)	Funds Raised from Market (100 million yuan)	34 981.65	22 716.05	25 119.83
普通股	Common shares	8 056.45	7 578.06	6 113.96
首次发行	IPO	1 017.23	1 376.55	864.93
再次发行	Additional Issued	7 039.22	6 201.50	5 249.03
优先股	Preferred shares	1 378.00	200.00	1 225.00
债 券	Bond	25 547.20	14 937.99	17 780.87

表 18.11 上证各类指数概况(2018)
ALL KINDS OF INDEX OF SHANGHAI

指 标	Indicators	最 高 High	日 期	Date	最 低 Low	日 期	Date	收 盘 Close
上证综指	SSE Composite Index	3 587.03	1 月 29 日	29, Jan	2 449.20	10 月 19 日	19, Oct	2 493.90
上证 180	SSE 180 Index	9 507.40	1 月 29 日	29, Jan	6 694.16	12 月 25 日	25, Dec.	6 808.80
上证 50	SSE 50 Index	3 202.47	1 月 24 日	24, Jan	2 256.47	12 月 25 日	25, Dec.	2 293.10
上证 380	SSE 380 Index	5 773.27	1 月 8 日	8, Jan	3 647.57	10 月 19 日	19, Oct	3 858.01
红利指数	Dividend Index	3 317.83	1 月 29 日	29, Jan	2 401.37	10 月 19 日	19, Oct	2 486.08
治理指数	Governance Index	1 196.94	1 月 29 日	29, Jan	854.83	12 月 25 日	25, Dec.	867.04
A 股指数	A-Share Index	3 757.20	1 月 29 日	29, Jan	2 564.94	10 月 19 日	19, Oct	2 611.38
B 股指数	B-Share Index	6 502.37	1 月 29 日	29, Jan	253.22	10 月 19 日	19, Oct	271.05
基金指数	Fund Index	7 670.68	1 月 26 日	26, Jan	5 465.12	12 月 25 日	25, Dec.	5 499.31
国债指数	T-Bond Index	169.88	12 月 28 日	28, Dec	160.89	1 月 4 日	4, Jan	169.88
企业债指数	C-Bond Index	225.78	12 月 28 日	28, Dec	213.61	1 月 2 日	2, Jan	225.76

表 18.12 主要年份上证综合指数 THE SHANGHAI COMPOSITE INDEX IN MAIN YEARS

年份 Year	开盘 Open	最高 High	日期 Date		最低 Low	日期 Date		收盘 Close
1990	96.05	127.61	12月31日	31,Dec	95.79	12月19日	19,Dec	127.61
1991	127.61	292.75	12月31日	31,Dec	104.96	5月17日	17,May	292.75
1992	293.74	1 429.01	5月26日	26,May	292.76	1月2日	2,Jan	780.39
1993	802.14	1 558.98	2月16日	16,Feb	750.46	12月20日	20,Dec	833.80
1994	837.70	1 052.94	9月13日	13,Sep	325.89	7月29日	29,July	647.87
1995	637.72	926.41	5月22日	22,May	524.43	2月7日	7,Feb	555.29
1996	550.26	1 258.69	12月11日	11,Dec	512.83	1月19日	19,Jan	917.02
1997	914.06	1 510.18	5月12日	12,May	870.80	2月20日	20,Feb	1 194.10
1998	1 200.95	1 422.98	6月4日	4,June	1 043.02	8月18日	18,Aug	1 146.70
1999	1 144.89	1 756.18	6月30日	30,June	1 047.83	5月17日	17,May	1 366.58
2000	1 368.69	2 125.72	11月23日	23,Nov	1 361.21	1月4日	4,Jan	2 073.48
2001	2 077.08	2 245.44	6月14日	14,June	1 514.86	10月22日	22,Oct	1 645.97
2002	1 643.49	1 748.89	6月25日	25,June	1 339.20	1月29日	29,Jan	1 357.65
2003	1 347.43	1 649.60	4月16日	16,Apr	1 307.40	11月13日	13,Nov	1 497.04
2004	1 492.72	1 183.01	4月7日	7,Apr	1 259.43	9月13日	13,Sep	1 266.50
2005	1 260.78	1 328.53	2月25日	25,Feb	998.23	6月6日	6, Jun	1 161.06
2006	1 163.88	2 698.90	12月29日	29,Dec	1 161.91	1月4日	4,Jan	2 675.47
2007	2 728.19	6 124.04	10月16日	16,Oct	2 541.53	2月6日	6,Feb	5 261.56
2008	5 265.00	5 522.78	1月14日	14,Jan	1 664.93	10月28日	28,Oct	1 820.81
2009	1 849.02	3 478.01	8月4日	4,Aug	1 844.09	1月5日	5,Jan	3 277.14
2010	3 289.75	3 306.75	1月11日	11,Jan	2 319.74	7月2日	2,July	2 808.08
2011	2 825.33	3 067.46	4月18日	18,Apr	2 134.02	12月28日	28,Dec	2 199.42
2012	2 212.00	2 478.38	2月27日	27,Feb	1 949.46	12月4日	4,Dec	2 269.13
2013	2 289.51	2 444.80	2月18日	18,Feb	1 849.65	6月25日	25,jun	2 115.98
2014	2 112.13	3 239.36	12月31日	31,Dec	1 974.38	3月12日	12,Mar	3 234.68
2015	3 258.63	5 178.19	6月12日	12,June	2 850.71	8月26日	26,Aug	3 539.18
2016	3 536.59	3 538.69	1月4日	4,Jan	2 638.30	1月27日	27,Jan	3 103.64
2017	3 105.31	3 450.50	11月14日	14,Nov	3 016.53	5月11日	11,May	3 307.17
2018	3 314.03	3 587.03	1月29日	29,Jan	2 449.20	10月19日	19,Oct	2 493.90

表 18.13 上海证券交易所有价证券成交总额(2015~2018)
TOTAL VOLUME OF PRICED SECURITIES TRADING IN SHANGHAI STOCK EXCHANGE

单位:亿元(100 million yuan)

指　标	Indicators	2015	2016	2017	2018
总　计	**Total**	**2 663 691**	**2 838 724**	**3 063 862**	**2 646 249**
股　票	Shocks	1 330 992	501 700	511 243	403 184
#A　股	A Shares	1 323 231	496 880	507 215	401 575
B　股	B Shares	2 357	984	555	390
债　券	Bond	1 228 534	2 247 175	2 473 418	2 169 458
基　金(含 ETF)	Fund	103 814	89 360	78 170	71 651

表 18.14 上海证券交易所股票账户开户情况(2015~2018)
ACCOUNT-OPENING BY INVESTORS IN SHANGHAI STOCK EXCHANGE

单位:亿元(100 million yuan)

指　标	Indicators	2015	2016	2017	2018
累计开户总数	**Total Accounts Accumulated**				
总　数	Total	13 751.31	16 994.84	19 500.11	21 447.87
个　人	Private	13 698.94	16 936.51	19 435.80	21 379.04
机　构	Institution	52.37	58.33	64.31	68.83
A 股累计户数	**A Shares Accounts Accumulated**				
总　数	Total	13 586.32	16 828.33	19 332.64	21 279.91
个　人	Private	13 536.32	16 772.45	19 270.85	21 213.67
机　构	Institution	50.00	55.88	61.79	66.24
B 股累计户数	**B Shares Accounts Accumulated**				
总　数	Total	164.99	166.51	167.47	167.96
个　人	Private	162.62	164.06	164.95	165.37
机　构	Institution	2.37	2.45	2.52	2.59
当年新开户总数	**Newly Opened Accounts During the Year**				
总　数	Total	4 013.79	3 243.53	2 505.27	1 947.76
个　人	Private	4 007.47	3 237.57	2 499.29	1 943.24
机　构	Institution	6.32	5.96	5.98	4.52
A 股新开户数	**Newly Opened Accounts of A Shares**				
总　数	Total	4 005.59	3 242.01	2 504.30	1 947.27
个　人	Private	3 999.38	3 236.13	2 498.40	1 942.82
机　构	Institution	6.21	5.88	5.90	4.45
B 股新开户数	**Newly Opened Accounts of B Shares**				
总　数	Total	8.20	1.51	0.97	0.49
个　人	Private	8.09	1.44	0.89	0.42
机　构	Institution	0.10	0.08	0.08	0.07

上 / 海 / 统 / 计 / 年 / 鉴

主要统计指标解释

■ 存　款

机构或个人在保留资金或货币所有权的条件下，以不可流通的存款凭证为依据，暂时让渡或接受资金使用权所形成的债权或债务。

■ 贷　款

机构或个人在保留资金或货币所有权的条件下，以不可流通的借款凭证或类似凭证为依据，暂时让渡或接受资金使用权所形成的债权或债务。

■ 上证综合指数

以在上海证券交易所上市的全部股票（A股和B股）作为样本计算的股票价格指数。

■ 市场筹资额

企业在上海证券交易所通过发行股票和债券所筹集的资金总额。

■ 原保险保费收入

指保险人与投保人之间直接签订的原保险合同中确认的保费收入，不包括再保险保费收入。

■ 原保险赔付支出

指保险企业根据保险人与投保人之间直接签订的原保险合同中确认的赔付款项，不包括再保险赔付支出。

SHANGHAI STATISTICAL YEARBOOK

EXPLANATORY NOTES TO MAJOR STATISTICAL INDICATORS

□ Deposit

Deposit refers to the creditor's rights or debt formed by temporary lending or receiving funds in condition of institutions or individuals to retain the ownership of funds or monetary and based on the non-negotiable certificates of deposits.

□ Loan

Loan refers to the creditor's rights or debt formed by temporary lending or receiving funds in condition of institutions or individuals to retain the ownership of funds or monetary and based on the non-negotiable certificates of loan or similar certificates.

□ SSE Composite Index

SSE Composite Index is a stock price index, which is calculated by the price of all stocks (including A stocks and B stocks) in Shanghai Stock Exchange.

□ Market Financing

Market Financing refers to the total amount of fund which enterprises raise by issuing shares or bonds in Shanghai Stock Exchange.

□ Premium of Primary Insurance

Premium of Primary Insurance includes the insurance premium which is entered into the original insurance contract signed directly between the insurer and the insured, and reinsurance premium is excluded.

□ Payment of Primary Insurance

Payment of Primary Insurance includes the insurance payment which is entered into the original insurance contract signed directly between the insurer and the insured, and reinsurance payment is excluded.

第十九篇

CHAPTER 19

2019上海统计年鉴 SHANGHAI STATISTICAL YEARBOOK

房地产业

REAL ESTATE

简要说明

一、本篇资料的主要内容

本篇资料反映上海市房地产业生产经营和发展情况。主要指标有房地产开发投资额、房屋施工面积、商品房销售面积、房屋征收户数、存量房成交面积等。

二、本篇的资料来源

本篇中房地产开发投资和到位资金情况、房屋建筑面积、商品房销售和出租情况根据上海市统计局制定的《房地产开发统计报表制度》调查汇总提供。

本篇中房屋征收情况、存量房交易情况由上海市住房和城乡建设管理委员会提供。

本篇中土地使用权出让情况由上海市规划和自然资源局提供。

三、本篇资料的统计调查方法

本篇中涉及房地产开发统计资料采用全面调查的方法，由全市房地产开发经营法人企业通过联网直报的方式上报取得。

BRIEF INTRODUCTION

I. Main Contents

Data in this chapter reflect business operation and development of real estate industry in Shanghai. Main indicators include investment in real estate development, floor area of construction, sold area of commodity, quantity of expropriation (resettlements), and registration areas traded of second–hand houses.

II. Sources of statistics

Data on real estate development investment and capital in place, construction area, commodity housing sold and leased are compiled in accordance with Statistical Reporting System on Real Estate Development and Operation made by Shanghai Municipal Statistics Bureau.

Data on buildings resettlement and the registration of second–hand houses transaction are provided by Shanghai Municipal Housing and Urban and Rural Construction Management Committee

Data on lease of land plot tenure are provided by Shanghai Municipal Bureau of Planning and Natural Resources.

Ⅲ. Survey Methodology

Data on development and operation of real estate adopt comprehensive reporting system, being collected from data directly reported by the city′s real estate development and operation enterprises with legal person status through the Internet.

表 19.1 主要年份房地产开发企业投资和到位资金情况
INVESTMENT IN REAL ESTATE DEVELOPMENT ENTERPRISES AND AVAILABILITIES OF CAPITALS IN MAIN YEARS

单位:亿元(100 million yuan)

指 标	Indicators	2010	2015	2017	2018
房地产开发投资额	**Total Investment**	**1 980.68**	**3 468.94**	**3 856.53**	**4 033.18**
按开发用途分	By use				
住 宅	Residence	1 229.83	1 813.32	2 152.40	2 225.92
#别墅、高档公寓	Villas and Apartment	373.67	381.48	540.75	493.63
办公楼	Office Building	224.46	654.54	642.20	692.71
商业营业用房	Commercial Building	244.70	467.67	506.71	461.42
其 他	Others	281.69	533.41	555.21	653.14
本年新增固定资产	**Newly Increased Fixed Assets This Year**	**964.27**	**1 890.67**	**2 110.17**	**1 955.84**
到位资金合计	**Total Capital in Place This Year**	**4 443.85**	**7 483.72**	**8 099.77**	**8 127.16**
上年末结余资金	Balance at End of Previous Year	1 214.56	1 951.86	2 715.11	2 796.70
本年实际到位资金	Capital in Place This Year	3 229.29	5 531.86	5 384.65	5 330.46
国内贷款	Domestic Loans	819.57	1 516.59	1 393.78	1 326.02
利用外资	Foreign Capital Utilized	96.05	33.92	5.22	0.11
自筹资金	Self-Financed Capital	1 070.88	1 519.99	1 549.20	1 896.42
其他资金	Other Capital	1 242.78	2 461.36	2 436.45	2 107.91

表 19.2 主要年份房地产开发企业房屋建设情况
CONSTRUCTION STATUS OF REAL ESTATE DEVELOPMENT ENTERPRISES IN MAIN YEARS

指 标	Indicators	2010	2015	2017	2018
房屋施工面积（万平方米）	**Floor Area of Construction (10 000 sq.m)**	**11 295.03**	**15 095.33**	**15 362.25**	**14 672.37**
住 宅	Residence	7 313.85	8 372.12	8 013.80	7 520.39
#别墅、高档公寓	Villas and Apartment	1 584.11	1 647.69	1 748.88	1 575.03
办公楼	Office Building	1 103.18	1 978.49	2 282.08	2 139.02
商业营业用房	Commercial Building	1 292.96	1 944.02	2 016.16	1 876.24
其 他	Others	1 585.04	2 800.70	3 050.22	3 136.72
房屋新开工面积（万平方米）	**Floor Space of Newly-started Buildings (10 000 sq.m)**	**3 030.59**	**2 605.08**	**2 618.00**	**2 687.17**
住 宅	Residence	2 111.11	1 560.28	1 402.91	1 473.17
#别墅、高档公寓	Villas and Apartment	389.84	208.55	251.70	155.01
办公楼	Office Building	147.39	304.87	368.84	310.84
商业营业用房	Commercial Building	298.10	307.57	297.68	206.93
其 他	Others	473.99	432.36	548.57	696.23
房屋竣工面积（万平方米）	**Floor Area Completed (10 000 sq.m)**	**1 941.25**	**2 647.18**	**3 387.56**	**3 115.76**
住 宅	Residence	1 396.05	1 588.95	1 862.74	1 730.27
#别墅、高档公寓	Villas and Apartment	328.00	340.65	348.14	392.25
办公楼	Office Building	150.69	219.23	444.83	413.46
商业营业用房	Commercial Building	176.41	306.45	387.73	341.05
其 他	Others	218.09	532.55	692.27	630.98
房屋竣工价值（亿元）	**Value of Building Completed (100 million yuan)**	**779.93**	**1 488.32**	**2 054.31**	**1 941.04**
住 宅	Residence	536.66	881.17	1 020.42	1 019.36
#别墅、高档公寓	Villas and Apartment	178.27	285.39	251.84	278.70
办公楼	Office Building	74.23	174.90	336.02	307.62
商业营业用房	Commercial Building	87.13	176.58	321.96	291.16
其 他	Others	81.91	255.67	375.90	322.89

表 19.3 主要年份房地产开发企业商品房销售和出租情况
COMMODITY HOUSING SOLD AND LEASED OF REAL ESTATE DEVELOPMENT ENTERPRISES IN MAIN YEARS

指 标	Indicators	2010	2015	2017	2018
商品房销售面积（万平方米）	**Sold Area of Commodity Housing (10 000 sq.m)**	**2 055.53**	**2 431.36**	**1 691.60**	**1 767.01**
住 宅	Residence	1 685.35	2 009.17	1 341.62	1 333.29
#别墅、高档公寓	Villas and Apartment	341.71	390.97	212.04	179.77
办公楼	Office Building	162.89	197.41	124.10	147.08
商业营业用房	Commercial Building	125.56	113.70	79.33	101.75
其 他	Others	81.72	111.08	146.55	184.89
商品房销售额（亿元）	**Sales Volume of Commodity Housing (100 million yuan)**	**2 959.94**	**5 093.55**	**4 026.67**	**4 751.50**
住 宅	Residence	2 395.35	4 319.93	3 336.09	3 864.03
#别墅、高档公寓	Villas and Apartment	852.62	1 462.81	1 153.49	1 176.74
办公楼	Office Building	307.67	488.68	394.07	484.83
商业营业用房	Commercial Building	197.57	227.89	208.23	269.37
其 他	Others	59.34	57.05	88.28	133.27
商品房出租面积（万平方米）	**Commodity Housing Leased (10 000 Sq.m)**	**1 262.47**	**1 202.42**	**1 646.30**	**1 868.11**
住 宅	Residence	85.72	120.59	110.15	128.60
#别墅、高档公寓	Villas and Apartment	76.18	66.26	55.43	54.91
办公楼	Office Building	516.18	501.86	692.42	753.40
商业营业用房	Commercial Building	373.34	367.02	542.09	630.83
其 他	Others	287.23	212.95	301.63	355.28

表 19.4 房屋征收情况(1995~2018)
BUILDINGS EXPROPRIATION

年 份 Year	征收户数(户) Quantity of Expropriation (unit)	其中 of which #居民住宅 Residence	征收面积(万平方米) Floor Area Expropriated (10 000 sq.m)	其中 of which #居民住宅 Residence
1995	75 777	73 695	322.77	253.90
1996	89 132	86 481	342.95	258.86
1997	79 857	77 388	479.67	363.16
1998	78 205	75 157	452.22	343.94
1999	75 185	73 709	342.50	248.17
2000	70 606	68 293	365.77	288.35
2001	73 728	71 909	515.65	386.66
2002	101 097	98 714	644.53	485.00
2003	80 858	79 077	584.93	475.47
2004	42 415	41 552	308.40	232.52
2005	75 857	74 483	1 222.53	851.85
2006	81 126	76 874	1 516.85	848.35
2007	51 354	49 092	825.00	690.00
2008	53 583	51 288	1 028.53	753.71
2009	68 286	65 439	927.63	612.56
2010	39 721	38 441	585.70	389.87
2011	23 112	22 349	333.83	182.83
2012	21 910	21 262	219.42	127.27
2013	30 921	30 322	159.57	123.18
2014	26 799	26 334	118.58	95.81
2015	23 062	22 801	78.52	69.83
2016	28 426	27 063	136.47	86.00
2017	19 148	18 456	76.60	64.38
2018	16 763	16 215	62.77	52.46

表 19.5 各区房屋征收情况(2018)
BUILDINGS EXPROPRIATION IN DIFFERENT DISTRICTS

地 区	District	征收户数(户) Quantity of Expropriation (Resettlements) (unit)	其中 of which #居民住宅 Residence	征收面积(平方米) Floor Area Expropriated (Resettled) (sq.m)	其中 of which #居民住宅 Residence
总 计	**Total**	**16 763**	**16 215**	**627 724**	**524 601**
#浦东新区	Pudong New Area	43	32	6 358	1 536
黄 浦 区	Huangpu	6 826	6 706	188 403	184 350
徐 汇 区	Xuhui	7	6	787	583
长 宁 区	Changning	771	767	32 977	32 833
静 安 区	Jing'an	1 956	1 792	101 262	58 892
普 陀 区	Putuo	565	563	18 366	18 307
虹 口 区	Hongkou	4 433	4 280	154 802	147 254
杨 浦 区	Yangpu	2 121	2 030	98 435	78 611
嘉 定 区	Jiading	1	1	42	42
奉 贤 区	Fengxian	1	1	85	85

表 19.6 土地使用权出让情况(2018) LEASE OF LAND PLOT TENURE

指 标	Indicators	出让地块(幅) Leased Plot (piece)	出让面积(万平方米) Leased Area (10 000 sq.m)
总 计	**Total**	**298**	**1 316.10**
商业服务	Commercial Service	47	138.96
住 宅	Residence	150	672.29
工业仓储	Storage of Industry	92	459.04
公共建筑	Public Buildings	9	45.81

表 19.7 存量房交易情况(1994~2018) EXCHANGE OF SECOND-HAND HOUSES

年 份 Year	成交套数(套) Houses Traded (set)	成交面积(万平方米) Areas Traded (10 000sq.m)	其 中 of which		
			#住 宅 Residence	办公楼 Office	商业营业用房 Commerce
1994	2 821	31.76	10.59		
1995	4 176	60.87	19.70		
1996	4 689	82.29	25.09		
1997	9 180	162.40	87.68	23.95	14.95
1998	24 501	315.23	197.56	21.49	18.28
1999	44 234	510.84	336.69	37.63	14.61
2000	96 348	778.52	648.23	39.48	21.65
2001	164 598	1 422.43	1 031.48	56.99	57.24
2002	204 239	1 790.50	1 341.60	65.70	91.80
2003	263 297	2 306.28	1 807.57	105.14	114.28
2004	303 291	2 726.70	2 222.24	117.12	121.39
2005	189 896	1 971.50	1 608.20	88.10	78.00
2006	184 194	1 706.81	1 375.22	67.35	46.53
2007	213 733	1 992.59	1 715.05	49.73	36.34
2008	142 224	1 413.41	1 107.17	40.61	42.04
2009	312 857	2 809.45	2 490.58	48.19	43.59
2010	202 511	1 966.86	1 522.21	68.31	70.61
2011	146 151	1 398.67	1 058.71	62.87	51.21
2012	157 585	1 446.77	1 136.17	57.34	46.71
2013	291 176	2 575.70	2 228.02	65.59	47.18
2014	177 083	1 586.14	1 324.18	52.61	40.90
2015	303 414	2 647.83	2 351.30	52.27	41.62
2016	347 667	3 219.80	2 225.42	450.89	261.04
2017	179 385	1 563.53	1 264.13	80.75	60.26
2018	175 061	1 549.12	1 229.01	77.45	58.47

上 / 海 / 统 / 计 / 年 / 鉴

主要统计指标解释

■ 房地产开发投资

指房地产开发企业本年完成的全部用于房屋建设工程、土地开发工程的投资额以及公益性建筑和土地购置费等的投资。

■ 施工面积

指房地产开发企业本年施工的全部房屋建筑面积。包括本期新开工的面积和上期开工跨入本期继续施工的房屋面积，以及上期已停建在本期恢复施工的房屋面积。本期竣工和本期施工后又停缓建的房屋，其建筑面积仍计入本期房屋施工面积中。

■ 新开工面积

指房地产开发企业本年新开工建设的房屋建筑面积，以单位工程为核算对象。不包括在上期开工跨入报告期继续施工的房屋建筑面积和上期停缓建而在本期复工的建筑面积。房屋的开工以房屋正式开始破土刨槽(地基处理或打永久桩)的日期为准。

■ 竣工面积

指房地产开发企业本年按照设计要求已全部完工，达到住人和使用条件，经验收鉴定合格或达到竣工验收标准，可正式移交使用的各栋房屋建筑面积的总和。

■ 商品房销售面积

指房地产开发企业本年出售新建商品房屋的合同总面积(即双方签署的正式买卖合同中所确认的建筑面积)。

■ 商品房销售额

指房地产开发企业本年出售商品房屋的合同总价款(即双方签署的正式买卖合同中所确定的合同总价)。该指标与商品房销售面积同口径。

■ 商品房出租面积

指年末房地产开发企业出租的商品房屋的全部面积。

SHANGHAI STATISTICAL YEARBOOK

EXPLANATORY NOTES TO MAJOR STATISTICAL INDICATORS

□ Investment in Real Estate Development

Investment in Real Estate Development refers to investment entirely used for building construction project and land development project by real estate development enterprises, and investment in public buildings and purchase costs of land.

□ Floor Area of Construction

Floor Area of Construction refers to total floor space of all buildings constructing by real estate development enterprises during the reference period, including floor space of newly started buildings during the reference period, floor space of construction extended from the previous period to the current period, and floor space of construction suspended during the previous period and resumed in the current period. Floor space of construction completed in the current period, and floor space of construction started and then suspended in the current period are also included in the floor space under construction of the current year.

□ Floor Area of Newly-started Buildings

Floor Area of Newly- started Buildings refers to the floor space of buildings newly started to construct by real estate development enterprises during the reference period, one unit project was considered as a calculating unit. Excluding the floor space of buildings started in last period or stopped or delayed in last period and restarted in this period. The date of start construction refers to the beginning of breaking gouging (foundation treatment or permanent pile).

□ Floor Area Completed

Floor Area Completed refers to the floor space of all buildings completed in the reference period, which have been appraised and accepted (or come up to the designed standards) and have been transferred to the owners for use.

□ Sold Area of Commodity Housing

Sold Area of Commodity Housing refers to the total area of new commodity housing sold by real estate development enterprises in the reference period (the construction area confirmed by formal contracts).

□ Sales Volume of Commodity Housing

Sales Volume of Commodity Housing refers to the total sales volume of new commodity housing sold by real estate development enterprises in the reference period (the sales volume confirmed by formal contracts). The caliber of this index is same to Sold Area of Commodity Housing.

□ Commodity Housing Leased

Commodity Housing Leased refers to the total area of commodity housing leased by real estate development enterprises at the end of the reference period.

第二十篇

CHAPTER 20

科学技术

SCIENCE AND TECHNOLOGY

简要说明

一、本篇资料的主要内容

科技统计资料主要内容包括:全社会以及工业企业、政府部门属研究机构、高校的研究与试验发展(R&D)活动情况;技术市场交易情况;科技成果情况;科技型企业情况;科协系统科技活动情况;专利申请和授权情况等。

二、本篇资料的统计范围

科技活动统计资料范围为全社会有研究与试验发展(R&D)活动的企事业单位,具体包括工业企业、政府部门属研究机构、普通高等学校以及研究与试验发展(R&D)活动相对密集行业(包括农、林、牧、渔业,建筑业,交通运输、仓储和邮政业,信息传输、软件和信息技术服务业,金融业,租赁和商务服务业,科学研究和技术服务业,水利、环境和公共设施管理业,卫生和社会工作,文化、体育和娱乐业等)中从事研究与试验发展(R&D)活动的企事业单位。

三、本篇的资料来源

全市综合资料、企业及有关行业企事业单位的研究与试验发展(R&D)活动情况资料由上海统计局调查提供;政府部门属研究机构资料由上海市科学技术委员会、上海市经济和信息化委员会调查提供;技术市场资料、科技成果、科技型企业状况由上海市科学技术委员会调查提供;高校资料由上海市教育委员会调查提供;科协系统科技活动资料由上海市科学技术协会调查提供;专利资料由上海市知识产权局调查提供。

四、本篇的调查方法

研究与试验发展(R&D)活动情况采用全面调查取得;科协、专利资料采用抽样等多种调查方法取得。

五、统计资料口径变化

2000年以前科技活动统计资料只包括大中型工业企业、政府部门属研究机构、普通高等学校,2000年及以后年份扩大到了全社会范围。

BRIEF INTRODUCTION

I. Main Contents

Data on science and technology mainly include: data on scientific and technological activities, R&D activities all over the country, including industrial enterprises, scientific and technological institutions under government departments, universities and colleges; data on technological markets; data on science and technology achievements; data on scientific and technology enterprises; data on the scientific and technological activities in the system of associations for science and technology; patents application accepted and granted.

II. Statistical Range

Data on science and technology include research and development (R&D) activities of enterprises and institutions all over the country, mainly including industrial enterprises, scientific and technological institutions under government departments, universities, colleges and relatively R&D-intensive industries (such as agriculture, forestry, animal husbandry, fisher, construction, transport, storage and post, information transmission, software industry and information technology service, financial intermediation, leasing and business services, scientific research and technical service management of water conservancy, environment and public facilities, health and social work, culture, sports and entertainment).

III. Data Sources

Data on citywide aggregates and R&D activities of various enterprises and institutions are from Shanghai Municipal Statistics Bureau; data on scientific and technological institutions under government departments are from Science and Technology Commission of Shanghai Municipality、Shanghai Municipal Commission of Economy and Informatization; data on technological markets, scientific and technical payoffs, scientific and technology enterprises are from Science and Technology Commission of Shanghai Municipality; data on scientific and technological activities in universities and colleges are from Shanghai Municipal Education Commission; data on the scientific and technological activities of associations for science and technology are from Science and Technology Commission of Shanghai Municipality; Shanghai Intellectual Property Administration provides data on patents.

IV. Statistical Methodology

Data on R&D activities are collected through complete surveys. Data on scientific and technological associations and patent applications are through sample surveys and other surveys.

V. Changes of the statistical coverage of data

Before 2000, data only included large and medium-sized industrial enterprises, scientific research institutions under government departments, and universities and colleges. Since 2000 (inclusive), data have covered all industries.

表 20.1　主要年份科技活动主要指标
MAIN INDICATORS OF SCIENTIFIC AND TECHNOLOGICAL ACTIVITIES IN MAIN YEARS

年　份 Year	科技活动人员（万人） Personnel Engaged in Scientific and Technological Activities (10 000 persons)	研究与试验发展（R&D）人员全时当量（万人年） Full-time Equivalent of R&D Personnel (10 000 person-years)	研究与试验发展（R&D）经费内部支出（亿元） Expenditures on R&D (100 million yuan)	研究与试验发展经费支出相当于上海市生产总值比例（%） R&D as Percentage of Gross Domestic Product (%)	地方财政科技经费支出（亿元） Local Fiscal Expenditures on Scientific and Technological Research (100 million yuan)	科技经费支出占地方财政支出比重（%） Percentage of Expenditures on Scientific and Technological Research in Local Fiscal (%)
1990	19.34		10.13	1.30	2.44	3.2
1995	18.25		32.60	1.29	5.12	2.0
2000	20.17	6.31	76.73	1.59	10.08	1.6
2001	17.57	5.20	88.08	1.68	12.39	1.7
2002	17.89	5.02	102.36	1.77	15.25	1.7
2003	17.59	5.62	128.92	1.91	19.84	1.8
2004	18.25	5.73	170.28	2.09	39.32	2.8
2005	19.67	7.07	213.77	2.28	79.34	4.8
2006	20.07	8.01	258.84	2.41	94.89	5.2
2007	22.79	9.03	307.50	2.43	105.77	4.9
2008	23.08	9.75	362.30	2.54	120.27	4.6
2009	33.90	13.29	423.38	2.77	215.31	7.2
2010	33.46	13.50	481.70	2.76	202.03	6.1
2011	37.53	14.85	597.71	3.06	218.50	5.6
2012	38.91	15.34	679.46	3.31	245.43	5.9
2013	43.16	16.58	776.78	3.49	257.66	5.7
2014	45.10	16.82	861.95	3.58	262.29	5.3
2015	44.81	17.18	936.14	3.65	271.85	4.4
2016	49.88	18.39	1 049.32	3.72	341.71	4.9
2017		18.35	1 205.21	3.93	389.90	5.2
2018		18.81	1 359.20	4.16	426.37	5.1

①本表部分数据由上海市财政局等部门提供。
②2018 年“研究与试验发展经费支出相当于上海市生产总值比例”根据 2018 年上海市生产总值快报数计算。
❶Data in this table are mainly provided by Shanghai Municipal Finance Bureau.
❷In 2018, the R&D as Percentage of Gross Domestic Product is calculated according to the 2018 Shanghai GDP express report.

表 20.2　主要年份研究与试验发展(R&D)经费内部支出按执行部门分类
EXPENDITURES ON R&D GROUPED BY EXECUTIVE DEPARTMENT IN MAIN YEARS

单位：亿元（100 million yuan）

指　标	Indicators	2000	2010	2017	2018
总　计	**Total**	**76.73**	**481.70**	**1 205.21**	**1 359.20**
科研机构	Research Institutions	25.58	105.35	320.49	347.57
高等院校	Institutions of Higher Education	7.43	45.80	109.20	124.91
企　业	Enterprises	41.44	321.31	747.54	857.73
#工业企业	Industrial Enterprises	34.78	274.05	540.00	554.88
#大中型工业企业	Large and Medium Industrial Enterprises	30.98	237.75	450.86	453.04
其　他	Others	2.28	9.25	27.98	28.99

表 20.3 主要年份研究与试验发展(R&D)活动情况
BASIC STATISTICS OF RESEARCH AND DEVELOPMENT (R&D) ACTIVITIES IN MAIN YEARS

指标	Indicators	2000	2010	2017	2018
有 R&D 活动单位数(个)	**Quantity of Science and Technology Institutions (unit)**	**1 070**	**1 782**	**2 808**	**2 923**
科研机构	Research Institutions	125	113	111	106
高等院校	Institutions of Higher Education	41	68	117	123
企业	Enterprises	820	1 453	2 441	2 556
其他	Others	84	148	139	138
R&D 人员投入情况	**Personnel Investment on R&D**				
R&D 人员(万人)	R&D Personnel(10 000 persons)		17.75	26.23	27.12
R&D 人员全时当量(万人年)	Full-time Equivalent of R&D Personnel(10 000 person-year)	6.31	13.50	18.35	18.81
基础研究	Basic Research	0.60	1.42	2.04	2.17
应用研究	Applied Research	1.92	2.29	2.54	2.85
试验发展	Experimental Development	3.79	9.79	13.77	13.79
R&D 经费投入情况	**Expenditure on R&D**				
R&D 经费内部支出(亿元)	Intramural Expenditure on R&D (100 million yuan)	76.73	481.70	1 205.21	1 359.20
按活动类型分	By Activity Types				
基础研究	Basic Research	4.98	31.05	92.51	105.69
应用研究	Applied Research	18.18	68.99	152.32	169.45
试验发展	Experimental Development	53.57	381.67	960.38	1 084.07
按经费来源分	By Source of Funds				
政府资金	Government Funds	24.22	142.78	429.45	471.25
企业资金	Self-raised Funds by Enterprises	33.76	318.28	719.80	839.53
境外资金	Offshore Funds	4.79	6.80	17.17	11.61
其他	Others	13.96	13.83	38.78	36.82
R&D 项目(课题)情况	**R&D project**				
项目(课题)数(万项)	Quantity of Projects (10 000 item)	2.07	5.56	8.31	9.01
项目(课题)参加人员(万人年)	Personnel Engaged in Projects (10 000 persons year)	5.42	11.89	16.93	17.78
项目(课题)经费内部支出(亿元)	Inner Expenditure on Projects (100 million yuan)	54.31	379.37	1 083.68	1 168.53
科技活动产出情况	**Output of Science and Technic Activities**				
新产品产值(亿元)	Production Value of New Product(100 million yuan)	1 401.62	5 870.02	9 159.91	8 609.79
新产品销售收入(亿元)	Sales Revenue of New Product(100 million yuan)	1 398.54	6 543.07	10 068.15	9 796.73
专利申请数(件)	Patent Applications(piece)	11 337	71 196	131 746	150 233
#发明专利	Invention Patents	4 713	26 165	54 633	62 755
专利授权数(件)	Patents Granted(piece)	4 050	48 215	72 806	92 460
#发明专利	Invention Patents	304	6 867	20 681	21 331
有效发明专利数(件)	Effective Invention Patents(piece)		23 843	100 433	114 966
发表科技论文数(篇)	Quantity of Science and Technic Papers Published(case)	37 216	87 971	102 139	114 114
出版科技著作(种)	Science and Technic Works Published(piece)	2 614	3 329	3 010	2 929
商标申请注册数(万件)	Register Applications for Trade Marks (case)	0.95	6.02	34.40	40.89
商标核准注册数(万件)	Registration approved for Trade Marks (case)	0.62	7.04	19.30	29.17
科技成果登记数(项)	Quantity of Achievements Registered in Scientific and Technological Activities(item)	1 102	2 318	2 028	1 618

注：本表部分数据由市知识产权局和市科学技术委员会提供。
Note: Data in this table are partly provided by Shanhgai Intellectual Property Service Center, and Shanghai Municipal Science and Technology Commission.

表 20.4 国有企事业单位专业技术人员基本情况(2018)
PROFESSIONAL AND TECHNICAL PERSONNEL IN STATE-OWNED ENTERPRISES AND INSTITUTIONS

单位:万人(10 000 persons)

类别	Types	合计 Total	其中 of which	按学历分 by Education Background		
			#女性 Female	大学本专科以上 College and University above	中等专业 Specialized Secondary School	高中及以下 Senior Middle School and below
总计	**Total**	**103.84**	**52.64**	**98.69**	**3.08**	**2.07**
高级岗位	Senior	11.98	4.70	11.92	0.04	0.02
中级岗位	Medium	31.55	17.13	30.96	0.44	0.14
初级岗位	Junior	30.58	17.30	28.40	1.63	0.54
未聘人员	Not Appointed	29.73	13.52	27.40	0.97	1.37

表 20.4 续表 continued

单位:万人(10 000 persons)

类别	Types	合计 Total	其中 of which	按学历分 by Education Background		
			#女性 Female	大学本专科以上 College and University above	中等专业 Specialized Secondary School	高中及以下 Senior Middle School and below
总计	**Total**	**103.84**	**52.64**	**98.69**	**3.08**	**2.07**
工程技术人员	Engineering	29.03	6.52	27.37	0.88	0.78
农业技术人员	Agriculture	0.56	0.18	0.49	0.05	0.03
科学研究人员	Scientific Research	2.89	1.10	2.85	0.03	0.01
卫生技术人员	Medical Professionals	11.92	8.96	11.20	0.69	0.03
教学人员	Teaching	19.81	14.49	19.69	0.10	0.02
经济人员	Economic	27.45	13.87	25.73	0.83	0.89
财会人员	Financial Accounting	7.13	4.77	6.63	0.33	0.16
统计人员	Statistical	1.02	0.57	0.96	0.03	0.03
翻译人员	Translator	0.08	0.05	0.08	0.00	0.00
新闻出版、播音人员	Media, Publishing & Announcer	0.92	0.54	0.90	0.01	0.01
艺术人员	Culture & Art	0.59	0.28	0.48	0.07	0.04
其他专业人员	Others	2.44	1.31	2.31	0.06	0.06

注：本页数据由市委组织部提供。
Note: Data on this page are provided by Shanghai Municipal Party Committee Organization Department.

表 20.5 主要年份各类技术合同项目
VARIOUS TECHNOLOGICAL CONTRACTS IN MAIN YEARS

单位:项(item)

年 份 Year	项 目 Item	其中 of which 技术开发 Technological Development	技术转让 Technological Transfer	技术咨询 Technological Consulting	技术服务 Technological Service
1991	25 023	3 038	1 992	3 203	16 790
1995	21 213	1 915	775	3 672	14 851
1996	20 074	1 841	823	3 821	13 589
1997	18 863	1 643	1 037	3 569	12 614
1998	18 364	1 206	919	3 235	13 004
1999	19 721	1 158	937	3 993	13 633
2000	20 974	1 561	888	3 905	14 620
2001	23 816	2 385	1 294	5 012	15 125
2002	26 010	2 984	1 156	4 983	16 887
2003	27 292	3 512	2 112	5 306	16 362
2004	27 327	4 398	2 453	4 814	15 662
2005	30 290	5 256	2 444	4 753	17 837
2006	28 191	6 165	2 172	3 592	16 262
2007	27 742	6 425	2 133	3 086	16 098
2008	28 713	7 154	1 749	3 873	15 937
2009	27 109	8 071	1 549	3 034	14 455
2010	26 185	8 894	1 370	2 685	13 236
2011	29 332	10 771	1 317	3 277	13 967
2012	27 998	10 974	1 170	3 026	12 828
2013	26 297	10 057	1 102	3 094	12 044
2014	25 238	10 187	1 201	2 876	10 974
2015	22 513	9 579	1 050	2 458	9 426
2016	21 203	9 141	1 041	2 211	8 810
2017	21 559	9 498	912	1 819	9 330
2018	21 630	10 694	1 203	1 140	8 593

表 20.6 主要年份各类技术合同成交金额
TOTAL CONTRACTED VALUE IN VARIOUS TECHNOLOGICAL CONTRACTS IN MAIN YEARS

单位:亿元(100 million yuan)

年 份 Year	成交金额 Contracted Value	其中 of which 技术开发 Technological Development	技术转让 Technological Transfer	技术咨询 Technological Consulting	技术服务 Technological Service
1991	9.33	2.15	1.90	0.55	4.72
1995	23.04	4.14	1.57	2.12	15.21
1996	25.65	4.38	1.50	2.81	16.97
1997	28.76	5.72	2.14	3.28	17.61
1998	31.41	4.55	2.58	2.44	21.85
1999	36.63	3.68	3.50	3.24	26.21
2000	73.90	9.96	36.44	3.51	23.99
2001	106.16	28.24	50.71	4.63	22.58
2002	120.22	45.40	46.18	4.63	24.01
2003	142.78	50.96	50.79	6.11	34.92
2004	171.70	61.31	42.32	6.00	62.07
2005	231.73	87.47	110.08	6.42	27.76
2006	344.43	142.79	165.18	7.60	28.86
2007	432.64	181.50	212.49	5.50	33.15
2008	485.75	213.24	229.53	6.41	36.57
2009	489.86	266.30	174.34	5.39	43.83
2010	525.45	264.68	213.86	4.93	41.98
2011	550.32	328.25	164.49	5.40	52.18
2012	588.52	297.14	223.48	5.17	62.73
2013	620.87	267.33	230.15	7.40	115.99
2014	667.99	299.83	221.99	5.95	140.22
2015	707.99	321.49	296.99	5.32	84.20
2016	822.86	309.39	338.00	9.69	165.78
2017	867.53	513.91	271.59	5.35	76.68
2018	1303.20	683.16	311.57	3.44	305.03

注：本页数据由市技术市场管理办公室提供。
Note: Data on this page are provided by Shanghai Technology Market Administrative Office.

表 20.7 科技成果(2000~2018)
ACHIEVEMENTS IN SCIENTIFIC AND TECHNICAL RESEARCH

单位:项(item)

年份 Year	科技成果 Achievements in Science and Technology	按成果水平分 By Level of Achievements			
		#国际领先 Being First Created in the World	国际先进 Attaining Advanced World Levels	国内领先 Being First Created in China	国内先进 Attaining Advanced Domestic Levels
2000	1 102	45	462	452	117
2001	1 338	78	542	444	116
2002	1 418	65	603	463	106
2003	1 508	71	532	481	155
2004	1 629	147	669	480	155
2005	1 701	123	629	588	189
2006	1 953	250	675	655	191
2007	2 396	180	761	938	254
2008	1 866	125	664	663	226
2009	2 166	260	651	831	247
2010	2 318	188	698	724	202
2011	2 388	211	598	568	158
2012	2 415	177	572	596	142
2013	2 490	125	462	548	164
2014	2 384	108	423	531	149
2015	2 356	125	367	467	155
2016	2 245	122	364	438	189
2017	2 028	102	349	437	131
2018	1 618	101	298	330	106

表 20.7 续表 continued

单位:项(item)

年份 Year	按成果分 By Type of Achievements				
	基础理论成果 Fundamental Theory Research Results	应用技术成果 Application of Technological Achievements	其中 of which		软科学成果 Soft Scientific Achievements
			已推广应用 Been Populized	未应用 Not Been Populized	
2000	79	953	809	144	70
2001	81	1 196	940	256	61
2002	110	1 250	961	289	58
2003	97	1 281	1 045	236	130
2004	70	1 488	1 204	284	71
2005	61	1 555	1 261	294	85
2006	52	1 799	1 506	293	102
2007	139	2 162	1 724	438	95
2008	115	1 695	1 337	358	56
2009	94	2 009	1 747	262	63
2010	152	2 104	1 824	280	62
2011	182	2 137	1 943	194	69
2012	218	2 112	1 914	198	85
2013	248	2 152	1 872	280	90
2014	263	2 023	1 798	225	98
2015	239	2 040	1 764	276	77
2016	272	1 909	1 654	255	64
2017	181	1 788	1 638	150	59
2018	190	1 357	1 219	138	71

表 20.8 主要年份科研机构研究与试验发展(R&D)活动情况

BASIC STATISTICS OF RESEARCH AND DEVELOPMENT(R&D) ACTIVITIES OF SCIENTIFIC RESEARCH INSTITUTIONS IN MAIN YEARS

指 标	Indicators	2000	2010	2017	2018
有 R&D 活动单位数(个)	**Quantity of Science and Technology Institutions (unit)**	**125**	**113**	**111**	**106**
R&D 人员投入情况	**Personnel Investment on R&D**				
R&D 人员(人)	R&D Personnel(person)		26 550	32 821	32 522
R&D 人员全时当量(人年)	Full-time Equivalent of R&D Personnel(person-year)	19 802	23 241	29 331	29 055
基础研究	Basic Research	2 675	3 781	6 090	4 913
应用研究	Applied Research	8 873	8 771	9 450	10 353
试验发展	Experimental Development	8 254	10 689	13 791	13 789
R&D 经费投入情况	**Expenditure on R&D**				
R&D 经费内部支出(亿元)	Intramural Expenditure on R&D (100 million yuan)	25.58	105.35	320.49	347.57
按活动类型分	By Activity Types				
基础研究	Basic Research	3.06	13.87	39.43	42.19
应用研究	Applied Research	9.84	34.51	74.03	87.68
试验发展	Experimental Development	12.68	56.97	207.02	217.70
按经费来源分	By Source of Funds				
政府资金	Government Funds	18.89	88.98	285.59	310.90
企业资金	Self-raised Funds by Enterprises	1.09	6.61	5.25	11.57
境外资金	Offshore Funds	0.69	0.54	0.83	1.01
R&D 项目(课题)情况	**R&D project**				
R&D 项目(课题)数(项)	Quantity of Projects(item)	3 190	5 933	9 395	10 497
R&D 项目(课题)人员全时当量(人年)	Personnel Engaged in Projects (person-year)	14 015	18 799	25 836	26 817
R&D 项目(课题)经费内部支出(亿元)	Inner Expenditure on Projects (100 million yuan)	8.56	58.99	249.45	276.62
科技产出及成果情况	**Output of Science and Technic Activities**				
发表科技论文数(篇)	Quantity of Science and Technic Papers Published(case)	6 831	7 896	10 003	10 281
出版科技著作(种)	Works of Science and Technology Published(kind)	187	197	222	254
专利申请受理数(件)	Number of Patents Applications(piece)	425	1 864	4 239	4 476
#发明专利	Inventions	275	1 593	3 526	3 842
专利申请授权数(件)	Number of Patents Application Granted(piece)		817	2 458	2 486
#发明专利	Inventions		502	1 969	1 903
有效发明专利数(件)	Effective Invention Patents(piece)	779	2 732	10 501	12 247

表 20.9 主要年份获得科技成果奖励情况
ACHIEVEMENTS AWARDED IN SCIENTIFIC AND TECHNOLOGICAL RESEARCH IN MAIN YEARS

单位：项(item)

指 标	Indicators	2000	2010	2017	2018
科技成果获奖总数	**Quantity of Achievements Awarded**	**287**	**298**	**330**	**347**
获国家科技成果奖	National Award	21	58	58	47
国家最高科学技术奖(人)	State Supreme Science Award		1		
国家自然科学奖	Natural Science Award	3	6	6	3
国家技术发明奖	Technological Invention Award	1	4	11	7
国家科学技术进步奖	Science and Technology Progress Award	17	46	39	37
中华人民共和国国际科学技术合作奖	China International Science and Technoloty Cooperation Award		1	2	
获上海科技进步奖	**Shanghai Award**	**266**	**240**	**272**	**300**
# 国际科学技术合作奖(人)	International Science and Technology Cooperation Award		1	2	1

表 20.10 主要年份区级属研究与开发机构状况
RESEARCH AND DEVELOPMENT INSTITUTIONS AT DISTRICT LEVEL IN MAIN YEARS

指 标	Indicators	2000	2010	2017	2018
机构数（个）	Quantity of Institutions (unit)	35	18	16	15
从业人员（人）	Quantity of Employees (person)	1 261	1 015	887	740
# 从事科技活动人员	Personnel Engaged in Science and Technic Activities	736	764	760	686
科技活动经费内部支出（万元）	Inner Expenditures on Science and Technic Activities (10 000 yuan)	7 343	15 482	35 650	36 094

表 20.11 主要年份高等学校研究与试验发展(R&D)活动情况
RESERCH AND DEVELOPMENT(R&D) ACTIVITIES OF HIGHER EDUCATION IN MAIN YEARS

指 标	Indicators	2000	2010	2017	2018
有 R&D 活动单位数(个)	**Quantity of Science and Technology Institutions (unit)**	**41**	**68**	**117**	**123**
理工农医	Science, Engineering, Agriculture and Medicine		38	60	65
人文社科	Humanity and Social Science		30	57	58
R&D 人员投入情况	**Personnel Investment on R&D**				
R&D 人员(人)	R&D Personnel(person)		38 175	46 207	52 904
R&D 人员全时当量(人年)	Full-time Equivalent of R&D Personnel(person-year)	10 816	21 565	24 625	28 323
基础研究	Basic Research	3 015	9 026	12 792	15 266
应用研究	Applied Research	6 378	10 387	10 763	11 479
试验发展	Experimental Development	1 423	2 152	1 070	1 579
R&D 经费投入情况	**Expenditure on R&D**				
R&D 经费内部支出(亿元)	Intramural Expenditure on R&D (100 million yuan)	7.43	45.80	109.20	124.91
按活动类型分	By Activity Types				
基础研究	Basic Research	1.44	15.19	50.64	60.07
应用研究	Applied Research	4.50	24.71	51.93	55.54
试验发展	Experimental Development	1.49	5.90	6.63	9.30
按经费来源分	By Source of Funds				
政府资金	Government Funds	3.26	27.33	73.36	90.24
企业资金	Self-raised Funds by Enterprises	3.38	15.47	32.36	30.93
境外资金	Offshore Funds	0.31	0.67	0.36	0.52
R&D 课题情况	**R&D Projects**				
R&D 课题数(项)	Quantity of Projects(item)	12 525	36 656	56 674	62 717
R&D 课题人员全时当量(人年)	Full-time Equivalent of Personnel in Projects(person-year)	15 945	21 541	24 611	28 316
R&D 课题经费内部支出(亿元)	Inner Expenditure on Projects (100 million yuan)	7.28	32.96	69.16	74.31
科技产出及成果情况	**Output of Science and Technic Activities**				
发表科技论文(篇)	Quantity of Science and Technic Papers Published(case)	25 896	70 290	84 386	89 017
出版科技著作(种)	Works of Science and Technology Published(sort)	2 206	3 020	2 648	2 563
专利申请数(件)	Number of Patents Applications(piece)	527	6 828	10 517	12 613
#发明专利	Inventions	385	4 834	8 576	10 147
专利授权数(件)	Number of Patents Application Granted(piece)		4 035	6 276	6 629
#发明专利	Inventions		2 169	4 740	4 579
有效发明专利数(件)	Effective Invention Patents(piece)		11 558	21 534	24 159

表 20.12 高等学校科技活动人员(2018)
SCIENTIFIC AND TECHNOLOGICAL PERSONNEL OF INSTITUTIONS OF HIGHER EDUCATION

单位:人(person)

指 标	Indicators	合 计 Total	其 中 of which 自然科学 Natural Science	工程与技术 Engineering and Technology	医学科学 Medical Science	农业科学 Agriculture Science	其 他 Others
总 计	**Total**	**63 980**	**6 779**	**17 200**	**36 836**	**474**	**2 691**
#科学家和工程师	Scientists and Engineers	61 267	6 538	16 797	34 946	467	2 519
按职称分	**By Professional Title**						
高 级	Senior	21 972	3 728	8 213	9 238	221	572
中 级	Medium	24 228	2 401	6 911	13 405	168	1 343
初 级	Junior	14 758	332	1 484	12 291	72	579

表 20.13 高等学校研究机构和课题情况(2018)
RESEARCH INSTITUTIONS AND PROJECT OF HIGHER EDUCATION

指 标	Indicators	合 计 Total	其 中 of which #自然科学 Natural Science	工程与技术 Engineering and Technology	医学科学 Medical Science	农业科学 Agriculture Science
研究机构数(个)	Research Institutions(unit)	343	56	160	65	59
机构 R&D 人员(人)	Institutions Personnel of R&D(person)	4 195	1 108	2 100	647	320
机构 R&D 经费支出(亿元)	R&D expenditure of Institutions (100 million yuan)	6.32	3.14	2.40	0.40	0.37
课题数(个)	Quantity of Projects of R&D (unit)	43 655	6 672	20 720	15 240	1 023
课题投入人员(人年)	Project Personnel(person-year)	26 137.90	2 822.00	9 499.50	13 278.40	538.00
课题投入经费(亿元)	Project Funding(100 million yuan)	123.76	22.39	71.91	27.87	1.58
课题经费支出(亿元)	Project Expenditure(100 million yuan)	87.99	14.77	53.08	18.95	1.19

注:本页统计范围是指高等学校中理工农医类口径。
Note: Figures of this page refer to those of science, engineering, agriculture and medicine of higher education.

表 20.14 主要年份专利申请量和授权量
PATENT APPLICATIONS AND CERTIFIED IN MAIN YEARS

单位：件(item)

指标	Indicators	2000	2010	2017	2018
专利申请量	**Patent Applications**	**11 337**	**71 196**	**131 746**	**150 233**
#发　明	Inventions	4 713	26 165	54 633	62 755
专利授权量	**Patent Certified**	**4 050**	**48 215**	**72 806**	**92 460**
#发　明	Inventions	304	6 867	20 681	21 331
有效发明专利	Effective Invention Patents		23 843	100 433	114 966
PCT 国际专利受理	PCT International Patent Application Accepted		735	1 760	2 105

表 20.15 科协系统出版物和科技服务情况(2018)
PUBLICATIONS AND CONSULTATIVE ACTIVITIES OF SCIENCE AND TECHNOLOGY ASSOCIATIONS

指标	Indicators	合计 Total	其中 of which: 市级科协 Municipal Level Associations	区(县)级科协 District and County Level Associations	市级学会 Municipal Level Societies
出版物	**Publications**				
主办科技期刊(种)	Scientific Journals (sort)	74	2		72
科技期刊总印数(万册)	Total Printed (10 000 copies)	360	25		334
编著科技图书(种)	Science and Technology Books (sort)	271	222	5	44
科技图书总印数(万册)	Total Printed of Science and Technology Books (10 000 copies)	72	56	2	14
主办科技报纸(种)	Technology Newspaper (sort)	5	2		3
科技报纸总印数(万份)	Total Printed of Technology Newspaper (10 000 copies)	391	388		3
咨　询	**Consultation**				
提供决策咨询报告(篇)	Decision Consultation Reports (sheet)	105	29	47	29
#获上级领导批示报告(篇)	Marking by Superiors (sheet)	25	9	7	9
举办决策咨询活动(次)	Decision Consultation Activities (time)	111	25	61	25
参加决策咨询活动专家数(人次)	Experts Participating in Decision Consultation Activities (person-time)	1 227	446	335	446

表 20.16 科协系统科普活动和科技培训情况(2018)
PROMOTING SCIENCE ACTIVITIES AND TRAINING PROGRAM ORGANIZED BY SCIENCE AND TECHNOLOGY ASSOCIATIONS

指标	Indicators	合计 Total	其中 of which 市级科协 Municipal level Associations	区(县)级科协 District and County Level Associations	市级学会 Municipal Level Societies
举办科普宣讲活动(次)	Science Propaganda Activities (time)	1 480	32	700	748
科普宣讲活动参加人次(万人次)	Participants in Science Propaganda Activities (10 000 person-times)	324.85	32.91	217.12	74.82
举办实用技术培训(次)	Practical Technical Training (time)	442	16	314	112
实用技术培训参加人数(万人次)	Trainees of Practical Technical Training (10 000 person-times)	8.16	0.10	6.80	1.26
举办青少年科技竞赛(次)	Youth Science Competition (time)	260	4	218	38
青少年科技竞赛参加人数(万人次)	Competitors of Youth Science Competition (10 000 person-times)	71.23	3.72	23.66	10.45
青少年科技竞赛获奖人数(人次)	Winners of Youth Science Competition (person-time)	21 591	6 260	9 888	5 443
青少年参加国际及港澳台科技交流活动(次)	International and Hong Kong, Macao and Taiwan Technology Exchange Activities (time)	29	12	12	5
青少年参加国际及港澳台科技交流活动人数(人次)	Participants in International and Hong Kong, Macao and Taiwan Technology Exchange Activities(person-time)	1 274	500	584	190
举办青少年科学营(次)	Youth Science Camp (time)	71		57	14
青少年科学营参加人数(人次)	Participants in Youth Science Camp(person-time)	12 598		11 367	1 231
举办青少年科技教育培训(次)	Youth Science and Technology Education and Training (time)	238	16	177	45
青少年科技教育培训参加人数(万人次)	Trainees of Youth Science and Technology Education and Training (10 000 person-times)	26.72	0.98	19.12	6.63

表 20.17 各级科协机构和人员(2018)
INSTITUTIONS AND PERSONNEL OF SCIENCE AND TECHNOLOGY ASSOCIATIONS AT VARIOUS LEVELS

指标	Indicators	市级科协 Municipal Level Associations	区级科协 District Level Associations
机构数(个)	Institutions(unit)	1	16
人员(人)	Personnel(person)	60	169
各级学会在册个数(个)	All Levels Societies Registered(unit)	200	360

表 20.17 续表 continued

指标	Indicators	机构数(个) Quantity of Institutions (unit)	个人会员(万人) Individual Members (10 000 persons)	团体会员数(个) Organization Members (unit)	所属分科学会(个) Attached Associations (unit)
市级学会	Prefectural Societies	200	30.6	14 631	1 306

表 20.18 科协系统学术交流情况(2018)
ACADEMIC EXCHANGES OF SCIENCE AND TECHNOLOGY ASSOCIATIONS

指标	Indicators	合计 Total	其中 of which #市级科协 Municipal Level Associations	市级学会 Municipal Level Academies
国内学术会议	**Domestic Academic Conferences**			
举办次数(次数)	Times(time)	1 485	14	1 429
参加人数(人次)	Participants (person-times)	286 623	3 000	269 069
交流论文(篇)	Papers Exchanged (piece)	28 644		28 168
境内国际学术会议	**International Academic Conferences**			
举办次数(次数)	Times(time)	75	1	72
参加人数(人次)	Participants (person-times)	52 839	3 232	49 360
交流论文(篇)	Papers Exchanged (piece)	8 378	2 289	6 073
港澳台地区学术会议	**Quantity of Academic Meeting Related with Hong Kong, Macao and Taiwan**			
举办次数(次数)	Times(time)	7		7
参加人数(人次)	Participants (person-times)	946		946
交流论文(篇)	Papers Exchanged (piece)	127		127
参加国外科技活动人数(人次)	**Participants in Foreign Scientific and Technological Activities (person-time)**	**43**		**243**
参加港澳台地区科技活动人数(人次)	**Participants in Hong Kong, Macao and Taiwan Scientific and Technological Activities (person-time)**	**3 093**		**3 093**
接待国外专家学者(人次)	**Reception of Foreign Experts and Scholars (person-time)**	**1 388**	**124**	**1 262**
接待港澳台地区专家学者(人次)	**Reception of Hong Kong, Macao and Taiwan Experts and Scholars (person-time)**	**215**	**11**	**204**

表 20.19　主要年份科技型企业状况
SCIENTIFIC AND TECHNOLOGICAL ENTERPRISES IN MAIN YEARS

指　标	Indicators	2000	2010	2017	2018
机构数（个）	**Number of Institutions (unit)**	**12 316**	**18 008**	**15 459**	**16 873**
从业人员（万人）	**Employment (10 000 persons)**	**26.33**	**94.25**	**172.68**	**180.50**
#从事科技活动人员	Scientific & Technological Personnel	12.95	21.69	61.75	63.88
#高中级技术职称人员	Personnel with Medium and Senior Titles	8.90	12.12	14.35	
资产总额(亿元)	Total Assets(100 million yuan)	1 064.07	9 070.91	40 494.00	44 738.30
总收入(亿元)	Revenue(100 million yuan)	811.35	8 462.57	25 454	27 405.65
研究开发费用(亿元)	Inner Expenditure on Scientific and Technological Activities (100 million yuan)				1 861.63
当年形成用于研究开发的固定资产(亿元)	Annual Fixed Assets Formation on Scientific and Technological Activities (100 million yuan)				154.08
来自政府部门的研究开发经费(亿元)	Government Funds on Scientific and Technological Activities (100 million yuan)				123.89
工业总产值(亿元)	Gross Output Value(100 million yuan)	311.22	5 687.91	12 976.00	13 265.69
利润总额(亿元)	Total Pre-tax Profits(100 million yuan)	47.58	601.59	2 597.00	2 212.31
税金总额(亿元)	Total Tax and Duties(100 million yuan)	28.64	417.57	333.23	1 337.71
出口创汇(亿美元)	Foreign Exchange Income(100 million USD)	2.83	647.36	427.95	417.27
专利申请量(件)	Patent Applications(piece)	452	31 997	83 682	89 717
#发明专利	Inventions		11 259	38 095	40 620
专利授权量(件)	Patent Certified(piece)	1 169	15 052	49 616	57 791
#发明专利	Inventions		3 912	18 093	16 049

注：本表统计范围是符合《上海市科技企业界定参考标准》(沪科〔2015〕70 号)的本市科技型企业。

Note: The statistical range of the data in this table is science and technology enterprises complied with <The reference definition standard of Shanghai science and technology enterprises>(Shanghai Science (2015) No. 70).

表 20.20 主要年份规模以上工业企业研究与试验发展(R&D)活动情况
BASIC STATISTICS OF RESEARCH AND DEVELOPMENT(R&D) OF INDUSTRIAL ENTERPRISES ABOVE THE SET SCALE IN MAIN YEARS

指标	Indicators	2000	2010	2017	2018
有 R&D 活动单位数(个)	**Quantity of Science and Technology Institutions (unit)**	**327**	**1 193**	**2 057**	**2 174**
R&D 人员投入情况	**Personnel Investment on R&D**				
R&D 人员(人)	R&D Personnel(person)	26 253	82 095	120 229	120 599
R&D 人员全时当量(人年)	Full-time Equivalent of R&D Personnel (person-year)	20 576	69 077	88 967	88 016
基础研究	Basic Research			20	67
应用研究	Applied Research	764	244	317	1 363
试验发展	Experimental Development	19 812	68 833	88 630	86 586
R&D 经费投入情况	**Expenditure on R&D**				
R&D 经费内部支出(亿元)	Intramural Expenditure on R&D (100 million yuan)	31.15	274.05	540.00	554.88
按活动类型分	By Activity Types				
基础研究	Basic Research			0.09	0.27
应用研究	Applied Research	1.33	2.00	1.97	7.25
试验发展	Experimental Development	29.82	272.05	537.93	547.35
按经费来源分	By Source of Funds				
政府资金	Government Funds	0.37	16.77	32.64	33.28
企业资金	Self-raised Funds by Enterprises	20.19	253.75	502.94	514.72
境外资金	Offshore Funds		2.37	2.09	4.87
R&D 项目(课题)情况	**R&D project**				
R&D 项目(课题)数(项)	Quantity of-Projects (item)	2 412	9 240	12 557	12 442
R&D 项目(课题)人员全时当量(人年)	Personnell Engaged in Projects (person-year)		60 232	82 293	82 834
R&D 项目(课题)经费内部支出(亿元)	Inner Expenditure on Projects (100 million yuan)	28.14	247.29	539.51	521.17
科技产出及成果情况	**Output of Science and Technic Activities**				
新产品产值(亿元)	Output Value of New Products (100 millon yuan)	1 355.19	5 870.20	9 159.91	8 609.79
新产品销售收入(亿元)	Sales Revenue of New Products (100 millon yuan)	1 351.69	6 543.07	10 068.15	9 796.73
发表科技论文数(篇)	Quantity of Science and Technic Papers Published(case)		2 846	3 029	3 032
形成国家或行业标准数(项)	Becoming The Formation of National or Industry Standards (item)		630	793	669
专利申请受理数(件)	Number of Patents Applications Accepted (piece)	1 455	14 967	27 581	29 258
#发明专利	Inventions	221	6 474	12 329	12 541
有效发明专利数(件)	Effective Invention Patents(piece)	468	9 822	43 416	47 940

注：本表 2000 年数据统计范围为大中型工业企业。
Note: Statistics range of data of 2000 is large and medium-sized industrial enterprises.

表 20.21 主要年份规模以上工业企业 R&D 人员情况
PERSONNEL FOR RESEARCH AND DEVELOPMENT(R&D) ACTIVITIES OF INDUSTRIAL ENTERPRISES ABOVE THE SET SCALE IN MAIN YEARS

单位:万人(10 000 persons)

类 别	Types	2010	2017	2018
总 计	**Total**	**8.21**	**12.02**	**12.06**
按隶属关系分	**By Subordination**			
中央单位	Central Units	1.41	1.40	1.14
地方单位	Local Units	6.80	10.62	10.92
按登记注册类型分	**By Registration Categories**			
内 资	Domestic Funded	7.37	6.38	6.31
#国 有	State-owned	0.92	0.05	0.01
有限责任公司	Companies with Limited Liabilities	1.88	2.53	2.33
股份有限公司	Share-holding Companies with Limited Liabilities	1.54	1.30	1.08
港澳台商投资	Hong Kong, Macao and Taiwan Funded	1.56	1.46	1.61
外商投资	Foreign Funded	6.09	4.18	4.14
按企业规模分	**By Size**			
#大型企业	Large	5.74	5.42	5.34
中型企业	Medium	6.23	3.34	3.03
小型企业	Small	3.05	3.25	3.67
按行业分	**By Sectors**			
#高技术产业	**High Technology Industry**	**4.47**	**3.16**	**3.31**
信息化学品制造	Information Chemical Product Manufacturing	0.03	0.01	0.01
医药制造业	Medicine Manufacturing	0.58	0.53	0.59
航空航天器制造	Aviation and Aircraft Manufacturing	0.23	0.19	0.21
电子及通信设备制造业	Electronic and Communicantion Equipment Manufacturing	2.47	1.76	1.75
电子计算机及办公设备制造业	Electronic Computer and Office Equipment Manufacturing	0.55	0.23	0.27
医疗设备及仪器仪表制造业	Medical Machinery amd Measuring Instrument Manufacturing	0.61	0.44	0.48
#六个重点发展工业行业	**Six Key Industries**	**11.32**	**9.22**	**9.22**
电子信息产品制造业	Electronic Information Product Manufacturing	3.59	2.57	2.30
汽车制造业	Automobile Manufacturing	1.92	2.39	2.49
石油化工及精细化工制造业	Petrochemical and Fine Chemical Products Manufacturing	0.90	0.70	0.78
精品钢材制造业	Fine Steel Manufacturing	0.53	0.21	0.21
成套设备制造业	Equipment Complex Manufacturing	3.61	2.55	2.57
生物医药制造业	Bio-medicine Manufacturing	0.77	0.80	0.87

表 20.22　规模以上工业企业 R&D 经费内部支出来源构成(2018)
STRUCTURE OF R&D INNER EXPENDITURE SOURCE OF INDUSTRIAL ENTERPRISES ABOVE THE SET SCALE

单位:亿元(100 million yuan)

类别	Types	R&D 经费内部支出合计 Total of R&D Inner Expenditure	其中 of which #政府资金 Government Funds	企业资金 Enterprise Funds	境外资金 Foreign Funds
总　计	**Total**	**554.88**	**33.28**	**514.72**	**4.87**
按隶属关系分	**By Subordination**				
中央单位	Central Units	63.65	14.78	48.78	0.08
地方单位	Local Units	491.23	18.49	465.94	4.79
按登记注册类型分	**By Registration Categories**				
内　资	Domestic Funded	258.25	28.04	228.28	1.72
#国　有	State-owned	0.18		0.18	
有限责任公司	Companies with Limited Liabilities	104.38	24.82	79.36	0.13
股份有限公司	Share-holding Companies with Limited Liabilities	72.16	1.03	69.77	1.34
港澳台商投资	Hong Kong, Macao and Taiwan Funded	59.68	1.39	56.32	0.52
外商投资	Foreign Funded	236.94	3.85	230.12	2.63
按企业规模分	**By Size**				
#大型企业	Large	347.15	28.08	314.14	3.43
中型企业	Medium	105.88	2.40	102.23	0.98
小型企业	Small	101.06	2.79	97.58	0.46
按行业分	**By Sectors**				
#高技术产业	High Technology Industry	127.31	26.72	98.23	1.18
信息化学品制造	Information Chemical Product Manufacturing	0.07	0.02	0.05	
医药制造业	Medicine Manufacturing	25.82	0.89	24.52	0.40
航空航天器制造	Aviation and Aircraft Manufacturing	13.10	12.17	0.93	
电子及通信设备制造业	Electronic and Communication Equipment Manufacturing	64.93	12.11	52.09	0.65
电子计算机及办公设备制造业	Electronic Computer and Office Equipment Manufacturing	6.68	0.14	5.43	0.02
医疗设备及仪器仪表制造业	Medical Machinery amd Measuring Instrument Manufacturing	16.71	1.39	15.21	0.11
#六个重点发展工业行业	**Six Key Industries**	**464.03**	**32.15**	**425.83**	**4.31**
电子信息产品制造业	Electronic Information Product Manufacturing	77.30	6.91	68.34	0.81
汽车制造业	Automobile Manufacturing	196.86	1.07	192.80	2.61
石油化工及精细化工制造业	Petrochemical and Fine Chemical Products Manufacturing	31.63	0.46	30.83	0.23
精品钢材制造业	Fine Steel Manufacturing	18.41	0.46	17.95	0.01
成套设备制造业	Equipment Complex Manufacturing	103.51	21.24	82.02	0.23
生物医药制造业	Bio-medicine Manufacturing	36.32	2.01	33.89	0.42

表 20.23 规模以上工业企业办科技机构情况(2018)
SCIENCE AND TECHNIC RESEARCH INSTITUTIONS FUNDED BY INDUSTRIAL ENTERPRISES ABOVE THE SET SCALE

类别	Types	科技机构数(个) Technological Development Institutions (unit)	机构人员数(万人) Quantity of Personnel (10 000 persons)	机构经费支出(亿元) Expenditure of Institutions (100 million yuan)	机构仪器设备原价(亿元) Original Value of Equipment (100 million yuan)
总 计	**Total**	**628**	**6.47**	**441.48**	**257.12**
按隶属关系分	**By Subordination**				
中央单位	Central Units	43	0.97	58.67	49.81
地方单位	Local Units	585	5.50	382.81	207.30
按登记注册类型分	**By Registration Categories**				
内 资	Domestic Funded	390	3.65	200.69	129.36
#国 有	State-owned	1	0.00	0.04	0.02
有限责任公司	Companies with Limited Liabilities	134	1.73	81.40	58.20
股份有限公司	Share-holding Companies with Limited Liabilities	43	1.04	89.62	49.18
港澳台商投资	Hong Kong, Macao and Taiwan Funded	82	0.68	34.13	43.86
外商投资	Foreign Funded	156	2.15	206.66	83.90
按企业规模分	**By Size**				
#大型企业	Large	94	3.89	343.81	162.49
中型企业	Medium	198	1.59	65.64	65.84
小型企业	Small	332	0.99	31.94	28.71
按行业分	**By Sectors**				
#高技术产业	High Technology Industry	154	1.33	60.29	57.43
#医药制造业	Medicine Manufacturing	52	0.36	18.39	13.01
航空航天器制造	Aviation and Aircraft Manufacturing	2	0.08	3.72	11.29
电子及通信设备制造业	Electronic and Communication Equipment Manufacturing	67	0.77	30.80	27.90
电子计算机及办公设备制造业	Electronic Computer and Office Equipment Manufacturing	8	0.02	2.66	1.66
医疗设备及仪器仪表制造业	Medical Machinery amd Measuring Instrument Manufacturing	25	0.10	4.72	3.57
#六个重点发展工业行业	**Six Key Industries**	**417**	**5.22**	**381.00**	**202.99**
电子信息产品制造业	Electronic Information Product Manufacturing	91	0.79	29.58	33.74
汽车制造业	Automobile Manufacturing	69	2.22	231.60	92.10
石油化工及精细化工制造业	Petrochemical and Fine Chemical Products Manufacturing	53	0.26	10.67	8.78
精品钢材制造业	Fine Steel Manufacturing	4	0.07	21.48	13.11
成套设备制造业	Equipment Complex Manufacturing	122	1.43	65.14	39.38
生物医药制造业	Bio-medicine Manufacturing	78	0.45	22.53	15.88

表 20.24 规模以上工业企业其他技术活动费用支出情况(2018)
SPECIAL TECHNICAL PROJECT FUNDS OF INDUSTRIAL ENTERPRISES ABOVE THE SET SCALE

单位:亿元 (100 million yuan)

类 别	Types	技术改造经费支出 Expenditures of Technical Transformation	技术引进经费支出 Expenditures of Technical Introduction	购买国内技术支出 Expenditures of Buying Domestic Technology
总 计	**Total**	**185.19**	**145.04**	**46.50**
按隶属关系分	**By Subordination**			
中央单位	Central Units	88.94	20.54	41.20
地方单位	Local Units	96.25	124.49	5.29
按登记注册类型分	**By Registration Categories**			
内 资	Domestic Funded	102.85	24.41	42.70
#国 有	State-owned			
有限责任公司	Companies with Limited Liabilities	19.97	13.30	11.14
股份有限公司	Share-holding Companies with Limited Liabilities	79.32	10.98	31.49
港澳台商投资	Hong Kong, Macao and Taiwan Funded	4.66	0.86	0.00
外商投资	Foreign Funded	77.68	119.77	3.80
按企业规模分	**By Size**			
#大型企业	Large	160.42	139.49	44.62
中型企业	Medium	12.53	4.89	1.74
小型企业	Small	12.22	0.66	0.14
按行业分	**By Sectors**			
#高技术产业	**High Technology Industry**	**3.48**	**4.67**	**10.75**
医药制造业	Medicine Manufacturing	0.85	0.71	0.36
航空航天器制造	Aviation and Aircraft Manufacturing			9.90
电子及通信设备制造业	Electronic and Communicantion Equipment Manufacturing	2.63	3.58	0.39
电子计算机及办公设备制造业	Electronic Computer and Office Equipment Manufacturing			
医疗设备及仪器仪表制造业	Medical Machinery amd Measuring Instrument Manufacturing		0.38	0.10
#六个重点发展工业行业	**Six Key Industries**	**59.29**	**164.38**	**142.97**
电子信息产品制造业	Electronic Information Product Manufacturing	2.63	3.76	0.48
汽车制造业	Automobile Manufacturing	53.74	75.70	120.07
石油化工及精细化工制造	Petrochemical and Fine Chemical Products Manufacturing		8.21	0.19
精品钢材制造业	Fine Steel Manufacturing	0.07	70.78	6.39
成套设备制造业	Equipment Complex Manufacturing	2.00	4.95	15.48
生物医药制造业	Bio-medicine Manufacturing	0.85	0.98	0.36

表 20.25 规模以上工业企业新产品产出情况(2018)
OUTPUT OF NEW PRODUCTS OF INDUSTRIAL ENTERPRISES ABOVE THE SET SCALE

单位:亿元 (100 million yuan)

类 别	Types	新产品产值 Output Value of New Products	新产品销售收入 Sales Revenue of New Products	其中 of which #新产品出口 Exports of New Products
总 计	**Total**	**8 609.79**	**9 796.73**	**1 309.64**
按隶属关系分	**By Subordination**			
中央单位	Central Units	912.32	906.03	283.25
地方单位	Local Units	7 697.47	8 890.70	1 026.39
按登记注册类型分	**By Registration Categories**			
内 资	**Domestic Funded**	**3 463.92**	**3 830.54**	**546.45**
#国 有	State-owned	9.04	9.03	
有限责任公司	Companies with Limited Liabilities	1 553.18	1 801.30	367.34
股份有限公司	Share-holding Companies with Limited Liabilities	856.68	868.45	62.55
港澳台商投资	Hong Kong, Macao and Taiwan Funded	765.58	819.25	331.10
外商投资	Foreign Funded	4 380.28	5 146.95	432.08
按企业规模分	**By Size**			
#大型企业	Large	5 645.46	6 574.00	875.54
中型企业	Medium	1 746.37	1 933.87	297.48
小型企业	Small	1 215.19	1 286.08	136.21
按行业分	**By Sectors**			
#高技术产业	**High Technology Industry**	**1 386.71**	**1 409.65**	**588.31**
信息化学品制造	Information Chemical Product Manufacturing	0.76	0.82	0.01
医药制造业	Medicine Manufacturing	297.66	271.27	14.94
航空航天器制造	Aviation and Aircraft Manufacturing	53.09	62.00	0.15
电子及通信设备制造业	Electronic and Communicantion Equipment Manufacturing	833.85	878.43	480.13
电子计算机及办公设备制造业	Electronic Computer and Office Equipment Manufacturing	84.39	80.75	71.24
医疗设备及仪器仪表制造业	Medical Machinery amd Measuring Instrument Manufacturing	116.96	116.38	21.84
#六个重点发展工业行业	**Six Key Industries**	**7 190.95**	**8 259.36**	**1 052.58**
电子信息产品制造业	Electronic Information Product Manufacturing	1 081.66	1 145.46	558.96
汽车制造业	Automobile Manufacturing	3 742.91	4 589.38	92.73
石油化工及精细化工制造业	Petrochemical and Fine Chemical Products Manufacturing	290.84	339.07	10.11
精品钢材制造业	Fine Steel Manufacturing	200.00	193.31	21.09
成套设备制造业	Equipment Complex Manufacturing	1 525.96	1 670.24	348.05
生物医药制造业	Bio-medicine Manufacturing	349.58	321.90	21.64

注：新产品既包括经政府有关部门认定并在有效期内的新产品，也包括企业自行研制开发，未经政府有关部门认定，从投产之日起一年之内的新产品。

Note: New Products include new products certified by relevant government agencies within the period of certification, as well as new products designed and produced by enterprices within a year without certification by government agencies.

表 20.26 主要年份大中型工业企业科技活动情况
SCIENCE AND TECHNIC ACTIVITIES OF LARGE AND MEDIUM INDUSTRIAL ENTERPRISES IN MAIN YEARS

指 标	Indicators	2000	2010	2017	2018
企业办科技机构数（个）	**Science and Technic Institutions Funded by Enterprises (unit)**	**264**	**638**	**308**	**292**
从事 R&D 活动人员数（万人）	**R&D Personnel (10 000 persons)**	**2.63**	**6.64**	**8.76**	**8.37**
#研究人员	Researchers	–	2.26	3.60	3.52
科技活动经费支出情况（亿元）	**Expenditures on Science and Technic Activities (100 million yuan)**				
#R&D 经费支出	R&D Expenditures	30.98	237.75	450.85	453.04
#新产品开发经费支出	Expenditures on New Products Development	47.56	302.45	556.10	609.91
其他技术活动费用支出(亿元)	**Other Expenditures on Technic Activities (100 million yuan)**	**117.47**	**235.63**	**320.53**	**423.42**
技术改造经费支出	Expenditures on Technological Transformation	75.31	123.21	156.03	172.95
技术引进经费支出	Expenditures on Technological Introduction	39.00	61.09	95.66	144.38
用于消化吸收的经费	Expenditures on Technological Digesting and Absorbing	2.41	28.68	47.37	59.73
购买国内技术支出	Expenditures on Buying Domestic Technology	0.75	22.65	21.47	46.36
科技项目情况	**Science and Technic Project**				
项目数（项）	Quantity of Projects (item)	5 140	11 384	6 392	5 977
项目人员（人）	Personnel of Project Groups (person)	45 254	94 165	80 634	59 210
项目经费内部支出(亿元)	Intramural Expenditure on Projects (100 million yuan)	63.72	309.75	450.43	425.57
科技活动产出情况	**Output of Science and Technic Activities**				
新产品产值(亿元)	Output Value of New Products (100 million yuan)	1 355.19	5 504.38	8 187.05	7 391.84
新产品销售收入(亿元)	New Products Sales Revenue (100 million yuan)	1 351.69	6 180.81	9 014.65	8 507.87
#新产品出口	New Products Exported	197.41	1 023.11	1 187.29	1 173.02

注：本表 2016 年起科技项目为 R&D 项目。
Note: The Science and Technic Project is R&D Project since 2016.

上/海/统/计/年/鉴

主要统计指标解释

科技活动

指在自然科学、农业科学、医药科学、工程与技术科学、人文与社会科学领域(简称科学技术领域)中,与科技知识的产生、发展、传播和应用密切相关的有组织的活动。可分为研究与试验发展(R&D)、研究与试验发展成果应用及相关的科技服务三类活动。

R&D

R&D是“科学研究与试验发展”的英文缩写。指在科学技术领域,为增加知识总量,以及运用这些知识去创造新的应用进行的系统的创造性的活动。R&D包括基础研究、应用研究、试验发展三类活动。

基础研究

指为了获得关于现象和可观察事实的基本原理的新知识(揭示客观事物的本质、运动规律,获得新发现、新学说)而进行的实验性或理论性研究,它不以任何专门或特定的应用或使用为目的。其成果以科学论文和科学著作为主要形式。用来反映知识的原始创新能力。

应用研究

指为获得新知识而进行的创造性研究,主要针对某一特定的目的或目标。应用研究是为了确定基础研究成果可能的用途,或是为达到预定的目标探索应采取的新方法(原理性)或新途径。其成果形式以科学论文、专著、原理性模型或发明专利为主。

试验发展

指利用从基础研究、应用研究和实际经验所获得的现有知识,为产生新的产品、材料和装置,建立新的工艺、系统和服务,以及对已产生和建立的上述各项作实质性的改进而进行的系统性工作。其成果形式主要是专利、专有技术、具有新产品基本特征的产品原型或具有新装置基本特征的原始样机等。在社会科学领域,试验发展是指把通过基础研究、应用研究获得的知识转变成可以实施的计划(包括为进行检验和评估实施示范项目)的过程。人文科学领域没有对应的试验发展活动。

科技活动人员

指直接从事科技活动、以及专门从事科技活动管理和为科技活动提供直接服务,累计从事科技活动的时间占全年制度工作时间10%及以上的人员。(1)直接从事科技活动的人员,包括:在独立核算的科学研究与技术开发机构、高等学校、各类企业及其他事业单位内设的研究室、实验室、技术开发中心及中试车间(基地)等机构中从事科技活动的研究人员、工程技术人员、技术工人及其它人员;虽不在上述机构工作,但编入科技活动项目(课题)组的人员;科技信息与文献机构中的专业技术人员;从事论文设计的研究生等。(2)专门从事科技活动管理和为科技活动提供直接服务的人员包括:独立核算的科学研究与技术开发机构、科技信息与文献机构、高等学校、各类企业及其他事业单位主管科技工作的负责人,专门从事科技活动的计划、行政、人事、财务、物资供应、设备维护、图书资料管理等工作的各类人员,但不包括保卫、医疗保健人员、司机、食堂人员、茶炉工、水暖工、清洁工等为科技活动提供间接服务的人员。

R&D人员

R&D人员一般用折合全时当量来表示。即参加R&D项目人员的全时当量及应分摊在R&D项目的管理和直接服务人员的全时当量两部分相加计算。一个折合全时当量是一人年。例如,一个人在R&D活动上花费了30%的正常工作时间而70%的时间用于其他工作,则其折合全时当量为0.3。

科技活动经费支出

指企事业单位实际支出的全部科技活动费用,包括来自科研渠道的经费、教育事业费、基本建设投资、技术改造投资等实际用于科技活动支出的费用。科技活动经费支出分为内部支出和外部支出。

R&D经费内部支出

指企事业单位用于内部开展R&D活动(包括基础研究、应用研究、试验发展)的实际支出。包括用于R&D项目(课题)活动的直接支出,以及间接用于R&D活动的管理费、服务费、与有关的基本建设支出以及外协加工费等。不包括生产性活动支出、归还贷款支出

主要统计指标解释

以及与外单位合作或委托外单位进行R&D活动而转拨给对方的经费支出。

■ 专　利

是专利权的简称，是对发明人的发明创造经审查合格后，由专利局依据专利法授予发明人和设计人对该项发明创造享有的专有权。专利包括发明、实用新型和外观设计三种类型。

■ 发　明

指对产品、方法或者其改进所提出的新的技术方案。是国际通行的反映拥有自主知识产权技术的核心指标。

■ 实用新型

指对产品的形状、构造或者其结合所提出的适于实用的新的技术方案。反映具有一定技术含量的技术成果情况。

■ 外观设计

指对产品的形状、图案、色彩或者其结合所作出的富有美感并适于工业上应用的新设计。反映拥有自主知识产权的外观设计成果情况。

■ 新产品

指采用新技术原理、新设计构思研制、生产的全新产品，或在结构、材质、工艺等某一方面比原有产品有明显改进，从而显著提高了产品性能或扩大了使用功能的产品。新产品既包括政府有关部门认定并在有效期内的新产品，也包括企业自行研制开发，未经政府有关部门认定，从投产之日起一年之内的新产品。

■ 独立研究与开发机构

指有明确的任务和研究方向，有一定学术水平的业务骨干和一定数量的研究人员，具有研究、开发、开展学术工作的基本条件，主要进行科学研究与技术开发活动，并且在行政上有独立的组织形式，财务上独立核算盈亏，有权与其他单位签订合同，在银行有单独户头的单位。

SHANGHAI STATISTICAL YEARBOOK

EXPLANATORY NOTES TO MAJOR STATISTICAL INDICATORS

□ Scientific and Technological Activities (S&T Activities)

Scientific and Technological Activities (S&T Activities) refer to organized activities which are closely related with the creation, development, dissemination and application of the scientific and technical knowledge in the fields of natural sciences, agricultural sciences, medical sciences, engineering and technological sciences, humanities and social sciences (referred to as scientific and technological fields). S&T activities can be classified into 3 categories: research and development (R&D) activities, application of R&D results, and related S&T services.

□ R&D

R&D is an abbreviation which stands for ′ Science Research and Experimental Development′ , which means systematic and creative endeavors aimed at expanding the overall volume of knowledge and applying the knowledge in systematic creation. R&D includes basic studies, application research and experimental development.

□ Basic Research

Basic Research refers to empirical or theoretical research aiming at obtaining new knowledge on the fundamental principles of phenomena of observable facts to reveal the nature and law of movement of objects and to acquire new discoveries or new theories. Basic research takes no specific or designated application as the aim of the research. Results of basic research are mainly released or disseminated in the form of scientific papers or monographs. This indicator reflects the original innovation capacity of knowledge.

□ Applied Research

Applied Research refers to creative research aiming at obtaining new knowledge on a specific objective or target. Purpose of the applied research is to identify the possible use of results from basic research, or to explore new (fundamental) methods or new approaches. Results of applied research are expressed in the form of scientific papers, monographs, fundamental models or invention patents.

□ Experimental Development

Experimental Development refer to systematic activities aiming at using the knowledge from basic and applied researches or from practical experience to develop new products, materials and equipment, to establish new production process, systems and services, or to make substantial improvement on the existing products, process or services. Results of experiment and development activities are embodied in patents, exclusive technology, and monotype of new products or equipment. In social sciences, experiment and development activities refer to the process of converting the knowledge from basic or applied researches into feasible programmes (including conduct of demonstration projects for assessment and evaluation). There are no experiment and development activities in the science of humanities.

□ Personnel Engaged in S&T Activities

Personnel Engaged in S&T Activities refer to personnel directly engaged in S&T activities, in the management of S&T activities, and in providing direct service to S&T activities, who spend over 10% of the total working hours in a year in S&T activities. (1) Personnel directly engaged in S&T activities include researchers, engineers, technicians and other related personnel engaged in S&T activities in independent- accounting R&D institutions, institutions of higher learning, and in research institutes, laboratories, technology development centers and central experiment workshops under enterprises and institutions. Also included are people working in S&T information archiving institutes, and graduate students working on the design of their thesis. (2) Personnel engaged in the management of S&T activities and in providing direct service to S&T activities include senior management people responsible for S&T activities in independent-accounting R&D institutions, S&T information archiving institutes, institutions of higher learning, and in enterprises and institutions where S&T activities are undertaken. Also included are people responsible for the planning, administration, personnel management, financial management, logistics supply, equipment maintenance, information and library management that are related with S&T activities. People providing indirect services are excluded, such as security, medical ser-

EXPLANATORY NOTES TO MAJOR STATISTICAL INDICATORS

vice, drivers, plumbers, cleaners and those providing catering and related service.

□ R&D Personnel

R&D Personnel generally amount to the full-time equivalent. It equals the full-time equivalent of personnel engaged in the R&D projects plus the full-time equivalent of personnel directly manage and service the allocated R&D projects. A full-time equivalent refers to a person year. For example, a person spent thirty percent of common working time on R&D activities and seventy percent on other jobs, then the full-time equivalent is 0.3.

□ Expenditures on Science and Technical Activities

Expenditures on Science and Technical Activities refers to the total expenditures that the enterprises actually spent on science and technical activities. It includes expenditures on scientific research, education expenses, basic construction investment, investment on technical transformation. It is divided into internal expenditure and external expenditure.

□ Internal Expenditure on R&D

Internal Expenditure on R&D refers to the actually expense on R&D activities inside enterprises. It includes the direct expense on R&D projects, and indirect expense, such as management fees, service fees, basic construction investment and processing fees, on R&D activities. But it does not include the expenditures for productive activities, expenditures on repay the loans and the expenditures pay for the R&D activities entrusted to other enterprises.

□ Patent

Patent is an abbreviation for the patent right and refers to the exclusive right of ownership by the inventors or designers for the creation or inventions, given from the patent offices after due process of assessment and approval in accordance with the Patent Law. Patents are granted for inventions, utility models and designs.

□ Invention

Inventions refer to the new technical proposals to the products or methods or their modifications. This is universal core indicator reflecting the technologies with independent intellectual property.

□ Utility Models

Utility Models refer to the practical and new technical proposals on the shape and structure of the product or the combination of both. This indicator reflects the condition of technological results with certain technical content.

□ Exterior Designs

Exterior Designs refer to the aesthetics and industrially applicable new designs for the shape, pattern and color of the product, or their combinations. This indicator reflects the appearance design achievements with independent intellectual property.

□ New Products

New Products refer to new products produced with new technology and new design, or products that represent noticeable improvement in terms of structure, material, or production process so as to improve significantly the character or function of the older versions. They include new products certified by relevant government agencies within the period of certification, as well as new products that are not certified by relevant government agencies and are designed and produced by enterprises within one year since they are put into production.

□ Independent Research and Development Institutions

Independent Research and Development Institutions refer to the state-owned institutions which have direct mission and research purpose, a certain research level and quantities of personnel, favorable conditions for R&D and engaging in scientific research and technological development. The institutions also have their own independent organization, accounting system authority to sign contract with other units, and their own accounts in banks.

第二十一篇

CHAPTER 21

教育

EDUCATION

简要说明

一、本篇资料的主要内容

教育统计资料包括公办教育和民办教育、学历教育和非学历教育。具体有高等教育(研究生教育、普通高等教育和成人高等教育)、中等教育(高中阶段教育、初中阶段教育和成人中等教育)、初等教育(小学)、学前教育(幼儿园)、特殊教育(特殊教育学校和工读学校等)和留学生教育等资料。主要指标包括学校数、在校学生数、招生数、毕业生数、教职工数和专任教师数等。

二、本篇资料的来源

教育统计资料由上海市教育委员会提供。

BRIEF INTRODUCTION

I. Main Contents

Data on education cover the situations on education funded by government and non-government agencies, and the education with and without academic credentials including higher education (education of postgraduates, general higher education and adult education), secondary education (senior and junior high schools), elementary education (primary schools), preschool education, special education (special education schools and reformatory schools) and overseas education. The main indicators include the number of schools, the number of students enrolled, the number of new students enrolled, the number of graduates, the number of staff and workers, the number of full-time teachers.

II. Sources of Data

Data on education are provided by Shanghai Municipal Education Commission.

表 21.1 主要年份教育事业基本情况
BASIC STATISTICS OF EDUCATION IN MAIN YEARS

指 标	Indicators	2000	2010	2017	2018
学校数（所）	**Quantity of Schools (unit)**	**2 225**	**1 730**	**1 747**	**1 740**
普通高等学校	Regular Institutions of Higher Education	37	66	64	64
普通中等学校	Secondary Schools	1 133	869	912	925
中等专业学校	Specialized Secondary Schools	84	65	50	50
职业中学	Vocational Secondary Schools	60	26	25	23
技工学校	Technical Worker Schools	115	10	7	7
普通中学	Regular Secondary Schools	861	755	818	833
工读学校	Reformatory	13	13	12	12
普通小学	Primary Schools	1 021	766	741	721
特殊教育学校	Special Education Schools	34	29	30	30
教职工数（万人）	**Quantity of Teachers and Staff (10 000 persons)**	**22.73**	**21.42**	**22.44**	**22.85**
普通高等学校	Regular Institutions of Higher Education	6.01	7.42	7.39	7.51
普通中等学校	Secondary Schools	10.43	8.26	8.60	8.74
中等专业学校	Specialized Secondary Schools	1.27	0.91	0.74	0.72
职业中学	Vocational Secondary Schools	0.66	0.43	0.36	0.35
技工学校	Technical Worker Schools	0.77	0.13	0.10	0.09
普通中学	Regular Secondary Schools	7.66	6.73	7.36	7.54
工读学校	Reformatory	0.07	0.06	0.05	0.04
普通小学	Primary Schools	6.13	5.58	6.29	6.44
特殊教育学校	Special Education Schools	0.16	0.16	0.16	0.16
专任教师（万人）	**Quantity of Full-time Teachers (10 000 persons)**	**12.83**	**14.52**	**16.50**	**17.03**
普通高等学校	Regular Institutions of Higher Education	2.05	3.92	4.35	4.46
普通中等学校	Secondary Schools	6.26	5.97	6.56	6.76
中等专业学校	Specialized Secondary Schools	0.53	0.50	0.47	0.47
职业中学	Vocational Secondary Schools	0.39	0.29	0.28	0.27
技工学校	Technical Worker Schools	0.30	0.07	0.05	0.05
普通中学	Regular Secondary Schools	5.01	5.07	5.72	5.93
高 中	Senior Secondary Schools	1.42	1.67	1.79	1.84
初 中	Junior Secondary Schools	3.59	3.40	3.93	4.10
工读学校	Reformatory	0.03	0.04	0.04	0.03
普通小学	Primary Schools	4.43	4.52	5.47	5.68
特殊教育学校	Special Education Schools	0.09	0.11	0.13	0.13

注：2018 年，普通中学学校数中，完全中学 89 所，高级中学 143 所，初级中学 369 所，九年一贯制学校 204 所，十二年一贯制学校 28 所。

Note: In regular secondary schools in 2018, there are 89 whole secondary schools, 143 senior high schools, 369 junior high schools, 204 system schools of 9 years and 28 system schools of 12 years.

表 21.1 续表 continued

	指 标 Indicators	2000	2010	2017	2018
毕业生数(万人)	**Graduates (10 000 persons)**	**55.67**	**47.14**	**45.04**	**44.94**
普通高等学校	Regular Institutions of Higher Education	4.09	13.37	13.42	13.25
普通中等学校	Secondary Schools	32.76	21.24	17.23	16.59
中等专业学校	Specialized Secondary Schools	3.86	3.34	2.14	2.07
职业中学	Vocational Secondary Schools	3.99	1.38	0.70	0.61
技工学校	Technical Worker Schools	1.86	0.31	0.24	0.27
普通中学	Regular Secondary Schools	22.92	16.13	14.12	13.62
高 中	Senior Secondary Schools	7.18	6.24	5.13	5.19
初 中	Junior Secondary Schools	15.74	9.89	8.99	8.43
工读学校	Reformatory	0.13	0.08	0.03	0.02
普通小学	Primary Schools	18.73	12.44	14.31	15.03
特殊教育学校	Special Education Schools	0.09	0.09	0.08	0.07
招生数(万人)	**New Student Enrollment (10 000 persons)**	**52.23**	**50.66**	**51.02**	**54.03**
普通高等学校	Regular Institutions of Higher Education	8.13	14.46	14.28	14.34
普通中等学校	Secondary Schools	33.71	21.07	20.30	21.38
中等专业学校	Specialized Secondary Schools	3.00	2.99	1.90	1.80
职业中学	Vocational Secondary Schools	2.44	1.23	0.69	0.66
技工学校	Technical Worker Schools	1.68	0.42	0.28	0.38
普通中学	Regular Secondary Schools	26.46	16.33	17.38	18.51
高 中	Senior Secondary Schools	7.84	5.39	5.33	5.23
初 中	Junior Secondary Schools	18.62	10.94	12.06	13.28
工读学校	Reformatory	0.13	0.10	0.04	0.03
普通小学	Primary Schools	10.28	15.05	16.37	18.25
特殊教育学校	Special Education Schools	0.11	0.08	0.07	0.06
在校学生(万人)	**Student Enrollment (10 000 persons)**	**207.61**	**197.70**	**196.65**	**200.28**
普通高等学校	Regular Institutions of Higher Education	22.68	51.57	51.49	51.78
普通中等学校	Secondary Schools	105.53	75.47	66.22	68.04
中等专业学校	Specialized Secondary Schools	11.89	10.91	6.31	5.98
职业中学	Vocational Secondary Schools	8.48	3.77	1.97	1.99
技工学校	Technical Worker Schools	5.37	1.08	0.81	0.93
普通中学	Regular Secondary Schools	79.54	59.44	57.06	59.07
高 中	Senior Secondary Schools	23.94	16.89	15.89	15.82
初 中	Junior Secondary Schools	55.60	42.55	41.17	43.25
工读学校	Reformatory	0.25	0.27	0.07	0.07
普通小学	Primary Schools	78.86	70.16	78.49	80.02
特殊教育学校	Special Education Schools	0.54	0.50	0.43	0.44

表21.2 每万人口在校学生数、每个教师负担学生数(1978~2018)
STUDENTS ENROLLMENT PER 10 000 PERSONS AND STUDENTS TAUGHT BY EACH TEACHER

单位:人(person)

年 份 Year	平均每万人口在校学生数 Students Enrollment per 10 000 Persons				平均每个教师负担学生数 Students Taught by Each Teacher		
	大学生 Colleges and Universities	中专生 Speciallized Secondary Schools	中学生 Secondary Schools	小学生 Primary Schools	普通高等学校 Institutions of Higher Education	普通中等学校 Regular Secondary Schools	普通小学 Primary Schools
1978	46	14	908	789	3	17	18
1979	60	21	719	774	4	16	19
1980	67	24	544	742	4	13	18
1981	78	25	427	713	5	11	17
1982	71	28	451	665	4	12	16
1983	66	30	433	665	4	10	16
1984	74	37	404	686	4	11	17
1985	88	48	391	683	4	12	17
1986	94	55	387	693	5	11	17
1987	97	55	381	706	5	11	17
1988	100	51	355	764	5	11	18
1989	96	49	351	809	5	11	19
1990	90	46	362	826	5	11	19
1991	87	45	379	825	5	12	19
1992	88	47	401	830	5	13	22
1993	95	54	417	845	6	14	21
1994	100	66	468	815	6	15	21
1995	101	76	512	776	7	16	20
1996	102	68	525	734	7	16	20
1997	103	75	500	688	8	16	20
1998	108	81	483	630	8	17	19
1999	119	83	489	556	9	17	19
2000	141	74	494	490	11	17	18
2001	168	73	481	433	13	16	17
2002	194	74	461	393	14	17	17
2003	214	78	427	367	16	16	17
2004	227	77	451	293	15	17	14
2005	234	72	407	283	14	16	14
2006	237	70	362	272	14	15	14
2007	235	62	318	258	14	14	14
2008	235	56	289	276	14	13	14
2009	232	52	273	304	13	13	15
2010	224	47	258	305	13	13	16
2011	218	44	252	311	13	12	16
2012	213	42	248	319	13	12	16
2013	209	38	246	328	13	12	16
2014	209	32	241	331	12	11	16
2015	212	30	246	331	12	11	15
2016	213	28	236	326	12	10	15
2017	213	26	236	325	12	10	14
2018	214	25	244	330	12	10	14

表21.3 各级各类学校在校学生数(1978~2018)
STUDENTS ENROLLMENT BY VARIOUS SCHOOLS

单位:万人(10 000 persons)

年份 Year	普通高等学校 Institutions of Higher Education	普通中等学校 Secondary Schools	其中 of which 中等专业学校 Specialized Secondary Schools	普通中学 Regular Secondary Schools	职业学校 Secondary Vocational Schools	技工学校 Technical Worker Schools	普通小学 Primary Schools	特殊教育学校 Special Education Schools
1978	5.06	101.81	1.55	100.26			87.06	0.18
1979	6.74	90.80	2.42	81.72		6.66	88.00	0.18
1980	7.67	71.68	2.81	62.71	0.29	5.87	85.47	0.18
1981	9.11	58.82	2.94	49.93	0.45	5.50	83.22	0.16
1982	8.39	61.69	3.30	53.53	0.85	4.01	78.88	0.16
1983	7.87	60.53	3.61	52.04	1.71	3.17	79.82	0.23
1984	8.99	61.01	4.48	49.18	3.07	4.28	83.47	0.21
1985	10.79	63.50	5.92	48.23	4.69	4.66	84.18	0.23
1986	11.77	64.82	6.86	48.31	4.71	4.94	86.56	0.25
1987	12.25	64.50	7.03	48.21	4.08	5.18	89.35	0.28
1988	12.82	61.20	6.52	45.68	3.69	5.31	98.39	0.30
1989	12.61	61.01	6.45	46.10	3.54	4.92	106.02	0.32
1990	12.13	62.59	6.17	48.31	3.66	4.45	110.19	0.33
1991	11.69	65.92	6.01	51.24	3.97	4.70	111.38	0.35
1992	11.95	70.84	6.41	54.77	4.90	4.76	113.37	0.38
1993	13.10	76.54	7.58	57.69	6.39	4.88	116.70	0.44
1994	14.04	87.23	9.23	65.56	7.54	4.90	113.98	0.52
1995	14.41	96.38	10.85	72.40	8.64	4.49	109.78	0.57
1996	14.79	99.97	9.95	76.23	9.12	4.67	106.46	0.62
1997	15.38	100.81	11.10	74.43	10.29	4.99	102.44	0.63
1998	16.51	102.53	12.38	73.85	10.72	5.58	96.14	0.52
1999	18.63	105.66	13.06	76.69	10.21	5.70	87.16	0.53
2000	22.68	105.28	11.89	79.54	8.48	5.37	78.86	0.54
2001	28.00	104.37	12.12	80.23	7.48	4.54	72.28	0.48
2002	33.16	103.59	12.66	78.97	7.56	4.40	67.24	0.55
2003	37.85	100.71	13.69	75.47	7.04	4.51	64.83	0.55
2004	41.57	106.94	14.05	82.78	6.43	3.68	53.74	0.54
2005	44.26	99.24	13.67	77.02	5.76	2.79	53.50	0.52
2006	46.63	92.25	13.70	71.17	5.33	2.05	53.37	0.50
2007	48.49	85.17	12.81	65.60	5.20	1.56	53.33	0.50
2008	50.29	79.97	12.08	61.77	4.80	1.32	59.06	0.51
2009	51.28	77.07	11.50	60.37	4.14	1.06	67.12	0.50
2010	51.57	75.20	10.91	59.44	3.77	1.08	70.16	0.50
2011	51.13	73.96	10.22	59.17	3.52	1.05	73.11	0.49
2012	50.66	73.45	9.88	59.04	3.55	0.98	76.04	0.49
2013	50.48	72.63	9.23	59.35	3.24	0.81	79.25	0.47
2014	50.66	69.67	7.74	58.42	2.72	0.79	80.30	0.46
2015	51.16	67.39	7.24	57.05	2.32	0.78	79.87	0.45
2016	51.47	66.67	6.68	57.11	2.04	0.84	78.97	0.43
2017	51.49	66.15	6.31	57.06	1.97	0.81	78.49	0.43
2018	51.78	67.97	5.98	59.07	1.99	0.93	80.02	0.44

注：本表中普通中等学校在校学生数中不包括工读学校在校学生。
Note: Quantity of students enrollment of secondary schools in this table doesn't include those of reformatory schools.

表 21.4 主要年份各阶段教育实施情况
BASIC STATISTICS OF VARIOUS PHASES EDUCATION IN MAIN YEARS

单位:%

指 标	Indicators	2000	2010	2017	2018
小 学	**Primary Schools**				
小学学龄儿童净入学率	Enrollment Rate of Schoolage Children	99.9	99.9	99.9	99.9
初 中	**Junior Schools**				
初中学生净入学率	Enrollment Rate of Students in Junior Secondary School Phase	99.9	99.9	99.9	99.9
高 中	**Senior Schools**				
高中阶段新生入学率	Enrollment Rate ofStudents in Senior Secondary School Phase	97.0	96.5	99.7	99.4
普通高中招生比例	Recruit Students Rate of Regular Senior Secondary Schools	51	51	60	61

表 21.5 主要年份各级民办学校基本情况
BASIC STATISTICS OF CIVIL SCHOOLS IN MAIN YEARS

类 别	Types	2000	2010	2017	2018
民办高等学校	**Civil Institutions of Higher Education**				
学校数(所)	Schools (unit)	3	20	20	19
在校学生(万人)	Students Enrollment(10 000 persons)	0.67	9.37	10.82	11.03
专任教师(人)	Full-time Teachers(person)	304	3 906	4 993	5 082
民办中学	**Civil Secondary Schools**				
学校数(所)	Schools (unit)	155	109	129	131
班级数(个)	Classes(unit)	1 842	2 103	2 390	2 488
在校学生(万人)	Students Enrollment(10 000 persons)	8.48	7.87	8.05	8.37
高 中	Senior	4.54	1.68	1.59	1.45
初 中	Junior	3.94	6.19	6.45	6.92
专任教师(人)	Full-time Teachers(person)	2 400	4 583	6 813	7 505
民办小学	**Civil Primary Schools**				
学校数(所)	Schools (unit)	35	184	139	111
班级数(个)	Classes(unit)	987	3 747	3 094	3 004
在校学生(万人)	Students Enrollment(10 000 persons)	3.95	16.42	11.23	10.66
专任教师(人)	Full-time Teachers(person)	831	7 181	6 944	7 052
民办幼儿园	**Civil Kindergarten**				
学校数(所)	Schools (unit)	92	396	601	623
班级数(个)	Classes(unit)	636	3 584	5 925	5 973
在校学生(万人)	Students Enrollment(10 000 persons)	1.77	9.91	17.37	16.78
专任教师(人)	Full-time Teachers(person)	1 056	7 161	11 042	11 166

表 21.6 民办学校(园)基本情况(2018) BASIC STATISTICS OF CIVIL SCHOOLS

单位:人(person)

指标	Indicators	学校数(所) Schools (unit)	毕业生数 Graduates	招生数 Students Recruited	在校生数 Students Enrollment	专任教师数 Full-time Teachers
普通高等学校	Institutions of Higher Education	19	29 609	34 514	110 336	5 082
普通中学	Regular Secondary Schools	131	18 150	23 348	83 696	7 505
高　中	Senior Schools	63	4 958	4 260	14 457	18 350
初　中	Junior Schools	68	13 192	19 088	69 239	40 996
普通小学	Primary Schools	111	21 556	22 774	106 641	7 052
幼儿园	Kindergartens	623	58 621	53 293	167 834	11 166

注：根据《民办教育促进法》的新规定，民办中、小学统计口径中扣除了公立转制学校。
Note: According to new provision of Civil Education Advance Law, the scope of civil secondary and primary school excluded public schools transformed.

表 21.7 主要年份外国留学生情况 STATISTICS OF FOREIGN STUDENT IN MAIN YEARS

指标	Indicators	2005	2010	2017	2018
外国留学生人数(人)	**Quantity of Foreign Students(person)**	**13 691**	**17 340**	**31 941**	**34 005**
按费用来源分	By Tuition Resource				
中国政府资助	Chinese Government Sustentation	934	2 585	7 607	9 270
本国政府资助	Homeland Government Sustentation	15	347	406	378
国际组织资助	International Organization Sustentation			24	18
学校间交换	Inter-school Communion	463	1 570	3 602	3 971
自　费	Commoners	12 279	12 838	20 302	20 368
按地区来源分	By District				
亚　洲	Aisa	10 490	11 689	17 499	18 032
非　洲	Africa	289	969	2 475	2 769
欧　洲	Europe	1 927	3 023	8 078	8 760
北美洲	North America	766	983	2 921	3 131
南美洲	South America	129	477	644	697
大洋洲	Oceania	90	199	324	616

表 21.8　主要年份研究生人数
QUANTITY OF POST GRADUATE STUDENTS IN MAIN YEARS

单位：人(person)

年　份 Year	获博士学位人数 Quantity of Doctor's Degrees Obtained	获硕士学位人数 Quantity of Master's Degrees Obtained	研究生 Postgraduates 毕业生数 Graduates 普通高等学校 Institutions of Higher Education	毕业生数 Graduates 研究所(院) Research Institutions (Academies)	招生数 New Students Enrollment 普通高等学校 Institutions of Higher Education	招生数 New Students Enrollment 研究所(院) Research Institutions (Academies)	在读人数 Students Enrollment 普通高等学校 Institutions of Higher Education	在读人数 Students Enrollment 研究所(院) Research Institutions (Academies)
1978			9		1 072		1 253	
1980			6		410		2 696	
1985	57	1 371	1 543	37	4 264	83	8 163	170
1990	300	2 746	2 953	369	2 803	324	8 533	1 035
1991	342	2 739	2 936	320	2 717	302	8 020	949
1992	343	2 124	2 262	264	3 323	345	8 858	997
1993	368	2 489	2 569	315	3 919	363	10 037	1 008
1994	442	2 363	2 608	251	4 665	465	11 905	1 185
1995	606	2 742	3 038	317	4 776	525	13 378	1 335
1996	627	3 233	3 537	323	5 915	592	15 307	1 528
1997	890	3 585	4 117	358	6 163	562	16 841	1 619
1998	1 090	3 552	4 253	389	7 281	593	19 499	1 663
1999	1 323	4 288	5 196	415	8 758	655	22 656	1 764
2000	1 307	4 546	5 435	433	11 796	856	28 582	2 032
2001	1 487	5 330	6 380	437	14 751	1 075	36 528	2 515
2002	1 655	6 067	7 481	445	17 848	1 363	45 713	3 183
2003	1 994	7 683	9 501	578	20 767	1 757	55 092	3 998
2004	2 678	10 580	12 788	681	23 545	1 789	64 747	4 690
2005	3 119	13 245	15 857	884	25 845	1 847	73 557	5 171
2006	3 772	15 957	18 833	1 098	28 250	1 849	81 487	5 419
2007	4 355	19 250	22 691	1 235	28 748	1 862	86 177	5 586
2008	4 483	20 734	24 431	1 322	30 195	1 947	89 778	5 720
2009	4 661	23 622	26 949	1 342	35 418	2 007	97 639	5 853
2010	4 749	23 458	26 843	1 364	36 619	2 024	105 711	6 006
2011	4 610	25 568	29 431	1 385	37 971	2 109	112 902	6 115
2012	4 913	29 270	33 189	1 417	41 899	2 330	120 503	6 511
2013	5 077	30 311	34 148	1 521	43 659	2 564	127 803	6 996
2014	4 516	32 056	36 013	559	43 353	577	131 806	1 748
2015	4 490	33 378	37 289	579	45 400	605	136 539	1 748
2016	5 009	34 724	39 181	552	48 450	626	143 172	1 806
2017	5 513	34 912	40 425	557	58 906	613	151 536	1 785
2018	5 412	37 018	42 462	619	62 971	657	176 905	1 885

①2001 年前的获博士学位和获硕士学位的人数为当年毕业生人数。
②2014 学年起，中科院、煤炭院所属科研机构不纳入本市研究生培养机构统计。
❶Quantity of Doctor's and Master's Degrees obtained refer to Quantity of graduates in this year before 2001.
❷Since 2014 school year, subsidiary institutions of Chinese Academy of Science and Coal Research Institute are not included in the statistics of postgraduage training mechanism.

表 21.9 普通高等学校基本情况（2018）
BASIC STATISTICS OF INSTITUTIONS OF HIGHER EDUCATION

类别	Types	学校（所）Institutions (unit)	毕业生数（人）Graduates (person)	招生数（人）New Students Enrollment (person)	在校学生人数（人）Students Enrollment (person)	教职员工（人）Staff and Workers (person)	其中 of which #专任教师 Full-time Teacher	其中 of which #正、副高级 Senior and Associate Title
总计	**Total**	**64**	**132 508**	**143 428**	**517 796**	**75 115**	**44 585**	**22 865**
综合大学	Comprehensive Universities	4	15 033	16 504	67 748	25 164	11 737	8 096
理工院校	Science and Engineering	24	51 043	55 745	198 734	21 060	14 068	6 238
农业院校	Agriculture and Forestry	2	4 090	4 153	15 155	1 468	1 073	463
医药院校	Medical	2	3 581	4 648	15 126	2 108	1 236	482
师范院校	Teacher Training	2	8 278	8 576	34 912	6 907	4 228	2 723
语文院校	Linguistics and Literacy	3	5 376	4 493	14 850	1 913	1 247	498
财经院校	Economics and Finance	17	34 353	37 519	129 919	10 925	7 329	2 847
政法院校	Politics and Law	3	6 105	6 677	23 347	2 391	1 695	652
体育院校	Physical Culture	2	1 053	1 149	4 493	1 210	682	321
艺术院校	Art Schools	5	3 596	3 964	13 512	1 969	1 290	545

注：学生数中未包括在读研究生人数，在分类院校学生数中未包括成人高等学校中的普通本专科学生。

Note: Post-graduates are not included in the students enrollment. Undergraduates and junior college students in adult education schools are not included in the students enrollment by types of colleges.

表 21.10 普通高等学校分科专任教师数（2018）
FULL-TIME TEACHERS IN INSTITUTIONS OF HIGHER EDUCATION BY SUBJECTS

单位：人（person）

类别	Types	专任教师数 Full-time Teachers	其中 of which 正高级 Senior Title	副高级 Associate Title	中级 Junior Title	初级 Primary Title	无职称 Non-Title
总计	**Total**	**44 585**	**8 462**	**14 403**	**17 209**	**2 715**	**1 796**
哲学	Philosophy	999	190	283	416	65	45
经济学	Economics	2 413	417	857	930	101	108
法学	Law	3 385	547	983	1 414	265	176
教育学	Education	3 508	288	903	1 673	464	180
文学	Literature	6 735	779	1 873	3 323	423	337
历史学	History	590	183	179	206	12	10
理学	Science	5 064	1 624	1 827	1 381	93	139
工学	Engineering	12 397	2 973	4 559	4 056	483	326
农学	Agriculture	339	84	116	103	18	18
医学	Medical	2 387	531	756	855	152	93
管理学	Administration	3 786	564	1 273	1 514	252	183
艺术学	Art	2 982	282	794	1 338	387	181

表21.11 普通高等学校本科分科学生数(2018)
UNDERGRADUATE STUDENTS IN INSTITUTIONS OF HIGHER EDUCATION BY SUBJECTS

单位:人(person)

类 别	Types	毕业生人数 Graduates	招生人数 New Students Enrollment	在校学生人数 Students Enrollment
总 计	**Total**	**85 832**	**98 157**	**383 459**
哲 学	Philosophy	128	127	530
经济学	Economics	8 454	9 314	36 983
法 学	Law	5 479	5 929	22 786
教育学	Education	2 059	2 583	9 576
文 学	Literature	8 914	10 083	37 537
历史学	History	237	438	1 229
理 学	Science	4 862	6 056	22 700
工 学	Engineering	27 957	34 192	132 126
农 学	Agriculture	401	596	2 160
医 学	Medical	2 538	4 441	16 521
管理学	Administration	18 149	17 007	71 839
艺术学	Art	6 654	7 391	29 472

表21.12 中等专业学校基本情况(2018)
BASIC STATISTICS OF SPECIALIZED SECONDARY SCHOOLS

单位:人(person)

类 别	Types	毕业生数 Graduates	招生数 New Students Enrollment	在校学生 Students Enrollment	专任教师 Full-time Teachers in Professional Course	其中 of which: #正副高级 Senior and Associate Title	中级 Junior Title
总 计	**Total**	**20 715**	**18 029**	**59 779**	**4 691**	**1 143**	**2 324**
#土木水利工程	Construction and Water Conservancy Engineering	1 660	1 664	4 752	112	36	44
加工制造	Machining and Manufacture	3 297	2 926	10 326	428	126	207
交通运输	Transport	2 201	1 792	6 232	163	36	85
信息技术	Information Technology	2 096	2 232	6 839	340	76	169
医药卫生	Health	2 430	1 509	5 708	164	61	81
财经商贸	Trade and Tour	4 834	3 325	11 312	463	97	259
旅游服务	Finance and Economics	610	764	2 095	81	18	43
文化艺术	Culture and Art	1 205	1 023	4 149	283	76	146
体育与健身	Sports and Fitness	214	162	471	151	45	57
公共管理与服务	Society Commonality Business	215	364	913	21	7	10

表 21.13 各区普通中学基本情况(2018)
BASIC STATISTICS OF REGULAR SECONDARY SCHOOLS BY DISTRICTS

地 区 District		学 校 (所) Schools (unit)	毕业生数 (人) Graduates (person)	招生数 (人) New Students Enrollment (person)	在校学生 (人) Students Enrollment (person)	教职员工 (人) Staff and Workers (person)	其中 of which #专任教师 Full-time Teachers
总 计	**Total**	**833**	**136 214**	**185 100**	**590 712**	**75 398**	**59 346**
浦东新区	Pudong New Area	167	31 561	45 485	140 580	14 623	12 548
黄 浦 区	Huangpu	35	5 739	7 459	22 984	3 482	2 714
徐 汇 区	Xuhui	40	9 318	11 901	38 764	4 634	3 708
长 宁 区	Changning	26	4 059	5 118	16 887	2 893	2 036
静 安 区	Jing'an	51	8 510	10 332	34 367	4 900	3 677
普 陀 区	Putuo	48	6 259	8 641	27 906	3 930	3 039
虹 口 区	Hongkou	37	5 223	6 428	21 540	3 152	2 703
杨 浦 区	Yangpu	49	7 710	9 270	31 091	4 192	3 396
闵 行 区	Minhang	75	11 207	19 057	57 091	7 257	5 508
宝 山 区	Baoshan	68	9 981	13 477	43 458	4 589	3 988
嘉 定 区	Jiading	44	6 927	10 028	31 504	3 772	2 910
金 山 区	Jinshan	34	5 957	7 335	24 694	3 289	2 494
松 江 区	Songjiang	44	7 928	11 763	36 629	5 327	3 510
青 浦 区	Qingpu	33	5 260	6 958	22 997	3 052	2 412
奉 贤 区	Fengxian	45	6 480	7 260	24 402	3 261	2 644
崇 明 区	Chongming	37	4 095	4 588	15 818	3 045	2 059

表 21.14 各区普通中学初、高中学生基本情况(2018)
BASIC STATISTICS OF REGULAR JUNIOR AND SENIOR SCHOOLS' STUDENTS BY DISTRICTS

单位:人 (person)

地 区	District	毕业生数 Graduates		招生数 New Students Enrollment		在校学生 Students Enrollment	
		初 中 Junior	高 中 Senior	初 中 Junior	高 中 Senior	初 中 Junior	高 中 Senior
总 计	**Total**	**84 272**	**51 942**	**132 770**	**52 330**	**432 531**	**158 181**
浦东新区	Pudong New Area	20 105	11 456	33 825	11 660	105 572	35 008
黄 浦 区	Huangpu	2 521	3 218	4 320	3 139	13 778	9 206
徐 汇 区	Xuhui	5 074	4 244	7 920	3 981	26 303	12 461
长 宁 区	Changning	2 472	1 587	3 692	1 426	12 402	4 485
静 安 区	Jing'an	4 872	3 638	6 920	3 412	23 761	10 606
普 陀 区	Putuo	3 659	2 600	6 225	2 416	20 366	7 540
虹 口 区	Hongkou	3 071	2 152	4 350	2 078	15 156	6 384
杨 浦 区	Yangpu	4 126	3 584	5 863	3 407	20 464	10 627
闵 行 区	Minhang	7 316	3 891	14 549	4 508	43 944	13 147
宝 山 区	Baoshan	6 588	3 393	10 180	3 297	33 351	10 107
嘉 定 区	Jiading	4 709	2 218	7 537	2 491	24 385	7 119
金 山 区	Jinshan	4 003	1 954	4 998	2 337	17 711	6 983
松 江 区	Songjiang	5 434	2 494	8 986	2 777	28 484	8 145
青 浦 区	Qingpu	3 404	1 856	5 026	1 932	17 204	5 793
奉 贤 区	Fengxian	4 473	2 007	5 146	2 114	18 093	6 309
崇 明 区	Chongming	2 445	1 650	3 233	1 355	11 557	4 261

表21.15 各区普通小学基本情况(2018)
BASIC STATISTICS OF REGULAR PRIMARY SCHOOLS BY DISTRICTS

地 区	District	学 校(所) Schools (unit)	毕业生数(人) Graduates (person)	招生数(人) New Students Enrollment (person)	在校学生(人) Students Enrollment (person)	教职员工(人) Staff and Workers (person)	其中 of which #专任教师 Full-time Teachers
总 计	**Total**	**721**	**150 256**	**182 522**	**800 222**	**64 356**	**56 803**
浦东新区	Pudong New Area	162	39 613	44 593	200 262	13 901	13 076
黄 浦 区	Huangpu	29	4 016	4 739	20 822	2 159	1 799
徐 汇 区	Xuhui	43	7 820	10 095	44 212	3 155	2 730
长 宁 区	Changning	23	4 278	4 953	22 207	1 997	1 661
静 安 区	Jing'an	44	6 746	8 087	35 576	3 267	2 609
普 陀 区	Putuo	24	7 007	9 203	40 241	3 096	2 903
虹 口 区	Hongkou	33	4 396	4 994	22 719	2 175	1 981
杨 浦 区	Yangpu	42	6 035	8 912	37 905	3 200	2 914
闵 行 区	Minhang	66	17 490	21 658	94 572	7 238	6 273
宝 山 区	Baoshan	68	12 011	15 609	67 600	5 372	5 115
嘉 定 区	Jiading	42	8 323	11 870	48 749	3 610	2 973
金 山 区	Jinshan	26	5 065	5 693	24 703	2 305	1 935
松 江 区	Songjiang	37	11 086	14 645	62 010	4 958	4 126
青 浦 区	Qingpu	26	7 105	6 886	29 289	2 914	2 525
奉 贤 区	Fengxian	27	5 928	7 355	33 869	2 656	2 452
崇 明 区	Chongming	29	3 337	3 230	15 486	2 353	1 731

表 21.16 主要年份实验性示范性中学基本情况
BASIC STATISTICS OF SECONDARY CAMPUS SCHOOL IN MAIN YEARS

指 标	Indicators	2000	2010	2017	2018
学校(所)	Schools (unit)	84	128	148	147
班级数(个)	Classes (unit)	2 584	4 063	4 383	4 363
在校学生(万人)	Students Enrollment(10 000 persons)	12.10	14.67	15.26	15.56
教职员工(万人)	Staff and Workers (10 000 persons)	1.40	1.88	2.08	2.10
# 专任教师	Full-time Teachers	0.88	1.42	1.67	1.69

注：实验性示范性中学包括重点中学和寄宿制高级中学。
Note: Secondary campus school includs important secondary school and boarding high school.

表 21.17 主要年份幼儿园基本情况
BASIC STATISTICS OF KINDERGARTENS IN MAIN YEARS

指 标	Indicators	2000	2010	2017	2018
幼儿园(所)	Kindergartens (unit)	958	1 252	1 591	1 627
幼儿数(万人)	Children Enrollment (10 000 persons)	24.12	40.03	57.27	57.14
教职员工(万人)	Staff and Workers(10 000 persons)	2.52	4.09	6.66	7.06
# 教 师	Teachers	1.50	2.67	4.01	4.14

表 21.18 主要年份特殊教育基本情况
BASIC STATISTICS OF SPECIAL EDUCATION IN MAIN YEARS

指 标	Indicators	2000	2010	2017	2018
学校 (所)	Schools (unit)	34	29	30	30
毕业生数(人)	Graduates(person)	868	918	840	693
招生数(人)	New Students Enrollment(person)	1 141	776	734	481
在校学生(人)	Students Enrollment(person)	5 407	5 036	4 330	3 987
教职员工(人)	Staff and Workers(person)	1 584	1 596	1 623	1 641
# 专任教师	Full-time Teachers	943	1 143	1 268	1 286

表 21.19 网络教育本科学生情况(2018)
BASIC STATISTICS OF UNDERGRADUATE STUDENTS OF NETWORK EDUCATION BY SUBJECT

单位:人(person)

类 别	Types	毕业生人数 Graduates	招生人数 New Students Enrollment	在校学生人数 Students Enrollment
总 计	**Total**	**31 025**	**34 164**	**91 070**
#经济学	Economics	1 329	1 647	4 690
法 学	Law	1 045	554	1 588
教育学	Education	939	446	1 514
文 学	Literature	1 679	1 699	4 721
理 学	Science	240	313	720
工 学	Engineering	4 877	4 213	11 916
医 学	Medical	4 732	5 375	15 462
管理学	Administration	15 206	18 835	47 076
艺术学	Art	828	1 027	3 161

表 21.20 各级各类成人学校基本情况(2018)
BASIC STATISTICS OF ADULT SCHOOLS AT VARIOUS LEVELS

类 别	Types	学校数(所) Schools (unit)	毕业生人数(人) Graduates (person)	招生数(人) New Students Enrollment (person)	在校学生人数(人) Students Enrollment (person)	教职员工人数(人) Staff and Workers (person)	其中 of which #专任教师 Full-time Teachers
成人高等教育	**Adult Higher Education**	**14**	**46 168**	**45 574**	**128 566**	**1 425**	**728**
广播电视大学	Broadcasting and TV Universities	1				342	118
职工高等学校	Staff Higher Education Schools	10	1 457	1 792	5 387	792	496
管理干部学院	Institutes for Administrative Officials	3	284	106	577	291	114
普通高等学校办	Run by Regular High Education Institutions	55	44 427	43 676	122 602		
#函 授	Correspondence Programs	9	2 413	1 010	4 548		
业 余	Spare Time	46	42 014	42 666	118 054		
成人网络本、专科	**Adult Network Education**		**13 508**	**25 384**	**53 948**		
成人中等专业学校	Specialized Secondary Schools	12	5 130	4 961	13 569	264	113
成人职业技术学校	**Adult Technical Secondary Schools**	**631**	**1 703 741**		**1 781 765**	**14 051**	**7 914**

注:成人职业技术学校毕业生及在校学生数为培训半年以上人次数。

Note: Graduates and Students Enrollment of adult technical secondary schools refers to accumulative total number of students registered at schools who has been trained more than half a year.

上 / 海 / 统 / 计 / 年 / 鉴

主要统计指标解释

■ 学 校

指按国家规定的设置标准和审批程序批准设立的，招收适龄人口实施各级各类教育活动的教育机构。

■ 普通高等学校

指按照国家规定的设置标准和审批程序批准举办的，通过全国普通高等学校统一招生考试，招收高中毕业生为主要培养对象，实施高等教育的全日制大学、独立设置的学院和高等专科学校、高等职业学校和其他机构。

大学、独立设置的学院主要实施本科层次以上教育，高等专科学校、高等职业学校实施专科层次教育，其他机构是承担国家普通招生计划任务不计校数的机构。包括普通高等学校分校和批准筹建的普通高等学校等。

■ 成人高等学校

指按国家规定的设置标准和审批程序举办的，通过全国成人高等教育统一招生考试，招收高中毕业或同等学历的人员为主要培养对象，利用函授、业余、脱产的多种形式对其实施高等学历教育的学校。包括：职工高等学校、农民高等学校、管理干部学院、教育学院、独立函授学院、广播电视大学、其他机构等。

■ 中等专业学校

指经县或县以上教育行政部门批准设立，招收初中毕业生实施中等专业课程教育的教学机构。

■ 职业中学(职业高中、职业初中)

指经县或县以上教育行政部门批准设立，招收小学或初中毕业生实施中等职业技术教育的教学机构。按学校性质类别可分为：独立设置的职业中学(包括：职业初中、职业高中、职业初高中合设学校)；附设有普通中学班的职业中学。

■ 普通中学(普通高中、普通初中)

普通中学分为普通高级中学和普通初级中学两个阶段。普通初级中学是指独立设置的招收小学毕业的适龄人口进行初级中等基础教育的机构；普通高级中学是指独立设置的招收初中毕业的适龄人口进行高级中等基础教育的机构；完全中学是指普通初、高中合设的教育机构；一贯制学校是指在一所学校连续实施中小学教育的机构。其中包括实施九年义务教育的九年一贯制学校和实施高中教育的十二年一贯制学校。(说明：一贯制学校的办学条件如能划分为小学、初中、高中，则分开填报；如不能划分清楚，可按就高不就低的方法填入初中、高中报表中，不能重复填写。)

■ 普通小学

指由区或区以上教育行政部门批准，招收学龄儿童实施初等教育的教学机构。

■ 幼儿园

指招收三周岁以上(含三周岁)学龄前幼儿，对其进行保育和教育的单位。

■ 特殊教育学校

指本市独立设置的招收盲聋哑和智残儿童，以及其他特殊需要的儿童、青少年进行普通或职业初、中等教育的教学机构。

■ 小学学龄儿童净入学率

小学学龄人口中正在接受小学教育人数所占比重。

■ 初中学生净入学率

是指初中阶段教育(接受普通初中教育和职业初中教育)在校学生总数占初中阶段教育学龄人口数的比重。

SHANGHAI STATISTICAL YEARBOOK

EXPLANATORY NOTES TO MAJOR STATISTICAL INDICATORS

□ School Institutions

School Institutions refer to education establishments set up according to the government evaluation and approval procedures, enrolling population of the right age, providing various phase education activity.

□ Regular Institutions of Higher Education

Regular Institutions of Higher Education refer to educational establishments set up according to the government evaluation and approval procedures, enrolling graduates from senior secondary schools and providing higher education courses and training for senior professionals. They include full-time universities, colleges, high professional schools, high professional vocational schools and others.

Universities and colleges are mainly providing undergraduate courses; those high professional schools and high professional vocational schools are mainly providing professional trainings; and others refer to educational establishments, which are responsible for enrolling students but not covered in the total number of schools, including: branch schools of universities and colleges, and universities and colleges that have been proved and prepared to construct.

□ Institutions of Higher Education for Adults

Institutions of Higher Education for Adults refer to educational establishments, set up in line with relevant rules approved by the government, enrolling personnel with senior secondary schools or equivalent education, and providing higher education courses in many forms of correspondence, spare time, or full time for adults. Institutions of higher schools for adults include schools of higher educations for staff and workers, schools of higher education for peasants, colleges for management cadres, pedagogical colleges, independent correspondence colleges, Radio and TV universities and other educational establishments, etc.

□ Specialized Secondary Schools

Specialized Secondary schools refer to educational establishments set up according to approval and permission by educational administration department of district and above government, enrolling graduates from junior secondary schools and providing secondary professional education courses.

□ Vocational Secondary Schools (senior secondary schools and junior secondary schools)

Vocational Secondary Schools (senior secondary schools and junior secondary schools) refer to educational establishments set up according to approval and permission by educational administration department of district and above government, enrolling graduates from primary schools and junior secondary schools and providing secondary vocational education courses.

□ Regular Secondary Schools (senior secondary schools and junior secondary schools)

Regular Secondary Schools (senior secondary schools and junior secondary schools) are classified as senior secondary schools and junior secondary schools. Junior Secondary Schools refer to educational establishments enrolling graduates from primary schools and providing junior secondary educational courses. Senior Secondary Schools refer to educational establishments enrolling graduates from junior secondary schools and providing higher secondary educational courses.

□ Regular Primary Schools

Regular Primary Schools refer to educational establishments set up according to approval and permission by educational administration department of district and above government, enrolling graduates from children of school age and providing primary educational courses.

□ Kindergartens

Kindergartens refer to nursery and education establishments, enrolling children in 3 years old and above.

□ Special Education Schools

Special Education Schools refer to educational establishments set up independently, enrolling blind, deaf, dumb, amentia or other special children, and educational establishment, providing regular or vocational junior and senior secondary education for hobbledehoy.

EXPLANATORY NOTES TO MAJOR STATISTICAL INDICATORS

□ Enrollment Rate of School-age Children

Enrollment Rate of School-age Children refers to the proportion of school age children enrolled at schools to the total number of school age children both in and outside schools.

□ Enrollment Rate of Students in Junior Secondary School Phase

It refers to the proportion of total quantity of student in junior secondary school to the population of junior school age.

第二十二篇

CHAPTER 22

卫生、社会保障和社会福利业

HEALTH, SOCIAL SECURITY AND SOCIAL WELFARE

简要说明

一、本篇资料的主要内容

本篇主要反映卫生、社会保障和社会福利的发展情况。

卫生部分主要包括卫生机构、卫生技术人员、卫生机构床位、医疗机构诊疗入院、疾病死亡原因、婴儿死亡原因、三大死亡率、防病工作、家庭病床、妇幼卫生工作、公民献血用血、卫生总费用等情况。

社会保障部分主要包括城乡基本养老保险、城镇职工基本医疗保险、城乡居民基本医疗保险、城镇职工失业保险、城镇职工生育保险、城镇职工工伤保险、少儿住院基金等参保人数情况。

社会福利部分主要包括社会保障标准、社会福利事业机构、民间组织、养老服务、医疗服务和红十字会等情况。

二、本篇资料的来源

卫生部分资料由上海市卫生和计划生育委员会提供。社会保障资料由上海市人力资源和社会保障局提供。社会福利资料中，社会保障标准、社会福利事业机构、民间组织、养老服务资料由上海市民政局提供；医疗服务资料由上海市卫生和计划生育委员会提供；红十字会资料由上海市红十字会提供。

BRIEF INTRODUCTION

I. Main Contents

Data in this chapter mainly reflect the development of public health, social security, and social welfare.

Data on public health include mainly the number of medical and healthcare institutions, medical personnel, beds available at such institutions, in–patients medical treatment and death–causing diseases, infant death–causing diseases and composition, top three death–causing diseases, disease prevention, family sickbeds, work of gynecology and pediatrics, blood offered and used by citizens, total expenditure on health.

Data on social security include mainly the numbers of participants in urban basic pension insurance, urban employee basic medical care insurance, urban basic medical care insurance, unemployment insurance, maternity insurance, work injury insurance, rural social medical care insurance, and medical fund of children.

Data on social welfare include social security standards, social welfare institutions, civil organizations, services for aged people, medical services and basic statistics about the Red Cross Society of China Shanghai Municipal Branch.

II. Sources of data

Data on public health are provided by Shanghai Municipal Health and Family Planning Commission. Data on social security are provided by Shanghai Municipal Human Resources and Social Security Bureau. Of data on social welfare, data on social security standards, social welfare institutions, civil organizations, and services for aged people are provided by Shanghai Civil Affairs Bureau; data on medical services are provided by Shanghai Health and Family Planning Commission; data on Red Cross are provided by the Red Cross Society of China Shanghai Municipal Branch.

表 22.1 卫生事业基本情况(1978~2018)
BASIC STATISTICS OF PUBLIC HEALTH

年 份 Year	卫生机构数(个) Health Care Institutions (unit)	其中 of which #医 院 Hospitals	卫 生 技术人员(万人) Medical Professionals (10 000 persons)	其中 of which #执 业(助理)医师 Licensed (Assistant) Doctors	卫生机构床位数(万张) Beds in Health Care Institutions (10 000 beds)	其中 of which #医 院 Hospitals	每万人口医生数(人) Doctors per 10 000 Persons (person)	每万人口医院床位数(张) Hospital Beds per 10 000 Persons (bed)
1978	4 823	388	8.50	3.35	5.47	4.68	30	42
1979	5 627	394	8.88	3.58	5.56	4.78	31	42
1980	6 067	399	9.41	3.92	5.80	4.94	34	43
1981	6 337	403	9.57	4.37	5.84	4.99	37	43
1982	6 445	408	9.88	4.72	5.93	5.11	40	43
1983	6 451	415	10.09	4.87	6.00	5.20	41	43
1984	6 318	420	10.24	4.84	6.16	5.34	40	44
1985	7 245	405	10.42	4.85	6.02	5.32	39	43
1986	7 306	419	10.71	4.91	6.22	5.47	39	44
1987	7 330	431	11.00	5.05	6.38	5.60	40	44
1988	7 471	444	11.46	5.40	6.79	5.89	42	46
1989	7 550	460	11.65	5.73	6.87	6.04	44	46
1990	7 690	462	11.84	5.82	6.96	6.21	44	47
1991	7 554	463	11.92	5.89	7.01	6.31	44	47
1992	7 363	454	11.82	5.88	7.07	6.42	43	47
1993	6 077	486	11.53	5.75	7.12	6.75	42	49
1994	5 606	497	11.20	5.52	7.20	6.81	39	49
1995	5 286	485	11.06	5.37	7.10	6.69	38	47
1996	5 200	477	10.95	5.24	7.00	6.73	36	46
1997	5 028	474	10.89	5.13	7.00	6.78	34	46
1998	4 637	473	10.84	5.03	7.02	6.83	33	45
1999	4 620	465	10.81	5.06	7.24	7.06	32	45
2000	4 400	459	10.71	4.99	7.53	7.31	31	45
2001	3 813	432	10.51	4.85	7.88	7.63	30	47
2002	2 422	436	10.16	4.38	8.15	8.13	27	50
2003	2 319	452	10.22	4.41	8.44	8.11	26	47
2004	2 577	489	10.17	4.38	8.64	8.50	25	49
2005	2 527	487	10.35	4.40	9.08	8.93	25	50
2006	2 519	505	10.90	4.55	9.44	9.28	25	51
2007	2 646	288	12.24	4.88	9.59	7.54	26	41
2008	2 809	301	12.77	5.12	9.78	7.78	27	41
2009	3 013	296	13.09	5.11	9.97	7.95	27	41
2010	3 270	306	13.54	5.13	10.51	8.48	22	37
2011	3 358	308	13.91	5.21	10.71	8.75	22	37
2012	3 465	317	14.61	5.42	10.96	9.00	23	38
2013	4 929	328	15.64	5.81	11.43	9.47	24	39
2014	4 987	332	16.40	6.13	11.75	9.83	25	41
2015	5 016	338	17.02	6.31	12.28	10.35	26	42
2016	5 011	349	17.82	6.55	12.92	11.01	27	46
2017	5 144	363	18.80	6.83	13.46	11.59	28	48
2018	5 298	364	20.65	7.49	14.72	12.90	31	53

①2002 年开始,卫生指标按照新的《中国卫生统计调查制度》统计。
②2007 年开始,医院统计范围按照新的《2007 国家卫生统计调查制度》统计,不再包括社区卫生服务中心、妇幼保健院和专科防治院。
③2013 年开始,卫生机构,卫生技术人员和床位数中包含村卫生室相关数据。
❶Since 2002, statistics of health care has been based on “China Health Care Statistical Investigation System”.
❷Since 2007, statistics of hospital has been based on “2007 National Health Care Statistical Investigation System”, not including the community health care service center, maternity and child care hospital and special disease hospital.
❸Since 2013, data of health institutions, health technology personnel and beds contain the related data of village health rooms.

表 22.2 各类卫生机构、床位及人员数(2018) VARIOUS HEALTH CARE INSTITUTIONS,BEDS AND PERSONNEL

机构类别	Type of Institutions	机构数(个) Health Care Institutions (unit)	床位数(张) Beds (bed)	从业人员数(人) Personnel (person)
总　计	**Total**	**5 298**	**147 249**	**251 358**
#医　院	Hospitals	364	129 007	172 847
综合医院	Comprehensive Hospitals	176	72 758	116 391
中医医院	Hospitals of Traditional Chinese Medicine	19	6 164	10 049
中西医结合医院	Hospitals of Traditional Chinese and Western Medicine	10	4 626	6 737
专科医院	Special Diseases Hospitals	121	33 031	34 894
护理院	Nursing Homes	38	12 428	4 776
基层医疗卫生机构	Basic Medical and Health Institutions	4 729	16 042	62 283
社区卫生服务中心(站)	Community Health Care Centers	1 038	16 042	36 059
村卫生室	Village Health Rooms	1 162		1 929
门诊部	Policlinics	917		16 909
诊所、卫生所、医务室、护理站	Clinics, Health Centers and Infirmaries	1 612		7 386
专业公共卫生机构	Professional Medical and Health Institutions	108	1 337	12 568
疾病预防控制中心	Disease Prevention and Control Centers	19		3 048
专科疾病防治院(所、站)	Special Disease Hospitals and Institutions	16	34	1 191
健康教育所(站、中心)	Health Education Institutions	1		137
妇幼保健院(所、站)	Maternity and Child Care Hospitals and Institutions	20	1 303	3 152
急救中心(站)	First-aid Centers	11		2 931
采供血机构	Blood Collection and Supply Institutions	8		748
卫生监督所(中心)	Health Supervision Centers	17		1 209
计划生育技术服务机构	The Family Planning Technical Service Institutions	16		152
其他卫生机构	Other Health Care Institutions	97	863	3 660
疗养院	Sanatoriums	4	863	488
卫生监督检验(监测、检测)所(站)	Health Supervision and Inspection Institutions	1		210
医学科学研究机构	Institutions of Medical Science	9		511
医学在职培训机构	Medical In-service Training Institutions	9		258
临床检验中心(所、站)	Clinical Test Centers	27		1 281
其　他	Others	47		912

表 22.2 续表 continued

机构类别 Type of Institutions		#卫生技术人员 Medical Professionals	其中 of which: #执业(助理)医师 Licensed (Assistant) Doctors	其中 of which: 注册护士 Registered Nurses
总 计	**Total**	**206 468**	**74 948**	**93 478**
#医 院	Hospitals	144 302	47 132	71 928
综合医院	Comprehensive Hospitals	98 125	32 874	49 124
中医医院	Hospitals of Traditional Chinese Medicine	8 537	3 262	3 585
中西医结合医院	Hospitals of Traditional Chinese and Western Medicine	5 833	2 132	2 792
专科医院	Special Diseases Hospitals	28 172	8 125	14 690
护理院	Nursing Homes	3 635	739	1 737
基层医疗卫生机构	Basic Medical and Health Institutions	51 723	23 913	19 174
社区卫生服务中心(站)	Community Health Care Centers	30 427	12 905	11 446
村卫生室	Village Health Rooms	1 929	1 201	11
门诊部	Policlinics	13 453	6 441	5 647
诊所、卫生所、医务室、护理站	Clinics, Health Centers and Infirmaries	5 914	3 366	2 070
专业公共卫生机构	Professional Medical and Health Institutions	8 656	3 472	2 081
疾病预防控制中心	Disease Prevention and Control Centers	2 319	1 384	48
专科疾病防治院(所、站)	Special Disease Hospitals and Institutions	947	468	320
健康教育所(站、中心)	Health Education Institutions	43	26	
妇幼保健院(所、站)	Maternity and Child Care Hospitals and Institutions	2 652	1 013	1 249
急救中心(站)	First-aid Centers	1 250	549	150
采供血机构	Blood Collection and Supply Institutions	541	25	312
卫生监督所(中心)	Health Supervision Centers	891		
计划生育技术服务机构	The Family Planning Technical Service Institutions	13	7	2
其他卫生机构	Other Health Care Institutions	1 787	431	295
疗养院	Sanatoriums	346	144	133
卫生监督检验(监测、检测)所(站)	Health Supervision and Inspection Institutions	176	4	
医学科学研究机构	Institutions of Medical Science	305	100	9
医学在职培训机构	Medical In-service Training Institutions	38	15	16
临床检验中心(所、站)	Clinical Test Centers	558	62	7
其 他	Others	364	106	130

表22.3 各区卫生机构基本情况（2018）
STATISTICS OF HEALTH CARE INSTITUTIONS BY DISTRICTS

地 区	District	机构数（个）Health Care Institutions(unit)	床位数（张）Hospital Beds (bed)	卫生技术人员(人) Medical Professionals (person)	其中 of which #执业(助理)医师 Licensed (Assistant) Doctors	注册护士 Registered Nurses
总 计	**Total**	**5 298**	**147 249**	**206 468**	**74 948**	**93 478**
浦东新区	Pudong New Area	934	19 382	27 171	10 515	11 609
黄浦区	Huangpu	272	13 869	23 896	8 621	11 157
徐汇区	Xuhui	351	16 442	24 705	8 617	11 359
长宁区	Changning	252	7 878	12 015	4 232	5 695
静安区	Jing'an	308	13 485	19 803	6 821	9 281
普陀区	Putuo	204	7 746	10 622	3 867	4 837
虹口区	Hongkou	162	7 921	10 956	3 871	5 161
杨浦区	Yangpu	217	12 832	17 058	5 716	8 499
闵行区	Minhang	442	10 815	13 588	4 909	6 392
宝山区	Baoshan	279	8 767	9 543	3 422	4 221
嘉定区	Jiading	366	6 222	8 059	3 290	3 436
金山区	Jinshan	277	4 396	6 229	2 230	2 749
松江区	Songjiang	264	5 301	7 171	2 656	2 919
青浦区	Qingpu	346	3 993	5 540	2 122	2 241
奉贤区	Fengxian	268	5 134	5 796	2 283	2 274
崇明区	Chongming	356	3 066	4 316	1 776	1 648

表 22.4　医疗机构病床使用情况(2018)
STATISTICS OF HOSPITAL BED USAGE IN MEDICAL TREATMENT INSTITUTION

机构类别	Types	平均开放床位数(张) Average Beds Opened(bed)	病床周转次数(次) Turnover Times of Beds(time)	病床使用率(%) Usage Rate of Beds(%)	出院者平均住院日(日) Average Days to Inpatient in Hospital(day)
总　计	**Total**	**143 830.97**	**31.10**	**93.58**	**10.89**
卫生部门	Medical Institutions	105 238.69	36.81	97.39	9.74
#医　院	Hospital	87 798.88	41.60	99.47	8.74
#综合医院	Comprehensive Hospitals	53 513.11	47.17	99.64	7.74
中(西)医医院	Hospitals of Chinese (Western) Medicine	10 379.84	39.98	96.51	8.85
护理院	Nursing Hospitals	830.24	2.24	97.86	122.09
社区卫生服务中心(站)	Community Health Care Centers	15 744.67	4.38	87.99	77.05
其他部门	Other Departments	38 592.27	15.53	83.20	18.31

表 22.5　医疗机构诊疗人次和入院人数(2018)
PATIENTS TREATED AND INPATIENTS IN MEDICAL TREATMENT INSTITUTION

机构类别	Types	诊疗人次(万人次) Total Patients Treated(10 000 person-times)	其中 of which #门、急诊 Outpatients and Emergency Patients	入院人数(万人) Inpatients (10 000 persons)	每百诊次的入院人数(人) Inpatients per 100 Patient-times (person)
总　计	**Total**	**27 637.78**	**26 082.20**	**447.52**	**1.62**
医　院	Hospitals	16 524.22	16 435.90	425.28	2.57
综合医院	Comprehensive Hospitals	11 528.49	11 467.41	294.94	2.56
中(西)医医院	Hospitals of Chinese(Western) Medicine	2 489.09	2 485.09	41.49	1.67
传染病医院	Infectious Diseases Hospitals	63.60	63.60	2.74	4.30
精神病医院	Mental Hospitals	192.32	190.73	1.54	0.80
结核病医院	Tuberculosis Hospitals	121.71	121.71	10.25	8.42
肿瘤医院	Tumor Hospitals	162.29	162.29	9.71	5.98
儿童医院	Children's Hospitals	656.90	656.90	13.57	2.07
其他专科医院	Other Specialized Hospitals	1 228.33	1 207.21	48.31	3.93
护理院	Nurse Hospitals	81.49	80.96	2.73	3.35
社区卫生服务中心(站)	Community Health-care Service Centers (Stations)	8 577.62	8 384.84	6.85	0.08
妇幼保健院(所、站)	Maternity and Child Care Hospital	236.50	228.60	7.35	3.11
其他医疗机构	Other Medical Facilities	2 299.44	1 032.86	8.04	0.35

表 22.6 前十位疾病死亡原因和构成(2018)
THE TOP 10 DEATH-CAUSING DISEASES AND COMPOSITION

死亡原因	Cause of Death	死亡专率(1/10 万) Death Rate(1/100 000)	占死亡总数(%) Percentage of Total Death(%)
循环系病	Circulation Diseases	352.08	41.25
肿　瘤	Tumor	262.78	30.79
呼吸系病	Respiratory System Diseases	70.05	8.21
内分泌营养代谢病	Endocrine-Immunity-Metabolic Diseases	44.88	5.26
损伤中毒	Damnification and Poisoning	39.44	4.62
消化系病	Digestive System Diseases	19.44	2.28
神经系病	Nervous System Disease	12.83	1.50
精神病	Mental System Diseases	9.38	1.10
泌尿生殖系病	Genitourinary Diseases	7.55	0.88
传染病及寄生虫病	Infectious & Parasitic Diseases	7.13	0.84

表 22.7 婴儿前五位疾病死亡原因和构成(2018)
THE TOP 5 INFANT DEATH-CAUSING DISEASES AND COMPOSITION

死亡原因	Cause of Death	死亡专率(1/10 万) Death Rate(1/100 000)	占死亡总数(%) Percentage of Total Death(%)
先天异常	Congenital Anomaly	80.01	38.83
新生儿病	Neonatal Disease	75.62	36.70
损伤中毒	Damnification and Poisning	18.63	9.04
神经系病	Nervous System Disease	6.58	3.19
内分泌营养代谢病	Endocrine-Immunity-Metabolic Diseases	3.29	1.60

表 22.8 婴儿死亡率、新生儿死亡率、孕产妇死亡率(2015~2018)
DEATH RATE OF INFANT,NEW BORN,PREGNANT AND LYING-IN WOMAN

指　标	Indicators	2015	2016	2017	2018
婴儿死亡率(‰)	Death Rate of Infant(‰)	4.58	3.76	3.71	3.52
新生儿死亡率(‰)	Death Rate of New Born(‰)	2.27	2.05	2.12	2.17
孕产妇死亡率(1/10 万)	Death Rate of Pregnant and Lying-in Woman(1/100 000)	6.66	5.64	3.01	1.15

注：2016 年起，婴儿死亡率和孕产妇死亡率调整为上海地区口径，不再包含本市户籍妇女在外省市生育的数据。
Note: Since 2016, the statistic coverage of infant mortality rate and the maternal mortality rate has been adjusted to the Shanghai region, and no longer include data on the births of women in other provinces and cities.

表 22.9　主要年份防病工作情况
BASIC STATISTICS OF DISEASE PREVENTION IN MAIN YEARS

指　标	Indicators	2000	2010	2017	2018
传染病发病总例数（甲、乙）(万例)	**Cases of Contagious Diseases Reported (A,B) (10 000 cases)**	**3.58**	**2.22**	**2.32**	**2.11**
发病率(1/10 万)	Disease Rate(1/100 000)	271.66	161.17	161.31	145.66
传染病死亡总人数(人)	Quantity of Deaths Caused by Contagious Diseases (person)	179	127	96	92
死亡率(1/10 万)	Death Rate (1/100 000)	1.36	0.92	0.67	0.64
结核病登记病人数(千例)	T.B. Patients Registered (1000 cases)	3.09	3.26	3.35	3.74
登记患病率(‰)	Registered Disease Rate(‰)	0.23	0.23	0.23	0.26
结核病新发病人数(千例)	Newly Reported T.B. Cases(1000 cases)	5.18	3.76	3.62	3.83
登记新发病率(1/万)	Registered Newly Diseased Rate (1/10 000)	3.94	2.67	2.49	2.62
结核病死亡人数(人)	Quantity of Deaths Caused By T.B (person)	293	112	128	111
死亡率(1/10 万)	Death Rate (1/100 000)	2.22	0.80	0.88	0.76
牙病受检人数(万人)	Quantity of People Undergoing Tooth Disease Check (10 000 persons)	51.89	54.85	47.79	62.16
龋牙患病率(%)	Rate of Caries Patients (%)	28.28	38.61	34.89	34.21
小学生视力不良率(%)	Nearsight Rate of Students in Primary School (%)	26.0	36.1	37.6	44.4
初中生视力不良率(%)	Nearsight Rate of Students in Junior High School (%)	55.0	70.0	69.2	76.6
高中生视力不良率(%)	Nearsight Rate of Students in Senior High School (%)	78.5	85.7	85.8	89.5
免疫规划疫苗常规免疫接种率(%)	Conventional Vaccines of Vaccine Immunization Programmes Recipients Rate	99.7	99.8	99.9	99.8
乙肝疫苗全程接种率(%)	Hepatitis-B Inoculation Rate(%)	99.9	99.8	99.9	99.7

表 22.10　家庭病床情况(2018)
FAMILY SICKBEDS

机构类别	Types	开展工作机构数(个) Running Institutions (unit)	上门诊疗总次数(次) Total Times of Family Call (time)	年底实有病床数(张) Year-end Sickbeds (bed)	年内开设总病床数(张) Sickbeds Set up in 2018 (bed)
总　计	**Total**	**238**	**770 617**	**19 736**	**54 103**
医　院	Hospitals	4	25 092	408	1 174
社区卫生服务中心(站)	Community Health-care Centers	234	745 525	19 328	52 929

表 22.11 主要年份妇幼卫生工作情况
BASIC STATISTICS OF GYNAECOLOGY AND PAEDIATRICS IN MAIN YEARS

指 标	Indicators	2000	2010	2017	2018
妇女病普查人数(万人)	**Quantity of People Surveyed for Female Diseases (10 000 persons)**	**40.27**	**86.54**	**67.92**	**72.82**
患病率(%)	Sufferers Rate(%)	35.0	33.3	34.6	34.8
治疗率(%)	Patients Treated Rate(%)	91.1	98.7	93.9	91.2
胎儿娩出顺产数(万人)	Quantity of Smooth Delivery (10 000 persons)	4.05	8.81	10.51	9.1
顺产率(%)	Smooth Delivery Rate(%)	47.5	45.1	52.7	52.1
出生低体重儿(人)	Quantity of Low-weight Newborns (person)	2 567	6 961	8 952	8 857
占活产总数(%)	Proportion in All Deliveries (%)	3.0	3.6	4.5	5.1
出生缺陷人数(人)	Quantity of Newborns with Innate Problems (person)	764	2 496	2 157	2 436
出生缺陷率(‰)	Disabled Among All Deliveries Rate (‰)	8.96	12.80	10.08	14.00
0~6 岁儿童保健管理率(%)	Children of 0-6 Years Old under Health Programm Rate(%)	94.3	97.0	99.5	99.4
婚前检查人数(万人)	Quantity of People Undergoing Pre-marriage Checkup (10 000 persons)	17.36	8.53	3.23	3.74
婚检率(%)	Pre-marriage Checkup Recipients Rate(%)	98.4	35.4	17.9	19.1

表 22.12 主要年份公民献血、用血情况
BLOOD OFFER AND USE OF CITIZENS IN MAIN YEARS

指 标	Indicators	2000	2010	2017	2018
无偿(义务)献血(万人份)	Volunteer or Compulsory Blood Offer (10 000 person unit)	35.19	46.27	50.50	50.15
临床用血量(万人份)	Clinic Blood Use Volum (10 000 person unit)	34.70	42.02	49.01	49.25

表 22.13 主要年份社会保险参保人数
QUANTITY OF PARTICIPANTS IN SOCIAL INSURANCE IN MAIN YEARS

单位：万人(10 000 persons)

指 标	Indicators	2000	2010	2017	2018
城镇基本养老保险	**Urban Basic Pension Insurance**				
城镇职工	Urban Staff and Workers	431.27	522.44	1 020.68	1 032.08
个体工商户和自由职业人员	Individual Businessmen	9.82	20.43	38.35	39.30
领取养老金的离退休人员	Retired Veteran Cadres and Retired Staff and Workers with Pensions	234.23	352.02	489.19	501.99
城镇职工基本医疗保险	**Basic Medical Insurance for Urban Staff and Workers**				
城镇职工	Urban Staff and Workers	364.59	608.41	1 005.40	1 020.61
享受医保的离退休人员	Retired Veteran Cadres and Retired Staff and Workers with Medicare	202.14	391.33	491.38	504.21
城乡居民基本医疗保险	**Basic Medical Insurance for Urban Residents**		**259.17**	**344.63**	**342.76**
城镇职工失业保险	Unemployment Insurance of Urban Staff and Workers	434.86	556.20	961.84	977.20
城镇职工生育保险	Generational Insurance of Urban Staff and Workers		657.30	972.04	984.92
城镇职工工伤保险	Injured Insurance of Urban Staff and Workers		555.36	958.06	972.89
少儿住院基金	Medicare Fund of Children	212.47	197.19	224.77	227.03

①根据《中华人民共和国保险法》，2011 年对社会保险政策进行了调整。 原参加“小城镇社会保险”和“来沪从业人员综合保险”的从业人员被纳入城镇职工保险范围内，并对养老、医疗、工伤、失业、生育保险的相关政策作出了调整。

②根据 2016 年 1 月发布的《国务院关于整合城乡居民基本医疗保险制度的意见》，对城镇居民基本医疗保险和新型农村合作医疗两项制度进行整合，建立统一的城乡居民基本医疗保险制度。

❶According to Insurance Law of the People's Republic of China, the social insurance policy has been adjusted since 2011. Employees, who have participated in Town Social Insurance and General Insurance of Employment of Migratory Population before, are now within the range of insurance for urban staff and workers. Relative policies of pension, medical, injured, unemployment and generational insurances have also been adjusted.

❷According to Opinions of the State Council on the Integration of Basic Medical Insurance System for Urban and Rural Residents which is issued on January 2016, the two basic medical insurance systems of urban residents and the new rural cooperative medical service are integrated to establish a unified basic medical insurance system for urban and rural residents.

表 22.14 主要年份社会保障标准
SOCIAL SECURITY STANDARD IN MAIN YEARS

单位：元/月(yuan/month)

指 标	Indicators	2000	2010	2017	2018
职工工资最低标准	Minimum Standard of Wages of Staff and Workers	445	1 120	2 300	2 420
城镇居民生活保障最低标准	Minimum Standard of Urban Living Security	280	450	970	1 070

表 22.15 社会福利院、儿童福利院、社会福利医院和老年福利机构情况(1980~2018)

INSTITUTIONS OF SOCIAL WELFARE, CHILDREN WELFARE, SOCIAL WELFARE HOSPITALS AND SENIORS WELFARE INSTITUTIONS

年 份 Year	社会福利院 Social Welfare Institutions			儿童福利院 Children Welfare Homes		
	单 位 (个) Units (unit)	床位数 (张) Beds (bed)	年末在院人数 (人) Year-end Population Housed (person)	单 位 (个) Units (unit)	床位数 (张) Beds (bed)	年末在院人数 (人) Year-end Population Housed (person)
1980	9	1 555	1 337	2	600	559
1981	9	1 621	1 313	2	650	634
1982	9	1 525	1 495	2	650	672
1983	9	1 644	1 491	2	600	676
1984	10	1 948	1 635	2	600	633
1985	10	1 727	1 630	2	580	625
1986	10	1 697	1 648	2	550	612
1987	10	1 991	1 770	2	378	449
1988	13	2 189	1 790	2	387	458
1989	14	2 418	2 012	2	538	481
1990	15	2 679	2 019	2	589	586
1991	14	2 687	2 138	2	611	592
1992	14	2 776	2 431	2	665	651
1993	14	2 874	2 554	2	708	690
1994	15	2 931	2 648	2	878	862
1995	15	3 006	2 722	2	988	919
1996	17	3 294	2 866	2	988	943
1997	21	4 012	3 441	2	988	946
1998	24	4 596	3 678	2	1 004	984
1999	20	4 215	3 498	2	981	958
2000	23	4 884	4 137	2	1 100	1 092
2001	26	5 570	4 410	2	1 221	1 221
2002	27	5 590	4 760	3	1 491	1 429
2003	26	5 818	4 779	2	1 087	1 512
2004	26	5 876	4 848	6	1 300	1 893
2005	23	5 999	4 809	6	2 016	1 986
2006	25	6 583	5 024	6	1 252	2 142
2007	24	6 499	5 068	6	1 252	2 341
2008	26	6 864	5 215	6	2 490	2 454
2009	26	7 686	5 351	6	2 584	2 552
2010	25	7 944	5 774	6	2 454	2 423
2011	29	8 297	6 013	6	2 427	2 336
2012	30	8 703	6 200	6	2 455	2 289
2013	23	7 028	5 556	7	2 499	2 261
2014	23	7 434	4 937	3	2 133	2 053
2015	22	6 915	4 651	2	1 921	1 863
2016	22	7 095	4 780	2	1 921	1 786
2017	25	7 933	4 572	2	1 921	1 606
2018	24	9 119	4 609	2	1 921	1 517

表 22.15 续表 continued

年 份 Year	社会福利医院 Social Welfare hospitals			老年福利机构 Seniors Welfare Institutions			
	单 位（个）Units（unit）	床位数（张）Beds（bed）	年末在院人数（人）Year-end Population Housed（person）	机 构（个）Institutions（unit）	床位数（张）Beds（bed）	年末在院人数（人）Year-end Population Housed（person）	其 中 of which #老人（60 周岁及以上）Elders（60 and above）
1980	3	1 475	1 424	42		630	
1981	3	1 460	1 430	53		762	
1982	3	1 490	1 422	58		1 022	
1983	3	1 490	1 432	90		1 402	
1984	3	1 460	1 380	135		2 328	
1985	3	1 480	1 360	199	3 870	3 038	2 786
1986	3	1 510	1 354	249	4 655	3 446	3 100
1987	3	1 497	1 342	277	5 520	4 262	3 893
1988	3	1 497	1 313	322	5 969	4 754	4 429
1989	3	1 433	1 324	349	6 281	5 129	4 835
1990	3	1 497	1 298	332	6 275	5 031	4 452
1991	3	1 391	1 285	341	6 731	5 763	5 642
1992	3	1 510	1 404	351	7 002	6 035	5 655
1993	3	1 510	1 394	331	7 143	6 365	5 934
1994	3	1 510	1 392	333	7 533	6 838	6 541
1995	3	1 510	1 409	330	8 576	7 405	6 633
1996	3	1 510	1 429	333	10 270	8 361	7 867
1997	3	1 500	1 452	323	11 253	9 295	8 647
1998	3	1 500	1 455	339	13 958	11 122	10 826
1999	3	1 710	1 703	331	16 526	12 698	12 013
2000	3	1 840	1 779	398	22 244	16 988	16 541
2001	3	1 894	1 894	378	23 627	17 363	16 923
2002	3	1 917	1 901	417	33 413	20 900	20 309
2003	3	1 680	1 881	422	36 791	23 451	22 682
2004	3	1 780	1 829	414	33 891	26 993	25 902
2005	3	1 811	1 811	450	43 131	31 301	30 181
2006	3	1 860	1 796	479	52 427	35 946	34 447
2007	3	1 852	1 806	536	64 115	42 665	40 731
2008	3	1 851	1 809	556	72 365	46 107	44 226
2009	3	1 842	1 808	589	84 714	51 974	49 789
2010	3	1 835	1 800	600	89 897	56 860	55 118
2011	3	1 821	1 776	602	93 599	58 660	57 597
2012	3	1 802	1 753	601	96 512	61 268	59 383
2013	3	1 783	1 734	609	102 097	65 030	63 152
2014	3	1 800	1 717	637	107 473	66 614	64 549
2015	3	1 800	1 680	607	105 284	69 280	67 286
2016	3	1 800	1 678	626	111 864	72 939	70 904
2017	3	1 780	1 634	648	120 260	76 518	74 161
2018	3	1 780	1 645	649	124 974	78 552	76 645

表 22.16 主要年份社会福利事业机构数和职工人数
QUANTITY OF SOCIAL WELFARE INSTITUTIONS AND STAFF AND WORKERS IN MAIN YEARS

指 标	Indicators	2000	2010	2017	2018
机构数(个)	**Total Institutions (unit)**				
收养性福利单位	Adopting Social Welfare Institutions	427	635	679	679
优抚类	Subsidy	1	1	1	1
福利类	Welfare	426	634	678	678
优抚安置单位	Subsidy and Arrangement Institutions	45	41	34	33
社会救助中心	Social Assistance Centers	16	22	7	7
婚姻登记服务单位	Marriage Register Service Institutions		16	17	17
殡仪服务单位	Funeral and Interment Service Institutions	68	79	73	72
福利彩票发行单位	Issue Institutions of Welfare Lottery	16	19	17	17
职工人数(人)	**Staff and Workers (person)**				
收养性福利单位	Adopting Social Welfare Institutions	7 793	19 966	25 585	31 349
优抚类	Subsidy	35	47	38	44
福利类	Welfare	7 758	19 919	25 547	31 305
优抚安置单位	Subsidy and Arrangement Institutions	745	714	669	720
社会救助中心	Social Assistance Centers	472	403	88	94
婚姻登记服务单位	Marriage Register Service Institutions		110	169	169
殡仪服务单位	Funeral and Interment Service Institutions	2 577	3 201	3 462	3 484
福利彩票发行单位	Issue Institutions of Welfare Lottery	86	87	248	281

表 22.17 主要年份民间组织情况
STATISTICS OF CIVIL ORGANIZATIONS AND CHARITY IN MAIN YEARS

指 标	Indicators	2005	2010	2017	2018
民间组织数(个)	**Quantity of Civil Organizations (unit)**	**7 556**	**10 104**	**14 929**	**16 208**
社会团体	Social Organizations	2 952	3 634	3 999	4 083
民办非企业	Civil Non-Enterprises	4 537	6 353	10 504	11 658
基金会	Foundations	67	117	426	467

表 22.18 主要年份养老服务
ENDOWMENT SERVICE IN MAIN YEARS

指 标	Indicators	2005	2010	2017	2018
机构养老服务	**Endowment Service of Institutions**				
机构数(家)	Quantity of Institutions (unit)	474	625	703	712
床位数(万张)	Quantity of Beds (10 000 beds)	4.95	9.78	14.04	14.42
#新增养老床位	Newly Added Endowmet Beds	1.01	1.08	1.11	1.06
养老床位占60周岁及以上老年人口比例(%)	Ratio of Endowment Bed in Population above 60 (%)	1.9	3.1	2.9	2.9
社区养老服务	**Community Endowment Service**				
社区老年人日间服务机构机构数(家)	Community Daytime Service Institutions for Aged People Quantity of Institutions (unit)	83	303	560	641
月均服务人数(万人)	Population of Monthly Service Aged People (10 000 persons)	0.21	0.90	2.30	2.50
获得政府补贴的老年人(万人)	Population of Aged People Gained Governmental Subsidy (10 000 persons)	3.94	13.00	12.02	8.20

表 22.19 主要年份老年医疗服务
MEDICARE SERVICE FOR AGED PEOPLE IN MAIN YEARS

指 标	Indicators	2005	2010	2017	2018
老年护理院	**Nursing Home for Aged People**				
独立老年护理院	Independent Nursing Home for Aged People				
机构数(所)	Quantity of Institutions (unit)	13	14	37	38
建筑面积(平方米)	Structure Area (sq.m)	59 742	101 048	321 316	331 223
床位数(张)	Beds (bed)	2 353	3 285	11 745	12 428
住院人次(人次)	Person-time in Hospital (person-time)	4 346	10 322	21 447	26 001
老年医院	**Hospital for Aged People**				
机构数(所)	Quantity of Institutions(unit)	3	4	2	2
住院人次(人次)	Person-time in Hospital (person-time)	9 124	15 520	1 449	1 863
家庭病床总数(张)	**Total Quantity of bed in home (bed)**	**40 745**	**43 880**	**52 257**	**54 103**

表 22.20 主要年份红十字会基本情况
BASIC STATISICS ON RED CROSS SOCIETY OF CHINA SHANGHAI MUNICIPAL BRANCH IN MAIN YEARS

指 标	Indicators	2005	2010	2017	2018
红十字会组织机构	**Institutions**				
基层组织(个)	Primary Institations(unit)	2 934	3 042	1 555	1 643
冠名红十字会医疗机构(个)	Medical Institutions(unit)	67	72	71	74
红十字会团体会员单位(个)	**Team Members(unit)**	**970**	**969**	**994**	**1 043**
红十字会会员人数(万人)	**Quantity of Members(10 000 persons)**	**61.62**	**86.52**	**65.42**	**71.39**
#青少年会员(万人)	Hobbledehoy Members(10 000 persons)	37.16	58.64	33.63	39.40
社区公益服务站点(个)	**Community Commonweal Service Stations (unit)**	**1 589**	**3 077**	**5 397**	**5 698**
组织各种宣传活动	**Times of Publicizing Activity**				
在报刊登载宣传文章(篇)	Articles on Newspaper and Periodical (piece)	831	609	160	112
电视台播报宣传节目(条/次)	Programs on Television (piece/time)	459	200	16	18
参加普及宣传无偿献血活动人次数(万人次)	Person-time Attended Publicizing Volunteer Blood Donation Activiies (10 000 person-times)		23.76	43.52	25.49
卫生救护工作	**Sanitation Rescue**				
应急救护知识普及(万人次)	Rescue Popularization Training (10 000 person-time)	24.72	37.35	54.92	61.73
造血干细胞捐献工作	**Contributing Trunk Cell**				
当年参加造血干细胞捐献库人数(万人)	Quantity of Subscribers (10 000 persons)	5.60	10.42	0.82	0.83
遗体捐献工作	**Contributing Reliquiae**				
遗体捐献登记站(个)	Register Centers(unit)	27	25	26	26
遗体捐献接收站(个)	Accepting Centers(unit)	8	7	6	6
全年接受捐献遗体登记(人)	Quantity of Contributing Reliquiae(Person)	1 284	1 170	2 561	2 846
全年接受角膜捐献登记(人)	Quantity of Contributing Cornea(Person)	133	73	1 070	1 326
社会救灾和救助工作	**Working on Social Relieving**				
救灾投入(万元)	Relieve Devotion (10 000 yuan)	10 635.36	19 267.76	519.67	1 334.74
救助款物投入(万元)	Salvation Devotion (10 000 yuan)	1 538.12	4 780.71	1 978.75	843.95
救助受益人次(万人次)	Quantity of Beneficiaries (10 000 persons-times)	2.87	4.11	1.75	2.07

①社区救助受益人次不包含外省市受益人次。
②2013 年起，“参加普及宣传无偿献血活动人次数”口径调整为红十字会主办活动人次数。
③根据 2017 年 5 月 8 日新修订实施的《中华人民共和国红十字会法》第七条“县级以上地方按行政区域建立地方各级红十字会”的有关规定，自 2017 年起“基层组织”的统计口径不再包含“居村红十字小组”。

❶Persons benefited from community salvation devotion do not contain people from other provinces and cities.
❷The statistical caliber of Person-time Attended Publicizing Volunteer Blood Donation Activities was adjusted to Person-time of participating in the activities organized by the Red Cross since 2013.
❸According to the relevant provisions of Article 7 of the “Red Cross Society Law of the People's Republic of China”, “Local Red Cross Societies at the County Level and Above by Administrative Regions”, which was implemented on May 8, 2017, the statistical caliber of “Basic Organizations” will no longer includes the “Village Red Cross Group” since 2017.

表 22.21　全市残疾人各残疾类别人数情况(2018)
THE NUMBER OF CASES OF EACH TYPE OF DISABILITY

单位:人(person)

地　区	District	总　计 Total	视　力 Vision	听　力 Hearing	言　语 Speech	肢　体 Limb	智　力 Intelligence	精　神 Spirit	多　重 Multiple
全　市	**Total**	**549 232**	**93 159**	**67 735**	**5 113**	**259 870**	**57 831**	**52 620**	**12 904**
浦东新区	Pudong New Area	32 267	8 888	4 825	267	11 310	2 570	3 650	757
黄　浦	Huangpu	23 711	5 787	2 820	178	8 836	2 387	3 095	608
徐　汇	Xuhui	22 634	3 658	2 750	189	11 651	1 396	2 217	773
长　宁	Changning	37 970	7 214	5 555	303	17 260	2 727	4 083	828
静　安	Jing′an	37 113	5 545	3 873	288	20 374	2 710	3 225	1 098
普　陀	Putuo	25 541	4 989	2 916	148	11 907	1 932	3 133	516
虹　口	Hongkou	44 300	6 735	4 778	326	24 970	2 772	3 646	1 073
杨　浦	Yangpu	33 433	6 071	4 525	253	14 899	3 707	3 272	706
闵　行	Minhang	34 686	6 201	3 897	310	16 381	3 529	3 694	674
宝　山	Baoshan	27 049	2 934	3 702	219	13 801	2 949	2 669	775
嘉　定	Jiading	103 477	19 105	14 606	1 103	43 072	13 023	10 230	2 338
金　山	Jinshan	17 493	2 219	1 345	624	7 545	3 364	1 917	479
松　江	Songjiang	22 830	3 039	1 811	185	12 860	3 201	1 551	183
青　浦	Qingpu	22 670	2 089	2 484	162	13 234	2 040	2 371	290
奉　贤	Fengxian	19 417	1 739	1 969	313	9 347	3 625	1 913	511
崇　明	Chongming	44 641	6 946	5 879	245	22 423	5 899	1 954	1 295

注：本表数据由市残疾人联合会提供。
Note: Data in this table are provided by Shanghai Disabled Persons′ Federation.

表 22.22 卫生总费用(来源法)(2001~2017) TOTAL HEALTH EXPENDITURE BY SOURCE

年 份 Year	卫生总费用(亿元) Total Health Expenditure (100 million yuan)	其中 of which			构成(%)			人均卫生费用(元) Per Capita Health Expenditure (yuan)
		政府卫生支出 Government Health Expenditure	社会卫生支出 Social Health Expenditure	个人现金卫生支出 Personal Out-of-Pocket Health Expenditure	政府卫生支出 Government Health Expenditure	社会卫生支出 Social Health Expenditure	个人卫生支出 Personal Health Expenditure	
2001	202.63	45.70	98.01	58.93	22.6	48.4	29.0	1 233
2002	220.31	40.65	121.14	58.52	18.5	55.0	26.5	1 356
2003	266.19	51.30	151.60	63.29	19.3	56.9	23.8	1 556
2004	315.48	59.54	170.14	85.80	18.9	53.9	27.2	1 811
2005	362.13	70.30	199.44	92.39	19.4	55.1	25.5	2 036
2006	401.46	77.13	226.39	97.94	19.2	56.4	24.4	2 212
2007	485.67	99.39	278.50	107.79	20.5	57.3	22.2	2 614
2008	559.83	135.82	314.97	109.04	24.2	56.3	19.5	2 965
2009	656.66	141.30	366.90	148.45	21.5	55.9	22.6	3 418
2010	751.99	177.20	419.82	154.96	23.6	55.8	20.6	3 266
2011	931.00	215.70	521.62	193.68	23.2	56.0	20.8	3 966
2012	1 092.35	232.49	646.51	213.35	21.3	59.2	19.5	4 589
2013	1 248.68	250.82	740.42	257.44	20.1	59.3	20.6	5 170
2014	1 347.79	275.29	792.51	279.99	20.4	58.8	20.8	5 556
2015	1 536.60	319.94	882.39	334.27	20.8	57.4	21.8	6 362
2016	1 838.00	430.73	1 061.74	345.53	23.4	57.8	18.8	7 596
2017	2 087.09	449.64	1 209.53	427.92	21.5	58.0	20.5	8 611

表 22.23 卫生总费用构成(机构法)(2001~2017) THE STRUCTURE OF TOTAL HEALTH EXPENDITURE BY INSTITUTION

单位:%

年 份 Year	卫生总费用 Total Health Expenditure	医 院 Hospitals	基层医疗卫生机构 Basic Medical and Health Institutions	药品零售机构 Drug Retailers	公共卫生机构 Public Health Institutions	卫生行政管理机构 Health Administrative Organization	其 他 Others
2001	100	62.9	18.3	10.1	5.3	0.3	3.1
2002	100	65.9	15.7	8.9	5.2	0.3	4.0
2003	100	65.6	13.7	8.1	5.1	0.4	7.1
2004	100	65.1	14.1	8.4	5.8	0.5	6.1
2005	100	63.6	14.6	8.4	5.8	0.5	7.1
2006	100	65.3	14.8	8.4	6.1	0.3	5.1
2007	100	66.5	14.8	7.5	5.2	1.7	4.3
2008	100	62.5	17.8	10.0	6.2	1.2	2.3
2009	100	64.9	17.3	8.1	6.3	1.1	2.3
2010	100	65.8	14.6	8.0	5.6	1.6	4.4
2011	100	68.1	13.0	7.4	3.2	1.9	6.4
2012	100	69.8	12.9	7.2	3.2	2.3	4.6
2013	100	70.7	13.1	7.2	3.5	2.6	2.9
2014	100	71.7	12.9	7.3	3.1	2.8	2.2
2015	100	71.8	13.4	7.1	3.2	2.4	2.0
2016	100	68.8	12.2	7.2	3.5	7.0	1.4
2017	100	69.3	12.8	8.5	3.9	4.1	1.4

上/海/统/计/年/鉴

主要统计指标解释

卫生机构

是指从卫生行政部门取得《医疗机构执业许可证》，或从民政、工商行政、机构编制管理部门取得法人单位登记证书，为社会提供医疗保健、疾病控制、卫生监督服务或从事医学研究和医学在职培训等工作的单位。

医疗机构

指从卫生行政部门取得《医疗机构执业许可证》的机构，包括医院、疗养院、社区卫生服务中心(站)、卫生院、门诊部、诊所(卫生所、医务室)、妇幼保健院(所、站)、专科疾病防治院(所、站)、急救中心(站)和临床检验中心，但不包括村卫生室(单纯统计)。

医　院

包括综合医院、中医医院、中西医结合医院、民族医院、各类专科医院和护理院，不包括专科疾病防治院、妇幼保健院和疗养院。

卫生技术人员

包括执业医师、执业助理医师、注册护士、药师(士)、检验技师、影像技师(士)、卫生监督员和见习医(药、护、技)师(士)等卫生专业人员。不包括从事管理工作的卫生技术人员(如院长、副院长、党委书记等)。

执业(助理)医师

一律按领取医师执业证书且实际从事临床工作的人数统计，不包括从事管理工作的医师。

优抚对象

优抚指政府对革命烈士家庭、病故残疾工作人员以及参战负伤致残的民兵、民工的抚恤和人民群众对其的优待。优抚对象包括革命烈士家属、因公牺牲和病故军人家属、革命伤残人员、现役军属、退伍红军老战士、红军失散人员、复员军人、退伍军人、在职退役军人、在乡退役军人、带病回乡退伍军人、复退军人精神病员、孤老优抚对象等。

社会福利事业单位

指集中收养社会孤老、残、幼的机构。包括由民政部门管理的社会福利院、儿童福利院、精神病人福利院和城镇集体办的福利院，以及农村集体办的敬老院。

基本养老保险

1.(参保)职工人数：指报告期末按照国家法律、法规和有关政策规定参加基本养老保险并在社保经办机构已建立缴费记录档案的职工人数，包括中断缴费但未终止养老保险关系的职工人数，不包括只登记未建立缴费记录档案的人数。

2.(参保)离退休人员人数：指报告期末参加基本养老保险的离休、退休和退职人员的人数。

3. 基本养老保险基金收入：指根据国家有关规定，由纳入基本养老保险范围的缴费单位和个人按国家规定的缴费基数和缴费比例缴纳的养老保险基金，以及通过其他方式取得的形成基金来源的收入。包括单位和职工个人缴纳的基本养老保险费、基本养老保险基金利息收入、上级补助收入、下级上解收入、转移收入、财政补贴和其他收入。

4. 基本养老保险基金支出：指按照国家政策规定的开支范围和开支标准从养老保险基金中支付给参加基本养老保险的离休、通休、退职人员个人的养老金、丧葬抚恤补助，以及由于保险关系转移、上下级之间调剂资金等原因而发生的支出。包括离休金、退休金、退职金、各种补贴、医疗费、死亡丧葬补助费、抚恤救济费、社会保险经办机构管理费、补助下级支出、上解上级支出、转移支出、其他支出等。

5. 基本养老保险基金累计结余：指截止报告期末基本养老保险基金收支相抵后的累计余额。

基本医疗保险

1. 参保人数：指报告期末按国家有关规定参加基本医疗保险的人数。包括参加保险的职工人数和退休人员人数。

2. 基金收入：指根据国家有关规定，由纳入基本医疗保险范围的缴费单位和个人，按国家规定的缴费基数和缴费比例缴纳的基金，以及通过其他方式取得的形成基金来源的款项，包括：单位缴纳的社会统筹基金收入、个人缴纳的个人账户基金收入、财政补贴收入、利息收入、其他收入。

3. 基金支出：指按照国家政策规定的开支范围和开

主要统计指标解释

支标准从社会统筹基金中支付给参加基本医疗保险的职工和退休人员的医疗保险待遇支出，和从个人帐户基金中支付给参加基本医疗保险的职工和退休人员的医疗费用支出，以及其他支出。包括：住院医疗费用支出、门急诊医疗费用支出、个人账户基金支出、其他支出。

4. 基金累计结余：指截止报告期末基本医疗保险的社会统筹和个人帐户基金累计结余金额。包括银行存款、财政专户、债券投资和其他。

■ 失业保险

1. 参保人数：指报告期末按照国家法律、法规和有关政策规定参加了失业保险的城镇企业事业单位的职工及地方政府规定参加失业保险的其他人员的人数。

2. 失业保险基金收入：指按照规定从企业、事业及其他单位筹集的失业保险费及其他并入失业保险基金收入的总额。包括单位和个人缴纳的失业保险费、失业保险基金利息收入、上级补助收入、下级上解收入、转移收入、财政补贴和其他收入。

3. 失业保险基金支出：指报告期内为保障失业人员和下岗职工基本生活、促进其再就业等支出的基金总额。包括失业救济金、医疗费、死亡丧葬补助费、抚恤救济费、转业训练费支出、失业保险经办机构管理费、补助下级支出、上解上级支出、转移支出和其他支出。

4. 基金累计结余：指截止报告期末失业保险基金收支相抵后的累计余额。

■ 工伤保险

1. 参加保险人数：指报告期末依据国家有关规定参加工伤保险的职工人数。

2. 享受保险待遇人数：指劳动者因工负伤致残、死亡或因患职业病致残，根据有关规定享受工伤保险待遇职工或供养直系亲属人数。包括伤残人数、职业病人数、因工死亡人数、供养直系亲属人数。

3. 基金收入：指根据国家有关规定，由参加工伤保险的单位按国家规定的缴费基数和缴费比例缴纳的工伤保险基金，以及通过其他形式取得的形成基金来源的款项。包括：单位缴纳的社会统筹基金收入、财政补贴收入、利息收入、其他收入。

4. 基金支出：指按照国家政策规定的开支范围和开支标准从工伤保险基金中支付给参加工伤保险的人员及供养直系亲属工伤保险待遇支出及其他支出。包括工伤医疗费、伤残补助金、工亡补助金、护理费、丧葬补助费、工伤预防费用、职业康复费用和其他支出。

5. 基金累计结余：指截止报告期末工伤保险基金累计结余金额。包括银行存款、财政专户、债券投资和其他。

■ 生育保险

1. 参保人数：指报告期末依据有关规定参加生育保险的职工人数。

2. 基金收入：指根据国家有关规定，由参加生育保险的单位按照国家规定的缴费基数和缴费比例缴纳的生育保险基金，以及通过其他方式取得的形成基金来源的款项，包括：单位缴纳的基金收入、利息收入和其他收入。

3. 基金支出：指按照国家政策规定的开支范围和开支标准，从生育保险基金中支付给参加生育保险的职工，因妊娠、分娩和计划生育手术而享受的待遇及其他支出。包括：生育津贴、医疗费用支出及其他支出。

4. 基金累计结余：指截止报告期末生育保险基金累计结余金额。包括银行存款、财政专户、债券投资和其他。

SHANGHAI STATISTICAL YEARBOOK

EXPLANATORY NOTES TO MAJOR STATISTICAL INDICATORS

□ Health Care Institutions

Health Care Institutions refer to the units which have been qualified the Certification of Health Care Institution by the administration of public health, or qualified the Certification of Corporate Unit by the civil affairs, administration for industry and commerce, commission office for public sector reform, and engaging in medical care, disease prevention and control, health supervision and inspection, medicine research and health professional education, etc.

□ Medical Organizations

Medical Organizations refer to the institutions which have been qualified the Certification of Health Care Institution by the administration of public health, including: hospitals, health centers, community health service centers (stations), health centers, clinics (health stations and infirmaries), women and children care agencies (centers and stations), special disease prevention and curing agencies (centers and stations), first-aid centers (stations) and clinic inspection centers, but excluding village health care rooms.

□ Hospitals

Hospitals includes comprehensive hospitals, traditional Chinese medicine hospitals, traditional Chinese and western medicine hospitals, ethnic minority medicine hospitals, various special disease hospitals and nursing homes, but excludes special disease prevention and curing agencies, women and children care agencies and health centers.

□ Medical Technical Personnel

Medical Technical Personnel includes licensed doctors, licensed assistant doctors, pharmacists (assistant pharmacists), inspection technicians, image technicians (assistant image technicians), health care inspectors and practice doctors (pharmacists, nurses, and technicians), excludes medical technical personnel engaging in administrative jobs.

□ Licensed Doctors (Assistant Doctors)

It refers to the medical workers who have obtained the license of qualified doctors (assistant doctors) and are employed by medical institutions, but excludes the doctors engaging in administrative jobs.

□ Special Care

Special Care is offered by the government to the family member of the martyrs, disabled or demobilized servicemen or laborers who were injured on duty. Entitled to the special care are family members of the revolutionary martyrs, family members of servicemen who dies on duty or died of an illness, disabled servicemen, family members of servicemen on active service, retired veteran Red Army soldiers, scattered Red Army soldiers, demobilized servicemen, ex-servicemen, servicemen who were demobilized while on duty, ex-servicemen back to their rural homes, ex-servicemen who were demobilized because of an illness and have gone back to their rural homes, ex-servicemen who suffer from mental illness and elderly persons with no family.

□ Social Welfare Institutions

Social Welfare Institutions refer to institutions taking care of old people without children, handicapped people and orphans. They include social welfare institutions run by civil affairs departments, children's welfare institutions, welfare institutions for mental patients, and collectively-run old people's homes in rural areas.

□ Basic Pension Insurance

1. Number of staff and workers covered refer to staff and workers participating in basic pension insurance programme in line with national laws, regulations and related policies by the end of reference period, who have already had payment records in social security management agencies, including those who interrupt payment without terminating the insurance programme. Those who have registered in the programme with no payment records are not included.

2. Number of retirees participating in basic pension insurance programme refer to number of retirees participating in basic pension insurance programme by the end of reference period.

3. Revenue of basic pension insurance refer to payments made by employers and individuals participating in pension in-

EXPLANATORY NOTES TO MAJOR STATISTICAL INDICATORS

surance programs in accordance with the basis and proportion stipulated in state regulations, and income from other sources that become source of pension insurance fund, including the premium paid by employers and individuals, interest income, subsidies from higher level agencies, income as transfer from subordinate agencies, transferred income, government financial subsidies and other income.

4. Expenses of basic pension insurance refer to payment made to those retired and resigned people covered in pension insurance program in terms of pension or compensation within the scope and standards of expenditure according to related national policies, and expenditure occurred due to shift of the insurance relationship or adjustment of funds among agencies, including pension for resigned people, pension for retired people, pension for people quitting jobs, various subsidies, medical fees, funeral subsidies, compensation pension, management fees for social security agencies, expenses on subsidies to lower subordinates, expenses as transfer to agencies at higher level, transferred expenditure and other expenditure.

5. Balance of basic pension insurance refers to the balance of basic pension insurance at the end of the reference period after deducting expenses from revenue.

□ Basic Medical Care Insurance

1. Number of people participating in the insurance programme refers to people participating in the basic medical care insurance programme according to related regulations by the end of reference period, including number of staff and workers and retirees participating in this insurance programme.

2. Revenues of insurance programme refer to payments made by employers and individuals participating in medical care insurance programs in accordance with the basis and proportion stipulated in state regulations, and income from other sources that become source of medical insurance fund, including income of social comprehensive funds paid by employers, income from individual accounts, government financial subsidies, interest income and other income.

3. Expenses of insurance programme refer to payments made from social comprehensive funds to those retired and resigned people covered in basic medical care insurance within the scope and standards of expenditure according to related national policies, and medical care payment made from individual accounts to staff and workers and retirees, and other expenses, including medical expenses of hospital inpatients, medical expenses for outpatients and emergency patients, payment from individual accounts and other expenditure.

4. Balance of basic medical care insurance refer to the balance of medical care insurance of social comprehensive funds and individual accounts at the end of the reference period, including bank savings, special fiscal accounts, investment in bonds and others.

□ Unemployment Insurance

1. Number of people covered refers to staff and workers in urban enterprises or institutions who have participated in unemployment insurance programme in line relevant policies and regulations, and other people who have participated according to local government regulations, by the end of reference period.

2. Revenue of unemployment insurance refer to payments made by employers and individuals participating in unemployment insurance programme in accordance with relevant regulations and other income contributed to this programme, including unemployment insurance premium made by employers and individuals, interest income, subsidies from higher level agencies, income as transfer from subordinate agencies, transferred income, government financial subsidies and other income.

3. Expenses of unemployment insurance refers to total expenses during the reference period to guarantee the basic livelihood of unemployed people and laid-off staff and workers and to encourage their re-employment. Included are unemployment relief, medical fees, funeral subsidies, compensation pension, training expenses, management fees for unemployment insurance agencies, subsidies to lower level agencies, expenses as transfer to higher level agencies, transferred expenditure and other expenditure.

4. Balance of unemployment insurance refer to the balance of unemployment revenue deducting unemployment expenses at the end of the reference period.

□ Work Injury Insurance

1. Number of people covered refers to staff and workers who have participated in work injury insurance programme in line with relevant national regulations.

2. Number of beneficiaries refers to staff and workers and their direct dependents who can, in line with relevant regulations, benefit from work injury insurance, as a result of work injury leading to disability or death of the staff/worker, or occupational disease leading to disability. Included in this category are

EXPLANATORY NOTES TO MAJOR STATISTICAL INDICATORS

number of injured and disabled people, number of people with occupational diseases, number of deaths at work places, and number of direct dependents.

3. Revenues of work injury insurance refer to payments made by employers participating in work injury insurance programs in accordance with the basis and proportion stipulated in state regulations, and income from other sources that become source of work injury insurance fund, including income of social comprehensive funds paid by employers, government financial subsidies, interest income and other income.

4. Expenses of work injury insurance refer to payments made from work injury insurance funds to those who participated in the work injury insurance programme and their direct dependents within the scope and standards of expenditure according to related national policies, and other expenditure, including medical fees for work injury, injury and disability subsidies, death subsidies, nursing fees, funeral subsidies, injury prevention fees, rehabilitation fees for occupational diseases and other expenditure.

5. Balance of work injury insurance refers to the balance of the work injury funds at the end of the reference period, including bank savings, special fiscal account, investment in bonds and others.

□ Maternity Insurance

1. Number of people covered refers to staff and workers who have participated in maternity insurance programme according to relevant regulation at the end of the reporting period.

2. Revenues of maternity insurance refer to payments made by employers participating in maternity insurance programs in accordance with the basis and proportion stipulated in state regulations, and income from other sources that become source of maternity insurance fund, including income of funds paid by employers, interest income and other income.

3. Expenses of maternity insurance refer to payments made from maternity insurance funds to staff and workers who participated in maternity insurance programme within the scope and standards of expenditure according to related national policies, expenses paid for pregnancy, child delivery or surgeries related to family planning, and other expenditure, including allowance for child bearing, medical fees and other expenditure.

4. Balance of the maternity insurance refers to the balance of the maternity insurance funds at the end of reference period, including bank savings, special fiscal account, investment in funds and others.

第二十三篇

CHAPTER 23

2019上海统计年鉴 SHANGHAI STATISTICAL YEARBOOK

文化和体育

CULTURE AND SPORTS

简要说明

一、本篇资料的主要内容

本篇主要反映文化、文物、广电、新闻出版、档案、体育事业发展情况。

内容包括全市艺术表演团体、艺术表演场馆、群众文化活动机构、文物机构、文化娱乐机构、公共图书馆、新闻出版机构、档案机构等单位的机构、人员、经费和业务活动情况;全市广播电视机构设施、制作播出节目时间情况;全市电影摄制、译制和发行放映情况;全市图书、期刊、报纸、音像电子出版数量情况;全市优秀运动员、教练员、体育系统职工、群众体育健身活动场所情况。

二、本篇资料的来源

文化、广电资料由上海市文化广播影视管理局提供;文物资料由上海市文物局提供;新闻出版资料由上海市新闻出版局提供;档案机构资料由上海市档案局提供;体育资料由上海市体育局提供。

BRIEF INTRODUCTION

I. Main Contents

Data mainly reflect the development of culture; cultural relics; radio broadcasting, films and television; news and publication; archives and sports undertakings.

Data mainly include: data on institutions and employed persons, funds and activities of art troupes, art venues, mass cultural institutions, heritage institutions, cultural entertainment institutions, public libraries, press and publications, archival institutions, etc; data and playing hours of television stations and broadcasting stations, data on production, dubbing and showing of films, data on books, periodicals, newspaper, electronic audio and video products published, data on excellent athletes, coaches, staff and workers in sports sectors, mass physical activities.

II. Sources of data

Data on culture, television and broadcasting are from Shanghai Municipal Administration of Culture Radio Film& TV; data on historical relics are from Shanghai Municipal Administration of Cultural Heritage; data on news and publishing are from Shanghai Municipal Press and Publication Bureau; data on archive institutions are from Shanghai Municipal Archives; data on sports are from Shanghai Municipal Sports Bureau.

表 23.1　主要年份文化机构数
QUANTITY OF CULTURAL INSTITUTIONS IN MAIN YEARS

单位：个(unit)

年　份 Year	图书馆 Libraries	群众文化活动机构 Mass Culture	艺术教育机　构 Art Education	文艺科研机　构 Research	文物机构 Agency of Historic Relics	档案机构 Archives Institutions
1978	23	364	3		7	
1980	21	367	2	2	8	
1985	46	369	3	2	9	
1986	49	403	3	2	11	
1987	50	407	3	2	13	127
1988	54	416	3	2	16	125
1989	52	405	3	2	19	134
1990	51	410	3	2	18	137
1991	31	397	3	2	18	671
1992	31	394	3	2	20	745
1993	31	376	3	2	21	720
1994	31	371	3	2	23	
1995	31	332	3	2	23	768
1996	32	348	4	2	24	674
1997	32	352	4	2	24	681
1998	32	355	4	2	23	643
1999	32	349	4	2	24	994
2000	31	340	4	2	24	792
2001	32	276	3	2	23	614
2002	32	270	1	2	26	652
2003	35	261	1	2	26	656
2004	28	251	1	2	99	513
2005	28	248	1	2	106	545
2006	28	250	1	2	106	439
2007	30	247	1	2	111	524
2008	29	245	1	2	111	524
2009	29	242	1	2	112	533
2010	28	240	1	2	115	707
2011	25	241	1	2	125	677
2012	25	240	1	2	115	734
2013	25	239	1	2	112	743
2014	25	238	1	2	114	818
2015	25	237	1	2	110	760
2016	24	237	1	2	135	725
2017	24	238	1	2	135	730
2018	23	239	1	2	142	727

注：自 2004 年起文物保护机构中包括系统外的机构数。
Note: From 2004, Agency of Historic Relics Preservation refers to total quantity of Agency Bureau.

表 23.2 影剧院、艺术表演场馆、艺术表演团体数(1978~2018)
QUANTITY OF CINEMAS,THEATRES AND ART PERFORMANCE TROUPES

单位:个(unit)

年 份 Year	电影放映单位 Film Projection Units	其中 of which #影、剧院 Cinemas and Theatres	艺术表演场馆 Art Performance Places	其中 of which #剧 院 Theatres	书场、曲艺场 Storytelling and Quyi Places	艺术表演团体 Art Performance Troupes
1978	803	109	31	26	4	17
1979	799	115	46	32	5	45
1980	770	119	47	43	6	48
1981	804	127	60	56	6	49
1982	815	134	31	48	6	46
1983	822	140	54	49	8	46
1984	815	146	54	48	8	44
1985	847	156	52	47	8	44
1986	859	169	53	49	9	42
1987	890	199	51	48	8	42
1988	734	215	53	50	8	40
1989	579	213	52	49	8	37
1990	577	211	49	46	8	38
1991	548	229	51	47	9	38
1992	530	249	51	47	9	37
1993	462	254	49	40	9	34
1994	462	254	47	39	8	35
1995	452	249	43	35	7	31
1996	488	280	45	38	7	31
1997	466	263	45	38	7	31
1998	445	242	44	39	5	29
1999	445	242	44	41	4	29
2000	445	242	44	39	5	29
2001	370	273	41	35	3	28
2002	370	273	37	31		28
2003	328	238	180	174	4	72
2004	311	225	177	163	7	75
2005	236	193	160	150	5	85
2006	245	186	148	137	2	97
2007	233	175	150	140	6	103
2008	235	172	139	134	5	107
2009	226	169	104	100	0	77
2010	152	136	97	86	2	89
2011	161	146	103	90	4	102
2012	153	140	111	99	3	138
2013	169	151	127	116	3	148
2014	189	172	93	81	4	158
2015	209	202	50	34	1	180
2016	245	238	47	27	7	205
2017	314	302	49	31	1	199
2018	348	339	45	31	1	254

注：自 2003 年起文化统计范围扩大到全行业。
Note: The scope of statistics to culture expands to total sectors since 2003.

表 23.3 主要年份主要文化机构从业人员数
QUANTITY OF EMPLOYEES IN MAJOR CULTURAL INSTITUTIONS IN MAIN YAERS

单位:人(person)

机构类别	Category of Institution	2000	2010	2017	2018
总　计	**Total**	**217 572**	**274 267**	**222 667**	**204 928**
艺术机构	Art	4 759	9 482	12 040	11 108
图书馆	Libraries	2 513	2 180	2 101	2 110
档案机构	Archives Institutions	2 330	3 822	4 520	2 240
群众文化活动机构	Mass Culture	3 874	4 702	4 985	4 990
文物机构	History Relic	1 136	2 558	3 104	3 209
文化市场经营机构	Cultural Market Operation Institutions	63 297	60 358	43 900	39 806
新闻出版机构	Institutions Engaged in News and Publishing	138 492	185 620	149 895	139 479
其他文化机构	Other Cultural Institutions	1 171	5 545	2 122	1 986

表 23.4 主要文化机构和人员数(2018)
MAJOR CULTURAL INSTITUTIONS AND PERSONNEL

机构类别	Category of Institution	机构数(个) Institutions(unit)	从业人数(人) Employees(person)
艺术机构	**Art**	**314**	**11 108**
艺术表演团体	Art Performance Troupes	254	9 130
艺术表演场馆	Art Centers	45	1 513
艺术教育机构	Art Education	1	71
文艺科研机构	Literaturde and Art Research	2	40
艺术展览创作机构	Art Education Creation Organization	12	354
图书馆	**Libraries**	**23**	**2 110**
#少儿图书馆	Libraries for Children	4	77
档案机构	**Archives Institution**	**727**	**2 240**
群众文化活动机构	**Mass Culture**	**239**	**4 990**
群众艺术馆	Mass Art Centers	1	73
文化馆	Cultural Centers	24	903
文化站	Cultural Stations	214	4 014
文物机构	**Historical Relic**	**142**	**3 209**
文物保护管理机构	Heritage management agencies	6	64
博物馆	Museums	131	3 036
文物商店	Cultural Relic Shops	1	61
其他文物机构	Other Historical Relic	4	48
文化市场经营机构	**Cultural Market Operation Institutions**	**3 484**	**39 806**
新闻出版机构	**Institutions Engaged in News and Publishing**	**6 204**	**139 479**
其他文化机构	**Other Cultural Institutions**	**71**	**1 986**

注：2018 年起，档案机构不再统计兼职人员数。
Note: Since 2018, the number of part-time employees will not be counted by the archives organizations.

表 23.5 群众艺术馆和文化馆(站)情况(2018)
MASS ART AND CULTURAL CENTERS

指 标	Indicators	合 计 Total	群众艺术馆 Mass Art Centers	文化馆 Cultural Centers	文化站 Cultural Stations
单位数（个）	Quantity of Units (unit)	239	1	24	214
从业人员(人)	Employees (person)	4 990	73	903	4 014
组织活动	Organizing Activity				
文艺活动（次）	Literary Activity(time)	69 949	25	8 642	61 282
理论研讨和讲座（次）	Theoretics Conference and Chair(time)	934	240	694	
举办训练班(次)	Conducting Training Courses(time)	63 526	52	11 062	52 412
举办展览个数（个）	Exhibitions Conducted (unit)	4 768	36	356	4 376
场地面积(万平方米)	Floor Space(10 000 sq.m)	142.52	1.90	18.45	122.18

表 23.6 艺术表演团体情况（2018）
BASIC STATISTICS OF ART TROUPES

类 别	Types	剧团数（个） Troupes (unit)	从业人员（人） Employees (person)	国内演出场次(场) Times of Domestic Performance (time)	观众人数（万人次） Spectators (10 000 person-times)
总 计	**Total**	**254**	**9 130**	**35 380**	**1 098**
按隶属关系分	**By Administrative Relationship**				
市 级	Perfectural level	18	3 212	10 020	332
区 级	District and County level	236	5 918	25 360	766
按剧种分	**By Type of Drama**				
话剧、儿童剧、滑稽剧团	Drama, Children's Play & Comedy Troupes	58	1 951	6 540	271
歌舞、音乐类	Opera, Dance Drama, Opera and Dance Troupes	62	2 837	6 270	205
京剧、昆曲类	Song and Dances Troupeand Light Music Orchestras	6	561	650	37
地方戏曲类	Orchestras and Chorus	55	1 867	14 670	328
杂技、魔术、马戏类	Drama Troupes	5	295	1 970	85
曲艺类	Quyi, Acrobatics, Puppet, and Shadow Play Troupes	5	128	660	19
综合艺术表演团体	Comprehensive Art Performance Groups	63	1 491	4 620	153

表 23.7 博物馆、纪念馆情况(2018)
STATISTICS OF MUSEUMS AND MEMORIALS

类 别 Types		机构数 (个) Quantity of Institutions (unit)	馆内藏品实际数量 Real Quantity of Collections (件/套) (piece/set)	#一至三级藏品 Collections of Class One to Three	展览活动 (个) Exhibit Activity (unit)	参观人次 (万人次) Visiting Person-times (10 000 person-times)
总　计	**Total**	**131**	**2 010 506**	**229 232**	**347**	**2 216**
综合性	Comprehensive	12	48 428	4 639	75	387
历史类	Historical	41	354 536	69 786	147	744
艺术类	Art	8	1 022 017	143 857	54	269
自然科技类	Natural Science and Technology	3	294 512	4 902	13	729
其　他	Others	67	291 013	6 048	58	87

表 23.8 主要年份文物保护维修情况
PRESERVATION AND MAINTAIN OF HISTORICAL RELICS IN MAIN YEARS

指 标 Indicators		2005	2010	2017	2018
保护维修项目数(个)	Items of Preservation and Maintaining (item)	44	45	39	47
#国家级	National	4	10	4	2
市　级	Municipal	18	6	21	27
维修面积(万平方米)	Area of Maintaining (10 000 sq.m.)	2.30	13.51	4.20	6.76
项目总预算(万元)	Aggregate Budget of Items (10 000 yuan)	19 650	20 555	41 000	137 278
#专项补助	Special Assistance	934	8 463	1 073	1 003
已拨入专项补助(万元)	Special Assistance Appropriated (10 000 yuan)	1 209	8 463	1 073	1 003
当年保护维修支出(万元)	Expend on Preservation and Maintaining (10 000 yuan)	19 571	20 554	23 000	45 759

表 23.9 主要年份广播电台、电视台情况
TELEVISION STATIONS AND BROADCASTING STATIONS IN MAIN YEARS

类 别	Types	2005	2010	2017	2018
广播电台	**Broadcasting Stations**				
中、短波发射台(座)	Relaying Stations of Medium and Short Wave Broadcast (uint)	4	4	3	3
发射功率(千瓦)	Transmited Power (kw)	390	240	227	227
公共广播节目套数(套)	Public Radio Programs (set)	21	21	22	22
付费广播节目套数(套)	Pay Radio Programs(set)	1	1	1	1
日均播音时间(小时)	Broadcasting Time a day (hour)	347	360	407	413
全年制作节目时间(小时)	Length of Programs Produced (hours)	83 665	85 262	82 366	129 330
电视台	**Television Stations**				
发射台(座)	Realying Stations (uint)	11	11	22	22
发射功率(千瓦)	Transmitted Power (kw)	170	172	72	102
公共电视节目套数(套)	Public TV Programs (set)	25	25	25	25
付费电视节目套数(套)	Pay TV Programs (set)	15	16	16	16
周均播放时间(小时)	Broadcast Time a week (hour)	2 871	3 361	3 708	3 734
全年制作节目时间(小时)	Length of Programs Produced (hours)	62 819	49 507	54 741	75 855
广播电视卫星地球站(座)	Satellite Earth Station of Radio and TV Programs (uint)	1	1	1	1

注：2015 年起，电视发射台与调频发射台合并统计，不再单独统计。
Note: Since 2015, the statistics of television transmitting station have merged with FM transmitting station, and are no longer separate.

表 23.10 电视和广播公共节目播出时间(2018)
PLAYING HOURS OF TELEVISION AND BROADCASTING PUBLIC PROGRAMS

单位:小时(hour)

类 别	Types	电视台 Television Stations			广播电台 Broadcasting Stations		
		合 计 Total	市 级 Municipal Level	区 级 District Level	合 计 Total	市 级 Municipal Level	区 级 District Level
总 计	**Total**	**179 210**	**120 299**	**51 873**	**150 620**	**94 796**	**55 824**
新闻资讯类节目	News Program	28 685	21 132	6 988	37 642	26 699	10 943
专题服务类节目	Subject Service Program	46 712	31 531	12 315	32 938	23 031	9 907
综艺益智类节目	Variety and Quiz Show	9 425	7 885	607	54 470	29 367	25 103
广播剧/电视剧	Radio Drama /TV Play	60 036	34 192	23 964	6 842	937	5 905
广告类节目	Advertising Program	16 819	11 357	5 338	8 936	6 732	2 204
其他类节目	Others	17 533	14 202	2 661	9 792	8 030	1 762

表 23.11 主要年份有线电视基本情况
BASIC STATISTICS ON CABLE TELEVISION IN MAIN YEARS

指 标	Indicators	2000	2010	2017	2018
有线电视总用户数(万户)	Quantity of Cable TV Users (10 000 households)	303	573	796	804
#数字电视用户	Digital TV Users		236	718	736
有线广播电视传输网络干线总长(公里)	Lines Total Length (kilometer)	604	36 211	48 219	47 815

表 23.12 电影摄制、译制和放映情况(1978~2018)
PRODUCTION, DUBBING AND SHOWING OF FILMS

年份 Year	摄制和译制电影片 Production and Dubbing		电影放映 Film Showing			
	故事片(部) Feature Films (film)	动画电影(本) Animated Film(reel)	放映场次(万场) Showing (10 000 times)	其中 of which #影、剧院 Cinemas and Theatres	观众人次(万人次) Spectators (10 000 person-times)	其中 of which #影、剧院 Cinemas and Theatres
1978	10	24	35	17	27 405	15 291
1979	14	25	40	20	32 763	29 743
1980	17	30	39	20	29 304	18 039
1981	17	32	38	19	26 823	16 203
1982	19	35	38	20	25 828	15 586
1983	19	34	37	20	25 204	15 124
1984	19	40	36	21	24 149	15 539
1985	15	43	34	21	21 885	14 748
1986	19	38	36	24	23 220	16 720
1987	17	38	37	28	21 985	17 067
1988	13	29	38	30	20 461	16 742
1989	17	29	37	32	20 776	18 216
1990	16	47	38	33	19 351	17 021
1991	17	37	36	31	15 766	13 615
1992	17	42	29	25	9 145	8 089
1993	16	35	16	14	3 862	3 332
1994	14	13	22	20	4 001	3 617
1995	17	37	23	20	4 419	3 913
1996	10	58	27	25	4 420	3 783
1997	11	17	25	23	3 670	3 023
1998	4	16	23	21	2 924	2 451
1999	17	10	20	19	2 055	1 678
2000	10	20	18	17	1 794	1 452
2001	12	2	18	17	1 553	1 315
2002	10	2	20	17	1 198	921
2003	9	10	20	19	971	870
2004	12	1	24	23	1 364	1 183
2005	13		28	26	1 509	1 323
2006	9		27	26	1 254	1 173
2007	9		33	32	1 385	1 277
2008	17	8	35	34	1 456	1 381
2009	11		44	43	1 938	1 844
2010	19	2	55	54	2 288	2 174
2011	25		76	75	2 792	2 668
2012	22	6	96	95	3 154	3 074
2013	27		132	120	3 793	3 618
2014	28	8	158	149	4 678	4 621
2015	34	10	190	190	6 810	6 797
2016	32	2	252	251	7 307	7 292
2017	67	6	337	336	8 306	8 289
2018	75	2	403	400	8 728	8 562

注：2012 年起，译制片的统计口径发生变化，单位由过去的“本”改为“部”。
Note: Since 2012, the statistical calibre of dubbed films has been changed from reel to set.

表 23.13 主要年份电影发行放映情况
BASIC STATISTICS OF FILM DISTRIBUTION AND PROJECTION IN MAIN YEARS

指 标	Indicators	2005	2010	2017	2018
电影放映机构(个)	**Movie Projection Agencies(unit)**		**117**	**314**	**348**
#电影院	Cinema		69	269	306
影剧院	Theater		42	33	33
开放礼堂、俱乐部	Open Auditorium and Clubs		2	12	9
放映场次(万场)	**Projection Times (10 000 times)**	**27.60**	**54.63**	**337.23**	**403.16**
#电影院	Cinema	22.20	51.72	328.83	393.87
影剧院	Theater	3.90	2.19	7.54	6.62
开放礼堂、俱乐部	Open Auditorium and Clubs	1.16	0.68	0.86	2.67
观众人次数(万人次)	**Quantity of Audience (10 000 person-times)**	**1 509.31**	**2 287.84**	**8 305.97**	**8 727.52**
#电影院	Cinema	893.92	2 052.62	8 123.52	8 411.17
影剧院	Theater	428.63	121.33	165.43	150.46
开放礼堂、俱乐部	Open Auditorium and Clubs	36.24	55.99	17.02	165.89
放映收入(万元)	**Projection Revenue (10 000 yuan)**	**27 192.03**	**93 875.11**	**350 171.18**	**369 243.47**
#电影院	Cinema	23 591.47	89 302.91	344 176.42	361 155.90
影剧院	Theater	2 389.52	2 697.84	5 350.24	5 048.10
开放礼堂、俱乐部	Open Auditorium and Clubs	1 009.58	1 807.88	644.52	3 039.47
平均每一放映场次	**Average on per Projection Time**				
观众人数(人)	Quantity of Audience (Person)	55	42	25	22
放映收入(元)	Returns (yuan)	985	1 718	1 038	916
日均放映场次(场)	**Projection Time a Day (time)**	**756**	**1 497**	**9 239**	**11 045**
日均观众人次(万人次)	**Average Audience a Day (10 000 person-times)**	**4.14**	**6.27**	**22.76**	**23.91**

注：电影放映机构数为正在活动的单位数。
Note: The number of movie projection agencies is the number of units being active.

表 23.14 文化娱乐机构基本情况(2018)
BASIC STATISTICS OF CULTURE AND ENTERTAINMENT INSTITUTIONS

类　别	Types	机构数（个）Quantity of Institutions (unit)	从业人员（人）Employees (person)	主营业务收入（万元）Major Business Revenue (10 000 yuan)	主营业务利润（万元）Major Business Profits (10 000 yuan)
总　计	**Total**	**1 624**	**13 598**	**252 573**	**21 304**
按市区级分	**By City and District**				
#市　级	Municipal Level	14	807	21 406	-2 669
区　级	District Level	1 610	12 791	231 167	23 973
按活动场所分	**By Place of Activity**				
歌舞娱乐场所	Entertainment Sites of Singing & Dancing	1 180	12 417	222 467	20 682
游戏电子游艺经营场所	Business Sites of Games	444	1 181	30 106	622

注：文化娱乐机构未包括互联网上网服务营业场所及经营性互联网文化单位。
Note: Culture and Entertainment Institutions do not include internet service business places and commercial internet cultural units.

表 23.15 公共图书馆情况(2018)
PUBLIC LIBRARIES

指　标	Indicators	合　计 Total	市　级 Municipal Level	区　级 District Level
机构数（个）	Institutions (unit)	23	2	21
从业人员（人）	Employees (person)	2 110	799	1 311
总藏量（万册、件）	Collection (10 000 copies)	7 894.21	5 735.39	2 158.82
#图　书	Books	3 599.64	1 600.76	1 998.88
报　刊	Newspaper and Magzines	395.31	359.50	35.81
本年新购藏量（万册、件）	Publications Newly Bought (10 000 copies)	796.26	10.46	785.80
建筑面积（万平方米）	Floor Space of Buildings (10 000 sq.m)	43.79	13.40	30.39
#书　库	Stack Room	8.18	4.57	3.61
阅览室	Reading Room	10.88	1.35	9.53
阅览座位（个）	Seats in Reading Room (unit)	23 099	2 280	20 819
书刊文献外借情况	Books Lending			
人　次（万人次）	Readers (10 000 person-times)	621.60	179.01	442.58
册　数（万册次）	Books (10 000 copy-times)	2 505.08	672.07	1 833.01
信息化装备	Information Equipment			
计算机（台）	Computer (unit)	6 285	2 324	3 961
#电子阅览室终端数	E-reading Room Terminals	2 987	600	2 387
为读者举办各种活动	Activities Held for Readers			
组织各类讲座次数（次）	All Kinds of Lectures (time)	2 221	156	2 065
参加人次（万人次）	Participants (10 000 person-times)	32	6	26

表 23.16 图书出版数量(1978~2018)
BOOKS PUBLISHED

年 份 Year	种 数 (种) Quantity of Publications (type)	其中 of which #新出版 Newly Published	总印数 (亿册) Total Printed (100 million copies)	总印张数 (亿印张) Total Printed Signatures (100 million signatures)
1978	1 666	1 332	3.92	12.19
1979	2 040	1 563	4.58	15.54
1980	2 338	1 804	5.62	17.73
1981	2 801	1 949	6.01	22.89
1982	3 395	2 057	6.07	21.76
1983	3 653	2 254	4.65	21.31
1984	3 848	2 328	5.37	25.58
1985	4 176	2 634	4.96	23.95
1986	4 531	3 045	3.66	17.81
1987	5 103	3 151	4.26	19.84
1988	5 538	3 658	4.33	19.04
1989	6 765	4 960	3.28	14.52
1990	7 767	4 887	2.98	14.66
1991	8 141	4 756	3.11	17.30
1992	8 095	4 179	2.75	17.19
1993	7 721	4 272	2.26	15.34
1994	7 812	4 382	2.35	17.01
1995	8 338	4 185	2.44	17.92
1996	9 234	4 445	2.79	20.10
1997	9 928	4 844	2.70	18.00
1998	10 718	5 083	2.83	18.69
1999	11 381	5 880	2.68	18.69
2000	12 682	6 936	2.54	19.05
2001	14 000	7 947	2.68	21.24
2002	14 537	8 156	2.59	21.38
2003	15 636	8 726	2.74	23.27
2004	16 449	9 391	2.67	23.54
2005	16 504	9 286	2.59	23.65
2006	17 283	9 338	2.54	24.86
2007	16 958	9 085	2.40	24.05
2008	17 780	9 945	2.64	24.97
2009	18 873	10 615	2.74	25.46
2010	19 519	11 241	2.89	26.34
2011	22 056	12 542	2.89	27.37
2012	23 792	13 142	3.35	31.35
2013	24 969	13 665	3.37	32.09
2014	24 676	13 193	3.26	30.47
2015	25 954	13 626	3.53	33.83
2016	27 462	13 905	4.17	36.26
2017	27 772	13 261	4.23	37.56
2018	30 009	14 227	4.81	44.90

表 23.17 期刊出版数量(1978~2018)
PERIODICALS PUBLISHED

年 份 Year	种 数 (种) Quantity of Publications (type)	每期平均印数 (万册、份) Average Publications Issued (10 000 copies)	总印数 (亿册) Total Printed (100 million copies)	总印张数 (亿印张) Total Printed Signatures (100 million signatures)
1978	42	459	0.47	1.12
1979	90	721	0.73	2.08
1980	126	1 061	1.22	3.37
1981	266	1 873	2.03	5.95
1982	308	2 203	2.31	6.37
1983	349	2 572	2.51	7.07
1984	402	3 502	3.10	8.56
1985	491	3 424	3.45	9.21
1986	541	3 073	3.03	8.17
1987	546	3 058	3.13	8.05
1988	535	2 624	2.66	6.63
1989	527	1 793	1.86	4.58
1990	522	1 735	1.73	4.24
1991	504	1 749	1.79	4.44
1992	527	1 794	1.84	4.59
1993	535	1 668	1.82	4.95
1994	556	1 569	1.72	4.87
1995	565	1 583	1.78	5.30
1996	582	1 530	1.66	5.14
1997	587	1 513	1.66	5.35
1998	591	1 503	1.65	5.81
1999	606	1 493	1.78	6.87
2000	613	1 489	1.85	7.38
2001	616	1 413	1.85	7.58
2002	621	1 332	1.80	7.77
2003	626	1 335	1.83	8.51
2004	612	1 184	1.93	8.94
2005	612	1 130	1.90	8.96
2006	616	1 125	1.83	8.76
2007	624	1 117	1.83	8.75
2008	623	1 105	1.90	9.27
2009	621	1 039	1.79	9.02
2010	632	1 019	1.78	9.04
2011	632	1 023	1.82	9.42
2012	626	938	1.76	9.67
2013	625	875	1.62	9.00
2014	627	804	1.45	8.10
2015	628	715	1.28	7.23
2016	628	653	1.12	6.37
2017	630	579	0.94	5.23
2018	630	528	0.85	4.56

表 23.21 期刊出版数量(2018)
PERIODICALS PUBLISHED

类 别	Types	种 数（种） Quantity of Publications (type)	出版期数（期） Quantity of Issue (issue)	总印数（万册） Total Printed (10 000 copies)	总印张数（万印张） Total Printed Signatures (10 000 signatures)
总 计	**Total**	**630**	**5 649**	**8 504.58**	**45 601.33**
综 合	Comprehensive	14	82	55.62	430.59
哲学、社会科学	Philosophy and Social Science	143	1 494	3 306.22	16 973.21
自然科学、科技	Natural Science and Technology	354	2 920	1 559.45	11 118.52
文化教育	Culture and Education	79	764	1 379.30	7 744.20
文学艺术	Literature and Art	40	389	2 203.99	9 334.82

表 23.22 报纸出版数量(2018)
NEWSPAPER PUBLISHED

类 别	Types	种 数（种） Quantity of Publications (type)	期 数（期） Issue (issue)	每期平均印数（万份） Average Publication Per Issue (10 000 copies)	总印数（万份） Total Printed (10 000 copies)	总印张数（万印张） Total Printed Signatures (10 000 signatures)
总 计	**Total**	**97**	**8 483**	**395.83**	**81 702.57**	**320 768.78**
综合报	Comprehensive	12	2 643	136.14	48 751.20	242 248.10
专业报	Specialized	85	5 840	259.69	32 951.37	78 520.68

表 23.23 音像电子出版数量 (2018)
AUDIO, VIDEO AND ELECTRON PUBLISHED

类 别	Types	种 数（种） Quantity of Publications (type)	出版数量（万张、万盒） Quantity of Publications (10 000 piece box)	发行数量（万张、万盒） Quantity of Issued (10 000 piece box)	发行总金额（万元） Total Values (10 000 yuan)
总 计	**Total**	**2 460**	**4 638.45**	**4 413.22**	**28 482.02**
电子出版物	Electronic Publication	560	1 306.73	1 080.17	24 166.39
数码激光视盘	DVD	120	41.92	42.47	23.41
高密度激光视盘	EVD	392	2 097.89	2 093.80	870.76
激光唱盘	CD	1 162	1 013.08	869.45	1 896.95
录音带	Tape	78	96.04	249.48	1 259.51
其 他	Others	148	82.79	77.85	265.00

表 23.24　档案机构基本情况(2018)
BASIC STATISTICS OF ARCHIVE INSTITUTIONS

指 标	Indicators	合 计 Total	档案行政管理部门 Archival Administrative Department	档案馆 Archives Library	档案室(处、科) Archives
机构数(个)	**Quantity of Institutions(unit)**	**727**	**25**	**70**	**632**
从业人员(人)	**Employees(person)**	**2 240**	**228**	**937**	**1 075**
馆藏档案	**Archives Collected**				
全 宗(个)	Overall Rolls(unit)	6 407		6 407	
案 卷(万卷)	Rolls(10 000 rolls)	4 308.17		1 598.37	2 709.81
以件为保管单位档案(万件)	Archives(10 000 pieces)	1 921.13		619.93	1 301.21
录音、录像、影片档案(万盘)	Recprd, Video and Film(10 000 disks)	114.90		4.21	110.69
照片档案(万张)	Photo Records(10 000 pieces)	242.88		173.93	68.94
底图(万张)	Base Maps(10 000 pieces)	1 540.49		16.99	1 523.50
微缩胶片(万幅)	Microfilm(10 000 pieces)	3 765.21		2 859.46	905.75
档案利用	**Records Utilized**				
已开放档案	Records Opened				
案 卷(万卷)	Rolls(10 000 rolls)	232.41		232.41	
案 件(万件)	Cases(10 000 cases)	6.18		6.18	
开放档案目录(万条)	Catalog of Records Opened(10 000 pieces)				
案卷级	Roll Grade	91.28		91.28	
文件级	Document Grade	414.43		414.43	
本年利用档案	Records Utilized during the Year				
卷次(万卷次)	Roll-times(10 000 roll-times)	160.60		64.93	95.67
人次(万人次)	Person-times(10 000 person-times)	62.28		40.93	21.35

注：2018 年起，档案机构不再统计兼职人员数。
Note: Since 2018, the number of part-time employees will not be counted by the archives organizations.

表 23.25　主要年份裁判员、优秀运动员、教练员情况
BASIC STATISTICS ON PEFEREES, EXCELLENT ATHLETES AND COACHES IN MAIN YEARS

单位：人（person）

指　标	Indicators	2000	2010	2017	2018
等级裁判员（人）	Certified Referees（person）	880	559	603	729
优秀运动员（人）	Excellent Athletes（person）	899	771	1 171	1 075
#女运动员	Women	402	371	567	533
专职教练员（人）	Full-time Coaches（person）			1 143	1 290
#女专职教练员	Women			361	430

表 23.26　体育系统从业人员(2018)
EMPLOYEES IN SPORTS SECTORS

单位：人（person）

指　标	Indicators	总　计 Total	其中 of which：#优　秀运动队 Excellent Sports Teams	体育运动学　校 Physical Education and Sports Schools	业余体校 Sparetime Sports School	体育场馆 Stadiums and Gymnasiums
总　计	**Total**	**4 973**	**538**	**293**	**1 095**	**942**
#专职教练	Full-time Coaches	1 290	94	76	794	85
管理人员	Administraive Staff	1 327	81	72	195	475
文化教师	Culture Teachers	137		76		
科研人员	Scientific and Technical Personnel	78	4	1	8	
医务人员	Medical Personnel	74	7	9	1	5

表 23.27　群众体育健身活动场所情况（2015～2018）
PLACES OF MASS PHYSICAL ACTIVITIES

指　标	Indicators	2015	2016	2017	2018
社区体育健身设施数（个）	Quantity of Community Fitness Facilities（unit）	12 000	13 398	13 653	14 462
#健身点	Fitness Centers	9 905	11 106	11 316	11 954
社区健身场地面积（万平方米）	Area of Community Fitness Space（10 000 sq.m）	452	458	521	547
社区公共运动场（个）	Quantity of Community Public Playground（unit）	390	390	395	467
社区公共运动场面积（万平方米）	Area of Community Public Playground（10 000 sq.m）	53.2	58.5	66.5	76.1

上 / 海 / 统 / 计 / 年 / 鉴

主要统计指标解释

■ 文化机构

是指专门从事文化工作具有法人资格，独立核算的事业、企业单位，以及单独核算，附属于事业单位的经营性专业文化活动单位。包括从事艺术、图书馆、档案馆、群众文化、文物保护、艺术教育、艺术研究、文化娱乐、新闻出版等机构，以及其他文化机构。

■ 电影放映单位

指具有放映机器设备、固定或不固定的放映场所与专职或兼职的放映技术人员，经有关部门登记批准，经常为一定的观众对象放映电影的机构。包括电影院、影剧院、开放礼堂、俱乐部、放映队、对内礼堂俱乐部。

■ 艺术表演团体

指从事戏曲、音乐、舞蹈、杂技等专业艺术表演，有独立账户的单位，不包括半工半艺、半农半艺和民间职业剧团。该指标主要反映上海专业艺术表演团体发展规模水平。

■ 艺术表演观众人次

指售票、包场演出或民族地区免费演出的艺术表演观众人次数，不包括彩排审查和内部观摩演出的观看人次数。该指标主要反映上海观看专业艺术表演团体演出的效益规模。

■ 等级运动员人数

指经考核正式批准授予等级运动员称号的人数。运动员等级分为国际级运动健将、运动健将、一级运动员、二级运动员、三级运动员、少年级运动员。该指标主要反映运动员队伍的技术质量水平。

■ 等级裁判员人数

指经考核正式批准授予等级裁判员称号的人数。裁判员等级分为国际裁判、国家级裁判、一级裁判、二级裁判、三级裁判。该指标主要反映裁判员队伍的技术质量水平。

SHANGHAI STATISTICAL YEARBOOK

EXPLANATORY NOTES TO MAJOR STATISTICAL INDICATORS

□ Cultural Institutions

Cultural Institution refers to undertaking and business institutions which specialize in cultural work and have legal personality and independent accounting system, and those professional cultural institutions attached to undertaking institutions and have independent accounting system. It includes institutions specialize in art, library, archives, mass culture, historical relic protection, art education, art research, entertainment, news and publication and other cultural institutions.

□ Film Projection Units

Film Projection Units refer to units with film projection equipments, full or part-time projectionists, permanent or non-permanent places, approved by related administrative departments to show films regularly for certain groups of audience, including cinemas, theaters, public auditoriums, clubs, film projection teams, and interior auditorium clubs.

□ Art Troupe

Art Troupe refers to the troupe which is engaged in drama, opera, music, dance, acrobatics or other art performance, opens independent accounts with banks and has self-supporting accounting system; excluding the troupes which are engaged partly in industrial or agricultural activities, partly in art performance and the professional troupes organized by the people. This indicator reflects the development of Shanghai' s professional art troupes.

□ Quantity of Spectators at Art Performance

Number of Spectators at Art Performance refers to the number of attendants at commercial shows, completely booked shows or free shows given in minority national areas, and does not include the number of spectators at rehearsals for examination and internal shows for study. This indicator reflects beneficial results of spectators at Professional Art Performance.

□ Quantity of Athletes in Grades

Number of Athletes in Grades refers to the number of athletes who have been given titles through examination. The titles of athletes include international masters of sports, masters of sports, first-grade, second-grade and third-grade sportsmen and young athletes. This indicator reflects skill of the athletes.

□ Quantity of Referees in Grades

Number of Referees in Grades refers to the number of referees who have been given titles after examination. They are classified as international referees, national referees and referees of the first, second and third grades. This indicator reflects the skill of referees.

第二十四篇

CHAPTER 24

法律、公证和其他

LAWS, NOTARY AND OTHERS

简要说明

一、本篇资料的主要内容

本篇主要包括公检法司的情况。

内容主要包括律师机构、公证机构、人民调解委员会的机构、人员、主要业务活动情况；公安机立案的刑事案件及查处的治安案件情况；交通事故和火灾事故的次数、伤亡人数和损失折款情况；检察院直接立案侦查案件、民事行政案件办理、申诉案件处理情况；法院各类案件办理、执行案件和各类案件结案情况。

二、本篇资料的来源

律师、公证和人民调解等资料由上海市司法局提供；刑事案件、治安案件、交通火灾事故等资料由上海市公安局提供；检察院相关案件资料由上海市检察院提供；法院相关案件资料由上海市高级人民法院提供。

BRIEF INTRODUCTION

I. Main Contents

Data in this chapter reflect statistics on public security,procuratorial,legal and judicial affairs.

Data include mainly general information, personnel, and main activities of law firms, notarizations and meditations; criminal cases registered and offense cases handled by the public security agencies; casualties, and losses in traffic or fire accidents, cases under direct investigation by procurator´s office, civil cases, administrative cases and appeals handled by procurator's offices; cases handled, executed, and closed by courts.

II. Sources of Data

Data on law firms, notarizations, and meditations are provided by Shanghai Municipal Bureau of Justice; data on criminal cases, offense cases, and traffic and fire accidents are provided by Shanghai Municipal Public Security Bureau; Data on procurators are provided by Shanghai Municipal People´s Procurator´s Offices; data on courts are provided by Shanghai Municipal Senior People's Court.

表 24.1 主要年份律师、公证及调解工作基本情况
BASIC STATISTICS OF LAWYERS, NOTARIZATIONS AND MEDIATIONS IN MAIN YEARS

指 标	Indicators	2000	2010	2017	2018
律师工作	**Lawyers**				
律师事务所（个）	Law Offices (unit)	415	1 064	1 469	1 605
律师人数（人）	Lawyers (person)	4 642	13 027	23 186	25 412
#专职律师	Full-time Lawyers	3 522	11 749	21 280	23 265
兼职律师	Part-time Lawyers	731	549	693	710
全年办理	Total Transacted				
民事案件诉讼代理（万件）	Civil Lawsuit(10 000cases)	7.05	7.69	16.11	21.68
刑事诉讼辩护及代理（万件）	Criminal Lawsuit and Vindication(10 000cases)	1.13	1.49	3.18	4.40
非诉讼法律事务（万件）	Non-litigation Action(10 000 cases)	2.65	3.32	8.26	9.33
公证工作	**Notarizations**				
公证处（个）	Notarial Offices (unit)	22	22	21	22
公证人员（人）	Notarial Personnel (person)	366	821	1 269	1 189
#公证员	Notaries	243	359	471	432
办理公证文书（万件）	Documents Notarized (10 000 cases)	47.72	40.76	53.17	37.64
国内公证	Domestic	12.79	18.54	27.19	17.38
涉外公证	Foreign	19.93	20.98	25.09	20.07
涉港澳台公证	Hong Kong, Macao and Taiwan		1.24	0.89	0.20
公证费收入（亿元）	Revenue of Notarial Fees (100 million yuan)	1.13	4.70	6.98	4.43
人民调解工作	**People's Mediation**				
专职司法助理员（人）	Full-time Judicial Assistants (person)	416	734	778	767
人民调解委员会（万个）	People's Mediation Committees(10 000units)	0.89	0.63	0.66	0.65
调解人员（万人）	Mediators (10 000persons)	3.55	3.41	3.02	2.80
调解民间纠纷（万件）	Civil Disputes Mediated (10 000 cases)	6.37	23.24	35.52	36.16
#调解成功	Successfully Mediated		22.81	32.97	34.18
#婚姻家庭	Family Disputes	1.97	3.63	2.37	2.42
邻 里	Neighbor Disputes	2.51	5.12	6.13	6.42
赔 偿	Compensation	0.25	3.02	2.77	2.84
房屋宅基地	Housing and Housing Sites	1.04	1.29	1.16	1.20

注：办理公证文件中包括涉及港、澳、台公证文件。
Note: The number of notarized documents handled included Hong Kong, Macao and Taiwan's.

表 24.2 公证工作情况(2018)
STATISTICS OF NOTARIZATION WORK

指 标	Indicators	2018
公证处(个)	**Notarial Offices(unit)**	**22**
公证人员(人)	**Notarial Personnel(person)**	**1 189**
#公证员	Notaries	432
公证文书总计(件)	**Documents Notarized(case)**	**383 432**
#合同(协议)	Contract (agreement)	15 304
继 承	Inheritance	30 705
委 托	Entrustment	29 394
声 明	Statement	19 823
赠 与	Presentation	168
遗 嘱	Will	9 564
现场监督	Field Supervision	1 011
婚姻状况、亲属关系、收养关系	Marital Status, Kinship, Adoption	26 063
出生、生存、死亡	Birth, Existence, Death	18 702
身份、经历、学历、学位、职务、职称	Identity, Experience, Education Background, Degree, Job Title, Professional Technical Title,	1 423
有无违法犯罪记录	Having or Not Having Illegal and Criminal Record	25 145
公司章程	Articles of Association	120
保全证据	Preservation Evidence	28 569
证书、证照	Certificate and License	80 276
签名、印鉴	Signature and Seal	7 339
文本相符	Text Consistency	48 121
赋予强制执行效力	Compulsory Execution Effect	31 954
执行证书	Grant Compulsory Enforcement Force	342
国内公证文书出证数(件)	**Number of Domestic Notarial Documents Issued(case)**	**173 799**
国外公证文书出证数(件)	**Number of Foreign Notarial Documents Issued(case)**	**200 673**
涉港澳台公证文书出证数(件)	**Number of Notarial Documents Issued Involving Hong Kong, Macao and Taiwan(case)**	**1 959**
涉台公证文书出证数(件)	**Number of Taiwan related Notarial Documents Issued(case)**	**7 001**
公证费收入(亿元)	**Notarization Fee Income(billion yuan)**	**4.43**

表24.3　主要年份公安机关立案刑事案件情况
CRIMINAL CASES REGISTERED IN PUBLIC SECURITY ORGANS IN MAIN YEARS

单位:起(time)

类 别	Types	2000	2010	2017	2018
总　计	**Total**	**104 946**	**119 691**	**203 246**	**242 594**
杀　人	Homicide	252	174	134	115
伤　害	Injury	1 553	2 545	2 293	2 121
抢　劫	Robbery	3 033	1 558	323	188
强　奸	Rape	396	448	476	518
诈　骗	Fraud	8 425	16 598	34 158	68 800
盗　窃	Larceny	77 912	78 322	137 152	139 261
其　他	Others	13 375	20 046	28 710	11 323

表24.4　主要年份公安机关查处治安案件情况
OFFENSE CASES AGAINST PUBLIC ORDER HANDLED BY PUBLIC SECURITY ORGANS IN MAIN YEARS

单位:起(time)

类 别	Types	2000	2010	2017	2018
总　计	**Total**	**194 141**	**566 607**	**514 960**	**366 757**
#扰乱公共秩序	Disturbing Work and Public Order	23 568	25 787	24 401	11 141
寻衅滋事	Gang Fighting or Picking Quarrels and Making Trouble	3 373	3 315	2 021	3 197
阻碍国家工作人员执行职务	Obstructing the Government Workers to Perform Their Duty	1 029	658	2 159	1 253
殴打他人	Beating Other Body	16 973	59 876	45 553	59 593
诈骗、抢夺、敲诈勒索财物	Defrauding, Snatching or Extoring and Racketeering Valuables	2 936	24 510	39 425	53 171
伪造、变造、倒卖有价票证、凭证	Forging and Fraudulently Selling Bills or Certificates	5 551	524	97	45
卖淫、嫖娼	Prostitution or Going Whoring	4 631	7 281	9 004	8 959
赌　博	Gambling	17 464	21 760	35 559	26 772

表 24.5　交通事故和火灾情况 (1980~2018)
BASIC STATISTICS OF TRAFFIC ACCIDENTS AND FIRES

年份 Year	交通事故 Traffic Accidents 发生数 (万起) Number (10 000 cases)	死亡人数 (人) Death (person)	受伤人数 (万人) Injuries (10 000 persons)	损失折款 (万元) Losses Converted -into Cash (10 000 yuan)	火灾 Fires 发生数 (万起) Number (10 000 cases)	死亡人数 (人) Death (person)	受伤人数 (人) Injuries (person)	损失折款 (万元) Losses Converted -into Cash (10 000 yuan)
1980	1.10	445	1.01	96	0.08	17	126	457
1981	1.18	507	1.06	119	0.09	33	81	202
1982	0.83	434	0.77	98	0.07	33	76	255
1983	0.73	443	0.70	99	0.06	24	67	533
1984	0.83	503	0.75	123	0.05	21	71	177
1985	0.71	687	0.57	318	0.05	30	74	374
1986	0.84	678	0.62	576	0.06	25	54	790
1987	1.01	811	0.67	959	0.06	51	56	575
1988	0.84	707	0.56	1 117	0.06	58	53	460
1989	0.75	652	0.49	1 137	0.03	30	30	394
1990	0.76	608	0.47	1 345	0.21	45	137	1 868
1991	0.75	594	0.45	1 530	0.17	38	112	937
1992	0.45	591	0.18	2 029	0.17	40	57	2 742
1993	0.81	699	0.29	4 652	0.14	73	128	2 252
1994	1.26	722	0.33	8 337	0.11	51	95	2 378
1995	1.67	788	0.38	12 077	0.11	47	86	2 100
1996	2.01	783	0.44	13 462	0.09	87	96	2 206
1997	2.16	780	0.58	13 682	0.74	51	138	2 639
1998	2.40	781	0.65	15 186	0.72	42	114	2 205
1999	2.61	726	0.78	15 924	0.66	43	90	1 487
2000	4.13	1 492	1.61	20 391	0.52	40	57	1 919
2001	4.21	1 503	1.57	23 883	0.32	31	65	966
2002	4.71	1 400	1.57	30 052	0.60	39	58	1 313
2003	5.42	1 406	1.12	39 721	0.58	47	85	1 724
2004	2.71	1 543	1.13	19 149	0.51	30	47	1 681
2005	0.92	1 393	0.88	7 961	0.43	54	84	1 731
2006	0.66	1 231	0.67	3 292	0.45	45	54	2 292
2007	0.40	1 171	0.38	1 943	0.42	50	45	2 650
2008	0.27	1 100	0.26	1 469	0.35	50	57	14 523
2009	0.28	1 042	0.27	1 226	0.61	63	41	3 990
2010	0.22	1 011	0.19	967	0.57	101	125	22 949
2011	0.21	944	0.18	1 349	0.58	43	46	11 000
2012	0.23	916	0.21	1 488	0.45	39	45	6 924
2013	0.20	914	0.15	988	0.96	73	79	12 417
2014	0.12	902	0.06	463	0.58	59	55	7 428
2015	0.10	868	0.05	470	0.46	52	41	14 000
2016	0.08	759	0.02	371	0.45	44	47	10 763
2017	0.07	676	0.02	363	0.42	54	50	7 823
2018	47.28	647	8.57	27 487	0.39	44	43	6 367

注：2018 年起，交通事故统计口径扩大范围，包含走简易程序处理的事故，以前只包含走一般程序处理的事故。
Note: Since 2018, the scope of traffic accident statistics which only including accidents handled by general procedures before has been expanded, and the accidents handled by simple procedures are also included.

表 24.6 交通事故情况(2018)
BASIC STATISTICS OF TRAFFIC ACCIDENTS

类 别	Types	发生数 (起) Number (case)	死亡人数 (人) Death (person)	受伤人数 (人) Injuries (person)	损失折款 (万元) Losses Converted -into Cash (10 000 yuan)
总 计	**Total**	**472 833**	**647**	**85 660**	**27 487**
#死亡事故	Death Accident	627	647	129	381
伤人事故	Injury Accident	472 188		85 531	7 663
#机动车	Motor-driven Vehicles	399 775	506	51 586	23 276
#汽 车	Automobiles	395 511	489	50 135	23 118
摩托车	Motorcycles	3 443	12	1 361	130
非机动车	Non-motor-driven Vehicles	69 918	108	32 543	2 121
行人乘车人	Pedestrians and Passengers	2 796	31	1 453	2 080

注：2018 年起，交通事故统计口径扩大范围，包含走简易程序处理的事故，以前只包含走一般程序处理的事故。
Note：Since 2018，the scope of traffic accident statistics which only including accidents handled by general procedures before has been expanded，and the accidents handled by simple procedures are also included.

表 24.7 交通违法情况(2018)
BASIC STATISTICS ON TRAFFIC VIOLATIONS

单位:万人次(10 000 person-times)

指 标	Indicators	2018
处理违法人次	**Dealing with Illegal Activities**	**1 850.42**
#教育人次	Education	65.17
处罚人次	Punishment	1 785.25
#罚 款	Fine	1 697.85
#机动车	Motor Vehicle	1 344.75
非机动车	Non-Motor Vehicle	435.55
行人和行车人	Pedestrians and Drivers	70.12

表 24.8 火灾事故情况(2018)
BASIC STATISTICS OF FIRES

指　标	Indicators	发生数(起) Number (case)	死亡人数(人) Death (person)	受伤人数(人) Injuries (person)	损失折款(万元) Losses Converted -into Cash (10 000 yuan)
总　计	**Total**	**3 856**	**44**	**43**	**6 367.2**
电气火灾	Electrical Fire	1 527	21	24	3 754.1
生产作业类火灾	Production Operations	117		2	1 327.5
生活用火不慎	Careless Use of Fire	860	3	5	247.3
吸　烟	Smoking	137	8	6	137.9
玩　火	Play with Fire	12			8.8
自　燃	Spontaneous Combustion	81			76.1
雷　击	Lightning	3			4.4
静　电	Static Electricity	2			0.4
不明确原因	Unexplained	36			38.5
放　火	Set Fire	46	7	1	171.7
其　他	Others	1 035	5	5	600.5

表 24.9 检察院民事、行政案件办理情况(2018)
CIVIL CASES AND ADMINISTRATIVE CASES HANDLED BY PROCURATOR'S OFFICES

单位:件(case)

类　别	Types	受　案 Cases Accepted	结案处理 Cases Settled	其中 of which: 提出抗诉 Appeals Rejected	不支持监督申请 pervision Application not Supported	终止审查 Consorship Terminaled
总　计	**Total**	**1 955**	**1 769**	**61**	**1 518**	**81**
民事案	**Civil Cases**	**1 279**	**1 155**	**57**	**916**	**81**
婚姻家庭	Marriages Disputes	72	61	2	53	2
继承纠纷	Inheritance Disputes	45	45		39	3
物权保护	Property Rights Protection	71	67	1	61	2
所有权争议	Ownership Disputes	53	53	2	49	1
合同纠纷	Contract Disputes	635	573	40	407	57
劳动人事争议	Labor and Personnel Disputes	180	157	2	144	1
其　他	Others	223	199	10	163	15
行政案	**Administrative Cases**	**676**	**614**	**4**	**602**	

表24.10 检察院申诉案件处理情况(2018)
APPEALS HANDLED BY PROCURATOR'S OFFICES

单位:件(case)

类别	Types	受案 Cases Accepted	审查处理 Cases Investigated	其中 of which 分送本院其他部门 Dilivering to Other Department of Such Procurator's Offices
总计	**Total**	**7 702**	**6 737**	**2 860**
#首次申诉	Appeals First Time	5 226	5 363	2 713
#不服不起诉	Appeals Against Non-prosecution	35	35	12
不服不立案	Appeals Against Rejection of the Case	123	263	127
不服逮捕	Appeals Against Arrest	6	12	2
不服刑事判决	Appeals Against Judgment of Criminal Case	553	309	1
不服民事行政裁决	Appeals Against Adminnistration Arbitrament of Civil Case	3 108	3 277	2 043

表24.10 续表 continued

单位:件(case)

类别	Types	其中 of which 移送其他检察院 Removing to Other Procurator's Offices	移送外单位 Removing to Other Departments	直接答复 Direct Reply
总计	**Total**	**1 081**	**81**	**1 391**
#首次申诉	Appeals First Time	540	38	1 152
#不服不起诉	Appeals Against Non-prosecution	9		13
不服不立案	Appeals Against Rejection of the Case	33	2	35
不服逮捕	Appeals Against Arrest	9		1
不服刑事判决	Appeals Against Judgment of Criminal Case	82	3	91
不服民事行政裁决	Appeals Against Adminnistration Arbitrament of Civil Case	358	2	828

表 24.11 法院各类案件办理情况(2018)
CASES HANDLED BY COURTS

单位:件(case)

类别	Types	收案 Cases Accepted	结案 Cases Settled	其中 of which 判决 Judgement	裁定 Arbitration	调解 Mediation
一审刑事案件	**First Trial Criminal Cases**	**27 869**	**27 666**	**27 440**	**225**	**1**
#侵犯公民人身权利、民主权利罪	Offences Against Citizens' Personal and Democratic Rights	2 628	2 653	2 579	73	1
侵犯财产罪	Offences Against Properties	10 280	10 155	10 107	48	
妨碍社会管理秩序罪	Offences Against Social Management of Order	8 004	7 986	7 914	72	
一审民事案件	**First Trial Civil Cases**	**531 232**	**527 155**	**132 501**	**309 075**	**85 572**
人格权纠纷	Personality Right Disputes	8 694	8 665	3 037	2 102	3 526
婚姻家庭、继承纠纷	Marriage and Family, Inheritance Disputes	36 080	35 971	9 411	9 259	17 301
婚姻家庭纠纷	Marriage and Family Disputes	25 119	25 181	7 980	7 381	9 820
继承纠纷	Inheritance Disputes	10 961	10 790	1 431	1 878	7 481
物权纠纷	Property Rights Disputes	12 957	12 895	4 935	4 823	3 137
合同、无因管理、不当得利纠纷	Contract, Non-management, Unjust Enrichment Disputes	364 680	362 877	83 282	245 036	34 559
合同纠纷	Contract Disputes	363 723	361 961	82 965	244 540	34 456
不当得利纠纷	Unjust Enrichment Disputes	944	904	311	490	103
无因管理纠纷	Non-management Disputes	13	12	6	6	
知识产权与竞争纠纷	Intellectual Property Rights and Competition Disputes	21 104	20 539	1 208	17 860	1 471
劳动争议、人事纠纷	Labor Disputes and Personnel Disputes	12 232	12 115	6 111	3 042	2 962
劳动争议	Labor Disputes	12 203	12 072	6 085	3 030	2 957
人事纠纷	Personnel Disputes	29	43	26	12	5
与公司、证券、保险、票据等有关的民事纠纷	Civil Disputes Related to Companies, Securities, Insurance, Negotiable instruments, etc.	12 215	10 996	3 558	5 053	2 385
侵犯责任纠纷	Infringement Liability Disputes	42 554	42 844	18 009	5 159	19 676
其他民事案由	Other Civil Cases	20 716	20 253	2 950	16 741	555
一审行政案件	**First Trial Administrative Cases**	**5 466**	**5 992**	**2 361**	**3 568**	**63**

表 24.12 法院执行案件情况(2018) CASES EXECUTED BY COURTS

单位:件(case)

类别 Types		收案 Cases Accepted	结案 Cases Settled	其中 of which 执行完毕 Execution Completed	终结执行 Execution Terminated	终结本次执行程序 Execution Procedure Terminated
总计	**Total**	**125 877**	**126 190**	**67 486**	**10 495**	**46 947**
刑事	Criminal Cases	4 318	4 288	2 771	404	1 087
民事	Civil Cases	104 675	105 176	55 657	9 315	39 547
行政	Administrative Cases	345	362	229	22	108
行政非诉审查与执行	Non-litigious Investigation and Execution of Administration	1 158	1 111	615	66	425
仲裁	Arbitration	14 007	13 852	7 510	604	5 227
公证债权文书	Notary Creditor's Rights	393	383	75	55	217
其他	Others	981	1 018	629	29	336

表 24.13 主要年份法院各类案件结案情况 CASES ENDED BY COURTS IN MAIN YEARS

单位:起(time)

类别 Types		2005	2010	2017	2018
总计	**Total**	**283 230**	**406 582**	**802 146**	**794 143**
刑事案件	Criminal Cases	17 353	22 137	31 975	31 774
婚姻家庭、继承案件	Marriages and Inheritance Cases	28 563	31 114	37 774	37 702
合同纠纷案件	Contract Disputes Cases	128 118	180 459	389 212	376 009
行政案件	Administrative Cases	3 016	2 135	10 880	9 908
申诉、申请再审	Second Trial on Appeals and Requisition	4 023	4 120	5 818	6 157
司法赔偿	Justice Compensation	6	1	45	64
执行案件	Executed Cases	70 998	102 221	133 696	126 190

©中国统计出版社有限公司　2019

版权所有。未经许可，本书的任何部分不得以任何方式在世界任何地区以任何文字翻印、拷贝、仿制或转载。

©2019 China Statistics Press Co.,Ltd.

All rights reserved. No part of the publication may be reproduced or transmitted in any form or by any means, electronic or mechanical, including photocopying, recording, or any information storage and retrieval system, without written permission from the publisher.

图书在版编目(CIP)数据

上海统计年鉴. 2019：汉英对照 / 上海市统计局，国家统计局上海调查总队编.
——北京：中国统计出版社，2019.12
ISBN 978-7-5037-8993-9

Ⅰ. ①上…
Ⅱ. ①上… ②国…
Ⅲ. ①统计资料—上海—2019—年鉴—汉、英
Ⅳ. ①C832.51-54

中国版本图书馆CIP数据核字（2019）第207440号

上海统计年鉴—2019

作　　者 / 上海市统计局　国家统计局上海调查总队
责任编辑 / 钟　钰　熊　威
装帧设计 / 吴琪辉
出版发行 / 中国统计出版社有限公司
地　　址 / 北京市丰台区西三环南路甲6号
邮政编码 / 100073
电　　话 / 邮购 (010) 63376909　书店 (010) 68783171
网　　址 / http://www.zgtjcbs.com
印　　刷 / 上海万卷印刷股份有限公司
经　　销 / 新华书店
开　　本 / 890mm × 1240 mm　1/16
字　　数 / 111万字
印　　张 / 32.5
版　　别 / 2019年12月第1版
版　　次 / 2019年12月第1次印刷
定　　价 / 480.00元

本书附同版本CD-ROM一张，光盘内容以书面文字为准。
如有印装差错，由本社发行部调换。